1 MONTH OF
FREE
READING

at
www.ForgottenBooks.com

By purchasing this book you are eligible for one month membership to ForgottenBooks.com, giving you unlimited access to our entire collection of over 700,000 titles via our web site and mobile apps.

To claim your free month visit:
www.forgottenbooks.com/free785748

ISBN 978-0-483-61397-3
PIBN 10785748

TABLE OF CONTENTS.

THE

MERCERSBURG REVIEW.

JANUARY, 1849.

NO. I.

ARTICLE I.—PRELIMINARY STATEMENT.—*Explanatory Letter from Dr. J. W. Nevin.—Apology to the Alumni.—Character of the Work.—Contributors.*

IT was announced in the Prospectus of this publication, that its editorial conduct would be in my hands. As it now appears under a somewhat different form, the case may be felt to call for a brief explanation.

So far as any engagement is concerned, I have considered myself exonerated in full, by the simple fact, that the general condition on which it was assumed, has not been fulfilled. My consent to edit the Review, was given with much hesitation, in the confidence that a certain number of subscribers would be secured and returned, according to determination, before it should be commenced. The very spirited movement made at the start seemed to carry in itself a guaranty, that what was proposed in this way would be accomplished without any difficulty. But there has been a disappointment. The time proposed for returns came and passed, without any such amount of available patronage being secured, as had been made the basis of calculation for the important experiment in the beginning. In these circumstances, I felt myself released of course from all obligation to act as editor, and was well satisfied besides, to be in possession again of my original freedom. I am very willing, to believe indeed, that the want of sufficiently prompt and full action to which I have just referred, in the case of the subscription list, may be the result of mere procrastination, rather than of actual indifference towards the enterprise in hand. There is a natural disposition with most persons, in every enterprise of this sort, to move slowly, and to wait for the actual appearance of the publication they are called upon to support, before yielding themselves in form to its claims. But however this might be allowed under other circumstances, it has seemed to me altogether unreasonable in the present case, so far at least as regards what may be called the primary circle of patronage, here relied upon for encouragement and support. My own interest in the object has been conditioned throughout, by the supposition that it was of interest also for others.   Much has been said, for years past, of the importance of having such a publication as that which is now proposed, under the general banner displayed at Mercersburg.   I have been personally urged from different quarters, by ministers, particularly in the German Reformed Church, to undertake such a publication on my own responsibility, with the assurance that they and others stood ready to second the movement with their most hearty and active co-operation.   Finally, the Alumni Association resolved to embark in the enterprise, placing it under the most desirable form, as it seemed to most persons, which the case could well admit.   It was fair in these circumstances, to calculate on so much of a response from the very start, as would fully justify and sustain the movement.   Why should a few persons be expected to com-mit themselves for the *whole* enterprise, if others, including some perhaps who had shown themselves forward in urging the general measure, saw proper to hesitate about the assumption of a mere *fraction* of it in the form of carrying out its subscrip-tion list? This reflection was sufficient at all events, to deter-mine my own course.   There seemed to be after all no such earnest and urgent demand for the publication in question, as could be said really to call for my services in the way which had been proposed.   There was room enough for a doubt besides, whether this very arrangement, instead of helping the general design, might not be operating rather in some degree to its prejudice; by seeming to throw the enterprise too much under my control, and so embarrassing its proper liberty and independence. Altogether, as already said, I have found it a privilege and relief, to resign my editorial trust back again into the hands of the Alumni themselves, as represented by their Publishing Committee.

Nor is this all. I have even gone so far, as to advise and recommend the abandonment of the whole undertaking, on the general ground which has now been mentioned. No one could blame the Committee, of course, for refusing to go forward, in the midst of such apparent disposition on the part of others to excuse themselves from action; and it has been with me a serious question, whether in view of all the circumstances of the case, this was not the only policy that could be prudently and safely pursued. My advice was accordingly, to give up the enterprise altogether.

But in this my judgment has been overruled by the more sanguine zeal of the Publishing Committee. Confiding not so much in the actual subscription already secured, as in the general pledges and promises which are expected to be fulfilled in its proper completion hereafter, and having great faith besides in the character of the enterprise itself as well as a high sense of its necessity and importance, they have resolutely concluded to go forward with the publication as at first proposed; and the first number of it is here issued accordingly in the execution of this design. My hope and trust is, that such success may crown the undertaking, as fully to justify in time to come the courageous spirit with which it was made to start. For I would not wish at all to make the impression by any thing I have said, that it is to be regarded as ill-advised and rash. On the contrary, I look upon it as starting under very favorable auspices, though not in such form of absolute security as in this case might reasonably be required. There is good cause to believe that the calculation on which it rests, will be found to have been judicious and safe; and it is hardly necessary to add, that, in these circumstances, no one is likely to be better pleased with the result than myself.

It seems to me now, at all events, that the present arrangement is decidedly better for the general object of the publication, than that which was proposed in the beginning. Its leading character will remain of course substantially the same. It will be devoted to the same interests, it will occupy the same relations, it will represent the same spirit and tendency. As a mere contributor to its pages, I expect myself of course to write for it full as much as I should do, if its editorial management were formally in my own hands. At the same time, the relation on both sides will be more independent and free; and more room will be allowed, or at least more immediate encouragement given, for the revelation of a suitably various and manifold life in the Review itself. There is less danger of its coming to be regarded in this way as my publication simply, rather than that of the Association in whose name it is issued. It is important that the Alumni should feel it to be truly and strictly their own; though of course always for the high purposes which are embraced in its original plan; and this requires that the whole responsibility of its character should be allowed to continue in their hands.

J. W. NEVIN.

MERCERSBURG, December, 1848.

APOLOGY TO THE ALUMNI.

AT their last meeting the Alumni of Marshall College resolved to publish and sustain a Review of a given character. They appointed and properly empowered a committee to actualize their will. They pledged to this committee such co-operation as the success of this enterprise demanded. The committee at once addressed themselves to the accomplishment of their task. In doing this, certain expenses were incurred; but, infinitely more than this, the public were assured that a want, which for several years has been pouring reiterated urgent cries into the private ears of Mercersburg, should at last be heard. Circulars and subscription papers were sent out to the Alumni, and also to others, and a time set, when they would be expected to return freighted with the promised co-operation. The result of this has already been told in the foregoing letter. The committee were thus brought to an issue alike unexpected and unprovided for. In this emergency, the letter of their instructions was indeed silent—but it was the silence of death to their enterprise. There was an hour of painful suspense. The expense already incurred, though comparatively trifling, was not to be despised. But, vastly more than this, how could the committee go back to that Egypt of false promises and resolutions, which has so often darkened certain places of our land, and thus re-enslave our Israel, without the hope of defence, in degrading bondage to the flesh pots of its cruel and insulting Rationalism? A sea of uncertainty was indeed before them, and—the hosts of Egypt behind them. At last the spirit of their instructions, clear-toned and joyous, bade them "go forward." This first number of the Review, is the "rod of Moses" now stretched upon that sea of doubt. The wind of approbation already blows; the sea begins to divide; Israel is safe; let Egypt beware.

Three hundred subscribers were required as a sufficiently secure basis, on which to build the success of this Review. One-third of this number was obtained in a. few hours on the morning of last Commencement; and, although there has been an almost total failure of returns since then, yet there seems to be a perfect moral certainty that far more than the number of subscribers required for a beginning, will be sent in before the second number is issued. In all probability the true cause of the failure here spoken of, has already been given in the preceding letter. In reality it is doubtless still the firm purpose of the Alumni and others, fully to redeem the pledge given to the public for the establishment of this Review. Though they have apparently deserted their committee and left them in the lurch before the public, yet otherwise the committee have not the least indication of a disposition on their part to "go back to Egypt." Though the committee have neither seen nor heard of them for many days; yet, beyond a shadow of doubt, they are merely scattered here and there, honestly and diligently redeeming their pledge—only it takes them a little longer than they expected. This being the case, had the committee dropped their undertaking, the whole association, and others with them, would have been left in a position of falsehood before the public —and that, too, without any real necessity in the case.

Again: The Alumni desired a publication of a certain character; and, in order to secure this, it was at the time supposed that a certain editorial control was necessary. But now it seems that this end can fully as well, if not more fully, be secured under the present than under the former arrangement; and this, for the simple reason that the fetter of delicacy, which the former arrangement imposed upon the chief pen, is now removed.

Thus, in these two respects, the spirit of their instructions bade the committee "go forward." Though literally and legally freed from the task imposed upon them, yet were they morally bound to rescue their own, and the honor of their masters from a disgrace that has of late become but too common in certain directions. This obligation, of course, was conditioned by the possibility and necessity of the case; for no one is bound to achieve a thing alike unnecessary and impossible. But both the necessity, demand or call for this publication, and the possibility of establishing it, are not one whit less now than on the thirteenth of September last; but, on the contrary, they are, if any thing, far greater; and have been rendered so, if by nothing else, at least by the expectation which has been created in the case.

Moreover, if such a Review, as is here contemplated, is ever to be established, it must be done now or never; for the present effort is one of the critical sort that can never be repeated—that must "either make or break"—that eventuate either in life or death. If this effort have not in itself enough of moral strength to give birth to this enterprise, after having been naturally generated, conceived, and brought to the birth-point in the historical womb of Want, it must, of course, perish at this point, never to be generated again. If this be a fact, (and the committee believed it to be such,) how could they do otherwise than they have done?

CHARACTER OF THE WORK.

THE *distinctive character* of this Review has already been made known through the Prospectus; but it seems both needful for the information of those who may not have seen it, and necessary as an outline of its prominent features, here in the beginning to republish the body of this prospectus in a permanent form

It is to be a Literary and Theological Journal, published in the name and by the authority of the Alumni of Marshall College.

"The objects of the publication will be such as come within the scope of religious Reviews generally, with free room at the same time for the interests of literature under a wider form. Altogether, it is deemed best that it should not be closely bound beforehand to any particular method or plan.

"The Review is expected, however, of course, to bear a distinctive and peculiar character. As the mere echo of what already exists in this way, it would have no right to challenge any regard. Its peculiarity is denoted by its title. It proposes to represent, in philosophy and religion, the system of thinking which has come to be identified extensively, in this country, with the Institutions at Mercersburg, though of far wider and higher force in fact, on both sides of the Atlantic. With the same field of survey that is spread out to other Theological Reviews, the stand point of its observations will be materially different. It is wished, in this respect, to supply, by means of it, a want which all other Reviews at the present time fail to supply. Did the way seem to be fairly open, in any quarter besides, for a full and free representation of the tendency in whose service it is to appear, it would not be commenced.

"In Religion, the publication will be made to rest throughout on the basis of the APOSTLES' CREED, taken in its own proper and original sense. Its motto, here, will be that of the profoundly philosophical Anselm of Canterbury: '*Non quæro intelligere ut credam, sed credo ut intelligam.*' The last evidence of all truth will be acknowledged to hold only in the person of Jesus Christ, out of which with irresistible necessity, all other articles of this wonderful symbol flow.

"But Faith, as thus going before understanding, seeks not to exclude it. It is properly in order to science. It will be assumed thus, always, by the Mercersburg Review, that the mystery of Christianity is objectively in full organic harmony with the constitution of the world as otherwise known, and that it is capable, accordingly, of scientific apprehension under such form.   Room will be made, in this way, for the idea of theology as a living process in the life of the Church, and not a tradition simply in its outward keeping.   It will be taken for granted, that theology is not yet complete; just as little as the same can be said of the new creation in Christ Jesus, in any other view.

"Science, so rooted in the realities of Faith, can accomplish its growth only as it remains perpetually bound, in the midst of all progress, to the authority of the past.   Christianity involves necessarily, as in the creed, the idea of one Holy, Catholic and Apostolic Church.   The proposed Review will be decidedly historical and churchly, then, in its character, and may be expected to lay emphasis on all that truly and properly appertains to religion on this side.

"It will be *Protestant*, of course, in opposition to the corruptions of Rome; but *Catholic*, at the same time, in striving to honor and save the glorious and sublime truths out of which these corruptions for the most part spring.   In its controversy with Rome, it will allow no companionship still with the radical and rationalistic spirit of the age, engaged ostensibly in the same cause.

"It lies in its conception, as now described, that the Mercersburg Review will bear no strictly denominational character."

CONTRIBUTORS.

BUT though this publication must and will possess a distinctive character, yet it will be a catholic rostrum or pulpit, whence any one may speak, provided only, that his subject be of sufficient moment, his style possessed of proper merit, and his manner graced with becoming decorum.   This being the case, its columns will, of right, be open first of all to the Alumni, from any and all of whom *fit* contributions are hereby particularly requested.   It is expected, moreover, that the Ministry of the German Reformed Church, who are not included in this number, will also speak; for they, too, have rights herein involved and invested, and, therefore, room will be made for them, as cheerfully as for the Alumni. Again: All beyond the circle of these two classes, whose wealth of indifference or bigotry, or of both, has not alienated them from all rights inhering in the objects embraced by this Review, are hereby invited and urged to come forward and claim these rights. In so doing, they will meet with a hearty welcome.

Thus, then, as already intimated, even those who are opposed to each other, whether seemingly or really, in their contention for the Truth, provided they be manifestly led by the Truth, and do not attempt to lead it, will receive an impartial hearing. This is not, indeed, to be a theatre where men are to contend with beasts. Neither are men by any means to be considered as the possessors, revealers, guardians, defenders, and saviours of the Truth. The branches bear not the Root, but the Root the branches; the branches are not the revealers, but the revelation, of the Root. Man, indeed, lives—and yet not he, but the Truth lives in him; and the life that he lives in the flesh, he lives by the faith of the Truth incarnate in the Son of God. Man, therefore, is the servant, not the lord of Truth; he is bound by it, not it by him; if he be true at all, it is only in so far as he is possessed, guarded, defended, saved, and revealed by the Truth. Never, with his logic claws, can he grasp it by the forelock, and drag it into view. It is the Truth that immortalizes man, not man the Truth. It is its own revealer; and yet, in so far as it is human, man is its revelation. But because of the sinful and discordant posture of man, Truth can now reveal itself only by a dialectical conflict with error. The field of this conflict, is the human personality, and the court where Truth is crowned, is the human consciousness. This is the case in the experience of every individual who makes any progress at all in true virtue. In his bosom, truth and error daily grapple in a conflict of life and death. By this means alone is he formed, not forms himself, into the image of God. The same conflict, only in its general form, is going on in the bosom of the Church, both in a theoretical and a practical way; and it is only when precocious bigotry assumes to be already sanctified, and impudent folly affects to be superior to the Truth, and so to guard, defend, and save it, that this conflict is silenced as the work of Satan. This being the case, whatever professes to be an organ of the theoretical part of this conflict, if it be at all true to its pretensions, will speak, not the tongue or dialect of a single family or tribe, but all the tongues and all the dialects of the whole Church. If any cry out that this will cause a chaos of sounds, let them know that, if they have no *chaos*, they can have no *cosmos*. It is because certain ones will have this latter without the former, that they get neither, but only a solitary voice, incestuously wedded to its own echo, and housed between the mountains of ignorance and schism, where it bloats on the stagnant pool of bigotry, and battens on the impudence that creams so richly there. *Nullum chaos, nullus cosmos.*

ART. II.—THE YEAR 1848.

WONDERFUL, and long to be remembered, has been the year 1848, now thrown into our rear. The outward end of much that is past, and the beginning, outwardly, of a great deal, that is to come. A year of revolution and change; of uncertainty, anxiety, and alarm; answering to the prophetic imagery of "signs in the sun, and in the moon, and in the stars;" the powers of heaven shaken, and the order of the world thrown violently out of course. A year of mystery for the nations; involving a deep burden, which the whole civilized earth is concerned to hear and understand. Who shall pretend to fathom its sense? Who shall tell the mighty secret, that lies hid within its sybil leaves?

It is not for any age or period, fully to understand itself. While events are passing, they cannot, for the most part, be fairly seen in their true proportions and relations. The part of history, which it is always most difficult to interpret, is that which is in the process of immediate actual evolution. The present throws light upon the past; while its own sense again, so far as it is in any measure original and new, can find its clear and sufficient commentary at last only in the life of the unborn future. We are in a much better position now, to comprehend the age of the Reformation, than were the men who themselves lived and acted in its stirring drama. We are better able than they were, to perceive the general force and bearing of the movement as a whole, to separate the merely accidental and transient from the necessary and constant, to reduce the tumultuating show of seemingly chaotic elements to system and reason. We are not overwhelmed and hurried along, as they were, by the wild tossing torrent of what was taking place at the time; but are permitted rather, as it were from some lofty height of observation afar off, to survey with full leisure, in a calm objective way, the entire tract of revolution, in its connections, both with the period going before and the period which has followed since. There are those, indeed, who do pretend still to exhaust the meaning of such an age, by looking into it under a purely separate view; as though history had no life of its own, extending forward perpetually from generation to generation, as the growth of a divine thought; but were made up of confused parcels only, each carrying its significance mainly in its own facts, and requiring no light besides, for its proper interpretation. But this is to insult philosophy and religion, in one breath. No man can possibly have any true knowledge of the sixteenth century, who sees not in it the product of forces long before at work in the bosom of the Catholic Church; and whose estimate of its meaning, at the same time, is not made to embrace also in one and the same view its historical consequences, as they lie exposed to observation now in the lapse of subsequent time. The history of Protestantism thus far, is the revelation of what lay hid, originally, in the great fact of the Reformation. So in the case of our own age. It can never be fully understood by itself, but only as it shall be seen hereafter, when its past and future connections are brought into view together, and made to explain the whole in its interior sense and design. Now we see through a glass darkly.

Still, we see enough, to make us profoundly solemn and thoughtful. So much has become clear for all thinking men, that the age in which we live, is not one of the merely common sort. History moves not with continuously equable stream towards its appointed end. Its progress rather, is by vast cycloids or stages, each fulfilling a certain problem within itself, and accomplishing its course under a regular given form, only to open the way finally for the general process to go forward again in a new way under some similar form. It goes, as we are accustomed, indeed, ordinarily to speak of it, by eras and epochs. There is a difference then, of course, between one age and another as regards significance, according to the place they occupy in the order of the world's life. So long as this life continues to move in a direction already fully settled, carrying out and completing simply the sense of some tendency established in the time which has gone before, it may be expected to proceed with comparative regularity and quiet, and there will be nothing special or extraordinary in the age, to which it belongs. Not so, however, where two great eras come together, (*contact of ages*, 1 Cor. x. 11,) the old having finished its circuit, and a new one being at hand to take its place. Such going out and coming in are never accomplished, without more or less of commotion and struggle. The breaking up of the old, however gradually it may be brought to pass, involves necessarily a certain degree of violence and agitation; while the introduction of the new carries with it unavoidably also, the sense of exciting revolution. The age, within which such change falls, must ever, of course, be one of more than ordinary prominence on the field of history. It will stand out to view, through all succeeding time, as the revelation of a new epoch in the life of the world; and it will be attended, while it passes, with the consciousness of some such mighty birth, more or less clear, in the pangs and throes with which it is accomplished. So, we say, our own particular age is felt by all, who exercise any sort of earnest reflection, to be in this way of far more than common significance. Predictions and prophecies, for a long time past, as we are told, have been looking towards it as a period of eventful crisis, and change. A very general presentiment of such world historical revolution, as something close at hand, has gained ground in our own day far and wide, even among those who exercise but little speculation on this subject, but are of such temperament only, as to sympathize actively with the general life that surrounds them, and carries them in its bosom.

Such wide-spread bodings that grow out of no clear ratiocination or reflection, but spring forth spontaneously from the inmost life, as it were, of the world itself, are always entitled to consideration and respect. They come not without reason; and they have been found, in fact, to attend all grand turning points in the progress of earth's history. In the case before us, moreover, they are seconded and backed by the most cool and far-reaching calculations of reason. The men who think most, and who, by their position, are best qualified to think to some purpose, are those precisely who, of all others, participate most decidedly, we may say, in the general impression of which we now speak. It is felt, that the lines and tendencies of history have been gradually working, for more than two centuries past, towards a common issue, which has now been reached; and in which they have gathered themselves into a sort of universal *knot*, that admits no further progress under the same form. The knot must be dissolved, whether with violence or without it, so as to make room for onward movement again, under some new and different form. One era is passing away, and another is on the eve of taking its place. Our age is emphatically the period of transition, in which the extremities of both are made to touch and meet. Such, at least, has become a very widely prevalent opinion; and we see no good reason for casting upon it any sort of doubt or discredit. The whole course of events rather, seems to be lending confirmation to it every year. Especially has this been the case with the developments of the year, *annus mirabilis* we may well style it, which has just been conducted to its close.

It would seem to form, in some sense, the very hinge of the vast and mighty world epoch, which is supposed to be taking place; not the beginning of its revolution, of course, and much less in any view its end; but a sort of central revelation in the midst of the movement, suddenly disclosing the awful reality of its power, and determining in an outward way the absolute necessity of its going forward to its appointed consummation. In this respect, there has been no year like it, at least since the period of the Reformation. The world may be said, within the last twelve months, to have passed the Rubicon of a revolution, that is destined to turn all its fortunes into a new channel for centuries to come. History is brought to occupy the summit level of a whole vast continent of time, from which slope in opposite directions, behind and before, the retreating past and far prospective future, as two broad tracts of life, which might seem to have no bond in common, save the everlasting mountain barriers that fling them asunder. Whatever of uncertainty might have attended the opinion before, now at least, it may be confidently assumed, and boldly affirmed that old things are passing away, and that all things are becoming new. A true crisis has been reached, in the revelations of the past year. The plot thickens; events crowd, with ever accumulating momentum, towards their appointed end; a thousand signs conspire to show that the funeral pile is already lighted, where from the ashes of a dying era another is prepared to take its wondrous birth, more bright and full of promise than any which has gone before. So much of significance, awful and vast, is comprehended in the history of the year now registered as 1848.

The idea of such a grand crisis or revolution, in the world's history, as we have now mentioned, implies two forms of action unitedly at work for its accomplishment. There must be, in one direction, the violent breaking up of what is old and ready to pass away, in the order of life as it has stood before; and there must be, at the same time, in another direction, the working of an inward nisus and an outward providence jointly, towards the new form of existence, in which the process is required to become finally complete. On one side, the spirit is compelled to forsake the house of its former habitation as no longer suited to its wants; while on the other, it is carried forth, by inward longings, and outward beckonings, after the still unknown future, to which it is thus forced to look for help. In other words, the

preparation that serves to usher in a new era, is at once negative
and positive; not negative simply, and not positive only, but
both these in union; the old making room by its own dissolution for the birth of the new, and the new foreshadowed and
prefigured in the womb of the old.

See, on the one hand, the late political revolutions in Europe.
When, in any age before, has the world beheld such a succession
of broad and mighty changes, compressed into the compass of a
single year! It is still as it were but the other day, since the nations were electrified by the tidings of the revolution in France.
It seemed to be an event large enough of itself, to occupy the
attention and speculation of mankind for years. And yet, how
completely has it been shorn of its stupendous singularity, by the
earthquake shocks that have since rapidly followed in its train.
Italy, Austria, Prussia, in a measure, we may say, all Germany,
have been suddenly seized with the same spirit of commotion,
and change; agitation has succeeded agitation, in all the great
centres of political life; the pillars of the social system have been
made to tremble, if not absolutely to give way, in almost every
direction. Never before was the aspect of the civilized world so
altered, within so short a time. It has been hard to keep pace
with the movement, even in imagination and thought. Astonishment itself has been paralysed, by the overwhelming vastness
of what has taken place; and we are apt to think of it still as a
sort of dream or dioramic show, something which has come and
gone in the way of inward vision, rather than as an actual part
of the world's outward waking history. It costs an effort of
reflection, only to see and feel where the nations now stand, as
compared with their posture on the first of January, 1848.

And yet it were a false view of the case entirely, to conceive
of it, for this reason, as a mere passing accident, that is to be
followed with no deep lasting effect upon the course of history.
Sudden and violent as it may seem, it is the product of forces
and tendencies, which have been steadily working towards this
result for whole centuries past. In this respect, it is fully analogous with the general moral explosion that startled the slumbers of Europe, at the opening of the sixteenth century. The
causes, which produced the Reformation, had been in powerful

operation for a long period before, gradually, but surely, preparing the way for what was to follow. The political, commercial, social, and religious relations of the world, all pressed towards this result, as the necessary outlet of their force, and only proper and sufficient expression of their sense. Earnest men saw, and felt long before, that a great and mighty crisis was drawing nigh. So, too, it has been evident enough for men of this sort, and, in the way of dark presentiment, we may say, it has been vaguely felt also by the popular mind, for a long time past, that some such crisis as that, to which we now have come, was preparing to break over men's heads. Ideas, principles, tendencies, and powers, have been deep at work in the whole structure of society, which could not fail finally, to reach this very issue, by springing the bands with which they were held, and demanding new forms of existence more adequate to the scope of their action.

It is all important here, to distinguish properly between two widely different sides of history, the merely human namely, and the divine. It is carried forward in one view by the free action of particular men, or classes of men, ruled, more or less, always by private purposes and aims; while in another, it obeys altogether the action of a deeper, universal, and objective law, representing at every point the mind and plan of God. It amounts to nothing then, against the historical significance of the late revolutions in Europe, as now asserted, that the motives, and principles, and personal character, of those who have been most forward in bringing them to pass, may not commend themselves to our confidence, and respect. It is not by any such measure, that we can ever try truly the interior sense and weight of history as a whole. (Isaiah x. 5—7; John xi. 49—52; Acts ii. 22—23.)

With one of the boldest, and best, writers of our time, we are well persuaded that the very worst elements have been at work, and are at work still, in the whirlwind, which has been let loose in the old world.* We see in it, not the true law of reason and right at all, as the animating soul of the movement, but, on the contrary, the spirit predominantly of human wickedness and

---

* See an admirable tract entitled, *The Revolutionary Spirit, a Discourse, by Taylor Lewis, Esq.,* New York, 1848.

passion. It is not possible to justify it, at the bar of Christianity.
It is not to be marvelled at, that many good men in Germany
should look upon it with dismay, as the coming, emphatically,
of Antichrist, or the letting loose of Satan in the last days. Un-
principled radicalism, in no sympathy whatever with the mind
of Jesus Christ, but inwardly full rather of diabolical hostility
to all truth and righteousness, might seem to be the main force
immediately concerned in what is going forward. The whole
theory of revolution here, whatever may be said of the right of
such violent change in other cases, is such as cannot for a moment bear examination. It goes on the assumption that a full
reconstruction of society may be forcibly introduced at any time,
when it is found practicable to bring it to pass. The right of
revolution, is taken to be the right in full of any man, or set of
men, to upset existing institutions from the bottom, to the best of
their ability. "The claim comes fully up to the spirit of the
word. It is the period of *revolution*, of *rolling over and over;*
and this right of revolution or rolling over, has no place or principle at which it can consistently stop." That even the *Christian*
world on this side of the Atlantic, should be so ready and forward
to clap its hands, in joyful exultation, over the revolution in Paris,
and other similar explosions, without the least regard to right or
wrong in the case, as though the simple work of destruction
were in and of itself something good and desirable, is, to say the
least, a melancholy exemplification of human weakness.

But, after all this admission, we are bound, at the same time,
reverently to acknowledge, as well as diligently to study, the
presence of a deeper divine law in the whole movement, by
which it is to be regarded as a sacred necessity in the progress of
our general human history — a necessity also, intimately and
vitally allied with the triumphant resolution, finally, of the great
problem of Christianity itself. It is not enough, to resolve it
pragmatically into all manner of bad motives and springs of
action, on the part of the men concerned in it; we must see in it
also the all-wise and infinitely glorious providence of God. Is
it true that a sparrow may not fall to the ground without his
notice and will? How then should cities and nations be thus
thrown into commotion, and thrones tumbled into the dust, apart

from his eye and hand? But the providence of God involves necessarily the idea of counsel, connexion and plan. This in the end is the true sense of history, the evolution of a divine thought or purpose in the onward flow of human actions and events. In such view accordingly, we say, that sudden and abrupt as the late European revolutions may seem, they have not come by accident, and are not to be regarded as the product of mere momentary passion and caprice. No mob could hurry a whole nation into revolution, if the necessity of revolution were not already at hand historically in the constitution of the nation itself. It is only in such case the throat of a volcano, which seeks vent uncontrollably in this way. The stunning sound of this European explosion is but the outburst of pent up forces, whose action has been powerfully struggling towards this very issue for a long time past. The rumbling premonitions of its approach, for such as had an ear to hear, might be distinctly perceived many years ago. In one sense, the principles and tendencies which have led to it, may be said to have been at work since the epoch of the Reformation. It is no accident, no work of merely human hands, but the product truly of the inmost life of history itself, the result of an organic process which has been going forward for centuries in the very heart of the world's civilzation.

Thus springing from the life of the past, it carries in itself necessarily the deepest significance also for the future. Whatever of wrong on the part of men the movement may involve, it is not to be imagined that this is to be corrected by the simple negation or setting aside hereafter of what has now taken place. This is no merely outward and superficial change, of such nature that the course of the world can be expected to fall back from it again, in the way of wholesome reaction, to its old established channel. Clearly, it is a grand historical fact, that is destined to remain of force in all coming time. It is idle and vain to dream of so vast and startling a step as this, being recalled and taken back, and made to become as though it had never occurred, in the onward march of the world's life. Europe can never be again, politically, the same Europe, which it has been previously to the year 1848. Even if the old order of things might seem to be restored outwardly, the inward life would not be the same. But it is not to be presumed that any such outward restoration itself, can take place. It is the disproportion of the old forms to the reigning spirit, which has at length caused their strength to give way, and no power or art can avail to reinstate them again in their ancient authority. This is a point, which deserves to be well understood and considered. The nations of Europe have been borne forward, during the past year, to new ground. A vast and mighty change has taken place in their whole constitution and posture; a change, involving a new order of political existence, and so, of course, a new period of history, for each of them separately, and for all of them collectively; a change which must affect, sooner or later, every sphere of their existence, the momentous solemnity of whose consequences no political wisdom can now measure or foretell; a change, from the power of which, in this form, there can be no recovery or retreat. Well may a thoughtful mind be filled with awe, as it looks out on the great and mighty sea of providence, here opened to its gaze, and ask to what unknown shore its waves and billows lead.

For the case will not allow us to feel, that the change has come to an end. Our faith in God rather, and 'in history, as God's work, requires us to be fully persuaded that it has only begun. It were no better than atheistic impiety, to conceive of the powers of history as working into the hands of the revolutionary spirit, now rampant in Europe, *for its own sake*. This, we have seen already, to be prevailingly radical, infidel, and ungodly, the very power of Antichrist, as it might seem, himself. As such it is doomed, of course, in due time, to pass away. Such salvation and help then, as the age needs, is to be reached, not by falling back to what is past, but by pressing forward towards something better, which is still to come. So far as there is hope in these overturnings, it is not, assuredly, in the overturnings themselves, (Luke xxi, 25—26,) but only in the sign they show of a new and better period at hand in the future, (v. 29—31). It is thus we may trust, that He, whose way is in the deep, who maketh the clouds his chariot and walketh on the wings of the wind, is leading the world forward, " with a mighty hand and an out-stretched arm, and with great terribleness, and with signs and with wonders," to a state of such spiritual freedom and prosperity as it has never yet known. The commotion and revolution now at work, are only the beginning of the end—the first convulsive shudder produced by the crisis which is passing. Other like spasms may be expected to follow. It is not without reason that some look for a general war in Europe, which shall turn throughout on the issue now joined between monarchy and republicanism, the principle of established authority on the one side, and the principle of subjective freedom on the other. "The present revolutionary period, it has been well said, "is in many respects *sui generis*. It is not so much resistance, even alleged resistance, to actual oppression, either foreign or domestic, as a war for abstract rights." Here precisely lies its profound and terrible significance. It is this consideration, above all others, which clothes with portentous solemnity the memory of the year just fled. Here, however, comes into view also, the true encouragement it offers to the eye of faith. In proportion as we see and feel the greatness of the crisis which has come, are we prepared to hail from beyond it the glorious instauration it may be expected to usher in hereafter.

The convulsions in Europe are made still more significant and impressive, when we consider in connection with them the course of events on this side of the Atlantic. Every attentive observer must see, that the relative importance of our own country, as comprehended in the general system of the civilized world, has been greatly advanced during the past year. It has been plain for a long time past, that the character and state of the world at large were likely to be powerfully affected in the end, by the progress of society in America. But no adequate sense of the truth has existed heretofore, either in Europe or among ourselves. It is wonderful indeed, how slow the European world has been, for the most part, to acknowledge the prospective bearing of our American life on the course of universal history. Even well informed scholars, only a few years since, were ready to laugh at the suggestion of anything like a problem for the whole world, comprised in what has been going forward in these ends of the earth. And we have ourselves shared so far in this feeling, as to have at least no very full confidence in the originality and independence of our separate mission. With all our self-glorification, we have been prone to lean on foreign authority, as if not entirely sure of our own stability and strength. The whole course of events, however, within the past year, has served powerfully to bring in a new sentiment on both sides. The vast significance of America has been made to loom into view, on the other side of the Atlantic, as never before. As the foundations of society are found to give way in the old world, men's minds are turned with increased attention and interest towards the new. In various ways, the unsettled state of Europe, involving as it does the failure of so much that has been trusted as permanently secure, is rapidly turning the scale of comparative promise and hope against itself, and in favor of our youthful republic. The rate of exchange, to speak in commercial phrase, has been suddenly reversed, by the terrible shock now given to all moral and political institutions in the trans-atlantic world; and both our credit and capital are made to rise, with the depreciation of so much spiritual property abroad. It has so happened besides, that the movement of history on our own side of the ocean, just at this juncture, has been such as wonderfully to justify and encourage such transfer of credit to our account. Never before has our country seemed to stand on so firm and solid a basis, as just at the present time. Never before have our institutions presented the same title to reverence and respect. Never before probably has the nation at large had the same sense of its greatness, the same consciousness of an independent world-embracing mission. The last year has done more than all years past, we may say, to emancipate the national spirit, politically and morally, from all foreign thraldom, in the way of true inward self-knowledge and self-possession. With this memorable year only, and not sooner, the American Republic might seem to have closed in full and forever the period of its minority.

It is not necessary to dwell in detail on the great and stirring events, which have passed in our history within the last three or four years, all resulting in the new posture which has now been settled and fixed in our territorial limits. Questions have come up, relating to Texas, to Oregon, to Mexico, that seemed to threaten in different ways the very existence of the Republic, filling the minds of sober men with apprehension, and seeming to turn into mockery all our dreams of enduring prosperity. The wisest statesmen have felt, that the experiment of our government was called, in these circumstances, to pass through a crisis more trying, in some respects, than any which it had ever been subjected to before. It seemed not unreasonable to fear, that the vortex of excitement and agitation into which the nation was so suddenly drawn, and from which it had no power apparently, to make its escape, would end in desperate revolution, overturning our old established state, and carrying our destiny in some new direction. Had it been divinely foretold in 1845, that the revolutionary spirit was to be let loose as it has been since among the nations, without mention of the field it should traverse, the most sagacious politicians, probably, would have been ready to locate, at least its central catastrophe, in America rather than Europe. It must have been felt, at all events, that no such general convulsion could well take place in Europe, without communicating itself by sympathy and contagion to the predisposition which seemed to be already at hand, on all sides, for the same thing in this country. And yet it has not been so. Texas has taken her place quietly, in the circle of confederate States. The Oregon boundary has been peacefully settled. The Mexican war has been conducted through a series of brilliant victories, that have filled the whole world with admiration, to a triumphant well consolidated peace. While the European world seemed to be meditating only the proper time and way for interfering with our affairs, all its energies and thoughts have been suddenly called into requisition, by the universal crash which has fallen upon it, like thunder out of a clear sky, at home. In the very midst of this vast and fearful commotion, we have been enabled to bring our own troubles, as a nation, to the happy termination just mentioned, and to take our position, with calm dignity, on the same political ground we occupied before. The nation has resumed its ancient course, only with a field of action vastly more broad and free ; and might seem, to have gathered fresh confidence and strength from its difficulties, coming out of them more recruited than exhausted, like a strong man girded for the race. It has indeed accomplished a change, that may be counted fairly parallel in magnificent meaning with the change that has taken place in Europe, and that will be found to have just as much to do in the end, no doubt, with the world-historical epoch which has been reached at this time; but under what different aspect and form! We might seem authorised, by the contrast, to compare the epoch itself with the mystic cloud at the Red Sea, which was all darkness, we are told, on one side, and on the other full of light. Its significance, in this view, may justify us in styling it emphatically, the American epoch.

It is hardly necessary to. say that our sense of the vast significance of the crisis, through which the nation has lately passed, is not conditioned at all by any opinion we may entertain of the right and justice of the measures by which it has been accomplished. With the political morality of the Mexican war, we have here nothing to do whatever; just as little as we found it proper to take our measure of history, in the case of the late revolutions in Europe, from any particular estimate of the actors immediately concerned in bringing them to pass. In this case, as in that, we must distinguish between what is human in history, and what is properly universal and divine. The first may be worthy of all reprobation, where we are still bound to adore the presence of the second. It is with the second only, the interior objective life of history, its true and proper world-sense, that we are concerned at all in our present contemplation.

Certain it is, in this view, that the great events which have occurred in our history of late, are just as full of significance for a thoughtful mind, as has now been represented. It is not easy, adequately, to express, how much is involved in the movement which has taken place, or in the general result which has been reached by its means. It has served to test the capabilities of the nation, and to make the world sensible of its resources and powers, beyond any other ordeal through which it has passed. The experiment of our republican institutions has been placed by it on a far more sure footing, than ever before. Much that seemed problematical has been settled and made sure. The mere fact of its being able to come so triumphantly through such a crisis, in the midst of so many disturbing forces at work on all sides, is an argument of utility and strength in the nation beyond any which has been exhibited before. The sudden expansion of its territory, is only in keeping with the development of its inward greatness; the moral holding equal step with the physical; the genius of the country, especially as set in contrast with the revolutionary spirit across the Atlantic, towering to an independent height, which is answerable, fairly, to the gigantic measure of its new bounds. Never before was it so respectable in the eyes of the world, never so sure of its own strength at home.

The sense of what has now been said in a general way, seems to have impressed itself strongly on many persons, in connection particularly with the occasion of our late Presidential election. Coming, as this did, on the heels of the Mexican war, with all the new relations and exciting prospects which have grown out of it, after a most earnest political campaign, and in full face of the tumultuating agitations of the European world, it might have been apprehended that such an issue joined at this time between the two great parties of our country, would bring into jeopardy at least the interests of order and peace in every direction. These considerations could not fail, at all events, to place in strong relief the significance of the experiment and example the nation was called thus to present before the eyes of the civilized world; and when this took place under the most triumphantly successful form, it is not strange that the spectacle should have produced a feeling of moral sublimity, and a sentiment of faith in the destiny of the republic, such as no occasion of a like sort in its history ever wrought before. No more impressive commentary can well be imagined, on the spirit of our institutions; no more emphatic answer to all scepticism or scorn, as exercised at their expense. The whole world beside has no such spectacle to show; the very posibility of it can hardly be imagined in any land but our own. The following statement of the case by one of our secular papers, well deserves here to be repeated and kept in mind.

"Only consider it. In the short space of less than twelve hours, the dynasty of a great nation was to be changed. Four millions of people, representing the opinions, and the will, of nearly twenty millions, were, by a simultaneous act, to decide for themselves, amid all their own diversities of sentiment, to what hands they would commit the direction of their country's mighty energies.   It must be a wonder to the millions of lookers-on, who are not imbued with republican influences, that the contest was decided so speedily, so quietly, with such an utter absence of un-reasoning passion; in fact, it may be said to have been governed solely by the inspiration of pure reason.   Imagine the attempt of a people living under a monarchy, to change, we will not say the principle of their government, but merely the dynasty, the human instruments representing or embodying that principle. Such attempts have been made in various countries, and with various success.   And everywhere the struggle has been pro-tracted, furious, anarchical, destructive; bringing into action the wildest and most ungovernable impulses of human nature, and filling the land with misery and desolation.   Here, under the benign influence and inspiration of republicanism, through the wholesome sway of matured republican habits, not only was the great work accomplished between the rising and the setting of the sun, but so calmly, in such perfect order, that no uninstructed observer could be aware that it was in progress.   The usual avocations, amusements, and enjoyments of every-day life were pursúed without a visible interruption.   All the marts of business were in their accustomed activity; carriages, public and private, went up and down the streets, as is their wont; fair women thronged the fashionable side-walks, gay in apparel, graceful in movement, giving themselves up to the pleasure or more serious purpose of the hour, as if utterly unconscious of the great political crisis ripening around them — of which, indeed, there was nothing to remind them.   Not that the magnitude of the crisis was not appreciated; not that the thousands and tens of thousands practically engaged in it were careless or indifferent as to the result; but simply because their sense of its importance was regulated and controlled by a corresponding perception of the dignity and beauty of good citizenship, which demands, first, the observance of order and decorum in all great public acts, and, second, a cheerful and hopeful acquiescence in every deter-mination of the people's will, lawfully manifested in due and proper form by a majority of the people."

The significance of what has taken place latterly on both sides of the Atlantic, lies not so much in the European or Ame-rican movement separately considered, as in the relation which the one may be seen evidently to carry towards the other. It is not possible, if God be indeed at the helm of history, that the course of things in the old and new worlds should not be

comprehended, in some way, in a common plan, and have regard thus to a single universal end; and it might reasonably be
supposed, that in proportion as the elements and powers at work
in each direction should acquire force, and seem ready to preci-
pitate themselves in their last result, the reality of this correspondence and the general form and bearing of it also, would
rise more and more into view. Accordingly, it is just here, in
fact, that the earnest and contemplative student finds most to
fix his attention and engage his admiration. The simultaneous-
ness of the two series of developments, which have burst so
suddenly and with such apparently independent process, on the
world's astounded sense, here and in Europe, may be said to
show, beyond all else perhaps, the solemn meaning of the age.
On one side, we have the breaking up of old institutions and
forms, in which has been comprehended for centuries, the central
power of the world's civilization; as though this order of life
had now finished its course, and the time were at last come for
it to be taken out of the way, in order to make room for another
stadium under some higher and better form. On the other side,
we behold suddenly springing into new importance and promise,
after long years of comparatively silent preparation, what might
seem to be here, in America, the very asylum that is needed,
and the best theatre that could be found, for the accomplishment
of so great a metempsychosis in the flow of universal history.
All indications on either side, point negatively or positively, precisely in this way. It is, in the first place, the spirit of America,
or if we choose so to call it, the genius of Protestantism, itself,
as it has come to identify itself with our American institutions,
that forms, however blindly and darkly, the propelling force in
the revolutions of Europe. They carry in themselves, under
all their whirlwind violence, the force of a deep hidden sympathy and affinity, on the part of the old world, with the political
tendency which has come to such successful experiment in the
new. This is well understood by European statesmen and
princes generally. The bent and effort of all these agitations
and throes, is not in any way towards what has been hitherto
the life of Europe, as such, but only and altogether towards the
new form which life is found to be assuming in America. This

itself speaks volumes in relation to the general nature of the crisis to which the world has now come.   Then, along with this, we have the arms of America opening on all sides—her territory suddenly adapting itself to the emergency—to welcome into her bosom the emigration, if need be, of entire nations.* With such opportunity and invitation, co-operate all sorts of difficulty and distress abroad, to make the emigration such as the world has never before beheld.   Nay, the very experiments which are made in Europe itself to satisfy the struggling

---

* It requires some effort of consideration, to have any tolerable conception at all of the territorial increase of our country latterly, and the field it now opens for the diffusion of our national life.   Take the following statement, from the late Presidental Message:

"Within less than four years, the annexation of Texas to the Union, has been consummated; all conflicting title to the Oregon Territory, south of the forty-ninth degree of north latitude, being all that was insisted on by any of my predecessors, has been adjusted; and New Mexico and Upper California have been acquired by treaty.   The area of these several territories, according to a report carefully prepared by the Commissioner of the General Land Office from the most authentic information in his possession, and which is herewith transmitted, contains 1,193,061 square miles, or 763, 559,040 acres; while the area of the remaining 29 States, and the territory not yet organized into States, east of the Rocky Mountains, contains 2,590,513 square miles, or 1,318,126,058 acres.   These estimates show that the territories recently acquired, and over which exclusive jurisdiction and dominion have been extended, constitute a country more than half as large as all that which was held by the United States before their acquisition.   If Oregon be excluded from the estimate, there will still remain within the limits of Texas, New Mexico, and California, 851,598 square miles, or 545,-012,720 acres; being an addition equal to more than one-third of all the territory owned by the United States before their acquisition: and, including Oregon, nearly as great an extent of territory, as the whole of Europe, Russia only excepted.   The Mississippi, so lately the frontier of our country, is now only its centre.   With the addition of the late acquisitions, the U. S. are now estimated to be nearly as large as the whole of Europe."

California and New Mexico, alone, surpass in extent the whole original thirteen United States, by an excess which is equal to more than three times all New England.   Adding Texas and the Santa Fe country, the new territory, without Oregon, is about equal to the *whole* territory *east* of the Mississippi, from the British provinces, to the Gulf of Mexico; or to the united territories of England, Scotland, Wales, and Ireland, France, Spain, Portugal, Italy, Prussia, Switzerland, Holland, Belgium and Denmark.   If inhabited as densely as Massachusetts, it would sustain 78,000,000 of inhabitants, or four times as many as the present population of the whole United States; or if as densely as England, it would sustain 232,000,000—nearly one quarter of the present population of the globe.

tendency of the age, seem likely, for a time at least, to turn attention only the more powerfully, through their own disastrous issue,
to the shores of America, as presenting the only field which is
fairly open for its own order of life.   Especially is such likely to
be the result, when the failure of such experiments comes to be
placed in broad contrast with the self-conservative vitality, by
which this life at home, and upon its own soil, is carried so
triumphantly through its complicated trials ; showing itself equal
to all emergencies, maintaining its identity through all changes,
and absorbing into its own constitution, with · overwhelming
assimilation, all elements and tendencies, however uncongenial
before with its own nature, or incongruous among themselves.
It would seem as if God were plainly showing, by this very
relation, the true sense of what is taking place; and that nothing
can meet the necessities of the time, but such a new period of
history as requires for its development, the winding up in
full of that which has gone before, and with it the shifting entirely of theatre and scene to make room for its transaction.
Should the course of things in Europe continue to be, for any
length of time, as little auspicious as it has been thus far, it is
quite possible that this reflection alone may become in the end
a more powerful stimulus to emigration than all other causes
now at work in this direction.   Altogether, with the increase of
inducement here, and constraining force at home, and easy
communication between, the transplanting process which has
now commenced, may easily enough assume hereafter, and that
too, in a comparatively short time, such a form as hardly any
imagination yet has ventured to dream.   The world may yet
see, in new form, another *Voelkerwanderung*, that shall be re-
cognised hereafter as parallel, in the history of Christianity and
civilization, with that which overturned, in the fifth century, the
old Roman life, to make room, through such chaos, for the new
creation which has since risen in its place.

We wish to be rightly understood.   When we read in the
present state of the world, the approach of a new historical period, whose character and course are to be determined prevailingly by the new order of life which reigns in America, we are
not so foolish as to conceive of this under the form of a simple

triumph of our national spirit, as it now stands, over the social and political institutions of the old world; as though all had been wrong on this last side, and all on the first side were wise, and right and good; so that the controversy between them must be considered a contest purely of light and darkness, the cause of God and human happiness arrayed in broad and open antagonism to the cause of Satan and human wickedness. To hear some persons talk, one might suppose the history of the world to have been without sense or reason, until men came to exercise some little intelligence here lately, in America. The social organization of Europe, as it has existed since the Reformation itself, even in Protestant countries, is regarded as a system of unmitigated abominations, which it is only strange the human mind should have been willing to endure for so long a time. In the vocabulary of this wholesale school, monarchy and tyranny are identical terms, while republicanism is only another word for freedom. The full civilization and proper happiness of the world, are supposed to demand the prostration of all monarchical institutions, as a corruption and abuse. Kings are to be hated, as usurpers of a power which has never been given to them of God. It is by a righteous retribution, accordingly, that, in the providence of God, they are now driven from their thrones, or made to sit upon them with fear and trembling. The salvation of the world turns upon its coming in this way to a just sense of its inborn rights and capabilities; and we may trust accordingly, that God is interposing at this time, in the revolutionary spirit of the age, to bring the whole civilized world into the true liberty of nations, as we have it here happily exemplified, under the most perfect form, in these United States. How far this way of thinking prevails, need not be said. We own, however, no sympathy with it whatever. As already intimated, the revolutionary spirit, as now at work in Europe, is entitled to no sort of confidence or respect. In its own constitution, it is from beneath rather than from above; and the work accordingly, which it is pretending to accomplish, may not be expected to stand. Its significance is not so much in itself, as in the yet undeveloped life towards which transitionally it points and leads. This lies in the direction which the course of history has already begun to take in America, and may be expected to come to its central revelation finally, by means of the theatre here opened for its use.   But we have no right to assume, in such case, that the ulterior life of the world, as it is to be reached in this way, will be simply our American state of society, as it now stands, substituted by universal exchange for every other political order; as though we had long since fallen on the perfect idea of both Church and State, and the rest of the world now were required only to throw away all its previous thoughts and habits, and come to our position.   This would be a most weak and extravagant imagination.   Of one thing we may be very sure.   If America be indeed destined to introduce a new order of life for the world, and to open the way for a new period of universal history, it will not be by standing over against the whole previous life of the world, as something false and bad.   History in any case, goes forward, not by the mere negation and exclusion of what is thrown into the rear, but by such a setting aside of this as serves, at the same time, to save its interior substance and sense under a higher form.   So, in the case before us, the problem to be accomplished is not, simply, the triumph of one existing order of life over another, in an outward way.   It is not America wrestling with the world, as Hercules overcame the serpent in his cradle; but it is the world itself rather, wrestling in its own inmost constitution, through the medium of American influence, towards a general and common end, which may be said to embrace the sense of its whole history for centuries past.

Nothing can well be more out of character here, than the sophomorical style of self-glorification with which we are assailed, in certain quarters, on this subject.   It betrays always a narrow vulgarity of mind, which is as far as possible remote from the true genius of the dispensation, whose advent it affects to trumpet in this Pharisaic way.   It is the exclusiveness of Chinese vanity, which dreams itself in possession already of the " celestial empire," and can only commiserate or despise the barbarian world that lies beyond; but which, for this very reason, is itself doomed to perpetual imprisonment in the treadmill of its own miserable pedantry and conceit.   If America be called to mediate and bring about a new historical period for the world, as so many signs seem to show, she must be the very opposite of China ; not walling out the life of the world in its other forms, but making room for it rather, and offering it hearty welcome in her broad and capacious bosom. She must be willing to receive and learn from all sides, as well as to communicate and teach. She must feel, not that she is the world herself, but that she is fast becoming the theatre on which the central power of the world's history is to be displayed. In proportion, precisely, as this comes to be more and more the case, she must cease more and more to appear as an isolated interest ; the substance of all previous history will be found pouring itself into the open channel of her life; and only in this way will she be prepared, more and more, with proper inward qualification on her own part, to become the organ of a new universal life for the nations. The activity of the old world, for the last three hundred years, has not been without purpose; and the results of it are not now to be set aside as null and void. Nor is it necessary, by any means, to suppose that the nations of Europe have yet completed their part in the great drama ; or that they are to save their importance, only by at once confessing their whole past life to have been a lie, and consenting to take a fresh start politically, in the footsteps of the American republic. The case calls for no such wild extravagant supposition. Europe is not to be set aside as a grand failure. The true wealth of her past life will be carried forward to the new state, in which her institutions are to be finally perfected in their own form, by means of this crisis; only to become thus more valuable, by growing accumulation, always for the service of the world at large.

The historical significance of America thus far, lies mainly in this, that the substance of its life, as it is to be hereafter, is *not* yet fixed, but in the process only of general formation ; under such condititions and relations as are needed to bring it finally to a character of universal wholeness and completeness, beyond all the world is found to have produced before. We cannot speak of our American nationality as a settled and given fact, in the same way that we may speak of the nationality of England or France. The nation is ruled indeed by its own independent genius, and carries in itself a certain inward law or

type, that may be expected to determine permanently the leading form of its history. But all is still in a process of growth;
and the circumstances of the country make it impossible to bind
this process to any outward lines or limits. Even if the idea
might have been entertained in any quarter hertofore, that some
certain form of thought and life had acquired the right of stamp-
ing the country forever with its own image and superstition, to
the exclusion of all besides, every such conception is in a fair
way of being effectually exploded by the course of things at the
present time. No pent up Utica of this sort, which might have
been tempted before to make itself the measure of the whole
world, can well fail to be put out of countenance now, by the
continental size of our territory, and the rolling tide of emigration, with which it is coming to be so rapidly occupied and
filled from the other side of the Atlantic. The day for " Nativ-
ism," in all its forms, is fast drawing to an end. Whether for
weal or for woe, the life of Europe is to be poured in upon our
shores without restraint or stint, till it shall cause the ancient
blood of the land to become in quantity a mere nothing in comparison. God is fast showing, by the stupendous course of his
providence, that this American continent was designed from the
start, not for the use of a single race, but for the world at large.
Here room has been provided, with all the outward necessary
conditions, for the organization of a new order of life, that may
be as broad and universal as the soil it shall cover; and now the
material out of which it is to be formed, the elements that are
needed for such world embracing constitution, are made to flow
together from every side, for the purpose of being wrought into
a new nationality which shall at last adequately represent the
whole. What will be the form precisely in which this nationality shall become complete, the historical substance in which it
shall come finally to proper harmony and consistence within itself, in art, manners, literature, science and religion, it is impossible now, of course, to foresee or predict. We know only,
that the social and moral character of America is not yet settled,
and that the greatness of the country and its true promise, are
comprehended in this fact. Its inward history is quite as young
as its outward history; having but just passed, as it were, the

stage of childhood, in its onward progress to mature life. It has been emphatically styled the land of the future; and so it is in truth. Its true significance, since the days of Columbus, has lain in its relations to coming time; and with all the actual importance now belonging to it, the full measure of its greatness is still comprehended in what it is soon to become, rather than what it has become already. All signs unite to show that a new order of world history is at hand, and that the way is to be prepared for it centrally in America. Here a theatre is already secured, sufficiently broad for the process; the conditions required for it are showing themselves to be more and more at hand; the elements to be used in it, are wonderfully brought together from all sides; while all the indications of God's providence are conspiring towards the grand result, in which it is to become complete.

It were a most arrogant presumption, contrary to all history and all true philosophy alike, to suppose that the new historical period required by the world, is to proceed from the life of this country, just as it now stands, in an outward mechanical way. The country offers simply the necessary basis and room, for the elaboration of what is wanted, a properly universal spirit, in which the contradictions of the past shall be made to pass away. All particularism is excluded from the process, by its very conception. It must involve the reciprocal action of manifold tendencies and powers. The result must be, not abstract Americanism over against the rest of the world, but such an incorporation of the true substance of history from all sides into the American character, as may fairly and fully qualify it to become the type of the world's life universally. It is not enough that the outward material of the nation be gathered from all lands; it must take up into its inward constitution also, what is of worth in the mind and heart of all lands; so as to be, not merely a mixture of the several reigning nationalities, but an inward reproduction of their true sense under a new organic and universal form. How much remains still to be accomplished for this purpose, in our literature and culture generally, it is not necessary to say. But the forces are already powerfully at work, whose vastly accumulated strength may be expected to prove fully sufficient in due time, for the accomplishment of so great an end; while the palpable destiny of the nation, in the view now under consideration, forms in itself, at the same time, a certain guaranty that it will not fail to be reached.

Did our limits allow, it might be interesting to notice in detail, some of the more striking indications or signs, in the form of single scattered facts, which go to confirm the general anticipation now presented. It lies in any just conception of the world, as the evolution of a divine plan, that every great change in its history, must be preceded by a certain amount of preparation in its whole system, revealing itself in many new facts, apparently unconnected, which serve, in different measure, to foreshadow what is coming. A number of such facts are known to have led the way for the great epoch of the Reformation. Among them may be mentioned, the fall of Constantinople, the invention of printing, the discovery of America, the revival of classical learning, and various changes to which the social and political systems of Europe had come in the process of their own action. These and other facts, were of force, not on the ground simply of any direct bearing they may have exercised on the event of the Reformation itself, but much more as their ultimate necessity and sense may be said to have lain far forward in the new period which was to follow. Their *significance* was in the future; and in such a future as the world could not then rightly comprehend. And in the same way, precisely, we may read the advent of the great period now in prospect, in many most significant facts of the present time, the full power and meaning of which, look plainly beyond the whole constitution of the world, as it now stands.

Here belong the wonderful discoveries and inventions of the age generally, which have been following each other for some time in such form as never before, and whose action is already undermining the existing order of things, quietly but surely, at so many different points. We are apt to lose sight of the broad difference that is coming to exist more and more in this way, between our own circumstances outwardly considered, and those in which the world has stood in former times; and we seldom appreciate properly the bearing of such change on the structure of society or the progress of history. It needs no great reflection, however, to see that this cause alone is carrying the world forward, with uncontrollable necessity, to a social and political state, in which our present modes of existence are likely to become as fully antiquated before long, as are to us now the social relations and forms of the period before the Reformation. The cause is one, moreover, which may be expected to grow continually upon itself, and to multiply its own powers indefinitely. The rate of improvement is accelerated by its own progress; every new invention but paves the way for another; and the first effects of the change also, in each case, are no adequate measure at all of the long train of results to follow. Only think of what has been already wrought by the agency of steam; and yet how small a part of its mission, in all probability, has it yet accomplished? The mastery of mind over matter, has been amazingly advanced within the present century. The resources and powers of nature have been brought into subjection and made subservient to the purposes of civilization in a way which it would have been madness to dream of in former times. Especially worthy of note is the conquest gained more and more over time and space; by which the different parts of the world are brought continually nearer together, and made to verge from all sides towards the idea of a truly universal life. Mountains fall, seas shrink, rough places are made plain, and crooked places straight, in preparation as it might seem, for the most free intercourse and union among the nations. The ends of the earth are contracted, and its most retired and inaccessible regions are laid bare and open. Old barriers and divisions are fast falling away. With the entire change of relations which is coming upon it in this way, the world as it has been is plainly ready to vanish away; and it is equally plain that its history hereafter must show such a character of consolidation and universality as it has never known before.

And it needs no very active imagination certainly, to see in these conquests over nature and time and space, a peculiar prophetic bearing on the mission of this country, as manifestly ordained of Heaven to lead the way in the new order of things which is thus at hand. The processes of improvement and culture, are thus made answerable to the vast scale of our resources and opportunities. The work of years is accomplished in as many days. The multiplication of wealth and power goes forward as by magic. Cities and states spring up like the creations of romance. And still this vast growth of the nation brings with it no unwieldiness or want of strength. On the contrary, with its increasing volume, it is becoming always only more and more compact. It is more present with itself in all its parts now, than it was at the time of the Revolution; and there is good reason to believe that, when its population shall reach from the Atlantic to the Pacific, the bond that holds it together will be still more close and sure than it is at the present time. Space and distance are more and more annihilated as they are brought into the way; and the horizon of the country falls in dynamically upon its centre, in proportion as it recedes from it, in the way of outward vision, on every side.

Who can estimate prospectively the bearings of the *Electric Telegraph* on the course of coming history? It is sufficient of itself, in time, to change the entire order of the world's life. Shall we dream of it as an accident only, in the economy of providence? Or are we not bound rather to see in it a prophetic intimation of what is near at hand in God's plan, a new historical period, namely, in which full room shall be found for its widest use? Does it not point to such concentration and universalness in the coming civilization of the world, as men have had no conception of in ages past? Its main significance undoubtedly lies, not in the present, but in the future. Like the art of printing, it carries unborn revolutions in its womb. Those silent posts and wires mean more than all the thunder of Napoleon's artillery. A thousand mobs of Paris or Berlin, are but as the drop of the bucket, or the small dust of the balance, in comparison.

One other American improvement, still only in theory, but destined, soon, we may trust, to pass into magnificent effect, deserves to fix for a moment, our most earnest attention. It is *Whitney's* project of a *railroad*, to span the entire continent, from Lake Michigan to the shores of the Pacific. We hardly know how to trust ourselves in speaking of this vast and stupendous design. Thought is confounded, and the very imagination

itself is made to stagger, in looking down the long vista of results
which it opens to our gaze, more like the tales of the Arabian
Nights, than the sober realities of experience as it now stands.
And yet the whole thing lies as much within the range of plain
rational calculation, as any Yankee economist could desire. The
practicability of the measure is clear for all who choose to make
it a subject of examination. It is equally clear, that all providential signs are urging at this time towards its accomplishment.
The sense of our late acquisition of territory, can be made complete in no other way. Oregon and California can be held for
the nation, only by this road. Thus the true significance of
America for the world, would seem to hang upon its construction. Let no one say that this is making too much of the merely
outward and physical, for human history. The outward and
physical, here, are the force of mind itself, yoking nature to its
chariot wheels. Who that knows anything of history, can be
ignorant of the power which has been exercised upon it in all
ages, by the course of commerce? A new channel opened for
trade, has ever been sufficient to throw the kaleidoscope of nations into new form. Kingdoms rise and fall with the change
of mercantile routes and marts. Tyre, Alexandria, Palmyra,
Venice, what a lesson do they not read on this subject! But of
all levers that have ever been applied in such way to the course
of civilization, none can be named as fairly parallel with this
railroad to the Pacific. Its consequences must be boundless for
the entire globe. By no possibility can the world after its accomplishment continue to be the same. Europe and Asia must join
hands across the American continent. We will be in truth the
centre of the world; and not simply its centre in an outward
view, but the great beating heart we may say of humanity itself,
through which shall circulate the life blood of its nations, and
that shall serve as a common bond to gather them all into one
vast brotherhood of interest and love. New York will be brought
within twenty-five days travel of China. The commerce of the
whole earth will fall under our command and control. We shall
become thus a thoroughfare for the world, and its treasures will
be laid at our feet. At the same time, in thus connecting continents and oceans, we shall bind our own republic together with

such a bond as we can have under no other form. This bridge of nations will form also the arch of the American union, and the world's weight always passing over it will serve only to render it continually more solid and firm It is utterly impossible to calculate at present the immense results that must flow from the accomplishment of this single work, for America and for the earth at large. All social and political relations, art, literature, science and religion, in one word, the universal course of history must be brought by means of it to assume an entirely new form.

While Europe and Asia are in the way thus of coming together in the bonds of a new commerce mediated by America, it is most interesting to see the door opening apparently for a similar junction of our American life with the dark continent of Africa. Liberia is still an infant experiment; but the proportions of a Hercules already begin to show themselves in its limbs.— The experiment has proceeded so far, that prejudice itself is forced to look upon it with respect, as carrying in itself now every guaranty that could well be asked of an ultimate success, whose measure shall equal or perhaps transcend the largest calculations of its friends. It is no chimerical dream at present, to look forward to the day as by no means remote, when a flourishing and powerful nation, politically sprung from the American republic, and in close, active correspondence with its life, shall be found spreading far and wide along the shores of Africa, and carrying the blessings of civilization and religion towards its benighted interior. The results of this for Africa itself and for the world, it is not necessary that we should here pretend to foretell. Every one may see that they must be immense. What is mainly interesting, however, and worthy of note, is the concomitance in which this prospect stands with the signs of coming vast revolution in the entire order of the world's life on other continents, and the way in which it conspires with these signs from every side, to indicate prophetically the central relation of America to the period of universal history which is to follow. The world is fast coming together from the four ends of heaven ; it is urged from all sides towards a new system of existence, under such a character of consolidated universality as it has never yet known ; and it would seem plain that the organic law by which all this is

to be reached, is to proceed from the United States mainly, as the
land through which, in God's plan, all the nations of the earth are to
be blessed.   In such view it is that we feel ourselves authorised to
speak of the present crisis as emphatically the AMERICAN EPOCH.'

It has beome an established maxim in the philosophy of history
that the culture of the human race moves with the course of the
sun, from east to west.   " *Westward* the star of empire takes its
way."   Art, literature, science, politics, philosophy and religion
started in Asia, and their inward development from the beginning
has been accomplished by means of a corresponding outward
emigration ever since towards the setting sun.   Now they are in
the process apparently of entering upon a new stadium on this side
of the Atlantic; which, by analogy, may be expected to be more
complete than any which has gone before.   But, with the completion of our American civilization, the circuit of the globe will
be fulfilled, and the end brought round once more to the beginning.   Will the old movement then be gone over again under a
higher form?   Hardly.   The world will be brought so together as
to leave no room farther for the idea of any such successional cycle.
All betokens rather the abrogation of this law, as one that shall
have finished its necessary course, by making room for the inte-
gration of all stages of the world's life ultimately into the conception of its proper *manhood*, as this is to be revealed in the
new universalized culture, towards which so many signs are
pointing and so many powers struggling at the present time.
But we venture here on no farther speculation.

Let no one think, however, that we make too much of the outward progress of the age, in inferring from it the approach of a
new order also of culture and civilization.   We know very well
that the triumph of mind over matter is not of itself an advance
in morality and religion ; that a supreme devotion to material
interests is at war with the higher ends of the spirit ; that there
may be a titanic mastery over nature, which is at last in league
only with the powers of hell against the law of heaven.   But
we know too, that this is not the true constitution of our life.
Man is formed to rule the world in the image of God and for
God's glory.   The great problem of morality is to be fulfilled
by the complete subjugation of nature to its high behests.   The

last sense then of all outward improvements in the state of the world, lies necessarily in their final subserviency to its moral culture. It is not possible thus, with any faith in God, to look upon the signs of revolution with which we are now surrounded, as either without meaning altogether for man's spiritual history, or as significant only of coming evil. It is not by accident, surely, that so many new powers and resources are coming to be developed at this time, or that the outward relations of the world are so rapidly passing into new shape. All these things belong to a divine plan; and this, in the nature of the case, has regard to the highest end of humanity as comprehended in the religion of Jesus Christ. The victory of Christianity will be no Vandal barbarism, exercised at the cost of all outward civilization; but the free and willing homage rather of all art and science at its feet. However adverse then, under any particular aspect, the present course of things may seem to be to spiritual Christianity, we are bound to see in it notwithstanding, not negatively only, but positively also, a glorious preparation for such a reign of the Spirit as has not yet been known. Indeed, there is no alternative here for Christianity, but conquest or defeat. It must keep pace with the onward movement of the world—a movement that cannot be put back; or else stand openly exposed, as impotent altogether for the accomplishment of its own mission. The accelerated, concentrated, consolidated action of the world's outward life, must lead in some way to a corresponding energy in its moral organization. Otherwise it must perish titanically, through the wanton exercise of its heaven-climbing powers. How all is to come to pass, it may be hard for us now to see; but in the end, the physical or merely natural maturity of our race, will bring along with it also a parallel ripeness in its spiritual constitution. Such a new order of things as we see to be at hand, is at once the argument and guaranty of a new advance to be made in universal civilization.

As our article is already too long, we conclude with some general reflections, rapidly and briefly thrown together, in the way of hint merely, and stimulus for farther thought to such as know how to think.

1. There is a woe pronounced in the Bible, on those, (Isaiah,

iv. 12,) that "regard not the work of the Lord, neither consider the operation of his hands." And surely it must be taken as the mark of an irreligious and brutish mind, at this time, not to be affected by the tokens of God's presence with which we are surrounded, or not to be roused by them to some earnest and profound thought. For the judgments of God are not merely to be gazed at with passive animal stupefaction. They are instinct with the light of reason, and are so many challenges to the exercise, first of faith, and then of manly, vigorous speculation. It is a poor thing, to be so immersed in material interests and forms, as to have no eye for the far more magnificent realities of the spirit. It is a sad business to be so occupied with the mere outward sound and show of history, as to have no sense for the divinity it enshrines within. To believe in God truly, one must see him in nature and history; and this implies an earnest apprehension of both, as full of infinite wisdom and love. To look upon history as chaos, without form and void, is such a sin against faith, as it were to banish in thought all order and reason out of nature in the same way. And yet to this it comes at last, where men either deny openly and at once the idea of a universal plan and process in the course of the world's life, or at least deride all endeavors to understand it, as idle, if not presumptuous mysticism. From all such rationalistic *frivolousness* of the common understanding, deliver us, good Lord!

2. One great cause of such unbelief is found in the general selfishness of our nature, which prompts us to subordinate the general and universal to our own petty particularities. We are bound accordingly, in the case before us, to widen our thinking and interest, as much as possible, into some correspondence with the universal character of the crisis to which the world appears to have come. One great advantage of such a crisis is, that it naturally tends to produce this spiritual enlargement. Our constitution is such that universal interests are fitted to move us more deeply than any that are merely private, lying as they do indeed more intimately near the proper foundation of our life. It behooves us then to make room for their action in our souls. and not to shut it out by the stubborn egotism of our thoughts. We must not dream of bringing the course of universal history

into subserviency to *our* particular interests and aims as such, as though God were concerned, in all the revolutions of the age, only to play into our hands, and were pleading the cause of American politics, American opinions, &c., as such, against all the rest of the world. In religion, for instance, we have no right to assume that all the truth of universal Christianity is gathered up into our particular sect or system, Methodism, Puritanism, or any other like narrow interest, and that all variant systems, past or present, are to the same extent false, needing simply to be perfected by an unreserved translocation over to *our* ecclesiastical camp. All such pedantry is ridiculous, and directly at war at the same time with the true sense and meaning of the age. The first condition, we may say, for understanding or fulfilling our duty is, that it should be fully laid aside. So in the case of literature, science, and philosophy in general.

3. As the present course of things invites to wide and comprehensive thinking, so it is also eminently suited to confound and put to shame all narrow theories and schemes. Mere insular traditions must give way; not only such as belong to the old world, Germany, France, England, &c., but those also which have already begun to assert their tough life in the new. The idea that the form of existence which is to rule the world hereafter, is at hand here, as a given fact, in some corner or section of America, under this or that phase of thought and life, however it may have been able to keep itself in countenance heretofore, is in a fair way now of being effectually put to rest. Outward formulas, hereditary notions, mechanical stereotype rules of any sort whatever, will not answer for the time that is now at hand. Only living intellect and waking will, may be expected to carry with them any force.

4. And still the revolution which is coming will not be radical, in such a way as to break with past history. In bursting the bonds of particular forms and traditions, it will yet seek to incorporate into itself the sense of the universal past. This is implied by the way in which it is coming to pass. All particularism is excluded for the very purpose of securing for it a universal character; and the powers of the world's life are made to flow together in its service, from every quarter. Not as an abrupt

rupture with the previous civilization of Europe, but only as the true historical continuation of it under a higher and more world embracing form, will it be entitled at all to confidence and respect. Radicalism may mix itself with the course of history—is doing so at this time largely in Europe; just as blind traditionalism may mix with it also in a different direction. These two, indeed, are apt to be coupled closely together, and strangely enough involve at bottom very much the same falsehood. But history itself is neither radical nor traditional. It always moves away from the past, and still at the same time, never leaves it behind.

5. In the midst of the general revolution which is coming, the *Church* will be brought to assume a new form. The year 1848, has done more to shake the outward organization of the Church, than any year before or since the time of the Reformation. Romanism is made to tremble in the very heart of its own empire. Its ancient pillars seem ready to give way. The Church of the Reformation, on the continent of Europe, is threatened with universal dilapidation. It must pass through a process of reconstruction, in order that it may at all continue to stand. Just now the pressure of political intersts weighs down the question of the Church. But it will come forward in due time, with overwhelming interest. Nor can the posture of the Church in this country, be considered by any means as settled and complete. Our sect system is not the normal form of Christianity. No intelligent man is willing to stand forward openly in its defence, under any such view. In some way, sooner or later, it must come to an end. The *Church of the Future* cannot be the same in this respect with the Church of the Present.

6. In what form the Church will surmount finally her present trials, in the new period which appears to be at hand, we may not venture now of course to predict. The tendencies of the age seem on first view, it must be confessed, unfavorable to the idea of any outward catholic organization. But this is not at once to be taken for granted. What we see may be only the negative side of a process, whose ultimate sense is very different. One thing is clear. The way is opening for an universal consolidation in the general life of the world, far beyond all that has been seen in previous ages; and this of course must embrace

Christianity and the Church as well as other interests. Is it to be supposed that the Church, in these circumstances, will be less united and compact within itself than it has been heretofore? Or will it be imagined that its unity is to resolve itself into a mere invisible sentiment? And yet the *idea* of the Church seems to involve unity, catholicity, and visibility, as its necessary elements wherever it has come to be felt as an object of faith. To God we commit the mighty problem. May he resolve it soon in his own glorious way.

MERCERSBURG.   J. W. N.

ART. III.—THE RULE OF FAITH.

THE great interest taken of late, in subjects supposed to have been fully settled ages ago, has been a source of no trifling embarrassment to some of our Protestant theologians. Having no faith in the historical development of theology, they are half tempted to suspect that the ecclesiastical chronometer must be in advance of time by a few centuries. At least the awkward attempts occasionally made, to account for the "alarming fact" that one of these subjects, the Authority of Tradition, or the Rule of Faith, has called forth, within a few years past, so many books* and so much discussion, indicate a considerable degree

---

* The following to the writer's knowledge:—In England—1. *Tracts for the Times*, Oxford;—2. *Keble's Sermons*, Oxford;—3. *Palmer's Aids to Reflection*; 4. *Newman on Romanism*;—5. *The Divine Rule of Faith and Practice*, by Wm. Goode, Cambridge;—6. *Not Tradition but Scripture*, by Dr. Shuttleworth, Oxford;—7. *The Authority of Tradition in Matters of Religion*, by George Holden;—8. *Tradition Unveiled*, by Bader Powell, Oxford;—9. *Essay on Omissions*,—and 10. *The Kingdom of Christ Delineated*, by Archbishop Whately, Dublin. In Germany—11. *Philipp Melanchthon der Glaubenslehre*, Von F. Del-

of alarm and perplexity. True, one writer[*] upon the subject, seems to form an exception in the case. He thinks it by no means "difficult to account" for the fact above stated. And his reason is rendered with a confidence that anticipates no contradiction. Of course this reason is found in Romanism. Quite a convenient method of cutting knots, with this Roman sword! Convenient in view of the readiness of a great portion of the Protestant church to denounce Popery as the root of all our troubles. And, must it not be added, especially convenient when it might be somewhat unpleasant for an ultra-protestant to confess the truth! There is marvellous consolation in being able to blame a foreign agent as the guilty cause of all our griefs! "The serpent beguiled me, and I did eat!"

But what is gained in the end by daubing over the sore places of Protestantism with such untempered mortar? If, after all, the sores have not come from contagion, but are the breaking out of an inward impurity, will not some enemy do double mischief by exposing the self-deception or deceit? Are, moreover, the excellencies and attractions of our system so few and superficial, that its defects must be painted over, or concealed, to secure it from derision? If this be so, alas, for the Reformation and for Protestantism! But we have more faith in the great legacy bequeathed by the spiritual heroes of the XVIth century, than to think such artifices requisite. It is too glorious a legacy to be darkened by a few specks upon its face; (though they, like those of the sun, be mountains;) or to be really injured by any attempts to magnify and expose those specks, made by enemies

broeck, Bonn, *answered* by Sack, Nitzsh, Lueche and others;—12. *Von d. Tradition als Princip d. protestant. Dogmatik*, von Pelt;—13 *Theologische Controversen*, von Dr. H. A. Daniel, Halle, (to be esteemed for its candor and research but otherwise very objectionable.) This of course is a very deficient list of German works on the subject, but the writer has access to no better at present. In the United States—14. *Biblical Repertory*, Princeton, 1842;—15. *A Dissertation on the Rule of Faith*, by Dr. Spring, New York;—16. *Lectures on the British Reformation*, by Bishop Hopkins;—17. *Daillé on the Right use of the Fathers*, republished by the Presbyterian Board;—18. *Geneva and Oxford*, a Discourse by Dr. Merle D'Aubigne, translated by Dr. Baird.

[*] *Princeton Theological Essays, First Series, Essay I.*

that love to have Protestantism looked at through smoked lenses. The Catholic Church of the Reformation, bears her specific name, from the loud and decided *protest* she has always raised against error in every form and wherever found. Should then the same church, in the XIXth century, be false to her characteristic zeal, by refusing to recognize and uproot those errors which may still cling to her policy or creed?

What answer then shall be given to the question touching the deep and general interest taken in discussions upon this subject? How did it come to be renewedly agitated? And how did it happen to create and keep up till now, such prevailing interest? The reason assigned in the article alluded to, is believed to be erroneous. It is there wholly *assumed* that the recent unusual efforts of Popery have awakened these new discussions, or that any influential connection exists between the operations of Rome and the Oxford Tracts, and still less between the former and the interest taken in the subject by those who do not belong to the Oxford school. The novelty of the thing cannot be thought to have caused this agitation. How many discussions, Tracts intended for the Times, new schemes and theories advocated by Quarterlies, and profound dissertations on " vital subjects," are cast upon the waters to sink without a ripple! Why then should this occasion so much commotion? If we shall answer candidly to these things, must we not say, that the entire discussion sprang up spontaneously from the bosom of the Protestant Church, and that it awakened the degree of interest which immediately ensued, in consequence of the extreme position occupied upon the subject by that church? Is it not reasonable to suppose that, if the foundation on which Protestantism was believed to rest in regard to this subject, had not been thought hay and stubble, or something equally combustible, the fire brand cast into its midst would have been allowed to die out for want of fuel? Would the sentinels have sounded an alarm if they thought their citadel secure?

This we believe is a nearer approximation at least, to the true cause of our trouble. It cannot be thought strange that when men begin to suspect the firmness of the foundation on which they stand, they should take deep and common interest in whatever exposes its weakness, or increases its strength. And if *Faith* be what evangelical Protestantism makes it, then nothing can be of greater moment, than to *know certainly what to believe*, and consequently to possess a *certain Rule of Faith.*

It is with these convictions, and with the hope of contributing somewhat to the determination of this subject, that the present essay is undertaken.

I. And in order to make the examination of our subject the more intelligent and pleasant a work, let us first agree upon a *just definition of the terms in which it is expressed.* Much confusion, and more contention might undoubtedly have been saved, but for the neglect of determining at once the precise point in debate. This will be evident upon reference to some of the more prominent essays upon this vexed question. When one* incidentally, and by the collection of the several separated parts from different pages into one sentence, defines the Rule of Faith to be a rule *"fit to direct every one that will make the best use of it, in reference to all the material objects of faith, so complete as to need no addition, and so evident, that it needs no interpretation ;"* and another,† *"the authority by which our Faith must be governed ;"* and a third,‡ *" that by which our faith is to be directed and measured ;"* and when most others proceed without any definition formal or incidental, and with at best very vague intimations of what they regard as a proper definition ; it is little to be wondered at, that whatever else their discussion of the subject may have determined, the real point at issue is as widely open as ever. That one or another theory, or conceit in reference to the matter, may in this way be exploded,§ will hardly compensate for the false impression under which many are left, supposing the entire case finally and satisfactorily disposed of, whilst only one error has been routed. Proving Oxford and Rome to be wrong, will hardly in itself make the advocate of another view right, unless it had been previously demonstrated

---

*Chillingworth's Works, Philadelphia. 1841. p. 111, 109, 108.

†Bishop Hopkins on the British Reformation. p. 11.

‡Prot. Quarterly Review, April 1847, p. 106.

§As that of Oxford, by the Princeton essay referred to above.

that the choice lay between the three. And yet may not an oversight of what is really to be understood by the Rule of Faith, and of what is actually needed under that term, have led to the opposite conviction, and have encouraged some to believe, that because Dr. Spring or Dr. Hodge had successfully contended against the Tracts for the Times, and the Council of Trent upon this subject, therefore, the view now prevailing, or at least professing to prevail in the Protestant Church, must be the only alternative?

But some will say that in so plain and simple a case there is no need of a definition. To which it may be replied, first, that the discussion of the subject, as carried on for years past, does not favor this objection; and secondly, that definitions are often given of simple terms.

In making out a proper definition of our subject, there are several considerations deserving notice. *One* is, that when we speak of the Rule of Faith, *we do not mean something that is such in an abstract, but in a relative sense.* In the *former* sense none but a Romanist or Tractarian would consider any thing as "co-ordinate, or subordinate, or subservient to, or blended with,"* the Holy Scriptures. In themselves considered, those scriptures unquestionably contain a complete and perfect system of truth. They lack nothing in regard to clearness or sufficiency. They are altogether what their Divine author designed they should be. Upon every doctrine intended to be revealed, there is shed sufficient light to make it as clear as it was intended to make it; that is, clear enough to be ascertained upon certain conditions on the part of those possessing the divine word. And every page of it bears proof, not only of a superintending influence, but of plenary inspiration. In itself, therefore, it is Rule, and Judge, and Sentence. So that if it were our business to determine what was an abstract Rule of Faith, we should only need to prove the authenticity of the Bible. This sacred book however does not in reality occupy an abstract position. It stands at every point in the most intimate relation to those for whose benefit it was given.

---

*Oxford veiw, quoted by Whately—Kingdom of Christ. p. 61.

And it is *in this relative sense* that we need a Rule, by which
to determine whether views and opinions, professedly derived
from the Bible, may be approved or must be condemned.
Whether the Bible alone is, in this sense, the only Rule of
Faith, shall be considered in the proper place.

Another thought not to be overlooked, and one to be inferred
from what has just been said, is that the *Rule* required *is not at
the same time to be the judge and jury in the case.* For however successfully this may be insisted upon in an argument with
Romanism,* or Puseyism, it is certainly a petitio principii in the
present case. And inasmuch as what is needed, is a Rule by
which to be assured that certain interpretations of the Bible are
to be accepted or rejected, it will certainly not be thought adequate to appeal to the same book *alone*, either for their maintenance or suppression. It were a novel thing, or at any rate
puerile, for a Lawyer to defend a disputed opinion of a law, by
simple reference to the law itself. The question, therefore,
being in every case where a Rule is needed and applied, " what
is the true interpretation of this or the other set of Bible passages," must we not have a Rule which is different from those
scriptures themselves? And must not they who use this Rule discharge the part of judge in the case, the rule being that according
to which they decide? For since it is upon the true *import of
the sentence of scriptures* that judgment is to be passed, in reference to any private or individual opinion of its doctrine, neither
the person holding such opinion, nor those examining it, can
satisfactorily rest, with a simple reference to what may appear to
the one or the other, to be the true meaning of the words separately in which that sentence is expressed, or to their sense collectively considered.

Our Rule of faith *must* further *not be an arbitrary law*,
enacted and enforced by a spiritual despotism, (of which Rome
unquestionably furnishes the most fearful specimen,) for the purpose of securing outward union, and slavish conformity to a creed
formed in an equally arbitrary way. On the contrary, it must
rest upon the broad basis of reason and truth. To none other

---

*As is done most ably by Chillingworth, Works—p. 111—115.

4*

are rational and responsible men bound to submit. On the other hand however *it must set proper limits, and impose requisite restraints upon the lawless exercise of private judgment.* For with all the eloquent boasting and debate upon the *right of private judgment*, it is presumed no one will contend that it extends beyond the privilege of *judging aright.* No man possesses the right, either from God or his fellows, of exercising his private judgment in a wrong way. Just as little as it would be allowed a convicted criminal, to dispute the justice of a law which all honest men approved, but under which he lay condemned, would it be permitted any one to demur against the true Rule of Faith, whatever that may be, and wherever found, by which his creed when tried might be pronounced heretical. Not by any means that *the Rule* can be higher than the Divine truth involved in the case, but that it is *above the particular interpretation of it to be decided upon.*

With these cautions then, we may proceed to the consideration of our subject, with the understanding, that whilst the Bible, abstractly considered, contains all that is essential to salvation, and needs no additions to render it complete, we still require a *rule by which to test private opinions of its doctrines.* It need hardly be added that this Rule, besides having all the qualities belonging to rules in general, must possess such other features as the nature of the case may require. Only let it be kept distinctly in view, that it is not a rule by which to judge the Bible, that we are inquiring after, but one by which to determine the character of the divers private opinions of the contents of that sacred book.

II. Having thus endeavored to make a practical statement of our subject, we will next *briefly sketch its history.* For whether the men of this enlightened XIX. century, enjoying "the light of experience and the maturity of gray hairs," will consent or not, to learn at the feet of "the young and inexperienced christianity of the first ages;" or "to ascribe to the child the authority of the old man,* they may nevertheless find it at least amusing

---

* See D'Aubigne's Discourse on Geneva and Oxford. But for the *source* of these witticisms of the popular historian, they would unquestionably be thought puerile, not to say profane! Good reasons must be scarce where such ridicule is preferred.

to look at the *grotesque opinions* of the past! Children occasionally say things that are not only laughable but shrewd. And by searching closely the surviving fragments of such *boys (?)* as Polycarp, Papias, Justin Martyr, Irenaeus, Tertullian, and Cyprian, of the more "*juvenile*" ages of the Church, with a host of others, whose names it might be thought contagious to print, belonging to later history, the wisdom of this happy age might possibly, here and there, hit upon something worthy. of at least a corner in its well furnished cerebrum!

Concluding then, for this reason, if for no better, to give the testimony of primitive days a passing consideration, we cannot but express regret at the outset, that instead of having the sentiments of the earlier witnesses in their own books and proper connection, we must depend upon quotations found in writings of a later generation. Thus the first of the known views of the Apostolic Fathers upon the subject before us, is that of Papias, quoted by Eusebius. Not, however, that we are left in ignorance of their practice: for, besides knowing that they did not possess the Scriptures in their collected form, and consequently could not have possessed a perfect Rule of Faith, if the Bible alone be such, it is abundantly attested that during the first two centuries, the Church possessed numerous and important Apostolic traditions which were generally acknowledged to be pure. And not only were they possessed and accredited, but appealed to as authority. Shall any significance be attached to this fact? Are there no genuine links connecting the Apostles' Creed with these esteemed traditions? Touching the other matter, however, Eusebius reports * the following historical facts:

When Ignatius, (Elder of Antioch, from A. D. 67—107,) was carried away to Rome, he " exhorted the churches (through which he passed) to adhere firmly to the traditions of the Apostles; which for the sake of greater security, he committed to writing."—

Irenaeus, speaking in commendation of *Polycarp*, (the Elder [Angel, Rev. ii. 8—11,] of Smyrna, A. D. 108,) says, he always

---

* Eusebius Eccles. hist. B. III, c. 36.

taught what he had *heard* from the Apostles, *what the Church had handed down,* and what is the only true doctrine."[*]

Papias (Elder of Hieropolis, A. D. 116,) is quoted by Eusebius[†] in the following words, taken from the preface to his discourses: "But I shall not regret to subjoin to my interpretations also for your benefit, whatsoever I have at any time accurately ascertained and *treasured up in my memory, as I have received it from the Elders,* and have recorded it *in order to give additional confirmation to the truth by my testimony.* For I have never like many, delighted to hear those that tell many things, but those that teach the truth, neither those that record foreign precepts, but *those that are given from the Lord, to our faith, and that came from the truth itself.*"

To these quotations may be added the remark of Eusebius, that when Saturninus and Basilides, disciples of Menander, endeavored to corrupt the Church with their heretical doctrines, there arose " many ecclesiastical writers, (about A. D. 132,) who contended for the truth, and *defended the doctrine of the Apostles and the Church.*"

Whether any stress should be laid upon the passage of Clement of Rome, quoted by Dr. Spring, from the Epistle to the Corinthians, must be determined by the reader. It is as follows: "The blessed Paul did verily admonish you *by the spirit.*" The italics are by Dr. Spring. We must honestly confess, however, that we do not see why those words have been thus emphasized. For whether Paul admonished by *letter* or *orally,* does not appear.

From the paucity and character of these quotations, it will be seen that the original sources of testimony for the greater part of the first two centuries must be scarce.[‡] For from the date of

---

[*] Ibid, B, IV, c, 14.   [†] Ib. B III. c. 39.

[‡] A few facts in proof of this may be interesting to some readers. They are gathered from "Clarke's succession of Sacred Literature," London, 1830. Of twenty writers of any credit, during the first two centuries, and whose writings are known to have been numerous, by far the greater part are lost to us. Thus of the Apostolical Fathers, nothing remains but the Epistle of Barnabas, the Epistle of Clement above referred to, the Pastor of Hermas, the epistles of Ignatius to the Ephesians, and Polycarp's

the opinion above quoted from Eusebius, to the time of Tertullian, (A. D. 200,) the only passages that bear at all upon the subject, are (1.) that usually quoted from Irenaeus:—"We have received the method of our salvation from no others but from them by whom the gospel came to us; which gospel the Apostles first *preached*, but afterwards, by the will of God, *delivered in writing, to be for the future the pillar and foundation of our faith;*"* and (2.) those quoted by Dr. Daniel, from the same author:—"All who desire to know the truth, *have the tradition of the Apostles published to the world*, spread out before their eyes (Irenaeus, B. I. 2). This is *preserved in the Churches by their successive teachers*: (B. I. 3) in this order and succession has the preaching of the truth reached us. The Apostles gathered into the Church with full hands, as into a rich treasury, whatever might promote the truth, that each one who would, might draw out of her the water of life. Whenever, therefore, disputes occur upon unimportant questions, *the matter must be referred to the oldest churches, in which the Apostles ruled*, that it may be ascertained from them what has been decided upon the disputed question. The proper knowledge of the truth is therefore contained in the teaching of the Apostles, in the old

epistle to the Philippians—all of which it is presumed could be printed in three numbers of an ordinary newspaper.

If we turn to the writings of the primitive fathers, it looks but little better. Of five books *known* to have been written by Papias, (116,) only a few fragments are preserved by Eusebius. Of Justin Martyr, (140,) we have indeed a fairer specimen; but the probability is, the greater and more important part of his writings are also lost. Of eight epistles by Dionysius, (170) only a few fragments in Eusebius. Of Tatian's (172) numerous works nothing survives but the "Oration against the Greeks." Of a History of the Church, by Hegesippus, (173) only a few fragments. Of twenty books, &c., known to have been written by Melito, (Elder of Sardis, anno 177,) nothing is known but the *titles.* Of Irenæus, (178) only the five books against heresies are known. Of Athenagoras, (178,) who was most probably a voluminous writer, only two works remain. Of Miltiades, (180,) nothing is preserved excepting the testimony of Eusebius, that his writings are "monuments of his zeal for the Divine oracles." To all which may be added a few works of Theophilus, Clement of Alexandria, and a small tract of Hermias (199), The reader is left to his own inferences from these facts.

* Spring's Dissertations, p. 40.

and universal church-system, (*sustema*,) in the impressions or
views received by the body of Christ (*i. e.* the Church) through
the succession of Bishops.   These received the succession from
the Apostles, and by the pleasure of the Father, the gracious
gift of infallible truth.   They should be obeyed by the members
of the Church. (B. IV. 43; III. 5.)   Many barbarian nations
have *received the faith without the Scriptures*, carefully preserved
the tradition, and salvation was written upon their hearts without
ink, by the Spirit."[*] (III. 3.)   Quite significant passages, these
quotations of Dr. Daniel!   So much so, as to excite surprise at
their oversight by so many English and American writers.

Thus much then for the testimony of the Apostolic and primitive fathers of the Church during the first two centuries, the
period during which the canon of scriptures was fully collected
and brought to its completion, a few demurrers excepted.   And
as we have now to do only with the historical part of our subject,
the reader is left to answer for himself such questions as these
concerning this testimony: Was the Bible the only Rule of
Faith for the primitive Church? Was tradition of any authority,
and to what extent? Does the practice then prevalent, seem to
have been thought only a temporary one? Did the primitive
Church belong to the Roman, Oxford, or modern Protestant
school, or to neither upon this subject?

Towards the beginning of the third century the canon of the
New Testament being pretty generally settled, was possessed in
some collected form by many of the writers of that age, as
appears from frequent references to the several books composing
it. This fact might naturally be expected more or less to modify
their views in reference to a proper and sufficient Rule of Faith.
And such modification, whatever it may be, can hardly be without its influence upon the honest inquiring mind. How much
more the discovery, should such be made, that no modification
took place? So long as the echo of the Apostolic voice still
reverberated through the Churches, and could be clearly recognized as such, it would not appear strange if tradition should be
thought co-ordinate with scripture, especially since that scripture

[*] Theologische Controversen, pp. 48, 49.

was possessed only in unconnected fragments! But how shall it be when they possess the sacred oracles entire? Here again the testimony, as far as within our reach, shall be given without partiality.

First of all, a general remark upon the subject by an accurate (though not quite orthodox) Church historian.[*] Referring to the controversies carried on in this age of the Church, he says: "In opposition to worldly wisdom and heretical arcana, the Church held up *the letter of the Holy Scriptures.* But to the refutation of Heretics *tradition alone seemed adequate,* which, in the opinion of the times, was: *The doctrine of the Church delivered orally by the Apostles to the first bishops, and handed down uncorrupted to their successors;* in truth: *the substance of whatever the Christian consciousness of every preceding age had, by a public expression of opinion, affirmed against reigning errors.*" The controversial writings of Irenaeus and Tertullian are referred to as instances in point. How far this view of Hase is sustained, may be seen by considering the following quotations:

Clement of Alexandria[*] (An. 191—220) in his introduction to the Stromata says: "'These books were not fabricated as a work of ostentation, but that they may serve as an antidote to forgetfulness, and a treasury of recollections, to be as it were an image and sketch of those animated discourses, and truly praiseworthy men, whom it was my high privilege to hear. * * * * *For those men, preserving the genuine tradition of the blessed doctrine which they had received from as far back as Peter, and James, John and Paul,* as a son from his father (though but few children resemble their father) reached down to us through the grace of God, and scattered the primitive Apostolical seed."

Tertullian, a cotemporary of Clement, as quoted by Dr. Wiseman,[†] uses this language: "What will you gain by recurring to Scripture, when one denies what the other asserts? Learn rather who it is that possesses the faith Christ; to whom the Scriptures

---

[*] Hase, Kirchengeschichte. Zweite Auflage, p. 90.
[*] Eusebius (Cruse's translation) B. V. 11, Daniel's Theol. Controv. p. 38.
[†] Hopkins' Brit. Ref. p. 76. And still more fully in Daniel's work.

belong; from whom, and by whom, and when that faith was delivered, by which we are made Christians. For where shall be found the true faith, there will be the genuine Scriptures, there the true interpretations of them, and there all Christian traditions. Christ chose his Apostles, whom he sent to preach to all nations. They delivered his doctrines and founded Churches, from which Churches others drew the seeds of the same doctrine, as new ones daily continue to do. Thus these, as the offspring of the Apostolical Churches, are themselves esteemed Apostolical. Now to know what the Apostles taught, that is, what Christ revealed to them, recourse must be had to the Churches which they founded, and which they instructed by word of mouth and by epistle. For it is plain that all doctrine which is conformable to the faith of these Mother Churches is true; being that which they received from the Apostles, the Apostles from Christ, Christ from God; and that all other opinions must be false."

Dr. Spring makes no allusion to this passage in his essay, neither have we ever seen it quoted in any of the articles in the Protestant Quarterly Reveiw, upon this subject!

On the other hand, however, the distinguished Roman Catholic, Dr. Wiseman, appears to be wholly ignorant of the existence of such sentiments as the following, from the same learned author above cited[*]: "Adoro scripturae plenitudinem, quae mihi et factorem manifestat et facta. Scriptum esse doceat Hermogenis officina. Si non est scriptum timeat vae illud adjicientibus aut detrahentibus destinatum.[*] (adv. Hermog. 22.) And again (adv. Marcion): "Hac quidem scriptura non dicit—non recipio quod extra scripturam de tuo infers."[*] And once more (de virg. velat. c. 1.): "Christus veritatem se non consuetudinem cognominavit: *Quodcunque adversus veritatem sapit, hoc est haeresis, etiam vetus consuetudo.*"[*] And finally, (de Praescript. 14): "Qui ergo nec sibi sunt christiani quanto magis nobis? qui per fallaciam veniunt, qualem fidem disputant? Cui veritati patrocinantur qui eam a mendacio indicunt! *Aliunde scilicet suadere*

---

[*] See also Hopkins for other passages, pp. 80, 81.

[*] Daniel's Theol. Controv. pp. 42, 43.

non possent de rebus fidei nisi ex literis fidei."[*] But it may be thought time to bid adieu to Tertullian.

To what effect then is the *testimony of Cyprian*, (248,) the next witness that meets us. First, he says:[†] "Whence have you that tradition? Comes it from the authority of the Lord and the gospels, or from the Apostles? For God hath testified that we are to do those things that are written. If it be.commanded in the gospels, or contained in the epistles, then let us observe it as a divine and holy tradition." In another place[‡] (Epist. 74): "If a river, that once flowed abundantly, suddenly sinks, do we not go back to its sources to ascertain the cause of its disappearance? Thus must the priests of God do now, if any uncertainty exists with regard to truth. They must go back to the source, which is the Lord himself, back to the tradition of the Evangelists and Apostles. We must do that which is written: for this is God's will."[§]

Origen, (202—254,) a cotemporary of Cyprian and pupil of Clement, expresses himself upon this subject in the following manner:[‖] (in the preface to the 4 books of Principles,) "That only is to be held for truth which varies in nothing from the doctrine of the Church and the Apostles. This however should be understood, that when the holy Apostles proclaimed the Christian faith, they made known some points which they thought essential to all, even to those who did not exhibit much interest in the investigation of the divine science; and, what is particularly worthy.of notice, directed them that they should inquire for the true ground of every doctrine of those who were prominently possessed of spiritual gifts, and had received the gift of eloquence, wisdom, and knowledge, immediately from the Holy Spirit."

The council of Nice (325) seems to have been too deeply concerned in the settlement of the Arian controversy, to give any attention to our subject; or to have regarded the question

---

[*] Daniel's, ib.

[†] Dr. Spring's Dissertation, pp. 40, 41.

[‡] Ib. pp. 43, 44.

[§] For another important passage from Cyprian, see Hopkins, pp. 82—3.

[‖] Daniel Theol. controv. p. 50.

as settled. At least scripture and tradition were both appealed
to without contradiction. And whilst speaking upon this point
we may add, that a similar remark will apply to all the general
councils. Such sentiments as the following are incidentally met
with : "Whoever, therefore, presumes to think or teach otherwise than our churchly traditions teach, or, like ungodly heretics, to despise those traditions, or to introduce another doctrine
* * * shall be excommunicated." (Act. VII. Nic. II.)* "Cum
simus debitores omnes sacras literas custodire, et eam quae dicit,
in unaquaque ecclesia oeconomos esse, modis omnibus inviola-
bilem conservare debemus." (Nic. II. Can. XI.)* "Igitur
regulas, quae sanctae catholicae ac Apostolicae ecclesiae tam a
sanctis famosissimis Apostolis, quam ab orthodoxorum universa-
libus, nec non et localibus conciliis, vel etiam a quolibet Deiloque
patre ac magistro ecclesiae traditae sunt, servare ac custodire
profitemur." (Constant. Can. I.)* So much then for the
Councils until 1438. Shall their silence be thought significant?

To return to individual testimony, *Athanasius* (326), the
Apollas of the Roman Bishop Alexander at the Council of Nice,
and the *Wortfuehrer* in all the harangues against Arianism,
assures us that "The holy and divine scriptures are sufficient
for the preaching and exposition of the truth."† (Cont. gent.
I. p. 1.)

Hilary (354), "It is well if we are satisfied with what is
revealed to us in the Scriptures." (De Trin. 3, 23.)†

Basil of Cesarea (370): "It is the clearest proof of ungodli-
ness, and the surest sign of pride, for any one to reject what is
taught in the Scriptures, or to introduce something not there
found. The Lord hath said: My sheep hear my voice, another
will they not follow." (de fide 224.)†

The same author however in another place: "Of the dogmas
preserved in the Church, some are handed down in writing,
others we have received as mysteries through the tradition of
the Apostles. * * * I also regard it as apostolical to adhere to

---

* *Eisenschmidt* ueber die Unfehlbarkeit, d. Allgemeinen Concil. pp. 277,
285, 354.

† Daniel, p. 44. For valuable quotations from Cyril see Hopkins 83—84.

that tradition which is not written. I. Cor. xi. 2. I. Thess. ii. 14." (de spirit. sanct. c. 27 sqq.)[*]

Chrysostom (400). "Those belonging to christianity, must bind themselves to the Holy Scriptures; nothing else can be the touchstone of genuine piety; beyond this we are to have nothing else. It contains every thing essential to salvation in overflowing fullness. And heretics are to be resisted only with the Scriptures."[*] (Homilies.) But he also says, (upon I. Thess. ii. 14, 15.). "From this it appears that the Apostles did not deliver every thing in writing, but much in an unwritten form. This also is worthy of belief. It is tradition; ask for no more. (Hom. II. Thess. ii. 14—15; II. Tim. i. 3.)[*]

Gregory of Nyssa (394), contemporaneously with the above, writes:—"Let no one object that the doctrine we profess, must first be confirmed by proofs. In proof of our doctrine, the tradition received of the fathers is sufficient, which is given to us as an inheritance transmitted by the Apostles through the succeeding Saints." (Contr. Eunom. lib. 4.)[*]

Jerome (350—420), also a cotemporary, writes: "The Church ● ● ● has never left the limits of the Holy Scriptures. Whatever may have been spoken after the days of the Apostles, is dismissed, it has no authority. The sword of the divine word strikes all that fabricate any apostolical tradition, that is without the testimony and authority of the Scriptures." (Comment.)[*]

Ambrose (400), "How can we receive what is not in the Holy Scriptures?"[*] (de offic. 1, 23.)

Epiphanius (367—403) writes: "Not all Scriptures are to be understood allegorically, but as it stands. ● ● ● And in order to get the true meaning of every sentence, it will be necessary to make use of tradition, for not every thing can be derived from the Bible alone. Therefore the holy Apostles delivered some truths in writing, others by tradition. Hence the Church has received its tradition from the fathers." (adv. Apost. c. 6.)[†]

The course of this testimony has led us, as will be perceived, to the age of the learned, zealous, and influential *Augustine*, the man that with the greatest independence of mind weighed

---

[*] Daniel, 51, 44, 52, 52, 44, 45.   [†] Daniel, p. 52.

every thing in the balance of reason and truth before giving it the sanction of his heart or voice. The commanding position he occupies in the history of the Church, makes it desirable, if not important, that the weight of his opinion might be secured for whatever view is advocated. No wonder then that his works are courted assiduously, to obtain from them some smile of approbation. And upon no subject has more of this been done than that before us. Let us then hear him speak for himself.[*]

"I dare not appeal to the Council of Nice, nor you to that of Ariminium, as though the controversy were thereby ended. Neither of us is bound to such authority. *Scripturarum auctoritatibus res cum re, causa cum causa, ratio cum ratione certet.* Neither are the Bishops of the Catholic Church to receive our assent, when they fall into error, and advance something contrary to the Scriptures. * * * Such authorities are to be carefully distinguished from the authority of the canonical scriptures. For we do not listen to: Thus say I, or: Thus sayest thou :—but to, *Thus saith the Lord.* We yield ourselves to the divine books, with them we agree, *in them we seek the Church,* in them the proofs of our arguments. * * * Every thing must be weighed in the divine balance of the Scriptures, for without the authority of these the Lord does not require us to believe."[†] Yet the same Augustine says in another place: "The Apostles have given no written directions concerning infant baptism; but the custom took its origin, as we may readily believe, in Apostolic tradition. *For there are many things, held by the whole Church, which have not been instituted by Councils, but believed to be directed by the Apostles, though nothing can be found in their writings concerning them,* (de bapt. 5, 23: 4, 24.) *And I truly would not believe the Gospel, if the authority of the Catholic Church did not constrain me to do so."*[‡]

Peter Chysologus (Bishop of Ravenna 450), "As an otherwise salutary and sanative potion may cause the greatest misery if

---

[*] Bishop Hopkins quotes (p. 79—80) many excellent sentiments from Augustine, upon the preciousness of the Scriptures, but they have only an indirect bearing upon our question. Augustine may nevertheless have valued tradition.

[†] Ib. 45.   [‡] Ib. 53.

not taken at the proper time, and according to the prescription of the physician; so the Word of God heard by an over-curious hearer, and apprehended in a sense contrary to the doctrine of the Church, and the principles of faith becomes an occasion of death, instead of being the source of life."[*]

During the same period with the writer last quoted, *Vincent of Lerins* (440—450), an island in the south of France, published a work entitled, "*An admonition against the Profane Novelties of Heretics, in defence of the Antiquity and Universality of the Catholic Faith.*" It consists of *two parts*. In the *first* he shows how, upon the most careful inquiry, he was assured by all consulted, that the safest way of avoiding the snares of error was: *to abide by the authority of the Divine Law, and by the Tradition of the Fathers.* In the *second* he endeavors to prove the necessity of connecting tradition with Scripture, in order to a right understanding of it.[†] The work is in high esteem in the Romish Church. Of course our Vincent was canonized a saint! The only passage from this author to which we have access is the following: "Perhaps some one will say: If the Scriptures are perfect, why do you place the authority of an ecclesiastical interpretation along side of them? But as the Scriptures are so elevated and profound, all do not understand them alike. * * * Therefore it is necessary that the writings of the Apostles and Prophets should be explained according to the interpretation of the Catholic Church. * * * The Holy Scriptures must be interpreted according to the tradition of the church universal, and the rule of the Catholic dogma."[‡]

One more passage shall close the testimony of the ancients. It is from *Gregory the Great* of Rome, (590—604,) which is valuable as indicating the sentiment of the age immediately preceding the reign of the Popes: "*Fines Benjamin regulæ sanctarum scripturarum sunt, de quibus profecto finibus scriptum est: Ne transgrediaris terminos, quos posuerunt patres tui.*"[§]

The doctrine of the Roman Catholic Church, from this time

---

[*] Ib. 53.

[†] Clarke's Succession of Sac. Lit., vol. II. p. 218.

[‡] Daniel, p. 53—54.   [§] Daniel, 46.

forward, upon her authority as an interpreter of the Scriptures, is too·well known to require the testimony of particular writers. Only this needs to be remembered, that there was never a day from Gregory to the glorious Reformation, in which the spiritual usurpations of the Papacy, advancing, as they did, from point·to point, until a dogma was adopted never dreamed of by the early fathers, were not bravely resisted and denounced as utterly unscriptural. Hosts of such witnesses for the truth, might be cited if it were necessary.* But we must for this occasion forbear.

One temptation, however, we cannot resist, even though all credit for prudence and a proper love of life be forfeited. It is to seize a knight errant's sword and mace, and plunge into the midst of the dismal darkness of the middle ages! If our friends think it too madly rash to follow us, they are entreated to wait patiently for our return, unless, indeed, the mists should be so thick that we stick fast! Perhaps some treasures may be found to compensate for all the dangers undergone! * * * *

Well, we are safely back, and lo! what riches! First, a gem from the *Libri Carolini* (790)†: " Nos denique propheticis, evangelicis et apostolicis scripturis contenti et sanctorum orthodoxorum patrum, qui nullatenus in suis dematibus ab eo qui est via, veritas et vita deviarunt, institutis imbuti omnes novitates vocum et stultiloques adinventiones rejicimus."‡

Second, a nut§ from John Scotus Erigena (858): " Sanctae siquidem scripturae in omnibus sequenda est auctaritas, quum in ea veluti quibusdam suis secretis sedibus veritas sedet." (de div. nat. I. 66.)

Next, a pearl from Bernhard of Clairvaux (1140): " Non me sanctorum potest carere conventus nec loci corporisve distantia privat prorsus a concilio castorum, illo praesertim concilio in quo non hominum traditiones obstinatius defensantur aut superstitiosius observantur sed diligenter humiliterque inquiritur quae

---

* See *Moehler's Wahrheits-zeugen.*

† For the history of these books see Gieseler Eccles. Hist., vol. II, p. 35, where some valuable extracts on other subjects may also be found.

‡ Daniel, p. 74.

§ Which Oxford might find somewhat hard to crack.

sit voluntas Dei bono et bene placens et perfecta (ep. 91) volun-
taria sunt quae inventa a homine necessaria qua divinitus
instituta, (tract. de praecept.)

And finally, some rich and sweet clusters gathered from vines
growing even in this *dismal swamp* (?) of the benighted Church!

"The sacred writers stand before us like Watchmen of the
Church. They trace out the various tempers of men, discover
the passions and diseases which consume them, and penetrate
the recesses of all their thoughts. As often as I read them I
feel myself condemned. Their warnings make me tremble,
and I am wounded in positions which I thought firm and secure.
The veil of hypocrisy, ignorance and forgetfulness is torn off,
and the garment of vain-glorying is removed. In the light of
their descriptions I recognize my own stains, and by the thunder
of their words the inner door of my heart is burst open. Oh!
how salutary is this for me! For when I see no more beauty
in myself, and can no more rest in my own goodness, I am
drawn upward with deep longings of love to Jesus my Lord."[*]
Gilbert (1150).

"God comforts men in a twofold way: by temporal blessings
and by His word. Of these the latter deserves the highest
esteem, for it proceeds from the mouth of God, whilst creatures
are made out of nothing. Just as the bride rejoices more at the
voice of the bridegroom than in his gifts, as the loyal subject
feels himself more highly favored if his monarch speaks to him,
than by the reception of a reward, and as an affectionate son,
prefers the society of his father above all the sustenance afforded
him; so must we esteem the Holy Word of our God, far above
all creature gifts bestowed." Raymond (1375).[*]

If it were necessary or expedient, such sentiments might be

---

[*] See *Geistliche Stimmen aus d. Mittelalter v. Galle*, p. 191—192. Are these
really such lights as are not to be "put under a bushel," or only Will-o'-
wisps from the dark bog? How marvellous that with such men to rock
the cradle, through the gloomy night, the Reformation should not have
"slept until the crack of doom!!" Will those who see nothing but ghosts
in black when they look to the centuries next preceding the Reformation,
permit these beautiful and devotional collections of Galle to be recommended to their perusal?

multiplied. But enough has been said for our purpose. And
we are confident that if the opinions which have been collected,
are interpreted according to the rules usually applied in such
cases, there will be but one sentiment as to their import. If
the circumstances under which they were severally written, the
prevailing philosophies of their day, the extent of other outward
influences, the natural effect of their education, and whatever
else the rules of a fair hermeneutics suggest, are duly considered,
all discrepancies of sentiment, and contradictions of doctrine that
are of any moment can, it is believed, be honestly harmonized.
It will be found that, whatever the sound of the words may be,
Tertullian and Augustine did not contradict themselves, nor
each other, nor yet the views of others whose sentiments upon
this subject have been quoted.   From first to last the testimony
of these venerable and learned men agrees in opposing on the
one hand, a growing tendency to a superstitious regard for *vain*
traditions; and on the other, the attempts made to introduce the
innovations of infidelity by spurning altogether the instructions
and authority of tradition.

But it is objected to our laying any stress upon this series of
testimony, or any other like it, that *it is the testimony of only
a few men, and is derived only from fragments of their writings.*
This fact is of course admitted, but by no means the inference
intended to be deduced from it. For though the number of
our witnesses is small, yet it is honorable.   The writers quoted
will be admitted by all to have been *amongst* the leading spirits
of their day, and in some cases *the* leading spirits.   Why then
object to their being regarded in the same light in which prominent men are regarded now?   Are not the writings of Calvin
and Melanchthon of their day, of Charnock and Owen of their's,
and of Henry and Doddridge in their's, allowed to stand as fair
representations of orthodox views then prevailing?   And would
not the General Assembly consent, that in eighteen centuries
hence the excellent writings of the venerable Dr. Alexander, or
the Commentary of the Romans by Dr. Hodge, should be taken
as a pretty fair specimen of their theology upon whatever points
are handled?   Why then refuse to admit the surviving testimony of a Papias or an Irenæus, because we may known only

of their's? Or if the *mere fragments* possessed be the objection, then it may be said, upon the supposition, that the rest of their writings did not flatly contradict the sentiments contained in these fragments, that they deserve consideration as far as they go, and, like the isolated bones of Cuvier, may help the skillful to construct their whole system. But, at any rate, the objection would not be made with regard to living writers. There are single sentences, for instance, in the Princeton Repertory's article on Trancendentalism, (1839,) which, however desirable it might be thought to have the whole transmitted, would be allowed to go down to the latest generation, as an expression of its views of the philosophy of Fichte, Kant, or Hegel. And so of other articles and books. Why then ridicule any for applying the same principle to the precious fragments of former centuries!

But then *many of the primitive fathers thought and wrote much that was puerile and superstitious,* and therefore their views on other subjects merit but little estimation. A fine reproach indeed, to come from the posterity of the *Pilgrims!* Undoubtedly we should smile in reading Chrysostom's treatise on Virginity, and still more over Theodoret's lives of thirty remarkable monks; (especially that one who *dried up the spring* in which some industrious housewives were washing clothes, because the good women were so busy at their work as to forget to let down their tucked up garments while the modest monk was passing; and of him, who, living in a secluded cave, fed himself but once a week, having no time to spare from singing David's Psalms;) but still the "Priesthood" of the one, and the "Incarnation" of the other, will command respect and admiration. Who would throw away the "Essays to do good," or his other three hundred and eighty-two books, because some of them prove that *Cotton Mather, D. D., believed in witchcraft,* and because history testifies that he was prominent in having those believed to be "possessed," *delivered* by death?

But why meet objections more childish than the puerilities they profess to expose? Such objections refute themselves to the candid mind; whereas no reasons can silence prejudice.

Having seen our subject into the *dark ages,* it would be proper and interesting to trace, minutely, the several steps by

5*

which it emerged again, and consider, somewhat at length, the process by which, on the side of the Papists and that of the Reformers, it reached the definite shape which both dogmas then exhibit. But as this part of the essay has already passed the limits designed, we must be permitted at once to leap at the conclusions adopted in either case.

That to which the Reformed Church came, after various discussions is, we think, most explicitly stated in the latter Helvetic Confession, Art. II., and in the Tetrapolitan, chap. 14. We shall quote only from the former: " Proinde non probamus interpretitiones quaslibet: unde nec pro vera aut genuina scripturarum interpretatione agnoscimus eum, quem vocant sensum Romanae ecclesiae, quem scilicet, simpliciter Roma-ecclesiae defensores, omnibus obtrudere contendant recipiendum : sed illam duntaxat scripturarum interpretationem pro orthodoxa et genuina agnoscimus, quae ex ipsis est petita scripturis, * * * * *, cum regula fide et charitatis congruit, et ad gloriam Dei hominumque salutem eximie facit.

" Proinde non aspernamur sanctorum patrum Graecorum Latinorumque interpretationes, neque reprobamus eorundem disputationes ac tractationes rerum sacrarum, cum scripturis consentientes: a quibus tamen recedimus modeste, quando aliena a scripturis aut his contrarie adferre deprehenduntur. Nec putamus illis ullam a nobis hac re injuriam irrogari, cum omnes uno ore nolint sua scripta aequari Canonicis, sed probare jubeant, quatenus vel consentiant cum illis, vel dissentiant, jubeantque consententia recipere, recedere vero a dissentientibus. Eadem in ordine collocantur etiam Conciliorum definitiones vel canones."*

That the Reformed Churches would express themselves in the clearest and strongest terms upon this subject, and that too chiefly against the errors advocated by the Papists, is well understood. And it would be doing the greatest injustice to their real sentiments, to put the most extreme construction upon words and expressions intended, when taken in their mildest sense, to set forth all that they meant. They, undoubtedly, went to the

* Niemeyer's Ref. Confess. p. 469.

utmost limits of their belief in stating, as they did, those doctrines especially which stood opposite to some gross error on the Romish side. If, therefore, the circumstances of the case are duly considered, the frequent expressions of respect for the interpretations of the fathers which are every where met with, not in formal confessions only, but in private writings, are deeply significant, and must always be allowed to modify their expressions with reference to the sole authority of the Divine Word. Hence when we read in the Bohemian Confession, (Art. I.) "Scripta autem Doctorum ecclesiae, praecipue veterum itidem pro veris fideque dignis haberi, utiliaque esse ad instituendam plebem dicunt," it should be considered, as it really is, a caution against supposing that, because the false witnesses of the Papacy were discarded, they wholly despised the authority of the Past. Instead of interpreting this class of passages by those which hold up the divine sufficiency of the Holy Scriptures, as is usually done, the latter should be explained by the former. That such expressions as: "attamen in quibus a divinis Scripturis non dissident," should be used, whenever the opinions of the earlier Church are referred to, creates no difficulty to those who consider that Luther rejected the epistle of James for the same reason, and who themselves would not assent to a passage of *Scripture* which stood in flat contradiction to all its other teaching, but at once pronounce it an interpolation or typographical mistake.

Whilst the evangelical doctrine of the Church thus assumed a more definite and complete form, that of the Papacy could not be permitted to remain in its undetermined state. For whatever sanction the Romish view had from long custom, it had never ripened into an established canon. To bring it to this, was part of the difficult work of the Council of Trent. This Council aware of the necessity of great caution, seems to have been anxious to hide its true meaning under a multitude of oracular terms. The substance of the whole, however, is summed up in the following words:* "ut nemo   contra unanimem

---

* Also quoted in the Principle of Prot., by Dr. Schaf, and from which, in the absence of a copy of the Decrees of Trent in the original, the above sentence is taken.

consensum Patrum ipsam scripturam sacram interpretari audeat," which, in proper English, means, that whoever dares to interpret scriptures contrary to those traditions of the Fathers, which the Romish Church approves, and *in that sense of these traditions which it determines,* shall be anathema. And to this decree the Church of Rome to this day responds, amen!

As it is our intention to review this dogma of Rome, in connection with others now maintained, in a future article, nothing farther is added now.

EASTON, PA.   J. H. A. B.

ART. IV.—THE APPLE AS A CRITERION OF TASTE.

I OWN that I am sometimes distressed at the manner in which, during these latter days, we are too prone to look upon our fruits. By this last appellation I would, of course, comprehend at present not all vegetable productions, but only those variously tinted, rounded, succulent, and, in many cases, redolent esculents which are dependent from our trees. Among their manifold qualifications we are too apt to overlook the highest, thinking them to be addressed to merely one of our senses, and that not the most refined. We regard them, therefore, not with full appropriate affections. When placed before our visions, the orgasm of our palates after them do become so inordinate, it seems to me, that we lose sight, in a great measure, of their outward superior beauties, and certainly all sensation of their fragrance.

The apple, considered as a nosegay merely, without any refe-

rence to its edible contents, every person, one would suppose, who
had his senses in proper harmony, should acknowledge to be most
delectable.   The flute, of all musical instruments, is allowed, I
believe, to be the most charming to the ear, on account of the striking consonance of its tones to those of the human voice.   The apple,
with equal propriety, I would think, should be regarded, not only
of all fruits, but also of all flowers, as the most pleasing object to the
eye, on account of the striking resemblance of its contour and complexion to the human cheek.   Into what varieties too, considered
as a species, it is divided, to suit every taste!   Divesting yourself,
if you can, of all prejudice on account of their profusion, just cast
your eye on one of those "mellow hangings," as Shakspeare calls
them, in the month of October.   What plumpness of shape!   What
richness of tints!   What deliciousness of breath!   How much has it
improved on its own blossomage!   How far superior to the rose!
The most expressive emblems of our affections certainly are those
things which, by their striking resemblance in hue and shape to the
outward manifestations of the feelings themselves, as seen on the
human countenance, seem to sympathise with them.   What fruit
or flower then is better qualified for being the most eloquent interpreter of even our tenderest emotions, than the mellow, plump,
healthful, blushing-cheeked apple?   But who, nowadays, can understand its language?   Apples with us have lost the best half of their
significance.   We no longer present them to our dear friends for
the sake of awaking up kindred feelings.   It is only for being man-
ducated.

I would, by no means, have it supposed, however, that I am utterly
opposed to the eating of apples at all.   It is their ultimate design
and consummation.   Their prosaical destiny.   It is what they must
all come to in the course of nature, if not to some worse end.   But
before this, I maintain they have important duties to perform.   Their
principal mission into this world, is to give satisfaction and inspiration to our imaginations, through the media of our olfactories and
visual organs.   I love not their smack the less, but their odor and
aspect more.

How superior to ours were the notions of the ancients respecting
them!   How did they dote on the form, complexion and fragrance
of apples!   What renders this the more surprising too, is, that whilst,
in the course of ages, horticulturists, have, by means of propagation
and peculiar cultivation, been adding to the species almost innume-

rable varieties, for the sake of improving them as esculents, nature has no doubt, at the same time, been endowing them with additional beauty and fragrance; yet so far as we are concerned, all this remains in a great measure, unseen or wasted on the desert air. Some persons here will perhaps suggest that it is not unlikely, during the earliest ages, apples had advanced but a few removes in taste from their original progenitor, the wild crab, and therefore the ancients deserve not to be extolled so highly for having feasted their eyes and noses on them in preference to their mouths, inasmuch as, had they attempted to regale the latter, "the biter bitten," it would have been with a vengeance. But this rests altogether on a false hypothesis. Fewer varieties there were, it is true; but some of these, as the *melimelon*, for instance, or honey-apple, and the *amerinum* or winter sort, among the Greeks and Romans, were, in all likelihood, equal in relish to the choicest of our own. It is well known too, that, of the latter people, this fruit was the principal dessert—*usque ad mala*—wishing to have its flavor lingering about their palates after eating, as being the most delectable.

That this taste too, was not acquired by them artificially, from highly wrought civilization, but that it is natural to humanity, is evident from our meeting with some of the most striking instances of it among the most unsophisticated classes. Shepherds, surely, cannot be charged with over refinement, and yet it was among these especially, that, we find in ancient times. the apple was properly appreciated. Open any of the Idyls of Theocritus, the best delineator of rustic manners among the ancients. In almost any one of these you will discover some allusion to the fruit. Not to its saporosity, forsooth, but to its beauty and fragrance. Maidens he calls applecheeked. The Loves he likens to blushing apples. His robust young serenaders he describes, when sallying forth of nights, as bearing in their bosom-folds, well-chosen apples; which were more eloquent offerings than even their music. Should their mistresses accept of these, they would thereafter be placed in predicaments bordering very closely on betrothments. Polyphemus, I confess, is eccentric in this particular. Being a man of immense proportions, perhaps he could not find fruit large enough to express his affections. In those lamenting, unfortunate, unrequited addresses of his to his scornful, bewitching Galatea, he thinks proper to employ nothing but his roar of mouth. He is represented as doing everything in his own uncommon way. Roses and apples and ring-

lets, the poet tells us, he did not choose to make use of. By tell-
ing us this, however, the poet, at the same time, unweetingly lets
us know that, in his day, undoubtedly all sane wooers did make
use of these things. The Cyclops he cites as a most extraordinary
exception.

The silent eloquence of this fruit, however, was not peculiar to
pastoral life. It was felt also in urbane society. It was not a dialect of shepherds merely, and confined to Sicily. It was used also
by the polished and erudite, and understood throughout all Greece.
" Love and cherish," says Aristophanes in his Wasps, which were
presented before the refined people of Athens—" Love and cherish
only those poets, my friends, who are fresh and original in their
inventions; and be sure to preserve the thoughts of such, treasuring
them up in your chests, with your apples; which if ye do," he
adds, " an odor of cleverness, throughout the year, will be issuing
from your garments." Here apples and poetry are placed in their
proper conjunction. They are both recommended for imparting an
air of gentility to clothes. This fruit with the ancients, was redolent
of literary associations. How well could it be otherwise to a truly
Grecian nose? In most of the old heroic tales of Greece, we find
it employed as the principal instrument. Need I refer the classical
reader to those trees of the Hesperides, of whose golden fruit, to
obtain a specimen, occasioned some of the most difficult labors of
Hercules? Need I mention to him those apples of Meilanion, which
he threw down before his swift-footed cousin Atalanta, which while
she stooped to gather up, he escaped her spear and won from her
the race, and in consequence her beautiful hand? Need I remind
him of the fruit which Paris gave to Venus, causing the ten years'
siege and ultimate destruction of Troy? These to him are all familiar
as household words. He remembers besides, the story of Acontius,
how coming from his native Cea to Delos, for sacrificing to Diana,
he fell in love with the beautiful Cydippe; but that on account of
her high rank and his own poverty, he could not expect, by fair
means, to obtain her hand. He therefore had recourse to stratagem.
It was a sacred law in Delos, that whatever was promised in the
temple of Diana, must inviolably be performed. Having written
therefore on an apple, he cast it before her as she stood in the temple ; which her maid having taken up and handed to her, she read
aloud: " By Diana, I will marry Acontius." Of course, she was
no longer at liberty to become another's, even had she so inclined.

That oranges, citrons, or quinces were intended in one or two of
the above incidents as narrated by the poets, some discontented com-
mentators have labored very hard to substantiate; but even letting
them have their own way in this matter, these being still respectable fruits, in our own case, it would derogate not a whit from the
argument.

The Romans, it must be confessed, in their intellectual relish for
apples, fell considerably short of the Greeks.   They were too much
given up to the demolishing of human features with the sword, to
be deeply struck with dangling resemblances of these from trees.
The favorite organ with the Greeks was emphatically the eye.   Those
creations of art which sprang almost perfect from their imaginations,
were intended mostly to please this one sense.   How eminently
did they excel in sculpture, architecture and dramatic plots!   The
highest compliment they thought it was to the ear to compare its
gratifications to those of that transcendant organ.   If music was
good, they said it *shone*, or if a voice was sweet, they declared it
to be *splendent*.   The Romans, on the other hand, went in more for
the practical and the edible.   At their feasts their comestibles were
seasoned more highly than their conversation, and their wine was
more sparkling than their wit.   Still, they were not wanting in æsthetical taste, and from admiring the arts and literature of the Greeks,
in time, they became in this acutely sensible and refined.   Full of
imitations, however, their literature is not always to be taken as a
sure criterion of their own prevailing taste.   Of foreign manners it
sometimes smacks more distinctly than of their own.   Thus Virgil's
pastorals have more of the spirit of the old Sicilians about them
often, than that of his own countrymen; he having drawn them in
a great measure, from the Idyls of Theocritus.   With one thing,
however, we cannot help being well satisfied.   He has drawn along
with them also, most of the apples.   More than this, in one case
he has actually inserted some trees of his own; thus improving on
the original.   Transferring from the mountain-side the scene of early
impressions, to the more congenial orchard, he has put them in the
place of hyacinths.   It is in the following well known lines:

Sæpibus in nostris parvum te roscida mala
(Dux ego vester eram) vidi cum matre legentem;
Alter ab undecimo tum me jam acceperat annus;
Tum fragiles poteram ab terra contingere ramos.
Ut vidi, ut perii! ut me malus abstulit error!

Within our hedge-rows once I saw you, Sweet,
(I was your leader bold) a little girl
Gathering dewy apples with your mother.
Another year from my eleventh then
Had taken me. I was just able up
From the ground to reach me and crack the boughs.
How, as I saw, how was I stricken! how
Did mad delusion carry me away!

Cicero too, in his work, De Natura Deorum, has a handsome compliment for apples:

Hominum igitur causa eas rerum copias comparatas esse fatendum est; nisi forte tanta ubertas et varietas pomorum, eorumque jucundus non gustatus solum, sed odoratus etiam et adspectus dubitationem affert, quin hominibus solis ea natura donaverit.

For man's sake therefore has this abundance of things been provided, it must be admitted; unless forsooth, such a profusion and variety of apples and the pleasantness not only of their taste, but also of their odor and aspect, should bring suspicion that nature has not intended them for man alone!

He certainly here has a side eye especially on the pigs, who are too apt to be putting in their claims for a share of our fruits after they have fallen from our trees. Instead of being intended to promote their glory, however, the author well observes that they themselves were formed for our especial eating. It is the sole object of their creation.

Sus vero quid habet præter escam? Cui quidem, ne putresceret. animam ipsam pro sale datum dicit esse Chrysippus.

Your porker, what has he but his meat? Into whom, to keep him from spoiling, life itself has been put instead of salt, says Chrysippus.

If therefore he eat our apples, it is only to have them converted into pork and presented afterwards on our tables in that transformed shape. Their odor and aspect, of course, must be enjoyed, if at all before the metamorphosis.

But—*paula majora canamus*—let us take a sample from Hebrew poetry. "As the apple tree," says Solomon, speaking for the Church; and who was better qualified than he for choosing the most appropriate comparison, being familiar with trees from the cedar tree that is in Lebanon, even unto the hyssop that springeth out of the wall?—"As the apple tree among the trees of the wood. so is my beloved among the sons."

In Eden too, we know, our first parents were not forbidden to regale themselves on the fragrance and beauty of the fruit that was

in the midst. Their transgression was connected with their eating
of it.

But my lucubrations are becoming too leafy. I must come down
to modern literature. By the old Italian poets a disposition is too
often shown to sink the metaphor of apples, from the features,
down to the ivory breast. They are not satisfied with heads; they
must give us busts. A sufficient sample of this for us will be found
in the passage, from the Orlando Furioso of Ariosto, descriptive of
Alcina, with a translation by its warm admirer Leigh Hunt:

> Bianca neve e il bel collo, el petto latte ;
> Il collo e tondo, il petto colmo e largo ;
> Due pome acerbe, e pur d'avorio fatte,
> Vengono e van come onda al primo margo,
> Quando piacevole aura il mar combatte.

> Her bosom is like milk, her neck like snow ;
> A rounded neck ; a bosom where you see
> Two crisp young ivory apples come and go
> Like waves that on the shore beat tenderly
> When a sweet air is ruffling to and fro.

A taste for sculpture this displays, no doubt; and even our own
Theocritus, in one instance, stands blushingly convicted of the
same allusion; but the Greeks were certainly better pleased with
the superior, intellectual, facial resemblance. This might be shown
by quotations from their own bucolic writers and others, *ad libitum;*
but one statement will suffice. Not only in poetry, but in common
parlance, among the Greeks, the convex sides of beautiful faces, it
is well known, came at length to be called without a figure, *tá málà,*
the apples. That, on this point, it strikes me, is a clincher.

In old English poetry, while groping our way through obsolete,
rugged verse, sometimes having well nigh lost the track of thought,
to see at length, out from surrounding ruinous verbage, peering forth
the bright side of some appeol and catch its well known scent, how
swote it is! Consorted it will alway shew itself with goodly company; not with eatables nor with table garniture forsooth, but with
odor of flowers, twynkeling of harp, blast of musical instrument now
unknown, or, mayhap, set up, for comparison's sake, with youthful
cheek or ruddiest, sweetly breathing lip. Thus in Adam Davies'
Lyfe of Alisaundre:

> Mury is the blast of the styvor
> Mury is the twynkeling of the harpour;
> Swote is the smeol of flour
> Swete hit is in maidenes bour
> Appeol swote berith faire colour
> In treowe love is swote armour.

Or in language better understood, being more polished by the progressing age and his own superior genius, let us listen to Chaucer, whilst throwing off one of his life delineations, drawing, as his wont is, his comparisons not from books, but immediately from the farm or surrounding nature.　Hear, for instance, a part of his description of the young wife, as set forth in the Miller's Tale:

> Full brighter was the shining of hire hewe
> Than in the Tour the noble yforged newe.
> But of hire song it was loud and yerne,
> As any swalow sitting on a berne.
> Therto she coude skip, and make a game,　　　•
> As any kid or calf folowing his dame.
> Hire mouth was swete as biaket or the meth
> Or hord of appels laid in hay or heth.

These wrote in the Romantic age.　Jousts and tournaments were then in fashion throughout the land; and fair and virtuous ladies were highly and properly estimated.　No wonder then that apples were so also.　In the utilitarian times, however, that succeed, we find them less appreciated.

In books on Husbandry, it is hardly to be expected, I admit, that much poetry be found, as their main and professed design is to be practical; but being conversant also about trees and plants, they cannot well come forth from the hands of a true poet without containing some.　A large portion too of a country's people being generally employed in agriculture, by observing what poems their wants have called forth, and with which they are best pleased, we can form some estimate of their taste.　Virgil's Georgics are eminently practical, but at the same time, beautifully imaginative throughout.　His boughs he never strips of their natural bloom and foliage.　His grafted tree, on observing its foreign fruit, is affected with true poetic feeling.　Tusser, the old English rhymer, on the other hand, in his Five Hundred Points of Good Husbandry, which were once universally popular, has no fancy, no wit.　He is all practical.　An apple he regards with the same cold, calculating eye that he does a potato:

> Fruit gathered too timely will taste of the wood,
> Will shrink and be bitter and seldom prove good;
> So fruit that is shaken or beat off a tree,
> With bruising in falling, soon faulty wlil be.

Any one with Adam Davies' or Chaucer's eye, would have called them apples or pears; not fruit. There is no vividness in generic terms. But perhaps from his careful directions you will fancy at first sight that he regards his fruits with some tender, affectionate feelings. On looking closer, however, you will discover this to be a mistake. His tender mercies are cruel. They are no better than those of the butcher who abstains from striking his ox with a pole, when he is driving him to be slaughtered, not out of any admiration or humane compunctions, with regard to the animal, but for fear of bruising his meat. Philips has written a whole poem on cider; as if any poetry could be crushed out of apples. From grapes, I admit there may be some of a Bacchic sort; their juice in time becoming ruddy and inspiring to the fancy, though deleterious in its consequences; but in cider none.

> Lo! for thee my mill
> Now grinds choice apples, and the British vats
> O'erflow with generous cider.

Its inspirations fall even below those of malt liquor; and " he that drinks beer thinks beer."

As the useful arts are progressive, all poems founded on them that are purely didatic, of course, in time, become obsolete. They are superseded, in a great measure, by others better adapted to the improved state of the age. Of Tusser and Philips, therefore, the glory has departed; and, in England, works on husbandry and making cider are now more appropriately written in prose. Poetry, on the other hand, being addressed to the feelings and imagination, can never become superannuated. Like its own Muses, it bears with it always the beauty and freshness of the morning.

Some persons, however, will perhaps charge me now with partiality. Among the Greeks, they will remind me, it was in pastorals I met with the finest specimens of apple poetry; whereas in English Literature I am looking for it only in didactics. The fact is, however, the English have no pastorals. What they call such are mostly allegories or ideal scenes, the like of which were never transacted in their own or any other country. Oreads, hamadryads and satyrs are continually shewing themselves; though these belong not to their mythology. Those of Gay are generally considered the most graphic and natural; the customs introduced being wholly English; yet even these are for the most part, mere travesties on Virgil. In his Spell, thus Hobnelia sings, while "using up" an apple:

> I pare this pippin round and round again,
> My shepherd's name to flourish on the plain.
> I fling th' unbroken paring o'er my head,
> Upon the grass a perfect L is read;
> Yet on my heart a fairer L is seen
> Than what the paring makes upon the green.
> With my sharp heel I three times mark the ground,
> And turn me thrice around, around, around.
>
> This pippin shall another trial make.
> See, from the core two kernels brown I take;
> This on my cheek for Lubberkin is worn;
> And Boobyclod on t'other side is borne.
> But Boobyclod soon drops upon the ground,
> A certain token that his love's unsound;
> While Lubberkin sticks firmly to the last;—
> Oh, were his lips to mine but joined so fast!
> With my sharp heel I three times mark the ground,
> And turn me thrice around, around, around.

That the ceremonies here described are not fictitious, but drawn from actual observation of the poet in his day, is evident from their being still in vogue. Not, however, are they confined to shepherds nowadays, but observed in the most refined society. At a large party of young folks, this winter, in the house of my friend L——, at which it was my rare privilege to be present, not as a frolicksome guest forsooth, but, as besuited my years, as a quiet looker-on, the same manœuvres punctiliously gone through with, I witnessed, as above described; barring only the turning round on the heel. Indeed some other conjurations I saw that evening performed, by means of counting the seeds of a dissected apple and determining from their number, whether high or low, the impending happiness or misery of individuals of different sexes; all of which serves to to show that the natural poetry of the fruit is not utterly unfelt. But what a perversion of its promptings! what a misunderstanding of its meaning! How can the language of love and beauty be discovered in an apple after all its loveliness and beautifulness have been pared off and its fair proportions cut up into quarters! Verily

we are living in a country and, I fear, an age, given up to analysis
and dissections. How few of us nowadays have any eyes for organisms or the rounded completenesss of a whole!

Far be it from me to say that the poetry of apples is now utterly
unappreciated by any individual. Every true descriptive poet, in
his private walks, feels its influence, even though he may have had
no occasion to mention it in his public works. Who, for instance,
would say that Cowper in his rambles was not touched by its sweet
appeals from the trees, though he does not tell us this expressly in
his poems? How, indeed, could he be otherwise than affected;
steeped as he was in classic lore, and his very muse being nature?

> Nature, in all the various shapes she wears,
> Frowning in storms, or breathing gentle airs,
> The snowy robe her wintry state assumes,
> Her summer heats, her fruits, and her perfumes:
> All, all alike transport the glowing bard,
> Success in rhyme, his glory and reward.
> O Nature! whose Elysian scenes disclose
> His bright perfections, at whose word they rose,
> Next to that power who formed thee, and sustains,
> Be thou the great inspirer of my strains.

Thompson, too, was certainly under its influence, as, indeed, under
that of all fruits:

> Bear me, Pomona, to thy citron groves ;
> To where the lemon, and the piercing lime,
> With the deep orange, glowing through the green,
> Their lighter glories blend.   Lay me reclined
> Beneath the spreading tamarind that shakes,
> Fann'd by the breeze, its fever-cooling-fruit.

Thus he sings in the heat of the summer.   Let us hear him also in
the Autumn:

> Hence from the busy joy-resounding fields,
> In cheerful error let us tread the maze
> Of autumn, unconfined ; and taste revived
> The breath of orchard big with bending fruit.
> Obedient to the breeze and beating ray,
> From the deep-loaded bough, a mellow shower
> Incessant melts away.

There is poetry for you, both ocular and nasal. I own that, on one
occasion, he is represented as having been spied under circum-

stances somewhat suspicious.   Beneath a peach-tree, know he is
described as having been seen, standing "more fat than bard beseems," with his hands thrown behind his back, being too lazy to
lift them up, and his mouth elevated, and applied to the sunny side
of a peach that was still attached to its bough; but, although other
things are added, it has always struck me that, in all likelihood, he
was doing nothing more than kissing it.   Leigh Hunt, too, though
unfamiliar with the country, yet, from reading classics, is passion-
ately fond of apples, in a proper sense; and Tennyson, in his
translations and paraphrases, alludes to them sometimes even more
beautifully than the ancients.

In the earliest ages the practical and poetical were thoroughly
interfused and blended.   Then, works on theology, science, history,
and even law were often written in verse.   In the present stage of
advanced letters, however, this is not the case.   While the poetical
has generally retained its garb of verse, the practical has gradually and appropriately assumed that of prose.   My complaint is,
however, that mankind also have divided themselves into two
corresponding but most disproportionate classes; a few confining
themselves nowadays to aesthetics, while the whole mass are taken
up with merely what is useful.   They do not remember that their
intellectual and moral, as well as their physical parts must be fed.
Pastorals are now defunct.   Men and women are more pleased
with excitement and bustle, than with quietude and repose.   Hurled
abroad in cars and steamboats, their object seems to be to arrive at
the practical and productive as being the all essential.   For aesthetics, or what is beautiful, or sublime, in nature and art, they have
no eyes.   For "the breezy call of incense-breathing morn," they
have no noses.   With artificial scents and savors of rich ragouts,
they appear to be better pleased.   Their sympathies are all on the
side of edibles.   Indeed, some noses, nowadays, of my acquaintance,
have lost for etherials all relish whatever, and are no longer presented with such by their too indulgent owners.   With the tangible
and the titillating, are they rather served and delighted as contained in finely pulverized tobacco.   How far short do such fall of
the poets's olfactories, which are all awake to nature's breezes, and
so finely strung that, touched with fragrance from abroad as with
music, they call up before his imagination ideal scenes more beautiful than those in Araby the blest.

ART. V.—THE PRISONER OF LAZARE;
Or, *How the World Awards Honor*

BY ROB'T P. NEVIN.

NAY, lay the page aside, John,
    Nor heed the treacherous tale,
That deeds, which most accrue to fame,
    May best for fame avail.
To live in story is not all,
    For story sets at rest,
That they live best who least adorn,
    And least who merit best.

Staunch men of worth have been, John,
    With men of emptier mould,
Though those be writ in lines obscure,
    And these in lettered gold.
But not the glare, which vests a name,
    Confirms the claim implied;
Stars, seeming least, are mightiest,
    And nearer heaven beside.

Now heed, while I relate, John,
    And mark the lesson well,—
Yon tottering cripple, ghast and gray,
    Will witness, what I tell.
Go, where he leans upon his crutch,
    Salute his fading ear,
And learn, if such a chance e'er fell,
    Be known in his career.

There lived upon a time, John,
    A man wide known of men,—
A HERO;—many such have been,
    And oft will be again.
With armed might he held his march,
    Traversing to and forth
The sunny lands of southern climes,
    And snow-fields of the north.

And still, his standard waved, John,
   Triumphant where he passed;
For, though contending zeal might strive,
   'Twas forced to yield at last.
In vain devoted breasts opposed
   A bulwark firm and true,
With ruthless hand and reckless blade,
   He hewed his passage through.

The blood, that warmed the hearts, John,
   Of such as you and I,
In reeking gushes bathed the soil,
   Empurpled with its dye.
The homes of happy ones were spoiled,
   Towns stormed and seized a prey,
And cities of a thousand years
   Made ashes in a day.

No pestilential scourge, John,
   No plague far-dealing harm,
E'er wrought the tithe of ill that crowned
   The havoc of his arm.
And all, for what? — that vain applause
   Might ring in after time;
As though the incense of our breath
   Could sanctify the crime!

Now, further heed, I pray, John;
   There was, when terror reigned,
And murder stalked at will abroad,
   Unhindered, unrestrained,
Within the proud metropolis
   That owned the horrid sway,
A man, devoted 'mid the mass,
   Ordained to die, one day.

Arraigned, adjudged, condemned, John,
   And spotless of offence,—
Though ruling law, then most contemned,
   Spoke purest innocence,—

6*

Himself, to shield another's fate,
  Vicarious offering made ;
Assumed the fault his comrade due,
  And perished in his stead.

Now, tell me, pondering well, John,
  And fairly, in thy heart,
Which of the twain, by loftier deed,
  Achieved the nobler part ?
Who merits, for high valor proved,
  The prouder wreath to wear,
The HERO of a hundred fields,
  Or PRISONER OF LAZARE ?

And yet, in annals penned, John,
  Rarely and brief assigned,
A nameless line to hand *him* down,
  Is all the note you find.
But volumes for the conqueror-chief,
  Are found, when filled too few,
To trace the race from MONTENOTTE
  To bloody WATERLOO !

Then lay the page aside, John,
  Nor heed the treacherous tale,
That deeds, which most accrue to fame,
  May best for fame avail.
To live in story is not all,
  For story sets at rest,
That they live best who least adorn,
  And least who merit best.

PITTSBURG, November, 1848.

ART. VI.—T<small>RUE AND</small> F<small>ALSE</small> P<small>ROTESTANTISM.</small>

1. *Das Princip des Protestantismus, dargestellt von Philipp Schaff, Prof. d. Theol.*, Chambersburg, 1845.
2. *The Principle of Protestantism, as related to the Present State of the Church.* By Philip Schaff, Ph. D. Chambersburg, 1845, pp. 215.

This book has not yet received, by any means, that measure of attention to which it is fairly entitled. It speaks but little indeed for our general interest in theological science, that it should have been allowed so easily to pass out of notice. This we trust will not remain the case always. We are sure indeed that it cannot, if our theological and church life be destined to wake into a manly activity, that shall be at all commensurate finally with the greatness of our character in other respects.

It cannot be pretended, that the work itself, by its plan and execution, is undeserving of regard. The best judges have pronounced it, in this respect, admirably complete. No one even of its blindest enemies, has been carried so far in his blindness, as to call in question seriously the learning and ability with which it is written. But its title to attention is presented under a still more commanding form, in the vast practical moment of the general subject with which it is occupied, and the solemn interest of the great questions which it seeks to solve. Were the treatment of its theme far less able and thorough, and worthy of the cause of Christian science, than we know it to be in fact, the theme itself would still merit at all events, the most earnest consideration; and any work in which it was brought forward in a serious manner, might reasonably claim a hearing, so far at least as to open the way for a more competent discussion in some different quarter. It has been but too plain, in the present case, that the cold reception given to the book, resolves itself into a want of interest, on the part of our American church generally, in the subject of which the book treats. It is in such view, that we speak of it as by no means creditable to our existing theological science; and it is the same reflection which leads us to trust that the neglect will not always continue. We are not willing to believe that the vast central question of Protestantism here brought into view, will have no power sometime hereafter, in spite of all present indifference, to engage as much attention, at least in the religious world, as the question of a national tariff. How can it ever be possible for us, under any such supposition, to cultivate a truly living theology in any direction? It may not so remain. There are indications enough already, on all sides, that a more auspicious day is at hand. Our theology will yet wake to the character of a science. The reign of tradition, will give place to the power of living thought. When it comes to this, the grand question which is handled with so much ability, in the work before us, by Professor Schaff, cannot possibly fail to command respect. The difficulties belonging to it, will be understood and acknowledged. The vast interests suspended upon it, will be appreciated according to their true worth. Every attempt to meet it in the way of earnest scientific inquiry, will be looked upon with becoming respect. And then must this work itself also come into new and more enlarged notice. It may be possibly only to make room for other works on the same subject, more deserving of regard. But still, to be thus superseded, it must be duly noticed. It belongs to the literature of the question to which it is devoted, and it cannot be left out of sight in any movement by which this question is to be carried forward hereafter to its proper solution.

When we complain of the reception which has been given to Prof. Schaff's work, we wish to be distinctly understood. We do not mean to say at all, that it has fallen without effect on the community. We have had abundant evidence of the contrary, in the angry noise and clamor raised against it, in the ranks of those who have felt their prejudices uncomfortably disturbed by its light. This, we all know, has not been confined to such as have read the book, much less to such as have understood it. For one actual reader of this sort, there have been ten critics probably, who have felt themselves qualified on mere report, to visit it with wholesale condemnation. It has been widely slandered, misrepresented, and abused, by men who knew nothing

about it, except as they had been told that it ran counter to some
of their own favorite traditions; and no pains for a time, were
considered too great, to bring its author out of all credit and influence in the religious world.   Such zeal, at once so virulent
and so blind, may be taken as a very fair argument of more than
common force and point in the book.   It served to show that it was
a word spoken to the age, and so spoken as to be in some measure
heard and felt.   There is good reason to believe too, that some,
perhaps many, have been directly benefitted by its influence.
If has assisted at least, to bring sound thoughts into clearer form
and wider circulation.   It has stimulated inquiry, and suggested
new points for reflection.   Action of this sort, is naturally silent
and for the most part out of sight.   But it is none the less important on this account.   Altogether, the *Principle of Protestantism,* we have no doubt, has done good service to the cause
of truth, and exercised a wholesome power, of which its immediate popularity is not to be taken at all as the true measure.   It
is seldom indeed, that either the actual worth or the actual effect
of any work, are fairly shown by any such criterion.

Is it necessary to say still farther, that our complaint in the
case before us looks not at all to the mere want of agreement,
in any quarter, with the general theory of the work now under
consideration?   It was not expected of course by the author himself, that this would prove generally satisfactory.   The object
of the publication was not to echo simply the easy preconcep-
tions of those to whom it was addressed; and the nature of its
subject was such, that it could hardly fail, if it might merit attention at all, to challenge opposition and discussion.   To oppose,
however, is not necessarily to treat with disrespect.   Much less
does it imply any wrong to the general cause in hand.   On the
contrary, if the opposition be manly and fair, it deserves to be
acknowledged always as the best tribute which an earnest mind,
in the circumstances, can render to its claims.   It is the very
contrary, we may say, of indifference and neglect.

The thing to be complained of in the present case, is not that
Prof. Schaff's work should have been condemned and opposed,
but that no attempt has been made to meet it in the way of scientific criticism and answer.   It has been the subject of several

notices and reviews; but among all these, no one can be said to have grappled in earnest with the mighty question it has endeavored to discuss. Of what account is it in such a case, to be magisterially informed from the editorial tripod, whether of a common newspaper, or more dignified quarterly, that a book is not approved and endorsed, while the critic finds it convenient, at the same time, to observe a profound silence, in regard both to the matter of his censure and to its reason? It was not necessary at all that the work in question should be blindly accepted as sound and good; but this is no reason certainly, for its being blindly rejected, or overlooked. The case called for examination and discussion, not blind opinion merely, in any shape. Here is an open, manly, and able inquiry into the true nature of Protestantism, and its present posture, in serious conflict at various points with the current popular creed and practice. Dissent and contradiction follow naturally enough, on various sides. But our theology has no right, on a question of such momentous and far-reaching interest, to rest in a merely negative protest. Dissent and contradiction here owe it to themselves, so far as they may still lay claim to any scientific character whatever, to show in what respects the theory they oppose is unsound, and to state distinctly also, in what different form the truth is to be regarded as holding. How far from all this has been the actual course of things, in regard to the *Principle of Protestantism*, need not here be said. We have had in opposition to it, an abundance of hearty negations, but very little indeed in the way of actual contrary position. The book still waits for a truly scientific criticism on the part of its adversaries. It has been contradicted; but no one will pretend that it has been at all answered. No answer, in the proper sense, has been so much even as attempted. This we hold to be, in such a case, a just ground for complaint. It is moreover, as before said, a reproach upon our American theology, which we should be glad to see fairly wiped away.

The force of this reflection will become more apparent, if we direct our attention in a general way to the leading positions of the book, as they come before us in the solution of its general problem. We shall find them to be of such a character, that they imperiously challenge an earnest and distinct response at our hands. We have no right to overlook them, or to leave them unanswered; unless indeed, we choose to give up our boasted Protestant prerogative itself, and substitute for reason and science in religion the weight of mere outward authority, the prejudice of uninquiring and unthinking tradition.

We have a curious, almost laughable, illustration we might say, of the character of a certain portion of our modern Protestantism, in the hue and cry which was raised by some of its more zealous representatives against Prof. Schaff's work, when it first came out, on the score of its supposed *Romanizing* tendency and spirit. When we compare this charge with the actual structure of the work as a whole, we can easily understand how such a man as Krummacher, surrounded with other relations altogether, might be led to say rather harshly, that a man must be either a fool or a knave, of weak head or bad heart, to prefer it in serious form. Such a sweeping judgment, we have no wish to endorse; for we are well satisfied that many persons of good mind, in this country, by reason of a certain wrong cast in their religious education, might very well fall into such an error as that now mentioned, without any malignity of spirit whatever. With such persons, the mere fact that any word should be spoken in favor of Romanism, or in censure of Protestantism, must serve as an occasion of jealousy and alarm. The case before us, however, deserves to be remembered always, as a singular exemplification of the peculiar Protestant habit now mentioned, in the form of what may be styled a regular anti-popery panic. The book was proclaimed, first more quietly, and then in a sort of loud scream, a treasonable assault upon the very foundations of Protestantism. It was made to smell of Puseyism and Popery on every page; by distortion and exaggeration, all sorts of abominable doctrine were found lurking within its leaves; and those who knew least of it by actual inspection, showed themselves most fully convinced in many cases that it was rotten to the very core. A serious suspicion seems indeed to have prevailed with some, that the worthy author was himself in truth no better than a crafty Jesuit in disguise, a real body and soul emissary of Rome itself, who had contrived by some legerdemain to palm himself off on the German Reformed Church in this country, as a theological professor, for the express purpose of working with more success, in such insidious style, for the overthrow of our American Protestantism. Happily the Synod of the German Church had moral force enough, not to give way, in so high a case, to this spasmodic pressure. Opportunity was furnished to try the book, and bring its hideous features fairly into the light. But now, as in all similar cases of fright, the fictions of the imagination resolved themselves rapidly into unsubstantial air. Giant spectres, on close probation, shrank into dwarf realities; and the sounds that terrified men's ears, were found to be only the sense which their own fears had put into the murmurings of the hollow wind. The panic has passed entirely away. Few now would venture to repeat its exploded accusations, against Dr. Schaff's work. May we not trust besides, indeed, that a more wholesome tone of thought altogether has since come to prevail. Three years, at times, bring with them a great change of opinion. Hereafter it may be still harder to understand even, how it could ever have been possible for Protestant zeal to have such poor trust in the cause of the Reformation, as to see any danger to it in the concessions of this book.

The openly professed object of the work, to which it shows itself honestly and ably faithful throughout, is to vindicate the right of Protestantism to be owned and obeyed as the religion of Jesus Christ over against the exclusive pretensions of the Church of Rome; by referring it to its true and proper *priniciple*, in the constitution of christianity itself, so as to determine in this way its necessary existence, and the real character of its mission in the world.

It is not proposed, in this article, to follow in detail the general argument of the book; but only, as already intimated, to notice some of the leading positions embraced in it, as challenging and meriting a more vigorous attention than they have yet received.

1. It is assumed in the work throughout, that Christianity is *historical.* By this is not meant merely, that it has passed through different hands, and experienced various outward fortunes in coming down from the age of the Apostles to the present time. History in its true sense, is the evolution of some form of life, hu-

man life, which in the midst of continual progress, remains still, with unbroken continuity, always one and the same. Christianity, in such view, is a new order of life, starting in Christ himself, which as such has an independent being in the world, that requires for its completion, like all life, a steady evolution of its contents in the actual onward flow of our human existence. This real historical constitution of the new creation in Christ Jesus, by which it is clothed with an objective and enduring character so as to be properly an object of divine faith, as we have it in the Creed, is precisely what we are to understand by the *Holy Catholic Church.* Were this an abstraction only, or a creature of mere reflection and thought, it could be no such reality as faith necessarily requires. It is however no abstraction, but a concrete revelation of the fact of christianity itself under an outward and in all respects truly human form. Hence of necessity its historical character. Christianity has its very being in the form of history; showing itself thus through all ages, a single whole; the present bound always indissolubly to the past, and carrying in its womb, with like necessity, the life of the future. This process includes the most inward interests of the Church, as well as the most outward. Every doctrine has its history, without which it is not possible that it can ever be adequately understood.

This whole view however, as we all know, is opposed to a large amount of thinking at this time current in the christian world. Romanism when true to itself, allows no proper history to christianity, in the sense now described. It admits no development, but claims for itself the character of unvarying stability from the beginning. Newman mistook its nature, in seeking to establish a different theory in its favor. Protestantism also, however, to a wide extent, is found taking substantially the very same ground; not questioning indeed the fact of vast changes in the progress of church history; but holding these for the most part to have been no better than diabolical corruptions, which need only to be thrust out of the way, in order that the church may fall back again to what it was in the beginning, and what it was bound to have observed and kept as its standing traditional shape through all ages. Christianity, in this view, is no living process in the concrete life of the world, and has no objective being strictly under a historical form. We are to get it wholly from the Bible and God's Spirit; each man for himself, and all in a direct original way. Its continuity in the world holds in this only, that some in all ages have been under its saving power; while the way has always been open, by means of the scriptures, to bring it into view in its original character; which however was not done to much purpose till the age of the Reformation. So in brief, runs the theory, destroying in truth the article of the Holy Catholic Church. In room of this, it acknowledges only the phantom of an invisible abstraction which it chooses to dignify with such high name.

Now we have here, as all must see who care to think, a most interesting and momentous question, lying very near the ground of christianity itself and necessarily conditioning the view we may take of its constitution at almost every point. Are we bound to admit a truly historical character in the case of the Church, or are we not? In the Principle of Protestantism, it is assumed throughout, as already said, that we are. The whole argument of the work is based on the supposition that christianity has had a real objective being in the world under this form from the beginning; and that Protestantism must be vindicated, if successfully vindicated at all, on this ground and no other. Any vindication, it is taken for granted, would be insufficient and unsatisfactory altogether, that might proceed on any different view of what is included in the idea of the Church. The opposition which has been shown towards the book, on the one hand, has always involved the assumption that the Church, as such, has no strictly historical being in the world. And yet, strange to say, this primary fundamental question is never met, from that side, in an open and manly way. No one seems prepared to come forward with a formal denial of the historical character of the new creation, and an attempt to make good this position in the way of scientific argument against Dr. Schaff; although the case plainly requires the controversy to start here, and what should thus be boldly asserted and proved is in fact constantly assumed without proof as the ground of almost every objection that is made. This of course is most unreasonable and unfair. Our theology, if it pretend to have any opinion at all on the general subject here discussed, is bound to meet in some manly style the main view on which the whole discussion rests.   It will not do, to treat this question of the historical nature of christianity as though it were of no account; to be silent in regard to it, or to hold it in abeyance, and still presume to pronounce judgment on the merits of the case in debate.   The argument of the Principle of Protestantism begins here; it holds, in its subsequent progress, only with those who admit the preliminary idea of a truly divine historical constitution in Christ's Church ; for those who call this in question, it can of course be of no value or force ; and if they think it worth while to meddle with it at all, consistency requires that they should grapple first of all with this primary question, and bring it if possible to some satisfactory resolution.   Prof. Schaff has a right to complain that this has not been done. Among all his assailants, no one has had courage to come out and say : Your main position is false ; christianity is no such historically human fact as you pretend ; and there is no reason in the world, why we should think it necessary to bring our Protestant revolution into agreement with any theory of this sort ; enough that we see our way clear to accept it, as a fresh con- struction of the church, by our own private judgment, out of the Bible ; this, and this only, is the religion of Protestants.   So much most of the opposition made to Prof. Schaff's book *means;* but it has not been found willing thus far to commit itself dis- tinctly to any formal vindication of its own cause, under such aspect, in the way of open argument.

It would be vastly desirable, in the present posture of the Church, to have this primary point brought into discussion in some able and truly scientific style; and we see not indeed, how our reigning Puritanism can well avoid the responsibility of so taking it in hand.

2. In necessary conformity with the idea of a truly historical character belonging to christianity, it is assumed by the Principle of Protestantism throughout that the stream of its life, before the Reformation, lay mainly in the bosom of the Roman or Papal Church.   The case requires, that it should be allowed to have come down, under a strictly continuous form, from the time of

the Apostles; that no huge break or chasm should be admitted in the proper outward and visible life of the Church, cutting off its later existence from the existence which it had in the begining; that it should not be thought of as a phantom ship merely, appearing and disappearing, at long intervals, on the ocean of the world's history. In such view, we are bound plainly to allow the presence of Christ's true Church in the old Catholic system, as it stood through the middle ages and down to the great crisis of the sixteenth century. More than this; it lies in the conception of the Church, as a divine institution, that this portion of its history could not have passed away without reason or meaning. Christ's promise to be in the Church to the end of the world, may not be taken to have gone into oblivion or sleep, from the sixth century to the sixteenth, or from the eighth even to the fourteenth. For one who has come to know what it means to believe in a Holy Catholic Church, "against which the gates of hell shall *never* prevail," any such supposition must be felt to be absolutely impious. There is no escape then from the consequence that God was with the Church through the middle ages, gloriously carrying forward by its means the vast problem of christianity, with steady progress, towards its appointed end. We may admit a great apostacy from the truth, in its general history; we may, if we please, refer the beginning of this apostacy to the second century; but let us beware, in God's name, of affirming or supposing a pure or total apostacy, such as must involve the dissolution of the church itself, and make it necessary for it to try its own experiment over again, with fresh start from the beginning. There is something horrible in any such thought as that. The Church has never so succumbed to the power of hell. The mystery of iniquity has never so trampled in full over the mystery of godliness. Christ has not lain thus, for whole centuries, underneath the iron heel of Satan. We believe in his Church, as a real, divine, historical constitution in the world; and by this faith we feel ourselves shut up to the joyous conviction, that all through the night of long, laborious transition from the old Roman civilization over to the far higher culture of modern Europe, this same Church has been, not lost in the billows that seemed to overwhelm it, but from first to last actively wrestling with the fulfilment of its own mission, and making its way, through vast corruptions, to a higher and better state in the future. All along it was the central power of the world's tumultuating life, the ark in which was carried the last hope of humanity for all coming time.

All this, however, is virtually denied by much of our reigning Protestantism at the present time. The opposition made to Dr. Schaff's work in particular, may be said to involve throughout a different theory of the old catholic church entirely. The theory indeed is very hard to reduce to any distinct positive shape; but so much is clear with it *negatively*, that this old church is not to be regarded as in any way concerned at all in the actual onward flow of true christianity in the world. A long tract of what is popularly known as church history, must be viewed in truth as a blank at best, if not something much worse, in the actual progress of Christ's kingdom. The christian life, if we are to believe this theory, unfortunately missed its way almost from the very start; got unnecessarily entangled with Pagan philosophy and Jewish tradition; fell, from century to century, into continually more deplorable aberrations; lost sight of its original mission at last altogether, so as to put a yoke on the neck of the nations for the very purpose of leading them into perpetual captivity to the Devil; God all the while contemplating the wholesale failure of his own work, with a sort of passive surprise, and waiting for the sixteenth century to bring all back once more to a new experiment, under better auspices, of the same divine enterprise as it stood in the days of the Apostles, and some fifteen or twenty years *possibly* after their death.

This general theory, we say, plainly enough underlies the whole thinking of a large portion of our modern Protestantism, and on many occasions projects itself into the air, (like a black porpoise,) in sporadic bursts of zeal against the "whore of Babylon;" and yet, characteristically enough, it is not willing commonly after all, to come into the light of quiet scientific discussion, in order that its pretensions may be fairly tried and known. Who among the opposers of Dr. Schaff's work for instance, all ready to take it for granted, as it would seem, that Romanism has been a pure lie, ("Satan's masterpiece,") from the beginning, has felt it necessary to stand forward, at the same time, and face with any rational answer the profoundly momentous practical interrogations, which in that case need to be met and solved by christian science in the service of christian faith? How cheap and easy is that championship of Protestantism, which just plants its heel on the article of a universal christian church, at the very outset of its polemic crusade, and then carries the whole question, caricatured to its own content, to the bar of common sense, there to be settled in pure lynch law style, without the least regard to the mystery of christianity, as a past fact in the history of the world. We should like to see one of these wholesale dealers with Romanism, of some proper capacity for the purpose, required to come up boldly to the mark of distinctly asserting, and at least trying to prove, what they usually count it enough to take in the way of blind unthinking trust. Let him be compelled, for instance, to answer definitely some such questions as these: Can the Church, as a continuous body in the world, ever perish? If the corruptions of the nominally christian world must be allowed to have involved a total falling away from Christ in the middle ages, how far back must such fatal apostacy be carried?* Is Christianity to be regarded as a failure substantially, for one thousand, or six hundred, or three hundred years? What becomes, in such case, of Christ's word: "Lo, I am with you always to the end of the world;" and again: "On this rock I will build my Church, and the gates of hell shall not prevail against it?" Did it after all disappear in the middle ages? If not, where was it, and what world-mission was it then employed to fulfil? Such questions deserve an open and manly answer. It will not do to say: We have no opinion in the case, and do not count it material to express any definite judgment one way or another. The case is one that we are bound to have some settled judgment upon, if we pretend to have any voice whatever in regard to the general question handled in Dr. Schaff's work. For men to affect a full

---

* Few stop to inquire or consider, how far, in many cases, their darts hurled at Rome reach back into the life of primitive christianity. Roman baptism, we are told, is invalid, because its superstitious accompaniments are made to turn it into another rite altogether. But, alas, these spring from the *second* century. Has there then been no valid baptism in the Church since that time?

mastery of this question, in such way as to decide it for themselves and every body else in a few sweeping sentences, while
still unprepared to express any tangible view of what lies *back*
of Protestantism in the history of the Church, is just to show
themselves totally insensible to the claims of science, as well as
to those of charity and common honesty, in regard to the whole
subject.

3. Another position taken in the Principle of Protestantism is,
that the Reformation must be viewed as the product strictly and
truly of the previous life of the Church under its Roman Catholic form. This again flows necessarily out of the general view
of christianity already noticed. If the Church be truly historical, a constant genesis of new forms out of those that have gone
before; and if its proper continuity be found in the Roman communion before the Reformation; it follows of course, that the
legitimacy of Protestantism turns altogether on its title to be regarded as the true and proper succession of this old catholic life.
To make it, in any way, an original product of the generation
by whose agency it was brought to pass, or to derive it from any
quarter out of the Church as it stood before, is nesessarily to call
in question the historical being of the Church itself, and to resolve it into a mere creature of human thought and human will.
Where accordingly the least sense of the Church, as a divine
perpetual constitution, the proper object of faith, has come to
prevail, not only will it be allowed that Protestantism has its
root in the Church of Rome, but it will be felt to be indispensable to its full vindication, that this point should be clearly established against all cavil or doubt.

Here of course various false conceptions of the nature and
meaning of Protestantism, are at once excluded. It is not allowed
to stand essentially in mere opposition to Rome. To reject the
errors of the papacy, is not as a matter of course to be in league
with Christ's truth. No protest here can be of any account that
does not spring from the positive life of christianity itself; and
this life must hold in living connection with the old catholic
faith. Mere negation is no better in the end than infidel slang.
Protestantism involves no rupture with the old faith as such;
requires no new start to be taken in the life of christianity, in

such a way as to break all continuity of existence with the life
it had before ; on the contrary, it is genuine only in proportion
as it remains rooted, with its inmost consciousness, in the sense
of an imperishable christianity, which is felt to have come down
through the medium of Christ's outward historical Church, from
the time of the Apostles. It affects not to spring direct from the
clouds, or out of the brain simply of the sixteenth century. It
is the life of the old Catholic Church itself, reaching over thus
by inward historical development, to a new and higher form.
To refer it to any other source—to pretend its derivation from
some different quarter altogether, is to be guilty of sore treason
towards the whole cause which it may be attempted ignorantly
to uphold in this way.

But all this falls not in, by any means, with the view of many,
who are in the habit of considering themselves the best Protestants in the country, and who see a Romanizing tendency, as
they call it, in everything that betrays a particle of sympathy
with what the Church was before the Reformation. They make
a merit of placing Romanism always in the worst possible light,
for the purpose of showing off Protestantism to so much the more
advantage. They can see in it no meaning or reason whatever ;
it is purely the work of hell, cunningly contrived in the service
of a lie ; in the case of which one knows not at which most to
marvel, the barefaced absurdity of the imposition on the one
hand, or the dumb stupidity that could engage the world so long
to submit to it on the other. All bad epithets are heaped upon
the whole system unsparingly, oftentimes in true billingsgate
style, to make it odious and abominable. How then should
Protestantism be allowed to have any life in common with such
unmitigated apostacy? *Whence* exactly it may be supposed to
come, this zealous school is not prepared harmoniously to say ;
the necessity of referring it to any positive principle whatever,
has not been possibly thought of at all ; but one thing is fixed ;
be the source of it where it may, Protestantism owns no inward
historical connection with the Roman Catholic Church. It is
anti-popery in its very essence ; it is eternal enmity to Rome, by
its first definition. What it *is not*, in this view, is held to be of
far more consequence than what it *is*, or rather its proper exist-

ence is taken to stand in this negation, as its own true sense and reality.

Thus we have two perfectly contradictory schemes of Protestantism, either of which of course can never comfortably endure the other. All must see, that the view presented in Dr. Schaff's work can never find any favor in the eyes of those who carry in themselves the "fixed idea" that Romanism is purely and wholly the concoction of hell. On such necessarily, all argument and science in this direction are thrown away. The book is at once in conflict with their whole position; and they instinctively denounce it as dangerous and false. *Where* precisely the wrong lies, it may not be so easy to make plain; but its whole bearing is felt to be injurious and offensive. Men who feel their *craft* in danger, stop not to weigh reasons. Enough here to cry out: Popery! No fellowship with the Beast! or some other slang catch word, in the same Ephesian style.

It were to be wished, that the subject *could* be met in some more manly style. The question: Is Protestantism a continuation strictly of the life of the Church as it stood before, or does it spring wholly from some different quarter, is one that deserves and solicits a rational answer. Those who assume the second position, and build upon it so large a part of their polemic divinity, are bound surely to put their theory into a clear and open shape, and stand forward with at least a show of science in its defence. Let them tell us, up and down, that there was no living inward connection between the Reformation and the central stream of christianity, as it flowed previously in the Church of Rome, and then explain its origin and constitution in some more satisfactory way, if they can. Till this be done, or attempted, their blustering talk about the great subject discussed in the Principle of Protestantism, is entitled to exceedingly small respect.

4. From the historical view of Protestantism, as now stated, grows in the next place the necessary conclusion, that it is something more than a mere retrogression, on the part of the Church, to the position which it occupied in the beginning. Such an imagination, however popular it may be with many Protestants, is only in fact the old Roman fiction of stability and immobility over again, under a new phase, and with new power of prejudice and mischief. In the first place, it were a most gloomy reflection surely, to conceive of Christianity as doomed to fall back, in this bankrupt style, to its own primordial state, for the purpose of setting itself right from the universal blunder of a thousand years. The very thought, for a thoughtful mind, is one that tends to scepticism. But then again, the hypothesis refuses obstinately to come into harmony, in any view, with the actual form and shape of things. Protestantism consists, we are told, in going

back to primitive christianity. But where, in truth, is this
resurrection of antiquity to be found? Is Protestantim identical
at all, in figure or complexion, with ancient christianity, as it
stood in the fifth century, or in the second? Every true scholar
knows that it is not. In what contradiction then are we involved,
when the opposite notion is accepted as of necessary force, and
every sect feels itself bound accordingly to set itself up as a full
and complete model, image or facsimile, of what the Church
was in the beginning. Not one of our sects can make good any
such pedantic pretension; and the effort to do so runs out inevitably at last into more or less conscious hypocrisy and sham. So
terribly disastrous, in a moral view, is this doctrine of a stationary
christianity, as applied to the great fact of Protestantism. We
never understand it, and we can never do it justice in the way of
rational vindication, till we come to see and say openly: It is
not the nullification of christian history for more than a thousand
years; it is *not* a mechanical return simply to the ecclesiastical
life of the fifth century, or of the third, or of the second; it is
vastly more than all this, the conservation namely of that ancient
life, advanced now, by the long deep world-struggle of a thousand
years, with the gain of incalculable new wealth secured in the
process, to new and higher ground, such as the Church has never
occupied before, and never could have been brought to occupy
in any different way. No defence of Protestantism can be successfully maintained, as it seems to us, that is not maintained in
this form.

5. Professor Schaff, in natural harmony with the whole theory
of church history thus far brought into view, allows the fact of
an inward movement in the life of Protestantism itself, reaching
from the sixteenth century onward to the present time, and
involving the revelation of serious and alarming evils in its constitution. That there has been no small change in the posture
of the general interest, since the age of Luther and Calvin, would
seem to be too clear to admit any dispute. It is very easy to see,
for instance, that Puritanism includes a material advance, whether
right or wrong, on the original spirit of the Reformation. It is
just as little a strict copy of primitive Protestantism, as it may be
snid to be a transcript of primitive Christianity. Still broader
deviations however are presented to us, under other forms.
There can be no question either as to the bad character of much
that has come into view in this way in connection with Protestantism. The wide prevalence of Rationalism in Europe, and
the rampant reign of Sectarianism in this country, are palpable
demonstrations in proof of the assertion. These evils show an
inward affinity, it must be confessed, with the Protestant movement; they plead the principle of it in their own favor, and are

found growing forth from it actually at least in an outward way. All this the book now before us openly and fairly admits. The objection of the Romanists here is permitted to carry with it such weight, as of right belongs to it. No attempt is made to keep it out of sight or to evade its point. Protestantism is allowed to have faults; and these not simply accidental, but in a certain sense inherent in its very nature; constitutional diseases, we may say, that require to be worked out of it by the course of its own life. The very antagonism in which it stands with the Roman system, has involved danger to it in the opposite direction, from the beginning. Rationalism and the spirit of sect, (different sides only of one and the same evil,) are the form in which this danger has in fact come widely to triumph. They are both to be greatly deplored, and call loudly for redress. Still they do not at once convict Protestantism itself of falsehood. They show only that it is neither infallible nor absolutely complete. That the historical evolution of its principle should include along with what is good, much also that is objectionable and wrong, was to have been expected from the beginning, and is only in agreement with the general law of history as it stood before. Let the evils in question be acknowledged and laid seriously to heart, as they ought to be, and at once the advantage taken of them by the Romanist is shorn of half its weight.

All this however does not suit the high toned anti-popery school, to which we have before referred. It will hear of no process in Protestantism; and any evils that may be found in connection with it, here and there, are to be taken as accidental simply to its history, and no part properly of the movement itself. Its justification is supposed to require, that it should be counted infallible, identical with the absolute idea of christianity, the whole religion of the Bible, without fault and without disease.

Here now is a great question, that ought to be met in a manly way. Has Protestantism in truth been stationary in its form and character, from the beginning? Has it no tendency, in its own nature, to run into disease, on the side of the individual judgment and individual will? Has it not done so in fact? Can the modern sect system, (to say nothing of its theoretic counterpart,) be vindicated at all as in harmony with the spirit of Christ and the genius of his Church? A most momentous inquiry truly, which the position of the school just noticed might seem to urge imperiously into consideration; and yet it is met, on this side, with no clear and distinct answer.

6. Finally, the "Principle of Protestantism" applies its idea of a historical christianity still farther to the life of the Church, in such a way as to make room for the prospect of something far better and more glorious than its present condition, in time to

come.   In this view, it is openly admitted that Protestantism, in
its present form, is not the full end of christianity.   How can
that be supposed, in the face of the diseases and defects that are
so plainly incorporated in its system.   As it answers not strictly
to primitive christianity, so neither may it be taken as at once
the form of millennial christianity.   Its present state must be
regarded as interimistic, a period of transition over to some new
and higher order in which finally its present deficiencies shall be
supplied and its present diseases healed.   It is to be fully vindicated at last, by so completing the solution of its own problem, as
to overcome and surmount fairly all the disorders necessarily
incident to the movement, till the whole sense of it shall have
been brought into view.   The general nature of this higher state
of the Church moreover, may be argued from a proper consideration of what is needed to complete the mission of christianity.
It must take up into itself the whole life of the world on all its
sides, art, science, government, &c., fulfilling thus the old dream
of the Catholic Church ; but all at the same time in a free spiritual way, according to the genius of the true Protestant Church.
The Catholic and Protestant tendencies must come together,
with inward organic union, and in this way be delivered severally
from the hurtful aberrations to which each must ever be exposed
in a separate view.   This implies of course no return to Romanism; it is all involved rather in the onward movement of
Protestantism itself, and is simply the necessary form of its ultimate completion.

Those who reject the idea of historical christianity throughout,
must be dissatisfied of course again with the whole view now
stated.   They hold it a dangerous concession altogether, to say
of Protestantism that it needs any improvement, or may ever
be expected to pass over into any higher form of church life.
Especially are they unwilling to admit, that its perfection can at
all require any such improvement, as seems to them to be implied in the conception of anything like a reconciliation of the
Protestant and Catholic tendencies, as the true normal form of
christianity.   Protestantism, as they take it, needs no such higher
character.   It is already identical with christianity in the absolute
sense, either in the character of some single sect, or as exhibited
by the body of evangelical sects generally; and no absurdity is
felt in the imagination, that it is altogether sufficient in this view,
to take possession of the whole world and bring the christian
mission to an end.   To talk of a " Church of the Future " in
which the full sense of Protestantism itself shall find room hereafter to come to its proper expression, is regarded as an abandonment of faith in the church as it now stands, or as it has stood
heretofore.

No one will pretend that the question here brought into view, is of small interest or importance. But in what quarter do we find it submitted to any earnest and thorough discussion? Who among all the critics of Dr. Schaff has ventured to lay hold of it with any sort of vigorous grasp, and to come thus to an open and clear issue with him on scientific ground?

It may now be understood what we mean, when we complain of the general treatment of the work before us, as at once unfair to the high and solemn theme with which it is employed and discreditable to our reigning theology. The several positions at which we have glanced, as they are here bound together in the form of a learned argument for Protestantism, are not of such a character surely that we can have any right to pass them by with indifference; unless it be such right as we may claim to take no interest in theology whatever. They are of central significance, and it is not possible to be intelligently awake to what may be considered the great life question of the age, without feeling their weight. It is notorious besides, that they are in conflict with a large amount of our religious thinking; and just with that part of it too which is apt to be most confident and self-complacent in its own different view, as the only true theory of Protestantism and Christianity. In these circumstances, the points in question ought to be met and if possible settled in some truly scientific way. Mere presumption and dogmatic assertion here, are not by any means enough. We need evidence, argument, light. It is the glory of Protestantism, to court investigation, and to be able to give a reason of the hope that is in it, with earnest humility and faith. All blind tradition is at war with its inmost nature and life.

As the case now stands, we have no hesitation in retorting on the opponents of Dr. Schaff, the very charge, which some of them have so industriously tried to fasten on his book; the charge, namely, of ministering " comfort and help," indirectly, to the cause of Romanism, by placing the Protestant interest on false and untenable ground, in face of the war that is waged for its destruction. The true allies of Rome, in the Protestant ranks, are the men who think to put down Romanism by mere noise and rant, without pretending to go to the bottom of a single question involved in the movement of the Reformation; who take it for granted from the start, that the whole controversy is so shallow as to need no investigation, the merits of it lying open at once to any school-boy of common sanity and sense; who undertake, accordingly, to settle it, for themselves and for the whole world besides, by a few wholesale propositions, drawn from the most popular abstract understanding; who have no power to perceive or appreciate a single catholic idea or truth;

and who, in consequence of all this, so manage their opposition to Popery, that it becomes, in truth, a war at the same time, on the very life and substance of catholic christianity itself, in the sacred form which it has carried from the beginning. It has been well observed by a profound thinker, that no one is prepared successfully to combat a difficult error, who has not himself so entered into it, as to feel its power, and thus rise superior to it in an inward way; and so in the present case, emphatically, we may say, any argument against Romanism, must be counted weak as water, that is not made to rest on this condition. We have no patience with those who set out in their defence of Protestantism, with the assumption, open or implied, that the Roman system, as a whole, is destitute of all meaning or sense—a mass of sheer absurdity, or a pure creation of Satan. Every such assumption is arrogant and monstrous in the extreme, and is enough to destroy all confidence in any argument or declamation with which it may be joined. It is an outrage on all common sense, most disrespectful to man and God, to suppose that such a system as that presented to us in the Roman Catholic Church, the most magnificent and imposing organization the world has ever seen, at least in an outward view, should have so grown up in the bosom of christianity, towering to the very heavens in majesty, and filling the whole earth with its presence, through a long succession of centuries, and yet be at last the thin texture *only* of a huge diabolical lie, to which the stupid world was blindly sold for a thousand years, in the style represented by some of our nut-shell polemics. History is not so crazy as all that The gates of hell have carried no such disastrous triumph into the very heart of the christian Church. The great and good men of other days, the Bernards and Anselms of the dark ages, were not so wretchedly dumb as this sophomorical judgment would imply. The old champions of the Reformation—giants as they were themselves in intellectual and moral prowess, were not thus guilty of mistaking windmills for giants on the opposite side. It were more rational, certainly, in this case, to suspect our modern wholesale critics, who feel strong enough to prostrate Bellarmine with a harlequin's wand, as being themselves possibly the true sham, "made manifest" to all angels at least, if not to all men, by such exhibition. It is more likely, on the whole, that they are themselves in a crazy posture, mentally, than that all history over against them, should be so terribly out of joint, and the Church so hopelessly chaotic, down to their time. We have no mind at least, to listen to their oracular decisions, pronounced under such doubtful relation, and betraying such vast superiority to all difficulty or doubt. They do not understand the controversy with which they are so soon and so easily done.

Let them first comprehend the true sense of the ancient Church, and come to some sympathy with old catholic ideas, and learn some proper reverence for history, and master in a word the inward life of Romanism, as it reigns in truly pious minds, (not scouting the possibility of honest piety under any such form,) and *then* address themselves with insight and proof to the vindication of Protestantism, and we are prepared to give them a respectful hearing. Short of this, they do not deserve to be heard. Their false and shallow strategy serves only to betray the interest, on whose side they pretend to stand and fight. *

In contrast with all such powerless assaults on Romanism, Dr. Schaff's work stands before us in the character of an earnest and vigorous plea for the principle of the Reformation. It grapples with the subject in earnest; goes to the bottom of it; allows the opposite interest every advantage which it can legitimately claim ; does full justice to the truth involved in Romanism ; shows all proper reverence for history and the idea of the Church; admits in full the bad points of Protestantism itself, without any attempt

---

* Take, in illustration of the pseudo-protestant spirit here described, the following precious morceau, from the N. Y. *American Protestant*, for December, 1848 :

"REV. DR. NEVIN AGAINST PROTESTANTISM.—The U. S. C. Magazine publishes the discourse of Dr. Nevin, on the Spirit of Sect, under the head of 'Protestant Evidence of Catholicity.' The argument of Dr. N., is in accordance with the views of the Roman Catholic Hierarchy, and is sanctioned by them. Why should it not be, when he attempts to prove that all the Protestant sects are antichrist. Strange views are these, for a man who is without the pale of the Roman Catholic Church."

Of course the Am. Prot. has not *read* the tract here denounced. All goes in such a case, by *intuition.* Any tirade against Rome, is entitled to its reward, as such, in the way of glorification. Any word that Rome can lay hold of in its own favor, must be set down as contraband. The great offence with this tract is, its firm utterance of the article, *One Holy Catholic Church*, in the old sense of the Apostles' Creed; and its condemnation of the *sect system* as at war with the true spirit of the same. The Am. Prot. will have it, (if it mean *anything,*) that Protestantism is constitutionally sectarian, and that sects are not to be deplored as its curse, but gloried in as its peculiar privilege and ornament. That is, it sets Protestantism in full, plump contradiction to the whole idea of catholicity, as held by the ancient Church. The same Am. Prot. notices lately the outbreak of *Rongianism* in Vienna, as a revival of Religion ; *Ronge again in his glory ;* the times of Luther returned, &c. No amount of exposure, it seems, can put down the credit of this infidel movement, with a certain part of our religious press. It has a life as tough as that of Monk Leahey, which, howeve effectually killed in one place o-day, is sure to come to a glorious resurrection, through the *gullibility* of the popery mania, some where else to-morrow. We have no mind however, for our part, to graduate our idea of Protestantism, by the despotic censorship of any such self-constituted inquisition ; whose sympathies are so widely foreign from the spirit of the ancient Church, while they fall in so readily with the frivolous rationalism of this Rongian reformation, as bearing the same divine signature with that of the immortal Martin Luther.

to cover them with disguise or excuse; and yet at the same time, valiantly wrests from the hands of the imperious foe, all the most trusted weapons of his warfare, and rescues triumphantly the cause of the Reformation from his proud grasp. It is our deliberate persuasion, that no work has appeared previously, in our American theological literature, in which is contained at once so fair and able an argument against the high-toned pretensions of the Roman Church. This will be understood hereafter, if not now. One such tract of this sort, going to the bottom of the discussion, is worth a whole cart load of the ephemeral trash on the subject of popery, which we find so industriously trumpeted on all sides, in our common sectarian press, as the quintessence of polemic power and skill. What are a score of nicknames and anecdotes to a single argument? What are a hundred appeals to popular prejudice and passion, as weighed with the smallest amount of true christian reasoning, based on true christian ground? Much noise has been made about *Kirwan's* Letters to Bishop Hughes, as forming an epoch in the history of the Roman Catholic controversy; and we are ready to allow them the credit of a much higher respectability than what belongs to the mass of the popular reading now noticed. They are characterized by great readiness, vivacity and point, and have undoubtedly carried the victory *as against Bishop Hughes.* But as regards true force and value for the vindication of Protestantism, they can bear no sort of comparison with this treatise of Professor Schaff. And yet the first work is lauded to the skies while the second is looked upon widely as a sort of semi-jesuitic stab to the whole cause it pretends to support. So much for the *discrimination* of a large portion of our Protestantism. The Romanists themselves know better. They may catch at separate concessions made in such a work as the Principle of Protestantism; but they have no mind to grapple with its argument as a whole. Such a man as Brownson, understands well enough the advantage he has, in contending with those who set out by a rejection of all truly *catholic* ideas, as no part of the faith once delivered to the saints; but he is sufficiently prudent also, at the same time, not to meddle with an argument which allows to these ideas their full force, while it vindicates however their true and real possession to the cause of the Reformation. This is to plant the controversy on different ground altogether. Mr. Brownson promised some time since, to take up this view of Protestantism; but like a number of Protestant critics, he has found it convenient thus far, to forget his praiseworthy purpose, occupied in his own imagination, perhaps, with more *weighty* matters.

J. W. N.

THE

MERCERSBURG REVIEW.

MARCH, 1849.

NO. II.

ART. VII.—The Apostles' Creed.

To understand properly the religious significance and value of this most ancient Christian symbol, we must take into consideration, first, its *outward history;* secondly, its *constitution,* or *inward form;* and thirdly, its *material structure,* or *organism.* All this may be regarded as forming a proper introduction to the study of its actual contents, the glorious world of truth which it throws open to our contemplation.

I. *Outward History of the Creed.*

The title of the symbol seems, at first sight, to refer its authorship at once to the Apostles; and it has been in fact a very widely prevalent opinion in the Church, resting in long tradition, that it came originally complete in every part, as we now have it, from their hands. In the Romanist communion, it has been looked upon almost universally indeed, as profane to call this in question; and many in the Protestant world, have made it a part of their religion to believe the same thing. The first distinct statement

of the opinion, we find in Rufinus, a church father of the fourth
century; who speaks of it, however, as a common belief, handed
down from an earlier time. According to this tradition, he says,
the Apostles, before separating to their different fields of service,
that they might not fall into any confusion subsequently, met
together, and under the guidance of the Holy Ghost, by joint
contribution of views, framed and adopted this compend, as a
rule of faith, to be everywhere received by the infant churches.
Some allusion to such joint composition, was found in the Greek
name *symbol* itself, which signifies, primitively, a collation or
throwing together of different things; and it is in conformity
with the same thought, that we find the tradition elsewhere so
far improved, as to refer to each Apostle, separately, a distinct
article or clause of the creed, as his particular quota contributed
towards its formation.

This whole opinion, however, is one which cannot be maintained with any tolerable show of success. Not only is it destitute of all positive historical foundation, but insuperable difficulties stand in the way of it on every side. No such apostolic
creed or rule is mentioned in the New Testament. Some, indeed, have pretended to find it in St. Paul's "analogy or proportion of faith," Rom. xii. 6, the "good deposit" committed to
Timothy, 2 Tim. i. 14, the "first principles of the oracles of
God," mentioned Heb. vi. 12, the "doctrine" on which so much
stress is laid by St. John 2nd Epis. v. 10, and "the faith once
delivered unto the saints," as noticed by St. Jude, Ep. v. 3.
But there is nothing in these passages to require any such interpretation. Still more significant is the silence of the early church
writers. None of the fathers before Rufinus, Greek or Latin,
make any mention of the tradition to which he refers; and in
all their controversies and discussions, we meet with no appeal
whatever, to any such single and fixed form of words, as of
established authority from the time of the Apostles. On the
contrary, the way in which they touch the subject, shows clearly
that no fixed form of this sort was in existence. They refer
frequently to a christian rule or canon of faith, and occasionally
give us the sum of its contents; but this always with such free
variation, as plainly implies that it was regarded as standing in

substance of what it taught, rather than in any particular
rms of expression.   Nay, the testimony of Rufinus himself,
conclusive as regards this point.   He affirms expressly, that
e form was not the same precisely in all the churches; but that
ditions were made to it, in some cases, in opposition to particu-
r local heresies.   He himself chose to follow, as he tells us,
e form to which he stood pledged by his own baptism in the
urch at Aquileia.   This, of course, he accepted, as of apostoli-
, authority; and yet he admits, that it contained one article
hich was not found in the Latin or Greek symbols generally,
in use elsewhere at that time.   This was the article on Christ's
scent into hades.   It has been made clear besides, that the
ticle on the communion of saints, was wanting altogether, and
e article on the life everlasting, to a very considerable extent,
the symbols of the first four centuries; the truth asserted in
ch case, being held only, as something involved in the article
ing immediately before.   Such variations in the form of the
eed, forbid the supposition of any fixed system of words, recog-
ized and received as the composition of the Apostles.   For no
e, surely, would have felt at liberty to alter any such normal
heme of faith; and the use of other different forms altogether
Gaul, Spain, Alexandria, Antioch, Jerusalem, &c., must be
unted in this case a problem admitting no rational solution.

Against such weight of evidence, the mere *inscription* of the
mbol cannot be taken as of any particular force.   It is called,
deed, the *Apostles'* Creed.   But this title might have come
to use gradually, under a mistaken idea of its being derived
om the Apostles', when it had no such origin in fact; or the
le may be taken as referring, in its original application, only
the substantial contents of the creed, and not to its particular
raseology and form.   The last supposition, we have every
son to assume as true and correct.   The testimony of Rufi-
s himself, while it shows that there was a current general tra-
tion in the Church at that time, referring the authorship of the
eed to the Apostles, indicates clearly enough at the same time,
at this was to be understood only of its soul and substance,
d not of the very terms in which it might happen to be uttered
any given case.   For he does not pretend to confine the cha-

racter of apostolic dignity to any single form of it, as then in use, to the exclusion of all the rest; but takes it for granted, rather, that all the churches enjoyed in this respect, the same advantage. He seems to allow, indeed, a certain central normality to the creed as used at Rome; but chooses, nevertheless, as we have just seen, to abide by the form it carried in his own church at Aquileia, as strictly answerable to his idea of apostolical authority, although including a clause, which by his own confession, had no place in it as it had been in use to that time in other places. This shows plainly, in what sense he took it to be from the Apostles; and it was no doubt only in the same view, that the title which it now bears, came in the first place into general use.

The title indeed, was by no means confined originally to this particular symbol, as distinguished from others; but was applied frequently also to other symbols, that of Nice for instance, that of Constantinople, &c.; since with all their difference, they were regarded as alike embodying and representing in a true form, the one catholic faith of the Church as it had been handed down from the Apostles.

In this way, we are prepared at once to meet the vanity of those who affect to run away with the point now granted and proved, as though nothing more were needed to overthrow the apostolical credit of the Creed entirely, and turn it into the character of any mere ordinary human composition. Of the two extremes, it is hard to say which in this case most deserves our commiseration; the superstition, which in the face of all historical evidence to the contrary, still clings to the dream of an outward construction of the symbol as we now have it, on the part of the Apostles; or the shallow frivolity, that in detecting the untenable character of this prejudice, is ready at once to chuckle over its great discovery as the revelation of a " pious fraud," which it feels itself at liberty ever afterwards to scout from its presence as deserving of no regard whatever. With such mechanical *illumination*, that is so soon and so easily conducted to the end of its subject, it becomes us of course to have no patience or correspondence. Its superior wisdom is, after all, in the case before us, of a most sophomorical complexion. " What men call the Apostles' Creed," this spirit exclaims, " though very ancient, was no more an apostolical invention than was Christmas-pie."[*]   Admitted, so far as any particular outward structure is concerned.   But is *this* a discovery to be paraded in such style, over against the ancient fathers and the belief of the early Church?   The puerility here falls not on the fathers, but on the modern rationalism, that thinks to dispose of the whole question in such poor outward style.   Even Rufinus himself, refers the Creed to the Apostles, only in such a way, as to leave room for much liberty and variation in its external form.   But all this was not felt, either by him or by the Church in general, to conflict at all with the reigning tradition, which carried back its origin to the time of the Apostles.   The true power and value of the symbol were felt to stand, not in a given fixed version established for its universal use, but in the divine substance of its contents, which was capable of retaining its identity under very considerable changes of expression.   So far as this was concerned, the christian catholic world considered itself in possession always of one and the same faith, however much freedom it might see fit to exercise with the utterance of it in different places.   It was known well enough, that the general symbol admitted an utterance more or less full, as circumstances might require; that particular additions had been made to it with the progress of time, which did not belong to it in the beginning; and that it was not the same thing precisely, as to all its details, in any two leading provinces of the Church.   And yet, notwithstanding all this, it was felt that the Church had but one Creed, and that this was of truly apostolical dignity and authority.   It expressed not only the same faith that was held by the Apostles,

---

[*] See notice of Dr. Bushnell's address at Andover, in the October number of the Boston "Observatory," for 1848, p. 479: "We are at a loss to understand what is meant by the boasted progress of theological science. So far as we can see, the foot-prints of this progress are all *back-tracks*. The Puseyites are advancing stern-foremost towards the Dark Ages, and Dr. Bushnell is backing up to what he calls the 'Apostles' Creed,' which, though very ancient, was no more an apostolical invention than was Christmas-pie. Such hind-part-before 'progress,' like the 'man with his head turned,' with his reversed stridings and grotesque backslidings, does not promise that the 'new era of christianity,' which is said to be at hand, will be any improvement on the past." This may be allowed to be sufficiently *smart;* but is it not also sufficiently profane?

but it was their faith itself handed forward thus, under a living character, in the good confession of the Church from age to age. It was no product of private thinking here and there, as though the churches being left all to frame their several creeds in a separate way, had simply happened to come so near together, without yet reaching a full harmony; but it was something that came to them from a common source and under a common character, and which in this view was of broader and deeper force than any merely private confession as such. The unity of the Creed was determined by the realness of its contents, and the relation under which these were appeehended by all parts of the Church alike. It stood bound thus to the new order of life, which was revealed by Christ, through the Apostles, in the Church. Its stability was not in the outward letter, so much as in the inward spirit. It was written and preserved, as one of the fathers expresses it, not on plates of metal or stone, but on "fleshly tables of the heart," by the Spirit of the living God.*

In this way then, the old church tradition, as it is has passed down to us from the earliest times, is still entitled to our earnest respect; and we may easily see in fact, how with all its changes and variations, the symbol before us may be said to have taken its rise in the very age of the Apostles, and in a certain sense, under their very hands, and to have represented from the beginning, the one unvarying faith of the universal christian world. It needs no very close inspection to perceive that the manifold ways in which it was uttered come all to the same thing at last, and fall back always to a single fundamental formula as their general and common ground. They are at most, different translations, more or less full, of one and the same creed, comprising in itself the sense of the new creation in Christ Jesus.

It lies in the nature of the case, that the christian profession must have involved some common rule of faith from the beginning. "The word is nigh thee," Paul says, "even in thy mouth and in thy heart, that is the word of faith which we preach; that if thou shalt confess with thy mouth the Lord Jesus, and shalt

---

* Jerome, ep. lxi. as quoted by Bingham: Ab apostolis traditum, non scribitur in charta et atramento, sed tabulis cordis carnalibus.

believe in thy heart that God hath raised him from the dead, thou shalt be saved. For with the heart man believeth unto righteousness, and with the mouth confession is made unto salvation." Rom. x. 8, 9. Faith comes to its proper completion only in the way of utterance; the inward word to be truly real must pass over into the form of an outward word; which becomes thus, at the same time, the bond of union and fellowship with others who have been made to partake of the same grace. Such an utterance of christian faith, in what may be considered its primary central form, is presented to us in the memorable confession of Peter: "Thou art the Christ, the Son of the living God;" or, as we have it in another place: "To whom shall we go but unto Thee? Thou hast the words of eternal life; and we believe and are sure that thou art that Christ, the Son of the living God." (Matt. xvi. 16; John, vi. 68, 69.) The whole Creed, as we shall see hereafter, is in truth wrapped up in this foundation article, and grows forth from it with inward necessity. Afterwards we have it, more full and clear, in the form of baptism, as presented by our Saviour himself: "Go teach all nations, baptizing them in the name of the Father, and of the Son, and of the Holy Ghost." Christ is the revelation of God, under the three-fold character here brought into view; and this revelation may be said to constitute the sum and substance of christianity, as the object of the faith we profess in coming into his Church. To be baptized into Christ, is to be baptized into the whole mystery of the Trinity, as inseparably joined with his person; and the formal acknowledgement of this mystery accordingly, in the way of solemn response or confession, was associated with the ordinance, no doubt, from the beginning. It is allowed almost universally, that reference to such a confession is made by St. Peter, where he speaks of the answer of a "good conscience," (1 Pet. iii. 21,) as necessary to be added to the outward washing of water, to complete the idea of baptism. The good profession of Timothy "before many witnesses," (1 Tim. vi. 12,) is taken by many to refer also to the same thing. It is not necessary to suppose, that the profession thus required of all who came into the Church, was even in the age of the Apostles, under the same invariable form. It was sometimes more and sometimes less full, but it always carried in it, explicitly or by implication, a full assent to the contents of the baptismal formula. How far it may have become usual, before the death of the Apostles, to connect with this foundation the secondary clauses of the Creed as it now stands, cannot be clearly determined. But no one familiar with the early history of Christianity, can well fail to see that this must have been the case, at least to some extent; and the probability is certainly strong, that early in the second century, if not before, nearly all the particulars now embraced in it were found more or less in current use.

Still, as before said, the current use itself remained irregular and free. Each church considered itself at liberty to employ its own particular style of expressing its faith; just as each exercised the same sort of liberty in its general liturgy; while at the same time the faith itself was considered to be of a common character, belonging alike to all the churches and handed down from the Apostles. The variety and freedom thus allowed, were not suffered to trench upon the unity of the general tradition or rule. In the midst of it all, this was still felt to be one and the same, and is frequently appealed to accordingly, by the early writers as of acknowledged and easily intelligible authority.

Irenaeus speaks of such an "immoveable rule of truth," belonging to every christian by his baptism; and describes it as proclaiming: "One God, the Father Almighty, maker of heaven, earth, the sea, and all that they contain; one Jesus Christ, the Son of God, incarnate for our salvation; and one Holy Spirit, who by the prophets preached the dispensations and the advents; the generation from the Virgin, the passion, the resurrection from the dead, and the ascension with the flesh into heaven of our Lord Jesus Christ, the Beloved, and his coming from heaven in the glory of the Father, to gather all things together into one and to raise all human flesh, that to Jesus Christ our Lord, and God and Saviour and king, according to the good pleasure of the invisible Father, every knee may bow of things in heaven, and things on earth, and things under the earth, and every tongue confess, and that he may execute just judgment upon all; remanding wicked spirits, and sinning apostate angels, and the impious, unrighteous, disobedient and blasphemous among men, into eternal fire; but on the righteous, and holy, and such as have kept his commandments and continued in his love, some from the beginning and others from their repentance, bestowing life, the gift of immortality and everlasting glory."[*] Irenaeus does not mean, of course, to quote literally in this case, any certain formula, as of established and fixed use in the churches. His whole manner implies the contrary, and may be taken as evidence that no fixed formula of this sort, as afterwards settled in our present Apostles' Creed, was then in ecclesiastical use. But he appeals nevertheless to what he regards as a well defined and clearly intelligible rule of faith, as forming the substance of the christian profession; and it is easy enough to see, that this agrees entirely with the contents of the Creed now mentioned, showing it to reach back in the use of the Church, so far as these are concerned, to the age in which he lived. We have his testimony moreover, that it was in this view of apostolical and universal authority. The Church, he tells us, disseminated throughout the whole world, held it from the Apostles and their disciples, keeping it carefully, as though she occupied but a single house, accepting its contents everywhere as with one heart and soul, and preaching them as from one and the same mouth. " The dialects in which it is uttered are different; but the tradition is in force the same. The churches founded in Germany, have no other faith and doctrine; nor those in Spain; nor those among the Celts; nor those in the East; nor those in Egypt; nor those in Lybia; nor those of more central situation; but as the sun, God's workmanship, is over the whole globe one and the same, so also the evangelical truth shines everywhere and illuminates all who are willing to come to its light."

The testimony of Irenaeus is very important, as illustrating both sides of the true doctrine concerning the origin of the Creed. It started with no such fixed form of words, in the beginning, as it carries in its repetition now. Irenaeus, and the Church in his time, knew of no apostolical tradition in this outward form, and none should be pretended by any part of the modern Church.

---

[*] Adv. haeres. lib. 1. c. x. Quoted in full by Bingham, Orig. Ecclès. lib 10. cap. iv.

But Irenaeus, and the Church in his time, were perfectly familiar notwithstanding, with the idea of a christian *regula fidei* or creed, of universal force, and in actual use among all the churches. Still more, this rule was regarded as strictly and truly the *Apostles' Creed*. It was no product of private opinion, and it stood not at all in articles of convention and agreement adopted by the general christian body. It was accepted everywhere as a system handed down from the Apostles; not merely as supposed to be in the spirit of their teaching, but as carrying forward in the faith of the Church, the very substance and contents of the divine revelation itself, which they were sent to proclaim. Finally, we gather from Irenaeus, that this Rule of Faith, in living use with the universal Church of his time, embraced in itself, under a free character, all the leading features of the Apostles' Creed, as afterwards settled in its present form; in which view it may well continue to challenge the reverential homage of all Christendom still, and onward to the end of the world, as a true apostolical symbol. This testimony of Irenaeus, it is well always to bear in mind, carries us back to the second century, and into close proximity thus with the immediate disciples of the Apostles themselves.

Tertullian appeals frequently, in the same free way, to the christian Rule of Faith, and recapitulates several times its general contents, always in harmony with the sum of it as given by Irenaeus, for the purpose of confuting and confounding the heretics of his own time. His recapitulations are indeed always different, sometimes more and sometimes less full, showing that the Creed was more life than mere word; but they assume throughout, notwithstanding the clear identity belonging to it, as a single apostolical tradition.* The amount of it is always: One God, the almighty maker of the world; his Son, Jesus Christ, born of the Virgin Mary, constituted Messiah, crucified under Pontius Pilate, raised the third day, exalted to heaven and set at the right hand of God, from whence he shall come to judge the quick and the dead; the Holy Ghost sent forth vicariously, according to his promise, to sanctify those that believe in his name; the res-

* " Regula fidei una omnino est, sola immobilis et irreformabilis."

urrection of the flesh, the damnation of the wicked, and the reception of the righteous into eternal life and the blessedness of heaven.* This rule, he says, instituted by Christ, allows no questions, other than such as spring from heresy and go to make heretics; it is older than all heresies; their novelty, as exposed by it, serves to establish its antiquity; to know nothing beyond it, is to know all that is necessary.†

Origen, in like manner, gives a summary statement of the heads of christian doctrine, "as plainly received by apostolical tradition," which corresponds in substance with the same rule.

From Cyprian, we have an insight into the general Creed of the Church in Africa, as it stood in his time. The Novatians, he admits, proposed the same questions at baptism that were used in the Church catholic, calling for faith in God the Father, his Son Jesus Christ, and the Holy Ghost. But still, he contends, that as schismatics, their rule and interrogation could not be regarded as the same; "for when they say: Dost thou believe the remission of sins and eternal life through the holy Church? they interrogate falsely, since they have no Church." This shows that the whole Creed, nearly as we have it now, was in common use in Africa, at this time, as an apostolical rule of faith, in connection with the baptismal service.‡

These private testimonies show the presence everywhere in the early Church of an evangelical tradition, agreeing in its general contents with the Creed as it now stands, and accepted as of strictly apostolical origin and weight. They show also, that this tradition was regarded, not as a slavish form of words, but a free doctrine rather, that might be uttered in various ways. Still it would be a great mistake, to conceive of it as wholly loose and floating, in the style of these notices. In the nature of the case, the different churches must have held it from the beginning, under some regular and standing form. This may have varied some with the progress of time, as circumstances seemed to call

---

* De veland. virg. c.i De praescript. adv. haereticos, c. xiii. Advers. Prax. c. ii. Quoted in full by Bingham, Orig. Eccl. lib. 10. cap. iv.

† "Nihil ultra scire, omnia scire est."

‡ Epist. lxxvi. ad Magnum.

for new points and specifications; and in this way, there would be room of course, for considerable peculiarity in the several churches, compared one with another; but the reigning type of the creed in each case must have continued always the same. So much may be said to lie in the primitive design of the thing itself. It was the profession of faith that accompanied the sacrament of baptism, and that grew originally out of the baptismal formula as spoken by our Lord in its institution. Its use in the first centuries, was specially for those who were about to be introduced into the Church by this holy sacrament, after having gone through all proper previous steps, in the way of preparation for the solemnity. It was first delivered to the catechumen by the bishop, *(traditio symboli)* orally as it would seem, though possibly at times, also in writing; and then afterwards, in the course of a few days, publicly spoken back again and returned, *(redditio symboli,)* as being effectually laid up in the meantime in the candidate's memory.* This was followed by an open solemn profession on the part of the candidate, at the time of his baptism itself, in the way of response to distinct interrogatories embracing the symbol in its several parts. Such an " answer of good conscience," is referred to by the earliest ecclesiastical writers wherever the subject comes in their way, and is to be regarded as starting undoubtedly in the practice of the Apostles themselves. All this implies, however, a short standing form, of established use in each particular church. Cyprian gives us a glimpse into the general African formula, as it was everywhere of force in the first part of the third century. Other sections of the Church had similar standing forms; some more full perhaps than others; those of the East different from those of the West; but all handed down from the earliest time, and palpably expressing one and the same faith, as they belonged to one and the same baptism.

In the fourth century, these public formularies begin to come

---

* The brief form of this confession, says Neander, as a matter of course, did not need a written communication; it was to pass over into the soul of the catechumen, out of *the living word into the life;* it must be the utterance of his own conviction. Christianity stands primarily, not in letter, but life. So Augustine: Hujus rei significandae causa, audiendo symbolum discitur, nec in tabulis rel in aliqua materia, sed in corde scribitur.

more distinctly into view; always, however, in such a way as to show them in full, actual, and undisputed possession of the authority they claim, as of the most ancient right and force. Take for instance, the symbol then in use at Rome. It is not specially presented to us, before this time. But what could well be more monstrous, than to fancy that it was for this reason of any comparatively recent date. It meets us in no such form; it tolerates from us no such doubt. We might just as well question the antiquity of the church itself in Rome, as question the antiquity of its creed. We meet it not in the fourth century, as a new thing, the creation, possibly, only of that age, or the one going before; it is the old baptismal symbol, as all the world then might know it to have been in use there from time immemorial; it is the christian rule of faith, the creed of the Apostles, in the particular form in which it had come to be woven into the very life of this ancient church from the beginning. So with the church at Aquileia; and so with the churches generally. Their particular creeds are regarded always as dating, in their main character, from the most remote christian antiquity.

The very early origin of nearly all the elements presented in these church symbols of the fourth century, is shown not merely by the outward tradition going along with them in each case, and their general agreement with one another, but very strikingly also by the historical relations that are found imbedded as it were in their own form. The Creed is, of course, primarily positive, and not simply negative, in its contents. It affirms a substantial reality, which is not produced in any way by the mere denial of the various errors and false doctrines to which it stands opposed. At the same time, to be thus positive and affirmative, it must include in itself, from the start, a steady protest against such false doctrines as they came in its way. The christian consciousness can evolve itself only by a process of continual critical separation, by which all that is foreign to its true life is sundered from this, and made to stand over against it as its antichristian opposite and contradiction. It lies moreover in the nature of this process, that the errors which are thus cast out will not come into view confusedly and by chance, but must be conditioned and determined always by the posture which has been reached by the christian consciousness itself at the time of their appearance. In the history of the Church, accordingly, each age has its own forms of heresy, as well defined, we may say, as the successive geological formations that show themselves in the structure of the earth. The "fossil remains" of each period, are found wrought into the solid rock by which it is represented for all subsequent time.

In this way, the Apostles' Creed, aside from all outward historical evidence in the case, falls back plainly, in its main composition, to the earliest period of the Church. Its various propositions carry in them, beyond all doubt, a reference to certain false tendencies, which at the time of their original utterance, were actively at hand, and working towards the overthrow of the christian faith. This has been very generally seen and felt; and great pains have been taken by such writers as Vossius, Pearson, Basnage, King, &c., to identify the relation of the several clauses of the Creed, in this way, to specific forms of heresy mentioned in early church history. Thus one clause is explained as springing out of opposition to Ebion, Cerinthus, and others; a second, as in contradiction to Menander, Cerdo and Saturninus; and so most of the rest, as directed against Gnostic, Montanistic, Novatian, or other errors. Walch in his *Introd. in Lib. Symb. p.* 101, justifies this view in a general way, while he considers, at the same time, that it has been carried by some quite too far. Bull and Grabe are disposed to dispute its correctness a good deal farther; the latter especially, holding that all the clauses of the Creed, with the exception of those on the *descent into hades* and the *communion of saints*, (possibly also that on *the church*,) came into use in the age of the Apostles themselves, by their authority, or at all events, with their knowledge and approbation, and are to be explained out of relations existing at that time. The question cannot be brought probably to any such absolute determination as this; but in any case, a proper familiarity with the early history of the Church, must lead us to feel that we have no right to come lower than the first part of the second century, in order to fix, to the extent just mentioned, the rise of the several parts of the Creed. The errors excluded by them, are such as lie close around the inmost life of christianity. They

ong to the very first stage of the process by which this life was
quired to unfold itself in the form of history. They come in
a way of that process, by a sort of inward necessity, from the
ry start. We meet them, accordingly, under full revelation,
the second century. There is no occasion then to descend
ver than this, for the rise of the Creed. It was *needed* for the
cond century; it forms the proper utterance of the christian
a as it then stood, in the face of all sorts of Gnostic and Ebio-
ic unbelief. Still more; we have good evidence that those
rious forms of thinking were actively at work in the century
ere. Gnosticism, as it meets us in the second century, sprang
t abruptly and with a single stroke, like a full armed Minerva,
the arena of church history. We have traces enough in the
w Testament, of the chaotic workings at least of the same
ichristian spirit in the very age of the Apostles. Indeed, to
ert itself at all, the christian life must be supposed to have
en brought into conflict with the substance of these primitive
ms of heresy from the beginning. It was then practically an
erance of faith from the first, answerable to these circumstan-
; and no good reason can be shown, why the utterance should
t have passed over, in the apostolic period itself, to a free form
words also in substantial agreement with the ancient symbol
it now stands. Let any one but have in his mind a lively
se of the terrible aberrations from the truth, that are revealed
as darkly from the first days of the infant Church, in the wri-
gs of Paul and John and Peter and Jude, and he will not be
ily to feel that there is any necessity whatever for coming down
he heresies of a later time, as broached by Cerdo, Marcion,
urninus, Valentinus, Basilides, &c., much less to the age of
Novatians, or that of the Donatists, in order to explain the
se and force of the testimony here handed down in the Apos-
;' name. Was not the same testimony, at almost every point,
led for by the relations of the Church in the first century? And
so, what right have we to overlook these altogether, and refer
origin mainly to another time? No one, at all events, can
dy attentively the structure of the Creed, without finding in its
ole formation clear monumental evidence of the very highest
ristian antiquity.

With the advance of time, as the aspects of heresy changed, the old elementary style of the Creed was made to undergo naturally, in different quarters, partial and circumstantial modifications, in the way of direct testimony over against such new errors. Thus, for instance, in the church at Aquileia, the first article read in the time of Rufinus: I believe in God the Father Almighty, *invisible and impassible ;* with clear reference to the Sabellian and Patripassian heresies, which affirmed that it was the Father himself who had become incarnate and suffered under Pontius Pilate. This symbol also included the article on the *descent to hades,* as we have before seen, when it had no place, as Rufinus supposed, in the other creeds generally existing in his time. In the Oriental Church, the tendency of the Creed to adjust itself, by expansion and modification, to new necessities, prevailed more actively than it did among the Latins; by reason of the manifold phases and forms, in which false doctrine was always starting into fresh life, on that field, during the first ages. Thus we find in Cyril, the creed of the church at Jerusalem, as it had stood before the Council of Nice, bearing upon it such significant amplification at various points.[*] Still, different from this again, was the old creed used at Caesarea, in Palestine, recited by Eusebius, in the Nicene Council, as the formula of faith which he had received there at his baptism. It approached closely to the symbol adopted by this Council. It is a probable supposition, that the Nicene Creed was made to embrace the reigning type of the older Oriental symbols, with such additions only as were needed to meet effectually the false doctrine of Arius.[†] As issued at Nice, however, (a. 325,) it was made to close abruptly with the article of the Holy Ghost, leaving out all that should follow

---

[*] "I believe in one God, the Father Almighty, Maker of heaven and earth, maker of all things visible and invisible: And in one Lord Jesus Christ, the only begotten Son of God, begotten of the Father before all days, the God, by whom all things were created, who was incarnate and made man; was crucified and buried, the third day rose from the dead, and ascended into the heavens, and sat down at the right hand of the Father; who shall come to judge the quick and the dead, and of whose kingdom there shall be no end. And in one Holy Ghost, the Paraclete, who spake by the prophets; in one baptism of repentance for the remission of sins; in one holy catholic church; and in the resurrection of the flesh and in life everlasting."

[†] Walch. Introd. in Lib. Symb. p. 20.

concerning the Church and the course of the new creation in
Christ Jesus; by which some have been led to question the presence of these concluding topics in the earlier creeds altogether.
But we have ample evidence to show the contrary; and the
omission here is accounted for very easily, by the consideration
that the object of the Nicene Creed was simply to repel the
errors of Arius and his party in regard to the Trinity. The
topics following had not been called in controversy, and were
left to stand untouched accordingly, as already found in the
creeds generally. Subsequently, by the second general Council,
(held at Constantinople, a. 381,) this omission was formally supplied, and the Creed re-adopted, with some other improvements,
in the form in which it is now known and used; with the exception only of the clause that makes the procession of the Holy
Ghost to be *from the Son,* as well as from the Father, which
was added at a later period by the Latin Church. The older
Oriental creeds naturally gave way to this œcumenical Nicene,
or rather Niceno-constantinopolitan, symbol. It passed very soon
into general use, as it would seem in the administration of baptism; and was adopted subsequently into the stated liturgical
church service. It is agreed on all hands, however, that the
practice of reciting it in this way, was not introduced before the
middle of the fifth century.[*]

Among the earlier symbols of the Western Church, which
differed somewhat among themselves, as we have already seen,
though their reigning type was always the same, a sort of central dignity and pre-eminence was gradually claimed and allowed
in favor of the formula used at Rome.[†] When speaking of the
occasional slight variations of the Creed, in different churches,
Rufinus tells us, that nothing of this sort was to be found in the
Roman church; a fact which he accounts for in this way, that
no heresy had started there, and that those who were to receive
baptism were required always to repeat the creed before the whole
congregation, which stood ready at once to object to the slightest

---

[*] See Bingham, Orig. Eccl. Lib. x. cap. 4. § 14, 16, 17.
[†] Credatur symbolo apostolorum, quod ecclesia Romana intemeratum
semper custodit et seriat.—*Ambrose, Ep.* 81.

innovation in its terms.　Still Rufinus chose to abide by his own symbol, as he held it from the church at Aquileia; and whatever the stability of the Roman formula might have been previously, we find it at a later period consenting to complete itself by the admission of a little material at least, which did not belong to it from the beginning.　As it stood in the time of Rufinus, it lacked the articles on the *descent to hades*, and the *life everlasting*, as well as the title *catholic*, in connection with the Church. In reality, however, of course, the descent to hades was involved in the clause on *Christ's death and burial*, and the life everlasting in the idea of the *resurrection ;* while the Church, as an object of faith, includes the conception of catholicity as an attribute inseparable from its constitution.　When precisely the Roman creed was brought to include, in common use, the separate distinct utterance of the points now noticed, is not known. They were, however, in due time fairly installed in their place ; and in this form, having come in the fifth and sixth centuries into general use, it has come down to us, with the veneration of the whole christian world, as the standard edition of the ancient rule of faith, the best and truest representation of the fundamental realities of the christian religion, the proper Apostles' Creed.

In this character, it forms the basis of all sound christian profession, in the Protestant Church no less than in the Roman Catholic.　In the great religious revolution of the sixteenth century, its credit and authority remained inviolate and unimpaired.　The object of the Reformation was, to sweep aside the rubbish which threatened to smother the life of the ancient faith, not by any means to bring this faith itself out of the way.　Both divisions of the Protestant Church accordingly, the Lutheran and the Reformed, united in acknowledging the binding authority of the ancient oecumenical symbols, and especially the root of all symbols as found in the Apostles' Creed.　They did not pretend to abjure all connection with the past, but professed to build on a foundation already laid, and to carry forward a work already long since begun.　In the Lutheran Church, the three primary Creeds, (Apostolical, Nicene and Athanasian,) are made to precede the Augsburg Confession, in the Form of Concord ; to show, says Walch, "that Lutherans embrace not a new doctrine, but such

as is old and apostolical, and profess thus the truly catholic faith."
How fully it lay at the foundation of all christianity with Luther
himself, we all know.   It was part of his piety, a necessary means
of grace with him, he tells us himself, to repeat the Creed with
the Lord's Prayer, throughout his life, in the spirit of a little
child.   His sense of the authority that belongs to the ancient
catholic faith altogether, was very earnest and deep.   " It is dangerous and terrible," he writes in his memorable letter to Albert
of Prussia, " to hear or believe anything, against the united
testimony, faith and doctrine of the universal holy christian
Church, as held now and from the beginning, for 1500 years,
throughout the world."   The Creed, of course, occupies a conspicuous plcae in his catechism.   In this, however, we see only
an image of the universal Protestant feeling in that age.   Every
such formulary of religious instruction was expected, as a matter
of course, to take in the Creed, along with the Lord's Prayer
and the Ten Commandments.

The Reformed Church here was of one mind with the Lutheran.   Thus in Calvin's Catechism, the first section treats of
Faith; which is said to have the sum of its contents in the " formula of confession held in common by all christians; commonly
called the *Apostles' Creed*, and always received from the beginning among the pious; as being either derived from the mouth
of the Apostles, or faithfully collected from their writings."
After this it is recited and expounded in full.   So in the admirable symbol of the Palatinate, the Heidelberg Catechism, " it
is the articles of our catholic undoubted christian faith," as comprehended in the same Creed, which are made to underlie the
doctrine of salvation from beginning to end.   It formed part
of the regular church service, in the Reformed liturgies, accompanied their baptisms, and entered into their celebration of the
holy eucharist.   The Gallican Confession, art. 5. approves the
three Creeds, Apostolic, Nicene and Athanasian, as agreeing with
the written word of God.   " We do willingly receive the three
creeds," it is said in the Belgic Confession, art. 9, " namely, that
of the Apostles, of Nice, and of Athanasius; likewise that which
conformable thereunto, is agreed upon by the ancient fathers."
In the Helvetic Confession, art. 11, the symbols of the first four

general councils, together with that of Athanasius, are cordially
approved and professed. The three Creeds are endorsed in the
Articles of the Church of England, as worthy of all reception.
In the Declaration of Thorn, we are said to be all baptized into
the Apostles' Creed, as a compendium of the christian faith; and
the Nicene and Constantinopolitan Creeds are taken still farther
as a sure interpretation of the same heavenly doctrine, forming
thus the common ground on which all who profess Christ, must
of necessity come together, and the one firm foundation against
which the gates of hell shall never prevail. It is part of the true
Protestant faith, undoubtedly, as held by the Reformed Church,
no less than the Lutheran, to abide by the ancient christian Creed.
Whatever else it may include, it starts from this and rests in it
throughout, as its sure and necessary foundation.

It must be acknowledged, however, that the honor thus put
upon the Creed in the original Protestant Confessions, has undergone, practically at least, no slight eclipse, in a wide portion of
the modern Protestant world. So far as Rationalism has had
power in Europe, the authority of the ancient church faith, of
course, fell into discredit; and it is felt now by those who seek
the revival of pure christianity, that all turns on the power of the
Church to intone with full emphasis again, in her public formularies and services, every single article of the *symbolum apostolicum*, most especially those of the incarnation, the descent into
hades, and the resurrection of the body. But the low esteem
for the Creed, of which we now speak, has not been confined to
Rationalism, technically so styled. We see it widely displayed
in other sections also of the Protestant world, which we are accustomed to distinguish as orthodox and evangelical. The other
great disease of the Protestant system, the spirit of *Sect*, shows
a striking affinity here, no less than at other points, with the Rationalistic tendency of which it is the natural counterpart. Sects,
in proportion as they *are* sects, that is in the same measure that
they lack all sympathy with the idea of the Church, and substitute sectarianism for catholicity, will be found all the world over
to have no taste for the Creed. They may possibly extend to
it some cold token of respect, as a venerable relic of early christianity; but it has not their heart, falls not in with their habit of

christianity, and is admitted to no place of course in their worship, public or private.

More than this, *Puritanism*, which we do not wish to confound certainly with Rationalism and the Sect System, although it carries in itself undoubtedly a more direct tendency towards both than can be said to lie in original Protestantism, being in truth, an advance on this, whether for weal or for woe, and such an advance as places it in closer natural proximity to the evils now mentioned; Puritanism, we say, taking the term in the broad sense, to designate a special form of the religious life, which is just as well defined in history as early Protestantism itself, may be said to carry with it this universal character, that it makes no account practically of the Apostles' Creed. The remark is not made here of course in the way of censure or reproach, and ought not to be taken as disrepectful in any way to the system in question. We are dealing simply with the history of the subject; and the fact now stated, is one which no well informed person will pretend to call in question. It matters not that the authority of the Creed may be recognized, in some general way, in this or that old confession still retained in the Church; so far as the Puritan spirit in its modern form is found to prevail in any ecclesiastical body, all actual use of the Creed, and all hearty interest in it, are to the same extent wanting. It is not used, for example, in the religious education of families. Children, generally, are not made to lay it up in their minds, as the sum and substance of the christian faith. It comes not into view in catechetical instruction; if indeed this itself be still upheld, under any form, in regular use. It is not repeated of course in public worship; the minister who should take upon him any such innovation as that, would be suspected of some secret hankering after Rome. It is not made in any way a rule of christian profession or public teaching. It is quite common, for instance, in Congregationalist churches, to make use of " covenants," or forms of profession and engagement, when members are received into full communion, each congregation varying the form to suit its own taste; but it would be hard to find one among all, that would be content to make use of the Apostles' Creed in this way, or even to be

guided by it at all in the construction of its own formulary.[*]
The feeling is, plainly enough, that this old symbol has had its
day, and is now antiquated if not absolutely obsolete; that it
bears upon it the marks of a rude and imperfect christianity, not
without some touch of tendency towards superstition; that the
evangelical faith of the present day may be more clearly and satisfactorily expressed, in other schemes and summaries altogether,
any one of which, as taken from the Bible and common christian
experience, is to be held just as much entitled to honor as that
which is thus falsely ascribed to the Apostles.　It is felt to be on
the whole a loose and careless production; without much plan or
method, and governed by no principle in the choice of its articles;
introducing some points of no necessary importance, and leaving
out several others that should be counted indispensable.　One
thing is beyond all controversy certain, that if Puritanism were
called upon to form a fundamental, universal christian creed, it
would fall on something very different from this ancient symbol,
both in conception and style.　All this, as before said, is noticed

---

[*] A striking exemplification of this independence is furnished in the manufacture of a new confession of faith, a few years since, for the use of the
Protestant Armenian Church, lately started, under the auspices of our New
England missionaries, in the city of Constantinople.　In other ages, the
casting of a creed for a whole church has been counted an enterprise of no
common size and weight; but here, it was the work of one or two hands
only, brought happily to a full conclusion in the course of a few hours!
To expedite the business, and guard against all outward bias, the precaution
was adopted, we are told, of shutting out from all consultation whatever had
been adopted by any part of the Church as of symbolical authority previously, (the primitive foundation Creed of the Oriental Church, of course,
along with the rest,) so as to draw the whole by purely *original* deduction
direct from the Bible, *as traditionally understood in New England*.　Not a syllable accordingly does this new confession contain, in recognition of the ancient symbol of universal Christendom.　The greatest marvel of all, perhaps, is, that this bold way of going to work in so momentous a case, should
be quietly accepted so generally, (by the whole American Board for instance,)
as nothing out of the way, a mere matter of course.　So, it will be remembered, the late World Convention at London, in undertaking to construct an
œcumenical platform for the union of *evangelical* sects, found it necessary
to ignore the Apostles' Creed in full, and brought in a new set of articles altogether of its own invention, as better suited for the purpose.

here neither in they way of blame nor of praise, but simply as a matter of history which is open to common observation. In this view, however, it is entitled to earnest attention. The fact, in its own nature, is curious. Nor can it easily be allowed to be of only small significance. Such variation from the mind and posture of the ancient Church, in regard to the Creed, implies necessarily a serious variation from the life of primitive christianity in general. The difference between Puritanism and original Protestantism here, argues necessarily a very considerable remove in the whole inward habit and being of the first from the proper spiritual constitution of the second. Such a fact has a right to challenge notice. Whether it be looked upon as right or wrong, an occasion for gratulation or a reason for censure and complaint, it is entitled at all events to earnest consideration, and should if possible be fairly understood and explained.

The force of what is now said will become still more evident when we take into view the interior constitution of the Creed, its rise and structure in the living sphere of faith, to which it primarily and natively belongs.

J. W. N.

ART. VIII.—The Progress of Ethnology. *An Account of recent Archæological, Philological and Geographical researches in various parts of the globe, tending to elucidate the physical history of man.* By John Russell Bartlett, Cor. Sec. of the American Ethnological Society, and foreign Cor. Sec. of the New York Hist. Society. Second edition; New York: Bartlett & Welford, 7, Astor House. 1847.

No department of inquiry which tends to confirm the truth of Sacred Scripture, ought to be regarded as trivial. All researches therefore into the records of nations long since passed away, or which now exist in a state of degeneracy, must be replete with interest to the student of the Bible, that most ancient *thesaurus* of facts pertaining to the original inhabitants of the earth. It has long been the practice of infidels to scoff at the statements of the inspired penmen, and sneeringly to inquire what proofs can be adduced of the truth of many of their assertions, especially, in relation to tribes whose very names seem to have become extinct. But we are happy to perceive that the science of Ethnology has stepped forward and confirmed the truth of statements which could not otherwise have been so satisfactorily established.

The book before us, has given us a brief outline of such researches in various parts of the globe, especially during the year preceding its publication. It was laid before the New York Historical Society, (a society which has done much to draw forth the talent and enterprise of our country,) and, although not strictly a historical subject, is yet sufficiently so, to come within the scope and design of that excellent institution.

It has long been a well-known fact, that throughout most of the Western and Southern States, especially in the valley of the Mississippi, there exist monuments and ancient remains of a people, who seem to have far transcended the present Indians, in intelligence, skill, and the arts of civilized life. But little was done until "two gentlemen of Ohio, Dr. Davis and Mr. E. G. Squier attempted to explore the region of the Scioto valley. Their labors seem to have been crowned with abundant success; and they have been enabled to show that the tumuli which abound in those regions, are divided into three grand classes, viz: 1st. Tumuli of sepulture, each containing a single skeleton, enclosed in a rude wooden coffin or an envelope of bark or matting, and occurring in isolated or detached groups. 2d. Tumuli of sacrifice, containing symmetrical altars of stone or burnt clay, occurring within, or in the immediate vicinity of enclosures, and always stratified. 3d. Places of observation, or mounds, raised upon elevated or commanding stations." Within these tumuli have been found implements and ornaments of silver, copper, lead, stone, ivory, and pottery, and sculptures of animals, birds and reptiles. Rocks too, have been found, on which are cut the outlines of the human figure, and of birds and animals. These researches, says our author, "show that a people, radically different from the existing race of Indians, once occupied the valley of the Mississippi.'' Perhaps we are not far from the truth, in supposing them to be identical with the tribes of Central America, whose magnificent remains are so fully described by Mr. Stephens. We are farther informed of the successful labors of Dr. Dickeson, in the South-western States; he having examined no less than one hundred and fifty mounds and tumuli, one of which contains on its summit, a superficies of eight acres, having within vast numbers of skeletons, vases, ornaments, &c. The north side of it is supported by a wall of sun-dried bricks, two feet thick. To the different kinds of mounds, he assigns the names of *telegraphs or look-outs, temples, cemeteries, and tent mounds.* Many of these are built with mathematical precision, in the shape of squares, triangles, and circles. Wells and reservoirs, lined with burnt clay, were also found. And what is not a little remarkable, heads were discovered in which artificial teeth were found, as well as teeth which had been plugged, thus showing that the art of dentistry was known among them. In a long list of antiquities found by Mr. Dickeson, we note the following: arrow points of jasper, quoits, weights, corn-grinders, stone statues, beads, war-clubs, bracelets, handled saucers, earthen lamps, copper medals, jars, cups and vases in every variety. These mounds are easily distinguished from those of modern Indians; and one mound was found to be the work of three different periods. At the top were the remains of the present Indians; digging lower, he found ancient Spanish relics, and still lower, were the relics of the primitive race. Much interest was formerly excited, which still continues, in reference to certain characters inscribed upon a tablet found in the Grave-creek mound, Virginia, noticed by Mr. Schoolcraft, in the first volume of the Transactions of the American Ethnological Society. M. Jomard, of the French Institute, and Mr. Hodgson, have both expressed their decided opinion that these characters are Numidian, being the same with those found on the monument of Thugga, and with those used by the Taurycks, at the present day; constituting part of the Lybian alphabet. This would seem to confirm the tradition of certain Phœnician or Carthagenian ships having, at a remote period, visited America, by the way of the Canaries and other islands lying between Africa and this country; and it is worthy of remark that a strong affinity exists between the ancient names of men and animals in those islands and certain Carib words. We doubt not but that researches of this kind will ultimately establish upon a firm basis, the assertion of the Bible,

Another curious statement respects the Indians found in California, or New Mexico, in the province of Sonora, called the White
Indians or Munchies, who are far superior to other Indian tribes.
In the same province, are found the Navijos, "possessing a civilization of their own," and having never yielded to Spanish authority.
The arts of weaving and dying are understood among them, and
there is much reason to believe them identical with the ancient Az-
tecs or those semi-civilized races found in Mexico, by Cortez, at
the time of its first discovery. Such is the opinion of Baron Humboldt, and the tradition of the Indians themselves, favors this opinion.

The account of the vast region between the Rocky mountains,
Upper California, and Oregon, by Col. Fremont, of the U. S. Corps
of Engineers, has been pretty generally read, while the explorations
made by Mr. Hillert, in the isthmus of Panama, have done much
to show the best mode of constructing a canal and railroad across
the isthmus of Darien.   He has examined many plants in that
region, and describes an anti-venomous herb, with which, if the
hands be rubbed, scorpions, &c., may be handled with impunity.
This gentleman has discovered some ancient monumental edifices,
besides an ancient canal cut through the solid rock in the interval
between the rivers Atrato and Darien.

The researches in Greenland too, (a country first discovered in
877, and colonized in 986,) have been greatly extended by the labors
of the Rev. George T. Joergensen, at the firths of Igalikko and Tun-
nudluarbik, where important ruins are situated.   In vol. III. of the
Royal Society of Northern Antiquaries, may be found a vast deal
pertaining to this subject, from which it appears that Greenland too
abounds in ancient ruins of much interest.   The "Scripta Historia
Islandorum," by the same society, gives much valuable information
in regard to Iceland, Greenland, and other northern regions.   Sir
John Franklin spent at least two years in the Arctic regions, and the
Hudson's Bay Company have fitted out an expedition to the same
end.   Also the Hon. Albert Gallatin and Mr. Hale, philologist of
the United States' Exploring Expedition, have employed their pens
in regard to the Indian tribes beyond the Rocky mountains.   The
latter has issued a volume, entitled "Ethnology and Philology."
In South America, a French expedition under Count Castlenau, has
been for three years engaged in examining the country between
Rio Janeiro and Goyaz, on the head waters of the river Araguay, the
desert of the Chavantes, the diamond mines near Cuyaba, the sources

a remarkably beautiful race, having large eyes with long lashes, a long black beard and aquiline noses, and wearing hats made of hides.

The Count traversed also the country between Paraguay and Brazil. and examined the great lake Uberava, the limits of which have not yet been defined by geographers. From this place, he proceeded to Vera Cruz, Chuquisaca in Bolivia, Potosi and Lima. In Peru, Senor Nieto has discovered certain ruins in the province of Chachapoyas, of which "the principal edifice is stated to be an immense wall of hewn stone 3600 feet in length, 560 feet in width, and 100 feet high. It is solid in the interior and level on the top, upon which is another wall 600 feet in length, of the same breadth and height as the former, and like it solid to its summit. In this elevation, and also in that of the lower wall, are a great many rooms eighteen feet long and fifteen wide, in which are found neatly constructed niches, containing bones of the ancient dead, some naked and some in shrouds or blankets." A plane gradually ascends to its summit, on which is a small watch-tower commanding a view of eleven leagues. The cavities of the adjoining mountain, contained many skeletons wrapped in shrouds made of cotton of various colors. Other expeditions by the English and French governments are about to be sent out, and by this time have probably made many new discoveries.

In Africa, great zeal has been manifested, and the result of the expedition of the Landers, in ascertaining the mouth of the Niger, has led to recent efforts in regard to the sources of the Nile, by M. d'Abaddie, Dr. Beke, Isenberg, and others, but without success. M. Jomard has given a vocabulary of the language of Darfur. Also in Senegal, Mr. Thompson has made some important observations. In a journey performed by Mr. John Duncan, from Cape Coast, through Dahomey, that traveller witnessed a "review of six thousand female troops, well armed and accoutred." A grammar of the Pongwee tongue has been commenced, and it is said that this language is "one of the most perfect of which the missionaries there have any knowledge. It is not so remarkable for copiousness of words, as for its great and almost unlimited flexibility." Considerable discoveries have been made in the interior of Africa, by Mr. James Richardson, M. Raffencl, of the French navy, and Lieutenant Ruxton, of the Royal navy. Some valuable contributions have been made to our knowledge of Africa, by Mr. Cooley and Mr. Mc-

Queen, in works written by these gentlemen. It is to be regretted that Mr. Maizan, a young officer in the French navy, who set out from Zanzibar, in 1845, and had reached the village of Daguela-mohor, was there barbarously murdered by a chief named Pazzy. The desert of Sahara, it seems, has for a long time been erroneously regarded as a barren waste; the name signifying a country of pastures, it being in fact one vast Archipelago of oases or fertile spots. Among the interesting ethnological facts pertaining to Algiers, is that "of a white race inhabiting the Aures mountain, (mons Aurarius,) in the province of Constantine, having blue eyes and flaxen hair, which some believe to be the remains of the Vandals driven from the country by Belisarius. But the most interesting discovery in this part of Africa is, that of the Libyan alphabet, (to which allusion has been already made,) by M. F. De Saulcy, member of the French Institute. "This curious result has been produced by a study of the bilingual inscription on the monument of Thugga, which is published in the first volume of the transactions of the Ethnological Society of New York. The reading of the Phœnician part of this bilingual inscription having been established, the value of the Lybian or Numidian letters of the counterpart, has been as clearly proved as the hieroglyphic part of the Rosetta stone has been established, from a comparison with the Greek text of that bilingual inscription. By this discovery a vast progress has been made in the ethnography and history of ancient Africa. Two facts of the greatest consequence have been established by it:—that the Libyan language was that of Numidia at the early period of its history, when the Phœnicians were settled there; and that the Numidians of that early day, used their own peculiar letters for writing their own language." And it is a remarkable fact, that the Tuarycks, or present Numidian or Berber race, inhabiting the desert of Sahara, make use of these same characters at the present day. For this discovery also, we are indebted to M. De Saulcy. There is reason to believe that the Berber tongue was the original language of that region, and coeval with the ancient Egyptian.

In Madagascar, important results have been attained by M. Guillian. Several works have appeared or are about to apppear, upon this subject, especially those of the above gentlemen and of M. De Froberville.

But by far the most interesting part of Africa, is Egypt, in which since the days of Champollion, astonishing discoveries have been made in reference to the hieroglyphics used in ancient days, in that country; and the page of history has consequently received much light. And it is a delightful fact, (although it is one which every Christian confidently anticipated,) that the statements of the inspired penmen have found signal confirmation. We regret, however, to see an apparent *tendency*, (to say the least,) in some men, who rank high for learning and genius, towards a chronology at variance with the manifest tenor of inspiration. We know indeed, that the chronology established by Archbishop Usher, is not necessarily absolutely correct; but we deem it impossible that the period of 4004 years, usually allowed for the interval between the Creation and the birth of Christ, can be consistently extended to more than 6000 or 7000 years. But we are still more concerned, when we see a man of the learning and ability of Mr. George R. Gliddon, who has done so much to give us an interest and delight in the subject of Egyptian antiquities, favoring the idea, unless we have mistaken his meaning, that Moses, the inspired historian, did little more than give us those traditionary notions of the Supreme Being, which had been handed down from the earliest ages of the world, and preserved by the Egyptians. We do not pretend to deny that *some* things recorded in the Bible, as matters of history, were known to the Egyptians, and that Moses, being skilled in all the wisdom of the Egyptians, has related some facts thus derived; but we do assert, that he was indebted to the Spirit of God for the power of discerning the truth from mere traditional falsehood; and also, that the main part of the Pentateuch was a direct revelation from God.

The immense work published by Napoleon, has been followed by those of Champollion, under the French government, and of Rossellini, by the Tuscan government. Besides these, is the great work of Lepsius, who has brought from Egypt the result of three years' laborious explorations, at the expense of the king of Prussia. The French have also sent out M. Prisse for a new survey and exploration of Egypt.

"As regards the eminent men who have won brilliant distinction in the career of Egyptian studies, it must suffice to state, that all have marched boldly along the road opened by Champollion; and that the science which owed its first illustration to Young, to the Champollions, to the Humboldts, to Salvolini, to Rossellini, to Nestor L'Hote, and to whose soundness the great De Sacy has furnished his testimony, counts at this day as adepts and ardent cultivators such scholars as Letrone, Biot, Prisse, Bunsen, Lepsius, Burnouf, Pauthier, Lanci, Birch, Wilkinson, Sharpe, Bonomi, and many more." Quite recently, Prof. Schwartze, of Berlin, has been engaged in publishing a work on Egyptian philology, entitled "Das Alte Ægypten." De Saulcy too, has made great advance in decyphering the demotic text of the Rosetta stone. This stone, as most are aware, is a block of black basalt, found by Mons. Bouchard, a French officer of engineers, in August, 1799, when digging the foundations of fort St. Julien, between Rosetta and the sea, containing an inscription in three different characters, the Greek, the hieroglyphic, and the demotic, or common language of the Egyptians. By a comparison of the Greek with the other inscriptions, the value of the different hieroglyphic characters was slowly, and at length, satisfactorily unfolded; and it was found that each symbol represented a letter of the alphabet: as, for instance, the figure of an eagle stood for *a*, this being the first letter of the word *akkom*, which, in common parlance, meant an eagle.

A discovery has recently been made by Arthur de Riviere, at Cairo, who having separated the leaves of an ancient Coptic manuscript, found that, in addition to a portion of the Old Testament, it contained a work on the religion of the ancient Egyptians. These discoveries have enabled us to read the inscriptions on the obelisks, statues, sarcophagi, &c., of the Egyptians, and have thrown much light on some hitherto very obscure portions of ancient history.

We owe much to the lectures and chapters of Mr. George R. Gliddon, who has rendered the study of Egyptian antiquities familiar by his admirable illustrations of monuments and sculptures. In regard to chronology, our author well remarks, "we do not fear these investigations—truth will prevail, and its attainment can never be detrimental to the highest interests of man;" and we may add, will always be found on the side of the Bible.

A similar discovery has lately been made in Lycia, in Asia Minor, a country often mentioned by Greek and Roman authors, as well as by inspired penmen. Captain Beaufort had discovered many ruins on the coast, and in 1838 and 1840, Sir Charles Fellows visited the interior, and found it rich in historical monuments, the remains of amphitheatres, churches, cathedrals, temples, aqueducts, and sepulchres; and a pointed arch was found, of a description of which the ancients had previously been supposed to be ignorant. But the most interesting discovery was that of a "bilingual inscription, in

ın and Greek, and similar inscriptions subsequently discovered,
ı have furnished sufficient materials for ascertaining the values
ı several letters of the alphabet, which consists of twenty-seven
s, two of which are still doubtful.   Able disquisitions on the
ıage have been written by Mr. Sharpe and Prof. Grotefend.''
e of these inscriptions, the name of Harpagus, or his son, ap-
, who lived about 530, B. C.   "The language belongs to the
family as the Zend and old Persian."   It is thought that this
ıage was introduced by Cyrus, when he subjected the country.
dotus, in speaking of the subjugation of Lycia by Cyrus and
ıgus, says: "When Harpagus led his army towards Xanthus,
ıycians boldly advanced to meet him, and though inferior in
ıers, behaved with the greatest bravery.   Being defeated and
ıed into their city, they collected their wives, children and
ble effects into the citadel, and there consumed the whole in
ımmense fire.   Of those who now inhabit Lycia, calling them-
ı Xanthians, *the whole are foreigners*, eighty families excepted.''
a still more interesting discovery has been made in Persia, of
neaning of the arrow-headed inscriptions which had so long
d the efforts of antiquarians.   For more than twenty centuries,
ria, Babylonia and Persia have been a mere blank on the page
story, and all that had been known of them was the brief ac-
ı contained in Scripture and given by the Greek historians.
terally have the prophecies been fulfilled in regard to Babylon,
ıothing but vast heaps of rubbish of tumuli, and traces of nu-
us canals, remains.   Extensive ruins have been found also at
ıpolis, Pasargadæ, and Nineveh.   M. Grotefend and De Sacy
ı the first successful attempts to decypher some of the arrow-
ıd inscriptions found among the ruins of Persepolis.   At this
. is a large ancient edifice, containing many inscriptions; one
rticular, placed over the portrait of a king, as was sufficiently
ınt from his dress.   M. Grotefend naturally conjectured that
nscription contained the name and titles of this king, stating
ı same time, the name of his father, as was common in ancient
iptions.   "These names could not be Cyrus and Cambyses, as
wo names did not begin with the same letter;" nor Cyrus and
xerxes, as the latter name is too long for the inscription, and
örmer too short.   There remained, therefore, only the names
ırius and Xerxes, of the dynasty of the Achæmenides (to which
ıhe edifice was naturally referred).   As the ancient Greek does

not give the precise phonetic value of names, it was necessary to
ascertain the true sound as derived from the Zend language, formerly spoken in Persia, which is *Kshershe* for Xerxes, and *Darewsh*
for Darius; also he found that *Kshe* or *Ksheio* meant "king." The
groups of characters corresponding with these names were then
analysed and the value of each character ascertained. It was found
in fine, "that various combinations of a mark, shaped like a wedge
or arrow-head, together with one produced by the union of two
wedges, constitute the system of writing employed by the ancient
Assyrians, Babylonians, Medes and the Achæmenian kings of Persia."   M. Grotefend's labors were succeeded by those of Professor
Rask, who added two characters to the alphabet; also by those of
M. Burnouf, Prof. Lassen and Major Rawlinson. The last named
gentleman applied his mind to the great Behistun tablet, in Persia,
and by a knowledge of the Zend and Sanscrit, succeeded to a wonderful degree in translating these ancient records, and in presenting
"a correct grammatical translation of nearly four hundred lines of
cuneiform writing, a memorial of the time of Darius Hystaspes;"
and "this great inscription is sculptured in three languages and in
three different forms of the arrow-head character. In the midst of
these records, is a piece of sculpture in relief, representing Darius
followed by two of his officers, with his foot upon a man, who raises
his hands before him, and nine other figures representing the rebellious leaders whom he had severally conquered, connected by a
rope around their necks and having their hands tied behind them."
Professor Westergaard has added much to these discoveries. At
Nineveh, very interesting researches have been made by MM.
Botta and Flandin. The mound examined, contained a series of
halls and chambers, the walls of which were covered with paintings.
"The men were more athletic than the Egyptians, wearing long
hair combed smooth over the top of the head and curled behind.
The beard is also long and curled. Their dresses are exceedingly
rich, and profuse in ornaments and trimmings." Mr. Layard also
laid open a mound of much larger size, and found it "to contain a
palace consisting of many rooms, covered with sculptures and cuneiform inscriptions. Among them is a pair of winged lions with human heads, the execution of which is admirable." These labors
of Mr. Layard have been continued, and "he has opened fourteen
chambers and uncovered two hundred and fifty sculptured slabs.
They afford a complete history of the military art of the Assyrians,

and prove their intimate knowledge of many of those machines of war whose invention is attributed to the Greeks and Romans; such as the battering ram, the tower moving on wheels, and the catapult." Only a small part of this vast mound has yet been explored. These discoveries have remarkably confirmed the accounts both of the ancient Grecian and sacred historians.

Arabia, called in Scripture, Hazarmaveth, notwithstanding the glowing descriptions of Greek and Roman authors, had been for a long time much neglected; but an interest was awakened by the celebrated Pococke, in 1650, and perpetuated by such men as Lieut. Wellsted, Capt. Haines, Adolphe Baron Wrede, M. Arnaud, M. Fresnel, and Rev. T. Brockman. These men have made us acquainted with many interesting facts, especially in regard to places in the valley called Wadi Doun, and in reference to the Himyaritic inscriptions, an alphabet of which has been nearly if not quite constructed by comparing the inscriptions with the Himyaritic alphabets, in some Arabic manuscripts, and with the present Ethiopic alphabet. The *Cane Emporium* of Ptolemy, and the *Caripeta* of Pliny seem to be satisfactorily ascertained.

It appears also that " M. Grigorowitsch, professor of the Sclavonic tongues in the Imperial University of Kasan, has returned, after two years' journey in the interior of Turkey, bringing with him facsimiles of many hundred inscriptions, and 2138 Sclavonian manuscripts, 450 of which are said to be very ancient and of great importance." Also an exploration has lately been made of the steppes of the Caspian Sea, the Caucasus, and of Southern Russia. We are indebted also to Mr. Brooke and Capt. Keppel, for important facts concerning the Dyaks of Borneo, who are the aboriginal inhabitants of that island, and to Count de Strzelecki, Capt. Stokes, Dr. Leichardt, and others, for valuable information respecting Australia.

In Siberia, the labors of Prof. Von Middendorff stand conspicuous, from which it appears that the inhabitants are partly of Finnish and Mongol descent. In India, the labors of Missionaries are too well known to need an enumeration here, and the decline of Boodhism and the extension of Christianity, are cheering facts in relation to Siam. "The vast regions of Manchuria, lying north of Corea, are inhabited by various tribes, speaking different dialects, and subsisting principally by hunting and fishing. Their written characters are derived from the Mongols, but have undergone many changes." The journey of the Rev. Mr. Hue into Mongolia, shows that "this vast country, covering a million of square miles, consists of barren deserts and boundless steppes. The people live in tents without any permanent residence." The inhabitants of the Loo Choo Islands, are intimately connected with the Japanese. Their language is the same, (with unimportant variations of dialect,) and Chinese letters and literature are in like manner cultivated by both. In personal appearance, however, the two people are very unlike. The Japanese, Coreans, Chinese, and Cochin Chinese, owing to the common language used, have been called the *Chinese language nations.* "The Chinese ascribe the invention of their characters to Tsang Kieh, one of the principal ministers or scholars in the reign of Hwangti, about 2650 years before Christ. The characters first depicted, were the common objects in nature, such as the sun, animals, a house, &c., and were probably drawn with sufficient accuracy to be detected without much, if any explanation. They were all described in outline, and generally with far less completeness than the Egyptian symbols, and none of them contained any clue to the sound, and were all monosyllabic. The necessity of incorporating some clue to the sound of the thing or idea denoted, became more and more evident. But not only was the increase of inhabitants, as we suppose, a reason for making the symbols phonetic ; the need of reducing the ever growing list, and the difficulty of distinguishing between species of the same genus, and things of the same sort, was a still stronger motive. This was done by the combination of a leading type with some other well understood character, chosen quite arbitrarily, but possessing the *same sound* as the new object to be represented. These remarks will perhaps explain the general composition of Chinese characters. But by far the greater part of them are now formed either of the original pictorial symbols greatly modified, or of those joined to each other in a compound character, partly symbolical and partly phonetic. The former part is called the *radical*, the latter the *primitive*. Out of 24,235 characters, (nearly all the different ones there are in the language,) 21,810 of them are phonetic," and are to be learned by committing the sound as received from an instructor.

A remarkable Syrian monument was found A. D. 1625, in China, covered with rubbish, commemorative of the progress of Christianity in China, and is believed to be the work of a Christian missionary. It was erected in the year 718 of the Christian era.

In conclusion, we would remark, that the method adopted in the

review of our author, was the only one which seemed adapted to
give the reader an idea of the contents of this highly interesting
book.   We have sometimes quoted the precise language of the author, sometimes have given the substance of his remarks, (as far as
could be done in so brief a space,) and have sometimes interspersed
remarks of our own.   We know of no book containing so much on
this subject within the same compass as the volume before us; and
where no direct information is given in the text, we are referred to
a list of the best authors on the topics treated.   The arrangement
of the subject is systematic, and the style of the author chaste and
perspicuous.

PRINCETON, N. J.   G. W. S.

ART. IX.—ANGLING FOR TROUT.

IN the *Complete Angler*, on no occasion doth Izaak Walton wax
more frolicksome and fond of poetry, than when discoursing with
his companion and disciple concerning trout.   It is immediately
after the capture of one of these delectable fishes and inspirers of
his fancy, that on his way with his proselyte and scholar towards
Bleak-hall, to spend the night, he plyeth and induceth the milkmaid
and her mother, whom he hath encountered in the field a-milking,
to regale them with two or three of their choicest ballads; and when
arrived at the inn, it is after having partaken of that same trout,
with his scholar and two other companions there met, that himself
and one of them, Coridon the countryman, throw us off some of
their best songs.   It was not, certainly, the mere relish of the served
up trout, in itself considered, which excited, either anticipatingly
or from reminiscence, the old gentleman's fancy.   Of good eating
he was properly fond, I am willing to acknowledge; but he was
certainly none of your gourmands nor epicures.   Neither was it
the mere external beauty of the fish abstractedly beheld, its fresh
bloom when first plucked from the waters—though, of course, for

this he had an eye—that inspired him with all his cheerfulness and merriment on the occasion. The gratification from this source he places behind even that of its gusto. "Come, my friend Coridon," he cries aloud at the table, "the trout looks lovely; it was twenty-two inches when it was taken, and the belly of it looked some part of it as yellow as a marigold, and part of it white as a lily; and yet, methinks, it looks better in this good sauce."

Its rich associations then for the old gentleman, some one will suggest, were perhaps derived from the skill displayed in its capture. What dexterity and circumspection are required to draw out one of these sly lurkers from their native element, especially if you essay it with a fly! What care must be employed in the preparation of the accoutrements beforehand! How suitably to the season, the water and the whims of the versatile fish, must be adapted the color and pliancy of the rod and line, and the wings and shape of the artificial insect! What adroitness is required for the continual casting and recovering of your fly, so as to impart to it that rapid, quivering motion which seemeth to tickle the water's surface, and which to effect, methinks, mere art cannot teach, but yourself must be qualified in part by nature! Then, in fine, when your efforts are crowned with success; when at length the desperate fish springing up siezeth the lure and is diving off with it again towards its old haunts, but is suddenly checked by the tension of your line, and drawn along slowly but surely, fluttering and floundering, towards your eager hand, how complete the joy! How exquisite the consummation!

The fact is, however, Izaak Walton was no fly-fisher. That activity and continual watchfulness to the absorption of the whole man, required in order to succeed in this mode of angling, were not in accordance with his contemplative habits. He was better pleased with your stationary or sedentary fishing. Having cast his line into the water, he delighted rather to stand on the bank, holding his rod horizontally, himself upright and immovable as a statue; or having fixed it on a forked supporter as a fulcrum, with a stone on the grounded butt end, to keep it firm, he chose rather to step back and cast himself carelessly and shepherd-like *sub tegmine fagi*; or, mayhap, should a spring shower be passing over, to recline beneath a protecting honey-suckle hedge, musing alone, or conversing with some Meliboean companion concerning the beauty and grandeur of the works of nature and Providence. On this account, therefore,

was that he was fond of trout; because that fish frequents always
the most pellucid streams, and such, of course, as are overshaded
by the most bewitching scenery. Having a poet's eye, therefore,
is no wonder that, like a poet, he had his favorite haunts and di-
ctions of rural places. As on the Doon, Alloway's old haunted
kirk, and on the Ouse, Olney with its lofty spire, have been forever
consecrated by the poetry of Burns and Cowper, so on the Lea, Am-
wellbury, with its surrounding scenery, remains forever hallowed
by the graphic prose delineations of Izaak Walton. In a poem descriptive of that beautiful village thus singeth John Scott, Esq., 1782:

> It little yields
> Of interesting art to swell the page
> Of history or song; yet much the soul
> Its sweet simplicity delights, and oft
> From noise of busy towns to fields and groves
> The muses' sons have fled to find repose.
> Famed Walton, erst th'ingenious fisher swain,
> Oft our fair haunts explored; upon Lea's shore,
> Beneath some green tree oft his angle laid,
> His sport suspending to admire their charms.

To the American editor of the *Complete Angler*, for the biblio-
graphical information bestowed in his preface, and the additional
charm thrown around, not only the book itself, but the art which it
teaches, by his superadded lore and instruction, every lover of ang-
ing and poetry must feel himself forever obligated. Nevertheless
I cannot help expressing my regret that he has shewn us so little of
himself in his descriptions; that he has not permitted us to detect
some of his own partialities and characteristics, as we certainly would
have done had he described more fully some of his favorite American streams and inland fishing places.

I am aware, however, that our largest streams, unlike those of
the same class in England, are not frequented by trout. These fish
with us are like naiads. They prefer to be near the fountain heads.
They are to be met with only in our retired brooks and clear branches
of creeks. A bard or angler, therefore, I must admit, who neglecting our magnificent rivers, would bestow on these his descriptions,
instead of bringing them thereby into notice, would, more likely,
be left himself unnoticed on account of their insignificance.

I know not how my taste will be regarded after the confession,
but I must say, that I have always had a liking for the diminutive

in waters. From my boyhood I still retain a sort of sneaking partiality for brooks, rivulets and milldams. Your mighty rivers, with their surrounding grandeur, fill my soul, like any other's, with awe and admiration; but the innocuous, retired brooks lay hold on my affections. Wanting they are, it is true in majesty and might, but about them, methinks, is more of playfulness and beauty. In the breast of a mill-dam is sympathy with even the touch of a swallow's wing, the springing up of a trout or the leaping in of a grasshopper. Of all streams too containing trout—while at confessing I may as well speak it out—with none am I better acquainted and perhaps more smitten, than with one of little note, which sometimes I visit in my vernal holidays, secreted in the heart of Cumberland county, in the State of Pennsylvania, known by the unpretending name of *Big Spring.*

Thus named I imagine it has been from the potent but noiseless gush with which at its source it issues up from beneath the base of a woody hill, filling at once a mill-dam and putting in motion a grist mill only a few paces below. Indeed its whole pilgrimage, being northward and nearly three miles before it reaches the Conodoguinnet, is made up of dams at considerable distances, each backing up its water almost to the base of the next above; whereby, whilst in reality one of the most hard-working little streams in the county, it has imparted to it withal the appearance of indolent repose. Big Spring is it called throughout its course, I suppose, on account of its continued spring-like lucidness, and mayhap to distinguish it *par excellence* from other minor fonts oozing into it occasionally from its limestone ledgy sides. Above its last dam, that calm sheet of water, at any rate to an observer from its eastern bank, is the most instructive, bending around and reflecting the opposite graveyard, as, with its many slabs and headstones, it rises gently up towards the old stone church that tops the hill, behind which lies unseen and almost unheard, the little bustling village of Newville.

As by the rivers of Babylon the sweet singers hanged their harps, brought from Judea, upon the willows in the midst thereof, so, not in sorrow but in gladness, not around the pendent but sprightly wilows and other trees along the banks of Big Spring, do I always feel disposed to throw, at least so far as suitable, derived from other sources, all my piscatory songs and associations.

Apart from public travel for many years this stream had lain secreted, the turnpike road, then the great thoroughfare through the

valley, passing along some distance above its source. At present,
however, by the bridge on which rests the railway of later construction, it is sped over about a quarter of a mile above Newville.
Across this the majority of passengers, on other things intent, are
whirled unknowingly. By the watchful angler in the Spring, however, its proximity is ever sweetly felt. While the cars, at the
depot hard by, stop for being replenished with wood and water, out
he letteth himself carefully with his fishing accoutrements and tackle,
and while standing before the inn adjoining he catcheth of its bright
waters below and the tops of the willows near, delightsome glimpses,
off whirring the while the cars and leaving him behind, he carroleth
forth or whistleth to himself, in the plenitude of his joy, some such
ode as this from the "Angling Remeniscences" of Stoddard:

> Sing, sweet thrushes, forth and sing!
>   Meet the morn upon the lea ;
> Are the emeralds of spring
>   On the angler's trysting tree?
>   Tell, sweet thrushes, tell to me!
>   Are there buds on our willow tree?
>   Buds and birds on our trysting tree?
>
> Sing, sweet thrushes, forth and sing!
>   Have ye met the honey bee
> Circling upon rapid wing
>   Round the angler's trysting tree?
>   Up, sweet thrushes, up and see!
>   Are there bees at our willow tree?
>   Birds and bees at the trysting tree?
>
> Sing, sweet thrushes, forth and sing!
>   Are the fountains gushing free?
> Is the south wind wandering
>   Through the angler's trysting tree?
>   Up, sweet thrushes, tell to me!
>   Is there wind up our willow tree?
>   Wind or calm at our trysting tree?
>
> Sing, sweet thrushes, forth and sing!
>   Wile us with a merry glee,
> To the flowery haunts of spring,
>   To the angler's trysting tree.
>   Tell, sweet thrushes, tell to me!
>   Are there flowers 'neath our willow tree?
>   Spring and flowers at the trysting tree?

But "good wine needs no bush," and Big Spring needs no willows to draw customers after her trout. The fact is, she has always had too many customers for the safety and preservation of her fish. To protect these, therefore, many years ago public interference was necessary. Wherefore, then enacted it was by the Commonwealth of Pennsylvania, and the law continueth still in full force, that no angler shall cast a line into these waters save only during those four gentle, summer months, whose names are not roughened with an *r*. Moreover, as this was hardly sufficient, even during this favored season, the proprietors of mill-dams still extend their kind protection over certain select portions of these, within their jurisdiction, forbidding to angle therein all strollers save only themselves.

To your fully equipt angler, however, I must say, with his landing-net, his ferules and his creels, and what not, who cometh up mayhap from Philadelphia, the hospitable proprietor of the mill-dam is ever gracious, revoking for the time all restrictions, and furnishing him with his flat-boat and every useful information besides, remarking, however, I must confess, to some bystander, when the bold aspirant has pushed off into the deep, that with such paraphernalia he never saw much harm done to the fishes. To the home-bred fly-fisher, however, with his well-spliced rod, without any extra trappings, who is familiar with every nook and crook in the stream and the habits of the trout besides, he is not always so complaisant. Him, should he apply for his boat, he will often put off with excuses, saying that it is sadly out of repair, or, mayhap, that himself or some of his boys think of launching it out presently for fishing a little themselves.

Among these domestic anglers stands pre-eminent, being six feet and some inches in his shoes, the portly colored gentleman ycleped Joe. Loitering along the stream he may be seen, of any pleasant summer day, with his rod in hand and so noiseless in his tread that even the turtles, basking on the sunny sides of fallen logs protruded from the water's surface, do not care to edge themselves down side-long into their protecting element as he passes by, so familiar has he become to their fancies. Fortunate is the zealous youth whom he receiveth under his tutelage, for he will certainly bring him forth in the end a complete fly-fisher. His first lessons he doth not permit his pupil to practice on the water; but taking him up into a high clover-field apart, he letteth him expend his fury, in the first place, on the clover-heads, to the alarm and scattering merely of the grasshoppers or, mayhap, of some startled hogs in the adjoining field. Then conducting him down again, his second exercises he putteth him through over some stagnant recess of the dam frequented only by bull-frogs and water-turtles. It is not till after his having acquired some agility of hand and delicacy of touch, that he permitteth him to tickle, with his properly adapted rod and fly, the surface of the water within whose depths are gamboling the wary trout. Some of the best anglers in the county, who visit this stream in its season, owe their present proficiency in a great measure to the first lessons in this way imparted by honest Joe, the colored Izaak Walton of Big Spring.

For my own part, when I go a-fishing, I generally contrive to place myself under the care of one of the practised anglers of the neighborhood, some of whom I have the pleasure of reckoning among my choicest friends; and while he on the water performs the agile part of the business, as I am really "no fisher but a well-wisher of the game," I make out, however, on the bank to do the contemplative. Admirably adapted have I always found the stream, at any rate in the fishing season, from its fountain-head throughout, for inspiring sprightly thoughts and in some places also pensive. On the sequestered eastern bank especially, above the lowermost dam, it has often struck me that even Izaak Walton, were he still living and with us, would throw himself, in the spring season, with pleasure beneath its broad oaks, conning over some of his gravest madrigals. Not a shower nor a weeping willow would he need there to render him properly melancholy. The graveyard opposite would be sufficient.

> ———"Or we sometimes pass an hour
> Under a green willow,
> That defends us from a shower,
> Making earth our pillow;
> Where we may
> Think and pray,
> Before death
> Stops our breath;
> Other joys
> Are but toys,
> And to be lamented."

Not painfully melancholy, however, on a placid summer's eve, are the thoughts suggested on that bank by the opposite graveyard and church. Indeed, on the contrary, as they are shone over by the mellow fading twilight and we look down at their reflected images in the water, our musings become pleasingly pensive. They are lighted up with joy and hope, and we can almost fancy that beneath the tombs we are permitted to have, through hallowed openings, a soft, refreshing glimpse into the secret, peaceful Hades of the blessed.   **W. M. N.**[*]

ART. X.—Sartorius on the Person and Work of Christ.

1. *Die Lehre von Christi Person und Werk in populairen Vorlesungen vorgetragen von* Ernst Sartorius, *Doctor der Theologie. Fuenfte Auflage. Hamburg*, 1845.

2. *The Person and Work of Christ. By Ernest Sartorius, D. D., General Superintendent and Consistorial Director at Koenigsberg, Prussia. Translated by* Rev. Oakman S. Stearns, A. M., Boston, 1848.

The second work here named offers itself to the world, as a translation of the first. If by a translation, however, we are to understand a true transfer of the sense and spirit of a book out of one language into another, it is wholly a misnomer to apply the term to this case. The original work of Sartorius is one which comes up in full, both in sentiment and style, to the wide reputation, which has carried it in Germany through five editions, and made it a favorite with all who take an interest in practical piety under a manly and substantial form. No one can read it understandingly, without admiration and respect; and the heart must be dull indeed, that is not made to kindle, under its simple though profound devotional eloquence, into some corresponding

---

[*] Writer of "The Apple as a Criterion of Taste," in No. I., the signature having been inadvertently omitted.—Pub.

glow of christian edification. But of all this, it would be hard to form any conception from Mr. Stearns' *translation*. This is neither elegant, nor intelligent, nor edifying. A most lame, clumsy performance throughout, it presents no single attraction either in thought or expression, no redeeming quality whatever, save in the broken fragments of truth and beauty that still look forth here and there upon the beholder, in spite of the general desolation with which the work has been overwhelmed as a whole. It is indeed Sartorius *in ruins ;* a spectacle, whose re-mains of greatness serve only to render more affectingly sad, the chaotic dreariness in which its exhibition mainly consists. Mur-derous translations are by no means uncommon ; but we have seldom met with one which could be said more effectually to kill the life of the author it pretends to honor, in this way.

In the first place, Mr. Stearns evidently has had no sufficient knowledge of the German language, and no proper mastery of the English either, to do justice to any undertaking of this sort. His own English, as we have it in his short preface, is anything but easy and smooth. Were his knowledge of the German ever so complete, he lacks altogether the freedom and pliancy of style that are required to make a good translator. But he has brought with him no such advantage to his task. It is only a smattering acquaintance with German, he can be said to possess at best. His knowledge of the language shows itself to be throughout, mechanical, superficial, and in a great measure merely external. He has never entered at all into its true genius and life ; its idio-matic soul remains, to a great extent, foreign from the view of his understanding. Still less can he be said to be at home, in the peculiarities of German thought. There is not a page of his translation accordingly, we might say indeed hardly a sen-tence in its connections, which does not betray some want of insight, more or less, into the true living sense of the original work. Take as a specimen, the following extract, which is made to pass for the preface of Sartorius to the last German edition :

" Several years have passed away since the first appearance of this little volume, and now the Fifth Edition is deemed neces-sary by the continual demand for it. It is absolutely necessary that the doctrine of the incarnation, by the union of divinity and humanity in it, and the re-union of both by it, which was rejected by many theologians out of the historical churches, and had become foreign to and far from the educated and uneducated in general, should be transferred in this artless, familiar manner, from the department of learned theology, to the more common orbit of faith and life, and should be brought to the Christian conscience of readers of every grade, as the basis of all Christianity and of all salvation.   Great storms have been raised during this time respecting the proper field of the church, and they have been particularly directed against this fundamental doctrine. They have endeavored to turn away the testimony of the church and its judgement, thereby expecting to tear it asunder and destroy it.   Some have spoken of the incarnate Jesus as the Lord of humanity, in the loose generalities of the multitude, and thereby robbed him of the excellence by which he was to increase to a confederate head, and by which he should become the reconciler of everything which sin had separated, even the fountain of life and love from which every favor and power of renovation should flow   He has a very narrow conception of the thing who expects to remove from Christ the concentration of the fulness of the Godhead.   He most assuredly misunderstands himself, because if in him all fulness dwells, every favor, even grace for grace must come from him, and by means of him we become partakers of the divine nature.

"These storms, however, have to a great degree blown over or turned out to be mere wind.   Indeed, the church has strengthened itself, established itself, and made itself fast during the roar of the storm, clinging the more tenaciously to the reconciliation of heaven and earth by faith in Jesus Christ, the mighty God eternally generated from the Father, and the mighty man generated from the virgin Mary.   This union of time and eternity cannot be removed.   The denial of the divinity of Christ humbles him to an idol or a demi-god, and leads to a heathenish idolatry, or it degrades him to a mere man, and thereby sinks his religion behind Judaism.   Very evidently everything spiritual and human becomes him who is the king of the heavenly kingdom, who was exalted from the cross to the right hand of the majesty, not to conquer, but to receive the name which the Father has given, by virtue of which he shall obtain the homage of both angels and men.

" In spite of the stormy movements of the time, therefore, while the world renews the evidence of the Scriptures and the church respecting the Son of God, and the Son of man the mediator between God and man, Jesus Christ our Lord, who though in the image of God, humbled himself, and took upon himself the form of a servant, was obedient to the death of the cross, and from his humiliation is now exalted for us over all the world to his praise and for our salvation, this discussion will remain immovable by the side of that which is old and unchangeable. Neither the contents nor the form of this little book ought to suffer any material change. The circumstances of the time seem to demand the very same things. Indeed, they present themselves as another proper occasion for giving the book both in Germany and in other lands, by means of translations, a larger circle of readers. Its design is to meet not so much the wants of a theological public as those of a Christian public. Accordingly, the Fifth edition appears with every essential correspondence to the earlier ones. As I would not, however, omit any amount of care manifest in the other editions, I have inserted when and where it was proper, individual additions and emendations, and thereby increased the pages somewhat.

" May this work receive the blessing of him concerning whom it treats. May it receive the sanction of the Lord who renovated the condition of the world by reconciling it to himself. May it aid in establishing the Christian reader upon the precious cornerstone, without which every church organization founded upon some other basis than the rock of confession, which was first testified to by the apostles before the Lord gave to them the shutting up of the heavenly kingdom, is founded only upon the sand. This is the first and chief thing to be done by the church, that worshipping in the name of Jesus, every knee may bow, and every tongue confess that he is the Lord to the glory of God the Father."

To be properly estimated, this should be compared with the original German text. As however a large part of our readers must be supposed unable to try it in that way, we subjoin the true sense of the original in a different version. It will be easy to see, by the comparison, first that the "translation" just quoted has in part no clear sense whatever; and secondly, that such sense as it has, is materially different from that intended by Sartorius :

" Fourteen years have elapsed since the first appearance of these lectures, of which the continued demand now calls for a *fifth* edition. The doctrine of the *God-man*, of the union of divinity and humanity in him, and the reconciliation of both through him, (a doctrine by many theologians long since thrust out of the church into mere history, and that had grown strange to the Christian community, cultivated as well as uncultivated,) by these unpretending lectures, came forth again from the sphere of scientific theology into more general contact with faith and life, and was anew brought nigh to the christian consciousness of readers of every standing as the foundation on which christianity with its whole salvation rests. Great storms have swept since that time, over the field of the Church, and have directed their strength in particular against this foundation, bearing witness thus to its true character in this view, while seeking to unsettle it, and so to overthrow the church built upon it. It has been pretended to dissolve the God-man Jesus, the Lord of humanity, into the loose generality of the human race; robbing this thus of the head, from which the whole should grow up into a well compacted body, (Eph. iv. 15f,) of the mediator through whom is to be reconciled all that has been separted by *sin*, (Col. i. 20,) and of the fountain of life and love from which all should draw grace and power of renovation. The concentration of the fulness of the Godhead in the One Christ, (Col. ii. 9,) it was affected to set aside as something poor and narrow; while in truth such judgment was itself too narrow to see, how all fulness dwells in *him* for this reason precisely, that all may receive thence grace for grace, and become through *him* partakers of the divine nature (John i. 16; 2 Pet. i. 4).

" Those storms have to a great extent blown over, or are sunk at least into common winds; in the midst of their raging, however, the Church visibly gained strength, planting herself with new and more firm resolution on the rock of her all-reconciling faith in Jesus Christ, 'true God begotten of the Father in eternity and also true man born of the Virgin Mary.' She cannot recede from this ground which binds eternity and time into one; since the denial of Christ's divinity either sinks him to the character of an idol or demi-god, leading in this way to heathenish idolatry, or else reduces him to a mere man, and so falls back into Judaism. Assuredly all the spiritual and fleshly powers of the world will be found unable to prevail over the king Messiah who has been exalted from the cross to the right hand of majesty, or to take from him the name which is given him of the Father, so high and glorious as to compel the homage of angels and men.

" In the face accordingly of all the stormy agitations of the time, these lectures have stood immovably fast to the firmly settled, ancient (though never old, but rather always world-renewing) testimony of the Bible and the Church, concerning the Son of God and of Man, the Mediator between God and man, our Lord Jesus Christ; who being in divine form equal with God, nevertheless emptied himself and took upon him the form of a servant, and became obedient even to the death of the cross, and now is exalted from such humiliation over all the world for his own glory and our salvation (Phil. ii. 5ff). No material change therefore has been made in the contents of this little volume, as it has passed through different editions, nor even in its form; for this, as it had from outward popular occasion adapted itself to a wide christian rather than theological public, was just what procured for the work its extensive circulation, and this indeed not in Germany only, but by translations also in foreign lands. So this fifth edition also appears in substantial agreement with those which have gone before; only I wished to show my continued interest in the earlier work, and for this reason have introduced single additions and improvements, as it seemed worth while, which have increased somewhat also the number of pages.

"Under his blessing now of whom it treats, under the blessing of the Lord, who has brought into the world not so much a constitution as an atonement, may this little book still farther contribute to build christian readers on that precious foundation and corner-stone, without which all church organization, the great concern of the present time, will be built upon the sand, and not on the rock of that confession, (Matt. xvi. 16ff.) which the Apostles were required first to make, before the keys of the kingdom of heaven were given to them by the Lord. This it is which the Church needs first and above all, that at the name of Jesus every knee should bow in worship, and every tongue *confess* harmoniously with his people, that he is Lord to the glory of God the Father.

Koenigsberg, Passion week, 1845."

This will be sufficient, for all readers, to justify in full the sweeping censure we have allowed ourselves to pronounce on Mr. Stearns' translation. Harsh and exaggerated as the judgment might seem, on first view, it will easily be perceived that it falls not a whit short of the sober truth. The translation is no translation whatever, but a miserable travesty and caricature rather of the respectable work in whose name it appears. It is such a wrong indeed upon the character and reputation of Sartorius, that under any proper system of international literary law, he would be authorized to sue for heavy damages, as a grossly misrepresented and slandered man "The translation," we are told in the preface, "is designedly free, and as expressive of the views of the author as the time and means of the translator would allow." A good translation must be in any case *free;* that is not bound slavishly to the letter at the expense of the spirit and sense. But in the case before us, the freedom is such as flows from weakness and not from strength. It is helplessly, wilfully, and for this reason slavishly independent. Its liberty stands only in the power it has to go wrong, without understanding the fact. A strange freedom truly, that turns words and sentences continually from their proper sense, misled by its own mechanical dictionary-guided ignorance, and turns an author on every page into a shape, which can hardly be said to reflect a single feature of his native face. If the "time and means" of Mr. Stearns allowed no more than this, it had been better, we think, to turn his resources to some other work. It is no apology for such a wrong as this, that the doer of the work could do it no better. Why should he, in such case, feel bound to try it at all? The world would not have suffered any irreparable loss—Sartorius himself might well have borne the disappointment—if the little book in question had been left to go untranslated; at least till some more competent hand, with proper "time and means," had offered itself for the purpose. The thanks of the translator are tendered, in conclusion, to the Rev. Dr. Sears, President of the Newton Theological Institution, for suggesting the translation, "and for any aid he has generously afforded him during the progress of it." No doubt Dr. Sears recommended the work as worthy of being translated, as any one would who was able to appreciate its value; but it is not to be imagined for a moment, that he is responsible in any way for the character of the translation. He is known to be one of the most accomplished German scholars in the country; and to involve him even indirectly in the endorsement of such a production, must be taken as a wrong to his reputation, only less flagrant than the wholesale slaughter of poor Dr. Sartorius himself. How such a work could pass muster with the common religious press, might seem strange; for it abounds in sentences and entire passages that have no sense whatever, and as a whole is made exceedingly tasteless and dull; but newspaper notices, we all know, are not generally in such cases the fruit of much consideration or care. They go by presumption, far more than by insight. This has been well illustrated, in the present case.*

---

* Even the scholarly editor of the Methodist Quarterly Review, (Dr. M'Clintock,) is so far misled, on the faith probably of the respectable publishing firm, " *Gould, Kendall & Lincoln, Boston,*" as to say: " The translation appears to be faithful, and is in general well expressed."

Our interest, however, in this translation is something deeper than its merely literary character. As a bungling attempt to turn a good German author into English, its merits fall so low that it might seem scarcely worth while to make it the subject of criticism; although even in this view there is such a wrong involved in it, as ought not to go unnoticed and unrebuked. But along with the literary defect of this translation, must be taken into consideration also a general theological defect, which goes of course so far as it prevails, to aggravate the other evil. Some illustration of this may be found in the two phases of the preface already presented; which indeed have been given in full, for the purpose partly of bringing into view what is now stated.

The truth is, the religious theory of Mr. Stearns differs very materially from that of the author whose work he has here undertaken to translate. Of this he is himself aware, to some ex-extent. Sartorius, he tells us, is a Lutheran, with certain peculiarities, which he of course, as a New England Baptist, is not prepared to endorse or accept. It is plain enough, however, at the same time, that his sense of such difference between himself and his author, remains always in the end very partial and narrow. The peculiarities in question are taken to be in part verbal only, technical forms of different schools, and, in other cases, mere outward and accidental excrescences, (traditional *crotchets*,) rather than living and necessary elements in the inward constitution of the system to which they belong. It is quietly taken for granted accordingly, that this system is ,in all substantial respects, one and the same with that of the translator himself. Mr. Stearns has been honestly persuaded, in his own mind, that his general scheme of evangelical religion is identical with the scheme of Sartorius, and the *evangelical* German school generally, to which he belongs—barring only a few old-fashioned European prejudices, now fast going into disuse; and he has set himself to translate this work, and carried through the undertaking as he best could, without the least imagination probably that he was bending the inward habit of the work throughout to a form of thinking altogether strange and foreign from its own. And yet it is so in fact. Without the least *consciousness* of any such wrong, and much less with any malicious intent to bring it to pass, he has, nevertheless, contrived to surround Sartorius with a theological nimbus, or *cloud*, which, so far as it can be seen through at all, makes it very difficult, if not indeed absolutely impossible, for any merely English reader, to catch even a dim outline of his true German person.

The great object of the work, as is shown by the preface to the fifth edition already quoted, is to assert the glorious mystery of the incarnation, with its necessary consequences, as the one only sure and immovable foundation of religion, over against the rationalistic and pantheistic errors, with which it has been opposed, particularly in modern Germany. This mystery is of course accepted by all evangelical bodies in this country also, from the most churchly away out to the most unchurchly, as the foundation of the gospel, in opposition to all sorts of Unitarianism. Mr. Stearns accordingly finds no difficulty, in making common cause with Sartorius, on this ground. A tract on the Person and Work of Christ falls in easily with his theory of religion, as based on the conception of a supernatural redemption wrought out by his death; and no hesitation is felt about taking it in the sense of this theory, leaving all awkward *inconcinnities* to fetch themselves right as they best can. Here, however, is a grand mistake. The mystery of the incarnation in its relation to christianity, is something very different to Sartorius, from all it is made to be, or felt to be, in the Baptistic theology of Mr. Stearns. There is a stress laid upon the fact, a deep sense, a world of significance and force, made to go along with it, in the one case, which come not into view to any similar extent in the other. It is after all a different *christology*, that comes before us in the two cases.

With Sartorius, christianity is a new order of life that has its ground in the christiological fact itself. The incarnation is viewed not simply as an outward contrivance, to open the way for the work of redemption, but as the real foundation in which the entire mystery not only starts, but continues also to hold from beginning to end. It is the union of divinity and humanity in Christ, which not simply qualifies him for the work he was appointed to perform, but of itself involves in his person that reconciliation between heaven and earth, God and man, which the idea of redemption requires, and for which there could be no room in any other form. He is in his very constitution our PEACE,

in whom first the sundered worlds just mentioned are made one,
for the very purpose of bringing them together afterwards in the
way of a general salvation. It is in virtue only of what he is
in this view, as the head of our human life, that it becomes possible for the race beyond him, through union with his mystical
body and by conjunction with him as its centre and head, to
partake also of the divine nature. Thus it is, that " this ground
binds eternity and time into one," reconciles heaven and earth,
not circuitously and instrumentally only, but immediately and
at once, in Jesus Christ. This is very distinctly stated by Sartorius in the preface to the first edition of his work, which it may
be well to give here also in full :*

" After the example set by Professor Struve, at the beginning
of the year before, the following lectures were delivered during
Passion week of the present year, in aid of the poor supported
by the Benevolent Society of this place, in the large lecture room
of our university, before a mixed audience, which gave them
encouraging attention to the close. They are now printed, partly

---

* Travestied in Mr. Stearns' translation as follows :

"The subject herein discussed was originally presented to a mixed assembly in the form of lectures. Lectures on another subject had already been
given by Prof. Struve, by whose very kind assistance and instigation the
poor were accommodated during Passion-week in the great lecture-room of
our university. I now give them to the public, partly because others desire
it, and partly because I myself wish by these unassuming discourses to establish a fixed and determined knowledge of the peculiar evangelical doctrine of salvation, in a larger circle than that in which it is now found, even
among such laymen as err concerning true Christianity rather in knowledge
than in good will, Of these there are at the present time more than is generally supposed. I have, therefore, discussed the doctrine of the incarnation of the Son of God, the more extensively, because I wished to show
intelligibly, that the work of redemption, as connected with the divine bene-
volence, depends upon a personal union in Christ of divinity and humanity.
Moreover, this great doctrine is peculiarly practical and requisite in an age
when an unchristian rationalism is striving to destroy it by a foolish indifference, and is making bold efforts to deny the revealed truth of the Bible.
This discussion, besides furnishing a correct knowledge to the laity, will, it
is hoped, contribute to the purity, importance and completeness of the doctrine as believed by the church, maintaining as it does the only true and
self-evident medium between two antagonistic errors. Finally, if the publishing these Lectures shall remove any unavoidable mistake in a single
passage during their delivery, or shall give any proof in this time of jealousy with respect to evangelical Christianity, that there is in this doctrine
no new-fangled mysticism, but only the firmly-settled Bible-Christianity
of our fathers; which is to stand as long as the Augsburg Confession shall
have a lawful existence in our church, then my object will be accomplished.
Though the times may degenerate, and many may fall away, truth itself
never changes, but will continue when the heavens and earth have passed
away,"

to satisfy the wish of others, and partly from my own desire that their unpretending form may serve to promote, in more remote circles also, a definite and practical acquaintance with the peculiar saving truths of the gospel, among those of the laity, who are often wanting in right knowledge far more than in good will towards true christianity: and of whom there are more at the present time than is generally supposed. I have accordingly dwelt at large on the doctrine of the incarnation of the Son of God, as I wished to show, for common apprehension, how his work of redemption, together with all his benefits, rests for us throughout upon the union of divinity with humanity in his person; and of what practical moment and how necessary to salvation therefore this great doctrine is, which an unchristian rationalism, with stupid indifference and in plain contradiction to the Bible, is endeavoring to bring out of credit. The work may contribute besides to bring the purity, consistency and completeness of the church doctrine, which ever maintains the alone true and sure medium between opposite errors, into proper acknowledgment also with the laity. Finally, the publication of the lectures will remove any misunderstanding of single passages, such as is unavoidable with mere oral delivery, and furnish clear proof at the same time to such as share the reigning prejudice against evangelical christianity, that no new-fashioned mysticism has been presented here, but only the old, well authenticated bible christianity of our fathers, which alone can claim, as long as the Augsburg Confession stands, a legitimate authority in our Church. However many may have fallen from it, the truth itself is not for this reason fallen, but shall continue to stand when heaven and earth even pass away.

Dorpat, May, 1831.

In carrying out his design, Sartorius dwells at length in the first place, on the nature of the great mystery of godliness, "God manifest in the flesh," the way and manner of the union of divinity with humanity in Jesus Christ, as the basis on which rests the whole superstructure of the christian salvation. In the next place, the value and power of the fact for the purposes of redemption are shown. Finally the process is explained, by which all is made to pass over to the actual benefit of the human race.

The mystery of the incarnation is presented to us, as "the assumption of the human nature by the Son of God into the unity of his person." It throws us back at once on the eternal sonship of Christ, and the doctrine of the divine trinity. This, however, is not absolutel   culiar to revelation. Some trace of it at least is to be found in philosophy and heathen mythology. The God of the mere deist is a lifeless abstraction "There is hardly any ancient system of religion, in the East or West, which reveals not some glimmering of the doctrine of the trinity; the traces of it are to be met at the opposite poles, in India and Scandinavia." Peculiar to revelation rather, as its foundation truth is the announcement that the eternal Word has become flesh, under a personal historical form, in Jesus of Nazareth, the Son of the Virgin Mary. "The latest enemies of christianity, (Dr. Strauss and his followers,) have assailed it by asserting a general incarnation of God in humanity as a whole, in such way as to deny it under an individual separate form in Jesus Christ, nay, to repudiate the idea of this as narrow particularism. This is a gross error, which sees not in the first place, how estranged from God the human race has become by sin, so as to be wholly incapacitated within itself for a re-union with divinity without a mediator; and in the second place, does not consider that, in the perfect Mediator all the fullness of the Godhead dwells, just for this reason, that out of his fullness all may receive grace for grace, John i. 16., and not by any means that it may remain selfishly shut up in his person. So in the body of the sun, light is not concentrated, to remain there fixed, but rather that all the world may be enlightend by it; whereas when many stars twinkle in place of the one orb of day, we have at best but the dusk of night. Into such night dusk would those lead us, who rob the planets of their sun, while in room of the one God-man, who is the Saviour of all and the Light of the world, they affect to proclaim *all* men, and especially, the heroes of the race, an incarnation of deity. They deny both, the personal oneness and glory of Christ, as well as his true universality; for the last consists just in this, that as the *one* divine head of his Church, he comprehends under himself *all* its members, (Eph. iv. 15, 16,) and communicates to them his truth, grace and righteousness, forming them thus into one body. Where on the contrary the royal head is made to fail, the members fall asunder in helpless broken disorder, and there is no room to speak farther of a kingdom of Christ or a Church of God, or of any redemption and salvation of the human race. Here, then, if anywhere, it behooves us to abide by the Scriptures, which in most direct contradiction to this modern wisdom or folly expressly assure us, Col. i. 19: It pleased the Father that in him (in Jesus Christ) should all fulness dwell; and ii. 9: In him dwelleth all the fullness of the Godhead bodily."*

The incarnation under this personal, historical character, is shown to be an act of *free* condescension on the side of God. It implies no essential *change* in the divine nature. At the same time, the human nature assumed by the Son of God, must be allowed to be in all respects real and complete. It was no phantom or show only, but a true body joined with a reasonable soul. Lastly, the union of the two natures, while it leaves them distinct, must be regarded as organic, involving a strict personal unity in the form of a common undivided consciousness. " Without such a personal union of divinity and humanity, no redemption could be accomplished; for the very nature of it stands just in this, that grace brings together what by nature and sin are sundered, namely, God and man; a mere man could of himself as little redeem the world as he could create it; and God of himself, though able to create, uphold and govern the world, cannot either make reconciliation for it, since this requires a union of the sundered parts, and such a free satisfaction for sin as he only can render, who stands at once over the law and under the law. The error before us is accordingly at war with the whole Bible. Throughout, in the entire life of our Lord, we are confronted with only one personality, one *I*, one undivided, though in its contents, most manifold self-consciousness."

Sartorius next considers how the two natures, in this personal union, condition and affect each other. There must be, through the medium of the common consciousness in which they meet, a mutual communication, to some extent, of states and properties. Only so can the divine and human be regarded as coming fully together, in such way as the idea of a true and proper redemption and reconciliation requires. Hence the most opposite predicates can be affirmed of the common person. Secondly, the

---

* This fine passage, so intimately related to the deep significance of the christological mystery as held by Sartorius, his translator entirely omits; connecting what goes before and what follows, in a continuous paragraph, with a violence that fairly kills the original, to make out, what is, after all, only an *apparition* of sense.

properties of the divine nature attach, through the central consciousness, to the human.   Thirdly, the properties of the human
nature attach, in the same way, to the divine.*   With such constitution, the mystery of the Saviour's person, in order that it
may be still more fully understood, must be followed through
the successive stages of his humiliation and exaltation, till all
becomes complete finally in the glory of his second coming.

The way is opened thus, at length, for contemplating the *work*
of Christ, the end in which the mystery of his person reveals its
meaning and power.   This occupies the sixth, seventh and eighth
lectures.   All is made to grow out of the fact of the incarnation.
"So closely is the whole joined with this as its root, that to describe the wonderful constitution of Christ's person, is itself to
set forth in some measure its object.   If we cast a retrospective
glance over the entire portrait of the God-man, as presented to
us in both his natures, in their union and in his different states
of humiliation and exaltation, so as to bring all as much as possible to one grand impression, we must at once feel that the end
and purpose of it is to effect the inmost union and fellowship of
divinity and humanity, and in this way to glorify the love of God
as well as secure the happiness and salvation of men."   Man is
formed for religion, as the perfection of his being.   This holds
only in union with God, whose love is the ground of all good.
Sin sunders us all naturally from his presence.   Our salvation
requires that it should be taken out of the way.   This is accomplished only through the satisfaction of Christ, which, in virtue
of his inward living relation to the race, and the theanthropic
mystery of his person, carries with it a true reconciling and saving force for all mankind.

The next inquiry regards the application of this grace to particular men, the transition of what is accomplished primarily in
Christ, over to his people.   This leads to the consideration of the
means of grace, namely, the word and sacraments, as they have
been divinely lodged in the keeping of the Church for this pur-

---

* Mr. Stearns, with amusing awkwardness, makes Sartorius say here just
the same thing in his second and third conclusions; in the first case, "by
means of the communicated union of consciousness, the attributes of the
divine nature belong to the human," while in the second, "by means of the
reciprocal consciousness, the human nature receives also the attributes of
the divine nature."

pose. Next follows a view of the several stages in the process of salvation; after which the whole discussion concludes with a brief survey, in the last lecture, of the prophetical, priestly and kingly offices, as executed by Christ in the character of Mediator.

Throughout, thus, the person of the Saviour is represented as lying, inwardly and truly, at the foundation of the whole christian salvation. "Christ is himself the living substance of christianity;" which accordingly, from first to last, serves but to unfold or bring out the deep contents of his life. His work holds always and only in the mystery of his person, and is of force for others in no other way than as they are brought to have part in this as its constant support and ground. "In him dwells all fullness; all the predictions of the prophets, all the ideals of sacred poetry, all the deepest thoughts of true philosophy, are fulfilled and ac-actualized in him, in whom God became manifest in the flesh, (I. Tim. iii. 16.) that we might behold his glory, as that of the only begotten Son of the Father, and receive from his fullness grace for grace, John i. 14–18:" *In him*, not *by* him simply, all things which are in heaven and which are on earth, are reconciled, united and comprehended under one head, (Eph. i. 10., Col. i. 20.).

All this, rightly apprehended, is something materially different, we say, from the christology of Mr. Stearns. Without being aware of the fact, he has in his mind throughout, quite another conception of the theanthropic mystery, and quite another scheme accordingly of the christian salvation. Sartorius is a Lutheran, honestly and earnestly true to the substance of Luther's faith, though now in the bosom of the United German Church. Mr. Stearns is a Baptist, immersed all over in the unmystical element of his own creed. These two systems are by no means the same; and the difference is not simply accidental. It falls back, in the end, to the idea of Christ's person, and in this way necessarily conditions the theory and life of religion throughout. The Baptistic Christ is not in full the Lutheran Christ. He may be acknowledged in the same terms to a certain extent; but his constitution is not the same, and he stands in a different relation to the work of redemption. The Baptistic christology is not itself the new world of grace, in which the whole gospel stands revealed as a living fact, but forms rather the outward machinery which heaven has contrived for saving men.   The *work* which was required to take away sin, needed indeed a conjunction of divinity with humanity in Christ, to qualify him for its execution; but once executed, it carries with it an independent and separate value in the divine mind, and may be set to the account of men as a mere abstraction in this way, apart from Christ's life altogether.   The person of the Saviour is not viewed as the principle and root strictly of the whole christian salvation, but only as its outward occasion or instrument, brought in gloriously to make way for the action of grace under another form; just as the electric telegraph is employed as a medium for bringing a word to pass a thousand miles off, which could not be made to take effect in any other way, although it is in no sense itself the very form and substance of the word so spoken.   So regarded, the hypostatical union itself assumes a more or less shadowy and unreal character, leaning at one time towards Gnosticism, or at another saving itself again only in the form of Nestorian dualism.   The sense of an inward, *organic* union is, in a great measure, wanting. The true *universalness* of Christ's humanity comes not into view. The *reconciliation* of heaven and earth, which lies in the mystery of the incarnation itself, and involves potentially and necessarily all the atonement and redemption that follow, is not perceived. The deep, rich, overwhelming sense of the living *fact*, is not understood or felt.   In place of it, we have only an orthodox abstraction.   Then the redemption which follows, is of course apprehended under a corresponding character.   Christ executes all his offices in a comparatively outward way, parallel thus in kind with the Old Testament prophets, priests and kings, only rising above them in degree, "*primus* inter pares."   He reveals truth, buys righteousness, and exerts power, all in an external instrumental manner; instead of being in fact, as he always claims to be, in the very constitution of his own person, *the* way, *the* truth, *the* resurrection and *the* life, all in the most real and absolute sense, in whom, as well as by whom only, it is possible for any of the children of men to be saved.   An abstract conception of the work of redemption again brings with it necessarily also, a like abstract idea of the way in which men are made partakers of its grace.   The process is lifted into the sphere of pure thought.   All turns on supernatural acts of God on one side, and

the exercises of individual experience on the other, that come
after all to no steady union in the way of spiritual life. The
mystical, sacramental interest in religion, is practically underval-
ued, or we may say, rather to a great extent subverted altogether,
in order to make room more effectually for what are conceived
to be the far higher claims of piety under a different form.

It is easy enough to feel this want of congruity between Sartorius and his translator throughout; but it comes to its most
glaring exposure, where the subject of the sacraments is brought
forward. In the nature of the case, this could not be left out of
sight in the original work. No christology, no scheme of christianity, can be *Lutheran*, which leads not to the idea of sacramental grace, the *mystery* of Christ's presence in the sacraments,
as an essential, inseparable element of the gospel. Sartorius accordingly devotes a whole lecture mainly to this subject—a rich,
instructive and edifying discourse, for any one whose mind is
prepared at all to sympathize with the ancient faith of the Church.
But what now becomes of this most unbaptistic chapter of the
work, in the hands of Mr. Stearns? The whole of it is quietly
suppressed, with only the following explanation, in the way of
a short note, at the beginning of the next lecture: "The previous chapter discusses the Lutheran view of baptism and the
Lord's Supper, but is omitted in the translation as inapplicable
to the ideas upon that subject held by christians generally on this
side of the water."

Let us now look for a moment to the lecture in question, that
we may understand how much is involved in the summary renunciation, thus made in behalf, not only of the Baptist body,
but of the American churches in general.

The means of grace, according to Sartorius, have their force
only in the Church, constituted by the Holy Ghost, to hold them
in charge and administer them as organs for men's salvation.
They are, first, the *word*, in the two-fold form of law and gospel; then the two holy sacraments, *baptism* and the *Lord's supper*. These are not properly *our* works, but acts of grace performed towards us by Christ, through the Church, which we are
required to accept believingly in this character. Baptism is the
seal of our ingrafting into Christ. We are born under the curse
of original sin; but grace interposes, through Christ, to bring us

out of that state, extending to us, even in infancy, the visible pledge of such deliverence in this holy mystery. "Hence it is called the laver of *regeneration*, Tit. iii. 5; because by it the child, though at first still unconscious, passes out of the kingdom of the world and its spirit into the kingdom of God and his Spirit, and from a child of the flesh becomes a child of grace, on whom is impressed anew the seal of his original destination to the image of God and the inheritance of eternal life, while in the Church of Ohrist, of which he is a member, all means and helps are furnished for reaching this end." The objective value of it is not affected, in the case of infants, by the consideration that they cannot at once appropriate it by faith. It remains always at hand, as a divine fact, notwithstanding, for their use and appropriation through the whole of their lives. Does a man become truly and properly the child of his natural parents, only when he wakes first to the clear sense of what is comprised in such relation? Baptism, in this case, comes to its completion of right in *confirmation.* Again, as the christian life begins in this first sacrament, so it is fed and supported by the second, the holy supper. Here Christ imparts to us his flesh and blood, that is, the power of his own divine-human life; for he is, in truth, the living bread, of which all must partake or perish. There is, indeed, no change of the bread and wine into the substance of Christ, as the Roman Church teaches; but still there is a real union between them, above sense, according to his own word. "We will not envy those," says Sartorius, "who see in this meal only an outward figurative memorial of an absent Christ, which makes nothing more of him to be present, than what they may think along with it out of their own minds. Such, verily, would do better to contemplate a crucifix, or an *ecce homo*, or some other image of Jesus, than to eat a piece of bread and drink a sip of wine, destroying thus the recollection sign in the very act of its reception."

All this, of course, is at full variance with the system of Mr. Stearns. He allows no such efficacy to baptism, and dreams of no such mystery in the Lord's Supper. It is easy thus to see and understand, why he should be disposed to set aside the whole chapter as out of date. What, however, must we think of the *honesty* of such conduct? Be the merits of the suppressed lecture what they may, it is certain that for Sartorius himself, it has

been of indispensable account in the discussion of his general
subject. It goes necessarily, with him, to make out the completeness and integrity of the book; he would not be willing at
all, as a good Lutheran, to stand charged before the world, with
a christological theory, from which, by any possibility, the idea
of sacramental grace could be divorced in such wholesale style.
The probability is, that he would prefer decidedly the suppression of the whole work, to any mutilation so terrible as this must
appear to be in his eyes. What right then, we may well ask,
has any translator, standing in a wholly different system of religious thought, to mutilate the book in this way, and still publish
it *in Sartorius' name?* It may be proper, in certain cases, to
abridge another man's work, for more general popular use;
though, even then, to be at all honest, the abridgement must be
published *as such*, and is bound besides to be true to the sum
and substance of the full work. It is, however, quite another
thing, to change or expunge a single passage or even a single
word, by which the true sense and spirit of the original is expressed at any point, in such a way as to bring in another sense
quite foreign from the author's mind. This is spiritual forgery,
which deserves to be abhorred of all good men. No small noise
was made a few years since, about certain liberties of this sort,
taken with D'Aubigne's History of the Reformation, by the
American Tract Society. But that wrong, generally condemned, we believe, was small indeed as compared with the high-
handed violence here perpetrated on Sartorius; and it must be
regarded as a sign of the general obtuseness of the American
Church to the claims of the high interest here concerned, that
so glaring a wrong should be able to proclaim itself, with so little
danger of shocking the common sense of christian propriety. Let
the case be put into a new shape. Suppose a Baptist tract, gut-
ted of its baptistic peculiarities, or some good Puritan work *catho-
licized*, for the use of the Roman Church, by the careful oblite-
ration of a whole section on justification by faith, and we should
not soon hear the last of the stealthy-footed, cowl-mantled stratagem. Can it be less *jesuitic* to play the same game, under a
Protestant evangelical guise? We think not.

But this is not all. The case reveals a radically wrong conception of the entire theological system represented by Sartorius,

and of its relation to the theory of religion, in whose service he is here enlisted. It is quite common, we know, for all evangelical sects, as the Church now stands, not excepting Baptists of every hue and name, to claim inward affinity with *Luther* as the father of the Reformation, and to glory in his doctrine as only carried out to its purest form in their own faith and practice. His prejudices about the sacraments, and some other things, they, of course, have consigned to the tomb of the Capulets, (with due indulgence to the dormitancies of so great a Homer,) but only to stick the faster to the true life and marrow of his divinity, as found in the doctrine of justification by faith. But only see the contradiction which all this carries upon its very face. " Saul among the prophets!" was not, surely, a greater incongruity than the idea of Luther quietly seated among these various sects ("die himmlische Propheten") and consenting to be taught " the way of God more perfectly," at their feet. What a compliment, moreover, to the cause of the Reformation, to conceive of its great leaders generally, and most of all, the very Moses of its glorious exodus, as having no power to discriminate between the essential and the accidental, in so clear a case as this of the sacraments is now taken to be; but actually filling all Europe with their noise about it, as though it belonged in some way to the very core of christianity, when any child may now see that they were driving at a shadow from first to last. The whole conception is absurd. The sacramental doctrine of Luther, so far as the substance of it is concerned, was no outward fungus upon his system. It lies imbedded in its inmost life. To part with it, is to give up the cause of the Reformation itself, as it stood in his mind, and to turn his whole theology into a new and different shape. To think of the Baptistic theory of religion as one and the same with the evangelical Lutheran, *only* divested of his sacramental doctrine—as though this were an old cocked hat, to be kept on or laid off at pleasure—can only show the shallow character of the whole theology, for which any such thought is possible. So in the case before us, to drop the chapter on the sacraments, and yet pretend to be satisfied with the rest of the book as sound and good, must be taken as a gross inconsistency. Any christology that can admit the idea of a Church with no divine powers, no grace in its sacraments, no room in its bosom

for infants, no mystical presence of Christ's life in the Lord's
supper—be its claims to respect in any other view what they
may—must be counted utterly foreign from the entire mind of
Sartorius, and cannot possibly be the same that is presented to
us in this little book.　However it may be with others, *his* view
of Christ's person, (like that of Luther,) necessarily involves such
a conception of the christian salvation, as brings along with it in
the end all that the sacramental interest includes.　His scheme
of religion thus, in the nature of the case, is materially different
througout from that into whose service he is here forcibly *translated* by Mr. Stearns.

Still farther.　The Lutheranism of Dr. Sartorius, as presented
in this work, is by no means of the rigid extreme sort; so that
in the case before us, it might seem to be set aside in favor simply
of the old Reformed or Calvinistic doctrine of the sacraments,
as this stood in the sixteenth century.　Even in that case, the
wrong would, of course, still merit sharp rebuke.　But the opposition here, is not between the two forms of the original Protestant doctrine.　There are a few sentences, perhaps, in Sartorius,
to which a true follower of Calvin might demur; but the body
of his doctrine, beyond all doubt, is the same that is most distinctly taught in the writings of Calvin, and embodied in all the
classic confessions of the Reformed Church.　There was a difference between the two creeds, of course; but such as it was,
it lies away beyond the Baptistic horizon, with which we are
here concerned.　Both sides of the old Protestantism intended
to hold fast to the substance of the ancient sacramental doctrine,
as it had stood in the catholic Church from the beginning.　Both
held the sacraments to be *mysteries*, regarded them as *organs* of
grace, looked through them by faith to the *presence* of Christ's
life, as objectively and truly comprehended in their solemn transaction.　All this grew too out of a corresponding christology, by
which room was made for the idea of a concrete Church, with
divine resources and capabilities, commensurate, in all respects,
with the entire extent of our human fall, and fitted in this way
to cover the case of infants no less than that of adults.　All this,
however, and nothing more than this, is just the conception which
Mr. Stearns, true to his Baptist feeling, undertakes to expunge
from the doctrine of Christ's Person and Work, "as inapplicable

to the ideas upon that subject held by Christians generally, on this side of the water." This deserves to be well considered and borne in mind.

But now finally; what are we to think of the declaration here made of Christians generally, on this side of the Atlantic? The reference is, of course, not simply to the Baptist body, but to the so-called evangelical denominations in general. It is taken for granted, that they have collectively fallen away from the old doctrine of the sacraments, as here represented; that their system of religion excludes it; that it has come to be, in short, on all sides, obsolete and out of date. Is this representation correct? We fear that there is but too much reason for it, in the actual state of the Church. It is sometimes resented indeed, as harsh and unkind, to speak of any falling away from the original Protestant ground, in the posture of our modern churches. But the evidence of the fact, so far as the general Puritan and Methodistic tendency is concerned, is too clear in the case of the sacraments, to bear any controversy; and it can only be by making no account of the interest in consideration, that the reality and momentous significance of the fact are so generally thrust out of sight. This, however, is itself, one of the strongest evidences of the very change, which it is affected in this way to overlook or despise. It is the want of the old faith in the sacraments, precisely, which makes the question of the sacraments, and along with this the whole subject of the Church, to be for so many, of so little interest and meaning. With all this agrees, but too well, the low style, in which these divine mysteries are spoken of in every direction, and the determined resistance which is made to the idea of everything like sacramental grace. It would seem, indeed, as if Mr. Stearns had good reason to say of the old doctrine, both Lutheran and Calvinistic, (for *his* repudiation of Sartorius excludes it in both forms,) that it no longer suits the reigning faith of this country. The statement has called forth, so far as we have noticed, no contradiction or exception, on the part of those who have noticed his book. His monstrous wrong done to Sartorius, and to the theme of his book, on this plea, is suffered to pass without rebuke. Even the Lutheran Church, whose whole significance is here at stake, and whose dignity and glory it should be to stand forward, especially at such a time, as the bulwark of the sacramental interest, has lost, unfortunately, to a great extent, the power of entering any effectual protest in so grave a case. The "Lutheran Observer," which represents at present the reigning mind and life of that church, actually took notice of this mutilation of Sartorius, not long since, with a chuckle of delight, as a broad sign of the entire *antiquation* which has happily overtaken, here in evangelical America, the whole sacramental dream of the sixteenth century. The sympathies of this *organ* of Lutheranism fit it for making love ecclesiastically to the Cumberland Presbyterians, and other such sects, much more than for coming up to the help of its own proper faith in the hour of distress and danger. Could there well be however, a more grinning irony on our existing sect system, than is presented to us in such a spectacle—the creed of Luther, the faith of the Augsburg Confession, thus mortally wounded, in favor of the Baptists, in the house of its own professed friends!

It is all right, in this case, that the doctrine of infant baptism is made to share a common fate with the mystical presence in the Lord's supper, and the idea of sacramental grace generally. The baptism of infants can have no meaning for those who allow no objective value or force in the sacrament itself. Such may still hold fast to the rite, on the ground of old church tradition; but they do so with inward contradiction to their own faith; they are baptistic in principle, and to be at all consistent, should fall in fully also with the baptistic practice. This lies also necessarily in the christological theory, and their corresponding view they take of the Church. Only where the christian salvation is seen and felt to be a fact, primarily made real, under a concrete form for the benefit of the whole world, in the person of Christ, can there be any proper consciousness of its enduring objective character in the Church, and its necessary relation in this form to the *whole* tract of our human existence, from the cradle to the grave. The idea of a Christ, whose life is not formed to take up into itself the entire fact of humanity, (of which infancy is just as necessary a constituent as full age.) is such a contradiction as no sound christological feeling, no true sense of the Church, can ever comfortably endure. But let all resolve itself into a mere outward and mechanical salvation, and the case is quite changed. The whole mystical, sacramental side of christianity is given up as no better than superstition; and along with the loss of all faith in the grace of holy baptism, as well as in that of the holy supper, the right of infants to be comprehended in Christ, by any such laver of regeneration, is thrown into an unsubstantial unmeaning shadow.   J. W. N.

ART. XI.—ORGANIC CHRISTIANITY.

THE object of this article is, to exhibit *the relation of baptized children to the church.* It is assumed, that baptized children do hold some peculiar relation, and unless baptism is a mere ceremonial, a work of supererogation and unauthorized obedience, this must be true. In other words, there is significancy in this rite. It is not a matter of mere expediency or human origin and authority, which may be observed or neglected at the option of individuals.

Allowing this postulate, and with those who deny it, we have at present, no controversy, the question is, what is that relation? On this point, the mind of God, as given in our apprehension in the Scriptures, the mind of the whole church, from its organization till a few centuries ago, and the mind of that branch of the church, particularly, to which the writer has always belonged,* may be briefly and intelligibly expressed. Baptized children, are in the church, and not out of it: members, in fact, who are not to come from the world into the church, but, who, being already in the church, if they change their relations, must go from the church into the world. In this brief statement, the whole marrow of the subject is involved, either in the way of pre-supposition, or of legitimate inference. At this precise point, the two great antagonizing schemes of opinion and practice, in regard to the matter before us, diverge, and by this radical idea,

* The writer is a Presbyterian.

all minor differences in the different systems are governed and may be explained.

According to our apprehensions, there are two, and omitting minor points, but two schemes of thought in regard to the church, its nature, membership and modes of propagation and increase. One of these, we would denominate *Individualism;* the other, Organic Christianity. 1. First, there is the scheme of opinion and practice, which, without designing anything invidious, but as characterizing its great leading idea, may be termed, individualism. This theory denies that any one is, or can be, or ought to be considered a member of the church of Christ, but one who has personally exercised faith and repentance, as the fruit and evidence of regeneration. This, of course and of design, excludes from the membership of the church, all but adult and actually regenerated persons.

On the other hand, there is the scheme of opinion and practice, which, for the want of a better term, and also as expressing its leading idea, we would denominate *organic christianity*, in distinction from individualism. This holds as one of its vital ideas, that membership in the church of God, may exist, and the privileges and blessings pertaining to it, may be enjoyed, in the case of those who have not exercised, and, in fact, are not capable of exercising faith and repentance. In other words, that infants, in virtue of the faith of their parents, or in such a case, of one of their parents, are, and of right ought to be considered, members of the church, entitled to its privileges, till, by their own act, or refusal to act, they forfeit these privileges and voluntarily identify themselves with the world and God's enemies, and are cast out of the church. One of these schemes represents christianity, as in its nature and by the plan of its founder, possessing organic power, operating really, and in many instances, efficaciously, irrespective of the choice or agency of the individual. It represents the church as a nursery. Its appliances as eminently educational, and growth, its great law of progress.

The other, represents christianity as addressing itself only to and operating upon individuals, after they have arrived at the period of personal choice and voluntary agency. It represents the church characteristically, as an armory; its appliances, as essentially aggressive and belligerent, and its law of progress, conquest.

With such antagonistic views of the nature of christianity, of the church, and of the right mode of its preservation and propagation, there must necessarily be diversity in regard to the point now before us, viz : the component elements of the church. Infants and children will, of course, be regarded in a very different light as one or the other of these views is adopted. Men of loose thinking and illogical habits, may confound or try to blend these two schemes, take a part of one and a part of the other, and out of the heterogeneous elements, endeavor to construct what they denominate a system. But it is impossible. Like the iron and clay of the toes of the great image, they will not cohere. To be symmetrical, the leading idea either of individualism or organic christianity, must run through the whole, and govern the separate parts of every system.

Having thus endeavored, honestly and impartially, to set forth these two great leading schemes of thought and practice, as they bear on this subject, and to state what we believe is the great point of divergence between them, the question of moment now, is, *Which of these is true?* Which correctly represents God's mind in the case, and ought consequently to govern the opinions and practice of his people ?

Subsidiary to the proper settlement of this question, and though confessedly secondary, by no means, in our view, unimportant, let us ascertain the view, taken in the symbolical books of the church, on the point before us. For all practical purposes, we may take the standards of the Presbyterian church, as embodying the antecedent and contemporaneous sentiment of the church, in the apprehension of their framers, and without obtruding our personal preferences, may consider them as expressing the siprit of Protestant symbols. Old-fashioned Presbyterianism, as we apprehend and feel bound to expound and maintain it, goes with its full weight against the scheme of individualism, and can be explained, as a consistent and symmetrical system, as beyond all controversy it is, whether we allow it to be true or not, only on the idea of organic christianity, as we have endeavored to explain the term.

For example, in regard to the composition of the church, considered as universal or particular, the idea of the Westminster standards embraces all that we have denominated the organic character of christianity. Their language, concerning the universal church, is, " The universal church consists of all those persons, in every nation, *together with their children*, who make profession of the holy religion of Christ, and of submission to his laws." Again, in the same spirit, they represent a particular church thus : " A particular church consists of a number of professing christians, *with their offspring*, voluntarily associated together for divine worship and godly living, agreeably to the holy Scriptures, and submitting to a certain form of government." In these fundamental views of the nature of the church, it will be perceived that the church is represented as altogether different from a mere aggregation of individuals. The church is held forth as having precisely the same organic character, and embracing the same elements as the state does, whatever be its specific form of administration. A nation, be its government monarchical or republican, embraces in its elements the infant and unconscious offspring of its members, and by this means, its identity is preserved and its perpetuation and progress secured. These grow up in connexion with it, are entitled to its protection, enjoy its privileges, and without any other specific act, are considered as in its allegiance. When foreign elements, indeed, come to be incorporated with this body, by their own act of choice, a special form of allegiance and recognition is necessary. And very properly, for then citizenship and allegiance are transferred. But in the case of native born citizens, their citizenship stands in their connexion with their parents and is assumed and continued, till by some act of their own, it is forfeited and annulled. Precisely so, the symbols alluded to, represent the elements of the church. Children, the offspring of parents professing submission to Christ—the baptized portion of the congregation, are, *de facto*, members, entitled to its privileges, and can only be deprived of them by their own fault or the exercise of the church's prerogative of discipline.

The same idea is involved in the teachings of these standards on the subject of baptism. Baptism is represented as " a sacrament of the New Testament, ordained by Jesus Christ, for the solemn admission of the party baptized, into the visible church," and "not only those who actually profess faith in and obedience unto Christ, but also the infants of one or both believing parents are to be baptized"—tantamount, according to the definition already given, to being solemnly admitted into the visible church.

So again, "Baptism is not to be administered to any that are out of the visible church, and so strangers to the covenants of promise, till they profess their faith in Christ and obedience to him." This is designed to meet the case of adult admissions, analogous to the introduction of foreign elements into civil society; "but infants, descending from parents either both or only one of them professing faith in Christ and obedience to him, are in that respect within the covenant and are to be baptized." The unbelief of one party, as we shall see in another part of this subject, being sanctified and its exclusive influence counteracted, in God's constitution, by the faith of the other party.

The faith of parents, or of one parent, as the case may be, always enures to the benefit of the unconscious child, brings it into important relations, surrounds it with important associations, and is the ordinary channel along which decisive influences come to it, long before it is capable of performing any act, to which personal accountability attaches. On this plan, the question of preference is to be settled, not *by the child*, in the exercise of its free agency and individual choice, but *for the child*, by those who stand in organic relation to it. Children are not to be held, *in equilibrio*, as some preposterously contend, till they come to exercise the grand prerogative of personal choice, a thing, in the nature of the case, impossible and absurd, as well as undesirable, but so influenced, that the exercise of choice shall be right and in accordance with truth and safety from the beginning. The system now under consideration, knows nothing of that idea of religious vagrancy, (we know of no other name for it,) popular with infidels and worldlings, which is so jealous of the rights of private judgment and of undue influence, that a child, with all its admitted and hereditary tendencies in the wrong direction, must be left uninfluenced and uncommitted in its plastic period, lest its freedom of opinion and choice should be thereby compromitted—a plan equally indicating folly on the part of parents, and imposing peril unspeakable on the child, "as if," as one has strikingly said, "after producing the egg of immortality, the church, like the Nubian ostrich, should leave it in the sands, exposed to the tread of every passer by." (Dr. Bushnell.)

These views, we think, distinctly convey the organic character of the church and the true law of its propagation and progress, as the existing sentiment of the framers of these symbols. While they make provision for the incorporation into the church of foreign elements of adult age, by the exercise of faith and repentance and voluntary profession of obedience to Christ and the laws of his kingdom, just as nations do, the great principle for securing the perpetuation and expansion of the church, is the incorporation into it, of those who belong to its families, and the extension of these nurseries of the church, by the influence of the christian over the unbelieving portion of the family structure, securing by the faith of one party, the whole of the offspring to the side of christianity, and the enjoyment of its privileges and influences. Whenever the gospel is brought into contact with heathenism, and its institutions are to be founded anew, it must have to do primarily with the adult population. This was the case when christianity overleaping the limitations of the Judaistic institute, was brought to bear upon the Gentile nations in the first centuries. And this will serve to explain much in the epistles of Paul, addressed to churches, formed out of Gentile material, which otherwise seem adverse to the views we are suggesting. But when the church is founded, and is to progress by the laws of its own vitality, and such we conceive is the state of things contemplated in the standards of the church, then the extraordinary and exceptional gives place to the ordinary and permanent methods of progress.

The views now given of the relations of children to the church, involve some exceedingly important and practical results, the consideration of which will show that proper speculative views on the point now under discussion, should be carefully formed. According to these views, for example, the children of believing parents, as members of the church, and within the pale of the covenant, should grow up as christians; not as outcasts and rebels.

The children of the church need not, as many seem to imagine, grow up in sin, to be converted, if at all, after they come to mature age; but may and ought to open on the world and its active duties, as spiritually renewed, loving and practising what is good from their earliest years—"springing up as among the grass," which by living reproduction has been perpetuated from creation till now, and "as willows by the water courses," putting forth in early spring-time, the evidences of vitalizing power within.

Christian education too, should conform to these views. They should be trained up "in the nurture and admonition of the Lord." On the ground of covenant relation, recognized by baptism, parents are privileged to realize the new relations of the Trinity to their children as well as themselves.

They may and ought to regard God as being to their children a reconciled Father, through the mediation of Jesus Christ; Jesus Christ, as an actual and all-sufficient Saviour, and the Holy Ghost as a sanctifier, not on the ground of any goodness existing in them, for there is none, but as the means of awakening goodness, of producing faith and gratitude, and consecration in their hearts. Parents are privileged to act on these truths, in educating their children, to make these representations to them as realities, as soon as they are capable of comprehending them. And still further, and more practically, they should aim to incorporate these ideas into their minds and hearts, by a process of training, beginning long before personal accountability commences—by the assimilative power of the eye and countenance and temper and spirit. By these means, children might be and should be expected, without any conscious period of unregeneracy, to be brought under their sanctifying power. In such a case, just as in the case of adults after regeneration, such children would still recognize in themselves the law of sin and death, derived from apostacy and inherited corruption. "The flesh would lust against the spirit." "The law in the members" would still be in antagonism against "the law of the mind," and sometimes one, and sometimes the other would overcome. But their earliest exercises would be of that mixed character of genuine christianity, which belong in every period, even the most advanced, to the truly regenerated, and the really, though at best, imperfectly sanctified. The new principle would sometimes more, and sometimes less, powerfully assert its existence, by its appropriate effects, and at last grow up to supremacy, habitual and controlling. Seasons of torpor, sometimes apparently of death, just as in adults, would be manifest. Darkness, coldness and estrangement, and then life, and warmth and enjoyment would alternate, according to outward circumstances or inward influences, and as children have no hypocrisy, would be more evident in them than in adult christians; but the reality of grace, "the incorruptible seed that liveth and abideth forever," would be there, as truly as in those of adult conversion and mature experience.

It will be seen further, from these representations, that there is no absolute necessity, in the case of infant members of the church who have been properly trained according to the normal acting of the christian church, and the general design of God in its organization, for the *conscious* experience, much less for the recognition of the precise period, of what is called conversion, or obtaining a new heart, as it is familiarly termed. Observe, we do not say, the *experience,* but the *conscious* experience. Believing parents are not to take it for granted, that their children when they grow up, will necessarily have undividedly wicked hearts, and put forth perpetually and only, overt acts of rebellion against God and ingratitude to the Saviour. They need not and ought not, as many are accustomed to do, put them on the mystifying search after evidences of "a new heart." The great object and true result of parental training, should be, to bring them into the exercise of new hearts, in view of the new and glorious relations of the Holy Trinity to our race, which the Scriptures plainly reveal, and which the ordinances of the church certify and seal as realities, to all that intelligently engage in them, admitting fully and freely, as they must, the fact of original sin and inherited depravity in their children, from their connexion with the first Adam, existing, as all admit, without their personal agency and choice; of course, parents are privileged to expect along with the faithful use of appointed means, regenerative and sanctifying power from the second Adam, the counterpart in this respect of the first, also without their conscious agency, and previous to the period of personal accountability.

The theory of christianity, embodied in these standards, takes for granted, this regenerative and sanctifying process, anterior to all conscious and accountable exercises, in the case of infants dying in infancy, and on that fact, rest the hopes of parents, that the "early lost" are the "early saved." This truth sheds a lovely light on their little graves. "Elect infants dying in infancy."

We believe all dying in infancy are elect—"are regenerated and saved through the Spirit, who worketh, when, where and how he pleaseth." They are fitted for heaven, without personally exercising faith and repentance, for the simple and sufficient reason, that they are incapable of exercising these otherwise indispensable graces. Here the fact of the efficacious influence of the Spirit, in implanting the principle of life, in the unconscious period, is plainly asserted, and on no other ground can an intelligible and satisfactory account be given, (in the case of infants dying in infancy) allowing them to be originally corrupt, and consequently disqualified, of the process of preparation for future glory. Is there a parent who ever lost an infant, that is willing to deny that regenerative power is exerted, and has been exerted on the part of the Spirit, and experienced on the part of the child, anterior to the period of personal accountability? When children grow up amidst the congenial influences of glory, the germ of a new life, derived from Christ, through the Holy Ghost, is developed in the lovely forms of perfected piety, in the skies, why may not and ought not, the influences of the family and the church, if rightly exerted, result to some extent, at least in the same way here? The theory of organic christianity demands that the law in regard to infant members dying in infancy, and those who grow up to adult years and the period of accountability in the church below, should be the same, and that the absence of these regenerative influences, resulting in actual christian affections, is the exception. Instead of expecting, as a matter of course, therefore, that children will grow up enemies of God, "aliens from the commonwealth and strangers to the covenants of promise," without love or gratitude to Christ, or influence of the Spirit, making indispensable a period of conviction and conversion conscious to the individual, and a passing over from the world to the church, as, of course, is necessary, in the case of unregenerated adults, the fact of membership in the church, and a participation in the blessings of the covenant, and the guarantied power of the spirit, operating previously to the period of free agency, and the quickening grace of the second Adam, which is as real and operative as the polluting efficacy of the first, all conspire to encourage parents that their children, if properly trained, may grow up, and will grow up, as christians, and that their first conscious acts and exercises will be those of new hearts, and their subsequent lives with the alter natures already noticed, will be in correspondence with these christian beginnings. When a different result takes place, as, alas! it often does, there has been either some wrong view of the relations of the child, some wrong influence from the parent, or a want of true faith in the covenant promise of God. It is not for want of sufficient grace treasured in Christ and designed usually to be communicated through proper parental training. In accordance with this view of the case, the Presbyterian Directory for worship declares, " children born within the pale of the visible church, and dedicated to God in baptism, are under the inspection and government of the church, and are to be taught to read and repeat the catechism, the Apostle's creed and the Lord's prayer. They are to be taught to pray, to abhor sin, to fear God, and to obey the Lord Jesus Christ; and when they come to years of discretion, if they are free from scandal, appear sober and steady, and to have sufficient knowledge to discern the Lord's body, they ought to be informed it is their duty and privilege to come to the Lord's supper."

Such is the scheme of christianity, directly asserted, or everywhere assumed, in Presbyterian standards, with its special bearing on the point now under discussion—an interpretation, possibly, which seems new and unauthorized to some who have adopted these standards, which may convict some of gross practical departures from their professed formularies, and condemn some of the appliances heretofore deemed of paramount, if not exclusive importance, in building up and extending the kingdom of God and the church of Christ in our world. Be it so. It is with truth only, not its consequences, that we are concerned. If truth condemn us, let its condemning power excite us to rectification. If our past course has been founded in misconception, and unsuccessful because fallacious, let us try to gain better speculative views, and thus be guided into better and more successful practice.

Presbyterians ought to be in no doubt in regard to the relation of children to the church. On the faith of one or both parents, they are in the church, entitled to its privileges, and may ordinarily be expected to be savingly influenced by its institutions. Parents should act on the presumption furnished by these relations. They should present God to their children, as already reconciled, for the sake of Christ, and by means of this truth in the hands of the Holy Ghost, effect the state of actual, subjective reconciledness to him, confidence in him, and love to him, on the part of their children, which this new and glorious relation is designed and adapted to develop. The first, and sweetest, and most influential lesson they are privileged to teach them, is embodied in the phrase, "Our Father." So they should fix the first affections of their children on the Lord Jesus Christ, not as willing at some distant day, to be their Saviour and Redeemer, or in consequence of goodness or the possession of a new heart, or any previous exercise of grace; but, as being actually their Redeemer, who loved them and died for them, who loves them now, and by this love, in its manifestations on the cross and its present pulsations on the throne, designing to evoke reciprocal love to him, amongst the earliest exercises of the infant heart. So they should present the Holy Spirit, also, not as exerting a mysterious and talismanic, but a soul-felt, agency—a real, living, enlightening sanctifying power.

The children of the church, thus trained, when admitted to the discriminating privileges of the church, especially the Lord's supper, would regard it, not as an act of translation from the world and a state of rebellion, but as a grateful recognition, on their part, personally, of relations existing before, and whose influence by God's arrangement and blessing, they have felt in their hearts. It ought to be solemnly and constantly asserted, whatever practical difficulties may attend it, that membership in the church, must be forfeited or annulled by the party himself, or it exists, with all its responsibilities, and that the discipline of the church has its legitimate sphere of operation on baptized members, as well as others. In a settled state of the church, we ought to regard the families that belong to it, or may be added to it, as its nurseries and grand sources of supply, and means of extension, instead of trusting to periodical accessions from those confirmed in unregeneracy and sin. In the perpetuation and expansion of the church, we should primarily regard the law of progress which God has established, while, of course, we should stand ready to engage earnestly and believingly in those more strictly aggressive movements, which it has always pleased him to employ to repair the wastes of the church's faithlessness, and sometimes, indeed, entirely to transfer the seat of the church's existence.

Assuming, however, that these are the views of the symbols, and that they correctly represent the sense of the Scriptures, according to the honest apprehensions of their framers, this will not be sufficient for some. They may say, this is Presbyterianism or churchianity; but is it christianity? With some of the members, and alas! even officers of the church, it is of comparatively small moment, that a doctrine is set forth in the formularies they have embraced and profess as their creed. It is not enough, for example, that the combined wisdom of the Westminster assembly, or of the most learned and pious of uninspired men, ever convened since the time of the Apostles, has been expressed in regard to any point. Their individual judgment or preconceived opinion, or cherished theory, or previous practice, outweighs all this. There are men, too, whose minds are so constructed, or prejudices so confirmed, that whatever is old and established, is to them *prima facie*, suspicious and erroneous, and on the contrary, whatever is new, especially the result of their own independent thinking, is valuable and correct. This is one of the incidental evils, growing out of one of the confessedly great blessings and privileges, of the age, and one of the sad exemplifications too, of the tendencies to extremes to which the human mind has been prone, in all past times, and in none more than our own. It is not enough to find out what our fathers thought, what has been the common faith of the church in past ages, the embodied result and embalmed testimony of the past piety of God's people, every man, though with almost infinitely smaller advantages, must find out for himself the truth in the case.

In what remains of our article, therefore, we shall attempt to show that what we have denominated organic christianity, as contradistinguished from individualism, and of course, the relation of children to the church, inseparable from that idea of the genius of christianity, is the doctrine of the Scriptures, as really as of the symbols; in other words, that the framers of these formularies, in this respect, have truly, as well as honestly, given the sense of the Scriptures.

This part of the discussion will necessarily lead us back to the first organization of the church of God. And here, we presume, that none will question the fact, that the Old Testament church, as organized in the family of Abraham, and based on the covenant of circumcision, possessed this organic character. This feature is involved, we think, in the very nature of the organization and the terms of the covenant. The infant offspring of members, were included in the organization of the Old Testament church, and in the purview of the Abrahamic covenant. The plan of transmission and perpetuation, under the old Dispensation, too, was unquestionably, hereditary, as a general rule, allowing, in exceptional cases, of the incorporation of adult and foreign elements. The tenor of the covenant with Abraham, on which the church was then organized, is thus expressed: "I will establish," says God, "my covenant between me and thee, and thy seed after thee, in their generations, for an everlasting covenant, to be a God unto thee, and to thy seed after thee." Here is a plain distinction between the individual and the organic character of the covenant. "Between me and thee," and "unto thee," is individual. But what is "thy seed after thee, in their generations," but organic? "As soon as a new individual was generated from this seed, he was within the covenant, and God was his God," as really as the God of Abraham, and he had a right to the seals of the covenant, as a public ratification of his relation to God and his people, unless he chose to renounce them and the privileges thereto appended, "selling his birthright for a mess of pottage." Obviously, his right to church membership was a birthright, guarantied by covenant. He was sealed with its seal in infancy, surrounded with its influences, and committed to its formatory power, from his earliest being, and forfeited them only by his own act of voluntary self-exclusion, or by the process of excision in certain contingencies made and provided.

This was the genius of the church, and the original plan of transmission chosen and ordained by God. If we apprehend it aright, this was also designed to be perpetual. Such, as all must allow, continued to be the principle of perpetuation and transmission, through all the ages of the old Dispensation, from the time of Abraham to the coming of Christ. The organic character of the church, the fact that infants composed a part of its membership, that they were to be trained up as heirs of the covenant and entitled to its visible privileges, and could only be severed from its connexion by the process of excision, are so plainly exhibited in the Old Testament, that those who acknowledge the existence and organization of a church of God at all, anterior to the coming of Christ, cannot possibly deny that these were its peculiarities.

Let it not be said that this is aside from our purpose, and may all be granted, without any decisive influence on the question. It is of no small moment, to have these preliminaries rightly settled. For if this was the original organization of the church, if this organic feature was incorporated into it, at the beginning, the presumption is, unless specifically changed, these features were designed to continue. "The gifts and callings of God, are without repentance," or capricious changes of plan. What his wisdom selected and ordained, in view of the whole case and its contingencies at first, his wisdom may be supposed for the same sufficient reasons, to make perpetual.

The question then, is, did these peculiarities of God's covenant and church organization cease at the introduction of christianity? At that "epochal period," when the meeting and interaction of ages occurred, was a new church, on new principles, and with new modes of propagation and perpetuation inaugurated; or is the christian church a continuation only, with a new form of ordinances and wider range of influence, of that organized in the family of Abraham—based on the same covenant, distinguished by the same peculiarities, and designed to be perpetuated among men, and extending finally to all nations, by the same great means? Did the one original church, in passing from its Jewish to its Christian phase, from its preparatory to its permanent stage of being, put off its confessedly organic character, to assume the new feature of individualism; and were children, after being component elements of the church, by God's express direction and in virtue of an ordinance established by himself, from the beginning to that epoch, then formally excluded and placed out of covenant with God, and without the pale of his church, and a new plan of perpetuation and expansion established? These are important questions, bearing directly on the point before us. And, " what saith the Scriptures?" " How readest thou?" Just at this crisis, we hear the Master's own voice, saying: " Suffer the little children to come unto me, and forbid them not, for of such is the kingdom of heaven!" In this feature, the new dispensation is to be as responsive to parental affection and inclusive of infantile membership, as the old. " The God of Abraham," yearns yet with undiminished tenderness towards the lambs of the fold, and designs not that they should be excluded from his covenant blessings and provisions.

Again, at the memorable era of the Pentecost, the anniversary of the giving of the law, and designed by God as the period of the introduction of the better dispensation of the gospel, by the gift of the Holy Ghost, we would naturally look for confirmation or repeal of pre-existing privileges and peculiarities: does anything significant of confirmation or nullification occur at this transition period? Let it be borne in mind, that all the first materials of church organization at the day of Pentecost, were Jews—men brought up under the view of the Abrahamic covenant, already expounded, with hearts naturally solicitous in regard to the relations of their children, heretofore invariably associated with them in church privileges, and ready therefore to embrace with thankfulness, whatever it pleased the Holy Ghost, by the Apostles, to communicate on a point so near to their tenderest affections and dearest earthly interests. Now, what does Peter, speaking " as he was moved by the Holy Ghost," present in these circumstances to these Jews, as a ground or motive of baptism, or personal identification with christianity. " Repent and be baptized every one of you, in the name of the Lord Jesus, for the promise," the promise made ages before, unto Abraham, and designed to embrace all his seed, " the promise is unto you and your children, and all that are afar off, even as many as the Lord our God shall call." The gospel dispensation, in other words, is a ratification and confirmation, not a repeal or repudiation of existing privileges. In their circumstances, and to their state of heart, the words of the Apostle could have no less significance than this, and go utterly against the idea of the introduction of the individualistic theory at that time.

Further, the basis of the Apostle Paul's argument with the Galatian christians, is the hypothesis of one, original, perpetual church, organized in the family and covenant of Abraham. His object is to show that Gentiles, though not circumcised, are legitimate members of this church, and entitled to all its privileges. In doing this, he traces back the origin of the blessings now enjoyed by christians, to the promise made to Abraham. He contends that it was a part of the original plan of God, in organizing the church in the family of Abraham, "that the blessing of Abraham should come on the Gentiles by faith." " For they that be of faith, are blessed with believing Abraham," have the same blessing he enjoyed. " The Scriptures foreseeing that God would justify the heathen through faith," or foreshadowing or preintimating God's plan of justifying the nations or Gentiles through faith, after the coming of Christ, " preached before the gospel," or announced the glorious tidings " to Abraham, saying, in thee shall all nations be blest " The Apostle shows clearly that the episodical or interimistic dispensation, instituted at Sinai, did not touch at all the original covenant, but was designed to be subsidiary to it, till the fullness of time, when it was to have its full scope and influence. " The covenant confirmed before of God in Christ, the law which was four hundred years after, could not disannul, that it should make the promise of none effect." The Law, or Sinaitic dispensation, was introduced to keep up the succession of God's people, " till the seed should come to where the promise was made." It " was a schoolmaster to bring" the church to Christ, or the christian period—" a temporary constitution superadded to give effect to some of the provisions of the

covenant with Abraham and expired by its own limitations."
During this preparatory period, it is acknowledged that circumcision was the method of perpetuation, and was of force till Christ
came.   But the Apostle contends that in the covenant itself, on
which the church organization was based, it is provided, that
after Christ's coming, the exercise of faith should constitute an
individual a part of the seed to whom the promise was originally
made, and who have a right to all its blessings.   "We are all
the children of God, by faith in Jesus Christ."   "If we be Christ's
then are we Abraham's seed, and heirs according to the promise."
"They which are of faith, the same are the children of Abraham."   The existing church of God, according to the plan at
its organization, was to have a great expansion at the coming of
Christ.   "The abolition of those restrictions, which were suited
to a preparatory state, fitted her for universality," and now "all
nations" were to be embraced without destroying her unity or
original character.   In virtue of this provision, Gentiles, without
being circumcised, were, by the exercise of faith, incorporated
into the church.   Thus they form a part of the seed, with whom
"in their generations, an everlasting covenant" is made, and by
whom the existence of the church is to be perpetuated on the
original principles of its first organization.   Every one who in
adult age, from among the Gentiles, by the personal exercise of
faith in Jesus Christ, becomes an integral part of the church of
God, brings with him into that church, and has incorporated
with himself, into its membership, and entitled with him to its
privileges, all his infant family, just as the Jews, whose children
all along from the beginning, had an inalienable birthright in the
church, in virtue of the relation of their parents—a privilege
which, as we have seen, was ratified to them on the day of Pentecost, when they entered the christian church by baptism.   Whatever privileges of a personal or relative character belonged of right
to the members of the church of God, from the beginning, became
the right of every one, who from the heathen, by exercising faith
in Christ, was incorporated into the church.   Among the rest,
the right of having his children included in the covenant—a
right which had existed unquestioned, in all antecedent ages,
which the Jews always took for granted, and which the Gentiles

did not forego, because of the peculiarity of the mode of their admission, by personal profession of faith in adult age.

It will be perceived from what we have now adduced, that the Apostle's reasoning in behalf of the Gentiles, is based on the assumption of the unity of the church—the fact of its being founded on the covenant made with Abraham—of its having in its original structure a provision to meet this very case;—that the peculiar Judaistic institute was strictly interimistic, dating after the covenant four hundred years, and designed to cease as a provisional scheme, at the coming of the Messiah; whilst the true, original and perpetual organization of the church, on the basis of the covenant of promise, was to continue throughout all generations of the true seed of Abraham, and embrace every one who should exercise faith in Jesus Christ, with their children.

Allowing this to be a fair view of the Apostle's object and argument of the principles it involves, let us see what light is thrown upon it and our general subject, by his famous figurative representation of "the olive tree," in his Epistle to the Romans. He speaks of the church as "an olive tree"—of the Jews, as its "natural branches, broken off by unbelief"—that is, severed from connexion with the church. The Gentiles he represents as belonging to "an olive tree" also, but "wild by nature," and "grafted in, contrary to nature, into the good olive tree, and with them, partakers of its root and fatness." These original branches, "the natural branches" now broken off, "if they abide not still in unbelief," he says, "shall again be grafted in, for God is able to graft them in again." "Grafted into" what? "Their own olive tree"—the same church which exists still, though the members are changed. "The lopping off of diseased branches, destroys not the tree itself." What other possible interpretation will this allow, than this, that there was one, and one only, organized church, without any change in its essential features, into which the Gentiles were incorporated through faith, which is perpetuated according to the law existing at its organization, through all its changing dispensations, and into which, at some future period, the Jews are again to be introduced. In other words, christianity is a prolongation and expansion of a previously existing organization, but not a new church, except in its mode of dispensation, and a change in the form of its ordinances. Let us, also, recur for the same purpose, to a difficulty which would be of frequent occurrence in the primitive period of christianity, and which the Apostle specifically meets in his Epistle to the Corinthians. We mean the case where one of the united head of a family was a christian, while the other remained a pagan. The question would, here, naturally be suggested, in what light are the children of such parents to be viewed? In answering this question, the Apostle brings forward this interesting principle, exceedingly pertinent to our subject, viz: that the faith or piety of either husband or wife, as the case might be, even in the absence of christian principle or profession in the other party, secured the privileges of the church to their offspring. "The unbelieving husband is sanctified by the wife, and the unbelieving wife is sanctified by the husband." The faith of one party, prevents the injurious and otherwise exclusive influence of the other, so far as church privileges or the relation of their children to the church, are concerned. "Else were your children unclean," separated from the church, cast out into the common field of the world, without the pale of the covenant; "but now," in virtue of the faith of only one party, "are they holy," not in the sense of personal piety, but invested with the peculiar privileges and blessings pertaining to membership in the church of Christ; "holy," just as all the Jewish people were holy, separated unto God, visibly united to him and his church. To make "unclean," here mean illegitimate, as some contend, or personally unholy, is utterly indefensible on any correct principles of interpretation. The term "holy," expresses the state of a person or thing separated to the service of God, and "unclean," the state of a person or thing, not so separated, or which is "common." "Holy," therefore, in the Apostle's mind and time, would convey precisely what "a member of the church" does in ours, and could not otherwise have been understood by primitive christians. The position of the Apostle is that so far as the connexion of the children with the church is concerned, if one parent exercised faith and thus was constituted a part of "Abraham's seed and an heir according to promise," the faith of one party sanctified the other party, and brought the children into the

same relation to the church, that the children of the Jews held
in the old dispensation. The rite by which this relation in the
christian church is recognized, is different, but the relation itself
is the same. The rite is baptism; the relation, membership in
the church. Baptism perpetuates the original, and, as we apprehend, immutable, organic character of the church, and indicates
the great law of its perpetuation and progress in all dispensations,
to be the same. Except on the assumption of the unity of the
church, and the continuance of its organic character, and the
admission of infants to its membership, we cannot see how this
difficulty would ever have occurred, or that the Apostle has satisfactorily disposed of it, in the passage now considered.

Various other particular passages of the Epistles, convey the
same idea of the unity of the church and the perpetuation of its
organic feature, after the introduction of the new dispensation
and the Gentile element. In his Epistle to the Ephesians, for
example, Paul speaks of the Gentiles as being formerly " aliens
from the commonwealth of Israel, and strangers to the covenants
of promise;" but in virtue of faith in Christ, incorporated into
the church, " built on the foundation of the Apostles and prophets," who were Jews, " Jesus Christ himself being the chief
corner-stone," in whom these different parts of the one structure
were united together. " In whom all the building," the Jewish
part existing previously, and the part now added from Gentile
material, " fitly framed together, groweth unto an holy temple in
the Lord, in whom ye also are builded together, for an habitation of God, through the Spirit;" of course, when these new
elements were brought into the previously existing church, in
the absence of any specific repealing enactment, emanating from
the supreme authority in the church, they would come into possession of all the privileges previously and *ab initio* existing.
Had there been any such organic change as would have excluded
children from privileges accorded to them, in every previous age,
consequent upon the introduction of the Gentiles, a far fiercer
controversy than that about circumcision, would have been recorded in the " Acts of the Apostles." But we have not the
slightest intimation, in any part of the recorded history of the
early period of christianity, of such an idea or agitation; nor,

indeed, does the question of the relation of children to the church, occur at all, except as growing out of the difficulty, considered just now, during the canon of Scripture, nor, in fact, till a very late period of christianity. Individualism, was an idea utterly unknown and incomprehensible, by the Apostles and primitive christians, and the authors of the New Testament, who were all Jews.

It is, in this connexion and in view of this existing state of opinion, that the unquestioned fact of household baptisms, by the Apostles, assumes its true significancy. The households of the jailor, and of Lydia, and of Stephanus, baptized by Paul, came into the christian church in the regular and ordinary way, and were only specimens, incidentally recorded, we suppose, of what took place everywhere, when the word of God took effect on the adult population of heathenism at the head of families. Believers and their offspring became incorporated with the church, as soon as they renounced idolatry and identified themselves with christianity. And as the Apostles "went everywhere, preaching the kingdom of God," they "made disciples of all nations," as they were commanded, in families, by "baptizing them in the name of the Father, Son, and Holy Ghost." The church, through her ministry, "turning away from the Jews," when "they rejected the counsel of God against their own souls," though always, and in every place, giving them the first offer, "turned to the Gentiles." Thus they transmitted in a different line, the same glorious succession, a perpetuated, covenanted, organization. Organized christianity, notwithstanding all changes in nations, and the confusion of earth, exists on this principle to our day; and blessed be his name, we believe it will exist till the winding up of the whole scheme, purposed in the beginning. For "God's purpose shall stand, and the thoughts of his heart to all generations." "His ways are past finding out, and his judgments are unsearchable;" but his covenant is sure and faithful forever. "For of him, and through him, and to him, are all things, to whom be glory forever."

We maintain these views of organic christianity, and of the relation of children to the church, growing out of this idea then, not only as believers in the symbols of the church, but as believers in the Bible—taught there to recognize the church as one in all ages, notwithstanding the change of dispensations and ordinances. As warranted by the original covenant and church organization, which is still operative, we hold it our privilege to consider our children as with ourselves, members of God's church, constituting, organically, a part of that body, of which Christ is the head, and to which the precious promises and privileges of the original and unrepealed covenant belong, by God's own plan and purpose. On the Scriptural basis we have elucidated, we conceive it our privilege, also, not as a fiction or falsehood, but as a blessed fact, to teach them to say with us, " Our Father," at the family altar, and try to have them feel all the blessed efficacy of this appellation on their hearts. It is our privilege to train them up to regard their Father in Heaven, for the sake of their Elder Brother and Redeemer, as actually holding towards them a relation as real and tender as that of their earthly parents ; and exercising towards them, on the ground, not of goodness or excellence in them, but of the Saviour's interposition, feelings and affections, far more kind and compassionate than ever throbbed in the bosom of an earthly parent. It is our privilege, to bring up our children to exercise towards that glorious being, " the Father almighty, maker of heaven and earth," from the very beginning, the feeling of adoption, so that their first conscious exercises should be of reciprocated affection towards Jesus Christ, as a Person of ineffable loveliness and compassion. It is our privilege, along with the education influences, not only of direct instruction, but of our own spirit and temper and the whole manifested purpose of life, of our own hopes and joys and prospects, growing out of our own individual faith, to expect the efficacious and regenerative grace of the Holy Ghost, as really to make them christians in the church below, as that grace has fitted those taken from us in infancy, for the church above. Our children need not ever experience the feelings of unmitigated " enmity against God," except as we do ourselves, in our depraved nature, and must expect to do, till our dying day, though as a subjugated principle, rising and rebelling against, and sometimes conquering " the law of our minds," by which usually " we serve God." They need not occupy, at any conscious period of their being,

the position of rebels against God, " aliens and strangers," neces-
sitating a transfer of relations, and a terrible revolution in their
souls in adult age.   Being in the church and in covenant with
God, having the seal of God upon them, if, at mature age, they
prefer the world, and choose it as a portion, as many do, they
must do so by a deliberate act of renunciation.   They must give
up God their Father in heaven, and go out of the church, and
relinquish the privileges and blesssings of the new covenant, as
citizens of a nation renounce allegiance to one government and
go over to another.

The view we have thus given of the relation of children to
the church, is equally removed from " baptismal regeneration,"
as held by some churches, on the one hand, and the bald individualism, which we as unfeignedly reprobate, on the other, presenting, as we apprehend it, the right and safe medium.   It does
not say, that children have new hearts, because they are baptized
or will necessarily become christians and be saved, whether parents are faithful or not.   But it does affirm, that in the exercise
of faith in God's covenant and the faithful use of means, the
Holy Spirit may be expected to give to our children, the germ
of a new life, and that God's promises afford a blessed presumption, which we ought to cherish, on which we may act, and by
which we may be animated, that they will grow up christians, and
remember no definite time or set of conscious exercises, when and
by which they became children of God.   While it repudiates the
idea that grace is governed by ordinary generation, it does hold that
piety is preserved and was designed by God to be perpetuated,
ordinarily, in the line of family succession.   As the faith of Timothy, " dwelt first in his grandmother Lois, and then in his mother
Eunice, and last of all in him also," though " his father was a
Greek."   And as the piety of President Edwards, can be traced
up, in the ascending series, to a faithful preacher, in the days of
Queen Elizabeth, and in the descending series, has been transmitted to about seventy of the existing ministry of America,
besides other posterity, eminent for piety in other walks of life,
almost innumerable, and as, moreover, according to statistics,
which utterly refute the slander, that the children of ministers,
are usually the worst, at least one-fifth of the existing Presbyte-

rian and Congregational ministry of the United States, are descendants of "the tribe of Levi."

Such is christianity, as originally embosomed in the Abrahamic covenant—the christianity to which the Jewish institute served as a pedagogue or preparatory system—the christianity expounded by the great Apostle of the Gentiles, who regarded Abraham as the "the Father" alike of "the circumcision," or the Jewish branch, and of "the uncircumcision," or Gentile portion, "if they walked in the steps of that faith which Abraham had being yet uncircumcised"—who preached "Christ as the minister of circumcision, for the truth of God, to confirm the promises made unto the Fathers," and also of uncircumcision, "that the Gentiles might glorify God for his mercy."

From the beginning, through all its phases and dispensations, the church is one; organic in its character, embracing among its members, the infant children of believers. from whom eminently its growth is to be expected. It is a part of the plan of God to bring the law of family increase directly into the church, and make it also a law of spiritual increase, or in the words of Baxter, himself an exemplification of his profound remark, "Education, rightly conducted, is an ordinary way for the conveyance of God's grace, and ought no more to be set in opposition to the Spirit, than the preaching of the word."

Were these views as clearly apprehended and fully carried out as they might and ought to be, the great law of the church's progress and perpetuation, would be verified to the comfort of parents and to the illustration of divine faithfulness, to an extent seldom now, if ever witnessed. The reproach cast upon the church of God, of inefficacy and inferiority to other schemes of man's devising, would be wiped away, and the wisdom of God, in its original organization and immutable peculiarities, exhibited. Families would be the nurseries of the church. Faithful parental instruction, would secure the first buddings of the *plants of grace*, and pastors would only have to develop them by appropriate cultivation to "trees of righteousness," "filled with the fruits of righteousness, which are by Jesus Christ to the glory and praise of God." At the proper age, the infant members, recognizing their relations, would gratefully and intelligently assume the responsibilities involved in their early consecration by their parents, and thus from age to age, by a constant reproduction and increasing expansion, from this the primary source, in addition to all the aggressions made on the empire of Satan, and sin, and the votaries of the world, the church of God, would, as it was designed, go on, widening and deepening, till "the knowledge of the Lord would cover the earth as the waters do the sea." Piety, too, beginning early in life, would assume progressively lovelier and more influential forms of manifestation from generation to generation, so that "the child would die an hundred years old;" "the dew of youth," the strength of manhood, and the ripeness of age, would all be given to God and his cause. In virtue of this simple element alone, of internal vitality, independently of accretion from without, expanding by organic growth, not external conquest, the church of God, according to the tenor of the covenant, might soon fill the world. "I will multiply thy seed as the stars of heaven and as the sand which is upon the sea shore; and thy seed shall possess the gate of their enemies, and in thy seed shall all the nations of the earth be blessed." "For thus saith the Lord, this is my covenant with them, my spirit which is upon thee and my words which I have put in thy mouth, shall not depart out of thy mouth, nor out of the mouth of thy seed, nor out of the mouth of thy seed's seed, saith the Lord, henceforth and forever." In accordance with these covenant promises, "the mustard seed" grows till it "becomes a tree." "The leaven" spreads "till all is leavened." "The stone cut out without hands," becomes "a great mountain and fills the whole earth." "The handfull of corn on the tops of the mountains," multiplying by its law of reproduction, increases, till "its fruit shakes like Lebanon," and "they of the city," the church of God on earth, "flourish like grass of the earth," perpetuated and multiplied, from age to age, till it covers "the field which is the world," once filled with briers and thorns, "with its fresh and lovely verdure, and earth becomes again the Paradise it was at first, and which, the Son of God, became incarnate and shed his blood, to reproduce.

PITTSBURG, Pa.   D. H. R.

ART. XII.—False Protestantism.

We translate the following communication from a late number of Schaff's *Kirchenfreund.* It is too important, in our estimation, to be allowed to pass without attention. If there be any one evil among us, that deserves to be exposed, it is the disposition shown in so many directions to make common cause with any and every interest that proclaims itself in opposition to Rome. The worst sort of zeal for Protestantism, surely, is that which practically at least, seeks to turn it into a mere *negation,* the blind contradiction, simply, of all that is considered peculiar to Romanism; by which it is brought to regard all such contradiction, however rationalistic and radical, as so far good and desirable. It seems to be forgotten by many, that opposition to Rome *may* be at the same time hostility to all religion; and that the loss of the Pope is not necessarily, in and of itself, the gain of Christ. We have heard, indeed, of a distinguished minister openly preaching that infidelity itself is to be counted a less evil than religion under the Roman Catholic form; and we remember the case of another, (to our mind, a very *melancholy* case,) who took pains to show publicly, that his son had not sought the consolations of religion, when dying on the battle field, at the hands of a Roman Catholic chaplain—preferring, as it seemed, a death that left no hope to one that could offer it only in this form. But such diseased judgments carry with them no lasting or general weight. They caricature the true Protestant faith. This is not in league thus with Christ's enemies, against christianity under any form. The triumph of mere infidelity over Romanism, is not one which it can either desire or welcome. That is no true Protestantism, even when exhibited by otherwise good Protestants, which can take complacency in such a man as Ronge, or go off in a fit of sympathy with his so-called German Catholicism, whether in Europe or America. We all remember how this ungodly movement was greeted, at the beginning, by the most of our religious papers; and how few of them had honesty enough afterwards to utter any equally explicit denunciation of it, when its true character stood confessed finally before the whole world. What must we think, however, of the easy credulity of the same religious press, that after all this, could allow itself to be so readily imposed upon again by the very same spurious spirit presenting itself with the same pretensions on this side of the Atlantic. The movement referred to in the following letter, under the auspices of the notorious Giustiniani, was hailed in all directions, on the faith of our most respectable religious journals, as the outburst of a new reformation, which was likely to sweep the whole German Catholic population in this country, and turn it away forever from its allegiance to the Pope. No one cared, apparently, to sift very narrowly the positive character of this new church; enough that it showed itself ready, with open throat, to hate and curse Rome. And yet, as might have been easily foreseen from the first, it has all turned out to be just what Rongeanism was before, on the other side of the water, a hellish farce, a diabolical lie. This is, of course, sufficiently humiliating; but it is still more so, that the respectable and popular religious journals aforesaid, still lack nerve, as it would seem, to come out openly and confess the sham, which was thought so recently to deserve their high glorification; and judging by the past, there is too much reason to fear that a new outbreak of the same spirit in some new quarter, with the Rev. Giustiniani figuring at its head, would so throw them again off their guard, in spite of all that has gone before, that we should have the very same old song rung in our ears, from Dan to Beersheba, as though the whole movement had gone perfectly straight from the beginning.   J. W. N.

Letter in the Kirchenfreund.

In the November number of your Monthly, you have expressed your views freely, and for this very reason offensively to many, on the subject of *Free German Catholicism* in America. Will you allow a correspondent also, a few words, which may serve possibly to place your remarks in a still clearer light? When we speak of Free German Catholicism in America, we must now understand by it simply the efforts at conversion which are made by the American Protestant Society, through its missionaries and colporteurs, among the Roman Catholics; for the representative of the Rongean movement, Mr. Dowiat, who for a time created such a stir in New York, has already a good while ago, bid adieu again to this country,* and no trace whatever remains of his work. And what is it now that the American Protestant Society properly proposes in this case? Is it to transplant to America also, the movement started a few years since in Germany? So it is pretended; plainly, however, neither the nature of that movement is understood, nor the means needed, humanly speaking, for bringing it to effect. In truth, such a movement is at this time wholly impossible in America. Every one who knows anything of the general state of the case, knows that the Catholics of this country, so far as they retain any religious feeling and are not fallen into full indifferentism, are far more closely and stiffly wedded to the worship of their church, than those of the old mother country; that they are here much more under the authority and will of their priests and bishops, than in the old country, where the government has taken the regulation of ecclesiastical affairs into its hands, and the episcopal mandate becomes of force only through its *placet*. And the mass of the Roman Catholic people, belonging as they do almost entirely to the lowest class, and as such ignorant and superstitious, is perfectly satisfied with this state of things; neither the oppression of the hierarchy, nor the defect in doctrine or worship, are so felt as to create any longing after deliverance. And yet this is indispensable for any work of reformation, which is to stand. God himself must produce this feeling, this longing, however dark and unclear; so that the preacher standing forward in the service of such a people, shall have only to bring the dark want into clear consciousness, and show how it is to be satisfied; in other words, the fuel must be at hand, so as to need only the commencing spark to kindle the whole mass into a bright glowing flame. This was the case, unquestionably, with the Jews and heathen in the time of the Apostles, and with the Roman Church at the time of the Reformation; and inasmuch as nothing of the sort is found in the Roman Church of America, there is no room to think either of any result in this view. If the American Protestant Society wishes to do anything then for the benefit of Romanists, it should send pious and fit persons to visit them from house to house, who might converse with them in the spirit of love, proclaim to them the free grace of God in Jesus Christ, and so bring them to an inward dissatisfaction with their spiritual state. With the word of God in their hands, and the way to the throne of grace open, they would then soon find

---

* Condemned, Dec. 16, by the criminal court in Berlin, on a charge of riot, to six years' imprisonment.

the right way and come into union with some of the existing
denominations of the Protestant Church.   Such in fact was the
earlier design of the Society, till the notorious Giustiniani came
into it, and by his influence, with some of its more active members, brought about this unhappy change in its efforts.   Of the
fruit of the labors of its other misssionaries, almost nothing has
become known; though it has had several such, for longer or
shorter time, as Winkelmann, Reubelt, Lachenmayer, &c.; while
all noise has been made from time to time of Giustiniani, as
though the Roman Church in America, stood on the point of
falling to pieces under his hand.   How scandalously he has behaved, however, and how very foolishly the Am. Prot. Society
has acted in regard to him, must strike every one who is at all
acquainted with the case.   It is now just two years since he
made so much noise in New York; one hundred and eighty
conversions were reported, and the number of converts represented to be daily increasing.   But how soon did this soap-bub-
ble burst!   In June, of that same year, this flourishing congregation, under Giustiniani's own care, had melted down to fifteen,
and now no trace of it whatever is to be found.   The means
alone which had been resorted to, cut off all continued growth;
for not to mention that the greater part of those who had lent
their names to this farce, consisted of homeless Protestants and
unbelievers, no pains had been spared to win the few Catholics
included in it by fair promises, the prospect of profitable employment, and the assurance of having ministerial acts performed
without cost.   Is it any wonder, that all should go down under
such circumstances?   The Society boasts of a thousand conversions already wrought by its agents; but if it be with all as with
the hundred and eighty in New York, the thousand must melt
into less than a hundred.   With the state of things in New York,
the writer is fully acquainted, and can at any time prove any of
his statements.   According to report, the Free German Catholic
congregation in Newark, is also about breaking up; and Roch-
ester will form the exception to a rule, if within one year any
trace shall be left there of the same movement.   R.

Bi-monthly List of Recent Publications.

Robert Carter & Brothers, 285, *Broadway, New York.*

The Family Book. The genius and design of the domestic constitution, with its untransferable obligations and peculiar advantages. By Christopher Anderson. 12 mo. 75cts.

Bible Expositor. Confirmations of the truth of the Holy Scriptures; from observations of recent travellers, illustrating the manners, customs and places referred to in the Bible. 18mo. 50cts.

The Works of Charles Bridges, M. A., Vicar of Old Newton Suffolk. Comprising the "Exposition of Proverbs," "Exposition of Psalm cxix." "The Christian Ministry," and "Memoirs of Mary Jane Graham." 3 vols. 8vo $5 00.

Original Thoughts on Scripture; being the substance of sermons preached by the Rev. Richard Cecil, taken down by Mrs. Hawks, and now edited by Catharine Cecil. With a portrait of Cecil. 12mo. $1 00.

The Works of William Cooper. His life, letters and poems, now first collected by the introduction of Cowper's private correspondence. Edited by the Rev. T. S. Grimshaw, A. M. 1 vol. 8vo.

Scenes from Sacred History; or Religion teaching by example.— By Richard W. Dickinson, D. D. $1 00.

Gospel Sonnets. By the Rev. Ralph Erskine. 1 vol. 16mo. $1 00.

The History of the progress and termination of the Roman Republic. By Adam Ferguson, LL. D., Professor of Moral Philosophy in the University of Edinburgh. Complete in 1 vol. 8mo $1 50.

The Life of Philip Henry. 18mo. 50cts.

A Happy Home. Dedicated to the working classes. By the Rev. James Hamilton, author of "Life in Earnest," &c. Illustrated by Howland. 18mo.

Memoir of Mary Jane Graham. By the Rev. Charles Bridges. To which is added "The Test of Truth," and "The Freeness of Grace," By Miss Graham. 1 vol. 8vo.

Domestic Portraiture; or the successful application of religious principle in the education of a family, exemplified in the memoirs of three of the deceased children of the Rev. Legh Richmond. 12mo. 75cts.

Water Drops. By Mrs. L. H. Sigourney. Second edition. Revised and corrected by the author. 18mo. 50cts.

Modern Accomplishments; or the March of Intellect. By Miss Catharine Sinclair. 12 mo. 75cts.

Modern Society; or the March of Intellect. By Miss Catharine Sinclair. 12mo. 75cts.

The Works of Cornelius Tacitus. With an essay on his life and genius. Notes, supplement, &c. By Arthur Murphy, Esq. A new edition. With the authors last corrections. 8vo. $2 00.

The natural history of Enthusiasm. By Isaac Taylor. 12mo.

History of the Peloponnesian War. Translated from the Greek of Thucydides. By William Smith, A. M. A new edition. Corrected and revised. 8vo. $1 50.

The whole works of Xenophon. Translated by Ashley Cooper, Spelman, Smith, Fielding and others. Complete in 1 vol. 8vo. $2 00.

Notes on the Gospels, critical and explanatory, prepared to accompany the questions of the Sunday School Union, and incorporating with the notes on a new plan, the most approved harmony of the four Gospels. By Melancthon W. Jacobus. With illustrations. Per vol. 75cts.

Christ our Lord. By Caroline Fry.

The Young Disciple. A memoir of Anzonetta R. Peters. By Rev. John A. Clark, Rector of St. Andrew's Church, Philadelphia. author of the "Pastor's Testimony," "Walk about Zion," "Gathered Fragments," &c. 12mo. 88cts.

Comfort in Affliction. A series of meditations. By James Buchanan, D. D. 18mo. 40cts.

Phrenology examined and shown to be inconsistent with the principles of physiology, mental and moral science, and the doctrines of Christianity; also, an examination of the claims of mesmerism. By N. L. Rice, D. D., pastor of the Central Presbyterian Church, Cincinnati.

Lea & Blanchard, Philadelphia. Issued since Jan. 1, 1849.
1. AMERICAN WORKS.

Obstetrics, the Science and the Art. By C. D. Meigs, M. D., Professor of Midwifery, &c., in the Jefferson Medical College, Philadelphia. One vol. 8 vo. pp. 686, 121 wood engravings.

Western America, including Oregon and California, with maps of those regions and of the Sacramento valley. By Charles Wilkes, U. S. N., Commander of the U. S. Exploring Expedition. 8vo. price 75cts.

On the Cryptogamous Origin of Epidemic and Malarious Fevers. By J. K. Mitchell, M. D., Professor of Practical Medicine in the Jefferson Medical College of Philadelphia. 1 vol. royal 12mo. pp. 138.

2. REPUBLICATIONS.

Household Education. By Harriet Martineau. 1 vol. royal 12mo.

Outlines of English Literature. By Thomas W. Shaw, M. A. 1 vol. royal 12mo. pp. 438.

Introduction to practical Chemistry, including Analysis. By John E. Bowman, Demonstrator of Chemistry, King's College, London. 1 vol. royal 12mo. pp. 330, 97cuts.

Manual of Physiology, for the use of Students. By W. S. Kirkes and James Paget. 1 vol. royal 12mo. pp. 550. 118 wood cuts.

Haunted Man and the Ghost's Bargain. By Charles Dickens. 8vo. price 6cts.

A Practical Treatise on the Domestic Management of the more Important Diseases of Advanced Life. By George E. Day, M. D. 1 vol. 8vo.

NEARLY READY. 1. AMERICAN.

Authentic Narrative of the U. S. Expedition to the Dead Sea and Source of the Jordan. By W. F. Lynch, U. S. N., Commander of the Expedition. In one very handsome octavo volume, of about 500 pages, with numerous beautiful plates.

An Historical Sketch of the Last War with Great Britain. By C. J. Ingersoll, M. C. Vol II. 8vo.

Atlas to Dana on Zoophytes. Being vol. IX. of the Publications of the U. S. Exploring Expedition. 1 vol. large imperial folio, with about 60 colored plates.

On Some of the more Important Diseases of Infants. By C. D. Meigs, M. D. &c. vol. 1, 8vo.

2. REPUBLICATIONS.

Zoological Recreations. By W. S. Broderip, F. R. S., &c. 1 vol. Royal 12mo.

Practical Pharmacy; comprising the Arrangements, Apparatus and Manipulations of the Pharmaceutical Shop and Labratory. By Francis Mohr, Ph. D. &c., and Theophilus Redwood. Edited, with numerous Alterations and Additions, by Wm. Proctor, Jr. of the Phil. Coll. of Pharmacy. 1 vol. 8vo. of about 500 pages, with over 500 beautiful wood cuts.

Elements of Anatomy. By Jones Quaine, M. D. From the fifth London Edition, edited by Richard Quaine, F. R. S., and Wm. Sharpey, M. D. F. R. S. Edited with notes and additions, by Joseph Leidy, M. D. In two large octavo volumes, of thirteen hundred pages, with five hundred wood engravings.

Chemical Technology, or Chemistry applied to the Arts and to Manufactures. By Dr. F. Knapp. Edited, with notes and additions, by Dr. Edmond Rowalds and Dr. Thomas Richardson.— First American Edition, with notes and additions by Prof. Walter R. Jonnson. (Vol. I. lately published, with 214 engravings on wood) Vol. II. nearly ready, 8vo. about 400 pages, with 250 large wood cuts.

Lectures on the Diseases of Infancy and Childhood. By Charles West. M. D. (being published in the "Medical News and Library."

THE

MERCERSBURG REVIEW.

MAY, 1849.

NO. III.

ART. XIII.—THE APOSTLES' CREED.

II.—Its Inward Constitution and Form.

To estimate properly the merits and claims of the *apostolical symbol*, it is not enough to be acquainted with the facts of its history outwardly considered. We need still more to understand its interior history; its rise and progress under an inward view; the idea which is developed in its constitution, and the manner in which the development is to be regarded as taking place.

In the first place, the Creed is no work of mere outward *authority*, imposed on the Church by Christ or his Apostles. It would help its credit greatly in the eyes of some, no doubt, if it could be made to appear under this view. Their idea of christianity is such as involves prevailingly, the notion of a given or fixed scheme of things to be believed and done, propounded for the use of men, on the authority of heaven, in a purely mechanical and outward way. If there were evidence that some several of the Apostles together, or even the Apostle Paul, or the Apostle John alone, had formed the Creed as it now stands, and handed it over in this shape as something finished and complete, to the keeping of the Church, it would be looked upon, of course, as at once a divine tradition, the sacredness of which it would be no better than infidelity to doubt or call in question. It is plain, however, from the history already presented, that no such origin as this can be asserted in its favor. It is not in this sense it has claimed to be apostolical from the beginning. Its relation to the faith of the Church, is not that of an outward dead *traditum* or deposite, in any way. On the contrary, the idea of such a relation in the case, contradicts its whole nature. In no such form could it be the glorious christian *creed*, which we now find it to be in fact.

In the next place, it is no product of *reflection*, exercised on the contents of christianity, as an object of thought and study. This it might be conceived to have been, in two ways. We can suppose some gifted individual, well versed in the great truths of the gospel, to have addressed himself to the work of reducing them to the form of such a brief system or compend, in a merely private character; or we may imagine a body of competent persons met together for this purpose, as a council or synod, and furnishing the formulary as the result of their joint deliberation and discussion. This last view, especially, would suit the taste of many: more particularly if it could be made to appear that the Bible had been taken as the source and rule of all evidence in the case, and that the formulary was exhibited throughout as an extract simply, and summary, of what is to be found in its inspired pages. It would assist the respect of such persons greatly for the Apostles' Creed, if in the acknowledged default of a strictly apostolical *imprimatur*, it were possible still to refer to some ecclesiastical convention of this sort, in which with all due formality and deliberation it was brought out for the use of the Church, at the very beginning of its history; if that famous synod at Jerusalem, for instance, or some other solemnly convened for the purpose after the destruction of Jerusalem, were known to have taken the matter in hand, (after the fashion of the great *world convention* in London,) and to have produced finally, what they conceived to be, in this shape, a truly *scriptural* platform of christian doctrine. But it must be admitted that the ancient Creed comes down to us in no such form as this. We ask in vain for the private study or private theological brain to which it owes its birth; and we are equally disappointed when we think of tracing its origin to any more public theological or ecclesiastical source. In this respect, its rise is more obscure seemingly, than that of all modern confessions. It comes with far less "observation," than the Heidelberg Catechism, or that of Westminster. No trumpet tongue proclaims its "articles of agreement," for the whole world to hear, as in the case of the *late* "Evangelical Alliance." There is no evidence whatever, of plan, or calculation, or forethought, of any sort, in its production; not even to the extent of what is implied in the fabrication of a modern church "covenant," for the use of a single congregation. There is nothing in the case to match even the independent private manufacture of that new creed lately originated for the use of the Protestant Armenian Church, in Constantinople. We can see and understand easily how *that* was made: the missionary goes into his upper room, takes the Bible into his hands, forgets as far as possible all creeds besides, and so through the medium of his own head, with such theological shape as it has already at hand, contrives and puts together a scheme or plan of necessary christian truths; which in such form is presented, at the end of a few hours, all done and complete, and at once ready for use. All this however, we miss in the Creed which bears the name of the Apostles. No one can tell exactly whence or how it comes. Its beginning is vague and uncertain. It seems to spring up at different points, and its appearance is not at once well settled and defined. Plainly there has been no method or plan, no process of intellectual reckoning, no comparison of views and observations, no outlay of theological thought and reflection, in the production of the Apostles' Creed. The authorship of it, be it such as it may, does not hold at all in the form of any such relation to its contents as would be implied in this supposition. It is not the work of any mind, or set of minds, placing themselves over against the contents of christianity in the way of consideration, holding them off as it were objectively for the notice of thought, and so reducing them to logical statement for the understanding. We hear of no such process; and we read no trace of it in the formulary itself. That is not in any view its constitution and form. The Creed, it deserves to be well understood and well borne in mind, is not a confession in the common modern sense. It is not like a catechism. It is no summary of christian doctrine, no theory of divinity in miniature form. To be appreciated properly, it must be apprehended under a wholly different character.

We would not be understood, in what is here said, as undervaluing or disparaging at all, schemes of christian doctrine; as though the vital power of religion must be supposed to suffer, from any attempt to make it the subject of intellectual contemplation. There is a certain way, indeed, of using the understanding here, which is not to be approved; when its notions and abstractions, namely, are made to pass for the matter or substance of religion itself, as though this stood primarily in such mere acts of thought. To make reflection or intelligence, in this way, the principle of christianity, is to fall at once fully over into the arms of rationalism. But allowing the christian substance or reality to be already at hand, under a different form, there is no reason why it should not be made the object of thought, like any other material with which the mind is called to work. On the contrary, it lies in the very conception of christianity, that it should thus take possession of the thinking of men, as well as of their outward activity. It seeks continually to become objective, in the way of reflection and knowledge. Where there is no religious thought, no doctrinal scheme for the understanding, no theological science, it is in vain to expect that the life of religion can be truly prosperous in any other view. We undervalue not systematic divinity. We speak not a word against modern catechisms and confessions. They are all good and highly necessary in their place. Only we must not think of the Apostles' Creed, as belonging to the same order of ecclesiastical productions. It is no work of religious reflection, no product of the understanding, no digest in the form of thought. It holds altogether in a different element, and carries in itself quite another constitution.

What then is the true distinctive character of the Creed? How has it come to pass, and in what form does it now challenge our homage and respect?

We have the answer in its name. It is the *Creed*; that is, the substance of christianity in the form of faith. Here we reach at once its last ground and inmost constitution. It holds immediately and entirely in the element of *faith*, and it can be rightly appreciated only as it is apprehended under this view.

Are not, however, our ordinary confessions and catechisms, in this respect, of the same nature? Is it not precisely as compends or summaries of the christian faith, the things which christianity requires us to believe, that they are prized and counted sacred?

They are indeed, we reply, summaries of what is regarded as the christian faith, and it is only as the contents of this faith are truly represented by them, that they can deserve respect; but still they do not hold immediately and directly in the life of faith itself, as the very element and inward form of their representation. They give us the contents of faith, as projected in the first place from the mind which has them, and made the object of thought or reflection. This reflection is not itself faith, but something different from it altogether; which only in this case employs its force on what faith has caused to be at hand for its use. So apprehended, truth is before the mind not immediately, but mediately. The mind separates itself, as it were, from its own contents under the first form, and then turns round to gaze upon them, for the purpose of coming if possible to some clear knowledge of their sense. The process is indirect, circuitous, reflex; whereas in the first case, the apprehension is immediate, and without any intervening mental operation. The difference between such mediate and immediate apprehension, is very great, and is not confined of course to the sphere of religion. All knowledge starts in the second form, and from this passes forward into the first. So we have said already, the substance of christianity carries in itself the same necessary tendency. It requires to be translated into both thought and action. In this mediated form, however, it is no longer the same thing precisely which it was before. Thus it is, that our summaries of faith, in the form which they carry as the product of theological reflection, are always materially different from the Apostles' Creed. They represent christianity under a reflex view; whereas in the Creed we have it in its primitive form, as the direct immediate utterance of the christian faith itself.

The full import of this distinction requires, however, that we should now direct our attention more closely to the nature of faith. If our conception of this be defective and false, it must involve the whole subject for us necessarily in more or less confusion.

Faith, it is said, Heb. xi. 1, is the substance of things hoped for, the evidence of things not seen. With this agrees well the definition given of it in the Heidelberg Catechism : " True faith is not only a certain knowledge, whereby I hold for truth all that God has revealed to us in his word, but also an assured confidence, which the Holy Ghost works by the gospel in my heart, that not only to others, but to me also, remission of sin, everlasting righteousness and salvation, are freely given by God, merely of grace, only for the sake of Christ's merits." It is fully distinguished here from all mere fancy or opinion. It can hold only in regard to what is true ; it can never be sundered from the actual substance of that which it is called to embrace. The idea of faith in a falsehood, and the idea of faith in no actual union with its object, are alike contradictions, which come in the end to the same thing. Faith carries in its very nature its own warrant and guaranty. It is the "substance and evidence" of the realities it brings into view. Thus related to its object, it is no blind assent of course to mere outward authority. Just as little, however, can it be regarded, as the product of ratiocination. Certain knowledge, as the Catechism has it, even if such a thing could have place on other grounds, engaging us to give full credit to the declarations of the Bible, as we believe the Copernican system, or the facts of common history, would not come up at all to the conception. Our knowldge or conviction, in such view, springing from no apprehension of the things themselves, but based on something out of them and beyond them altogether, would be in fact no knowledge whatever, but a system only of unsubstantial notions and abstractions pretending to the name. It is just as impossible for ratiocination to do what is wanted here, as it is for mere outward authority and blind tradition. It is not by thinking of invisible realities, that they are made to be really present for the soul. This real presence is accomplished by faith, and by faith alone ; whose very nature it is to bridge over the chasm which divides the two worlds, and to bring them into actual substantial union, as the "hypostasis of things hoped for and the demonstration of things not seen;" and which for this very reason must ever go before, and not follow after, all true intelligence in the sphere of religion, according to the deep sense of our motto borrowed from St. Anselm, and through him we may say from St. Augustine: "*Neque enim quæro intelligere ut credam, sed credo ut intelligam.*"

Faith stands thus in the same relation to its objects, that holds in the case of sense. It brings the mind into direct communication with them, as actually present and at hand. Such is the apprehension we have of things immediately around us, in the world of nature, by means of our senses. As thus apprehended, they may be made the object of reflection and thought; but such reflection and thought are not themselves this primary apprehension. It goes before all thought, and lies at the ground of it, as that without which it could be of no force or worth whatever. In itself, it turns on no ratiocination, no intermediate bridge of any sort, between itself and the things to which it refers. It is in its own nature, the evidence of these things, the very form we may say, in which their existence is actualized and brought to demonstration. The relation of vision to light, for instance, is such as allows no room to intervene between them, no connecting link to bring them together. It is not in any sense external, but altogether inward. They are different sides only of the same fact, each being what it is wholly by the correspondence in which it stands with the other. Light asserts its character and power by means of vision; that is the form in which it comes to its revelation in the natural world. And so on the other hand, vision takes effect only through the presence of light; this constitutes the very matter or substance, by which it becomes real in the process of actual life. The light is in the eye, and not simply beyond it; the eye, or its capacity of seeing, is itself the power of what is seen, as made in this way to fill with its own immediate presence the mind that sees. It is the organ for light, which can never be exercised without it, and whose exercise then, of course, carries in itself the guaranty that its object is really at hand. In this, natural vision differs from all impressions of mere fancy, however vivid. It can have no place, without real natural light for its contents. The form here can

never be sundered from the substance, it is required to embrace.
To talk or think of sight, that sees nothing, is an absurdity.

And now parallel with all this, we say, is the connection that
holds between faith and the world of invisible realities, the true
home of the spirit, revealed and thrown open by its means. It
is the organ by which we perceive and apprehend the spiritual
and eternal; the telescope, through which our vision is carried
far over the confines of time and sense, into the regions of glory
that lie illimitable beyond; the very eye itself rather, that enables us to "look at things unseen," and causes their presence to
surround us as a part of our own life. Our nature is formed for
such direct communication with the world of spirit; carries in
itself an original capacity for transcending the world of sense, in
the immediate apprehension of a higher order of existence; and
can never be complete without its active development. Sin
indeed overwhelms this capacity and prevents its proper use;
natural men are said to do violence to the truth by their unright-
eousness, (Rom i. 18–20) closing their inward sense as it were, to
the revelation of it that surrounds them, and allowing it no room
in their minds; but the corruption of our nature in this respect,
is not its destruction. The great object of religion, accordingly,
is, to restore it to its proper freedom and power, by infusing life
into the spiritual sense of which we now speak. Thus called
into exercise by the power of the Holy Ghost, faith makes way
for the apprehension of divine things at once in their own light.
The barrier which had place previously between them and the
mind, is made of itself to fall away. They touch it, and make
themselves felt by it, on the side of its original capability for such
sense of the unseen; just as the things of the natural world touch
it also, and are felt, on the side of its corresponding sense for
what is outward and seen. As in the case of vision and light,
so here also the relation between perception and object, is of the
most inward and necessary character. It is the relation which
holds between contents and form. Faith is the form in which
divine truth comes to its proper revelation among men. As a
word in the Bible, merely, or upon the tongue, or in the brain
even, it is not made to be truly and fully in the world; only
where it is "mixed with faith in them that hear it," only where
it finds access to the living soul under this form, can it be said to

be revealed actually in its proper constitution. For truth is life; and it can hold as such only in an element answerable to its own nature. The words that I speak unto you, said our Saviour, (John vi. 63,) they are *spirit* and they are *life;* not letter for the eye only, nor sound for the ear, nor notion for the understanding, but truth whose very form is active power, and the apprehension of which accordingly is not to be imagined under any *other* form. The word lives, and is the word truly, only by faith. And so faith necessarily includes it also as its own proper substance and contents. Faith does not create truth; as little as our natural vision creates light; but without truth for its contents, it can no more be in exercise or existence, than the same natural vision can be where all light is wanting. As sense is developed by the world of sense, and subsists permanently only by union with it as its own substance; so faith is called into exercise only by the presence also of its proper objects, and can have no subsistence apart from them. Faith filled with fiction, is as great a contradiction as sight that sees nothing. It stands just in the apprehension of invisible things, in their own true and proper reality. The direct and immediate communication of our nature with this higher world, in virtue of its original capacity for such purpose, the state or activity in which this communication holds, is itself precisely what we are to understand by faith. It is the form or inward habit of a soul, in actual felt correspondence with things unseen and eternal.

The object of faith then, is always the supernatural; something that transcends nature, and is incapable of being reached in the way of mere sense and understanding. In this respect, it differs materially from common belief, such as we exercise continually in human testimony. This remains bound always to the things of this world. No amount of authority, no simply outward word, can bring into the mind under any such form, a real inward persuasion of the truth of things that belong to a higher world. Let a prophet come, doing miracles in proof of his mission, and then reporting to us invisible heavenly realities; and let us be never so well satisfied with his credentials, still the report, as such, can beget in us no actual faith. It might be fully sufficient to assure us of earthly things; but it cannot assure us in

the same way of heavenly things. These hold in a higher order
of life, and can be apprehended accordingly only where the capacity is at hand for perceiving them in this form. The testimony
of the prophet must be met with the power of faith on our side,
as the true inward sense for the supernatural already in force, in
order that it may be truly understood and received. By no possibility can faith in God, or in a divine word, be the consequence
and product simply of faith in man, or faith in nature. The
apprehension of divine things to be in any case real, must be in
virtue of a direct and immediate communication with them, as
something above nature and more than nature. This is faith;
and in this sense it is, we suppose, that Abraham is made to say
in the parable: " If they hear not Moses and the prophets, neither will they be persuaded though one rose from the dead."
Such an outward miracle could generate no faith, as men are
apt to think it might. It would be no better for this purpose,
we may say, than magic.

Faith looks at things unseen, things that transcend sense; eyes
the supernatural; apprehends the divine. Its general object in
this view, is the revelation of God; the being, and presence, and
glory of God, as they are made manifest for the knowledge of
men in his works and word. Such a revelation we have, to a
certain extent, in nature itself. " The heavens declare the glory
of God," we are told; " the invisible things of him from the creation of the world, are clearly seen, being understood by the things
that are made, even his eternal power and Godhead." But all
this is no part of nature itself, as it exists for mere sense. The
animal sees it not; and brutish men, as the Apostle tells us,
" change it into a lie." It is only by faith we are enabled to discern the supernatural in nature, looking through the sacramental
symbol and embracing the divine sense, which lies beyond.
" Through faith," it is said, Heb. xi. 3, " we understand that the
worlds were framed by the word of God, so that things which are
seen were not made of things which do appear." Some might
think mere natural understanding, reasoning from experience,
quite sufficient for this. But the philosophy of the Bible is deeper, and far more sound; the empirical understanding could never
bring us to any such result; we come to it, before all ratiocina-

tion, and in spite of it we may say, by faith. We understand *through* faith; not in order to it, but by its means; our creed precedes and underlies our intelligence. So in the case of history. God reveals himself here too gloriously, in the way of his providence. But the revelation is only for faith. "A brutish man knoweth not, neither doth a fool understand this." God reveals himself still more fully in the Bible. This is made up of many parts; but the whole may be regarded as one vast act of self-manifestation, by which he unfolds himself more and more for the view of the world, till at last the whole process comes to its consummation in the mystery of the *Word made Flesh.* Throughout, the general ·nature of faith remains the same. It is still the organ for the invisible and eternal, by which God and his relations to the world are apprehended, in the measure of the revelation actually at hand, at any given time, and under any particular form. It may have less or more range and horizon, but its relation to what this contains, is always the same; it remains throughout the *form,* in which the substance of what God reveals is apprehended; it is the light of the eye towards the higher world of the spirit, without which, emphatically, the whole body, the entire man, must be full of darkness.

Faith then admits of measures and degrees, from the bursting germ to the full corn in the ear. It could not be under the Old Testament, in this respect, what it is required to be under the New; and we have no right to try it in the child by the same standard, that may be applied to it in the case of the full grown man. With the same revelation, there may be very different measures of capacity (strong and weak faith) for its apprehension; and then the capacity must be conditioned objectively, by the amount of the revelation. Only a full revelation can make room for a complete faith. Thus it is, that true christian faith goes beyond all that faith could be under any other form, while at the same time it only completes the nature which belongs to faith universally. How could it be otherwise, if Christ be indeed the last and fullest revelation of God in the world, "the brightness of the Father's glory and the express image of his person." The soul of man, brought into felt contact with the presence and truth of the world invisible under such form, must be more completely open to the light of that world, than it could ever be possibly by any inferior revelation; which is only to say, however, in other words, that it can in no other revelation have the same perfection of faith.   Christ is the absolute and ultimate sense of all God's revelations; and so we say of christian faith, that it is the end of all other faith, the only form in which finally our correspondence with the invisible world can be made complete.   A fully developed faith, in our circumstances, can have place by the manifestation which God has made of himself in Christ, and in no other way.   This is the end, towards which it struggles from the beginning, and without which it must remain forever incomplete.   Any true *creed* must be in the end christianity.

Christianity then, is the absolute creed.   Its very form primarily is that of faith, in its highest and most perfect power, as called into exercise by the revelation which God has made of himself in his Son Jesus Christ.   The revelation can have place only in this way; it could not be made to the senses or to the merely natural understanding; it must hold in the element of faith.   It belongs to the conception of the supernatural, as it apppeared in Christ, that it should be apprehended, that it should come thus to a real and true *revelation*, by the form of existence we denominate faith, and in no other way.   Aside from this form and out of it, christianity might be objectively true in other respects, but it could not have any real existence in the world, it must be for men as though it did not exist at all.   To such real existence it comes only and wholly through faith, or the receptivity which makes room for it in the actual order of the world's life.   Others *saw* Christ in the days of his flesh, and had their *opinions* about him more or less shrewd; but to Peter it is said: "Blessed art thou Simon Bar-jona; for *flesh and blood* hath not revealed it unto thee, but my Father which is in heaven!"   The revelation was in the person of Christ himself, not as an outward fact for sense, but as the presence of a divine life for faith.

For christianity, it deserves to be well laid to heart, is in a deep sense identical with the life of Christ itself.   It is not the words he spoke, nor the works he wrought, as something sundered from his own person, but the living fountain of all these as introduced into the world in the mystery from which his person springs. He is the word itself made flesh; grace and truth enshrined in living *shekinah;* the life of God disclosed, to the fullest possible extent of revelation, in the very bosom of man's life. Christianity unfolds itself into a whole world of divine realities, (doctrines, promises and deeds.) to the eyes of angels even glorious to behold; but the inward substance of all this new creation holds continually in the mystery of the incarnation. It is no abstraction, no thing primarily of thought and notion; but a divine supernatural reality, brought into the world, revealed, made accessible and available for men through faith, and this the faith of our Lord Jesus Christ, by whom and in whom only life and immortality are brought to light. All comes to apprehension first, and has its true reality thus, only as Christ himself is apprehended in the spirit and power of Peter's memorable confession; in virtue of which, as the living appropriation of what it owned and saw, he is proclaimed a *rock* indeed, truly answerable to his own name. Christianity in this way is just as much a *living* reality, as Christ himself; and being like him above nature, the revelation of God in the world, its presence can be apprehended primarily only in the living form of faith. So apprehended, it may be made the object of reflection and science; but its whole reality stands first in this apprehension.

So it was regarded by the Church, in the beginning. Independently of all theoretical and practical use to be made of christianity, she knew herself to be in possession of its substance, as something real and constant, in a direct and immediate way. This was seen and understood to fall back on the person of Christ, as its ground. Not on this however, of course, as a mere outward historical fact; but on the mystery of the incarnation which it involved, and the world of truth and life here opened to the gaze of faith. Christianity in this form, was felt to be immediately and at once at hand, as a divine reality, which men were bound to admit and obey whether they might be able to understand it or not; just as the world of sense, made real to us by our senses, is to be accepted for what it is in such view, whatever may be required farther for its explanation in the way of science. This immediate substance of christianity, as it comes

to a real revelation in the first place directly for faith, forms the
contents, and furnishes us with the true idea, of the ancient
Creed.   It was never intended to be a theory of religion ; it was
not exhibited as a formulary imposed by outward authority, nor
as the result of any process of reflection.   It presented itself to
the world simply as a firm affirmation, on the part of the Church,
of what christianity was to her living consciousness in the way
of direct and immediate fact.   It embraces propositions, of course,
for the understanding ; which, moreover, it is quite possible to
accept, and repeat with the lips, in a merely notional way ; but
the propositions themselves are no product of thought, comparison and deduction ; they are the utterance only of what is immediately at hand in the proper christian consciousness itself ; and
they can be truly understood, only where this consciousness prevails.   This is the *form* of the Creed.   It has its very being in
the element and sphere of faith ; and it holds there, in the character of a direct spontaneous witness, with the mouth, to the
great central realities of faith as they are immediately felt in the
heart.

It is as though one should stand forward, with the full free
use of all his senses, in the midst of the world of mere nature,
and proclaim his faith in it as a fact actually present in such immediate view : " I believe in the sun, moon and stars, and this
solid earth on which I tread ; I believe in these towering mountains, and wide extended plains, and gently flowing streams :" &c.
We understand at once, without any difficulty, the nature of such
a confession.   It involves no reflection.   It takes the realities
of sense, as they are at hand, for the mind in their immediate
primary form, and simply affirms their presence accordingly.   So
here.   Faith turned towards Christ, as he stands revealed in his
own life, finds itself filled with the sense of a new spiritual world,
the proper consciousness of the christian Church ; and all this
comes to its right expression, under such form, in the solemn
language of the Creed.   This is christianity, that a man should
stand in Christ, in the new world which Christ creates, and say,
as in the other case : " *Behold* these heavens and this earth,
wherein dwelleth righteousness and everlasting salvation.   I believe in God, the Father Almighty, Maker of heaven and earth ;

and in Jesus Christ, his only begotten Son, our Lord; &c." The Creed affirms all this as a glorious reality, present not to sense, but to faith. It offers no problem, no hypothesis, no argument; but simply plants itself in the midst of the new order of things which is revealed in Christ, and proclaims its fundamental character and outline, with the force of an assurance that is felt to be identical with that of life itself. This, we say, is its constitution and form; this is its original meaning and force; to this it seeks to come always in the use of the Church. Its object is, not to lodge its articles as so many points of christian orthodoxy in the mind; but so to bring this rather into the very consciousness of what they affirm, that they may be appropriated by it, and made one with it, as a part of its own life.

It would be a mistake, however, to conceive of the Creed, as springing in the form now described, at once and in full, from the faith immediately of every single christian, separately considered. It owes its origin to the faith of the Church, as a whole; and it came to pass as we have seen, not at once, as a thing complete from the beginning, but in the way rather of free gradual progress and growth. These two points now require our consideration.

The Creed, we say, sprang in the beginning, not from the christian faith as something individual and single, but from the faith of the Church as a whole. It is the product of the early christian life, in its general and collective capacity. We shall not stop here to show how it is, that a collective life may originate and produce, in this way, without any outward consultation or reflection, forms of existence, to which no part of it can be considered fully equal when singly and separately taken. The fact itself is abundantly established, on all sides. Our single life is always borne and carried in the bosom of a broader social and public life, whose contents are not simply the arithmetical aggregate of its several parts, but a true spiritual unity rather, which as a single power pervades the whole, and as such, is always something deeper and more comprehensive than any portion of it separately viewed. So in the early life of nations, as it lies back of all history, we meet with creations continually, products of the spirit, that can be resolved into no single activity whatever and that come by no reflection, but seem to shoot forth spontaneously, by a sort of inward organic force, from the substance of the national mind itself. Language itself is such a production. It comes by no outward gift or command; it springs from no invention or compact; the single life, as such, could never reach it; it grows out of our nature, in its collective or solid capacity. And yet what an amount of intelligence does it not involve, even under the rudest form, far beyond all that may enter into the consciousness of any who speak it, through many generations. How often it happens, that a deep philosophical idea lies hid in the very etymology of a word, which has been made to enshrine it in this way, for the undeveloped popular mind, from the earliest stage of its existence. Think too of the institutions generally, in which society starts, its customs, maxims, and laws; think of the world of wisdom embodied, no one can tell when or how, in the proverbs of a nation, its old saws, its legends, its myths. Are they the fabrication of any single mind, condensing the result of its observations into such artificial shape, and so handing it over to the community for general use? Or have they sprung, perhaps, from a number of minds working together, with common counsel and agreement? Not at all. The national life itself, as a collective power, has produced them; making use, of course, of single organs, here and there, to bring them to utterrance and expression; but with a depth and wealth of sense, at the same time, which has seldom been clearly present, we may say, even to the consciousness of such individual organs themselves. In no other view, is it possible to do justice to such early creations of the human spirit. They are the spontaneous outbirth of mind itself, in its general or universal character. In some sense, this may be said of every production of true genius. Its proper ground lies back of its immediate authorship, in the power of a far broader and deeper life, (the spirit of the nation, the idea of the age,) which simply lays hold of this for the purpose of bringing itself to expression. Every true work of art is an outbirth, organically, of the general life to which it belongs.

All this may serve to explain what we mean, when we speak of the general life of christianity, in the beginning, as something more than the christian life added to itself in its simply individual forms; and when we say that the Creed is to be taken, not as the product of such single christianity separately considered, but as the full free outbirth rather of the christian faith as a whole.

The notorious Dr. Strauss, in his *Leben Jesu,* the most ingenious and complete of all infidel books, has endeavored to account for the whole fact of christianity itself, in this way. The life of Christ, as we have it portrayed in the four gospels, is nothing more, he tells us, than an ideal of the church, the product of its joint imagination, a magnificent myth, or rather a series of myths, (like the labors of Hercules,) made to cluster around the person of the man Jesus of Nazareth, and reduced to shape finally as they now stand, sometime during the second century. This, of course, is a most wild and extravagant hypothesis, which no amount of learning and ingenuity can ever rescue from contempt. The *idea* of Christ is itself something supernatural, and authenticates the reality of his life; and the main use of this work of Strauss, if it can be allowed to have any, is found just in this, that it serves, for a thoughtful mind, to make the mere letter of christianity, even as it stands in the New Testament itself, something secondary to its living substance as exhibited in the actual mystery of Christ and his Church. So much of truth, however, may be allowed to it, that this mystery is actualized, or brought to pass in the world, through the medium of the general christian life as such. It comes to its *revelation,* not to its creation, as a product only of human thought, (the Hegelian dream of Strauss,) but to its revelation as the supernatural in the form of faith, by means of the Church; and this through the activity of the Church, in its collective or universal character, the christian life as a whole. The primitive form of this revelation, is presented to us in the Creed. No man can be said to have composed it; it is no work of bishops or synods; it must be taken rather as the grand epos of christianity itself, the spontaneous poem of its own life, unfolded in fit word and expression from the innost consciousness of the universal Church. It is the direct image and transcript in word, of what christianity was as a living substance, at once historical and divine, for the faith and by the faith of the early christian world. It is christianity proclaiming its own immediate presence, as the new creation in Christ Jesus. That presence is the power of a supernatural or heavenly life in the Church; and the primitive necessary form of this is the living christian *Creed*, whose immediate utterance we have in this most ancient and venerable among all church symbols.

It will be seen then, that we are not disturbed in the least by the difficulty some urge against the Creed, on the ground of its outward history, as showing it to be vague and uncertain in its origin. Would it help the authority of what is called the Common Law of England, as we find it handled by Blackstone, if we were able to trace it back to some single source, and could lay our hand on a particular authorship of given place and date, to explain its rise? Who does not see, that as the product of the English mind itself, collectively considered, it must be a much more faithful transcript of the very substance of the nation's life, than it could ever possibly have been under any other form? So in the case before us, that the first christian symbol, the Apostles' Creed, should *not* spring from any particular source or authorship, but come down to us rather as the free spontaneous product of the life of the Church as a whole, the self-adjusted utterance of its faith, we may say, as it was felt to have stood from time immemorial; that no one can show exactly when or how it rose, and took its present shape; that its origin, in one word, is not mathematically definite, but confused and vague, and referable to no fixed time or place; all this, to our mind, is just as it ought to be, and rightly considered invests it with the highest title it could well have to our confidence and respect. It is in this character precisely of its organic relation to the life of christianity as a whole, that its authority may be said primarily and mainly to stand.

And so, of course, we accept also, without any hesitation, the idea of a gradual expansion and enlargement of the Creed, the other point already noticed, as claiming our attention. The outward history of it shows clearly enough that it did not pass at once into the complete form in which it became finally established. It came, not suddenly and at once, but in the way of *growth*. So come all such free creations, whose laboratory is the life of the spirit under a general and not simply individual form. It lies in a just conception of the true nature of the Creed, that it should come precisely in this way, and in no other.

There are two kinds of growth, or rather two ways in which what is called growth in this case, may be considered as taking place; by outward accretion namely, or accumulation, and by inward development. A stone grows in the first way; a plant, in the second. If the growth of the Creed had been by accumulation simply, one part added to another from time to time, without any inward reason, it might well be taken indeed, as a serious objection to its authority; for it would imply a mechanical production, the worth of which must depend, at every point, on the judgment and skill exercised in adding to it something new; and the process of its formation altogether would be felt to fall over in this way, into the sphere of common human reflection and contrivance. But we have seen already, that this is a false conception of the nature of the Creed. It represents, not a system of thought, but a system of life; and it comes into being along with this, as its direct, immediate revelation or expression in the way of word. It is the free spontaneous externalization of the christian consciousness, the substance of living christianity as a whole, in its primary form of faith. Its growth accordingly corresponds with that of the inward world it represents, the gradual amplification of the christian consciousness itself, or the determination successively of the grand facts it is found necessarily to embrace. This is no growth by mere outward addition or multiplication. It is such rather as belongs always to life, by its very nature; a growth from within; the evolution of hidden contents from a single root or ground, in which all have been comprehended from the beginning. Such growth implies no change, but is the argument rather of unity and sameness; it springs not from deficiency, but shows rather the presence of a complete whole. The Creed was not *made* not manufactured like a watch; it *grew*, self-produced, we may say, out of the great fact of christianity itself. The early Church was not the artificer that hammered it into shape, part by part, and one article after another; but the organ, through whose life as an actual fact it brought itself to pass. Its contents thus come from within, and not from without. In larger or smaller com-

pass, it remains throughout the same. As uttered by Peter, in
his rock-like confession ; as it meets us in the simple baptismal
formula ; as "the answer of a good conscience," more or less
full, in the apostolical churches ; through all its variations in the
second century ; and in the round symmetrical beauty of its last
settled form, as accepted formally by the universal Church ; it is
still always one and identical with itself, the same fundamental
witness and monument of the new creation revealed in Jesus
Christ.   All its articles gather themselves up at last into a single
root, and are throughout but the evolution, more or less full, of
what is found involved in this potentially from the beginning.
No view of the Creed can be taken as just, no interpretation as
sound and complete, in which this inward unity of organization
fails to make itself felt.

The very circumstances then, which go with some to invalidate the credit of the Apostles' Creed, in what regards the manner of its origin, we hold to be of special weight in its favor.
That it should be so free, as to outward form, and yet so fixed
and true to itself always, as to its actual inward substance ; that
it should rise into view gradually, now one article, now three,
and now twelve, and still show itself a single growth, the development of the same faith throughout ; that it should appear under
so many editions and phases, all more or less different in different regions and at different times, and be recognized notwithstanding on all sides as the one invariable *regula fidei* of the
whole christian world ; that it should be so loose a deposit apparently in the hands of the Church, from the first century to the
fourth, and after all, without negotiation or authority, by the
spontaneous voice of universal christendom, assume in the end,
the settled form it now carries, as its proper ultimate and constant
type ; could there well be, we may ask, a more convincing argument than all this, that the symbol is what it claims to be, a true
tradition, not dead but living, of the primitive christian faith,
the fundamental consciousness of the Church, the *Creed of the
Apostles!*   A very real and fixed substance, most assuredly, the
"rule" of christianity must have carried in itself, in the midst of
all its flowing freedom, to come at last in such free way to so
fixed and solid a result ; and we have no right, accordingly, to

quarrel with the early fathers, Irenæus, Tertullian and others, for appealing to it as they do, under this character, though their very appeal itself may be quoted in proof of the freedom now mentioned. They had no idea of a bound scheme of words, in the case, handed down from the Apostles; but they had a most distinct and strong sense of the actual contents of the christian faith as historically or traditionally carried forward from the apostolical age in the life of the Church; and to this they boldly and confidently appeal, and we may add triumphantly too, in opposition to all heresies, as a sure unity and firm universal fact, which no one could pretend to call in question. It is this *living* character of the ancient *regula fidei* precisely, its self-conserving and self-determining power, which clothes it with its chief title to respect. That such an apostolical rule, as to inward substance, existed and had force, as the unity of the universal christian faith, in the early Church, no one who does not choose to put out his own eyes, can for a moment doubt; and yet it is just as clear that this living rule embodied itself finally, and became permanent and fixed, in the Creed as we now have it. However it may have reached this precise form, the Creed is still, at all events, that old living tradition, nothing more or less, expressing itself in the one sense of the Universal Church. To reject it, is to reject the ancient faith; to make light account of it, is to make light account of the very substance of christianity, as it stood in the beginning. If the *regula fidei* of Irenaeus and Tertullian, is to have any reality or be of any force for us whatever, we must own its presence in the Apostles' Creed. We shall have for it most certainly but a figment of our own minds, if we pretend to find it anywhere else.

The true nature and constitution of the Creed, as now explained, may assist us in understanding its material structure, the organization under which its contents are presented to our view; while the right apprehension of this, at the same time, will serve to confirm and enforce still farther the representation of its character already given. It remains then, to consider the architecture, as it may be called, of this ancient creation of the Church, for the purpose of comprehending more completely its plastic reigning spirit and idea. ·J· W. N.

ART. XIV.—MINIATURE PAINTING.

I wonder what has become of my old friend Henry W——ns.
I sometimes fear that his promising genius has been struck down,
overturned and crushed, by the bright advancing car of modern
Improvement.

Many years ago, I knew him at Braddocksfield. He and I were
co-patriots and fellow-laborers on that classic ground. That there
we fought, bled and were defeated, under General Braddock, I
would by no means be understood to state. We date not so far
back in antiquity. At that rate, if not mere shades, which would
more likely be the case, but actual survivors of the carnage, my
friend at present would be one hundred and twelve years of age,
and myself one hundred and seventeen. We belong to a later era.
We are no such Methuselahs. It is not more than fifteen years
since he and I were quartered on that renowned battle ground.
What a change had then come over the spirit of its dream! How
unwarlike did look those quiet fields spread over the scene of its
former struggle, sloping gently down from the steep woody hill
above, to the broad meadows and primeval forests extended along
the banks of the flavous river below! How grass-grown too and
peaceful was the road, along which my friend and I often took our
morning and evening walks, across the very scene of the bloody mas-
sacre! No sharp volley of musketry, no dying shriek of Briton, no
exulting yell of Indian, saluted our ears. We heard only the gentle
lowing of kine in the meadows below, the sweet voices of thrushes
on the oaks around, or the merry laughter of maidens returning along
the road in bevies to the brick mansion adjoining, which was then
occupied as a female boarding school.

Military men then you cannot boast to have been yourselves, some
wary reader will interpose, inasmuch as you say the ground had lost
all its military character. Hangers on you must have been of that
ladies' seminary. Instructors, no doubt you were, in the rudiments
of the fine arts or of letters; thrummers on the piano or dabblers
in water colors; or, mayhap, you taught the accidence or made experiments in the gases.

We do own to something of the sort. It was our humor sometimes, to indulge in these things. Of having applied our hand,
however, to music or the gases, we plead not guilty. We dealt
not in things so evanescent and volatile. My friend was a connoi-

seur in paintings, an amateur artist.   He amused himself often with
delineations in oils.   For my own part, I was more charmed with
polite literature.   It was our pleasure to tarry a year or two at Braddocksfield, on account of its rich historical associations and beautiful natural scenery.   At the same time we did not grudge to bestow,
for a proper consideration, some of our superfluous knowledge on
the docile understandings of the far-gathered pupils of Edgeworth
Seminary, then under the supervision of an English lady, the bland,
accomplished, but now lamented Mrs. O———.

My friend had a keen eye for the picturesque.   In our walks he
was always on the look-out for striking lights and shades.   I was
better pleased with picking up a grapeshot or an Indian arrow-head.
My taste led me to seat myself of an evening, on that felled oak in
the field, against which, when upright and vigorous, had been leaned
the fallen General Braddock.   My comrade was drawn by his dilec-
tions further abroad into more retired places.

By hunters and others, he has often been descried and recognized
happily before any one of them had shot him for a panther, squatted,
in broad daylight, half way up some rugged cliff, beside some clinging tree, with his Bristol board and crayon, sketching off the sub-
tended landscape.   Not that he bore any resemblance whatever to
that ferocious animal—meek and gentle was he as a lamb—unless,
mayhap, in the keenness of his vision.   The delusion on one critical occasion, was more in the ear of the deceived one than in the
eye.   An unpropitious circumstance it was, at any rate, to the furtherance of the fine arts, and it spoke not well for advancement in
letters, that in that section of country, among the common people,
the name *panther* was always mispronounced *painter*.   An old hunter, therefore, stealing along through the glen, was startled by the
properly expressed, but incautious exclamation of his accompanying
boy :—"O! father, see the painter!"   In an instant his unerring
rifle was at his eye and directed towards the object pointed out, my
unfortunate friend, the abstracted artist engaged in his laudable vocation.   Perhaps at that very moment, unconscious of danger, he
had his eye fixed on the cruel marksman, thinking to appropriate
him, in his couched attitude and with his presented muzzle, as a
very peculiar and striking figure with which to set off his landscape.
Providentially, however, on that occasion, the humane, peaceful,
blue-coated form of my talented comrade was recognized befor
the drawing of the trigger.   By our being thrown together, I fan,

we were both improved.   From my always treating relics with that
regard and affection which besuits their rust and antiquity, he began
at length to see something of their worth.   On my part too, I must
acknowledge that, from his shrewd criticisms on nature, I received
and do still retain a keener relish for what is romantic in scenery.

His favorite study, however, was heads.   He was a passionate
admirer of the "human face divine."   Not to the mellowed likenesses of these depicted on canvas by ancient artists, did he confine his contemplations.   He was better pleased with living subjects.
A small man he was, compactly set, not above five feet in height,
and his own classic head was thickly clustered over with richly
waving auburn locks.   Methinks I can see him now, in his instruc-
ting room, standing in one of his favorite contemplative attitudes,
his arms folded across his breast, after the manner of a tragedian,
and his dark hazel eyes fixed with feasting admiration on the fair
features of some pupil engaged in drawing.   As

> Proserpine
> Gathering flowers, herself a fairer flower,
> By gloomy Dis was plucked,

so she studying heads, herself a fairer head, by abstracted W——ns
was studied.   Should she become aware, however, of his charmed
position and fancy his gaze was perhaps too ardent, or mistake it for
impertinence and therefore frown or flout at him from offended dignity, all unconscious of harm, the absorbed artist would only frown
or flout at her in sympathy.   Then drawing himself up for a while
like Othello, he would regard her with brows dark and lowering, till
suddenly a bright smile would flit over his expression from observing
in her features the fine artistic effect.   Nothing selfish was there in
his hallucination.   Passion it could hardly be called.   Jealousies
he had none.   He never thought of courtship.   How many admi-
rers his Madonna might have, and which she preferred, he never
cared.   His only ambition was to make the valued head his own by
transferring it, with all its life and expression, to his canvas.

Yet his portraits were never considered very striking.   Some
features of their originals you could discover in them, but the resemblances were far from being complete.   Some parts were exquisitely
touched, but as wholes they wanted keeping.   Other artists and
connoiseurs on looking at them would often shake their heads and
tell me in confidence, that they feared my friend had mistaken his
'alling.   Such fears they could never have entertained nor express-

ed had they seen him as I in his private walks and recreations. Deficient to some extent, I admit he was in the mechanical execution on canvas, but the whole pictorial imagery must have been vivid in his imagination. He was possessed of all the marks and eccentricities of genius. Like Sir Joshua Reynolds, he was endowed even with that gentle deafness, which was not so obtuse as to cut him off entirely from social intercourse, but it sharpened his visual perceptions, preserved him from all untoward noises, and permitted him to feast at leisure on the quiet beauties of nature, undisturbed. What led to the dilection I cannot tell, but all at once he applied the brunt of his genius to miniature painting. He bestowed his whole attention to portraying the fairy likenesses of features on oval pieces of ivory. His efforts were crowned with complete success. His genius had found its proper outlet. After only a few weeks' practice, his pictures began to excite attention. Striking, delicate creations they were! By artists, connoiseurs and all, they were soon pronounced excellent.

He presently left the fields and took rooms in Pittsburg, where he was patronized by the rich and beautiful. Afterwards he visited the eastern cities with equal success. At length I heard of his having embarked for England. This was nothing strange in his case, as he was a native of Wales. In childhood he had been conveyed thence by his parents to this our Land of Promise. He had inhaled his first inspirations from the towering cliffs of that ruinous, romantic, time-hallowed country. No wonder then that he was drawn back towards its remembered scenery. In England too, the fine arts are more highly estimated than with us. The nobility are pleased with pictures and they bestow encouragement on worthy artists. I confess I was half afraid that my friend's genius would not stand the test of their scrutiny. I was apprehensive that his fairy pencilings would not be appreciated by their too fastidious fancies. I did them wrong, however. I soon heard that his talents were immediately acknowledged; that he had depicted some of their proudest faces; that he had been received into court; that the Queen herself had been one of his gratified sitters. What further honors would have been thrown around his brow, I cannot tell, had not an unforseen occurrence intervened. The tasteful world were suddenly thrown agog in another direction. Daguerre had discovered his wonderful art. Operators soon sprang up in all civilized countries. In every city and village, before some doors, their glittering pictures were to be seen suspended as decoys. Likenesses by the aid of the sun were thrown off more expeditiously than dollars from the mint. Othello's occupation was gone. I have never heard of my young friend since. His profession had been stricken out of the fine arts.

The obsequies of a deceased king are soon lost sight of in the splendor of his successor's coronation. The case of miniature painting, however, was far worse. Its departure was entirely overlooked on account of the loud *eclat* on the coming in of daguerreotypes. When at the close of the silver age the divine Astræa winged her final flight from earth and became a noted constellation, mankind, we are told, lamented: poets sang her praises; but in this iron age —certainly not golden, notwithstanding all California's boasted resources, at any rate so far as taste is concerned—one of the fine arts has disappeared from our midst "unwept, without a crime!" When the seventh Pleiad, in olden times, withdrew her twinkling light from among her sisters, the inhabitants of earth were discomforted, and various were the fabled reasons assigned by poets for her bewailed departure: but for that soft Grace, in modern times, which did hang over the painter's brow, not far off and gazing coldly on him, like a star, but close at hand and sympathizing with his brightest, kindliest conceptions, inspiring him to catch the living expression and impaint it on the ivory, when frightened by the din of progress she spread her tiny wings and sped aloft forever gone, no tears were shed, no plaint was uttered; unless perhaps in secret by the few, her gifted but now forlorn followers!

I would not have it supposed, however, that I am at all disaffected towards the present dynasty. I do not know indeed, but that on the whole I would prefer a daguerreotype likeness of a friend, to one in painting. These stamp acts of the sun, these dark impressions of light, possess a stern reality, a sober truthfulness, which is very gratifying to an observer. Posterity will thank us for them. What a treat it would be for us in these modern times, to have the privilege of looking on a daguerreotype likeness of Shakspeare or of Homer; of Queen Elizabeth or of Helen; of any of the ancient worthies or beauties! How I would like to see one of king Solomon! From the many illustrious heads with which antiquity abounds it is somewhat difficult to select, but admitted into the cabinet, I think among the first, I would open the casket containing, on a single plate, the sweet, pastoral faces of Isaac and Rebekah. To a certain degree it would show us the true lineaments, the actual fashion of the countenance. No interpolations of the painter would it possess; no false touches; no flattery. As the magnetic telegraph, in these progressive times, has to a great extent annihilated distance and enabled us to communicate almost instantly with our dearest friends in the remotest regions, so the daguerreotype has, with magic nearly equal, annihilated time and bestowed on our posterity, when they shall have come upon the stage, the ability of beholding us, their respectable ancestors, almost face to face.

Still it must be admitted that, with all its correctness, this art, in some respects, falls short of the pencil. It is not capable of showing off the same variety of countenance. Some bright, sprightly expressions, often the most characteristic, and therefore seized on with avidity by the painter for his ivory, it cannot catch at all on its plates. They are too evanescent to wait out its awful half minute required of patient, head-supported, stationary sitting. A dread feeling withal, is apt to creep over the subject at the time, from the solemnity of his position. He feels conscious that he is holding up his face, not before a mirror for himself to see, but before a camera obscura, to be looked upon by his absent friends, and, in aftertimes, to be scrutinized, and, he hopes, admired, by the impartial eyes of posterity. Solemn occasion! He cannot help attempting to put on his most penetrating look, his most serious suit of features. The apparatus itself too, it must be added, has a strong tendency towards presenting the awfully dismal, which it is the constant endeavor of improvers to overcome. In the way of cheerfulness, it can seldom reach, in its pictures, beyond a pensive smile. Its plates, moreover, have not yet been divested fully of their metallic glare. In certain positions, with all their improvements, they still present us with a ghastly spectre, the sombre ghost of the original. The sun too, I would speak it respectfully, is not altogether impartial in his impressions. We can almost fancy we can detect something still of the old Phœbus in his disposition. Pindar surely knew his taste when he described him as having been smitten by the violet-colored hair and dark eyes of Evadne. The Muses too, that same poet tells us, were adorned with the same dark-colored tresses. No wonder then that, in his musical capacity, the golden-haired god of day was charmed with their society, and that, at the celestial banquets, he was wont to strike his lyre in unison with their singing. Can it be possible, because in modern times he has been deprived of that instrument, and because he is no longer invoked by poets and musicians as the inspirer of their lays and strains, that he has taken umbrage at their neglect, and to show that he really has a decided turn for the fine arts, he has assumed to himself the whole depart. ment of landscape and miniature sketching? Be that as it may, we know he still retains his old partiality for the same style of female heads. He prefers for his pictures the brunettes, the dark-eyed daughters of the South, his own favored clime. He may not absolutely flatter them falsely, but he takes care to show them off always in their best features. He is pleased with their pensive expressions. Towards your blonds, however, he is not so warmly drawn. Their blue eyes and light complexions he is disposed to disparage. Their freckles he blotches. He has a pique at their eyes. He cannot abide their mirth. He would not have posterity behold their dimples.

It must be borne in mind too, that this art, with all its beauties, can no longer be classed with those which are styled, *par excellence*, the Fine. All that was liberal about it has been assumed by the sun, and what is left for the operator, though requiring much taste and skill, is wholly mechanical. The man of plates feels not the same absorbing interest in your goodly looks. He does not, like the painter, by feasting on your features in fancy, make them his own and then recreate them, perhaps improved, on his ivory. For every advancement we are making in the useful arts, it seems to me, we are generally losing something in the romantic. For every actual possession we are acquiring in *Terra Firma*, we are giving up some ground in *Terra Fabulosa*. Let us not then plume ourselves too much on our present attainments. Let us still look back with reverence on the Past. Let us study its hallowed architecture, its rich poetry, its mellow paintings, its delicate miniatures. Not for the purpose of resuscitating their arts. In their pristine glory, at any rate, we can never recall them. They belong to ages that are gone. Nevertheless by feasting on their ambrosia, our humanities may be more fully developed, our imaginations may be strengthened: and hereafter, if not ourselves, our posterity at any rate may put forth improvements surpassing any that have gone before, on account of their partaking largely, not only of the physical and mechanical, but also of the æsthetical, the morally beautiful and sublime.   W. M. N.

ART. XV.—Kirwan's Letters.

Letters to the Rt. Rev. John Hughes, Roman Catholic Bishop of New York. By Kirwan. *First Series* 1847. *Second Series* 1849. *New York.*

The two small tracts which go under this title, have obtained. as is generally known, a very wide circulation. They appeared originally, as a series of communications, in the New York Observer, and were copied from this into a great many other religious papers. Their popularity led subsequently to their being printed as pamphlets; in which form they have been still more extensively scattered over the length and breadth of the land. They have been counted worthy of translation into other languages, and their fame may be said to have gone out to the ends of the earth. Vast praise has been bestowed upon them on all sides; to such an extent, indeed, that their author must have required no inconsiderable amount of grace, not to fall into the easy snare and condemnation of thinking more highly of himself than he ought to think. The religious press has rung the most flattering changes on the theme of his merits, one organ vying with another, apparently, in some cases, to show its own theological acumen, by heaping laudations on his head. His wit and learning have been trumpeted to the skies. He has been hailed as a second Junius in letters, more worthy of admiration in many respects than the first. All sects and parties have delighted to do him honor. A new era was supposed to have broken upon the history of Protestantism, by the bold onset of the "great unknown" on the pride and strength of the Roman Church. The whole controversy was made so level to the common understanding, so squeezed into nutshell dimensions, so shut up to the offhand alternatives of every-day sense, so bountifully sprinkled with the vivacity of the drawing room or the exchange; it seemed as though a full end of it were taken to have been made at once, and no room could be found for any farther argument in the case. The tomes of musty learning which had been given to it in other days, might have been necessary before; but all occasion for them seemed now to be fast coming to an end.

With a shepherd's sling, and a smooth small stone from the brook, Kirwan had gone forth to battle, and the philistine of Gath lay dead at his feet. To believe the puffs in the newspapers, his primers were worth, if not their own weight in gold, at least all the folios of Chemnitz and the Magdeburg Centuriators put together.

All this, of course, serves to clothe these "Letters" with importance. Their significance is not to be estimated by their size, we must look at their current reputation and credit. We feel bound also, to admit in their favor much more than a simply outward claim in this way to our notice and respect. They come, according to general uncontradicted acceptation, from a most respectable source; their author is one, whom we have long been accustomed to honor, and love, as an able and faithful minister of Christ. In the work before us, too, his general character stands in favorable contrast with much that we are doomed to meet in the current controversy with Rome, as conducted by other hands. The low bred vulgarity, the blackguard polemics, which, too, often come in our way under such form, (reminding one of the vagrant mendicancy of the Roman Church itself,) are not allowed to offend us from the pen of Kirwan. He bows throughout the air and bearing of a gentleman. As a general thing, moreover, he breathes a spirit of kindness; even when he may be unjust and harsh in fact, it is easy to see that it springs not from a directly malignant temper towards those who are wronged. He sins out of ignorance, in such cases, more than out of fanatical hate. He ceases not to be good-natured, however we may feel too often that he is neither sufficiently earnest nor fair. His frivolity carries with it a certain dignity, and sets upon him with well bred ease. It is not such as delights in the companionship of fools. His style abounds with sprightly vivacity and wit, and is well adapted to popular impression; though not exactly with an eloquence and earnestness to remind us, as his partial editor and *copy-right holder* remarks "of some of the most celebrated passages from the Irish bar." There is besides a tolerable amount of true and solid thought, embraced in the general argumentation of his Letters; which, it is to be hoped, may not fail to exert a good influence where they are read, and from whose value and force we have no wish certainly to detract. A certain degree of glory also has been reflected upon the whole position of the writer by the palpable advantage he has had over Bishop Hughes. This gentleman managed his part of the controversy badly, displaying in it but little of the tact and skill which he is generally supposed to possess. He could never have intended seriously to follow Kirwan in the details of his attack. Still, he seems to have felt it necessary to take notice of it in some way, at least indirectly. This, however, gave him the aspect, before the public, of one who had accepted the challenge he was here called to meet; and when the demonstration ended as it did, without being carried out apparently to its own proper end, it seemed naturally enough to betoken a sense of actual confusion and defeat, in the particular controversy he was thus found to waive. Such was, of course, the construction put upon the whole proceeding, by Kirwan and his friends. Bishop Hughes, the great champion of the Pope in America, was held to have been fairly silenced, because he had nothing whatever to say. He was taken all a-back by the prodigious novelty and power of this assault, and published his own shame by going to Halifax to hide it. All this, we say, has contributed to invest these Letters of Kirwan with a halo of glory, such as few pamphlets of the same size have ever been able to win and wear. The author comes before us like a conquering chief, with laurels on his brow, and roses in his path.

Kirwan's Letters, then, may be considered a very fair and respectable representation of the whole popular style of Protestantism, in whose interest they appear; and, in this view especially, they challenge respectful criticism, while they furnish at the same time a desirable opportunity for exposing at least some of the flaws and defects, under which this popular system labors. In dealing with Kirwan, we have to do, in fact, not with a couple of twelve penny pamphlets simply, but with the reigning tone of Protestant thought as it stands at present in this country; he has the mass of opinion and feeling, in all directions, on his side; this is the great secret of his popularity and credit. And all will admit, that the reigning fashion in this respect could not

well find a more worthy spokesman, to stand forward in its
name. It can have no right to complain of any criticism, which
lights upon it fairly, through its knightly representative in the
person of Kirwan.

We shall endeavour now to show, that the championship of
Protestantism here offered to our view, is wholly inadequate
and unsatisfactory. With all its brilliancy and eclat, it must be
counted a failure as regards its own cause. Whether viewed as
a vindication of the Protestant faith, or as a polemic assault upon
the Church of Rome, it falls far short of what such high argument legitimately requires. It is unfair and unjust to both the
interests, between which it pretends to mediate with chivalric
lance and sword. Romanism and Protestantism are alike
wronged by its intervention. As Rome was not built in a day,
so neither is it likely to fall by a flourish of trumpets, and if the
Church of the Reformation is destined to endure and prevail,
it must be on far other ground, than the foundation laid for it
in Kirwan's Letters.

A fatal presumption against them is found, at the very outset, in the air of easy overweening confidence, with which they
address themselves to their work; implying, as it does, an utter
miscalculation of the strength and power of the opposite cause.
A sling in the hands of David may prevail over the shield and
spear of Goliath; and the walls of Jericho, if God so please,
may fall before a blast of ram's horns. But it will not be by
imagining the giant, in the first case, into a Lilliputian dwarf;
nor by mistaking the walls, in the second, for a barricade of
pasteboard. We lay it down as a settled axiom, that no warfare
upon the Roman Church can be of any true force or weight,
which begins and ends with the assumption that it is a pure fiction throughout, which must crumble into ruins, or dissolve into
thin air, on the first application to it of a little common sense.

This assumption reigns, in most of our popular attacks on
Popery. To hear such crusaders talk, one might suppose that
all the powers of ignorance and sin had combined to work out,
in the Roman system, a hellish diabolical satire on the world
and its Maker, such as is to be found nowhere else in the whole
range of history besides. Here is a vast huge organization, fa-

vored by accident against God's proper plan, reaching through long centuries of blank chaos, filling the universal Christian world with its power, folding the tendencies of all modern history in its bosom, which yet, if we are to believe the view now noticed, is so full of absurdity in one direction, and so diametrically opposed to the Bible and all true religion in another, so void at once of all reason and all piety, that we need the conception of something like bedlam for the holy Church catholic, to understand how it could possibly subsist for a single day.

Kirwan, we are sorry to say, with all his general courtesy, is completely carried away also with the power of this wholesale fancy. It reveals itself as a sort of fixed idea, through his whole argument. He has been praised for his great urbanity towards Bishop Hughes; and it is easy enough to see, that he wishes to treat him with respectful politeness throughout. In reality, however, his style of address, on the score now mentioned and as measured from the position of the man addressed, must be regarded as insolent in the extreme; so that we wonder not in the least at the offence created by it in the bishop's mind. It is as though some English aristocrat should stand before us, and with cavalier genteel freedom allow us to see and feel every moment, through phraseology polite, that he took all Americans to be either knaves or fools. Romanism is for Kirwan a compound of miserable delusion and deceit, manufactured from the start by the joint activity of Satan and wicked priests; without any good design; in full opposition to the Bible, and in defiance of all common sense. *How* so bald an imposture should have come to such vast power on so poor a basis, he does not pretend to shew, not even probably to inquire; much less does he think it necessary to explain, *why* Christianity should have been doomed to such dreadful captivity for a thousand years. Enough that we have the fact staring us in the face. Confession, absolution, transubstantiation, the sacrifice of the mass, the celibacy of the clergy, &c., are all without a shadow of authority or sense in their favor. The case is taken to be so plain, that any child might see it. Everywhere Kirwan is ready to find with all ease, in this way, "a priestly device, to ensnare the conscience and to enslave men." All the peculiar doctrines and usages of the

Roman Church are referred to cunning policy and contrivance, on the part of bad men, for the purpose, consciously, of keeping the world from the knowledge of the truth, and binding it in chains of error. The Church has been plainly a hell-born conspiracy, to hold men in ignorance, and deprive them of their native rights, from the beginning. And all this, at the same time, under a form of such blunt and forward stupidity, as may be said to expose itself, by its very weakness, to scorn and contempt, as soon as it comes to any attentive consideration. All enlightened priests, of course, *know* that their religion is a sham and a lie. Bishop Hughes, in particular, it must be courteously taken for granted all along, is quite too well informed, and has too much American life in him altogether, to be at all honest or in earnest with his priestly trade. " What an outrage upon the common sense of the world to have men, dressed up in canonicals, teaching things as true, of which the beast that Balaam rode might well be ashamed." Bishop Hughes is no ass, we may charitably trust, and must, therefore, pass for a hypocrite. " Permit me to say, my dear sir, in reference to yourself," so Kirwan *graciously* speaks, " that I have far too high a regard for your intelligence to admit for a moment, that you believe in the absurd doctrines which your Church teaches. Like the ancient priests of Egypt, you must have one class of opinions for the people, and another for yourself. Will you say that this is harsh and uncharitable ? None knows better than yourself that history affirms it of popes, cardinals and bishops, that have lived before you. On no other ground can I possibly account for your remaining one hour in the Roman Catholic Church." So throughout, the bishop is respectfully begged to lay aside the priest, the acted part, and make room for his own honest convictions as a man.

All this, as we have said, is prodigiously insulting. It is not, however, in such view particularly, that we here make it the subject of notice. We refer to it, as illustrating the sense of immeasurable superiority, with which evidently the whole argument of these Letters is conducted against the Church of Rome. This, we say, constitutes a powerful presumption, from the start, against the force of the argument itself. Kirwan finds it quite too easy,

to end and settle forever this great controversy. He takes it for
granted, that he can bring it within the compass of an egg-shell,
and get to the bottom of it with a common tea-spoon. With the
aid of the Bible, and his own common sense simply to explain
it, he feels himself strong enough to storm all the entrenchments
of Romanism, as so many towers of ice cream or gingerbread.
They are felt, in his mind, to be creations only and wholly of
ridiculous folly and shame. All this, however, only shows that
he is not properly prepared for the task he has here taken into
his hands. He has no right acquaintance with the history of
the Roman Church; he is ignorant of its true genius and life;
he has never mastered, to any extent, its interior economy and
sense. No man who understands the Roman Church, and whose
voice deserves to be heard in opposition to its claims, can ever
think, or speak of it as a pure Satanic fiction. It is not in such
view, indeed, that even the errors of heathenism itself can be
rightly understood. They become intelligible, only as they are
admitted to include some fragments, at least, of religious truth,
and are studied in this way as comparative approximations towards religion in its perfect form, rather than as the denial in
full of its power. But if the history of religion, in such universal
view, be thus possessed of reason and order, how shall we dare
to question their presence to a far greater extent, in the history of
Christianity itself, under the form it is found to carry in the old
Roman Catholic Church! To conceive of this as taking the
place of the pure primitive faith, without any reason and in the
way of sheer Satanic corruption, by the art and craft of cunning,
wicked priests, to such an extent as to bind the whole Christian
world for centuries in bonds of nonsensical impious falsehood,
defeating the promise of Christ and virtually driving him from
the world; to conceive of all this, we say, as the true whole
sense and meaning of the Roman Catholic Church, is such an
outrage on reason, and such a libel on God's Providence, as no
one, who is brought to look at it rightly, can endure with a moment's patience. Away with the thought that such a system as
this, so magnificent and gorgeous in its whole structure, which
has nursed so many nations into maturity, which fills so large a
space in the history of the world's life, which has bred such a

multitude of souls for heaven, which so many of the profoundest minds, in different ages, have bowed down to with veneration
and respect—away with the thought, that such a system should
be, after all, the product only of chance or blind irrational wickedness, cunningly studying its own ends.　The whole imagination is monstrous, and becomes more so always, in proportion as
it is weighed in the balance of serious thought.　It overthrows
all faith in the Church.　It turns all history into chaos.　If our
defence of Protestantism is to be at all solid and sound, it must
proceed throughout on a different view of the Roman Catholic
Church.　Kirwan ruins his own cause, by making thus light of
the system he undertakes to oppose.　Romanism is not mere
nonsense, to be put down with an anecdote, or a pun.　It means
something; means, in truth, a great deal.　Every doctrine it
teaches has its bright side, as well as that which may be dark.
Only one who has felt its inward life in some measure, and is
prepared thus to do it justice, can ever be fully qualified to combat its pretensions and claims.　This is not the case with Kirwan.
True, he was raised in the Roman Church.　But he never understood its proper historical life, the peculiar meaning of religion
in the catholic form; and he has no understanding of all this
now.　If he had, he would have managed this controversy in
a very different style.

We can all see, readily enough, the vanity and weakness of
such sweeping prejudice, when exercised towards Protestantism
on the side of zealots for the cause of Rome.　Such can allow
no sense or truth of any sort, in the Reformation.　They will
have it, that it was all a work of blind wickedness, coming, not
from above, but from beneath, by the instigation of the devil
and the bad passions of unholy men. Zuingli, Luther, Calvin,
were all influenced, in their view, by the worst motives, and lent
themselves consciously to the service of a lie.　So the history of
Protestantism since, is taken to be wholly a blank, or a wild
horrid dream, in the world's life.　It includes, in such view, no
reason, carries in its bosom no truth, contributes nothing to the
cause of religion and human happiness, in any way; and so, of
course, is destined, in due time, to lose itself forever, like a
mountain torrent dispersed on all sides over a desert of sand.

Every such easy overweening imagination on the part of Romanists, we say, is enough of itself, to cut the sinews of any
argument against Protestantism with which it may be joined.
The movement of the sixteenth century is too grand; the crisis
involved in it for religion too clear; the epoch constituted by
it, too vastly significant; the actors, by whom it was brought
about, take quite too central a place in the drama of human life,
and are quite too imposing in the colossal proportions of their
intellectual and moral strength; the consequences of the convulsion are altogether too deep and broad, and far reaching, for
the entire life of the modern world, its literature, art, science,
politics, and social character; the entire course of Protestantism,
in one word, shows itself too profoundly *historical*, carrying
along with it evidently the grand central stream of the world's
civilization, and embracing in its bosom evidently the most active
and powerful elements by which this civilization is to take a still
higher form hereafter: the whole fact of the Reformation and
its results down to the present time, is too impressively overwhelming for any truly thoughtful mind, to be capable of being
rationally treated in any such summary way. We must thrust
out our own eyes, and lose all faith in history as God's work,
and abandon all manly trust in Christianity itself, to admit that
Protestantism is without meaning and power for Christ's kingdom in the world. Romanists must learn to do justice to its
actual greatness, before they can expect to be heard patiently in
opposition to its claims. One champion like the learned and
pious Mœhler, now with God, who knows how to admit the
historical significance of the Reformation, while he still tries to
show that it was unnecessary, who can speak respectfully and
honorably of such men as Luther, Melanchton, and Calvin,
while he holds them guilty of great wrong, who takes pains to
understand and represent fairly the Protestant doctrines, which
he yet labors to confute; one *such* champion is worth, on that
side, a full score of Auduns and Brownsons, who can see in
Protestantism no worth or meaning whatever. And just so, on
the Protestant side; any argument against Romanism must be
compartively powerless in the end, that refuses to do justice to
its historical significance. The Roman Catholic Church is a

great fact too, which only the blindness of bigotry can fail to see and acknowledge. It is just as monstrous to stultify the history of the Church, and make it mean nothing, or worse than nothing, from the ninth century to the fifteenth, as it is to abuse in the same way the period reaching from the age of Luther to the present time. How much more power, immeasurably, in defence of Protestant faith, is exhibited by such a man as Ullmann, the admirable and accomplished author of the "Reformers before the Reformation"! One *such* writer, we say here again, is of more account for the interest on whose side he stands, than a hundred tongues and pens let loose against Rome in the usual anti-popery style.

Kirwan's polemics are made up largely of particular facts discreditable to the Church of Rome, and *ad captandum* appeals to common sense. His facts are furnished, in considerable part, from his own experience and observation in Ireland. There can be no question that disgraceful exemplifications of Romanism, in the form of ignorant priests and irreligious superstitious practices in the name of religion, may be found in that unhappy country, to almost any extent. We may find large store of such argument also in Mexico, as well as in other lands; and it is easy to gather it in almost any quantity, from the history of christianity in past ages. We admit, too, that it is not without force when properly used. The corruptions in the Roman Church, in the sixteenth century, led to the Reformation, and may still be appealed to for its vindication. The comparative tendencies of Romanism and Protestantism, as exemplified in the history and present state of the countries in which they have respectively prevailed, furnish a very fair ground of argument against the overbearing pretensions of the first, and in favor of the moral superiority of the second. It requires, however, a very profound and comprehensive survey, with due regard to all circumstances and conditions, to conduct such a comparison to anything like a scientific issue; and then its results must be taken as of relative, rather than absolutely conclusive force, in regard to the main question. Much turns here on nationality and outward relations. Admitting it to show the superior power of Protestantism, that it falls in with the genius of the more active nations, and binds them to its service, it will not follow that the want of such spirit of action has been owing in all cases heretofore, or that is wholly attributable among any particular people now, to the want of Protestantism. No difference of this sort is sufficient to explain the difference between Mexico and New England. Institutions may be, to a certain extent, good in one age, that cease to be so altogether in another. It must ever be unsafe, in the case before us, to argue either the absolute corruption of Romanism, or the absolute perfection of Protestantism, from a comparative view of their tendencies at the present time. Especially must it be unsafe to lay such stress on isolated, fragmentary proofs and illustrations. The history of the Church abounds with abominations, we may say, from the beginning, which a writer like Gibbon can easily put forward in such style, that they shall seem to throw all her virtues into the shade. There are besides, abominations belonging to Protestantantism itself, taking it in the broad sense, which agree as little with true christianity as the worst errors of Rome; and seem clearly enough to show, at all events, that however superior it may be to the other interest, it is by no means entitled still to look upon itself as exclusively in possession of all truth. It is wholly unsatisfactory to bring forward particular abuses, however gross, which are found connected with Romanism in certain quarters of the world, and at once build upon such ground a sweeping and final conclusion against the whole system to which they belong; as though this must be held responsible for every corruption wrought in its name, and as though all had been contrived and designed in its case, just to run to such bad end. The premises are much too narrow for so broad a conclusion.

We mean not then to undervalue the argument from facts here, in its proper form; for we believe it to be, in truth, of great force. Neither do we dispute the importance of Kirwan's facts, in their right place. We say only that they fall far short of establishing legitimately, what they are employed to establish in his hands. He does not use them to exemplify simply the capabilities of evil that are lodged in Romanism, its wrong tendencies as springing from its wrong constitution; but applies them, directly and immediately, as tests of universal character, as though they were, as a matter of course, the very aim and drift of the system throughout. This is shallow. It proves nothing, except as it takes for granted all it proposes to prove from the start. It goes on the broad coarse supposition, that the whole structure of Romanism, is the senseless fabrication of wicked men and devils in league to deceive the world; which we have already seen to be absurd.

Kirwan's use of " common sense," is much of the same order with his use of " facts." It lies all on the surface, and turns on the most bald, first-best, hap hazard apprehension of its objects. No pains are taken to reach the interior sense of anything; all is estimated by the way it strikes the mind, under its first, most naked and outward presentation. It is easy to make almost anything ridiculous, by sundering it from its proper connections, and placing it in a false light; and the manifold abuses and superstitions that caricature, in every direction, the institutions of the Roman Church, may be said to lay them specially open to this mode of attack. Most easy is it in this way, to dispose of the doctrines of purgatory, penance, extreme unction, transubstantiation, and any other that is turned to bad purpose in the hands of ignorant or corrupt men; but our theological earnestness must be small indeed, if we can feel that we have gone by any such argumentation to the bottom of the subject, in any case, or disposed of it at all according to its true intrinsic merits.

Take it altogether, this *common sense* is a very ticklish and uncertain tool to work with, in matters of theology and religion. It is not the same thing in all hands. It is more like the weathercock that goes by the wind, than the steady compass turned always towards the same point. The common sense of the Quaker, sees only mummery and folly in all religious forms: that of the Baptist, derides the sprinkling of babies; that of the Unitarian, finds only the wildest contradiction in the doctrine of the Trinity, and the holy mystery of the incarnation. It is, indeed, where thought becomes most earnest and deep precisely, that common sense, in its ordinary acceptation, is least to be trusted as a guide. It plays sad havoc with philosophy, and we are warned against it in the Bible as the enemy of all sound religion. *Common sense*, the off-hand outside judgment of the natural mind, is no safe measure at all of spiritual christianity; it cannot discern the things of the Spirit of God, but is ever ready to cry out against them as foolishness. We mean not, of course, to say a word against the use of intelligence and reason, in the service of religion. God can never be pleased with the sacrifice of *fools*. We object only to the fashion of appealing, in Kirwan's style, to the first sense that comes to hand in the common mind, as conclusive on questions of religious faith and practice. No such standard is safe; no such judgment can be secure.

It needs no great depth of thought, to discover the insufficiency of this sort of argument, as actually managed in the hands of Kirwan. Where his appeals to common sense are most direct and bold, we find them, in some cases at least, most undeserving of all confidence and respect. So, for instance, in some of his interpretations of Scripture. He makes much of the Bible, as we all should. " With *me* the teachings of all your councils," he says, " weigh not a feather; give me, if you can, Bible authority.—With *me*, the authority of your popes and councils is not worth a penny. I would rather have one text of Scripture bearing upon the point, than the teachings of as many such as you could string between here and Jupiter." All very well. That sounds big and independent. But the man needs pretty heavy ballast, in the way of knowledge and sense, who thus plays off his own use of the Bible against that of the whole world besides, and holds the judgments of all councils more light than a feather as weighed against one text expounded by himself. He requires, if not downright infallibility, yet something not far from it, to justify such vast confidence; and we may well be struck with the inconsistency, if after all, his interpretations of Scripture betray no very profound insight into its sense. Kirwan, we are sorry to say, is by no means thus infallibly safe in this business of explaining the Bible. He will not allow the authority of popes and councils to be of the least value, for unlocking its meaning; but thrusts into our hands for this purpose, the key of his own common sense. To our view, however, this last pope is just as little to be trusted as any of the rest. He makes himself indeed, to be identical with the Bible, the personification of the divine text itself; but who does not know, that all other popes, and all councils too, have affected to do, more or less, the very same thing?

Kirwan finds no difficulty whatever, in getting at once in full to the bottom of the Lord's supper. The words of institution are plain, and it is only strange that the subject should ever have cost any body the least trouble. All resolves itself into the common-place thought, that the bread was to be a sign merely of Christ's body and the wine an emblem of his blood. "Just see," our cunning Daniel exclaims, "how a little common sense simplifies every thing!"—Simple of a truth, and no less *flat*.

The grand and solemn passage, Matt. xvi. 15–19, is disposed of in similarly facile style. Upon this *rock*, that is the confession of Peter that he was the Son of the living God, Christ engaged to build his Church. "How simple and common sense," cries Kirwan. Again, the kingdom of heaven means the visible church, and the *keys* are simply the power of admitting proper persons into it and excluding improper persons from it. "How simple and common sense is all this," once more cries Kirwan. To bind and loose is a figurative expression, to represent the instructions and regulations of the twelve apostles, for the use of the Church. "This, Sir, I believe,"—that is, *I*, Kirwan, who count all popes and councils as lighter than a feather over against my own dexterity in the use of Bible texts—"this *I* believe to be the common sense, the fair and just interpretation of a passage on which your Church has built up a priestly power, that has overshadowed the earth and enslaved nations. Where now, sir, is your supremacy of Peter—your power of the keys—your power of absolution? Gone, like the morning cloud before the sun. Blessed be God, you have not yet turned your keys upon the common sense of the world." Summary work of it, indeed, is made by this potent talisman, the world's common sense! It puts one in mind of the "*veni, vidi, vici*," of the old Latin general, so swift is its progress, so easy its triumph. But, alas! how it belittles all that is sublime, and turns the magnificent poetry of heaven into the tame prose of the most trivial every-day life!

Our limits, however, forbid details. It is more of account, besides, to direct our criticism towards what is general. In this view, we go on to say that the whole position of Kirwan, in these Letters, is such as to place him in a false relation to the truth. Whatever may be the justice of his cause as against the Pope and bishop Hughes, it is so managed in his hands as to become most unjust to Christianity. His defence of Protestantism, goes forward at the cost of the ancient faith; and his war upon Rome, to a fearful extent, is a war at the same time on all that is comprehended in the idea of the Holy Catholic Church.

The most general acquaintance with church history, is sufficient at once, to show that, in many cases at least, his argumentation proves a great deal too much. Instead of stopping with the proper Roman abuse, it runs back into the very life and heart of the early Church. It seems indeed, to proceed throughout on the assumption that the system it opposes, came in violently and abruptly, one tyrannical contrivance after another, displacing and superseding a quite different order of things which had prevailed before. "Yours is not the oldest religion," Kirwan says in his address to Irish Roman Catholics: "I could here give you the time, did the limits of a letter permit, when the distinguishing doctrines of your Church were introduced. The celibacy of the clergy came into the Church in the fourth century, purgatory appeared in the seventh, &c." There is room, certainly, for arguing against the errors of the Roman Church, on the score of their comparative novelty; and the subject is so important, that it would have been well to *force* more time into the task of doing it some sort of justice; but the argument is one, which to succeed at all, requires a most careful discrimination between all such corruptions and the earlier forms of church life, of which they are to be taken as an abuse. With Kirwan, as with the school in general to which he belongs, this discrimination is wanting altogether. He just lumps the whole argument into a single easy proposition, which his readers are then asked to accept as true on his own infallible authority. Romanism is a novelty, introduced by usurpation into the seat of ancient christianity, and all its institutions here condemned, are to be regarded as the product, root and branch, of this violent diabolical revolution. Never was there, in fact, however, a more untenable hypothesis applied to the course of church history. It cannot bear a moment's examination.

Take, for instance, the celibacy of the clergy. It came in, says Kirwan, in the fourth century. That itself is pretty far

back, for a purely *popish* error. But the root of the thing lies a
great deal farther back still. The idea of a peculiar merit or
spiritual worth in celibacy, adopted for the more unreserved service of Christ in the Church, falls back beyond all controversy,
to the very dawn of Christianity, and meets us in full force in
the second century. "A bishop *must* be the husband of one
wife," according to Paul in the hands of Kirwan. But the early
Church took that text differently; italicising not the "must," but
the "one," and seeing in it the exclusion of a second marriage;
as a widow, in parallel case, (1 Tim. v. 9,) was to be the wife
of one man; and, on this very ground, it was held improper for
a priest to marry after taking orders, however he might be allowed to continue a marriage into which he had entered before.
Kirwan, not to be outdone by the Council of Trent, hurls his
anathema against the whole business, as "a doctrine of devils,"
forcing the "common sense exposition," as he calls it, of 1 Tim.
iv. 3, into the face of Bishop Hughes, to reduce him to reason.
It is not, indeed, quite clear, how a regulation, making celibacy
a qualification for a certain service, which men are as free to enter, or avoid, as a military or mercantile expedition to China, is
tantamount at once to a Gnostic prohibition of marriage itself,
as something universally unclean. And one is bewildered still
farther in the case, when it is remembered, that the very same
Church, which has thus magnified the merit of celibacy, from
the beginning, as voluntarily embraced by the few for the sake of
the many; so far from falling in with the Gnostic condemnation
now mentioned, with no less emphasis from the start has always
denounced this, as contrary to the truth, and at full war with the
spirit of the New Testament; carrying her zeal for the sanctity
of marriage so far indeed, as finally to raise the institution into
the character of a divine sacrament. With all this, however,
we have here no immediate concern. Our object is simply to
illustrate the way, in which the rapier of Kirwan's common
sense, as plied against Romanism, runs itself too often, up to the
very hilt, in the bowels of primitive Christianity. As an idea,
or tendency at least, the institution of celibacy meets us from
the earliest days of the Church; and some regard must be had
to this fact, before we can pretend rationally to have disposed of
it in a truly rational way.

In the same manner, it would be very easy to show that the opposition made by Kirwan to Roman baptism, confession, absolution, transubstantiation, &c., is so conducted as to extend, for the most part, to realities that were held to be of sacred authority in the early Church. Whatever may be the *peculiarities* in the case that deserve to be stigmatized as strictly Roman inventions, abuses that are fairly chargeable to *popery* as a system in the way of defection from the earlier faith, no proper pains at all, are taken here to sever them out for our notice; but, as a general thing, they are confounded with forms of thinking that were notoriously in force from the earliest times before, by which means these are sweepingly involved in the same uncompromising censure and reproach. The argument at last, has regard, not so much to the Roman *form* of thinking, separately taken, as to the whole primitive substance, which it is found to caricature and misrepresent. In the case of baptism, for instance, it is not simply the superstitious accompaniments that attend it in the Church of Rome, that turn it into a fiction, (although, even in such view, the fiction would amount to a nullification of the Church since the third century); the whole idea of baptismal grace, as it has reigned in the Church most clearly from the time of the Apostles, is treated with derision. So the mystery of the holy eucharist. So the conception of supernatural powers belonging to the Church, in every form and shape. All, with Kirwan, is superstition and nonsense; "which," he says, "excite my wits as I may, I cannot understand; it is addressed to my ignorance." This may be all true enough; and our business, just now, is neither to explain nor vindicate any part of the mystery. We simply hold up to view the fact, that these things all entered into the faith of the early Church, and cannot be assailed therefore as exclusively popish. The argument, or declamation rather, of Kirwan, proves a great deal too much. In almost every case, it lays the axe at the root of an old catholic idea, while pretending only to lop off a Roman superstition, so that we are forced to cry out: Woodman, spare *that* tree! Let us not, to use a German proverb, tumble out the child with the bathing tub. Or, if that be our purpose, let us, at all events, see what we are about, and not pretend to be doing the one thing only, while we *are, in truth,* at the same time doing also the other.

It is quite likely, indeed, that Kirwan would not be greatly intimidated, if he even knew himself in this case to be at issue, not simply with the Pope and his servant Bishop Hughes, but with the whole ancient Church. The man, for whom one text of scripture, seen in the mirror of his own mind, is of more weight, than a string of ecclesiastical decrees reaching to the planet Jupiter, need not be much disturbed by the authority of all the fathers from Barnabas to Bernard. This, however, is not the ground. on which he openly professes to stand, in these Letters. He affects rather, to make common cause with primitive Christianity, as it reaches from the first century to the fourth; assailing the institutions and practices of the Roman Church, as wholesale innovations, having no shadow of reason in the proper life of the Church as it stood before. This broad-faced assumption requires to be met with flat contradiction. However true it may be that Romanism is something widely different from the christianity of the first three centuries. it is equally certain that this finds no proper representation whatever in Kirwan's Letters. Neither Irenaeus. nor Tertullian, nor Cyprian, nor Origen, nor a single father of all that galaxy of worthies that meet us from the age of Chrysostom and Augustine could at all take him by the hand as a true champion of the christianity for which *they* stood ready, every one of them, in their own time. to go joyfully into prison and to the stake. Most emphatically, rather, might they all be expected to exclaim: " Non *ta'i* auxilio; the faith of martyrs asks the *same* faith, for its vindication and defence!"

This brings us to a still more serious reflection. It would be strange indeed, if such disagreement with the early Church involved no actual defect in the system to which it belongs; for arm ourselves as we may, in the panoply of the Bible and our own common sense, it is not easy to admit the feeling that the vessel of Christianity. with Christ at the helm, missed its own true course out and out, from the very start. The whole supposition is monstrous; and the virtual consequence with which it stares out upon us from Kirwan's argument. at once enables and compels us to fix a charge of error on himself. One whole side of christianity never comes properly into his view; its sacramental, mystical side, namely; that by which it carries in itself the character of an objective, historical union of divine and human powers, in the form of the *Church*. Here, to our mind, is a grand defect, which like a dead fly, corrupts the whole odor of these famous Letters. Kirwan, as we read him, has no faith in the Church. Let us not be misunderstood. We know and admit that he professes the contrary, and we are willing to take this profession just at its own value. What we mean, however, is this, that he has no faith in the Church after the old church sense, as we find it expressed in the Apostles' Creed, and woven into the whole texture of christian thought during the first centuries. This he takes pains himself, unwittingly, to make clear, in a whole letter devoted expressly to this subject. The *idea* of the Church as it is presented to us in the Creed, is conditioned by its relation through the Holy Ghost to the mystery of the incarnation on one side, and to the full compass of the new creation on the other: As the object of *faith*, it is the real comprehension of supernatural powers under an outward historical form. It carries its own attributes with invincible necessity in its constitution. one holy, holy, catholic, and apostolical. So the entire ancient Church believed, in her own favor; and this faith is found entering, with broad ramification, into all her institutions and ways. She held that she was founded in very truth on the rock, not of a bible doctrine only, but of Christ's living word itself, incorporated into her own constitution; that she was the pillar and ground of the truth; that she was the organ and medium, by which God's presence was brought to tabernacle among men · that a true prophetical and priestly power, as well as a true kingly power, was lodged in her hands; that her ministerial acts were divine; that her sacraments conferred grace, her baptism being for the remission of sins, and the body and blood of Christ mystically at hand on her altar serving as food unto everlasting life. All this, we say, is comprehended in the article of the *Church*. as it stands in the ancient christian Creed; it is no product of popery, however it may be found to underlie all that is most monstrous in the pretensions of this system; on the contrary these pretensions become intelligible only when the faith now mentioned, is allowed to have been in full force before. But now of this faith, the living sense of a divine Church with su-

pernatural powers, according to the Creed, we seem to find no
trace whatever, in Kirwan. The Church, as he takes it, is either
an abstract word only to represent the general fact of religion
under a christian form, or else an outward simply human organization, or multitude of organizations rather, which Christ has
directed his people to form as a convenient apparatus for religious
ends. The marks of the Church unity, catholicity, apostolicity,
and infallibility, he finds to be a fiction in the case of the Roman
Church: but the fiction is so exhibited and exposed, that it is
virtually made to hold of the whole Church, as this has stood
from the beginning; no allowance being made, as it would seem,
for the difference between her actual history and her ideal inward
constitution. "My Bible tells me, sir," we hear him saying, "that
whosoever believeth in the Lord Jesus Christ, shall be saved.
The sincere believers in the Lord Jesus Christ, whether in your
church, or in other churches, or in no church, form a part of that
Church which Christ will present to the Father, without spot or
wrinkle or any such thing." The amount of this is, that the
church is to be considered something outward and accidental altogether to the christian salvation; Christianity stands essentially in the transaction of souls privately and separately with
God, through the medium of the Bible; the idea of a divine
power going along with its general outward constitution, in any
real way, deserves only derision. Kirwan has no conception of
a true union between the visible and the invisible, in the constitution of the Church, the very form of existence under which
she is made to challenge our faith, as a part of the general christian mystery, in the Creed. In this respect, he has fallen away,
not only from the old catholic ground, but from the original
ground also of his own denomination. He ceases to be a Presbyterian, and stands before us as a Baptist or Quaker.

There is no room, of course, for sacraments, in their true sense
where the Church is thus shorn of her proper supernatural character. The very idea of a sacrament is, the union of an outward
sign and the grace represented by it, in such a way, that the second shall be felt to be bound to the first mystically as its actual
body. Outward and inward enter conjointly into its constitution,
with like necessity and reality. Kirwan, however, knows of no

such sacrament. His artillery played off against transubstantiation, reaches *through* that to the very substance of the old catholic mystery on which the error rests. Baptism sinks with him into the character of a mere human sign or pledge. The notion of a real mystical grace in it, he turns into ridicule, as something that lies beyond his common sense; not considering, that it would be quite as easy to turn to ridicule, in the same way, the "brazen serpent" in the wilderness, or the "tree of life" in the garden of Eden. We marvel not, that bishop Hughes should pronounce him rationalistic, irreverent and profane; though our knowledge of the man, and the allowance we are bound to make for his position, make it easy for us to exercise a more tolerant judgment. The early fathers, of course, however, from Ignatius to Augustine, would be much of one mind here with bishop Hughes; and Luther himself, the immortal father of the Reformation, could not fail, as we all know, to throw the full power of his voice, were he now living, into the same scale.

An interesting, we might say somewhat amusing, exemplification of the wrong position of Kirwan, as now noticed, in regard to the Church, has been furnished by the little controversy into which he has fallen latterly with the Baptists, as represented by Dr. Cote of the Grand Ligne Mission in Canada, and the New York Recorder. Dr. Cote, himself a convert from Romanism, and a great admirer of Kirwan, was led in the simplicity of his heart, to quote the *argument* of this last against Roman baptism, as equally valid against the "sprinkling of babies" in every shape. "The apostles administered baptism," Kirwan had said, "to those who expressed faith in Christ; and through this sacrament we obtain a place and a name in the visible church. This all men can understand; but how you, or any mortal man, by the application of water in any or all ways, can wash away the original and actual sins of the sinner, infuse into his soul the habits of grace, and give him a title to heaven, I cannot comprehend." This, of course, says Dr. Cote, excludes the baptism of infants, who can make no such confession; the thing is without Bible authority, a mere tradition of the Roman Church; and Kirwan, to his credit, virtually unchurches all who use it, as having no true baptism at all. This, however, was more than Kirwan himself saw proper to admit; as he took pains to inform Dr. Cote, and the world, by a letter, more tart than strong, in the New York Observer. He complains of a *hocus pocus* mystification of his Letters; repudiates the unchurching dogma, in every form and shape; and welcomes to his communion table any and every friend of Christ, papist or protestant, baptist or paedobaptist. He treats the whole baptistic question as a "hobby;" a mere external; an accident of christianity at best, that should be held at arm's length from the true life of it, under its proper *unchurchly* form. The point really at issue, he leaves wholly untouched. No wonder, the Baptists should be put quite out of humor by such cavalier treatment. The Samson, that seemed so strong before, was suddenly shorn of his locks. It was plain that he was not fit to write about the Baptists at all. "For the sake of our common Protestantism," cries the New York Recorder, "we hope he understood Popery more truly when he wrote about *that*. A most unwelcome suspicion would come over us, as to that point, were not his representations corroborated by others who were born and nurtured in Romanism like himself, and who sustain his testimony by their own." This last reflection is soothing. The Recorder, in conclusion, still insists: "The passage quoted by Dr. Cote, from the Letters to Bishop Hughes, expresses precisely the faith of Baptists, and cannot be reconciled with that of the Presbyterian Church. Kirwan has adroitly passed that passage without an allusion, in his letter to the Observer." Quite recently, we have Dr. Cote himself again on the field, taking his "*dear* Kirwan" to task, more roughly still, in the same style; though with great regret, "on account of his laurels won in the controversy with Bishop Hughes." He knows not how to account for the sad change which has come upon him: *there* so strong, *here* so very weak. He seems to be Samson now, just up from the lap of Delilah—that "perfidious *tradition* of the Church of Rome," has turned the slayer of the Philistines into a common man. "When I came to read the fourth division of your letter, the paper fell several times from my hands, and as it dropped upon my desk, I said to myself: Were we to judge of the accuracy and correctness of Kirwan's assertions against the Church of Rome, by what he says so unjustly and so unfoundedly against the Baptists and their sentiments, certainly the verdict of public opinion would be against the man, to whom Bishop Hughes found it so difficult to respond " "The mightiness of your strength was never so well exhibited, as when, in your letters to Bishop Hughes, you demonstrated to that prelate the absurdity of his creed, and the contradictions of the tenets of his Church. But next comes *your* turn to expose your weak side, Kirwan, when you try to grapple with and overthrow the scriptural doctrine of believers' baptism; and when I behold your contradictions and misrepresentations, I must be allowed to exclaim, with an unfeigned regret: Kirwan! Kirwan!! O Kirwan!!! How is the mighty fallen."—"I feel sorry that your earlier Romish education, and your later Presbyterian training, allow you to fall into a strain of half-sarcastical and half-jeering expressions, when speaking of the mode of an ordinance established by Him, whose minister and servant you profess to be. I would like to find words strong enough to show you the undignified manner with which you treat so lightly, what so large a number of your Presbyterian brethren confess to be the original mode of administering baptism. What a powerful arm you have thus lent to Bishop Hughes, in your letters to whom you profess to have so much reverence for all the doctrines taught in the Holy Bible. Solemnity and respectful language would have been preferable to scoffing and light words. Really, I feel abashed, that a Presbyterian brother could expose himself in the way you have done." We are not sure, after all, that the levity thus castigated by Dr. Cote, differs materially from the "great courtesy, urbanity, and sprightly humor," which have been placed to his credit in the controversy with bishop Hughes. But in this last case, the sport was with Romanism *only*, while in the other case, game is made of the whole Baptist denomination. Circumstances, of course, alter cases. So much for the history of this rather curious affair.

There is not the least doubt, we think, but that Dr. Cote and the Baptist Recorder are right, in claiming the argument of Kirwan as legitimately and fully on their side. On his own principles, and with his own style of warfare, he can never make head successfully against their attacks. If the Church be no more than he supposes; if the sacraments are of such purely outward significance; if all is to turn so mechanically on the letter of the

Bible, with so little room for the authority of Christianity as a
living constitution; it were better to yield this whole question at
once, and pass over in form to the Baptist ranks. The very style
in which he talks about it, shows how little earnest value it has
in his eyes. He stands, in truth, himself on baptistic ground;
his theory of christianity is baptistic; his idea of the Church is
baptistic; and it is only by *tradition*, accordingly, that infant
baptism still keeps its place in his system. It is not a principle
with him strictly, but as Dr. Cote styles it, retorting upon him
his own term, a "hobby," which he holds against himself, in
the way of concession to the Romanists. The concession is two-
fold. Infant baptism cannot be established, in the first place, by
direct Bible proof; in the second place, it has no meaning aside
from faith in a divine grace-bearing Church. Kirwan will have
Bible proof, chapter and verse plump to the point, for every position; his motto is, the text, the whole text, and nothing *but* the
text; and yet here we find him, in a most important case, insisting upon a doctrine and practice, for which he is able to urge
no text whatever. If infant baptism be at all taught in the Bible,
it is by the sense and spirit of it, and not by the letter of a single
passage separately considered; and the sense and spirit of it, in
such view, are made out for us by the presumptive practice of
the Christian Church in the age of the Apostles, authenticated
by the known practice of the same Church in the age following.
But this is not all. Kirwan allows no sacramental grace in the
old sense, no Church as an object of faith according to the Creed,
no mystical objective power consequently in baptism under any
view. His conception of the Church, is that of a purely me
chanical organization added to the proper substance of christianity
from without, and of no real force any farther than this substanc
is supposed to be already at hand, in the way of christian expe
rience, under a different form.* Christianity is strictly for be-
lievers, and for such only; the entire world of infants accordingly

---

* Hear his own language :—"There is one other point to which I would
direct your special attention, because it is one upon which you have been
greatly deceived; I mean the Church. Every effort has been put forth by
our priests to mystify this topic, and to deceive you in reference to it. All

is excluded from it, by original insurmountable disqualification. God may save infants that *die* such, if he see proper, in some other way (by the mere magical *fiat* of his own will); but not by any real comprehension of them, as a living component part of our redeemed humanity, in the new creation brought in by Jesus Christ. *This*, Kirwan makes to be throughout, for "believers," and for such only. His church has no room in it for infants, except *catachrestically*, by making itself into a mere "pedagogium" for educational purposes. Thus the *idea* of infant baptism, at once falls completely to the ground. If infants cannot be comprehended organically in Christ, in the new order of life, introduced by the mystery of his incarnation, in the true living compass of his mystical body, the Church; why in the name of all "common sense," we may well ask with the unsacramental Baptists, should we so trifle with a divine institution as to apply to them the holy *sign* of baptism? The sign in their case, has no significance; while it goes directly, for this very reason, to foster the Roman imagination of its being something *more* than a sign only. Infant baptism is truly part and parcel of the old catholic idea of the Church, and without this is of no force whatever.

Kirwan, of course, has no power to be true and fair, in his

who truly believe in Jesus Christ, and practice the precepts of his word, are reconciled to God. They are adopted into the family of God; they are the sons and daughters of the Lord Almighty. A connection of such with any branch of the visible church, does not interfere with their connection with the family of God. No good man is lost, and no bad man is saved, because of their connection with any church. As a man may be a true Papist, and be a Jesuit or a Jansenist, or a monk of La Trappe, or a shorn friar, so he may be a true Christian, and a member both of the visible and invisible church, and be a Protestant or a Papist, and a member of any of the sects into which they are both divided, which hold to the true atonement of Jesus Christ."—How very roomy and convenient! Why not add: Let such a good christian include in his canon of scripture, *all* the books of the Bible, or only half of them, or only two or three, or even none at all, *provided* he do but hold fast still to the atonement of Christ, and all will be well. Strange Presbyterianism, of a truth; much like that which Dr. Potts once undertook to *defend*, to the edification of all concerned, in his memorable duel with Wainright.

controversy with Romanism. With the utmost honesty of intention in his own mind, his whole position is such as to disqualify him for understanding correctly, or representing justly, the system he undertakes to expose. His own theory of christianity is one-sided and defective : he has no sympathy with catholic ideas; his notion of history is fantastic; the interior sense of Romanism lies for him away out of sight. Hence the force of what is true and good in his Letters, is greatly weakened by the way in which it is mixed up continually with what is false and bad.

Take one broad, and truly glaring, illustration of this defect. To prove Romanism false, all pains are taken to make it out the systematic enemy of liberty and knowledge—a favorite topic, as we all know, with ordinary haranguers on this subject. As the foe of civil liberty, it has required nations and kings to hold its stirrup : as the tyrant of the mental world, it has not allowed men to suit the Bible to their own sense. And then what has been the effect of popery upon human *knowledge?* Kirwan answers: "When Christianity, like a new sun, rose upon the world. there was much that might be called education in the Roman Empire. The obvious effect of Christianity was to extend it. After the lapse of some ages, popery by gradual stages crept, serpent like, to the high places of power. How soon afterwards the lights of learning go out; how soon the dark ages commence and roll on as if they were never to end! And those centuries of darkness form the golden age of your Church. And what spirit did it manifest on the revival of learning in England, after the sacking of Constantinople, and at the Reformation? Leo X. prohibited every book translated from the Greek and Hebrew, &c." Again : "When the Reformation occurred, the retrograde movement of the world towards ignorance and barbarism and idolatry, had almost been completed. Had it not occurred, a radiance might continue to gild the high places of earth after the gospel sun had set—a twilight might be protracted for a few ages, in which a few might grope their way to heaven. but each age would have come wrapped in a deeper, and yet deeper gloom. until impenetrable darkness had fallen on the world."

When one reads such stuff, and hears it echoed on all sides as the shout that laid flat the walls of Jericho, he may be excused for calling to mind, at least, the indignant blunt remark of Johnson: "Let me tell you, Sir, no Church in the world has ever been so slandered as the Church of Rome!"

Could there well be a more gross insult put upon Christianity, than to make its triumph lead to the downfall of the old Roman culture and civilization? Even Gibbon has ventured on no assertion so bold as that. It does not help the case at all, to say: Christianity was indeed at first favorable to learning, but Popery came in stealthily under its name, and accomplished this great ruin. The Christianity, under whose presence the old Roman life fell, call it by what name we please, was the same substantially that conquered the empire in the fourth century, and that gave birth to the brilliant theology of the following period. It was, besides, the only Christianity in the world, the legitimate succession of all that had gone before, the whole Church as it then stood. And are we to be told, that this was the power which extinguished the lights of science for the ancient world, and thus made room for the dark night of ignorance that was to follow? Kirwan seems never to have heard of the universal revolution wrought in the Roman empire at this time, by the barbarous population poured in upon it from the North. Must we tell him and those who are forever harping on the same key, that the old civilization was overturned by Paganism, and not by Christianity; that the foundations of society were completely broken up, in the awful process; that universal chaos took possession of Europe; that a wild, tumultuating, savage life, prevailed on all sides; that a new course of culture was to be commenced; and that the Church was the ark, in whose bosom mainly was preserved all that was still left of value for this purpose, from the wreck of that great time which had gone before. Then follow the *incunabula* of modern society; the nations of Europe in swaddling clothes; the vast and mighty elements of a new civilization, wrestling not without terror towards the accomplishment of their great problem. Such a process of new creation, was never before seen. Still it goes forward. And in the whole of it the Church takes the lead. The world is again outwardly conquered, in the name of Christ, with a victory fairly equal to

that which won the throne of the Caesars in the beginning.
Dark ages indeed are to be gone through; a long night, comparatively speaking, of ignorance and superstition, violence and
wrong; for nations are not born in a day, and the great problems
of history ask centuries for their solution. But what then? Is
the Church to be held responsible for this necessity? So Kirwan would seem to think. Because she was not able to com-
press the work of ages into as many hours; because barbarous
nations did not at once become wise, and learned, and politically
free, under her magic hand; because her own constitution was
shaped and moulded, more or less, by the power of the rude life
with which she was called to deal; because, in one word, the
light and liberty, and institutions generally, of the nineteenth
century were not anticipated, under her auspices, in the ninth;
she is held up to reproach, as the very *mother* of all the darkness
and sin, through which the course of her history lay. What is
bad, is laid unsparingly to her charge; while all good is regarded
as going forward by some other force, and in spite both of her
power and will. Nay, we are told that no such onward movement can be allowed, in truth, to have taken place. It was all
one grand " retrograde" march, from the days of Alfred the Great
and Charlemagne, down to the sixteenth century; at which time
fortunately the Reformation occurred, to arrest the downward
tendency; just in season, apparently, to save the world from
universal barbarism, and a total extinction of the blessed light of
Christianity. So this precious theory runs!

It never entered Kirwan's head probably, seriously to compare
the actual civilization of Europe in the fifteenth century, with
what the same Europe was in the ninth and tenth centuries.
Had he done so, he would have found the rate of difference
quite as striking, in the way of advance, as any which has been
created by the progress of society since. The life of Europe,
in all that time, was neither stationary nor retrograde, but powerfully onward.

The entrance of the Middle Ages, as they are called, was in
the midst of universal chaos. With their going out, we behold
the presence of a new world; Europe reclaimed from barbarism;
forests cleared; lands cultivated; nations tamed and brought

under law; art, science, politics, trade, all actively awake; life as a whole, we may say, in universal motion. Academies and schools had multiplied on all sides. Of universities alone, as many as sixty-six were established before the year 1517, the date of the Reformation. Some of these were almost incredibly large. That of Paris formed a sort of commonwealth or state, within its own limits. Students and teachers were congregated there from all nations. Thought had acquired prodigious force, and stood ripe for the most brilliant exploits in literature and science. To talk of the revival of classic letters, the art of printing, the discovery of America, and other such agencies, as *originating* the scientific spirit of modern Europe, is infantile simplicity. Such powers were themselves possible only through the action of mind already awake, and only for such mind could they have been of any account. It required some culture, to welcome the learning of ancient Greece and Rome, when it was again brought to light. Men on the verge of barbarism take no pleasure in reading Plato; the songs of Pindar have no particular music for their ear; neither the strength of Thucydides, nor the grace of Herodotus, are apt to engage their taste. No importation of letters from Constantinople or anywhere else, would raise into enthusiasm the torpid mind of Mexico or China. "The very fact of the Reformation itself," as a distinguished Roman Catholic ecclesiastic has said, "presupposes a time, whose leading representatives occupied a very high grade of intellectual life; a period less awake, and possessed of only small furniture in the way of knowledge, could neither have produced it nor met it with proper support. Let any one compare with the Protestant Reformation the later dissensions of the Greek Church, and he must almost loathe their insignificance and want of character. The separation which took place from the Latin Church in the sixteenth century, on the contrary, both in the objects it sought, and in the principles from which it sprang, reveals something grand and full of meaning, reflecting thus a brilliant light, against its own will, on the Church it left behind, and in its very blame covering her with praise. Who can survey, without admiration, the polemic powers brought into action on both sides? Indeed the writings of Luther, Melancthon, Calvin, Chemnitz and Beza, on the one side, and the works of an Eck, Catharinus, Cochlaeus, Albert Pighius, Sadolet, Fisher, Thomas More, Reginald Pole, Vega, Andrada, and Bellarmine, on the other, in point of keen intelligence, eloquence and learning, afford a rare treat, which were it not embittered by other considerations, might be counted perfect. We know moreover, that the Reformers did not drop at once from heaven, when they first undertook to set the world right. It is no secret, where Luther went to school, whose instructions were enjoyed by Melancthon, who it was that put Calvin, still a little boy, into the use of a benefice, that the talent he saw in him might not go without means for its proper cultivation. The papal legate too is not unknown, to whom Zuingli was indebted, at the close of his academical studies, for a yearly pension, enabling him to enlarge his library."*

This way of looking at the subject, as it is infinitely more rational, seems to us also, we confess, to be vastly more complimentary to the Reformation itself, than the view we have just seen taken of it by Kirwan. The Reformation would be a very small affair, if it had sprung up like the mushroom of a night, from such a compost of pure ignorance and corruption, as his theory supposes the whole Church to have been before. The true glory of it, and its only sure vindication in the end, are found just in this, that it did *not* fall from the clouds, nor creep forth from a corner (the valleys of Piedmont for instance); but that it was the product of the old Catholic Church itself, and the very channel in which was carried forward the central stream of its history, the true significance of its life. The notion that all was dark before the sixteenth century, and that then all suddenly became light, however generally current at one time, is now fairly exploded. It is a fiction worthy only of the nursery, which, in truth, kills itself, and must sooner or later be hissed out of the world.

So far is it from being true that the Roman Church stood opposed systematically to learning, her zeal for it was urged against her at times, as implying a want of true interest in religion. Her

---

* Mæhler's *Schriften und Aufsætze.* Vol. II. pp. 12, 13. Considerations on the state of the Church in the fifteenth century and first part of the sixteenth.

theology was held to be too scholastic. Even Melancthon himself, at one time complained of the attention given to Plato in christian schools. It is generally made the reproach of Leo X. and his cardinals, that their taste for the classics spoiled all their relish for the Bible. The pope, at all events, ranked first among the patrons of polite learning. He it was, the scholar of Politian and Chalcondylas, the friend of Picus and Marsilius, who sent the Greek, John Lascaris, back to his own country, to purchase up manuscripts of the classics and of the Greek church fathers; who invited young men of talent, in large numbers, from Greece into Italy, to give instruction there in their native tongue; who made it his business to encourage so many deserving men, by pensions and in other ways, to devote their lives to the cause of science. The revival of letters was not a consequence strictly of the Reformation; just as little as we can say that our modern civilization in general, starts from it as its ultimate cause. It contributed powerfully, no doubt, to the whole course of mind since, and may be taken, indeed, as the indispensable condition of its universal progress; but the necessity for such progress lay far back of this particular revolution itself, in the previous state of the christian world. Europe could not wake into full life, without the Reformation; but the waking itself, was something more broad and deep, which simply came to its most signal expression in this great fact.

"A *reformation* in the higher sense of the word," it has been finely remarked by Ullmann, " is always a vast historical result; the outlet of a spiritual process that has extended through centuries; a deep all-constraining necessity, brought to pass indeed by the free action of great men as its chosen organs, which yet in its essential character rests on a comprehensive mass mind, that cannot be produced at will, but gradually forms itself with irresistible force out of the inmost wants of life. In such a continuous spiritual formation process, however, there must be before all things, an actuating positive soul or centre; for what is merely negative, doubt, rejection, the denial of what is at hand, is not sufficient by itself alone, to unite the minds of men in this massive way, and to hold them thus in tension through centuries, moving in a fixed direction. Neither in the physical world, nor in the moral, can any organic and enduring creation ever take place, except from the ground of a living fruitful germ, which holds in itself previously in the way of real power, all that is actually unfolded from its life; and this germ is always something positive, which first asserts its own existence, and only *then*, in order to win room for free growth, opposes and thrusts aside what is foreign and obstructive to its own nature. This general law we perceive also in every movement, that can at all lay claim to the dignity of a reformation in the sphere of religion. Reformation is a forming over again, a restoration of life. But in the conception of such a religious life-restoration, three things are essentially involved. *First*, it is a going back to something already given, and original; for a reformation, as distinguished from the first founding of a religion or ecclesiastical constitution, seeks not to make something entirely new, but only to renew what is already made; it moves always, accordingly, in a fixed historical sphere or tract, and loses its character when this tract is forsaken. *Secondly*, it is not a mere going back, a passive acknowledgment of the original, or a desire towards it, but above all an active *bringing* back of its power, a real renovation of that old faith in the form of life; this particularly constitutes its practical positive nature; it is a great historical fact, but one that rests on a given ground, clearly understood and acknowledged in the general consciousness, and which, for this very reason, forms itself again the foundation for farther development, new spiritual superstructure. *Lastly*, however, it lies also in the nature of a reformation, that it contends against what is false and sets aside what is out of date, that its "position" takes the form also of "opposition;" for the idea of renewing an original, implies that this original has in the course of time undergone distortion and falsification, that corruptions cleave to it which need to be removed; and to have free room for the new growth, what has run its course requires to be pruned away. Still a reformation, of the right sort, is never mere destruction as such, but always *creation*, involving destruction only as its unavoidable accident and condition." All these requirements meet, according to Ullmann, in the religious revolution of the sixteenth century. It was no accident, but an act which proceeded from the inmost

and deepest life of the world, and formed the grand turning point
of its universal modern history.   Such an act is not rationally
conceivable, without vast presuppositions.   " A world-historical
epoch of this sort requires, like a gigantic oak, deep, far reaching
roots, and firm solid ground, out of which to have grown.   It
betrays a poor sense of history, to seek the explanation of all
here in single personalities or transient interests.   These elements, indeed, must not be overlooked ; but the truly great, the
general, the enduring in history, springs from other and deeper
grounds.   Individuals make it not ; they serve it rather, and become great just by this, that they do so with clear conscious conviction and full resolution, and the greater and more powerful
always, in proportion as that is the case."   The grandeur, and
glory, and world-wide significance of the Reformation, stand
precisely in this, that the forces which finally brought it to pass,
had been maturing their strength and struggling in the same direction, for centuries before ; so that the sense of ages might be
said to become complete in the end by its presence.

In conclusion, with all becoming respect for the worthy author
of these Letters, and the fullest confidence in the integrity of
christian purpose with which they have been written, we are
bound to say that we think them suited to do harm rather than
good.   We like not their anti-catholic temper and tone, disguised
under the show of opposition merely to Popery and Rome ; the
rationalistic, nay, even radical, affinities and tendencies, that to
our mind at least, make themselves painfully prominent in their
whole character.   We deprecate the spread of such views and
feelings, in the holy name of Protestantism.   We must say, in
all solemn earnestness, we wish no such atmosphere of thought
ever to reach the education of our own children.   We would
train them rather to faith in the idea of the Church, and sympathy with the articles of the ancient Creed.   " Would to God that
you could see things as *I* see them," Kirwan exclaims in one
place, not without feeling, to Bishop Hughes.   The bishop
would say with equal earnestness, no doubt : " Would that *you*
could see them as they appear to *me*."   It is very certain, that
they move in different worlds, with little power on the part of
either to understand truly the position of the other.   The bishop

sees Protestantism in a false light; dwelling only on its abuses and errors; having no eye for the vast world of truth which it reveals, no sense by which to appreciate properly its inward significance and power. But it is no less clear, that Kirwan is full as much in the dark, as it regards the opposite side. The fundamental meaning of the Roman Catholic Church, is hid from his view. There is a whole region of Christianity there, which he has never yet been brought to explore or comprehend. He confounds Catholicism perpetually, as we have seen, with the abuses heaped upon it by Popery. However valuable his own form of piety may be, (and we wish not to dispute its worth,) there is another style of piety altogether, forming a complete *terra incognita* to his experience and beyond the horizon of his thinking, which we are yet bound to acknowledge as of high and necessary account also to the complete conception of the christian faith. The most comprehensive and significant designation for this order of religion, is found in the term *Catholic*; as we may employ the term *Puritan*, on the other hand, to express what we mean by religion under the opposite type. We use both terms in an honorable sense, and simply to express in brief the general distinction now noticed. Catholicism stands in the sense of the outward and objective in Christianity, as a supernatural constitution actually at hand in the world under a historical form; the idea of the Church, as the bearer of heavenly powers; submission to authority; resignation of individual judgment and will to the apprehension of a divine rule, embodied and made concrete in the Church as a whole; sympathy with the symbolical, mystical, sacramental interest in religion. It will not do to treat all this as an obsolete fiction. It has too much countenance from the Bible; it finds too much to appeal to in the inmost depths of our religious nature. Any scheme of piety, however excellent it may be in other respects, which breaks in full with the faith and devotional life of the entire early Church, eviscerates the Creed of its true force, and makes it impossible for us to feel ourselves at home in the society of such men as Ignatius and Polycarp, Irenaeus and Tertullian, Cyprian, Augustine, Anselm, Fenelon, and the ten thousand others whose saintliness had been more or less like theirs from the beginning; any scheme of piety that goes thus virtually, by its pretensions, to sap the very foundations of the Church itself, must be in its own nature defective and insecure. Puritanism must learn to do justice to Catholicism, before it can do full justice to itself. Its proper mission will be complete, only when the two forms of thinking are brought in some way to flow together, excluding on both sides all that is found to be incompatible with the idea of such a marriage.

We know full well, and have not forgotten for one moment, in all this review, that there is a Charybdis here as well as a Scylla, which we are bound on vast peril to shun and avoid. These Letters of Kirwan lie all on one side, covering at no great depth the treacherous *rock* we have now tried to expose; at some future time, if God permit, we shall take notice of the *whirlpool*, in an article, not on Bishop Hughes, but on "Brownson's Quarterly Review." J. W. N.

ART. XVI.—Zuingli no Radical.

The following extract is translated from Professor Ebrard's great work, on the History of the Doctrine of the Lord's Supper. It forms part of a somewhat extended vindication of the general character of the Swiss Reformer, against certain injurious views which have been entertained of it, in Germany particularly, and in the bosom of the Lutheran Church. He has been held up to reproach, as a man whose zeal for the Reformation was more bent on pulling down than on building up; and who was ruled by the cold mechanical abstractions of the understanding, more a great deal than by proper power of the christian faith. It has been the fashion widely to associate with his name, the idea of a somewhat rationalistic and revolutionary tendency in religion; which is supposed also by the high Lutheran school, to have communicated itself, as a reigning permanent distinction, to the entire Reformed Church. This whole supposition Dr. Ebrard meets, as being in the case of Zuingli, no

better than a pure fiction of fancy, or theological prejudice. He
insists upon it, that his theology was characterized throughout by a
regard to the inward positive life of christianity, in its supernatural
mystical form; and that even his sacramental doctrine itself, was
based all along on the assumption of a real participation in the *very life*
of Christ, as the necessary result of faith—something far deeper, of
course, than the rationalistic conception of a mere moral union with
him, which now so often affects to take shelter under the respectable authority of Zuingli's name. As for the notion of his being a
fanatical radical, in his reformatory action, it is treated as wholly
destitute of foundation. The extract here given, is intended to show,
and it must be allowed indeed to do so very triumphantly, that this
father of the Helvetic Reformation was, to say the least, full as con-
servative in his spirit as Luther, or any of the leaders of the same
movement in Germany:

If to some of our readers the quotations now presented may
perhaps seem too large and long for the end immediately in hand,
we would remind them that they all go not merely to meet particular complaints against our reformer, which have no direct
connection with the doctrine of the sacraments, but also at the
same time to give us an insight into the fundamental character
of his theology, *which is of the utmost consequence for the right
understanding of his view of the Lord's supper.* We see at
once, that Zuingli does not sunder faith scholastically from sanctification, but on the ground of his historical and biblical education apprehends both in their living organic union. Every
where he opposes the *totality of what Christ does,* to the totality
of what man can do without Christ, the decree of redemption
through Christ to all humanly devised ways of salvation, deliverance from guilt by Christ's death to satisfaction by good works,
sanctification by Christ's Spirit to the power of legal obedience.
The vicarious action of Christ appears thus in the most intimate
association with the vicarious passion of Christ. He makes good
our shortcomings, not simply by suffering punishment in our
stead, but also by *bringing to pass in us works* which we could
not bring to pass of ourselves. Sanctification is taken here not
as a subjective act growing out of faith, but as the immediate
operation of *Christ living in us;* and the oneness which holds
between the working of the *Holy Ghost* in us, and the life of

Christ himself in us, is thus apprehended in its deepest depth. With Zuingli accordingly, faith is not distinguished from sanctification, good works, the communion of the Holy Ghost, and the *mystical union*, but is regarded as the *totality of the new life*, which of itself involves all these from the start.

This will be very important for us hereafter. For the present we remark only how far Zuingli had entered into the true idea of Christian freedom. We see, that his opposition towards particular abuses proceeded not at all from the mere legal application of certain legally construed passages of Scripture, but from the most free and inward principle of faith. Allowing, however, the *ground* of this opposition to have been good, it is still asked whether the *manner* of it is not to be blamed as radical. Did he not mercilessly sweep away all that was old, even where it was free from harm?

Before we enter here upon the actual state of facts, it seems necessary first of all to clear out a whole Augean stable of prejudices and fables which busy *mythology* has contrived to throw around this part of the reformer's labors. To the Lutheran theologians, rather than to the Roman, belongs the credit of having vented their spleen upon him in the way of these ingenious imaginations; what one relates as dreadful, is made still a little worse in the hands of the next; and so the tattle runs through the polemical tradition, till it gains at last the show of well accredited history. What, did not Zuingli abolish everything! Not simply altars and images, but church music also, organs, ringing of bells, nay, the bells themselves, possibly even the steeples along? Is not the stale ory still in circulation, that he presented a petition to the Council for the suppression of church music, singing it himself, as he did so, to show practically the absurdity of using song in prayer—is not this flat story in circulation, we say, even in books and quite respectable theological journals, some of which we could easily name? Is it not the general impression that, while Luther retained all the old forms, and removed only what was doctrinally offensive, Zuingli made a clean sweep of the whole, and, then, constructed a poor scheme of his own in its place?

Against all this, at the outset, speaks the entire spirit of the good city, which Schiller has styled, not without reason, "the *old* Zurich." What is new in Zurich springs from 1830, or, at farthest, from 1790. It is questionable, if any German imperial city (Nuremberg even scarcely excepted) has retained its ancient manners, institutions, and usages, with so little change, for any like time, as Zurich. The small, narrow streets, whose hurdle-work still shows plainly, by towers, citadels, and remains of walls and trenches, the three several enlargements the city has gone through in the course of history, threw open the outermost ring of their gates and barricades, only a few years since, for free intercourse with the country. The old democratic usages prevailed universally down to 1830; and are still, at least, half in force. Even since the old corporations have lost their importance politically, they still continue to stand, as social fraternities, proud of their old guild houses, which, under different names, are familiar to every child. In a city, whose spirit has cleaved for centuries with such attachment throughout to what is old, it is not so easy a matter to make any such clean sweep as is here supposed. If now, however, we compare the Zuinglian changes with those of Luther and Calvin, we reach the surprising result, that, so far as *the principle and spirit* of the changes are concerned, Zuingli stands throughout on the side of Luther against Calvin. Calvin created entirely new forms; Zuingli, like Luther, retained all the old, and set aside only what gave offence. Only in *result*, not in principle, does he differ from Luther; in this namely that the images as such seemed to him doctrinal stumbling-blocks, while Luther made a more nice distinction between their edifying use as works of art, and their misuse as objects of idolatry.

It is regarded as an essential difference, that Luther retained the existing church organization; provosts, chapters, and archdeacons, parish priests, and deacons, all remained in their place; while Calvin proclaimed all ministers equal, and brought in with violent novelty the presbyterial and synodical system. We inquire not here which is best; we say simply, that Zuingli took the course of Luther. The cathedral chapter of Zurich, with its canons or prebendaries, stood till within a few years past, and the number of the members has not even yet died out, while the distinction between priest and deacon continues to this day in all its old legal force. The archdeacon too, or "chief

helper," has not become strange to the Reformed church of the
Zuinglian type.—Another small, but characteristic, difference,
is, that Luther retained in the Lord's prayer the old and more
hard form: "*Vater unser,*" which the Calvinistic Reformed church
of German tongue changed, (after Luther's own translation of
the Bible however,) into "*Unser Vater.*" Zuingli allowed, as
Luther, the old *Vater unser* to keep its place, and it remained there
in the Zurich church service till near the close of the last century.—Calvin set aside baptismal fonts; Luther and Zuingli allowed them to stand, and in Zurich, where all the children are
baptized in public service, they are still in use every week.—
Calvin abolished private baptism in extreme cases by midwives;
Zuingli, and Luther, did not; the Zuinglian Reformed church,
moreover, was more consistent with it, than the Lutheran, as not
permitting the baptism to be repeated in case the child lived.—
Another small but significant difference between the Calvinistic
Reformed church and the Lutheran, is shown in regard to the
renting of church sittings, a practice set aside by the first, while
it is retained by the last; here again Zuingli stands on Luther's
side.   The Calvinistic church eschews crosses in grave yards,
which with the Lutheran and Zuinglian are in general use. In
observing christening-days as family festivals, instead of birth
days, the Zuinglian church is even nearer to the Roman than
the Lutheran itself.—Let us look now, in full, to the Liturgy!
Calvin constructed a new liturgy, on a new plan, the greatness
of which, with all its simplicity, we have no wish to dispute.
Zuingli, in his work *De canone Missae,* has followed the mass
service, part for part, word for word, leaving out merely, or
changing, all passages referring to the sacrifice of the mass and
the worship of saints, so as to form a sacramental liturgy that
was afterwards subjected, indeed, to various contractions on account of its undue length, but which still rests throughout on the
old foundation, and breathes the spirit of antiquity; and which
continues in use to this day.   While the eucharistic liturgies of
Calvinistic type consist of a simple didactic address, which is
followed by a common extended prayer, and then by the dis
tribution of the elements, the Zuinglian form, or the contrary, is
made up of a number of smaller parts. It commences with the

ancient *introitus*, the translated *Dignum et justum est &c.*; then
1 Cor. 11, is read; after which the minister says (with the whole
congregation originally), "*Glory be to God!*" Next follows a
long responsory, now generally repeated by two ministers alternately. Then the familiar response between pastor and people:
"*The Lord be with you—'and with thy spirit;'*" then a lesson
from the sixth chapter of John; after another brief responsory, the
Creed; then a short exhortation; the Lord's prayer; a prayer
taken from the old mass service; the reading of the words of
institution; the distribution of the elements; the 117th psalm,
a closing prayer, and the benediction. In the same way, Zuingli
retained the old baptismal service, with proper pruning. We
find mention made of the chrisom cloth, on even to near the
end of the 16th century.

But he put away the bells? These still swing in their places,
and Zurich possesses verily a magnificent chime.—But they were
not used for years; Zuingli would not suffer them to ring? Not
for storms, true; otherwise bell ringing, in all its ancient classification, from the sound made at the beginning *and close* of divine
service, on through eleven o'clock, noon and vesper chimes,
down to the "coffee bell" at three o'clock in the afternoon, has
been religiously observed, in defiance of the Nurembergers,
through all centuries. Strange stories, indeed, are told of the
love of the Zurichers for bells. On one occasion, (if we mistake not, 1712,) they are said to have brought off from a war
with St. Gall, as *spolia opima*, a huge bell, transporting it in triumph to Zurich, with a team of forty-six horses!—But the cleri-
cal garments were abolished by Zuingli? The chasuble, (mass
dress,) true. In other respects, the ministers until within a few
years since, never appeared at regular church service, or at funerals
even, and in family visitation, otherwise than in gown and cap,
and with the large white ruff.—Has not Zurich, however, a synodical government? The Church, as of old, is divided into
deanries, which have their deans and camerarii, and stand under
the direction of the consistory or church senate, with the antistes
at its head. Once a year, the clergy in general, convene in a
synod, over which the same antistes presides, and which corresponds in its character more with the medieval councils than with

the Calvinistic synods.   By the antistes, besides, an episcopal
element has place in the system.—But the church psalmody?
the church psalmody? why did Zuingli abolish the church psalmody?   *What* church psalmody, we ask.   The chorals, perhaps?   Nothing of this sort was abolished by Zuingli, nor could
be indeed—since the Zurichers, as well as the Nurembergers,
" hang no one till he is first caught."   The chanted offices of
the convents and the Latin sing-song of the mass, Zuingli did
set aside.   Luther, it is known, did the same thing ; even the
pope wished this reform, and would have actually accomplished
it, had not Palestrina appeared with his new school.*   The light
in which the psalmody of that time was regarded, is briefly and
aptly represented by the Tetrapolitan Confession, (cap. 21,) as
follows : *(Cantiones et preces) a prima patrum consuetudine
usuque degenerasse abunde constat.*   An endless ringing of Latin psalms to trivial melodies, street ballads often, suited not the
purposes of christian worship.   Not long since we read, where
we would not have expected it, that Zuingli threw overboard the
glorious creations of medieval art.   It was forgotten here, that
the music, as well as painting, which we admire as old, springs
not from the middle ages, but is of the age of the Reformation
or later.   Palestrina, Durante, Orlando Lasso, Lotti, composed
their immortal hymns after Zuingli's time.   So with the paint-
ers ;   Raphael (†1520) was Zuingli's contemporary, Durer his
friend and secret adherent ; Corregio, (†1534,) Kranach, (†1553,)
Holbein, (†1554,) Michael Angelo, (†1564,) Titian, (†1576,)
Rubens, (†1640,) Murillo, (†1685,) all belong, with their main
labors at least, to the person after his death.   So the Nuremberg
proverb, that no one is hanged before being caught, may be applied also to the hanging of Raphael's and Durer's pictures, and
with slight alteration also to the church psalmody.   The true
state of the case is, that Zuingli abolished nothing save what Luther would also have abolished, the Latin singing, namely, of
the clergy ; but that Luther was able, sooner than Zuingli, to
substitute something new in place of the old which was set aside,
namely, the choral singing of the congregation.   In this, the last

* See *Thibaut's* work on the Purity of Music.

is indeed very clear of fault.   Luther was a poet; Zuingli made
some verses also, it is true, but poet he was not.   Thus Saxony
acquired a church psalmody *sooner* than Switzerland.   This
" sooner," however, is all that can be made of the matter.   As
soon as such psalmody made its way into Switzerland, it was
laid hold of with earnest, we might say even voracious desire.
As early as 12 Aug. 1526, Oecolampadius informed his friend
Zuingli with enthusiasm, how his congregation had of their own
accord begun to sing German psalms in the church.*   We see
how far the Swiss reformers were from any opposition to congregational singing as such.   In a short time it became universal
throughout Reformed Switzerland; and so it continues, in the
highest style of choral psalmody, to this day.

The only case then which remains at last, is that of the
images.   Here, too, we boldly undertake our Zuingli's vindication.

Professor Ebrard then goes into a historical review of the way,
in which the reformation in Zurich was carried forward in regard to
this subject.   The question, whether pictures, as works of Christian
art, might not be used, for exciting devotional feeling, in public
worship, was not one, he says, upon which any decision was called
for in Switzerland at this time.   The whole concern was in regard
to images only, which had been previously the *object of superstitious
veneration.*   What Zuingli says in opposition to images, is said
against them always in such view.   Luther contended against image
abolitionists, who made a sin of images legalistically as such, and
thought that everything was done, when they were outwardly
demolished; the great matter he saw, was to have them expelled
from the heart; the idol and the work of art must be properly
distinguished.   Zuingli, on the other hand, contended with such
as defended, not only the images, but image worship itself; in
a situation too, where the images had already become a shib-
boleth between Popery and the Reformation.   Here it was
necessary to insist upon it as a part of *Christian freedom,* that
the Church has a right to remove images.   In such spirit, the
opposition to them went forward in Zurich.   It was neither rash
nor radical. but considerate and sober throughout: showing all due
regard to the prejudices of the weak; advancing not a step outwardly, for which full room was not made previously in the way of
inward preparation.   About the end of Sept. 1523, a certain *Nicholas*

* Without doubt Luther's *"Psalmlieder"* as published by Wolff Koepphel,
in Strassburg, 1526.

Hottinger took it upon himself to break down a crucifix, in one of the suburbs of Zurich ; for which he was thrown into the prison, with Zuingli's approbation. A woman in Luzerne had set up an image, in fulfilment of a vow, which soon became a resort for many pilgrims ; on her conversion to the Protestant faith, she burned it with her own hand ; whereupon she was fined, and required to restore it again to its place. In this judgment Myconius directed her to acquiesce as just, she had no right to destroy thus what was no longer her own. The anti-image spirit was excited, not by Zuingli, but by *Ludwig Hetzer's* tract : "The Judgment of God, our Spouse : how to treat all idols and images, as drawn from the holy scriptures ;" a work, of which three editions, in the year 1523, were at once sold. Great commotion followed. A commission was appointed to investigate the question. A second conference took place, Oct. 26, 27, and 28, 1523, in the presence of 350 ministers and 450 laymen ; the result of which was a resolution, that no change should be made at that time, in regard either to images or the mass. Zuingli was directed to write on the subject, for the instruction of the people. This was done, and with good effect. The next year, a *third* disputation was held. Still no action was taken against the images ; they were allowed to keep their place a whole year longer, in accommodation to the prejudices of such as were still unprepared for their removal.

Finally, on Easter, 12. April, 1525, the Christian Lord's supper was celebrated in room of the mass—a solemnity of which *Gerdesius* has left us an impressive account ; and as a preparatory step, the images were removed. The three city ministers, with certain members of the council and the necessary workmen, went from church to church, and with closed doors took them all down, and brought them away to the Water church. The clear trash among them was afterwards burnt ; the better pictures are preserved to this day in the Water church, (now the city library). There is to be seen a coronation of Mary ; there are the patron saints, Felix, and Regula, all stiff productions belonging to the transition period from the Byzantine over to the old German school ; there again are some naked figures of martyrs, tortured with thorns, shocking to look upon ; above all, however, there is that wonderful saint, the smith Erhardt or Eligius, who cut off the legs of the horses, he was called to shoe, and having shod them in such style, restored them sound to their place, (a miracle, to which the coat of Treves is nothing !)—articles all, that must tend much, in truth, to the edification of Evangelical worshippers! We may understand from this, why it came so little in Zuingli's way to take his estimate of images, from the side of their artistic worth, their adaptation to produce feeling. If these pictures have any importance, it is only for the study of the history of art; and for this a library is altogether the most suitable place.

I must ask the indulgence of my readers, who have been carried along with me in this digression. It is not, however, my fault. So long as Zuingli remains as good as unknown, so long as he is absolutely misknown, so long as a caricature, a fanatical enthusiast and a man of mere dry understanding withal, is made to pass for him in the brain of the German theological public, so long also must it be a pure impossibility to apprehend the sacramental controversy between Luther and Zuingli in its true meaning and significance. It would be hard, indeed, to find the apprehension of a doctrine more intimately blended with the entire man, and his whole sense of Christianity, than just here in the case of Zuingli.

ART. XVII.—THE PERSON OF CHRIST.

The " Person of Christ," according to the Older Theologians of the Evangelical Lutheran Church. By Heinrich Schmid. Translated from the German and Latin by Chas. P. Krauth, Pastor of the Evangelical Lutheran Church, Winchester, Va.

[The title of the entire work from which this chapter is translated, is, "Die Dogmatik der Evangelisch-Lutherischen Kirche. Erlangen. 1843." It is designed to present the doctrines of the Lutheran Church as they were held when her faith was purest. Under each head, there is a summary statement of the doctrine of the church, by the author, and in the notes ample citations are made from the standards and standard authors of the church, to confirm and illustrate his general view. The arguments for the various doctrines can, therefore, only come in incidentally—the grand object being a display of the doctrines themselves. To those who have not access to the great sources from which these rich treasures are drawn, a work like this will be of very great value. To those familiar with the great teachers of the Lutheran Church, the work of Schmid would still form a valuable remembrancer and arranger, and to those who have a longing to drink at these wells of undefiled theology, this work, which is ably executed, would form the guide they need; for as old Quenstedt, to whom he would often find himself introduced, has well said, in the Preface to his great system of Didactic and Polemic Theology: "Scire, ubi aliquid possis invenire, magna pars est eruditionis." Tr.]

Chap. II.—*Of the Fraternal Redemption of Christ as another Element of Salvation.*

§. 31.

The redemption determined of God from eternity, was in time consummated(1) by his only begotten Son Jesus Christ, and of

(1) Holl.* "The Redeemer of the human race is Jesus Christ. The Redeemer is called Jesus, that is, Saviour, because he is to save his people from their sins. Matt. i. 21.—He is called Christ, that is, anointed, because he has been annointed by the holy Spirit as our king, priest, and prophet. John iii. 41.—The DD. declare farther that Jesus Christ is the 'true Messiah, in whom all the prophecies of the O. T. concerning the Messiah are fulfilled to the minutest particular.' " Holl. "Proof 1) whosoever is God, and man, is the true Messiah. But Jesus &c. The major is evident from 2 Sam. vii. 12, 13. Ps. cx. 1. Mich. v. 1. Jer. xxiii. 5, . . 2) Whosoever is born of the seed of Abraham, of the tribe of Judah, of the family of King David, and of a virgin undefiled, is the true Messiah. Major from Gen. xxii. 18. xlix. 10 2 Sam. vii. 12. Is. vii. 14. Minor from Luke ii. 23. 3.) Whatsoever ruler of Israel, as God, begotten from Eternity, as man, in the fullness of time, has been born at Bethlehem, 'is the true Messiah.' Major from Mich. v. 1.

---

* **Note by Translator.**—The following abbreviations are used in citing authorities:

Br.—J. G. Baier, Compendium Theologiæ Positivæ. Jena. 1686.
Chem.—Chemnitz, De Duabis Naturis in Christo. 1590.
DD.—Dogmatick Theologians.
Form. Con.—Formula Concordiæ. (I. Epitome. II. Solida Deebratio.) 1580.
Grh.—Gerhard. Loci Theologici. Jena. 1610—1625.
Hfrffr.—Matt. Hafenreffer, Loci Theologici. Holmiæ 1612.
Holl.—Hollazius. Examen, &c. Holmiæ. 1707.
Quen.—J. A. Quenstedt. Theologia didactico-polemica, &c. 1685.

this we here propose to treat. This doctrine involves a consideration I. of the person of the Redeemer: II. of the work, by which he has secured that redemption; III. of the different states involved in his incarnation.

1. *Of the Person of Christ.*

§. 32. *Unition—personal union.*

In Christ we observe a duality of natures and a unity of persons, in accordance with the expression: " in Christ, born of the Virgin Mary, are two natures, the divine nature of the Logos, and the human nature, so united that Christ might become one person." (Chemn.) If we regard this point with reference to its distinct parts, we would speak

　　I. Of the two natures in Christ;

　　II. Of the Person of Christ.

I. When we say of Christ, He is God and man, it is but another way of expressing the idea, that he exists in two natures, the divine and human.(1) Yet we must regard each of these na-

---

Minor from Matt. ii. 6. . . 4.) Whosoever at his coming hath his way prepared by a forerunner sent of God, he is the true Messiah. Major from Is. lx. 3. Mal. iii. 1. Minor from Mar. i 23. 5.) Whatsoever king of Zion enters Jerusalem poor and lowly, riding upon an ass, he is the true Messiah. Zach. ix. 9 . . 6.) Whosoever is Goel, or Redeemer, by right of consanguinity Job. xix. 25, a prophet like unto Moses Deut. xviii. 15, a king universal Zach. ix. 9. Ps. lxxii. 8, a priest according to the order of Melchizedek Ps. cx. 4, a priest interceding for sinners Is. liii. 12, to endure the last extremities Ps. xxii. Is. liii., to die Dan. ix. 26, to be buried Is. liii. 9, to be free from corruption, to descend into hell, and to rise again Ps. xvi. 10, to ascend to heaven Ps. lxviii. 18, to sit at the right hand of God the Father Ps. cx. 1, he is the promised Messiah. All which things the New Testament asserts of Jesus of Nazareth.

(1) Hfrlfr. "By the natures two principles, or parts (so to speak), are to be understood, of which the person of Christ is constituted, to wit: 'the divine and human nature.' Of *person* the remark is made—The person of our Redeemer is here considered not as ασαρκος or such as it was before the incarnation from eternity; but as ενσαρκος or such as it began to be in the fullness of time by the assumption of our human nature into its own divine hypostasis." (Holl.)

General Definition of *"nature"* and *"person"*: Chemn. "Essence, or substance, or nature, is that, which of itself is common to many

tures in its complete verity and full integrity,([2]) for Christ is true

individuals of the same species, and which embraces the whole essential perfection of each of them."

"Person, or Individual, is something singular, which has indeed an entire and perfect substance of the same species: but determined or limited by some characteristic and personal property, and thus being distinguished and separated, not in essence, but in number, from the remaining individuals of the same species, subsists by itself. For a person is an individual intelligent substance, incommunicable, which is neither part of another, nor is sustained by another, nor has dependence on another. Thus, therefore, $\theta\epsilon\acute{o}\tau\eta\sigma$, $\dot{\alpha}\nu\vartheta\rho\acute{\omega}\pi\tau\eta\sigma$, deity, humanity, divine nature, human nature, divine essence, human substance, are names of essence or of natures. God, man, are appellations of person"

On the distinction of meaning, when the word nature, or essence, is applied to God, and men. Comp. on the Trinity. Not. 11. Quen. "(Of the divine nature of Christ): The divine nature otherwise, signifies the divine essence one in number, common to all the three persons and entire in each, but in the article of the person of Christ it is not absolutely considered, in as far as it is common to the three persons of deity, but relatively, in as far as it subsists in the person of the Son of God, and is limited $\tau\rho\acute{o}\pi\omega\ \iota\nu\alpha\ \xi\epsilon\upsilon\varsigma\acute{\alpha}$ in the second person of the Trinity. Whence the whole divine essence is united to human nature, but in one of its hypostasis to wit the second."

(2) Holl. "Counc. of Chalcedon: We confess (him to be) true God, and true man, the latter consisting of a rational soul and a body, co-essential with the Father according to his divinity and co-essential with us according to his humanity, in all things like to us, sin excepted."

Quen. "With reference to his human nature is to be considered 1.) its verity; 2.) entireness; 3.) $\acute{o}\mu oov\sigma\iota\alpha$. The first denies it to be a phantasm, the second that it is partial, the third $\acute{\epsilon}\tau\epsilon\rho ovo\acute{\iota}\alpha\nu$."

Gerh. "In Christ is a true and perfect divine nature, and thence also Christ is true, natural and eternal God. We say not only that divine gifts, but that also a true and perfect divine nature, is in Christ, nor do we simply say, that he is, and is called God, but that he is true, natural and eternal God, that, in this way, we may more clearly separate our confession from the blasphemies of the Pholinians, and of all $\vartheta\epsilon o\mu\acute{\alpha}\chi\omega\nu$."

Gerh. "In Christ is a true, entire and perfect human nature, and thence, also, is true, perfect and natural man —By the *verity* of his human nature is understood, that the Logos did not assume a phantasm, or mere external appearance of human nature, but in very deed has become man. By *entireness* of human nature is understood, that he assumed all essential parts of human nature into unity of his person, not only a body, but also a rational soul, so that

God and true man.(3) As true man he partakes in all the natural
infirmities to which human nature is subject, not, however, in
consequence of a natural necessity, but in consequence of his
free will, in order to the promotion of his mediatorial commission ; for, inasmuch as he truly was born of man, of the Virgin
Mary, but was not begotten of a human father, his human nature
has also received nothing of all that which was the first consequence of Adam's sin.(4)　This does not prevent us from predi-

his flesh became animated flesh. Nor do we say alone, that he was
man, but that he still is, for what he has once assumed he never
has nor ever will lay down ''

(3) Holl. I. ''His true and eternal divinity is proved by the
most solid arguments, taken *a)* from the divine names (arg ονομασ-
τικοις); *b)* from attributes proper to the true God alone (arg.
ιδιωματικοις); *c)* from the personal and essential acts of God (arg.
ενεργητικοις); *d)* from religious worship due to God alone (arg.
λατρευτικοις); compare on the Trinit n 34.''
II. ''That Christ was true man is demonstrated *a)* from human
names, John viii. 40 1 Tim ii 5 ; *b)* from the essential portions of
man,　John ii 21. Hebr ii 14. Luke xxiv. 39.　John x. 15.
Math. xxvi. 38. Luke ii. 52　John v. 21.　Math. xxvi 39;
c) from attributes proper to true man, Math. iv 2 John xix 28.
Math xxv. 37 Luke xix. 41 Joh. xi. 33 ; *d)* from human operations, Luke ii. 46. 48 Math. iv 1. xxvi 55.; *e)* from the genealogy
of Christ as man (as to the ascending line Luke iii. 23, as to the descending line Math. i. 1,) ''
We must then distinguish a *''double generation,''* an *''eternal
generation,* through which he is Son of God'', and a *''temporal generation,* through which he is man, or son of man, Gal. iv. 4.''　(Br.)
(4) Chemn.　''Christ being conceived of the H. Spirit, assumed
human nature without sin, incorrupt.　Those infirmities therefore,
which, as penalties, attend sin, would not have been a necessary
condition in the flesh of Christ, but he could have kept his body
free from, and unexposed to, those infirmities.　For a flesh of sin
was not necessary to his being true man, as Adam, before his fall
without those penal infirmities, was true man.　But, on account of
us and for our salvation, Christ incarnate, that he might commend
his love unto us, voluntarily assumed those infirmities, . . . that so
he might bear the penalty transferred from us to himself and might
free us from it '' Hence Holl.: ''Christ assumed *natural infirmities*
common to all men placed in the natural state ; but he did not take
on him *personal infirmities,* arising from particular causes, far less
those implying moral evil.''—''*Natural common infirmities of men*
are, those found in all men after the fall, as to hunger, thirst, suffer

cating of Christ a true and complete humanity, like unto us, as the same may also be predicated of Adam, since the original sin which comes upon us in consequence of the sin of Adam, has not converted the nature of man into another; but it may well be a consequence of the special circumstances which by the birth of Christ had their being, and from the special relation which the divine λόγος has to this human nature, that special properties may be predicated of the human nature of Christ, in which it has advantages over that of other men. These are 1.) the ἀνυποστασία; 2.) the ἀναμαρτασία; 3.) the "singular excellence of soul and body."(5) The first is consequent on the special relation

fatigue, to be cold, hot, sorrowful, angry, agitated, to weep; which, since they are blameless, the holy Scripture attests, were assumed by Christ, not of force, but freely, not for his own sake, but for ours (Quen: that he might perform the functions of the mediatorial office, and become a sacrifice for our sins), not for ever, but for a time, to wit, in the state of exinanition, but not retaining them in a state of exaltation. Personal infirmities are, those which originate in particular causes, and have their source in a defect δυνάμεως πλαστικῆ, or of efformative power in the parent, as consumption, gout, or from a particular fault, as for example from gluttony or other excesses, as fever, dropsy, &c, or from a particular providence, or divine judgment, as disease in a family (2 Sam. iii 20) These were very far removed from the most sacred humanity of Christ, as to have assumed them was not expedient to the human race and would have derogated from human dignity."

(5) Holl. "Certain individual properties meet in the human nature of Christ, in which, as if ἱπεροχαῖς, or in certain prerogatives, he surpasses other men; of this kind are: a) ἀνυποστατὶ wanting proper subsistence, compensated by the divine hypostasis of the Son of God as far more eminent —If the human nature of Christ had retained its proper subsistence, there would have been two persons and consequently two mediators in Christ, contrary to 1 Tim ii. 5. The reason is: because a person by subsistence to the highest degree complete, is formally constituted, in its own being, and consequently from unity of subsistence unity of person, is to be estimated. It follows therefore, that one or other nature of those, which coalesce into one person, must be devoid of its proper subsistence: and since the divine nature, which is really the same with its subsistence, cannot be devoid of it, it is evident that to the human nature is to be attributed the want of a proper subsistence. From ἀνυποστασία we must distinguish the ἐνυποστασία: : Quen ἀνυπόστατον is, that which does not subsist by itself according to a proper

into which the divine λόγος has entered with the human nature; this, to wit: is at no time to be regarded as subsisting for itself and forming a person for itself, for the λόγος has assumed no human person, but only a human nature. The ἀνυποστασία is, therefore negatively predicated of the human nature, in so far as this human nature attains no proper personality, positively the ἐνυποστασία in so far as another hypostasis, that of the divine nature, participates in this human nature.

The ἀνυποστασία is expressly taught in many places of sacred

personality: ἐνυπόστατον however, that which subsists in another and has been made partaker in the hypostasis of another. When, therefore, the human nature of Christ is called ἀνυπόστατος, nothing else is meant than that it does not subsist by itself, and according to its own self in proper personality: but it is called ἐνυπόστατος, because it has been made partaker of another hypostasis, and subsists in the Logos."

Holl. notices the following objection: "You say, if the human nature is devoid of proper subsistence, it will be more imperfect than our nature αὐθυπόστατος, or subsisting by itself? Answ.: The perfection of a thing is to be estimated by its essence, not by its subsistence."—And there is weight in the observation of Gerh.: "That impersonality of flesh, which some assign as the *terminus a quo* of incarnation, which distinguishes between a subsistence, by which that mass from which the body of Christ was formed, subsisted as a part of the virgin, not by the proper and very subsistence of the virgin, and between a subsistence, by which the human nature from the sanctified mass, formed by the operation of the holy Spirit, began in the first moment of incarnation to subsist by the very subsistence of the Logos communicated to it, that is not be received in a sense that implies that, at any time whatever, the flesh of Christ was completely impersonal: but that, in our thought, the impersonality of such flesh, before its reception into subsistence of the Logos, is assumed, not in previous order of time, but of nature. That flesh and soul were not previously united into one person, but there were simultaneously a formation of flesh from the mass which had been operated and sanctified by the holy Spirit, the animation of that flesh thus formed, the assumption of the formed and animated flesh into subsistence of the Logos, the conception of the flesh formed, animated and subsisting in the womb of the Virgin."

b) Sinlessness (ἀναμαρτησία). Chemn. "'Therefore,' said Gabriel to Mary, 'the holy Spirit shall come upon thee, and the power of the Most High shall overshadow thee, that what shall be born of thee, shall be holy.' By the operation of the holy Spirit therefore, it was effected that the Virgin Mary, without the seed of man, con-

scripture, (2 Cor. v. 21, Heb. vii. 26, Is. liii. 9, Dan. ix. 24, Luke i. 35, 1 Pet. i. 19, ii. 22,) and follows also from the supernatural birth of Christ.   The "*singular excellence of soul and body* from his sinlessness.

II. The person of the Redeemer was formed by the union of the λόγος, the second Person of the Godhead, the Son of God, with human nature so closely and intimately, that the two united natures form only one person, that of the Redeemer, the God-man.(6)   The act itself, by which this was accomplished, is called "*personal unition.*"   Holl. "*A divine action, by which the Son of God took human nature into unity of his own per-*

ceived and became pregnant.   And that mass, which the Son of God in that conception assumed from the flesh and blood of Mary, the holy Spirit so sanctified and purified from all taint of sin, that, what was born of Mary, was holy. Is. liii. 9. Dan. ix. 24. Luke i. 35. 2 Cor. v. 21· Heb. vii. 26· 1 Pet. i. 19. ii. 22.   (Quen. I call the sinlessness inhesive, not imputative; for our sins have been truly imputed to him, and he has been made sin for us. 2 Cor. v. 21)."

c) "Singular excellence of soul and body.   Quen: Threefold perfection of soul, of intellect. will, and desire : (Holl. : the soul of Christ holds the elements of wisdom, Luke ii. 46. John vii. 46. . . of holiness).   Perfection of body : α. the highest ευκρασία, a good and equable bodily temperament; β. ἀθανασία, or immortality (Holl. : which belongs to him, as well on account of the integrity of a sinless nature, Rom. vi. 23· as on account of the indissoluble chain of the personal union. Christ, therefore, by reason of an intrinsic principle, is immortal, and the fact that he died, arises from an extrinsic principle, and according to a voluntary οικονομια·, John x. 17—18.   In that death, however, which he freely underwent, the body of Christ remained αφθαρτον, or free from corruption, Ps. xvi. 10. Acts ii. 31.); γ. the highest elegance and beauty of form, Ps. xlv. 3. (Holl. : The beauty of Christ's body is judged by the excellence of the soul that dwelt in it, and from the direct action of the Holy Ghost, by whose ἐπελευσει the most glorious shrine of the body of Christ was formed.   Quen : That he is said to be despised and rejected of men (vulg. most abject of men) Is. liii. 3. relates to the disfigurement consequent on the wounds of his passion)."

(6) Holl. "The divine and human natures existing in the one person συνθετω of the Son of God, have one and the same hypostasis, diverse, however, in the way in which it is had.   For the divine nature has it primarily, of itself, and independently; but the human nature secondarily, on account of the personal union, and therefore by participation."

son, in the womb of the Virgin Mary.(7)   This act has been
willed and determined by the entire holy Trinity; by them has
the mass been prepared, of which the human nature consists,
and by them has it been united with the divine nature; but this
act has been consummated by the second person of the Godhead, who alone has become man.(8)   This second Person of
the Godhead, the Logos, is so related in the act of union to the

(7) Br.   "The union of the human nature with the divine consists in this: that those natures are so conjoined, that they become
one person.   Synonymous expressions are: σάρκωσις, ἐνσάρκωσις, σα,-
κογευνησία, incarnation, inhumanation, and incorporation (ἐνανθρώπη-
σις κα. ἐνσωμάτωσις,) assumption (πρόσληπσις).
   Quen.   "The basis of this mystery: John i. 14.   Gal. iv. 4.
1 Tim. iii 16. Hebr. ii. 11. 13   Rom xi. 5."
   Definition: Holl.   "Incarnation is a divine act, by which the
Son of God, in the womb of his mother, the Virgin Mary, assumed
into unity of his own person, a human nature, consubstantial with
us, but without sin, devoid of proper subsistence, and communicated
to the same alike his divine hypostasis and nature, so that now the
ἐ ἀνθρωπος Christ subsists perpetually in the two natures, divine and
human, most closely united."

   (8) Gerh.   "The work of incarnation is said to be common to
the whole Trinity, as to the act: but proper to the Son, as to the
terminus of the flesh assumed, which is λόγου ἐνόστασις; the work is
called *ad extra*, and essential, or common, to the whole Trinity, as
to the effect or production: but *ad intra*, and personal or proper to
the Son, as to the termination, or relation   The act of assumption
proceeds from the divine power common to the three persons, the
terminus of assumption is a ὑπόστασις proper to the Son. —The
Father sent the Son into the world   The holy Spirit supervening
sanctified those drops of blood, and purified them from sin, from
which the body of Christ was formed, so that what should be born
of Mary, might be holy, and by divine power it might be wrought
in the blessed virgin that, apart from the order of nature, she might
conceive a fœtus, without virile seed.   The Son descended from
heaven overshadowed the virgin, came in the flesh, being made
flesh, by partaking of the same, manifesting himself in it, assuming
it into unity of his person"   (In Luke i. 35, by "power of the
highest" is generally understood the Son)   Holl. "Overshadowing
denotes a secret, and wonderful filling of the temple of the body
reared by the holy Spirit   To wit: the Son of God overshadowed
the Virgin Mary, whilst, in an unsearchable mode, he descended
into the womb of the virgin and, by a peculiar approximation, filled
and united to himself that virgin mass of blood excited by the holy

human nature, that he, the Logos, forms the person(9) as in general he is the efficient, through which the union is brought about; for it is he who has an active relation to human nature, who

Spirit, so that σωματικῶς he might dwell in it as his proper temple. — The conception Ἱεανθρώπου is appropriated to the holy Spirit Luke i. 35. *a)* because the whole work of fecundation is ascribed to him, Gen. i. 2; *b)* that the purity of that mass of blood, from which the flesh of Christ grew, might be more evident; *c)* that so there might be the same cause for the generation of Christ as man, and our regeneration, to wit, the Holy Spirit. The material principle, and that entire, of the conception and production of Christ the man, is Mary, a spotless virgin (Is. vii. 14.) of the royal stem of David, and, therefore, sprung from the tribe of Judah (Luke iii. Acts. ii. 30). The material principle, partial and proximate, is the animated seed of the Virgin Mary (Hebr. ii. 14. 16).''

(9) Chemn. "The human nature did not assume the divine, nor did man assume God, nor did a divine person assume a human person: but the divine nature of the Logos, or God the Logos, or person of the Son of God, subsisting from eternity in the divine nature, assumed, in the fullness of time, a certain mass of human nature, so that there would be in Christ the nature assuming, to wit, the divine, and the nature assumed, to wit, the human. But, in other cases, a human nature is always the nature of some particular individul, whose property it is to subsist in some certain hypostasis, which, by some characteristic peculiarity, is distinguished from all other hypostases of the same nature. So each man has his proper body and his proper soul. In Christ incarnate, however, a certain divine nature, before this union, subsisted by itself, and that, indeed, from eternity. But not thus did that mass of the nature assumed subsist, before this union, by itself, so that, before this union, it was the proper body of some particular and distinct individual, and a proper soul, i. e. a person peculiar and subsisting in itself, which afterwards the Son of God assumed. But, in that conception, the Son of God assumed that mass of human nature into unity of his own person, so that he subsists and is sustained in it; and, by assuming, made it proper to himself, so that the body is not the body of another individual, or of another person, but the proper body of the Son of God himself, and the soul is the proper soul of the Son of God himself —The 'Communication of hypostases, or of subsistence,' proceeds also from the Logos: Holl. 'Communication of hypostases is, that the Son of God truly and really brought his divine ὑπόστασιν to communion and participation of the human nature destitute of proper personality which he assumed, so that the same reaches a terminus, is complete in subsisting, and is constituted in the ultimate hypostatic *esse.*' "

assumes it, whilst the human nature stands to him in a passive relation.(10)   This close union then, of the divine and human nature, regarded as a state, is called " *the personal or hypostatic union.*" Holl. " *The personal union is the conjunction of the two natures, the divine and human, subsisting in one hypostasis of the Son of God, implying a mutual and indissoluble communion of each nature.*"(11) To wit: it is a result of this effi· ciency of the Logos, that the hypostasis of the divine nature has now also become a hypostasis of the human nature; i. e., the two natures have now one hypostasis, that of the Logos, and

(10) Quen. "But of these two extremes (of divine and human nature) one has regard to the agent, or to one who perfects, the other to the passive and perfectable. The former is the Son of God, or, simple person of the Logos, or, what is the same, the divine nature, determined by the hypostasis of the Logos: the latter is the human nature .   The former extreme is the active principle of the πιριχωρήσεως, which acts and perfects, the latter is the passive principle of the same πιριχωρήσεως, which is perfected, or receives perfections. Kg. 'Πιριχώρησις, immixtion, is that active permixtion, by which the divine nature of the Logos, perfecting within and completely around, pervades the human nature and communicates to the whole of it its entire self, to wit, in entireness and perfection of essence. Col. ii. 9.' Their operation is however this, that the fullness of divinity dwells within the human nature, and the two natures are ' to one another present by the closest presence.' "

(11) Gerh. "The state of union is properly and specifically called union, ἐνωσις ὑποστατικἡ, and is a most strict πιριχώρησις of two distinct natures in one person, most near in mutual presence, an impermixt and unconfused immixtion, on account of which one nature is not without the other, nor can be without the distinction of unity of person. The distinction between a state and an act of union is regarded as this: that the act is transient, but the state is permanent, and that the act is simply of one person, i. e. of the Logos, who, before his incarnation, was a simple person, on a nature, to wit, the human; but a state is between two natures, the divine and human, in ὑποστάσι συνθίτῳ, that the act consists in the assumption of humanity, made in the first moment of incarnation; but the state in that most close and ever enduring junction of natures."

Quen. "Formula of this personal union: *a)* participation, or communion, of one and the same hypostasis, 1 Tim. ii. 5; *b)* personal intimate, and perpetual presence, of the natures to one another mutually. John i. 14. Col. ii. 9."

form together one person, that of the Saviour, the God-man :(12)
in consequence then of this, the union of the two natures is so
complete and inseparable, that the one can no longer be thought
of without or apart from the other, but both at all times entirely
with one another,(13) yet in such a way, that both natures retain
their own essence and properties entirely unmingled with the

(12) Form. Conc. viii. 6 :   "Although the Son of God is of
himself an en ire and distinct person of the eternal Godhead, and,
therefore, was true, substantial, perfect God with the Father and
H. Spirit from eternity—yet, in assuming human nature into unity
of his own person, there were not two persons in Christ, or two
Christs, but Christ Jesus, now in one person, is at once true eternal
God, begotten of the Father from eternity, and true man." . . .

Chemn. "To the specific difference of the hypostatic union it
belongs, that those two natures are coupled and united to constitute
one ὑφιστάμενον in Christ incarnate, i. e., by that union the nature
inseparably assumed was so made proper to the person of 'the Word'
who assumed it, that, although the two natures are and remain in
Christ without confusion or change, the difference, both of natures
and of essential properties, being preserved, there are not two
Christs, but one.

Christ, therefore, since the personal union, is called a person σύνθετος. Gerh. "The hypostasis is called σύνθετος, not, because it was
composed by suffering, in itself, and of itself, any alteration or loss
of its own simplicity, but because, after the incarnation, there is a
hypostasis of two natures, when, before, there was a hypostasis of
the divine nature alone.   The person of the Logos, before the incarnation, was an αὐτοτελεστάτη, and simple ὑπόστασις, subsisting in
the divine nature only ; by the incarnation was made ὑπόστασις
σύνθετος, a constant nature at once divine and human, and so to the
integrity of the person of Christ, now incarnate, belongs not only
his divine, but also his assumed human nature :—Because the hypostasis of the Logos has been made the hypostasis of the flesh,
therefore the ὑπόστασις λόγου has been communicated to the flesh
(from whence follows the ' ἐνυπόστασία of the human nature')."

(13) Gerh. "For it is not a part united to a part, but the whole
Logos to the whole flesh, and the whole flesh to the whole Logos :
therefore, on account of the ὑποστάσεως ταυτότητα καὶ τῶν φύσιων εἰς
ἀλληλα περιχώρησιν, the Logos is so present to the flesh, and the flesh
to the Logos, that the Logos can neither be without the flesh, nor
the flesh without the Logos : but wherever the Logos is, there it has
the flesh most closely present with it, to wit, which it has assumed
into unity of person ; and whereever the flesh is, there it has the
Logos most closely present with it, to wit, into whose hypostasis it

other.(14) A perfectly exact conception, however, of the mode
and way in which these two natures are united in the one person,
cannot possibly be obtained, since the holy Scriptures, which certainly teach the union itself, say nothing of the How? of that
union.   We must, therefore, be satisfied with the ability to avoid
false conceptions of this union.(15) Consequently we may say,
that this union is *not* 1.) *essential*, by which two natures would
coalesce into one essence (in opposition to Eutychianism); 2.) not
natural, such as that of the soul and body in man; 3.) not *accidental*, such as is: *a)* between two or more separable accidents
coupled in one subject, (so whiteness and sweetness are united
in milk); *b)* between accident and substance (such as we have
in a learned man); *c)* between two substances but acciden-
tally united (as between the sticks in a bundle); 4) not merely

has been assumed. As the Logos is not without his deity, of which
he is a hypostasis: so also is he not without his flesh, finite indeed
in essence: yet personally subsisting in the Logos. For as his own
deity is proper to the Logos by eternal generation from the Father:
so to the same Logos the flesh has been made proper by the personal union.   Form. Conc. viii. 11.''

(14) Form. Conc. viii. 7. ''We believe that, now, in that one
undivided person of Christ, there are two distinct natures, to wit.
the divine, which is from eternity, and the human, which in time
has been assumed into unity of the person of the Son of God. And
these two natures, in the person of Christ, shall never be either
separated or confused, nor shall the one be changed into the other:
but each in its own nature and substance, or essence, in the person
of Christ, shall remain to all eternity. We believe . . . that each
nature also shall remain unconfused in its own nature and essence,
nor ever shall be taken away; so also each nature shall retain its
own natural essential properties, nor to all eternity shall lay them
aside.''

(15) Gerh. ''The mode of this union is wonderfully singular
and singularly wonderful, transcending the capacity not only of all
men, but of all angels, whence it is called ὑποσχουμεvῶς μεγα μυστη-
ριον. There are various and diverse modes of union, which are to be
regarded as different from the mode of personal union. For, as the
pious fathers say, that we can better know and say, what God is not.
than what he is: so also of that divine and supernatural union of two
natures in Christ we can, in truth, assert, that it is more easy to say
what is not its mode, than what is.''

From holy Scripture Gerh. vindicates the dogmatic conception

verbal, arising either from a title with no corresponding fact (as when a man is called counsellor of the prince, who in fact never gave him counsel,) or from an expression not literal, (as when Herod is called a fox); 5) not *habitual* or *respective*, which can subsist, although the extremes of this union are in fact separate and distant. (For there is respective union of various kinds, as moral between friends, domestic between married persons, political between fellow-citizens, ecclesiastical between members of a church.) On the other hand we may assert positively of this union, that it is 1.) *true* and *real*, because it exists between extremes truly cohering, the idea of separation or of distance being excluded; 2.) *personal* (but not of *persons*) and perichoristic; 3.) perpetually enduring. (Comp. notes 6—8.)

in the following: "The more important passages of Scripture, which speak of the union of the two natures in Christ, are these: John i. 14. Col. ii. 9. 1 Tim. iii. 16. Hebr. ii. 14—16. Since all these are paralell, they should be constantly united in the explanation of the union. John says, 'the Word was made flesh;' but, lest it might be thought, that the Word was made flesh, as water was made wine, Paul says, 'that God,' i. e. the Son of God, 'was manifest in the flesh, and that κεκοίνωνηκε (he became partaker) of flesh and blood'. But a κοινωνία involves at least a distinction of two, otherwise there would be μεταβολή και συμφυσις. God, is said by the Apostle, to have been manifest in the flesh; but, lest it might be supposed that there was such a φανέρωσις, as there was under the O. T. when either God himself, or angels, appeared in external forms, John says, that the Logos was made flesh, i. e., that he so assumed flesh into his own hypostasis, that he will never, in all time to come, lay it aside. The Son of God is said to have taken on him the seed of Abraham; but, lest it might be supposed, that it was such an assumption, as that of the angels who temporarily assumed corporeal figures, it is added that, forasmuch as the children are partakers of flesh and blood, he also himself likewise partook of the same. But it is evident, that the children partake in such way of flesh and blood, that flesh and blood, or human nature, is imparted to them by being born of their parents. The union is described by the Apostle, as a κατοίκησις λόγου in the flesh assumed; but, lest it might be thought that the Son of God dwells in the flesh assumed, in the same way that God dwells by grace in the hearts of believers, it is expressly added: that παν πλήρωμα της θεότητος dwells in the flesh assumed, and that indeed bodily, corporeally, as if a dwelling were denoted, or, personally, that the mode of union may be expressed."—The "negative properties" are very differently recounted by the theologians.

§. 33. *Communion of natures—personal propositions — com-*
munication of properties.

When now by the personal union the hypostasis of the divine
nature has at the same time also become that of the human nature, and so no longer a divine nature alone, but a human and
divine one is to be predicated of the person of the Redeemer, so
there has been constituted at the same time also, an efficient association of the two natures between one another, in consequence
of which the two natures are not related to each other in a barely
external way: for since the hypostasis of the divine nature is not
essentially distinct from that nature itself, but this hypostasis has
communicated itself to the human nature, it follows therefrom,
that a real and efficient communion and association between the
divine and human nature is established.(1) The first operation
of "the personal union" is also the "communion (also 'communication') of natures." Quen. "Comm. of nat. is that most
close and intimate κοινωνια and συνδυασις of the divine nature of

Besides that furnished in the text, the following are of principal
importance: "The union has been formed *a)* ασυγχυτως, without
confusion; *b)* ατρεπτως, in a way allowing no change; *c)* αδιαιρετως,
indivisibly: *d)* αχωριστως, inseparably: *e)* αναλλοιωτως, immutably:
f) αδιαλυτως, indissolubly: *g)* αδιαστατως, without distance. Ox:
not τοπικως, as formerly in the temple at Jerusalem: not ενεργη-
τικως, as in creatures, not χαριτως, as in the saints, not δοξαστικως,
as in the blessed in heaven, and the angels.'"

(1) Quen. "If the hypostasis of the Logos has been truly and
really communicated to the flesh assumed, there is absolutely a
true and real communication between the divine and the human
nature. which has been assumed, since the hypostasis of the Logos
and the divine nature of the Logos do not really differ. But that
exists. therefore also this does." Form. Conc. viii. 14.: "But we
are not to think of this hypostatic union, as though those two natures, the divine and human, are united in the way. in which two
pieces of wood are fastened together, so that really, or in very deed
and truly, they have no communication whatever, between them
For this is the error, and heresy, of Nestorius and Paul of Samosata.
heretics. who supposed, and taught, that the two natures are separate or distinct. and. in every respect. are by alternation or between themselves incommunicable. By this false doctrine. the
natures are separated and two Christs are supposed, of whom one
is Christ. the other God, the Logos, who dwells in Christ."

the Logos and of the humanity assumed, by which the Logos permeates* the human nature personally united to him by a most intimate and most profound περιχωρησις, perfects, dwells in, appropriates to himself, so that from each mutually communicating is made one incommunicable, to wit: one person."(2) But as in the act of union the divine nature is considered as the active one, and the divine Logos as that which has assumed the human nature, so is also the association of the two natures between one another to define it more closely, that between the two natures the active relation proceeds immediately from the divine nature, and this it is, which permeates the human. To obtain an adequate conception of it, would present the same difficulties as in the personal union, and we must be satisfied with analogies, which at least approximately give us a conception of it. Such we find in the binding together and association of soul and body, in the relation in which the three persons of the Godhead stand to one another or in the relation, which exists in red-hot iron between fire and iron. As soul and body bear to each other not merely an external relation, as for example, a man does to the

(2) Holl. "The communion of natures in the person of Christ is a mutual participation of the divine and human nature of Christ, by which the divine nature of the Logos having become partaker of human nature, permeates, perfects, inhabits, and appropriates it to itself; but the human, having become partaker of the divine nature, is permeated, perfected, and inhabited by it."

Br. "From the personal union flows the communion of natures, by which it comes to pass, that the human nature becomes a nature of the Son of God, and the divine nature a nature of the son of man. To designate this the word περιχωρησις, which, in its native meaning, denotes penetration, or the existence of one thing in another, began to be used: so, indeed, that the divine nature, is said, actively to penetrate, the human nature passively to be penetrated.—But in this we are to understand that all imperfections are removed. For

---

* "*Permeates.*" So Cudworth uses this word: "They (the three persons) are physically (if we may so speak) one also, and have a mutual inexistence, and *permeation* of one another."—*Intel. System. p.* 559.

"That subtile substance which *permeates* the whole world,"—*Do. p.* 456.

"God was conceived to permeate and pervade all things."—*Do. p.* 503.— Translator.

clothing which he has put on, or an angel to the body in which
he appears, but as the binding together of soul and body is an
operative, intimate and perfect one, so also is the binding together
and association of the two natures. As soul and body are inseparably united with one another and constitute the one man, so is
also the human and divine nature united most inseparably. As
the soul co-operates with the body and is bound together with it,
so that no commingling however, of the two is introduced, on
the contrary, the soul always remains soul, and the body always
remains body. So must we also contemplate the association
the two natures that each remains in its own integrity. As finally
the soul is never without the body, so also the Logos is always
to be thought of as in the flesh, and never without the same.(3)
As such a communion of natures actually exists, it follows therefrom:

I. That the two natures can also be reciprocally predicated of
one another, that we can with the same propriety say: " the man
(Jesus Christ) is God," as: " God is man," which expressions
have not naturally the sense, that God, in becoming man, had

the divine nature does not so penetrate the human, that successively it occupies one part of it after another, and by extension
diffuses itself through it; but because it is spiritual and indivisible,
the whole of it, at once, acts on and perfects every part of the human nature and the entire nature, and is and remains entire in the
entire human nature, and entire in every part soever of it. Here
comes in the passage Col. ii. 15."

Holl. "Περιχώρησις is not indeed a Biblical term; it is, however,
an ecclesiastical one, and began to be especially employed, when
Nestorius denied the communion of natures. But they did not
mean a περιχώρησις, which implied locality, or quantity, as a bucket
is said, to contain (χωρεῖ) water, but they employed it illocally
and metaphorically... In addition: περιχώρησις notes: 1.) that the
personal union is intimate, and most perfect; 2.) that the communion of natures is mutual; 3.) that the personal union and
communion of natures in Christ is ἀχώριστον, inseparable; 4) that
the communion of natures is ἀσύγχυτον, μικτον, καὶ ἀτρεπτον, that is,
implies no confusion, mixing, or transmutation."

(3) Form. Conc. viii. 19. "And indeed learned antiquity. to
some extent, set forth the hypostatic union, and the communication
of natures, under the similitude of the soul and body, likewise of

ceased to be God, but on the contrary, that the very Christ, who is God, is at the same time also man. (Holl. "The Son of God personally is the same, who is son of man, and the son of man personally is the same who is the Son of God.") So that the predicate man belongs as much to the subject God, as the predicate God to the subject man :(4) for if we deny this, we must at once discover, that, instead of two natures in Christ, we are thinking of two persons, of which each remains what it originally was, which would be Nestorian. From the " communion of natures," follow also the " personal propositions, that is, ex-

glowing iron. For the soul and body, (as also fire and iron,) not only as a phrase, or mode of speech, or verbally, but really, and truly, have a communication between themselves : nor, however, is there in this way introduced a confusion, or equalizing, of natures, such as takes place, when mead is made of honey and water, for such a drink is neither mere water, or mere honey, but a certain drink mingled of each. Far otherwise, assuredly, is it in that union of the divine and human nature (in the person of Christ) : for far more sublime and clearly ineffable is the communication and union of the divine and human nature in the person of Christ"

(4) Gerh. "The origin and foundation of the personal propositions consists alone and entirely in the personal union and communication of natures, from which entirely and immediately they take their rise, from which entirely also they are to be estimated and explained. For since the divine and human natures in Christ are personally united, since to these two natures personally united, an intimate περιχώρησις comes in, so that the divine nature of the Logos does not subsist out of the human nature assumed, nor the assumed human nature subsist out of the divine, thence and therefore God is man, and man is God. Since the hypostasis of the Logos is not only the hypostasis of its own divine nature, but also of the human : therefore God is, and is called man. Since the human nature assumed subsists in that hypostasis of the Logos, therefore man is and is called God."

Biblical examples : Jer. xxiii. 6. xxxiii. 16. Math. xxii. 42—45. Luke xx. 44. Ps. cx. 1. 2 Sam. vii. 19*. Is. ix. 6. Math. i. 21. 22. xvi. 13. 16. Luke i. 35. ii. 11. 1 Cor. xv. 47.

---

* There is no force in this quotation in the English version. But Luther has rendered the latter part of the verse thus : "That is the way of a man, who is God the Lord." "that is : Thou speakest to me of an everlasting kingdom, of which no one can be king, unless he be God and man, for he is to be my Son, and yet shall be a king forever, which can relate to God alone."—Tr.

pressions in which the concrete of the one nature (the one united) is predicated of the concrete of the other nature, that is, those
two truly distinct essences are enunciated of each other in the
concrete truly and really, but in a way altogether peculiar and
extraordinary, to express the personal union."(5)   To prevent
false conceptions about these personal propositions, they may be
designated more nearly, as : 1.) not "merely verbal," i. e., they
are not so to be understood, as if the name, but not the nature,
expressed by it, were affirmed of the subject, as Nestorius did,
when he said of the Son of Mary, He is the Son of God, in
which he attributes, as it were to the subject only a title, but will
by no means concede, that the very same, who is the Son of

---

(5) *a.* The expression "concrete" was used, when a personal
designation was sought for Christ, as one in whom are two natures.
If the personal designation was taken from one of his two natures,
it was called a 'concrete of nature': and, also, since Christ is in
two natures, a 'concrete of the divine nature,' when the designation
was taken from the divine nature ; 'concrete of the human nature,'
when taken from the human nature.   To the first class belong the
designations—God, Son of God, &c. ; to the other these—man, son
of man, son of Mary.   Holl. : 'Concrete of nature is a word, by
which is signified nature with a connotation of hypostasis.'   Br. :
'By concrete is understood a word, which signifies the suppositive
in its direct sense, the nature in its indirect sense.   So God denotes a suppositive. having a divine nature : man denotes a suppositive, having a human nature.'   From the 'concrete of nature'
is to be distinguished, however, the 'concrete of person,' which
expression is used, when the personal designation is taken no
so much from one of the two natures, as it serves, on the contrary,
to designate this distinct person, in whom the two natures are
united as in one person. by an expression derived elsewhere.   Br. :
'Concrete of person is a word. or name. of such kind. that it signifies. formally. a person. consisting of each nature, for example
Christ, Messiah, Immanuel, which names signify, in a direct sense
the suppositive : in an indirect sense. neither nature alone, but
rather both.'—In the present case only the 'concrete of nature
comes into use, for it is employed only in the cases, in which the
communion of natures is to be expressed in their personal designations.   To the 'personal propositions,' in a proper sense, those
'propositions' do not belong. in which a 'concrete of nature' is predicated of the 'concrete of person,' as is the case in such expressions as : Christ is God, is man, is God-man.   Gerh. : 'Because
these propositions express precisely, and formally, not so muc

Mary, is actually the Son of God; 2.) not "identical," as though the predicate which is affirmed of the subject were identical with it, and only embraced an affirmation of the subject, as would be the case if the truth: the Son of God is the Son of Mary, had been thus expressed: the man, who is united with the Son of God, is the Son of Mary; 3.) not "figurative or tropical," as would be the case in the predicate, which would express in regard to the subject, not the properties of its own actual nature, but would attribute only certain properties of this predicate to the subject, so that in a figurative sense it might be said, God is man, in the same sense that we say of a picture, that is a man, or a woman; 4.) not "essential and univocal," as if the subject were

unity of person, as duality of natures in Christ: for thence and therefore Christ is, and is called, man, since in him is human nature; thence and therefore he is, and is called, θεάνθρωπος, because in him is not only a human, but also a divine nature.'

It is farther understood, in regard to this, that these 'propositions' can only be employed on the presupposition of the personal union, and are not in general available, hence Holl.: "If the divine and human natures are regarded apart from the personal union, either God or man, there is a disparity; nor can the one be affirmed of the other. For as I cannot say: a lion is a horse,—so neither can I say: God is man. But if a union between God and man comes in, and a certain real union, such as in Christ, comes in between the divine and human nature, they can properly be mutually predicated in the concrete. The reason is, because by union the two natures constitute one person; the concrete of nature, whichsoever it is, signifies that very person. Since therefore the man Christ is the same, as he who is God, or this person who is God, is that very person who is man, it may be said, with propriety: Man is God, and God is man."

b. Finally also, in regard to the 'abstracts of nature,'—('an abstract is that, in which, indeed, there is a nature, but considered, not with respect to union, but in its own self, and abstracted from union or concretion, not in very deed however, but only in the mind:' Hrffr.) the parity does not hold, as in regard to the 'concretes of nature', nor could we say: 'Deity is humanity, humanity is Deity.' Quen.: 'The reason is, because the union is not made to one nature, but to one person σύνθετον; the difference of nature being secured, therefore the one nature is not predicated in the abstract of the other, but the concrete of one nature is predicated of the concrete of the other nature."

according to its essence, that which the thing predicated affirms
of it (God is man, would mean then : the essence of God is this,
that it is the essence of man). The "personal propositions" rather
are : 1.) "real," i. e., what is predicated of the subjects actually
and in truth appertains to them ; 2.) "unusual and singular," for
as the "personal union" has no farther example, so also the personal propositions have none.

But from "the communion of natures" follows—

II. That a mutual operation is established between the natures
towards themselves, and between the natures and the person.(6)
This is expressed in the doctrine of the "communication of properties. Br. Communic. of prop. is that by which it comes to
pass that those things, which, the two natures being compared
between themselves, relate per se and formally to one of them,
are also truly proper to the other nature, either in respect of concretes or in order to the nature itself looked at in the abstract."(7)
In accordance with this doctrine also, a property can neither be

---

(6) Gerh. "Whatever in the assumption of human nature comes
under the union, comes also under the communication. And, in
fact, the properties now come under the union, because no nature
is destitude of its own properties; since a nature without properties, would also be without existence, and two natures are united in
Christ, not bare, or stripped of their properties, but entire without
defect, having endured no lapse of what was proper to them. Therefore also the properties come under the *communication.*"

Holl. "No union can be perfect and permeant (perichoristica)
without a communication of properties, as the examples of animated body prove. A seeming union of two pieces of wood may
be made without a communication of properties, we readily admit,
because that degree of union is very low and imperfect. But, as
Scripture has defined it, the personal union of the two natures in
Christ, is most absolute, perfect, and permeant (perichoristica):
therefore, it cannot exist without a communication of properties."
So also can evidence be drawn from the communion of natures,
which involves the communication of properties as a necessary consequence.

(7) Holl. "Communication of properties is a true and real par
ticipation of the properties of a divine and human nature, resultin
from a personal union, in Christ, the God-man, denominated fro
either or both natures."
Explanation of the single ideas of communication and property
a) Gerh. "Communication is the distribution of one, which i

affirmed of one of the two natures, which is not a property of
the whole person, nor can an operation or action be affirmed of
one of the two natures, in which the other nature does not also
participate, naturally, but not in the same way, as when with the
properties or the operation proceeding therefrom at the same time,
also the essence which constitutes their basis, passes over to the
other nature.(8)   "A communic. of prop." is accordingly es-

common to many, into those many, which have it in common."
Quen. : 'Not that ἰδιώματα κοινά, become common, but that they become κοινωνητά, by, and on account of, the personal union.' *b*) 'Ἰδίωμα,
in Latin, proprium : Quen. 'By ἰδιώματα are understood those properties and differences of natures, by which, as marks and chara-
teristics, two natures (in verity of person) are mutually distinguished
and separated from each other.   But the word ἰδιωμάτων is taken
either strictly for those natural properties themselves, or, in a wider
sense, it comprehends also those operations themselves, by which
the properties, properly so called, exhibit themselves ; *in this place*,
properties, or idiomata, are taken in the wider signification, so that,
on account of the properties strictly so called, they embrace also in
their compass, actions, and passions, ἐνεργήματα καὶ ἀποτελέσματα,
since by ἐνεργείας and ἀποτελέσματα, the idiomata exhibit themselves.'
Gerh. 'Notice : the notion of divine idiomata is one thing, that of
human another.   The idiomata of the divine nature are the very
essence τοῦλόγου, and are not really distinguished from it.   The
properties of human nature are not the constitutives but the consecu-
tives of essence.'   As regards the justification for the establishment
of this doctrine Holl.: 'This phrase, communication of properties,
is not found αὐτολέξει (in so many words) in the sacred Scriptures,
but the thing itself has most clearly a Scriptural basis.   For as
often as the Scripture assigns to the flesh of Christ the actions
and works of omnipotence, so often, by consequence, omnipotence
is attributed to him as an *actus primus* (immediate act), from whom
the divine ἐνέργεια flows as an *actus secundus* (mediate act).   But
although the '*communicatio idiomatum*' was first used by the scho-
lastics : yet orthodox antiquity in the controversies with Nestorius,
and Eutychius, employed equivalent modes of expression.'   The
first complete development of this doctrine was made by Chemnitz
in his book ' De Duabus Naturis in Christo,' 1590.

(8) Hence the idea of the ' communication' is farther guarded,
by saving. that it is not a 'communication κατάμιξεξιν, or essential,
by which one passes over into the essence, and definite character,
of the other'; but a 'communication, κατα συνδίαςιν, i. e. such a
communication of the two natures, by which one of those united is
so connected with the other, that, the divine essence remaining, the

tablished between the natures and the person, and between the natures towards one another.(9) Thence the communication of properties is divided into distinct kinds, of which we enumerate three, (for the Holy Scripture makes distinct mention of this number,(10)) the "genus idiomaticum, majestaticum and apotelesmaticum."—The more particular consideration of these three genera is as follows:

I. *Genus.*—Since the two natures are actually united to one person, it follows that every property which immediately appertains to one of the two natures, may be predicated of *the whole person*; in general the properties of the divine nature as well as those of the human nature, must pertain to the person of the

one truly receives and assumes the property of the other, its power and effi·acy by and because of a communion made, without any confusion whatsoever.' (Quen.) So there might be given yet farther designations, as in the case of the 'personal union'. Gerh.: ·As the union is not essential, nor verbal merely, nor by σιγχυσι., or αλλο.ωσιν, or μιξιν, or παρατασιν, nor is προσωπικη, or sacramental; so also the communication is not such.'"

(9) Gerh. "Communication of properties is of nature to person. or of nature to nature."

Hfrlfr. ·"Communication of properties is a true and real participation of divine and human properties, by which, on account of the hypostatic union of the two natures in Christ, not only the personal properties of the joint nature, (which is at the same time God and man,) but also the things proper to one or other nature, are attributed to the other: that is, to the Logos human attributes, and to the humanity assumed divine. And, on account of the same κοινωνιαν, each nature operates with a communication of the other: the natures however, and the properties, being preserved uninjured."

(10) Quen. ·"Certain and distinct grades of the communication of properties are given: because, however the question concerning the number of grades, or *genera*, of the communication of properties relates not to faith, or its establishment. but to the τροπον παιδειας and method of teaching, some constitute two, others three. others four kinds of properties. A threefold arrangement pleases most of our theologians, inasmuch as, in accordance with a threefold mode of expression, it is observed in the Bible. It proposes, we say, three distinct kinds. though it does not number them." Some DD. receive "four kinds of communication of properties," inasmuch as they distinguish the "expressions, in which things proper to the human nature are attributed to the Son of God," from the "expressions, in which the properties of either nature are enunciated of the

Saviour. Since also the birth or the suffering is a property of the human nature, it can as well be said : " Christ, the God-man, was born, has suffered," as it could be said of him : " by him were all things created," although creation is a property of the divine nature.(11) For if we are unwilling to speak thus, but maintain that a property of the human nature may only be predicated of the concrete of the human nature, and a property of the divine nature only of the concrete of the divine nature, so that it should be expressed : " the man Jesus Christ has been born," " through Christ, who is God, all things have been created," the personal union would be destroyed, and it would seem as though not two natures, but two persons were supposed ; (12)

whole person of Christ ;" and also regard the proposition : "Christ suffered," as belonging to a different class, from the proposition : " God suffered." But most DD. declare themselves against thi division.—But the order, also, in which these three *genera* are introduced, is not the same in all DD. Quen.: "Some follow the *order of doctrine*, others the *order of nature*. The former (Form. Conc.—Chemn.) place the communication of official actions, as it is more easy, and less controverted, before the communication of majesty, which is chiefly controverted, and is to be more largely explained. The latter follow the order of nature, and place the communication of majesty before the communication of official actions, because that in nature precedes this."

(11) Gerh. "The basis of this communication of properties is the unity of person. For, since after the incarnation, the one person of Christ subsists in two, and of two natures, of which each is invested as it were, with its own properties, thence the things proper to each nature, whether the divine or human are predicated of the one synthetic ($\sigma\nu\nu\vartheta\acute{\epsilon}\tau\varphi$) person of Christ." Form. Conc. viii. 36. "Since in Christ there are two distinct natures, which, in their essences and properties, are neither changed, nor confounded ; but of the joint nature there is but one person : those things, which are proper only to one nature, are attributed not to the other person in itself, as if separated, but to the whole person, (which is, at the same time, God and man,) whether it be named God, or man."

(12) Chemn. "Nestorius, however, supposed such a communication, that divine properties might be attributed to Christ, the God, but to the man Christ only human, that the man, for instance, not the God, was born of Mary, was crucified, &c. Likewise, that the God, but not the man, had healed the sick, raised the dead ; but thus there would be one person of Christ as God, and another of Christ as man, and two persons, and two Christs, would be formed."

but the personal union directly displays itself as a positive thing, in this, that all properties which pertain to one or the other nature, are also equally properties of the person.   Since farther in virtue of the communion of natures and of the personal propositions following therefrom, it is all the same, whether we name Christ with reference to his two natures, or with reference to one of them, so can a property of one of the two natures be predicated equally well of the concrete of the one or of the other nature, it can be said with as much propriety : " God has died," as that : the man Jesus Christ is almighty.(13)

Nevertheless, though the properties of the two natures may be assigned to the concrete of the two natures, (Christ, the God-man,) or the concrete of one to the two natures, (God—to the man Jesus Christ,) yet does it not follow therefrom in any way, that the properties of the one nature become the properties of the other, for the two natures are not changed by the personal union as regards their substance, and each of the two natures retains its essential and natural properties.   In addition, it is *only of the person* that we can, without farther distinction, predicate alike the properties of the one or the other nature, but by no means can this be done of the natures in themselves in such a sense,

13) Chemn. "To show this very close unity of person, those things, which are proper either to the divine, or to the human, or to the joint nature, are attributed to that one hypostasis, or are designated by a concrete, or taken from the divine, or the human, or the joint nature.   Likewise : Because the union of natures, is made in the hypostasis of the Word, so that the person of each nature is now one and the same, subsisting, at the same time, in each nature : the concrete words, taken from the divine nature, as God the Logos, Son of God, when they are predicated of the incarnate Christ, although the denomination is taken from the divine nature, it yet signifies not the divine nature only, but a person subsisting now in two natures, to wit, the divine and human.   And the concrete words, taken from the human nature, as man, son of man, when they are predicated of the incarnate Christ, designate not the bare or mere human nature: but a hypostasis, subsisting both in the divine and human nature, and to which each nature bears a relation.   And hence it comes, that to the concrete words, signifying the person of Christ, whether taking their denomination from both natures, or one only, are rightly attributed all the properties, whether they are those of the divine or human nature."

as if each of the two natures singly no longer retained its essential properties.(14)   In order to avoid a misapprehension of this character, it is usual to employ expressions by which is particularly marked from which nature the Person derives the properties attributed.(15)

(14) Chemn. "True belief does not, however, with Eutyches and the Monotholites, confound that communication between the natures, with a conversion and confusion both of natures and properties, so that humanity is said to be divinity, or the essential property of one nature becomes the essential property of another nature in the abstract, or apart from the union, or in itself or of itself, in the union itself of the nature under consideration.   But the property agreeable to one nature is communicated or attributed to the person in the concrete." Hence Holl. 1.) "The subject is not abstract, but is a concrete of nature or of person." (We cannot say : 'Deity was crucified.') 2.) "The Predicate" (that to wit, which is affirmed of the subject, i. e. of the person ἐνσαρκος σύνθετος) "does not designate the very substance, whether divine or human, but a property of either nature."

(15) Form. Conc. viii. 37 : "But in this kind of expressions, it does not follow that those things which are attributed to the whole person, are at the same time properties of each nature : but it is distinctly to be declared, according to which nature anything is to be ascribed to the person."

Chemn. "Lest, however, it might be thought that the natures are confused, it is usual to add to the example from Scripture a declaration, to which nature the property belongs, which is attributed to the person, or according to which nature it is attributed to the person.   For the existence of the properties of one nature, does not prevent the presence of another nature with its own properties. Nor does it prevent the properties of the one nature from being attributed to a person subsisting in each nature.   Nor is it necessary that those things which in this way are predicated of the person, should be agreeable to each nature.   But it is enough, if according to one or other, whether the divine or human, they are agreeable to the person." Quen. "Such particles are, ἐν, ἐξ, διά, κατά, 1 Pet. ii. 24, iii 18, iv. 1 ; Rom. i. 3, ix. 5 : Acts xx. 28." By this additional closer designation is then expressed, how the predicate is attributed to the subject, since it also relates, because of the union of persons, to both natures, yet primarily belongs properly only to one of the two natures.   Hence, "the modus prædicandi" (the way and method, in which a predicate is made of the subject) is thus described : (Holl.) "It is a true and real thing, by which divine or human attributes are enunciated of the whole human-divine (θεανθρώπου) person, (for what are the properties of the humanity in themselves, those

General Definition: (Quen.) "The first genus of the communication of properties is, when things proper to the divine or

are truly and properly predicated of the Son of God, on account of
the personal union, and *vice versa*,) in such a way, however, that
by the discretive particles they are claimed for that nature to which
they are strictly proper, whilst they are appropriated to that nature
to which they belong, not formally, but on account of the personal
union." The "modus prædicandi" is illustrated in the following
examples: (Holl.) "The Son of God was born of the seed of David,
according to the flesh, Rom. i. 3. The *subject* of this idiomatic
proposition, is the Son of God, by which is denoted the entire person of Christ, assuming a title from the divine nature. The predicate is being born of the seed of David, which is a human property.
This is predicated of the concrete of the divine nature, to which of
itself it does not belong, but on account of the union of the divine-
human (θεανθρωπου) person. Hence by the limiting particle κατα, according to the flesh, the human property is claimed for the human
nature, to which a temporal nativity properly belongs: but yet the
divine nature is not excluded or separated from a participation in the
nativity, inasmuch as to it the being born of the seed of David relates
by appropriation." The proposition: "God has suffered," is thus illustrated: "The Son of God has suffered according to the human
nature subsisting in the divine personality. As, therefore, when a
wound is inflicted on Peter's flesh, it is not merely said that Peter's
flesh is wounded, but that Peter, or the person of Peter, was really
wounded, although his soul could not be wounded: so when the
Son of God suffers according to the flesh, not his flesh alone suffers,
or his human nature, but the Son of God, or the person of the Son
of God, truly suffers, although the divine nature be impassive
(απαθης)." The statement: God has suffered, dare not be resolved
with Zuingli into this: the man Jesus Christ, who at the same time
is God, has suffered, in which case the "modus prædicationis"
would be nothing "real or appropriate." Form. Conc. viii. 39.*
Zuingli calls this allocosis, when something is affirmed of the
divinity of Christ, which is however proper to the humanity and
the contrary. For the sake of example: when it is said in Scripture: ought not Christ to have suffered these things, &c., there
Zuingli trifles, by remarking that the word Christ in this place is to
be understood of the human nature. Beware, beware, I say, of that
allocosis. . . For if I could persuade myself to believe "that the
human nature alone suffered for me: surely Christ would not be to
me a Saviour of great value, but would himself in the end need a
Saviour. "

---

* These words are quoted in the Formula from Luther's Greater Confession on the Lord's Supper.—Tr.

human nature are truly and really attributed to the whole person of Christ, denominated from one or the other nature, or from
both."(16)

This genus the later DD. divide into three species, according
as the different properties are predicated of the concrete of the
divine nature or of the concrete of the human nature, or of the
concrete of both natures. These species are: *a*) ἰδιοποίησις, or
οἰχείωσις, appropriation, when human properties are attributed to
the concrete of the divine nature. Acts iii. 15, xx. 28, 1 Cor. ii. 8.
Gal. i. 20; *b*) χοινωνία τῶν θείων, when to the person of the incarnate word assuming a title from the human nature, divine properties are attributed on account of the personal union. John
vi. 62; viii. 58. 1 Cor. xv. 47; *c*) ἀντίδοσις or συναμφοτέρισμος,
alternation or reciprocation, by which divine as well as human
properties are predicated of the concrete person or of Christ denominated from each nature. Heb. xiii. 8, Rom. ix. 5, 2 Cor.
xiii. 4, 1 Pet. iii. 18.

II. *Genus.*—Since the divine Logos has taken upon him the
human nature, so that through the personal union the hypostasis
of the divine nature has also become that of the human nature,
it is a further and natural consequence therefrom that the human
nature has also therewith become partaker in the properties of
the divine nature,(17) for through the personal union not alone

(16) As appellations of this first genus, the following have been
introduced, whose origin has been referred to the old Church Fathers: "ἀντίδοσις, alternation, τρόπος ἀμτιδόσεως (Damascenus), ἐναλ-
λαγή καὶ κοινωνία ὀνομάτων, permutation and communication of names
(Theodoret), ἰδιοποι.α καὶ ἰδιοποίησι, appropriation (Cyrill), αλλοίωσις"
(but in a sense different from that in which Zuingli uses it), "οἰκεί-
ωσις, συναμθυτερισμός."—Examples from Holy Scripture: Hebr. xiii. 8.
1 Cor. ii. 8, Acts vii. 2, Ps. xxiv. 7, 8, Acts iii. 15, John viii. 58.

(17) Quen. "The basis of this communication is the communication of the hypostasis and of the divine nature of the Logos.
For since the human nature, assumed in the union, has also by the
union been made partaker of the hypostasis and divine nature of
the Logos, therefore also it has been made partaker truly and really
of the divine properties; for these do not differ from the divine
essence."

Chemn. "If the indwelling of God in the saints by grace, con-
fers many gratuitous divine gifts more than and beyond natural

the person, but, since person and nature cannot be separated, the divine nature also has entered into communion with the human nature, and indeed the communication of the divine attributes to the human nature follows in that very moment in which the divine Logos has united itself with the human nature.(18) But here no mutual operation takes place, for the human nature can readily become participant of the properties of the divine, and can thus have an increase of its essential properties, but not convertibly, for the divine nature according to its essence is unchangeable, and can sustain no increase.(19) The attributes,

endowments, and works many wonderful things in them, what impiety would it be, to be willing to believe that in that mass of human nature, in which the whole fullness of the God-head dwells bodily. only physical endowments are to be acknowledged. and noth ng of that which surpasses and exceeds the natural conditions of human nature when it is looked at in itself or by itself apart from the hypostatic union.''

(18) Quen. "For in the very moment in which the personal union is made, the communication of majesty is also made. For the divine nature of the Logos with its entire fullness has united and communicated itself to the flesh assumed, from the very beginning of the incarnation.''

(19) Quen. ''The *subjectum quo* is the nature. to which the communication has been made. But that is not the divine, since to it, in accordance with entire immutability, nothing can be added: but the human taken into the hypostasis of the Logos.'' John vi. 53, i º. Matt. xxvi. 28. Acts xx. 28. John v. 27. Phil. ii. 9. (Form. Conc. viii. 49, 51.) ''That it is not the divine but is the human nature which is the *subjectum quo,* is proved by the condition of the divine nature, which as most rich cannot be enriched, as most good it is impossible δοτοῦσθαι, as most high cannot be exal ed as most perfect cannot be perfected, as most glorious cannot receive an augmentation of glory.''—The ground, on which the human nature partakes of the idiomata of the divine, whilst the converse is not true, arises from the mode of the ''unition.'' Br. ''It amounts to this, that like as on the part of the natures, although the divine is personally united to the human and the human to the divine, this distinction yet intervenes, that the divine nature intimately penetrates and perfects the human, whilst the human does not in turn penetrate and perfect the divine, but is penetrated and perfected by it: so in the communication of properties, this distinction on the part of the natures intervenes, that the divine nature penetrating he human, makes in its own mode the same also, abstractly con-

finally, which in virtue of the personal union and of the communion of natures have been imparted to the human nature, are truly divine, but are also to be distinguished from the peculiar human prerogatives, which the human nature, assumed by the Logos, has beyond other human natures.(20)

sidered, partaker of its own divine attributes: but not so in turn the human nature, which neither permeates nor perfects the divine nature, and does not and cannot equally make it, abstractly considered, partaker of its own properties."

(20) Gerh. "We do not deny that besides the essential properties of human nature certain habitual endowments inhere in Christ the man, subjectively, which, although they are most excellent and far surpass the endowments of all men and angels, yet are and remain finite: yet we add besides these habitual and finite endowments, there have been communicated to Christ the man, endowments truly infinite and immense by the personal union and exaltation to the right hand of the Father." Holl. "By and on account of the personal union, endowments truly divine, increate, infinite and immense are given to Christ according to the human nature." And it may be in general affirmed: "all the divine attributes are communicated to the flesh of Christ," yet we are to distinguish: "attributes ἀνέργητα and ἐνεργητικά."

Quen. "The attributes which are ἐνεργητικά admit a secondary act or proceed by ἐνεργήματα and operations *ad extra*. Such are goodness, omnipotence, pity, omnipresence, &c., (and which do not involve anything which is entirely inconsistent with human nature. Br.)" "The attributes ἀνέργητα are those, which apart from the divine essence remain quiescent, and do not outwardly, by operations upon creatures, exert or present themselves to our cognition, as eternity, infinity, spirituality, immensity, &c. (involving something inconsistent with human nature. Br.") Of both it is said: "they are communicated to the flesh of Christ, which they inhabit and possess," but only of the first: "they are communicated so as *to be actually employed* and to be *immediately predicable*." Of the "attributes ἐνεργητ" it is affirmed that they are participated, "immediately," of the "attributes ἀνεργ," that they are participated "mediately or by the medium of an operative attribute." The DD. make special mention of "omnipotence," of "omniscience" (which, however, "he employed in his state of exinanition not always and everywhere, but freely, when and where he willed," of (omnipresence, (Form. conc. viii. 28. Br. which words, *solid. decl.*, manifestly describe that omnipresence, not as absolute, for a nude indistant nearness to all creatures, and without efficacious operation, but as it were modified or conjoined with an efficacious operation, and adapted to the exigency of that universal dominion which Christ exer-

Definition: (Holl.) The second genus of the communication of properties is that by which the Son of God truly and really communicates, on account of a personal union, the properties of his divine nature to the human nature assumed, so that there is a common possession, employment and denomination.[21]

cises according to each nature,") of " worship by religious adoration (that the flesh of Christ the mediator, is to be worshipped and adored in the same adoration with the divine nature of the Logos)." In regard to "omnipresence," Quen. farther remarks: " The human presence of the body does not here come into controversy, whether resulting from the proper character either of a natural ($\psi\upsilon\chi\iota\kappa\sigma\varsigma$) or of a glorified body. We grant that the body of Christ by act of nature was through exterior circumscription in a physical locality, from the first conception on to the resurrection, to wit, as long as it was a natural ($\psi\upsilon\chi\iota\kappa\sigma\nu$) body. We grant also, that after the resurrection and ascension into heaven, that very body as it is glorified, by act of nature is not everywhere, but determinately in its own celestial $\pi\sigma\iota$. not indeed by circumscription, but definitively, as in their own order and grade other glorious bodies are definitively in their own $\pi\sigma\iota$. But here the only inquiry is, whether the human nature of Christ, now raised to the right hand of God the Father, is in this glorious state of exaltation at the right hand of the divine majesty, omnipresent to all creatures in the universe. And, therefore, it is not in question, whether this divine presence is proper to Christ, in as far as he is man, from the proper character of human nature, for this we also deny; but whether it is to be attributed to him, through and on account of the personal union, even as this is inseparably connected with the exaltation of the humanity to the right hand of God the Father. The former modes of presence are, therefore, so to be set forth, that the infinite presence in the flesh assumed, shall not be denied."

Of the communication of these "divine attributes," to the human nature, it may in fine be observed: Br. "This communion is not made 1.) by an essential or natural effusion of the properties of the divine nature into human nature; as if the humanity of Christ could have them in themselves and separated from the divine essence, or (2) as if by that communication the human nature in Christ had at all laid aside its own natural properties, or (3) had been converted into the divine nature, or (4) in itself and by itself had been rendered equal to the divine nature, by its properties communicated: or (5) that the natural and essential properties and operations of both natures had become the same, or at least equal. But those words and phrases (real communication, really communicated) are employed in opposition to a merely verbal communication."

(21) Quen. "The second genus of communication of properties

III. *Genus.*—The whole aim of the incarnation of Christ is no other than the completion of the work of redemption by Christ in unity of the human nature. From the association of the two natures, which has been introduced through the personal union, it follows, that all operations, which proceed from Christ, cannot be referred exclusively to one of the two natures.(22) The operation proceeds it is true from one of the two

is that, in which the Logos with its own divine nature communicates its own proper glory and excellence to the humanity hypostatically united to it, on account of this very hypostatic union truly and really, and without any commixture or confusion of natures and properties so as to be possessed, employed and denominated in common."—Scripture evidence: "To the human nature majesty is communicated: Matt. xi. 27. Luke i. 33. John iii. 13; vi. 62. Phil. ii. 5. Heb. ii. 6. The man Christ seated at the right hand of majesty: Matt. xxvi. 64. Mark xiv. 62. Luke xxii. 69. Rom. viii. 34. Eph. i. 20. Hebr. vii. 26; viii. 1. Omnipotence: Matt. xxviii. 18. Phil. iii. 21. Omniscience; Col. i. 19; ii. 3, 9. Omnipresence: Matt. xviii. 20. xxviii 20, Eph. i. 22; iv. 10. Power of vivifying: John vi. 51. 1 Cor. xv. 21, 45. Power of Judgment: Matt. xvi. 27. John v. 27. Acts xvii. 31." Appellations: "Communication of majesty—genus majestatical, βελτίωσις, προσθήκη μεγάλη, ὑπερύψωσις, μετάδοσις, δόξασις, μετάληψις θείας ἀξίας, μετοχή θείας δυνάμεως, θέωσις, ἀποθιοσία, θεοποίησις. In sacred Scriptures: unction, viz., Ps. xlv. 8. John iii. 34. Acts x. 38.

(22) Form. Conc. viii. 46. "As to the functions of office, the person does not act or operate in or together with one or through one nature only, but rather in, with and according to and through both natures, or as the Council of Chalcedon expresses it, one nature does or effects, with the communication of the other, that which is properly its own. Christ, therefore, is our mediator, redeemer, king, &c. not according to one nature only, whether divine or human, but according to both natures." Gerh. "The Son of God thence and therefore assumed human nature, that in it, with it and by it he might carry on the work of redemption and the parts of his mediatorial office. 1 John iii. 8, &c. Hence, in the works of his office, he does not act as God only, nor as man only, but as θεάνθρωπος, and what is the same, the two natures in Christ do not in official acts operate dividedly, but unitedly. From unity of person flows unity ἀποτελέσματος (of effect)." Holl. "The remote foundation of this communication is the united person and intimate conjunction of the divine nature in Christ. The proximate foundation is the communication of properties of the first and second genus." Holl. "If the divine incarnate nature of the Logos (on

natures, and each of the two natures completes its own distinctive operation, but in such sense, that, during the manifestation of such an operation on the part of one nature, the other nature is at the same time not idle, but active ; that also, whilst the human nature suffers, the divine, which of course cannot suffer, yet assists the human, imparts power and strengthens it for the endurance of the burden laid upon it ;(23) that the human nature, then, is not to be contemplated simply as active through its essential attributes, but, in addition to these, through its essential attributes in virtue of the second genus of the communication of properties which its participated divine attributes enter into, with which it operates.(24)   For the divine nature cannot in itself

account of the communication of properties of the first and second degree) truly appropriates to itself those things which belong to the human nature, and communicates to it its own properties (omnipotence, &c.) to possess and employ them, it inevitably follows, that the divine nature appropriates to itself what the human nature performs in the mediatorial office, and the latter operates not only by a natural, but also by a communicated divine ενεργεια."

(23) Chemn. "When one nature in Christ does that which is proper to it, or when Christ does anything in accordance with the proper character of one nature, in that action or suffering the other nature is not idle, so that it either is doing nothing or is engaged in something else, but that which is properly of one nature, is and is done in Christ with the communion of the other nature, that difference being observed which is proper to each, so that when Christ in his human nature suffers and dies, this also comes to pass with the communion of the other nature, not that the divine nature also in itself suffers or dies, for this is proper to the human nature, but because the divine nature of Christ is present personally with the suffering nature, and wills that suffering of his human nature, does not avert it, but permits his humanity to suffer and die, strengthens and sustains it, so that it can bear the infinite burden of the sin of the world and of the entire wrath of God, and renders those sufferings precious before God and the source of salvation to the world."

(24) Chemn. "Because the offices and blessings of Christ our Saviour, are of such a character, that in many or in most of them, the human nature in Christ cannot co-operate by its natural or essential properties or operations alone, therefore beside and beyond the natural properties, there are numberless hyperphysical and paraphysical imparted and communicated to the human nature by hypostatic union with divinity."

alone give a ransom for the propitiation of the world, it must, in order to this, be united with the human nature, which, consisting of body and soul, can be given up for the redemption of men, and, on the other hand, there was much which the human nature could not accomplish, (miracles, &c.,) had not its properties obtained an accretion by the accession of the divine.(25)

Holl. "The mode of union and of mutual confluence consists in this, that the divine nature of the Logos not only performs divine works, but also truly and really appropriates to itself the actions of the flesh assumed; but the human nature, not only according to its natural powers, but also according to that divine virtue, which has been communicated to it by the personal union, sustains the office of Mediator." Quen.: We say by *means of the hypostasis*, (mediante ὑποστάσει,) it appropriates to itself the actions and sufferings of the humanity, for we do not say: the *divine nature* bled, suffered, died, as it is said: the human nature gives life, works miracles, governs all things, but *God* bled, suffered, died."

(25) Chemn. "The evidence of Scripture clearly shows, that the personal union of the two natures in Christ, was made in order that the work of redemption, propitiation, salvation, &c., might be perfected in each, with each, and through each, nature of Christ. For if redemption, propitiation, &c., could have been effected either by deity alone, or by humanity alone, to no end would the Logos have descended from heaven and become man incarnate for us and our salvation." Gerh. "The human nature indeed could suffer, die, and bleed, but the cruel sufferings and bloody death of Christ would have had no saving effect, had not the divine nature added a price of infinite value to those sufferings and that death, which the Saviour endured for us." The work of redemption, as well as each transaction of Christ, is consequently considered as one in which both natures in Christ participated. The expression which designates this is ἀποτέλεσμα ("a common work, resulting from a communicative* and intimate conflux of natures, or in the production of which the operations of each nature concur.")—(Quen.) Since, however, each distinct act proceeds from one of the two natures, from that to wit, of whose original attributes it is derived, the term for it is ἐνέργημα ("an effect proper to one nature"). Thus the shed blood of Christ is an operation of the human nature, for only the human nature has bled, the inestimable value which this blood possesses, is an operation of the divine nature. The propitiation for our sins,

---

* "Communicative." "For the Father and Spirit do dwell in his human nature, as he is now become one of the persons; the man, God's fellow, in their *communicative* society together.—*Godwin's Works*, vol. I. pt. iii, p. 35.—Translator.

Definition: (Gerh.) "The third genus of communication of properties is that by which, in official acts, each nature performs that which is proper to it, with a communication of the other. 1 Cor. xv. 3. Gal. i. 4; iii. 17. Eph. v. 2."(26)

however, which could be accomplished by the shed blood alone, is the work (ἀποτέλεσμα) of both natures, since both natures contributed thereto their own parts, the human nature to shed, the divine nature to give to that blood an infinite worth. The "apotelesmata of Christ," Holl. farther designates as of "two kinds. Some things the divinity of the Logos could not bring to pass apart from the conjunction with the flesh, for example, the atoning sacrifice, the life-giving death; some things of free εὐδοκίᾳ, or good pleasure, it wills not to produce without the flesh—as miracles, for example."

(26) Br. "The third genus of communication of properties consists in this, that operations belonging to the office of Christ, are not those of either nature alone, but common to both, inasmuch as each contributes to them its own part; and thus each acts with a communication of the other."

Closing Note by the Translator.

With the harmonious and glorious view of his Church on this great central idea of Christianity, the translator feels the profoundest sympathy. He believes that there is no consistent position between the essentials of this view and the dreary half-socinianism of Nestorius. The doctrine lives in the hearts of thousands of God's children, to whom it has never been imparted in the teachings of the theology to which they have been wont to listen. It is only the doctrine of a *true* incarnation which can lift us to the power of that adoring love which the Son of God, our Saviour, demands. It is this alone which can cause us to present, as the true homage of our souls, the prayer of the Church which found voice in that sweet hymn of Aquinas:

> "Adoro te, devote latens Deitas:
> ——Jesu Domine
> Me immundum munda tuo sanguine,
> Cujus una stilla salvum facere
> Totum mundum quit ab omni scelere."

ART. XVIII.—INNOCENCE.*

Well have I loved thee, little *Innocence,*
And fain would love thee more, would love thee more.
Sweet, sweet flower! image of our heavenly birth,
And sole memento of our perished bliss!
Amidst the ruins of Humanity,
More grand and awful than the broken arch,
Column and lofty architrave of that
Proud temple of the Sun in desolate
Palmyra, fresh thy lowly head appears.
The human spirit, reared so high and pure
That it did on its Father's bosom lean
In felt communion as a holy child
To drink the glory of his image in,
Fallen and crushed, its beauty, holiness
And grandeur gone, now sad in ruin lies:
But yet in thee, the stream of heavenly life,
From year to year and age to age flows on;
And, constant as the Spring, in endless youth—
In *innocence,* blooms on thy lovely brow.

Strange that the foul and tainting air of earth
Hath ne'er seduced thee from thy rectitude;
Bedimmed the lustre of thy heavenly eye;
Rude rubbed the blush from off thy modest cheek;
Hung down thy head in shame of conscious guilt;
Then reared it up in bold effrontery,
That blushes not to either God or man!
O whence that strange, unutterable power
That breathes so holy round thy lowly head?
O whence that smile which steals into the heart,
Startling that culprit into breathless awe?
That still small voice which wakens in the soul
A dim remembrance of a something lost,
Whose name and image, faded from the breast,
We toil in vain, with anguish and remorse,
Long, long to summon into life again?

" Child of the dust, no more; my answer's short:

" When your high Nature fell and thundered down,
It caused an earthquake such as ne'er had shook,
And hath not shaken since, the world below;
Nor yet like that, when once again its Lord

---

* *Houstonia cærulia.*

Shall shake both it and heaven—to close the world.
Then I and all things staggered 'neath the shock,
As if the day of doom had crushed the world,
And sickening Death crept gasping through our veins.

"Then Innocence, as lovely angel, sad,
Her last walk through the bowers of Eden took.
Nor eye of man, of beast, nor yet of flower,
(As they were wont, in other, holy days,)
Kindling with joy, her form reflected back.
Indeed it was a mournful scene—and hard
Her tender heart was wrung, to see those forms,
So lofty once, in ruin prostrate now.
Where her own spirit, as in heaven at home,
Communed with beauty in its holiness,
An exile now and utterly alone,
In earth's aceldema herself she found.
Her voice, with power mysterious in its tones—
Whose like hath never since been heard on earth,
Save in the sacred land of Palestine,
When Justice drank the blood from Mercy's veins,
And sent her Voice to wander o'er the world,
And call the sons of men to life again
Her voice, which led the Paradisic choir,
Was silent now; for chokings of the heart
Stood armed to guard the pass from out her soul,
And exit there was none.

　　　　　"She sought the gate.
As near it there and near the path I stood,
And life's last flutterings trembled on my cheek.
The blushing wonder caught her eye surprised,
And kindled up its sparkling joys again.
Upon me there she fixed its heavenly blue,
Called back my youth, restored my purity;
And gazed until the same celestial hue
Beamed and returned betwixt our mutual eyes.
She sealed that color with a fervent kiss;
And, as she spread her pinions to the sky,
With her last tear, baptized me—INNOCENCE.
A being strange, her living miniature,
Thus pencilled by her eye, she left me here,
That man may see, though with his outward eye,
What he has exiled from her home, his heart,
And from the world—till back recalled,
" *The Seed*" shall seat her in her throne again,
To rule in peace a ransomed, holy world."　　　A. J. M. H.

ART. XIX.—Publications.

A Dictionary of the German and English Languages; indicating the accentuation of every German word, containing several hundred German synonyms, together with a classification and alphabetical list of the irregular verbs, and a dictionary of German abbreviations. Compiled from the works of *Hilpert, Flügel, Griel, Heyse*, and others. In two Parts: I. German and English. II. English and German. By *G. J. Adler, A. M., Professor of the German Language and Literature in the University of the City of New York.* New York: D. Appleton & Co. Philadelphia: George S. Appleton. 1849.

We find this work favorably noticed on all sides; and so far as we can judge from a general examination of its plan and execution, it seems to be every way worthy of such distinction. Its outward appearance, in the first place, can hardly fail to create an impression in its favor, with all who have any sort of taste for good style in the manufacture of books. The paper, type, binding, are all of the best order; in its whole mechanical character, the work is such as to reflect honor on the publishers, and may be counted indeed an ornament to the American press. For one who has been accustomed to the dingy blurred aspect presented by our common German Dictionaries, it produces a feeling of relief and satisfaction only to look at the clean, clear page which is here offered to his eye. The whole has a bright, cheerful air about it, which carries with it also, in its way, an enlivening and pleasant influence for the mind. The main merit of the work, however, is something more a great deal than this goodly outward show. Its literary or scientific contents are in full keeping with the promise it thus holds out to the eye. Seldom, indeed, has a work been published that might be considered equally complete in its kind. It is all that could well be demanded as a German Dictionary, for popular use among an English people.

It has its general basis in the work published at London, under the name of Flügel, though in reality compiled by Heimann, Feiling and Oxenford. This is considered the most complete and judicious which has appeared in England. Still it is only the *basis* of this American publication. The German-English part in particular, which is here made to take the lead, as it should, for English use, has been carefully revised, much of it re-written, and the whole augmented by an addition of at least thirty thousand new words and articles, making almost the half of it, indeed, to be entirely fresh matter. In these additions, the editor has availed himself, with independent and full learning, of the best lexicographical helps supplied by modern scholarship in Germany. One great advantage of the Dictionary is, the accentuation of the German words, which it gives according to the system of Heinsius and others. Another very valuable addition is found in the *synonyms*, which it presents in an abridged and not unfrequently somewhat modified form, from Hilpert. The vocabulary moreover of foreign words, as used in art, science, and more and more always in popular conversation, also, is far more full than in our common German Dictionaries.

It is encouraging to find such a work received with so much interest and favor. We have no blind enthusiasm for German learning; no sort of disposition to yield implicit trust to its authority; not the least faith, we may add, in the capacity of the German mind, as such, for bringing to proper practical solution the great questions of the present time. We are equally sure however, that this solution will never be reached by any system of thinking that allows itself to overlook or ignore the philosophy and learning of Germany, requiring the world to take in stead its own separate circle of notions as the consummation of all wisdom. The activity of the German mind, the power of German thought, enter largely into the general movement of the world's life as it now stands, and must be respected accordingly. This plainly is coming to be more and more felt and acknowledged on all sides. Above all may the German life, in this way, lay claim to favorable regard on the side of the English. The two nationalities are closely bound together, by original inward affinity. One may be taken as in some sense the explanation and complement of the other. So as regards mere language. No man can understand the English fully, who has not some knowledge of its analogies with the German. And so then too, of course, as regards mind; for language is ever but the outward form of thought. To be truly and thoroughly English, is to be in sympathy at least with what is truly and thoroughly German at the same time. N.

God in Christ.—Three discourses, delivered at New Haven, Cambridge, and Andover. With a Preliminary Dissertation on Language. By *Horace Bushnell.* Hartford: 1849.

We acknowledge thankfully a copy of this work, received from the respected author; to a mere general notice of which however we find ourselves confined by our present limits. The Discourses made some noise when they were preached; and now that they are put into book form, they seem to be in a fair way to make a good deal more. The misery of it is however, with our theology, that a little *noise* is generally the end of any agitation to which it is brought in this way. Our theological controversies are apt to go off in a volley of newspaper squibs, with a few declamatory review articles, which in the end discuss nothing and settle nothing scientifically, but simply lay the whole subject at last on the shelf, to make room for some new excitement equally superficial and equally ephemeral. What has ever come of the great question broached in Dr. Bushnell's tract on *Christian Nurture*, at all answerable to the vital character of the interests involved in it? So it will be probably with this new work. This we may well regret. For however wrong Dr. Bushnell may be in his views, it is not enough to dispose of him in this summary style. We believe him to be wrong. But we are very sure, at the same time, that he is struggling in his spirit towards great truth, and that the things he is warring with in the actual theology of New England, are no spectres simply of his own imagination, but very substantial realities at bottom, that greatly need in some way to be dragged into the light and properly exposed. For this reason, we honor his book, and hope that it may do good. Even the errors of an earnest wakeful mind, battling with the problems of life in a living way, it has been well remarked, may be more deserving of veneration, than the true notions of those in whom all such earnestness is wanting. We trust that Dr. Bushnell is thus honest; and we know, that his thoughts and inquiries lie in the direction of what must be regarded as the great central interest of the age, the constitution of Christ's person, and, as determined by this, the true idea also of the Christian Church. We would fain hope too, that his true sense and meaning are far more orthodox, than to many his language as it now stands may seem to imply. He discards the article of the *Eternal Generation* of the Son. We are sorry for this ; it seems to us to overthrow the true doctrine of the Trinity. But New England Orthodoxy has done as much before, without allowing the necessity of any such consequence. Altogether, however, we have no taste for his toleration toward *Unitarianism*, as though it were part and parcel still of the ruptured New England *Church*. His view of the *Atonement*, if we get hold of it at all, seems to us to turn it into a pure fiction and we see not how his Christ can be considered along with it to have much more substance than a Gnostic phantasm. If an *æsthetic* salvation is all that we need, sin must resolve itself last into something less than the vast *moral* evil it is always represented to be in the Scriptures. We know very well the general false conception which it is the object of Dr. Bushnell to exclude ; but that may be done far more effectually, we think, in a different way. We dislike again his opposition to what he calls *Dogma* in christianity, which must include, if we understand him, all systematic or scientific theology. Christianity is indeed primarily life, not doctrine ; but it is such a life as requires to take full possession, in the end, of our whole human being. This includes knowledge as well as action ; and why then should not the contents of the new creation lay claim to our understanding full as much as to our Will ? Just here Dr. Bushnell falls into contradiction with himself ; his New England habit of thought gets the better of the right churchly tendency, that lies involved in another part of his system. It is just *because* Christianity is a new life, that it must work like leaven into our whole existence, generating a theology or theoretic religion in its own form, as well as a religion of mere feeling and practice ; and just for this reason, too, it must be a process going forward from one age to another. All life is *historical*, not a dead outward tradition, but an inward continuously active movement. Dogma then, historically taken, forms an essential element in the constitution of the Church. Christianity starts in the Apostles' Creed, and can be true in any age only as it continues to grow forth from this as its root ; but is not bound by any means confessionally, through all time, to the limits of Creed ; just as little as the man is required to take his measure from the child, out of which, notwithstanding, all his growth springs. Dr. Bushnell is not prepared to do justice to the historical objective character of Christianity, as it meets us in the Universal Church.

THE

MERCERSBURG REVIEW.

JULY, 1849.

NO. IV.

THE APOSTLES' CREED.
III. Its Material Structure or Organism.

THE articles of the Creed, in its full form, gather themselves up, in the first place, into three parts; the first treating, as our Catechism has it, of God the Father and our creation; the second of God, the Son, and our redemption; the third of God, the Holy Ghost, and our sanctification. Christianity rests throughout on the mystery of the Ever Blessed Trinity, as revealed for the apprehension of faith through the incarnation of our Lord and Saviour Jesus Christ.

In this way, however, the three parts of the Creed now mentioned, fall back ultimately upon a single proposition, affirming the fact of the revelation thus made by Christ. The whole Christian faith, as we have had occasion to say before, finds its primary central utterance in the confession of Peter: "Thou art the Christ, the Son of the living God." This accordingly must be taken as the foundation article of the Creed, on which its whole subsequent structure is to be regarded as resting from the beginning. This does not imply, of course, that Christ is in any way the ground or source of the Trinity itself, but only that the being and presence of God under this form come by him to an actual revelation in the world. He underlies in this way the entire mystery of the new creation, as it is in the process of being brought to pass through the Church; which is said accordingly to be built upon the foundation of the apostles and prophets, Jesus Christ himself being the chief corner-stone.

This confession of Peter is well suited to exemplify the true conception of the Creed, as it has been already represented and explained. It is no mere opinion, borrowed from others or the product of private reflection, to which utterance is thus solemnly given. It is the conviction of faith, as immediately exercised upon the living person of the Redeemer himself. Others might think him to be Elias, or Jeremias, or some other of the ancient prophets, but Peter *knew* him to be more than all this; the revelation of his higher nature, his immediate union with God, had made itself felt in the inmost soul of the disciple as a part of his own life; and so he was prepared to exclaim in the language, not of speculation, but of lively heart-felt creed, *Thou art the Christ, the Son of the living God.* That the confession carried in it this high character, we are expressly assured by our Saviour himself. "Blessed art thou, Simon Bar-jona," we hear him saying; "for flesh and blood hath not revealed it unto thee, but my Father which is in heaven."

The confession utters, in the most immediate and direct way, the fact of Christianity, the new order of life it has brought into the world, as apprehended under its most general character in the person of Christ. The object so apprehended by faith, and thus at once brought to utterance, is no doctrine or report simply concerning Christ, but the glorious reality of the incarnation itself, as exhibited in him under a historical and enduring form. Christianity resolves itself ultimately into this mystery. It has its principle and root in Christ's person. So are we taught most clearly and fully, in the New Testament. The Word reveals itself in him, not by outward oracle or prophecy, but by becoming *flesh :* he is the living comprehension of the truth he proclaims, the actual world of grace itself, which he unfolds and makes known. He is the way, the truth, and the life, by whom alone it is possible for any one else to come to the Father. He is the resurrection and the life; not the proclaimer simply of the doctrine of a future state and the soul's immortality, but the very ground and medium of the whole fact. The new creation which is, at the same time, the end and completion of the old, starts from the mystery of his person, and holds from first to last in the power of the indissoluble union, thus established between earth and heaven, eternity and time. The incarnation is the deepest and most comprehensive fact, in the economy of the world. Jesus Christ authenticates himself, and all truth and reality besides; or rather all truth and reality are such, only by the relation in which they stand to him, as their great centre and last ground. In him are hid thus all the treasures of wisdom and knowledge. He is the absolute revelation of God in the world; the brightness of the Father's glory, and the express image of his person. As all this, he is no object primarily of intellection, but can be apprehended only by faith; and in this form, he constitutes the sum and substance of Christianity, as it lives in the consciousness of the Church and finds its expression in the Creed.

It is easy to see here the difference between the contents of faith as actual, and its contents again as simply potential. Peter's christianity, at the time of this confession, fell far short of the sense he had of the new creation in Christ Jesus after the day of Pentecost. It included no apprehension of Christ's sufferings and death, of his resurrection and ascension, or of his glorious mediatorial kingdom. It brought with it no knowledge of the Holy Ghost as he works in the Church, no knowledge of the Church itself, or of its cardinal attributes, no distinct sense of the glorious prerogatives and privileges comprehended in its communion. We have no right to suppose, that the mystery, even of the holy Trinity, or the doctrine of our Saviour's true and proper divinity, as afterwards defined, came clearly into Peter's view, when he uttered his wonderful confession. It would have been hard for him probably, to say, what view he had precisely of Christ's person, or what exactly he expected from his life. He was simply overwhelmed with the felt power of God's presence, as it broke upon him, under a form transcending all other revelations, in the "glory of the only begotten of the Father, full of grace and truth." And yet his faith, in this form of primitive and undivided simplicity, was, in its own nature, universal and complete. In its apprehension of Christ, as a living reality, it embraced in truth the entire meaning and power of Christ, as set forth afterwards in the full Creed. All its articles were there, though still to a great extent only under a latent or potential form. As the new creation grows forth actually from the mystery of Christ's person, being from first to last the evolution or developement simply of capabilities, relations and powers, that are treasured up in him from the beginning; so the sense of what Christ is as the incarnate Word, when it enters the soul by faith, however circumscribed the horizon of its sight may be at the first, brings with it surely, in the end, by proper culture, all that the full idea of Christianity requires. The mere notion of Christ, or an abstract thought made to stand for him in the Unitarian sense cannot, of course, do this; but it is the very character of faith, as distinguished from all fancy of opinion, that it is called into exercise and determined in the nature of its action, by the supernatural object from which it is filled, as form, with its proper contents. As the *real* apprehension of Christ thus, it can embrace him only as he actually is, from the beginning, and must carry in itself thus an inward necessity of developement always under the same form and no other. Of all this we are indirectly assured, by the high honor put on Peter's confession when it was first spoken. This stands not simply in the marvellous and sublime benediction which was pronounced upon his faith, considered as his own, but still more in the proclamation made of its value and power for the future Church. "Thou art *Peter*"—now, indeed, first worthy in full of thine own name—"and on this *rock*," (the living Creed here incorporated with thy life,) "I will build my Church, and the gates of hell shall not prevail against it."* Narrow as the foundation

---

* Nothing can well be more miserable in its way, than the shifts which have been resorted to here to wrest this great passage out of the hands of the Romanists. Some turn it into a sort of pun or ambiguous play on Peter's name, in which Christ *pointed* to his own person, as he spake, to show the true sense of his riddle. Others make the doctrine avowed in Peter's confession, to be the rock on which the Church is built. All in full disregard of the context, as well as of the special stirring solemnity of the whole

might seem to some, this single article of the incarnation, "Christ the Son of the living God," really embraced by faith, bears up in the end the entire superstructure of Christianity. All Christian theology, as well as all Christian life, starts here, and flows forward from this as its all comprehending source. Here, as we have seen, the outward history of the Creed commences; and here also we find the power, from which is generated its entire structure, inwardly considered. This article, in the form of *creed*, or as made to be actually present in the life of the world by faith, is, in very truth, the ROCK, on which rests the Church, and that may be said to support the new heavens and the new earth themselves, through this as "the pillar and ground of the truth."

Out of this primary article grows, in the first place, generally, the faith of the holy *Trinity ;* as it comes before us, for instance, in the formula of baptism : " Go teach all nations, baptizing them in the name of the Father, and of the Son, and of the Holy Ghost." So we have it also in the apostolic benediction : "The grace of our Lord Jesus, and the love of God, and the communion of the Holy Ghost. be with you all." This threefold view of the divine nature, proceeds from the apprehension of Christ, as the Son of the living God. This does not mean, of course, that the fact of the Trinity commences with the incarnation; the

occasion as presented in the evangelical narrative. It is, indeed, a contradiction, against which all religion revolts, to found the Church, in the Roman sense, on the person of Peter separately considered; but neither can it be said to rest on Christ, or on the thought and confession of his name, in any like outward and separate view. The idea of the *Church* requires the flowing together of our common human existence and the higher life revealed in Christ. So long as they stand apart, the new creation must be without effect in the world. It holds altogether in the mystery, by which, through the capacity of faith on one side and the wonderful power of the Holy Ghost on the other, the fallen weak nature of man is so linked with the very life of Christ, "God manifest in the flesh," as to become one with it in a living way. This fact it is, the passing over of Christ's life into the life of the world, the comprehension of the last in the sense of the first, which forms the soul of Peter's confession; and on this living ground, of a truth, as it was now laid in him and his fellow-apostles, the Church, which binds earth and heaven together, was to be built to the end of time.

filiation of the Son, and the procession of the Holy Ghost, as
they hold in the being of God himself, are from eternity. Neither does it mean, however, simply, that the doctrine of the holy
Trinity has been published by Christ more clearly than before.
We meet with no such outward proclamation, in his ministry
and word. Some have objected to the doctrine on this very
ground, that being so mysterious, and so fundamental as the
Church pretends to her whole constitution, so little stress is laid
upon it, in the way of clear categorical statement, in the New
Testament. And there must be allowed to be no small force in
the objection, if the revelation of christianity be taken, as it often
is taken, to stand primarily in the form of word or thought for
the understanding. It only shows, however, in truth, that such
is not its original and fundamental form. It is not primarily a
a doctrine spoken by Christ, but a fact comprehended in his person; which as such, accordingly, is to be apprehended and appropriated by the world in the way of creed, before it can enter
truly into its intelligence or outward life. Christ then, is neither
the creator of the Trinity, nor simply its proclaimer; but the
form of its explication in the economy of time, the medium by
which it manifests itself for faith, and so for knowledge, in the
consciousness of the world. The economical Trinity, as it is
sometimes styled, in distinction from its immanent character, the
Trinity in its relations to man, as it goes forth from eternity into
time, for the accomplishment of our salvation—the only form in
which the mystery can be said at all to have for us any *rerela-
tion*—comes fully into view only and wholly by Christ. There
are indeed, adumbrations of the idea, what may be called a spiritual *nisus* towards it in the depths of the human spirit, in the
religion and philosophy even of the heathen world; and still
clearer intimations of it are to be found in the revelation of the
Old Testament, like streaks of light in advance of the rising
day; just as in all respects christianity completes the sense of
our universal life, by which, at the same time, thus its advent is
gloriously harbingered from the beginning. But still the absolute and proper revelation of the Trinity, is brought to pass at
last only in the person of Christ, and by the mystery of the incarnation. So it is expressly affirmed in the New Testament.

He is the brightness of the Father's glory, and the express image of his person: No man hath seen the Father, the only begotten Son which is in the bosom of the Father, he hath *revealed* him: No man knoweth the Father but the Son, and he to whom the Son shall *reveal* him. God had manifested himself to a certain extent, came forth in some measure from the awful solitude of his own absolute being, in the work of creation, and in the course of history as it stood before Christ came. But all this fell short immeasurably of the self-manifestation which took place in the *act* of the incarnation, when the everlasting Word became flesh, and linked itself into one life with the life of the world itself, as raised to its highest power in man. God came forth in this act, manifested himself, laid himself open in the form of life to the view of faith, as never in all revelations before. Only so was it possible for the mystery of the Trinity to bring itself out clearly in the apprehension of the world; and in no other form, than as thus apprehended, can the doctrine be of any true value or force. Never was there a greater mistake, than to conceive of it as primarily an abstract theory or speculation. It is the most practical of all truths; for it lies, in the form of *fact*, at the ground of the whole christian revelation, and is in truth the very form in which this revelation makes itself real, through faith, in the consciousness of the Church. This precisely is the mystery that faith finds in Christ. It lies at the foundation of christianity. To be baptized into Christ, is to be baptized into the holy Trinity. The faith and apprehension of God in three persons, Father, Son, and Holy Ghost, lie involved from the beginning, in Peter's confession—Thou art the Christ, the Son of the living God.

It is only by this view of the revelation of the Trinity, that we can at all maintain the credit of the doctrine as a part of christianity. Infidels and Unitarians are able easily enough to show, not merely that no pains are taken to affirm it with clear doctrinal precision, (after the fashion of our catechisms,) in the New Testament; but also that the doctrinal statements of the early Church in regard to it, continue to be for a long time very indefinite and insecure. We do not find the distinction of persons in the Godhead, and their several relations, clearly and fully apprehended from the beginning, in the form under which all was afterwards defined and settled. This has often embarrassed those whose conception of christianity requires it to start in the form of doctrine rather than in the form of life. With any right view, however, of its true nature in this respect, the difficulty is made at once to vanish. The Trinity unfolds itself, discloses itself as a fact, only in the historical process of the incarnation, the mystery revealed by Christ's person; and in this way, of course, only as this mystery is made to pass over truly, through faith, into the living constitution of the world, so as to underlie it and take possession of it as the power of a new creation. Thus revealed and apprehended, the entire fact might be in the life of the Church, long before it could be brought to any satisfactory representation in the form of thought. So we have it proclaimed from the start, in the Apostles' Creed. The Trinity is there, not indeed in full theological statement as afterwards settled, but still in the overwhelming sense of its necessary substance, as it looks out upon the world through the glorious fact of the incarnation, and completes its presence in the Church, "the fulness of Him that filleth all in all." The new creation stands throughout in the mystery of the Triune God, Father, Son, and Holy Ghost, historically brought to light by the union of the everlasting Word with our fallen flesh.

The Creed is the utterance of this mystery as it unfolds itself by Christ, in the consciousness of the christian world. All forms a single revelation, which takes effect, however, in the way of magnificent process, starting in the bosom of the Father, and completing itself finally in the full glories of the new earth and new heavens. The end accordingly, grows out of the beginning, and is comprehended in it from the start. The new creation commences with the Father, enters the world through the incarnation of the Son, and runs its course in the world's life subsequently, by the Holy Ghost constantly present and always active in the Church. Such is the order in which the three grand divisions of the Creed come into view; each forming a complete whole within itself, with more or less full utterance of its leading landmark facts; while the entire contents of the second are apprehended, as flowing in the way of derivation from the first; and then again, as coming to their full issue and last sense, only in the broad sea of glory which is thrown open by the third. In the case of each division, moreover, the characteristic points of fact which it is made to include, whether more or less full, follow each other to a certain extent, in the same way. They are not properly so many items of truth, separately propounded for our reception, as they are notes and characters rather that mark the onward progress of the great universal fact to which they belong, and by which they have place. The Creed rolls thus, like a lofty anthem, with continuous stream of music, rising and swelling throughout on the same key, from its commencement to its close. We may style it a panoramic view of the " pure river of water of life," the moving process of the world's redemption, as it starts from the throne of God and of the Lamb, and flows forward by successive stages, with paradise on its banks, to the region of light and immortality in which finally the Holy Catholic Church shall become forever complete.

All begins in "God the Father, Almighty, Maker of heaven and earth." This is not to be taken, of course, as an article here, of mere natural religion, which may be supposed to go before the revelation of Christianity and to make room for its presence. God does, indeed, reveal himself through nature, as the absolute ground of the universe. But Christianity does not simply take up this fact as thus previously at hand, and then go on to add to it new truths of its own. It goes beyond all previous revelations, and especially all merely natural religion, not only extensively in the amount of what it makes known, but also *intensively* in the depth and power of its apprehension. God in Christ is indeed the God of nature; but with such new self-manifestation of his interior life, as makes him to be, even in this last relation, a wholly different being for our faith, from all he seemed to be before. The revelation of nature is shadowy and superficial, as compared with that which has place in Christ; and it is only by means of this finally, that it comes to its own full significance and sense. Christianity then allows no simply natural religion in its bosom. " When that which is perfect, is come, then that which is in part shall be done away ;" the relative, as such, enters not into the composition of the absolute. So the Creed embraces God, even in his character of Creator, as he has now come to be known, not simply in nature, but in the person of his Son Jesus Christ; "by whom also he made the worlds;" and through whom alone, "in these last days," the full sense of that first creation is fairly brought to light. He is recognized thus, and worshipped, not merely as the author of nature, or as the supreme being, in the cold language of rationalistic deism, but as "the God and Father of our Lord Jesus Christ," who is disclosed to the vision of faith, *through him*, as *our* Father also, the fountain and source of the new glorious creation revealed in his person. In this way it is, we are encouraged to approach him in the Lord's Prayer; and in no other view can he be the object of a truly Christian faith. It is through the apprehension of Christ, as the Son of the living God, in the sense of Peter's confession, that the Creed throws us back to this first article as its own everlasting ground and foundation. "He that hath seen ME," our Saviour himself says, "hath *seen the Father.*"

In the second section of the Creed, this sublime revelation is represented as going forward, to the actual apprehension of faith, in the historical person of our Blessed Redeemer, Jesus of Nazareth, from the point of his miraculous conception and birth, onward to the completion of his glory finally at the right hand of God in heaven; where he reigns head over all things to the Church, and from whence he shall come at the last day to judge the quick and the dead. "The Life was manifested," says St. John, "and we have seen it, and bear witness, and show unto you that eternal Life, which was with the Father, and was manifested to us." The mystery of the incarnation is not strictly a fact, which is to be considered as complete all at once from the point where it commences. In any such view, it would be more magical than real. Our human life does not hold at all under any such stationary character; but is, in its very conception, a fact that accomplishes itself only in the way of historical process and growth. To become human at all then, to enter truly into the stream of man's life, it was indispensable that the Son of God should take humanity upon him, not suddenly and abruptly, but with progressive order, agreeably to the general law of all existence in time. His life as human, moreover, could not become absolutely complete, so as to display the full sense and meaning of its union with the divine nature, until it was brought, in the way of regular historical progress, to surmount in full the limitations of our present mortal state, thus triumphing over death and him that had the power of death, in the glory of the resurrection. Hence altogether, in the very nature of the case, the stupendous fact of the incarnation, resolves itself into a series or chain of events, a living historical process rather, by which the mystery enters more intimately and deeply always into the drama of the world's life; till finally it becomes complete, and is found to have its perfect work, when "Jesus was glorified," and the windows of heaven were opened thus, (John vii. 39,) for the power of his Spirit to descend in full measure upon the earth. Only under such view, can the faith, which the Creed requires us to exercise in Christ, be considered real and true. Hence the general fact comprised in his person, is drawn out in a succession of historical points, that mark and define its progress from the womb of the Virgin to God's right hand. These, we can see at once, might easily be more or less in number, without affecting the substance of the main article, or the general design with which they are brought forward. As the Creed now stands however, they are wonderfully pertinent and complete; as we shall see presently, when we come to speak more particularly of their significance as articles of faith.

The mystery of the incarnation, as it stands before us in the person of Christ, includes two sides, which must both enter steadily into our faith, to make it complete. We must apprehend, in the first place, the presence of a truly divine life in the fact, the entrance of God into the world as he had not been in it before; in the second place, this life must be admitted under a true human form, and in such relation to the previous constitution of the world, that it shall not violate its order, but be felt rather to fall in with it organically and complete its sense. Thus in Peter's confession, the power of his faith shows itself just in the firm combination of these two views. "The Son of the living God"—a new full manifestation of the divine life—"art *thou*," the living human Master, whom we follow and serve. This *felt* apprehension of the union of the divine and human, the infinite and the historical, in Christ's person, was that precisely which imparted to the faith of the disciple such high value in his Master's eyes.

So the Creed affirms first the full presence of God's life, in the awful fact which is here proclaimed. "I believe in Jesus Christ, his only begotten Son, our Lord." This is to be taken in direct continuation of what goes before; and asserts, in fact, that our faith in God the Father himself is conditioned by the real revelation, under which he is made known to us in Christ; as it is said in one place by the Saviour himself: "This is life eternal, that they might know thee, the only true God, and Jesus Christ whom thou hast sent" (John xvii. 3); and, again, by the Apostle John: "We know that the Son of God is come, and hath given us an understanding, that we may know him that is true: and we are in him that is true, even in his Son Jesus Christ. This is the true God and eternal life" (1 John v. 20). The Creed, in the strongest manner, asserts this identification of Christ with the contents of God's life, so far as this can be an object either of faith or knowledge for men; in full correspondence with what is said in the first chapter of St. John's gospel: The same Word which was in the beginning, which was with God, and which was God, in the fulness of time became flesh, and tabernacled among us, exhibiting his glory as of the only begotten of the Father, full of grace and truth; no man hath seen God at any time, the only begotten Son, which is in the bosom of the Father, he hath declared him.

Then follows however, at length, the assertion, no less clear and firm, of the true human and historical character of all this revelation, in the person of Jesus of Nazareth. The Son of the living God, who is here embraced as the object of faith, "was conceived of the Holy Ghost and born of the Virgin Mary." So the supernatural in him links itself organically with the existing constitution of the world, and lays the foundation thus within it for a new and higher order of life. The miraculous conception becomes a natural birth, making room and way for the coming of Christ in the flesh. Such a birth implies growth, development, progress in stature and wisdom (Luke ii. 52); and the life of Christ involves subsequently his full ministry and work. In this way, the Creed might include other dates and facts in his history, such as his baptism, temptation, miracles, &c., and still not suffer any material alteration. It does include all these points in truth, though only in a latent way, and as comprehended in the general fact; while its utterance confines itself to the great and necessary outline simply of the Saviour's history as a whole. In this way, we are carried at once to the close of his life under its earthly form: "He suffered under Pontius Pilate; was crucified, dead, and buried; descended into hell." His existence in the world was human throughout, rounded in as a living process from the womb to the grave. As he came into the world by a real birth, notwithstanding the divine sublimity of his nature as the Son of the living God, so he went forth from it at last by a real death. His was no fantastic manhood only, that played itself off on the eyes of men as true, when it was only a Gnostic shadow, or vision, in fact. He suffered under a Roman magistrate, openly, publicly, and with solemn form. and this passion ran out into a most real and full dissolution of body and soul; it was no sleep or swoon, but death; his body was laid in the grave, while his soul went into hades, the intermediate state. This last clause, as we have seen before, was introduced at a comparatively late period. It was, however, virtually a part of the Creed from the beginning: having no other object at last, than to affirm explicitly, what had been affirmed all along by implication, in the assertion of his death and burial. The descent to hades is indispensable to complete the conception of a full obedience to the law of mortality, comprehended in the problem which Christ came to fulfil. Short of this, his death could not be regarded as a historical fact.

The death of Christ, however, as an object of faith, is far more than the termination simply of a common human life. The person, of whom all this holds, is still the Son of the living God, the everlasting Word in union with our weak mortal flesh. The *reality* of this conception requires then, that the higher nature here at work should not allow itself to be overwhelmed and crushed in the process, but so enter into it, as to assert in the end its own superiority in the way of universal triumph over its terrific power. The sufferings and death of the Son of God involve thus necessarily, for faith, the idea of a *conflict*, the issue of which is a full victory over death and the grave, as well as over the power of sin from which they come. It was not possible, we are told, that he should be holden of death (Acts ii. 24); that he should sink to rise no more, in the catastrophe, which brought his mortal state to a close. This *impossibility* is perceived and felt by faith, even while it acknowledges his passion; the sufferings of the Son of God are proclaimed, as the very form in which he destroyed death, and him that had the power of death, that is, the devil, and thus brought in righteousness and immortality for all that believe in his name. So it follows immediately: "The third day he rose again from the dead; he ascended into heaven, and sitteth at the right hand of God, the Father, Almighty." All in continuation simply of the living process, on which he entered at his birth. The true universal significance of his life, as including in itself a deeper power than the law of mortality he came to abolish, now comes into view. The nature he had assumed, is made to surmount the limitations of its first state, and rises triumphant to the skies. Hades is shorn of its strength, the grave resigns its prey: he that descended into the lower parts of the earth (Eph. iv. 9, 10), is the *same* that is seen to ascend up far above all heavens, that he might fill all things. The old order of the world in his case, is brought to an end; he leads captivity captive; man, in his person, finds himself exalted finally to his proper supremacy over the whole inferior creation. All things are placed under his dominion, and he is head over all things, to the Church. In this character, he must reign till all enemies are put under his feet, and the whole world subdued into harmony with the order of the new creation. His mediatorial government extends, by the very nature of the case, from the hour of his exaltation onward to the end of time; and finds its necessary conclusion in the general judgment. So all is comprehended here again, as in the case of our Saviour's first state, within the extremes that bound the entire stadium on either side: and, with a single stroke, we have this part of the Creed complete: "From thence he shall come to judge the quick and the dead."

In all this representation of the Saviour's personal history, the outline of his life as it reaches from his introduction into the world on to the winding up of his mediatorial reign, we have, after all, it must be borne in mind, the evolution simply of the one single fact in which Christianity begins, as proclaimed in Peter's confession: "Thou art the Christ, the Son of the living God." The several specifications employed to set it forth, are not to be taken as so many independent propositions, asserted on separate evidence, and brought together in the way of collective sum; they might be more, or they might be less; but in any case they are to be taken as bound together in the constitution of one and the same great object of faith, out of which, in the end flows all their title to a place in the Creed. For instance, it would be a mistake to suppose that the miraculous conception, or the descent to hades, or the resurrection and ascension into heaven, are exhibited as articles of christian belief, which we may be expected to receive in the first place on their own proofs separately considered, and then lay away under this form in the general repository of our faith; as though the Creed were the accumulation merely of such theological conclusions and results. The only *ground* of all Christian faith, we have seen already, to be the person of the Lord Jesus Christ himself. To suppose now, however, that the miraculous conception, or the resurrection, might be made certain by themselves, in the first place, on proofs lying wholly out of Christ, is to contradict this conception in full. There is no such contradiction in the Creed. Every topic affirmed here of Christ's history, is an article of *faith* in the high christian sense; a reality that belongs not to the world of nature and sense as such, but to the new creation, in which heaven and earth are brought supernaturally together by the mystery of the incarnation; no outward witnesses and no common human reasons, impart to it its ultimate credibility; this lies in the relation in which it is felt to stand to the fact of the Saviour's person itself. The grand argument after all, for the great distinctive *memorabilia* of Christ's theanthropic life, and that without which no evidence besides could make them certain, is comprehended in his own presence. The first condition of all knowledge here, is an entrance, by faith, into the central fact of the Gospel, as

we have it presented to us in the living and moving form of the
Divine Word itself, incarnate for us men, and our salvation, in
the Virgin's Son.   Not as we stand on the threshold merely of
this sublime and magnificient temple, but only as we pass into
the awful bosom of the sanctuary itself, may we ever expect to
apprehend as they are the forms and proportions of its true interior structure.   Only in proportion as my faith is first overwhelmed with the sense of Christ's real divine majesty, as the
Son of the living God made flesh, can I be brought to admit
with firm faith, on any evidence, the astounding mystery of his
birth, or the no less astounding mystery of his resurrection. The
whole lies *beyond* nature, in the sphere of a new order of life
which is revealed in Christ and nowhere else; how then should
it be apprehensible at all, or creditable, under any other form of
observation?   But, on the other hand, let the sense of Christ's
majesty so overwhelm the mind, in the first place, and these
mysteries, astounding as they are, can no longer be repelled;
they are felt to be indispensable to the conception of his person.
Such a person could not come into the world by the ordinary
course of nature ; and equal violence is involved in the imagination of his yielding finally, like other men, to the power of
the grave.   The man Christ, as he stands before us there through
the medium of Peter's faith, is felt to be a fact that transcends the
whole course of nature, even while it discloses itself historically
in its bosom; it is the presence and power of a higher supernatural order of existence in union with nature, which cannot, as
such, be included and bound within its economy as it stood before, either first or last.   Faith in Christ, as the revelation of a
divine life in the world, cannot stand at all in connection with
the supposition, either of his being born, or of his remaining in
the grave, like other men.   In any such view, it would cease to
be this faith altogether, and the Christ of the Creed would no
longer exist, except as a phantom for the imagination.

Thus it is that all the points of this historical confession, however some of them might seem to be accessible to our knowledge
at least, to some extent in a different way, yet in the true force
and spirit of the Creed, are to be taken as supernatural truths,
which can be rightly apprehended and uttered only by faith in

full communication throughout with the grand primary fact to which they belong and from which they spring. Even the passion of the Saviour, his sufferings under Pontius Pilate, his bloody death and burial, are vastly more in this case than topics of natural intelligence; the apprehension of them, as entering into the life of Christ, the Son of the living God, lifts them at once into the supernatural sphere in which that life holds; and it requires accordingly the same sort of faith to say, " *Christ died,*" which we need to add immediately, " and rose again." The fact of the resurrection witnessed by *sense*, that is as a mere phenomenon in the world of nature, would not be its truth as asserted in the Creed; just as little as the sight and acknowledgment of Christ's miracles, in the days of his flesh, amounted, with the Scribes and Pharisees, to any true apprehension of his divine glory. The idea of Christ is not of itself his history; but it is only through the power of it, as actually at hand, for faith, that his history becomes intelligible and enters also into our creed under a corresponding mode of existence.

The great fact of the Creed, the revelation of the Ever Blessed Trinity in the mystery of redemption, completes itself finally in the Holy Ghost, through whose presence in the world the saving power of Christ's life is carried over to his people. A new region of glory is thus thrown open to the vision of faith, including as before, a flowing process, whose commencement is here joined at once with its magnificent end. The whole however, as already intimated, is but a continuation of the one stupendous mystery that goes before. Our faith in the Holy Ghost is not drawn from some other quarter, and then made to range itself as a separate and independent belief, along with our faith in the Incarnation; it grows forth from this as its necessary and only sufficient ground; it can have no value, no reality in truth, save as it is made to enter our minds in this way. So too our faith in Christ completes itself legitimately only in the faith of the Holy Ghost. A true christology, involving, as it must, a living sense of the true universal import of Christ's life, carries in itself a demand for the extension of its power, in some way, over to the race he came to redeem. The river of life which first opens upon our view in his person, must flow over these banks in the end, and become a sea of glory, filling the whole world. This can be accomplished only through the living activity of the Holy Ghost; whose proper personality and work, accordingly, faith is thus brought to apprehend, as the necessary complement, we may say, of what it has previously apprehended as the presence of God in Christ. We read of God's Spirit as present with a certain kind of action in the world, before Christ came; but it will not do to take this as identical at all with the form of his presence in the world since. We are plainly told, that the Spirit as he now works in the Church, could not be given till Christ was glorified; the mystery of the incarnation must complete its course in his person, before room could be made for the farther revelation of its power in the other form. This accordingly was the great promise for which his disciples were directed to wait, when he left the world; the fulfilment of which too, as we all know, took place on the day of Pentecost, and laid the foundations of the Christian Church. The article, "I believe in the Holy Ghost," has regard altogether to this revelation, the entrance of God's Spirit into the process of the world's life as the Spirit of Jesus Christ, under such form of existence and action as had no place before, and was first rendered possible only by the new creation brought to pass in his person. To accept the doctrine of the Holy Ghost as true on *other* grounds, and under a simply abstract form, can not satisfy at all the sense of the Apostles' Creed. The only faith in the Holy Ghost it knows, is that which is conditioned by faith in the sublime Christology that goes before, and which grows out of this as its cause and ground.

Forth from this divine spring-head now rolls, in conclusion, the full tide of Christianity, as it is found still pouring itself forward, age after age, in the Church. The topics or heads that follow, stand related again to the primary article, much as we have found the several clauses in regard to Christ to be related to the general article of the incarnation. They serve simply to draw out and define graphically the contents of our faith in the Holy Ghost. The Holy Ghost is apprehended in the Creed, not as an abstraction or thought merely, but as a fact actually revealing itself in the world; and the form of this revelation expresses itself comprehensively in the "Holy Catholic Church," where the new creation is exhibited in grand outline, as "the communion of saints, the forgiveness of sins, the resurrection of the body, and the life everlasting."

The article of the Church, then, of course, is not made co-ordinate in any way with the articles of the Father, Son, and Holy Ghost. We are not to believe *in* the Church, as we are required to believe in God; we believe it simply, as we believe the resurrection of the body and the life everlasting; it is something sure to us, as the form under which the Holy Ghost is apprehended, as historically present and active in the world. So the world itself may be an object of faith, (Heb. xi. 3,) when the revelation of God in it is truly seen and felt. It must be always kept in mind, however, that this involves far more than the knowledge of it by mere sense. The world does not properly beget our faith in God; but it is this faith, rather, which enables us to believe the world, as the true sacrament of his presence. And so the Church also, the new creation in Christ Jesus, notwithstanding the subordinate character now assigned to it, is still altogether an object, not of sense and natural knowledge, but of faith. However accessible it may be under certain aspects to mere outward observation, its actual reality and substance, as affirmed in the Creed, are ever to be acknowledged as something divine, of which no proper assurance can be had in any such outward way. The entire Creed has to do with realities that hold in a world above nature, (though not abstractly disjoined from it,) and that can be apprehended, accordingly, as they are, only by faith. To believe the Church, then, is something far more than to believe the presence of some certain, tangible and visible organization in the world, like the British Parliament, for instance, of which we can take the measure and gauge by direct outward inspection. Such palpability in the case of the Church, even if it were fully at hand, would not of itself bring with it what this article requires; just as little as the *sight* of Christ after his resurrection, might be taken as equivalent to the sense of it by faith. The invisible and supernatural here, as throughout the Creed, must be apprehended as going before the outward, underlying it, and filling it with its true and necessary sense. We rise not from the region of sense here, into the region of spirit; but from the region of spirit itself, rather, as we have come to be in it already by the faith of our Lord Jesus Christ, we descend into the region of sense and actual life; and by virtue of the same assurance with which we say: *Thou art the Christ, the Son of the living God*, are enabled and urged at the same time to exclaim: *We believe in the Holy Catholic Church*. The revelation of grace and truth which starts in the mystery of the incarnation, the great christological fact here disclosed to the view of faith, runs forward, of itself, into the mystery of the Church. We need no outward precepts and texts here to prop up our belief and make it rational; on this *rock*, the Church is built as a living necessary fact; and if it have no reality for our faith in such form, it is in vain to expect that it can ever be made an object of faith to us truly in any other way.

Thus apprehended in its ideal constitution, as the necessary outbirth of Christ's Mediatorial life, the Church waits for no definition from abroad, but proceeds at once to define itself, in the Creed, as One, Holy, and Catholic; which at once includes also the title Apostolical, as afterwards frequently introduced. These attributes come not from without, hang not at all on men's invention or consent, rest not primarily on any basis of empirical observation or induction. They are the necessary conditions of the *idea*, which is here laid hold of by faith, as something given and made sure through the mystery of Christianity itself. It will not do to cut and square this, with arbitrary violence, into our own shape; we must take it as it stands, and interpret it accordingly. To say that facts forbid such a construction of the Church, is only to say in other words, that the idea of Christianity presented in the Creed is a fiction, and along with this that its view of Christ's person is false; for the one conception flows with inward necessary deduction from the other. From the stand-point of the Creed, the attributes of the Church are just as fixed and certain, in its own sense, as the being which is felt to belong to it as the Body of Christ. It is this relation precisely in which it stands to his person, that fixes and settles its character in all the respects here under consideration. If it be in very truth the comprehension of a new and higher order of life for the world, the fountain of which is the Redeemer himself, it must require in its own nature unity, sanctity and catholicity. It must be such a positive whole, as owns nothing beyond itself, and can allow no schism within itself. As it is the most perfect form of human life, so it must claim authority also as the most universal. It must be apostolical too, or in other words strictly *historical*, a real continuously active constitution from the time of the Apostles on to the end of the world. All this is implied, for faith, in the lively sense of what is comprehended in Christ's person; as all skepticism or indifference, on the other hand, in regard to these necessary attributes of the Church, is a worm which may be said to lie at last very near to the core of Christianity itself.

The mystical supernatural character of the Church, as now described, is expressed in one word as the "communion of saints." The Creed means not by this, of course, to resolve it into the ordinary fellowship of kindred minds. The object is rather to lift the conception distinctly into a higher sphere. Nothing can be more real than this new order of existence, though the law which underlies it, and the bond that holds it together, be "not of this world" in the ordinary view. Its common universal character is membership in Christ, who is the one everlasting foundation of a life, more real, and deep, and solid, and enduring, than all that belongs to the world besides. To believe the *communion of saints*, as such a supernatural constitution in Christ, historically present in the world, binding all ages of the Church together as a single whole, reaching over into the intermediate state, and destined to break forth at last into the full triumph of the resurrection, amid the glories of the new heavens and the new earth, may well be counted something high and great, and worthy of the place it holds in the Creed. "*Fools* never raise their thoughts so high;" mere flesh and blood can bring us truly to no such revelation.

Within this mystery now of the new creation, is comprehended the process by which individual souls, from age to age, are gathered from ruin and made meet for eternal glory. To a vast deal of our modern thinking, the order observed here by the Creed must appear careless, at least, and ill-advised. It would be led far more naturally to say: I believe in repentance and conversion, then in the communion of saints, and finally, in some sort

of holy catholic church; putting the individual isolated christianity, in order of thought, before that which is general and collective. The early Church, however, had a different way of
looking at the matter; and the difference is here very plainly
graven upon- rock, in this old monumental symbol. The
Church is taken to be the Holy Mother, from whose womb, as
Calvin has it, we must all be born, and on whose breasts we
must all hang, in order that we may grow up unto everlasting
life. The general, objective, universal side of Chrittianity, starting as it does in Christ, although it can never be sundered from
individual religion in the Church, must not be viewed simply as
the product and consequence of this, but is to be apprehended
always by faith rather as the power that truly underlies and supports all its worth. The process of our salvation lies, not beyond
the Church and out of it, but directly in its bosom. We have
it measured here by its extreme ends, with all intermediate forms
of experience quietly included, of course, as parts of one and the
same historical fact. This starts in the "remission of sins," and
becomes complete fiinally, with the completion of the Church
as a whole, in the "resurrection of the body." The first clause
is no doubt one in sense substantially, with the Nicene article,
"one *baptism* for the remission of sins." No one at all familiar
with the life of the early Church, or in any way at home in the
true genius of the Creed, can hesitate at all or feel much embar-
rrssed, in regard to this point. The religion of the Creed is,
throughout, sacramental and churchly, in the right sense of these
terms. We may, if we choose, force into it a different meaning,
to suit our own different taste; but the meaning of the period
from which it springs, is abundantly clear, and we are bound to
respect it, at least so far as history is concerned. The Church is
here made an object of faith; a new divine economy is regarded
as permanently at hand in her constitution; she is the mystical
mother of saints; her sacraments convey grace, where the way
is open for its reception; the remission of sins, in order to a christian life, comes under God from her hand (Matth. xvi. 19, xviii.
18,); and the act by which the grace is sealed is holy baptism,
which it is the duty and privilege of all, accordingly, to embrace
with full faith, as carrying in it this divine force. All this was
liable to be greatly abused, and, as we very well know, was so

abused in fact. But still, rightly understood, it expresses deep and sacred truth; the force of which *we* also must acknowledge and feel, if we would not forfeit all lot and part in the Creed of the ancient Church.

The whole winds up with "the life everlasting;" which is simply the triumphant issue of the christian process, as it is to reach its conclusion finally in the resurrection. To some, the doctrine of everlasting life appears to carry with it an independent certainty, on other grounds; so far at least as the "immortality of the soul" is concerned, it is felt to be comparatively easy to accept the idea of a future state, on what are supposed to be the merely rational evidences of its reality. But the Creed knows nothing of any such abstract immortality. Its life everlasting is conditioned absolutely, by the resurrection of the body; it stands in the recovery of the man as a whole unity, from the law of sin and death which lies upon him in his present state; and all becomes real, only as a fact comprehended in the new creation which is brought to pass in Jesus Christ. Such plainly too is the view taken of it in the New Testament. The *immortality of the soul*, as it is called, in the common sense of the doctrine, is not taught in the Bible; on the contrary, it is heathenish, and tends to subvert the fundamental idea of Christianity. Life and immortality in the New Testament sense, are "brought to light" by Jesus Christ, as the result of his own mysterious union with our fallen nature, and in this form embrace at once body and soul together. To be in Him, is to have everlasting life, with the certainty of being raised up in virtue of it at the last day. He is the Resurrection and the Life. Thus it is that this article of the Creed as well as all the rest, is an object strictly and truly of *faith ;* and this the same faith at last by which we assent to the mystery of Christ's person. To hold it on other grounds is not enough ; we *believe* it truly, only when we embrace it as a fact which is felt to have its foundation and necessity in this living revelation, and in this alone.

Practical Reflections.

Such we conceive to be the general scheme and structure of the Creed. It is no such fragmentary, disjointed production, as it is often imagined to be, by those who have little or no sympathy with its true sense and spirit. Take it as it is in its own constitution; let it be apprehended and estimated, not as a work of outward theological reflection, but as a transcript of what may be styled the intuitional consciousness of christianity itself in its original fundamental form; let the true conception of christianity be at hand as a new life, and not simply a new theory, springing from Christ, and along with this the true conception also of faith as the very power by which it is substantiated and made to be present in the world; and it will be no longer difficult for any one to feel the divine force of the symbol, the grandeur of its idea, the unity and harmony and complete wholeness of its architectural design. It is in all respects single, rotund and full, within the compass of its own orb. It is a majestic tree that grows forth from a single root. It is a grand oratorio of the Messiah, and of the Creation, in which the full harmony of heaven pours itself along, like the sound of many waters, from beginning to end. It is a vast Gothic dome, whose massive symmetry, poised upon a single centre, seems to swim with aërial lightness in a world of its own, piercing at last the very heavens. No work of art could well be more finished and complete. Each part becomes intelligible, nay, as an object of *faith*, becomes real, we may say, only by its inward organic union with the whole; while this, on the other hand, includes and requires all the parts, from the beginning, as essential to its own constitution. Some have thought, that it would be an easy thing to *improve* the Creed, by throwing out some parts of it and adding to it various doctrinal propositions which are now wanting. There is reason to suspect, indeed, as already intimated, that with no small portion of our modern Protestantism, the task would be felt comparatively light, to construct a much better new Creed altogether. All such thinking, however, turns of course, on a radically defective sense of its true nature and design, and betrays besides a most unsafe apprehension of christianity itself; the very last that can deserve to be trusted, with all its imaginary orthodoxy, for the manufacture of any religious creed or confession whatever. The Creed, in its right conception, can admit no such improvement or alteration. There is no room to speak of different creeds as we may speak, for instance, of different catechisms or church covenants; as though the fact of Christianity might be cast into several totally diverse schemes of thought, and yet remain true to itself in this character. To be truly a *Creed* at all, it must be the very movement of the fact itself, as disclosed to the vision of faith. It must be one thus, and not many. There is room, as we have seen, for variations in the filling up of the outline or scheme. This may be more or less full. But there is no room for different outlines or schemes. The Creed, in this respect, is as much one as Christianity itself is one. It determines its own contents, and it determines also its own form. It literally makes itself, and it will allow no man to turn it into any other shape. Whatever else our Christianity may include, in the way of doctrine or practice, it must start under the form here proclaimed, if it is to be at all legitimate and worthy of trust. This, at all events, is Christianity in its most universal character, the glorious fact of the new creation by Christ Jesus, under its broadest and most comprehensive features. Under such view, it is admirably complete; and it must be the wildest extravagance ever to dream of improving it by taking from it, or adding to it, or re-forging it into any new shape.

We close with the following reflections, flowing more or less directly, in the way of corollary or suggestion, from the whole subject:

I. The Creed does not spring from the Bible. This is plain from its history. Its main substance was in use before the New Testament was formed. Peter's confession, " Thou art the Christ, the Son of the living God," had no such origin. It was produced from the living sense of Christ's presence itself. And so, we may say, the whole Creed which lies involved in that confession, is derived through faith out of the same living ground. It is, of course, in harmony with the Bible; for it has to do immediately with its central revelation, the mystery of the Word made Flesh. It comes not, however, circuitously, in the way of reflection and study, through its pages. The early Church got it not from the Bible, but from the fact of Christianity itself, which must be allowed to be in its own nature older even and deeper than its own record under this form. Strange that there should be any

confusion in regard to what is in itself so palpable and clear.
The Bible is not the *principle* of Christianity; nor yet the *rock*
on which the Church is built. It never claims this character,
and it can be no better than idolatry and superstition to worship
it in any such view; as much so as though the same worship
were directed towards a crucifix or the Roman mass. The one
only principle of Christianity, the true and proper fountain of its
being, is the person of Christ; not any written account or notion
of his person, but the actual living revelation of it, as a fact in
the history of the world. The Church rests immediately on this
foundation, and no other. The Bible is of force, only as it proclaims this revelation. In such view, it is of indispensable account for the preservation and advancement of the christian life;
it is the divinely constituted rule, by which, through all ages, it
must be measured and led. But still it is not this life itself; its
relation to it is, after all, that of a condition, rather than that of
a ground; and we are bound to see in Christianity always the
presence of the Word under another form, as the true substratum
at last of all its glorious power in the world. It is a Fact, independently of the Bible and before it, which, as such, has a right
to challenge our faith, whether we can show the Bible to be
inspired or not. Indeed our ability to show the Bible inspired,
must ever turn on our ability to prove in the first place, the reality
of the revelation. So in all our systems of divinity, we begin,
not with the inspiration of the sacred volume, as though this
could be established in any wholly *ab extra* way, but with the
truth of Christianity itself; feeling well assured that without this,
it must be worse than idle to think of bringing the other question
to any satisfactory issue. But what is this else than an acknowledgement that the Bible is not the principle of Christianity, but
that this has its being in the world under another form, which is
no less divine than the Scriptures themselves. Christianity is
not only a written word, but a new creation in the form of life,
starting from its founder Jesus Christ. In this last view, it *must*
have, if it be what it claims to be, a real historical substance,
which we are bound to respect as divine, no less than the Bible
itself. There is not merely room thus, but an absolute necessity,
for what may be styled a true christian *tradition* in the Church;

not as something against the Bible or foreign from it; but still not as a mere derivation either or efflux simply from its pages; a tradition which starts from the original substance of Christianity itself, as it underlies the Bible, and which in such form becomes the living stream into which continuously the sense of the Bible is poured, through the Holy Ghost, from age to age, onward to the end of the world. This divine tradition meets us under its clearest, most primitive and most authoritative character, in the Apostles' Creed.

II. The idea of the Creed, as now given, throws light on the true character of the Church, as related to Christ in one direction and to the Bible in another. The Creed represents the primary substance of Christianity, as it has passed over from Christ in the form of life, into the general consciousness of his people. This general life is the Church. It is of course, a divine fact in the world, and so of right an article of faith more immediately than the Bible itself. First the Church, and then the Bible. So in the Creed: "I believe in the Holy Catholic Church," instead of: "I believe in the Holy Inspired Bible;" not certainly to put any dishonor on this last; but to lay rather a solid foundation for its dignity and authority in the other article; for, after all, it is the Church, next to Christ, and not the Bible, save as comprehended in the Church, which according to St. Paul, is "the pillar and ground of the truth." Is this to throw Christ into the shade, as the opposers of the Church sometimes pretend? Just as little, we reply, as faith in the divine authority of the Bible tends to throw him into the shade. The Church *may* be so magnified as to wrong Christ; but it is just as possible, and at this time also, just as common, to magnify the Bible in a like bad way, at Christ's expense; as where men, for instance, insist on sundering it from the objective fact of Christianity itself, the life of Christ in the Church, and force it to become instead the vehicle only of their own private judgment and proud self-will. Neither the Church, however, nor the Bible, can be held responsible for any such abuse. In their own nature, they do homage perpetually to Christ. The Church is but the living revelation of his presence and power, from age to age, in the world. The Bible is his written word. In this view, both are required to go together. Christianity is the proper union of both. Neither can fulfil its mission, apart from the other. The Church, to be true to her vocation, must be ruled by the Bible; if any pretend to follow her voice, without regard to this, they will be led astray. But the converse of this is no less certain. The Bible to be a true word of Christ, must be ruled by the life of the Church; if any pretend to follow it without regard to this, they too will most assuredly miss the truth. Will it be said that this is a circle? Be it so. In such circle precisely, is it the divine prerogative of faith, at all times firmly and serenely to move.

III. Christianity, as such a divine fact in the consciousness of the Church, is historical. The idea of history is opposed both to dead tradition and to dead change. It moves; it lives; it grows. So the Creed originally came to pass. In its very conception thus, it makes room for a continuous historical evolution of the christian life on all sides. To take it as the end of all Christianity, is to mistake its nature entirely. It is only the form in which it begins. Christianity must be far more than such beginning. Its mission is, not merely to cover the earth with its outward presence, but to occupy and rule inwardly also the universal being of man. It must regenerate the thinking of the world and all its action; it carries in itself, accordingly, the possibility of becoming such a reconstruction or intensification of our universal life, from the start. The substance then which it exhibits primitively in the Creed, is by no means bound to that, either as a rigid shell or loose drapery; but widens itself continually, in the way of historical concrete growth, and unfolds its inward wealth in forms as manifold as the complex fact of humanity itself. So in particular it admits and requires a progressive theology; for why should not Christianity occupy our nature in the form of science, as well as in the form of action or feeling? Theology implies doctrines. These come, for the understanding, by gradual process. Hence each single doctrine has its history, and theology is historical as a whole. The history in this case is not something outward only, but enters into the very substance of the christian fact itself; so that in any right view of the case, it is just as necessary for theology to be historical, as it is for it to be biblical. History is one of the factors, by which it is brought to pass and made to have in itself a real existence. True faith in the Creed then, does not require us to renounce all interest in theology, and fall back on the primary christian consciousness as the *ne plus ultra* of the new creation; on the contrary, it is just what we need to overthrow the idea of all such stability, and fit us for the right appreciation of theology as a continuously progressive science. To have faith in the Church, is to have faith at the same time in History. The spirit of the Creed is not radical. It is the spirit of Sect, ever violent and abrupt by its very constitution, that seeks to nullify the whole christian process since the days of rhe Apostles. To a mind in sympathy with the Creed, that process is ever something sacred and divine, no less, we may say, than the primitive faith itself.

IV. With such historical character, all true theology, at the same time, grows forth from the Creed, and so remains bound to it perpetually as its necessary radix or root. History is not progress in the way of outward local remove from one point to another, but progress that carries the sense with which it is freighted onward and upwards always into new forms. It resembles the growth of a tree or the gradual evolution of our individual human life. It is a river, which carries itself forward with its own flow, ever changing and yet ever the same. The relation of the Creed then to the forms of sound christian doctrine which have since appeared, is simply this, that they are to be regarded as lying silently involved in it from the beginning, though some time was needed to bring them to clear and distinct utterance. The great articles of christian theology come from the Bible; but, at the same time, they are *mediated* or brought to pass for the mind of the Church, only through the presence and power of the primitive christian consciousness, (expressed in the Creed,) as something already at hand. It is no defect in the Creed, that it contains not several most important and necessary articles of a sound theology as the Church now stands, the inspiration of the Scriptures, for instance, or the doctrine of justification by faith. On the other hand, however, such articles lose no credit or authority whatever, by the fact of such omission. The only question is, do they flow from the substance of Christianity as given in the Creed, and do they hold in it and from it perpetually as their vital root. This, after all, is complete, under its own form, as an utterance of the primary *fact* of Christianity; and it only follows that other articles have their truth and importance, not in the same primary way, but all the more surely, for this very reason, in the way of derivation and outflow from what goes before. We reach thus this great practical conclusion, that the orthodoxy of every doctrine is fairly tested at last by its inward correspondence or want of correspondence with the Creed. It is not enough that it seem to be biblical from some other stand point: its biblicity must be evident, as seen *through* the fundamental substance of Christianity embodied in this universal faith of the Holy Catholic Church. It is not enough that a doctrine be sound in form; if it refuse notwithstanding to coalesce inwardly with the spirit of the Creed, it convicts itself of substantial falsehood. Take in illustration, the article of justification by faith, Luther's criterion of a standing or falling Church. It is not sufficient, surely, that it be accepted in a merely general and abstract way. Our sects, United Brethren, Albright Brethren, Winebrennerians, and a score of others to the same general tune, readily meet for the most part, on this ground; one trying to outdo another, in its zeal for this particular side of religion. And yet Luther would have denounced the whole of them, as a worse plague than the locusts of Pharaoh. Do we ask, why? With Luther, the article had firm and fast root in the Creed, the historical substance of the old catholic christian life; whereas, with these upstart sects, it is a mere abstraction or fancy, which makes no account of the old catholic faith whatever, and so proves itself to be the growth of some other soil, the product simply of the human brain. These sects have no sympathy with the Creed; they do not stand in it with their inward life; their theology starts not out of it at all, as its primitive ground. *Thus* held, the article of justification by faith ceases to be true, and is no longer safe, but full of peril for all the interests of religion. So would all the Reformers say, with one voice.*

* *Professor Tayler Lewis,* of the New York University, in his manly and truly able review of the Mercersburg School, as he calls it, published in Nos. 114 and 115, of the *Literary World,* expresses some apprehension of

V. **Regard** for the Creed then, may be taken as a fair measure of sound church character, as distinguished from the spirit of sect and schism.   In its whole conception and life, the Creed is catholic, inwardly bound to the true universal power of the Christian life, as it stood in the beginning.   Hence it will be found invariably, that the sect spirit, whose essential nature it is to be abrupt, violent, unhistorical and upstart, leads, if not openly, at least quietly, always, to the abandonment of the venerable symbol altogether.   Sect piety has no relish for the Creed; it cannot utter itself naturally in any such way; it makes no account, in truth of Christianity in that form.   The genius of Puritanism, as we have already seen, is also strikingly at variance with the same rule.   The fact admits no doubt.   It stares upon us in the almost universal neglect into which the Creed has fallen, wherever Puritanism prevails.   It will not do to say, that this neglect is more apparent than real, and that the substance of the Creed is still in honor, though not its particular form.   The difficulty is, precisely, that the form is such as will not easily allow another substance to be put into it, than that which belongs to it in truth; on which account, the use of it is felt to be uncongenial with the

the danger there is of wronging the forensic side of our salvation, in trying to make too much of Christ as the bearer of life for us in a real way. He allows both, but seems to think that the first interest forms for our faith the safety of the second. "The incarnation and the crucifixion," he remarks, "are the fundamentals of our faith. It may be admitted too, that the first is the necessary ground of the value of the second; but all ecclesiastical experience has shown, that for us, and to us, in our unrecovered state, the latter is the nearest truth, that it has the most of moral power, and that when vividly sustained, it has ever sustained the belief in the coördinate mystery." This we cannot admit. The forensic interest is full as liable to run wild, as the other. So we see in the case of our unsacramental sects, on all sides. The true order is, the mystery of the incarnation first, and then the atonement, as growing forth from this, and *only in such view.* Such is the conception of the Creed. Peter's confession is the rock that must underlie, in our minds, all other divinity. Protestantism can be of true and genuine growth, only as it grows forth from *catholicity,* the primitive substance of christianity as a fact, made to break on the sense of the soul through the apprehension of Christ's person. A sound *christology,* involving always the idea of a sound church life, is indispensable, we more and more believe, to all true orthodoxy at other points.

true life of Puritanism, as something which is, in fact, not inwardly harmonious with the life of the ancient Church. Hence such use in this case can never be easy, natural and free, but produces always some sense of awkward and stiff constraint. Puritanism must wrest the Creed into quite a different sense from its own original meaning, to be able at all to acquiesce in its several articles. Left to itself, it would fall on a very different scheme of fundamental and necessary truth. It can see no reason why the Creed carries just its present form, or why so much should be left out of it, that Puritanism is apt to think of first, in its own abstract way. The orthodoxy of New England, for instance, can hardly be said at all to grow forth organically from the primitive mind or consciousness of the Church, as embodied in this symbol. Is not this strange and startling fact entitled to some consideration? We are firmly persuaded that it will be felt to be solemnly significant, in proportion exactly as it is made the subject of earnest thought. An orthodoxy which owns no inward fellowship with the Creed, and which feels itself complete in a wholly different way without it, deserves to be regarded with distrust, and may well be asked to give a reason of the hope that is in it under such abstract and unhistorical form. We are free to confess, that, in our view, any scheme of Christianity to which the voice of the Creed has become thus strange, labors under a most serious defect; and we need no other proof than the general fact here noticed, to show what is shown by so many proofs besides, that Puritanism, with all its great excellencies and merits, involves a material falling away from the faith of the sixteenth century as well as from that of the early Church.

VI. For the settlement of our existing theological and ecclesiastical difficulties, the first and most indispensable necessity is a true and hearty inward submission to the authority of the Creed, according to its original intention and design. Not that this is to be taken as of itself the sum and end of all theology; but all sound doctrine and true church life, must proceed forth from a common faith here, as their only sure ground, and it is vain to dream of their being prosperously advanced in any other way. It is mere loss of time, for instance, to argue the question of election, or that of infant baptism, with those who are not imbued, in the first place, with a true reverence for the Apostles' Creed. It is, in truth, of very little consequence, in such case, whether it be the affirmative or the negative of any such question that is maintained; as growing forth organically, not from the primary substance of the Christian faith at all, but from some other ground altogether, the opinion whether right or wrong in its notional and formal character, is sure to be in its inward material constitution, unchristian and wrong. So, as we have just seen, the doctrine of justification itself, in its right outward shape, may become, through such divorce from the life of the Creed, in the highest degree false and dangerous. Election, the atonement, imputation, &c., can have no validity as christian doctrines, in an abstract view, but only as they can be developed from the concrete mystery here apprehended by faith. Theology in any other form, is always necessarily rationalistic, an effort to build faith on intellection, whereas the true order is just the reverse. This rightly understood and felt, would at once greatly narrow the field of theological controversy, as well as greatly facilitate the proper conclusion of its cardinal debates. How much, especially of our modern disputation, our *sect-fights*, we may say, generally, would be found by this rule to be little better than mere *skiomachy*, the battling of phantom shapes projected on the air. The first condition of all sound theology is, active sympathy with historical Christianity, with the idea of the Church, with the catholic mystery of the Creed. So also as regards all church questions; we do but run ourselves into endless talk, if we propose to settle them from any other ground, or in any other frame of mind. For instance, the question of using, or not using, a settled liturgy in public worship; how much of the argument on both sides, do we not find proceeding under a wholly different, and, therefore, wholly unsatisfactory form? The interest is vindicated or opposed on purely outward grounds, instead of being referred, as it should be, first of all, to the interior demands of Christianity itself, as embodied in the Creed. Or take the question of *Episcopacy*. It has been much the fashion to place it all round, on such *ob extra* proofs and reasons, as though the point were to make out a simply external warrant for or against it, independently altogether of the contents of the christian life itself. Thus Episcopalians often try to find it outwardly prescribed in the New Testament; a vain and hopeless task, which only serves to countenance the equally vain and fruitless attempt, on the other side, to overthrow it in the same mechanical way. To make Episcopacy the necessary hedge of Christianity, which we are to be sure of first on outside reasons, whether biblical or historical, in order that we may then be sure of the inclosed truth, is just again to subordinate faith rationalistically to the lower authority of the understanding; for how can such a purely outward and mechanical authority be a whit better at last, than any other form of thought and will which is not ruled by the very substance of the truth itself. Who may not see, that if Episcopacy be indeed the *first* thing towards a sound faith, it ought to come first also in the Creed, or, at least, to follow immediately the general article of the Holy Ghost; whereas, in truth, as we all know, it has no place in the Creed whatever. Are we then, at once, to infer from this, on the other hand, that Episcopacy is false, or that no definite organization is required as the normal form of the Church? By no means. Only this is not the way in which the question can ever be settled. What we need for that, especially just now, is a general hearty return to the catholic life of the Creed, as the necessary point of departure for coming to a true solution of all our church questions. This we firmly believe is something that *can* take place extensively, long before we are able to see at all to the *end* of the perplexing difficulties with which we are now surrounded; and that *must* take place, indeed, before a single step can be successfully made towards their proper practical resolution. It is the idea of the Church, the mystery of Christianity as it is made sure to us by faith in the Apostles' Creed, something older certainly, and deeper in its own nature, than any mere outward hedge surrounding it, which we are bound first of all to embrace; which alone is sufficient to draw after it any right theory or practice, as regards all other church interests; and which, therefore, we have it in our power to begin with, as an *a priori* foundation, for reaching in the end the results that the case requires. A convention of sects to negotiate a federal Church, is much like a convention of the blind to settle the laws of light. We must be in the Creed, and so have faith in the Church, in order to find it, or to settle its exact form and limits. This is the true method for bringing to an issue the sacramental question, the liturgical question, the question of festival days. An active revival of the consciousness expressed in the Creed, would in due time restore all these great interests to their pristine authority. And we will just add, in the way of friendly hint to Episcopalians, that if their favorite system of church polity *could* be vindicated as necessary, in this way, to the conservation of the great catholic ideas that enter into the primitive faith, it would be, in our estimation, an argument of more weight and force in its favor, than whole tomes of learning employed to establish its authority in an outward and abstract view. J. W. N.

ART. XXI.—The Rule of Faith. — *Concluded.*

Having defined our subject and glanced at its earlier history,[*] we shall next *notice the leading false theories of it, which more or less prevail,* and conclude with *a statement of the evangelical doctrine in the case.*

III. It has been the mournful destiny of the Church and her ordinances, from the first, to be perverted and scandalized by the false zeal or the depravity of those professing to be her sincere friends. Driven thus from one extreme to another, and tossed by the contentions ever connected with such movements, her history presents, in this view, an ever varying scene of agita-

---

[*] Which was explicitly stated to be the *sole object* of the former article, and more than which, consequently, no intelligent reader would expect to find in it. As to the *definition* given, it is hoped that those who did not discover it at first, have been so fortunate as to find it since, lying very quietly in simple *italics*, and in its proper place, about the middle of p. 50. If they have not, we really know of no better remedy than *pica!*

tions, giving full occasion for grief and wonder, fear and hope. Her constant subjection to abuse from human ignorance, pride, or passion, awakens sorrow and alarm, whilst the continual evidence we have that an Omnipotent Agency is overruling all for a most triumphant issue to these alarming conflicts, must call forth admiration of the mighty power of God, as exhibited in the Past, and inspire confidence in its all-sufficiency for the Future. No doubt but the end will prove that, as the *fall* was the necessary antecedent to Redemption, the suffering life and ignominious death of our Lord Jesus Christ, to the conquest of death and hell, and the falling away, and " blindness in part that hath happened unto Israel," to the gathering in of the Gentiles, so all these violent perversions of Christianity are essential to the working out of the great scheme of grace which God is executing by the Church.

An illustration of what has thus happened to the Church in general, is afforded by the fate of the subject in hand. For clear and well-settled as the primitive doctrine and practice in reference to the Rule of Faith must have been, tendencies to departure from it very soon began to work and show themselves. This is implied in the complaints of Paul already, concerning those on the one hand, " who opposed and exalted themselves above all that was called God," " departing from the faith, and giving heed to seducing spirits and doctrines of devils ;" and of those on the other hand, who were " lovers of their own selves, boasters, proud, * disobedient to parents, * * * traitors, heady, highminded. * * who, as James and Jambres withstood Moses, so they resisted the truth : men of corrupt minds, reprobate concerning the faith, * * deceiving and being deceived." With these complaints of Paul, others of Peter, James, and Jude fully agree, and all show that the mystery of iniquity did then already work. The aim and purpose of these departures from the creed of the early Church upon this subject, we are expressly told, was to loosen the hold of the faithful upon " the traditions they had been taught, whether by word or by epistle," and thus to turn them from following Paul (and the other representatives of the Church) as he followed Christ. But though their aim was thus *one*, the *forms* which they severally assumed, were almost as diversified as the instances of their occurrence were numerous. They may, however, be reduced to *three general classes,* to which those existing at the present day are intimately allied. They will also be found to stand in close inward relation to each other, (notwithstanding the apparent outward conflict,) whilst all of them cling to the Truth, like the gum and other excrescences of a wounded tree, seeking to rid itself of the worm deposited to feed upon its strength. And firm must be the sinews, and vigorous the life of that old vine, which has been able so long and successfully to contend against these and similar pernicious foreign elements, so likely to effect its ruin!

The *first* of these *false theories* that claims attention, is that which signalizes the Romish Confession, and which is, indeed, "the ground and pillar" of its strength. It consists in an extreme abuse of that side of the gospel principle which provides for the proper subordination of the part to the whole, of the members to the body, by perverting it into a despotic hierarchy, in which the christian principle is frustrated, because the rights of the individual are destroyed. This theory may be summed up in the following proposition: *In all matters of faith and practice, the traditions of the Roman Catholic Church, with its interpretation of them, are of divine authority, because the Church is infallible.* This is the substance of the decree of Trent upon the subject. That Council, at its fourth session, decided as follows: " Praeterea, ad coërcenda petulantia ingenia, docerint, ut nemo, suae prudentiae innixus, in rebus fidei, et morum, ad aedificationem doctrinae Christianae pertinentium, sacram scripturam ad suos sensus contorquens, *contra eum sensum, quem tenuit et tenet sancta mater ecclesia, cujus est judicare de vero sensu et interpretatione scripturarum sanctarum,* aut etiam contra unanimen consensum Patrum, ipsam Scripturam sacram interpretari audeat."* It is not our purpose in this brief review of false theories, to arraign and condemn the authors of them as being influenced only by the

---

* As it altogether suits the design of this essay better, the language of the decree is given in the original. Those who desire, may find a good translation of all the Decrees of the Council, (with the original appended,) in "Cramp's Text-book of Popery."

most wicked motives in their production and defence. Rather would we go upon the opposite presumption, and hope, that whatever may be true of some who advocate error upon this subject, others are sincere in believing it to be truth, and as such essential to the maintenance and furtherance of the gospel. But certainly, a more subtle mixture of truth and error, a more cunning wrapping up of the poison in sweet and precious truth, could hardly be conceived of, than is exhibited in this decree. For who will deny that "petulant minds" ought to be restrained? Or that "Christian doctrine should be maintained?" Or that any one should so "confide in his own judgment" as to "wrest the sacred Scriptures to his own sense of them?" Or that the Church is holy and our Mother, and hath held and still holds that which it becomes all to believe? In what, then, does the error of this doctrine of Rome consist? Let her own version and interpretation of it answer.

The creed of Pope Pius already furnishes a significant paraphrase of it: "Apostolicas et ecclesiasticas traditiones, reliquosque ejusdem ecclesiae observationes et constitutiones firmissime admitto, et amplector. Item sacram scripturam juxta eum sensum, quem tenuit et tenet sancta mater ecclesia, cujus est judicare de vero sensu et interpretatione sacrarum scripturarum, admitto; nec eam unquam, nisi juxta unanimem consensum patrum accipiam, et interpretabor."

If now we turn to accredited writers in the Romish Communion for a further exposition of their doctrine, we shall find the proposition laid down above, fully sustained by their own avowals. From a great abundance of evidence, we shall adduce the testimony of only a few witnesses, and those of the better sort.

Bellarmine affirms, in defence of the Romish doctrine, "that scripture is very often obscure and ambiguous, so that *unless it be interpreted by some one who cannot err, it cannot be understood;* hence it is not sufficient alone." (De Verb. iv. 4.) That "one who cannot err," is afterwards declared to be Tradition speaking through the Popes and Councils of the Roman Church.

Knott, in the memorable controversy with Chillingworth, asserts still more boldly, that the traditions of that church, with her interpretation of them, is the only and sufficient judge in all religious disputes, because of her infallibility, defending this position as the doctrine of his church. He says, after laboring to show that the holy Scriptures are in themselves insufficient, and that the Church is invested with infallibility to make up for this deficiency of the word: "I conclude, therefore, with this argument; whosoever resisteth that means which infallibly proposeth to us God's word or revelation, commits a sin, which, unrepented, excludes salvation: but whosoever resisteth Christ's visible Church, doth resist that means which infallibly proposeth God's word: Therefore, &c., * * * Now, what visible church was extant, when Luther began his pretended reformation * * *, is easy to be determined."* This he determines himself, in another place, to be none other than the Roman Catholic.

Pallavicini, one of the most esteemed and distinguished advocates of Rome, confirms this testimony when he declares: "The whole of our faith rests upon one indivisible article, viz: *the infallible authority of the Church.*"

Another eminent writer, whose notoriety has been rendered more extensive than was probably thought desirable, (though he is of standard authority in the Church,) tells us that the doctrine of the Church is, that "*divine tradition is a Rule of Faith, and whatever the Catholic (Roman) Church declares as such, is to be regarded as tradition.*" And again in reply to the question: "What is the judge of controversies concerning the faith and customs? The Church, whether scattered or assembled in general Council, and the Pope, the head of the Church." (Den's Theology, translated by Rev. Dr. Berg.)

But it is useless to multiply proofs in so plain a case. Indeed the doctrine, as set forth in the foregoing quotations, is so precious to every true Papist, that, rather than invalidate it by a denial, he would seek to corroborate it by additional testimony. So firm is the Church's determination to maintain this doctrine, and so zealous are her sons in their defence of it that we are warmly assured by a man of as much learning and seeming sincerity as Dr. Wiseman, that "the moment any Roman Catholic doubts, not alone the principles of faith, but any one of those doctrines

---

* "Charity maintained by Catholics." Chap ii. § 27.

which are thereon based, the *moment he allows himself to call in question any of the dogmas which the Church teaches, as having been handed down within her*, that moment the Church conceives him to have virtually abandoned all connexion with her."*

This, then, is the doctrine of Rome, concerning the Rule of Faith, the iron sceptre of its spiritual despotism over the millions that do patient, and, mostly, willing homage to its authority! And why should it not be true? Can it be, as some would persuade us, that it has nothing in it but the most irrational absurdity, and yet finds so many intelligent and some unquestionably pious advocates? Were it not every way desirable to have an infallible organ of Truth? Is not the Church of Christ the divinely constituted depository, channel, and exponent of God's revelations to men? Did not her exalted Head promise to her His own continual presence, and the constant assistance of the Holy Ghost, that she might be kept in the truth to the end of time? And do not the endless schisms and jarring discords, that seem to be necessarily consequent upon a denial of this authority of the Church, and to prevail most among those who reject this doctrine, all prove it essential to the preservation of the unity of the faith, and the peace of the Church, and the comfort and edification of her members?

To these and similar questions, honestly considered, there can be but one answer. And yet, though our reply be affirmative, we are by no means committed to the Romish dogma. For even waiving the consideration of all its fearful effects and the terrible consequences which have always, in fact, flown from the practice of it, as the history of the Papacy will testify, and which is strong circumstantial evidence against it, there are insuperable objections to it, as it stands, by which, upon its own principles, it is condemned. The *first* is found in *its peculiar form of Church Government.* The Council of Trent gives us no definition of the Church, and the creed of Pius IV. fails to supply the deficiency. But standard writers define it to be " a body of men united in the profession of the same christian faith, and

* Wiseman's Lectures. Vol. i. p. 65.

communion of the same sacraments, under the government of lawful pastors, and particularly of the Roman pontiff, Christ's only vicar on earth."[*] If now, according to the decree of Trent, already quoted, "the right to judge of the true meaning and interpretation of sacred writ," belongs exclusively to "Holy Mother Church," then according to the above definition, it belongs to those who constitute this church, or to such as they may delegate with such authority. The decision and judgment must be that of the whole "body of men (so) united"—*all* must be permitted to examine Scripture and tradition, in order to its being truly ascertained what the Church, of which each member is equally a constituent part, has held and does hold. But is any thing like this allowed in the Romish Church? Is there such a thing known as the right of the common membership to their part in the examination and adoption of doctrines and discipline? Have they any thing to say in the election of popes, the appointment of cardinals, the consecration of bishops, the ordination of priests, or even the admission to church fellowship of private members? Are they consulted in the calling of councils, or the appointment of delegates thereto, or in their debates and decisions when convened? Have they ever been? Will, or can they ever be, as long as the Papacy remains? If not, how does the Roman Catholic Church know what the Church holds or rejects as doctrine or tradition? And if it is necessary to know this, in order to our having a certain Rule of Faith, how can that Church lay claims to any, seeing she has ever denied the Church (according to her own definition of it) a voice in a single doctrine, sacrament, or custom, which she holds and imposes as divine?

But even if this difficulty were not in the way, the Romish doctrine can be refuted on its own principles, for that small aristocratic portion of the Church of Rome, which has usurped the prerogatives of the whole, has neither been *unanimous* nor *infallible* in determining upon or interpreting its doctrines and traditions. And yet they teach that unanimity and infallibility are essential to a sufficient Rule of Faith. Out of its own mouth therefore, it stands condemned here again.

---

[*] Bellarmine de Eccles. militante, c. 2.

The proof of this assertion will hardly be insisted upon. The history of Popery, with all its vaunted unity, unanimity and unchangeableness, is an almost uninterrupted chain of testimony to it. And the ever reiterated charges of the want of all these desirable qualities, brought against Protestantism by the friends of Rome, have provoked a longer and louder array of such proof than has been at all agreeable. One or two instances in point, under each head, is all that we shall give at present.

In the Roman Church, then, we have no *unanimity*. Tradition, in numerous cases, is arrayed against tradition. Thus in reference to the doctrine of *purgatory*, Cyprian is appealed to, among many others, as satisfactory traditionary authority in its favor. And yet, this church father expressly affirms : " When once we have departed hence, there is no longer any place for repentance, no longer any effectiveness of satisfaction. Here, life is either lost or held : here, we may provide for our eternal salvation by the worship of God and the fruitfulness of faith . . . To him who confesses, pardon is freely granted : to him who believes, a saving indulgence is granted from the divine pity: and immediately after death, he passes to a blessed immortality."

The same discrepancy exists in the invention of *image-worship*. The Council of Elvira (early in the fourth century) decreed that the testimony of tradition was totally opposed to the worship or adoration of paintings or images. And when, in the course of time, superstition and will-worship prevailed in the introduction and abuse of them, the Council of Constantinople (A. D. 754) reiterated this decree with additional remonstrances, appealing for authority to the accumulated testimony of tradition. But, only thirty-three years later, the Council of Nice reversed their decision, disowned and denounced the Council, and required all the faithful to " *salute and adore the unpolluted image of our Lord Jesus Christ, our true God, and the holy image of the holy mother of God who bore him.*" And all this was done in accordance with Tradition! Indeed the array of traditionary proofs brought forward at that memorable synod, was so overwhelming, as to convince and convert many that had gone to the Council for the purpose of opposing all image-worship as gross idolatry! In charity, however, to Rome, and to common sense, we shall not repeat the strange legends here, lest the sanity of the three hundred and fifty bishops composing that council might fall into suspicion! Still it is an important illustration of the open hostility in which tradition is made to stand against tradition.

Another instance, equally remarkable, is met with in what has and has not been, is and is not, the doctrine of the Romish Church upon the free circulation of the Holy Scriptures in the vulgar tongue among the laity. On the one hand, tradition and the decrees of councils are freely cited against it. This is done even by Fenelon in his letter to the Bishop of Arras, on " The Use of the Bible." On the other hand, however, the excellent L. v. Ess. occupies twenty-eight of the forty-four pages of the interesting and instructive introduction to his translation of the New Testament, with precious testimony, gathered from all ages of the Church, in favor of the free circulation and diligent study of the Holy Scriptures by all classes of Christians. By which of these traditions does the Roman Church abide, and by which would she be judged? Certainly, in view of facts like these, she can no longer support her claim to be sole arbiter in matters of faith and practice, upon the ground of *unanimity* in doctrine!

But her other prop of *infallibility* is equally frail, and breaks under the weight of her own anathemas. For whether the seat of this infallibility be lodged in popes, or cardinals, or councils, those of one age, though pronounced infallible in all their decisions, have been convicted of error by those of another. And this has been and is the case upon almost every doctrine peculiar to the Papacy. Gregory the great was but the mouthpiece of his age, when he vociferated : " *Whoever claims the universal episcopate, is the forerunner of Antichrist.*" And it would fill volumes to record the contentions and debates which attended the development of this doctrine. At length, however, the Council of Florence (1439) boldly and unequivocally ordains: " We define that the holy apostolic see, and the Roman Pontiff, *have a primacy over the whole world, * * * that he is the head of the whole Church, * * * and that to him, in St. Peter, was delegated by our Lord Jesus Christ, full power to feed, rule and govern the universal Church.*" The Catechism of Trent also proclaims him, "the father and governor of all the faithful, of bishops also, and of all other prelates, be their station, rank or power what they may." And on the strength of this Church authority, Bp. Hughes had the candor and courage, only a few weeks ago, to inform a New York audience that the Pope was considered ·subject to no man, be he king, or president."

Now both these doctrines, the one denying and the other affirming papal supremacy, cannot be true. And yet both are taught by an infallible Church!

If any more instances of such glaring contradictions are desired, we must refer those wishing to see a full investigation of them, to " Edgar's variations of Popery," where the whole subject is amply discussed.

The conclusion, therefore, to which this review of the Romish theory of the Rule of Faith leads us, is clearly this : *In matters of faith and practice, the traditions of the Roman Catholic Church, with its interpretation of them, cannot be the only or true judge, because they deny the Church a voice in their adoption, and because they contradict and condemn each other.* As long as this is the case, it is unnecessary to press other objections.

Doubtless, if the Papacy were found, upon examination, to adhere to the accredited doctrines of the Church, as held during the first four centuries, and always to have been consistent with itself in its decisions and decrees, many that now denounce it as an apostacy, would be numbered among its most faithful children. But it is precisely because *neither is true of Rome,* that Rome is what it is. Upon her own principle, her present doctrines and customs cannot be of divine authority, for they contradict those traditions which bear the stamp of her approbation; and her own mouth has condemned to-day as false, those very doctrines for *denying* which she banned and burned others not many days ago!

Indeed it had been well for the cause of truth and mercy, if the Papacy had ever remained faithful to its earlier traditions, and infallibly maintained and practised them. The most pernicious errors of Rome, those antichristian elements which are bound up in her very life, which have made her a blighting curse where she might always have been a blessing, date from her departure from the track of traditions previously acknowledged and revered. And we are free to confess that, to our view, the Romish Church seems more deserving of reprobation on this account than any other. Her huge heresies of Purgatory, and efficacious prayers for the dead, of image-worship, saint-worship, and satisfaction for sin, of papal supremacy, indulgences, transubstantiation, celibacy and persecution of heretics, which she now fastens with fetters of brass on the consciences of her members, as doctrines taught by divine traditions, are all modern inventions in comparison with those received as genuine in the earlier ages of her history. And shall we now receive those things as true which bear the brand of her own condemnation? Let her first reconcile these contradictions before she requires assent to her creed!

That a despotic dogma like this of Rome, would excite violent resistance, is in full harmony with the laws of our nature. Justice and humanity required that those precious rights of man, which it rudely trampled upon, should be vindicated and released. The very cause of truth and unity, which this dogma professed most securely to entrench and fortify against all encroachments and perils, demanded deliverance from a bondage that had *buried* both for their preservation. And moreover, if there existed a tendency on the one side to run one part of the gospel principle into the hierarchical extreme of the Romish theory, there existed an equally strong tendency on the other side to carry another part of that principle into an opposite extreme. The workings of this tendency are by no means confined to modern times. It is found exerting itself simultaneously with the other in all ages of the Church. We are now concerned, however, with it in its present form, and as it is advocated and practiced upon by a portion of our brethren of the Protestant Communion. And here we find it maintaining that "*every man has an inalienable right to test any doctrine by the sacred scriptures, and to adopt or reject it, accordingly,*" as he may suppose it to agree or disagree therewith. And though it is admitted that this right must "not involve the casting off of all respect for Church authority, nor contempt for the opinions of the venerable, learned and pious, nor denial of accountability to God"(?) still "it does reserve to him the liberty to form his own opinion at last," with regard *not to the less essen-*

tial only, but *all* the doctrines that may claim attention. This theory is sometimes more plausibly expressed, by affirming that "*the Bible is the only Rule of Faith*" for Christians. In such hands as those of Chillingworth and Tillotson, both of whom plant their foot upon it in opposing the Romish view, it is made to command respect, especially as contrasted in its bearings with those of the dogma against which it is arrayed. And in any honest and sincere hands, it must, if intelligently discussed, always commend itself as a bold rampart raised, with the laudable design, at least, of defending the rights of the weakest member of the Church, against the aggressions and impositions of a spiritual aristocracy.

The reasons usually assigned in favor of this theory, are fairly represented by the following, quoted from a recent article upon the subject, in which it is zealously defended: First, it is argued, "there is no good reason why this right (of judging for one's self) should be denied to some men and granted to others." Secondly. "It is impossible to find an authorized and infallible judge of the sense of Scripture." Thirdly. It follows from the fact "of every man's personal accountability." Fourthly. "The Scriptures themselves teach the right of private judgment." And finally, none of the objections arrayed against this doctrine are valid, whilst "history and the common sense of mankind sustain the opinion that we are a thousand times more likely to make infidels, by sending men for light to Church opinions and traditions, than by sending them directly to the Bible, and the Bible only."

An elaborate and a particular refutation of these several reasons is cheerfully assigned to those who may think it necessary. We shall say nothing else or worse of them, than they are certainly as weighty and forcible as any usually advanced on the Romish side, and vastly more rational than the arguments by which the 2nd Council of Nice defended their doctrine of image-worship! It is a pity, however, if the body of the theory is sound, that it has such weak legs! But we have a general objection to urge against it, which, if well-founded, will answer for all others. *This theory, in substance and effect, considers the individual christian as holding morally an isolated position with reference to the Church,* and *invests him, accordingly, with complete independence of all spiritual relations,* and full authority to act for himself in all matters of religion. The branch must receive such substance as belongs to the stock that bears it, and appropriate the light and rain of heaven, in accordance with the law of its species. But these twigs of the spiritual vine may set out upon an independent existence, if they think it best, i. e. if they choose, and bear what and when they please, without the risk of excision. The citizen of the state, if a good and orderly one, is expected to receive the law at the mouth of the properly constituted authorities, to whom he himself, in union with others, has delegated the requisite power, and he does not for a moment think of setting up his private judgment in vindication of his rights; but the citizen of our great spiritual commonwealth must let his hands and tongue be tied by no such fetters as these, but has guarantied to him the right to think and judge, untrammeled, for himself! True, there may be, and it is mostly expedient that there should be, VOLUNTARY *associations of those of one persuasion,* conglomerated under certain *freely adopted* laws of combination, to which those willing to be members, are bound *by their own free act of consent,* so long as they choose to continue in such voluntary companionship. But no one is bound to bow to such authority, nor obligated to curtail his moral liberties by any such annoying limitations, unless it be his good pleasure so to do! If a man, considered in a social aspect, should find no existing condition of society exactly suited to his taste or principles, and would, accordingly, withdraw from all human fellowship, to enjoy the sweet privileges of unbroken solitude, his peculiar fancy would be attributed to some mental derangement. But in his religious character he may, if, in his own best judgment, all existing creeds and confessions of christian communities around him, are thought erroneous, separate from all, and convert himself into a solitary anchorite, and so secure the glorious prerogatives of a christian freeman!

This is virtually the theory, with some of its legitimate inferences, which is warmly advocated by many sincere and intelligent protestants. It is held forth as the *beau ideal* of liberty in general, and as the glory of the Christian religion in particular!

Oh! the bliss of being permitted and encouraged to think for one's self, (even though it may never be done,) with the pleasant conviction that in doing so, we are sure to be right, though all others should be thereby proven wrong!

All this may sound very well to some ears. It is, no doubt, honestly considered by its advocates, to be the only theory that is in harmony with the truth and consistent with personal responsibility and duty. but it is certainly not the doctrine of the Bible, nor compatible with the true idea of the Church. In its zeal for the protection of the individual, it would sacrifice the rights of the whole body to which he belongs—a procedure which finds no countenance or palliation in the writings or doings of the holy Apostles and primitive Church. If this were the religion of Protestantism, our blessed cause would soon be its own destruction.

It is well, however, and worthy of special notice. that this view exists and prevails as it does, much more in theory than in practice. That with all the warm declamation indulged in favor of the right and duty of private judgment, comparatively few of those who advocate it in this form, ever think of reducing it to practice themselves, and still less expect others to do so. Though a long sermon may be delivered in praise of such christian liberty, at the end of it the application for admission to the church, or the candidate for ordination is expected to subscribe in good faith to every article of the Saybrook Platform or Westminster Confession. Freely as it is allowed to each one to search and see for himself, even some of those most ardent in contending for the privilege, will not hesitate to launch a fierce charge of heresy against all who may happen to see and embrace a view that openly conflicts with " the five points," or some one, even, of the less essentials of sound faith. Indeed those that are bold enough to act out their creed on this subject, are at once excluded from christian fellowship as schismatics and dangerous fellows! So that after all, in this case again, as practice and theory appear in such manifest contradiction, the theory nullifies itself.

We have thus named only the negative difficulties of this ultra-protestant view. For positive objections to it, we refer the reader to what shall be said in another place. But who does not see at once, that, though it is professedly arrayed in direct opposition to the Romish dogma, it is very nearly the same thing in another form.   Both systems agree in investing *one* individual with supreme authority, to judge and decide in all matters of religious controversy—in other words, *in setting up a papacy.*   Only in the one case it is the *Pope in Rome,* and in the other the *Pope in the belly!*

Unquestionably, if required to choose either of these theories, we should prefer the latter.   But only as *being the least formidable of two evils.*   For with all our aversion to it, and dread of its necessarily pernicious consequences, we must own a still greater aversion to a way they have in Rome, of removing practical difficulties to their theory by fire and blood!   And the number of those is probably scarce, who desire to be rid of their wrong opinions by losing their heads!   We may rejoice, however, in not being shut up to so painful a dilemma!

But rejecting these two apparently opposite and extreme dogmas, the one as doing violence to Christian equality and liberty, and the other as throwing down, theoretically at least, and trampling upon all Christian authority and subordination—the one as binding the hands and the feet, the other tying up the eyes and tongue of the body—and both as hostile to the true idea of the Church—shall we not find the true middle path by adopting as our rule of faith, *the doctrines and traditionary practices of the first three or four centuries of Christianity, insofar as they may be clearly ascertained and agreed upon,* not arbitrarily by popes and councils, and arch-bishops, but by the true catholic Church?   Had not the Church of those earlier times the best means of ascertaining the decisions of the Apostles and their immediate disciples, upon *all doctrines* about which there might be any dispute?   Did they not possess the best and all needful facilities for knowing the opinions and the practice of the Apostles, in reference to all the customs and rites of our Religion?   And is it not fairly presumable that, by the end of the fourth century, at farthest, all things pertaining to the theology and economy of the Church, would be finally settled and perfected?   And does not the history of the Church down to that period, and of the venerable and pious fathers, whom God seems to have raised up for the special purpose of effecting such a completion and settlement of the form and constitution of the Church, altogether favor these suppositions? If then, there is good reason for believing these things to be so, *will it not be best for us to adopt their creed and practices as our own, and submit to them as of binding authority?* Constrained to consent to their apostolic origin, shall we not yield then that respect due to such a source? Has the Church of the hoary and reverend Past, not a right to expect this of us? Will it not prove our wisdom to sit at their feet and learn the law at their lips? Can any safer resort be found? Could any object to such an appeal? Is there any modern division of the Church but would find an impartial umpire there? And would not thus, many of the schisms that now mangle the mystical body of Christ, be healed—would not the angry contentions that mar her peace, in this way be hushed—would not the proud pretensions and personal vanity of self-styled reformers, and the stormy agitations of fanatic zeal, which now bring so much grief and reproach upon Christianity, be rebuked? And might we not thus, soon realize the fulfilment of the day, when the Church, uniting all believers into one body, should come forth, " bright as the sun, fair as the moon, and terrible as an army with banners?"

Thus have the learned Doctors of Oxford, and their disciples, thought and taught. Professedly, and, as there is very good reason to believe, (in opposition to the suspicions cast upon their motives and aims, by some with whom this is the most powerful weapon they can use against those who may hold different sentiments,) *sincerely* lamenting the low state of piety in their own Church, and supposing all this, with the diversities of opinion prevailing, both with reference to doctrines and usages,* traceable to a silent but extensive departure from the original teachings and institutions of the Church, and apprehending a dismemberment of their communion, and a consequent influx and prevalence of infidelity, if the evils were not speedily checked, they have thrown themselves into the supposed breach, and lifted up

---

* " In the English Church, we shall hardly find ten or twenty neighboring clergymen who agree together; and that, not in non-essentials of religion, but as to what are its elementary and necessary doctrines." " If the people go to one church, they hear one doctrine, in the next, another."— *Newman's Lectures, p.* 365.

a loud and earnest voice in favor of their primitive institutions, and supported their appeals and remonstrances by the testimony of earlier traditions—affirming that their Church has ever taught what they now maintain and plead for—that "*acknowledging Scripture as her written charter, and tradition as the common law whereby both the validity and practical meaning of that charter is ascertained, venerates both as inseparable members of one great providential system.*"*

With the gross errors and popish squinting charged upon Puseyism, by its opponents, we have here, of course, nothing to do, and consequently nothing with the controversy upon the subject within the limits of the Episcopal church. But this much it is proper in passing, to say, that as with the subject in hand, so with all the other peculiarities of that system, a personal examination of them has produced impressions very different from those made by the perusal of the statements of those hostile to the Oxford doctrines! And surely insofar as those doctrines are false and dangerous, they need to be met with more powerful arguments than appeals to low prejudices, misrepresentations, and the defamation of those who advocate them!

But what shall we say to this Oxford theory of the Rule of Faith? Shall we reply in the tone and sentiment, which, in another instance, have been employed in reference to this system: 1.) That it "confounds the true Church, or the company of faithful men, with the external and visible Church;" 2.) that "the voice of all professing Christians, everywhere and at all times, it is impossible to ascertain;" 3.) that the decisions of councils, &c., are but of small authority, because "the Church Catholic does not admit of being represented"—and because "councils contradict each other," and especially because "there was no council having the least pretension to be called general, held during the first three centuries;" 4.) that "the unanimous

---

* No notice has been taken in this cursory review, of the charge of Romanism which it is usual to prefer against Puseyism, because whatever particular notions the latter system may be thought to hold in common with Popery on other subjects, there is very clearly no more connection between its theory of the Rule of Faith and that of Rome, than between that of ultra-protestantism and the latter.

consent of the fathers of the first three centuries, is (no) proof of the apostolic origin of any doctrine," inasmuch as "the remains of their writings are so scanty;" and they "are not trustworthy" witnesses, because "too credulous;" 5.) and finally, that the advocates of the Oxford school depart from their own theory, by the arbitrary manner in which they adduce the testimony of the age to which they love to appeal? If we did thus oppose their view, we should certainly raise up five very clever reasons against the system. But certainly, its grand error would be scarcely grazed, the roots of it would be left undisturbed. Plausible as they are in themselves, and worthy as most of them may be of consideration and approval, a skilful Puseyite would not only parry every stroke they might seek to inflict, but retort with biting effect. Their own language as quoted by no common adversary, could be made to tell with much more power than he imagines it possessed of. "Why should not the Church be divine? The burden of proof is on the other side. I will accept her doctrines, and her rites, and her Bible—not one, and not the other, but all, till I have a clear proof that she is mistaken. It is, *I feel*, God's will that I should do so; and besides I love these her professions. I love her Bible, her doctrines and her rites, and therefore I believe." Against the spirit of language like this, the objections above stated, in our opinion, patter with powerless fury. Indeed they hardly reach up to it at all.

Dark and dreary, indeed, were the retrospect, if all that is sometimes said, (and that in the way too of triumphant rejoinder to an opposite view,) of the state of the Church during the first *four* (not the first three) centuries, were true! Meagre and swampy truly, must have been its soil, if it could send up and nourish only such heavy headed bulrushes, or light reeds so easily "shaken by the wind," as are sometimes set forth as its best productions! How soon must the divine promise of continued divine presence and power, have been withdrawn or forgotten! How much more speedily must the Church, her first love being lost, have become recreant to the precious gospel trust committed to her, than were the Jews of old, to that less glorious one deposited in their hands! And all this too, under circumstances the more propitious to a persevering maintenance of the institutions committed to them, because of the fierce assaults made upon them by enemies from without, and false or self-deceived disciples within! It would surely be among the darkest of all the deep mysteries of our religion, were this so! But there is a sweet relief in knowing that it is not so—and still more in hearing those, who sometimes imagine that the defence of the truth calls for statements implying thus much, acknowledge that the presence of Christ and operations of His holy Spirit, were much more clearly and gloriously manifested during those very ages, than they have at times been willing to admit. Ah! yes, those were burning and shining lights, which then arose on the Church's horizon! And though, by reason of our distance from them, their number seems small, because (as with the more distant stars) those only that blaze most brightly can be seen, yet we have good reason to hope that the final day of revelation will prove our usual estimate of their number, far too low! That day may show that many who now seem to blind the eyes of the Church with the light of their learning, and the dazzling of their wit, are but flickering tapers in comparison with lights of those earlier times, whose rays have never reached us!

It is not, therefore, for its belief in the divine character of the Church, in the continual presence of divine grace and power in her midst, that we must differ from and oppose the Oxford dogma; neither for its fond and filial affection and *respect* for the **Past**, but because its faith in the one and its regard for the other, are sickly with sentimentalism, and inconsistent in their application with their own avowed principle.

This is evident in their reverence for the ancient institutions of the Church. Not all such reverence is of the right texture, nor even what it supposes itself to be. "There is," in language of which the source need not be given here, "a bondage to the power of the Past, by which it is as little honored, as it is by the revolutionary zeal that tramples its authority under foot. A bondage by which it is, in fact, arrayed against itself, and forced to become the grave of its own life. This appears wherever a disposition is shown to cleave to a given standpoint, as the absolute and ultimate perfection of life, and to withstand every tendency or effort by which it is attempted to advance to a new position. All change in such case is regarded, as in its nature, revolutionary, and the new is supposed to involve, as far as it prevails, the full sacrifice of the old. Hence fidelity to the old, is made to consist in a fixed immobility of spirit, by which, as much as possible, all thought and all life is held to the same traditional form." This is the bondage in which Oxford lies, and into which it would lead the entire Catholic Church. And this mistake is, at least, one fork of the tap-root of its romantic and sentimental system. The great law of progress and development which pervades the Church, in common with humanity and the world, is repudiated and opposed. Instead of falling in with the advancing and swelling stream of Christianity, it would push back the waters to their fountain-head, and linger there amidst the shade and poetic groves of the primitive ages of the Church. Instead of helping forward the "stone cut out of the mountain, without hands," and growing with its spread and increase, until it had subdued all opposition, and covered the earth, this theory would lead us back to Zion, or Gerizin, that gathering upon their rocks, a fortress might be built impregnable by our enemies, in which the Church might patiently and safely await its translation to high ground! Instead of so cultivating "the mustard tree," that it might shoot out its branches with continually wider stretch, until it had reached to the uttermost parts of the world, and extended its sheltering shade over the most distant islands of the sea, it would keep it closely trimmed in, and require all to find room, if they could, within its original limits! The garden of the Lord, in the prophet's eye, was so to extend its borders, as to convert the vast wilderness into a field of blooming and fragrant fertility. But according to this theory, the "ancient landmarks" of Eden, must not be moved by sacrilegious hands, and the wall inclosing it, be rather raised than lowered, that the wild beasts of the forests may be tamed and driven into its sacred enclosures! Thus then, as the theory last considered really curtailed and wronged the rights of the individual, by the very means by which it may have sincerely hoped to vindicate and restore them, so this doctrine of Oxford actually smothers and destroys the Past, by the profuseness of its affection and the warmth of its embrace.

There is, however, another objection to the Puseyite theory

of the Rule of Faith, also derived from its own concessions. It very justly contends for *the divine nature of the Church.* In this we are heartily ready to unite with another in taking Oxford by the hand, and fearlessly challenge either the ridicule or argument of opponents for doing so. Let them deny this attribute of the "kingdom of heaven" in its earthly pilgrimage, if they have the courage for it. The doctrine is a rock of hope and joy beneath our feet, and mocks derision or assault! But if Oxford really believes this, why not be consistent with itself in its belief? Is it the Church of the first four centuries only, that is divine? And was the enlightening and guiding presence of her Head withdrawn from her thenceforward? This will certainly not be for a moment pretended. But if it is admitted that her divine nature has been preserved and perpetuated through all succeeding ages down to the present, why not respect this fact in our theory of the Rule of Faith? The primitive Church nowhere claims the exclusive right of determining finally all matters of faith and of doctrine, and Oxford acts without authority or consistency in conceding it. Her dogma, therefore, cannot receive our assent.*

IV. Let us then turn in conclusion to a brief consideration of what may be termed *the evangelical doctrine upon our subject.* This title is given to it because it will be found, as is hoped, at least, to be *the view which the true Church has always maintained, either in theory or practice, against the errors represented by the false systems which have been noticed.*

Before making a formal statement of this doctrine, we will indicate the several facts or arguments upon which it rests—the steps by which it is reached.

1. The first is, that *the Bible was never given to be the only authoritative guide and directory for the individual Christian.* It has been so common to maintain the opposite of this, by some of the warmest and sincerest defenders of evangelical protestantism against the aggressions of Popery and Infidelity, that the assertion made may startle some of our friends. Others may use it for a sort of Treves coat, to create a panic with. But so long

---

* See Note, *ante* p. 363.

as we have the Bible itself, and their own ecclesiastical institutions and practice on our side in making it, there is not much need for fear. From the one, then, we learn that the preaching of the gospel by the Church, and its administration of the sacraments, and execution of discipline, are commended to those, and enjoined upon those, who could not possibly have been in possession of the sacred word. The Saviour's charge to the Apostles and the seventy, the Apostles' charges to such as they again ordained for the work of the ministry, and the directions of inspired epistles to Timothy, Titus, and established churches, all are indisputable proofs of this. Adding now to this, the fact that the most *republican church societies* always have acted in agreement with these directions, and exercised their authority in accordance, indeed, with their convictions of Bible teaching, *but still in accordance with their convictions, and not those of any one* who might happen to fall under their judgment, our assertion will surely not be so hastily denounced. Nay, the more Divine we regard the sacred Oracles, and the profounder the reverence we pay to their pure and exalted Source, the more ready will we be to pay deference to their explicit teachings upon this very point.

2. Another fact to be considered here, is, that *the Church is as truly divine as the Divine Word.* This again, we fear, is a position which may awaken dislike and murmuring. For, however willing professed believers may be to wake up the harmonies of the timbrel and the harp, and chime in with their own voices, in singing sweet songs in praise of Zion, and " speaking together in psalms and hymns," all manner of pleasant things about her celestial beauties, and divine attire, there is certainly a growing disposition in our day, and on the part of some, to let the matter rest with soft sounds. To such it may seem startling that it should be claimed that the Church is as really divine as the revealed Word. But why should we refuse to admit this? Is the Church a human institution, devised and framed by men? Is her life a merely human and earthly product? Is not her

---

* See besides other passages—Matth. xviii. 15; Acts xv. 1; I. Cor. v. 4–6; Gal. vi. 1; II. Thess. iii. 6, 14, 15; II. Tim. ii. 2; Titus iii. 10; Rev. ii. 2.

head a divine Head? Is not her spirit a divine Spirit? Are not her doctrines (as they were proclaimed before a syllable of them was recorded) divine doctrines? Are not her sacraments and rites of worship all from the same source? Are not her members divinely called and divinely renewed, and temples in which the Holy Spirit deigns to dwell? Is she not continually pervaded, in every artery and vein, in heart, and thought, and muscle, by the presence of Him who hath promised to be with her always, even to the end of the world? Is she, finally, not the Kingdom of God, of Heaven, of Christ? Can we say more than this of the Sacred Oracles?

We often hear it said, the genuineness and authenticity of the Bible, is proven by such and such outward and inward evidences. And are there not similar evidences in favor of the Church? Suppose a man who had heard nothing of either, should be called upon to examine the claims of the latter, without having the Bible to guide him, would he not be able to find such proofs—or could they not be pointed out to him with equal force and clearness, as those existing in favor of the divine origin of the word? It is not denied that there are mysteries and difficulties here. But neither will the existence of both in the other case, be disputed.

This is not the place, however, even if there were room and time, for a lengthy argument in vindication of the divine nature of the Christian Church. We simply wished to state the fact, and show that the statement had a good foundation. The inference from this fact, as to *the combined claims* of the Church and the Bible, will easily suggest itself.

3. A third fact in the settlement of our subject is, that *the Church is an animate body, a living organism, in which the several united parts, have mutual rights and duties, owed from and to each other, all separately considered, being subject to the whole.* If it were necessary to fortify this assertion, with reasons additional to those presented in proof of the Bible's not being the only guide, the Divine Word and the practice of the Church, might be made to furnish pages of testimony. The organization, constitutions, creeds, confessions, worship, and discipline of all regular Christian denominations, are based ultimately in this

fact, whether it be appealed to in their favor or not. Schism is no sin without it. Sectarists may plead everything in their favor apart from it. The fact is more real and necessary, if that be at all possible, than the living union and subordination of the several parts of the body to each other, which in the absence of any thing stronger, the Apostle uses as a fit figure of the constitution of the Church.

4. The last general fact bearing upon this subject is, that whilst the *Christian religion* is explicit and strict in defining and requiring assent to certain essentials in doctrine and practice, *it reduces these essentials to few in number, and allows free scope for Christian liberty and charity.* Whether this fact is acceded to or rejected by the reader, we are persuaded that it has been the bane of the Church, to disregard it. Ecclesiastical demagogues, fixing an ambitious eye upon some high seat among their brethren, have succeeded in multiplying and in hardening their chains of spiritual bondage, by persuading them to tear loose from the few silken cords by which the Church would fain have held them within safe limits. Thus whilst they were professedly defending themselves against the creed they had forsaken, they were really building up prison-walls for their own closer confinement. The effects of the spread of this selfish spirit, are seen all around, and occasion much grief, and yet, are only what must ever be expected from a departure from the true policy of our Religion. This spirit, too, is made to be its own tormentor. "Whatsoever a man soweth, that shall he also reap." How many schisms might have been healed in their incipient fomentations, but for the oversight of this fact! How much contention, and debate, and ecclesiastical warfare, and bitter bickering amongst believers, might have been wholly shunned!

As to its more immediate bearing upon our present question, the proper consideration of this fact would have saved much trouble and dispute. It teaches us in how far we can have and ought to seek a Rule of Faith, and defines its proper limits. And it exposes the mistake of those who, in inquiring after one, desire a Rule by which they may demand implicit assent to all the peculiar little lights and shades which may distinguish their particular draft of the Christian Religion; and who, without, perhaps, in every case, being aware of it, would only enforce their demand the more urgently, by pressing *the Bible only* into their special service! The bad company into which others may appear to fall, by the views they advocate, excites in them sincere abhorrence and pity. The pie-bald unbelieving crew which leads their van, inspires no dread or shame!

5. Taking these general facts together, and summing up their import, we shall find that the Christian Religion lays down the *combined testimony of the Word and the Church, past, present, and to come, to all fundamental doctrines, and essential ordinances, as the only true rule of faith.* To these all men are bound, on pain of eternal exclusion from all the privileges and blessings of the Church, here and hereafter, to yield hearty faith and support. And with reference to all things, not defined by these, all men are left to the upright exercise of their own judgment, enlightened by the faithful use of all the means of knowledge within their reach.

We have set forth and advocated this doctrine, as well as we could within such narrow limits, with the greater freedom and confidence, not because it was conceived to be something " new under the sun," or under the imagination that we were proclaiming a mystery hitherto hid from the heart of the Church, but directly under a contrary conviction. For we are fully persuaded, as has already been affirmed, that, in spite of all conflicting theories upon this subject, the practice of the great body of the true Church, has always been in accordance with the conclusion to which this essay has come.

" *In necessariis unitas, in dubiis libertas, in omnibus caritas.*" We will unite yet, finally, in the fervent prayer of thousands who mourn over the distractions of the Church, that the day may be hastened on when this unity shall be fully realized; when, throughout the whole earth, there shall be " one fold and one Shepherd."

Easton, Pa.   J. H. A. B.

ART. XXII.—CROMWELLIAN CHRISTIANITY.[*]

It is proposed in the subjoined remarks, to institute an examination into what we have chosen to denominate Cromwellian Christianity. Under this designation, we would have our readers to understand that form of religion, or imitation of religion, as we shall see hereafter, which we find embodied in the person of Oliver Cromwell, Protector of the Commonwealth of England. From the start, therefore, it will be remembered, that we have no particular reference to what is generally called Puritan Christianity. We cannot, by any means, coincide with Carlyle, when he represents Cromwell as the soul and life of Puritanism. Cromwell may have been closely connected with the Puritans during his whole life, and these latter may have coöperated with him in many of his movements, still we do not consider the connection so intimate, as it is represented by the above mentioned critic. Puritanism might have existed and run in pretty much the same channel, if Cromwell had never lived, though it is not likely that Cromwell could have flourished, had there been no Puritantsm. If our conceptions of Puritanism are correct, there is a fundamental difference between the one and the other. In the Protestant world, at least, there is no longer any doubt respecting the evangelical character of the ancient Puritans. Their names have been long ago recorded among the excellent of the earth, and their memories have been embalmed in the hearts of Christians in all parts of the world. They have left behind them a history of trials and tribulations for the cause of humanity, replete with edification to succeeding ages. Their martyrdoms are of as pure and elevated a character as have been offered anywhere at the shrine of Truth: their works, which do follow them, will endure when the monuments of the Pharaohs, and the trophies of art, shall have crumbled into dust. Their wood, hay and stubble will, doubtless, be consumed by the devouring element of time, but only that the durable material of their building may be brought more clearly to view. Thus much, however, cannot be said of Cromwellianism. Two

[*] Oliver Cromwell's Letters and Speeches, with elucidations, by Thomas Carlyle. New York, 1847.
The Protector: A Vindication, by J. H. Merle D'Aubigné, D. D. New York, 1847.

centuries have passed away, and its claims to a Christian character have not as yet been established. Its memory had been consigned to eternal ignominy, had it not af late awakened the sympathies of two of the most influential writers in Protestant Christendom—Carlyle in the literary, and D'Aubigné in the religious world. The weight of these two names when employed on the side of Justice and Truth, may be considered sufficient to resist any attacks made against an injured man: and Cromwell, if he were now alive, would have no reason to complain that wit and genius had all combined to hold his memory in execration, but on the contrary, to rejoice that the world is, at length, prepared to do him justice, whatever its decision is destined to be.

With reference to the office which Carlyle has performed, it is not our intention here to dispute or object. He certainly deserves our warmest thanks for his Herculean task, "for fishing up authentic utterances of the man Oliver, from foul Lethean quagmires, where they lay buried." As far as we can judge, he has successfully proved that "Stupidity" and "Dryasdust," favorite terms of his, have heretofore combined to denounce one of the greatest benefactors of the English nation: that Cromwell completely cut the sinews of Popery in England, and forever settled the question whether Protestantism should be established there on an impregnable basis, or yield at last to the intrigues of the Jesuits. Whilst Protestantism was struggling for a political existence on the continent, England was still storm-tost, and veering from Protestantism on the one hand, to Popery on the other. Queen Elizabeth did not establish Protestantism so immovably as she supposed. It was destined for Cromwell to complete what she had commenced. Popery was made, not only in England, but also on the Continent, to quail at the name of the Protector. If, then, the preëminence of England, in the old world, be owing to her Protestant faith, it is owing more, perhaps, to the policy of Cromwell, than to any other instrumentality, that Protestantism there found a home.

With the appearance of Carlyle's work on Cromwell, we believe, that the tribunal of history is solemnly invoked to review her former decisions, and to render a new one, that will be more in accordance with the dictates of truth and an enlightened age. As a consequence, we may expect the historic literature of England, to be revolutionized and to be written over again. It is more particularly, however, with the *inference*, which D'Aubigné has drawn from the performance of Carlyle, that Cromwellianism is Christianity, that we have here to do. We are disposed to honor the warrior and the states-man, whilst we are not able to award him the honored name of the Christian.

It must be admitted that many of our opinions on the most important matters, are mere prejudices, imbibed from the age in which we live, or inherited from former times. On this account it is extremely difficult to decide respecting the character of such an individual as Cromwell, from the mere impression which the facts of his life are calculated to make upon our minds. But every person possesses the remnant of a moral taste, that experiences a sensation of pleasure when confronted with moral beauty. Let this test be applied to the history of Cromwell, and what is the result? Is it the same as that which we experience in gazing at the Reformers, through D'Aubigné's graphic representations? The heroes of the Reformation awaken our sympathies for man, and invest human destiny with a dignity and glory of which we had no previous conception. The mind as it passes from scene to scene of that sprit-stirring drama, is elevated above the sphere of passion, and feels a kindred glow for all that is great and good in our common history. We feel ourselves involuntarily attracted to the cause of Freedom, Humanity and the Gospel, and prompted by an inward inspiration, we would descend ourselves into the battle-field, where Light and Darkness are disputing the ground. Can the history of the English Commonwealth thus enlist our affections, even when its darker side is left out of view, as is seduously done in D'Aubigné's life of Cromwell? Has the light which has been shed upon the life of Cromwell, for the last two centuries, created so warm an impression in its favor?

But the subject is one of importance and will not admit of being disposed of thus summarily. Let us endeavor to gain some idea of a pure Christianity, and then contrast it with its Cromwellian surrogate. If Christianity be anything at all, it is something more than a creed, a confession, or the triumph of a party. It is properly a new and spiritual creation. It is the same power which in the beginning called forth a world of created beings, and animated them with life, and form, and beauty. It is something more fundamental than any activity which is witnessed in the world of history or nature; it is the unity in which all finite beings are reconciled, and made to stand in their proper relations. Apart from such a living

connection with Christ, the world is still a chaos, or like a vessel
loosened from its mooring, lost by the wild, tempestous wave. But
Christianity is a thing of nought, until man becomes conscious of
it, and awakes to a sense of its power over himself and the world.
It then becomes the law of his being, imbedded in the depth of his
inmost soul, infusing life and health through his entire frame.—
When an individual experiences such an inward consciousness of
the vital character of religion, he is said to possess faith in the proper
sense, which with propriety is distinguished by theologians from
mere knowledge. A clear view of the spiritual nature of Christianity, therefore, must in the nature of things produce a conviction
of its capacity to penetrate every department of life. It is felt that
this may be effected without the destruction of the object it seeks
to subdue. It possesses a power to purify the world as it is, with
its infinite variety of languages, customs, governments, and degrees
of culture. In can thrive under an absolute monarchy, as well as
under a free republic. Sin being its only opponent, it asserts a sort
of divine authority for the constitution of the world at a given time.
It says, honor the kings, whether he be a Nero or a Trajan. It
never regards the world as absolutely the best, which the Divine
mind could produce, but the best for man in his present condition.
As the prison is the best place for the criminal, so the circumstances, favorable or unfavorable, with which he is surrounded, are the
best for man as a sinner. The world changes and improves, as the
spiritual condition of man is elevated; but such changes must not
precede the internal change, as the radical would have it, but are
always found to succeed it as a necessary result. The mild genius
of Christianity on this account does not ask for the fire and sword
to further its progress. It possesses a power which renders these
superfluous, and every one who possesses it must be conscious of it,
for he is taught of God. When individuals or ages then are found
to put confidence in human resources, in an arm of flesh, we may
reasonably conclude that they have no higher resort or hope.

Let us now apply the above remarks to the case in hand. Do
we meet with such a confidence in the divine power of Christianity,
as to render violence unnecessary? No doubt but that Cromwell
was under the evangelical spirit of his times. But how was his
zeal tempered by faith in the living energy of the divine word?
We shall seek in vain for this *sine qua non*, when Cromwell is excited to activity. His army and sword were in his estimation better

adapted to execute his ends than prayer or argument. With Cromwell, the Protestant faith was endangered by the reigning monarch, whose influence must first be curtailed, and whose life was at length sacrificed for the cause of Truth! or as he very sincerely no doubt thought, for the cause of God! In the next place, the parliament, which took the place and power of the king, seemed to stand in the way of the gospel, and this must necessarily be dissolved to make way for the army, to do the work of the Lord more faithfully. At length, however, the army itself in his view, was insufficient to finish the work so auspiciously commenced, and he begins to think that the whole protestant movement must be centered in his own person. Here it will be remembered, that we are not discussing the expediency or inexpediency of his political measures; they may have been justifiable or unjustifiable in a political point of view. But what are we to think of the Christianity which seeks to extend itself by the overthrow of an ancient constitution—the freest of the age, by the death of the sovereign, by the dissolution of the law-making-power, and by the concentration of all power within itself? When further, the progress of religion is set forth as the ruling motive—the grand inducement for such sudden and extensive changes? Is there faith here in Christianity as a grain of mustard seed? Or is it not a practical denial of Christ, and an implied unbelief in the purifying power of the Truth?

The spirit of the age might be plead as extenuating the matter, and doubtless the mere faults of an individual's piety may often be bolstered upon his age or associations. But such a plea is not of place, when the question has reference to the essentials of religion, and such is the issue which is made above. But let the objection have its weight. It will be admitted that Luther lived in a less enlightened age than Cromwell,—and yet we find him reposing the utmost confidence in the word of God to accomplish its ends. The elements of strife were present in Germany, and it would have required but little excitement to produce the explosion, which took place a century after, still he clings with all his soul to the unadulterated word of God, as the power which was to bring order and subordination amidst the general uproar. D'Aubigné himself in his History remarks of this, as a peculiar excellence in the Reformer's piety, that he did not wish to further the Reformation by arms, but by the simple preaching of the Gospel: but it excites no horror in the historian, when a contrary spirit is manifested by Cromwell.

This comparison might be considered unfair, as their circumstances differed so widely. Let us employ one that may be considered more equitable. The ancient kingdom of Israel was at one time in a condition similar to that of England at the time of Charles I. The king was unpopular, and was known to be wicked and forsaken of heaven. A youth, the son-in-law of the king, enjoyed the affections of the people, and it was, moreover, a general impression, that he was to be the future king—that he possessed the necessary talents to manage the affairs of the state. With all these circumstances in his favor, with abundant opportunities to destroy the king, and to seize the reins of government, solicited as he was on all hands by his followers, David was the last to commit an act of violence to Saul anointed of heaven to be king. He rather endured privations and sufferings, until Providence should open the way for the realization of the divine promise, nor have succeeding times been able to impugn his motives for thus conducting himself. Will centuries yet to come place the Protector on the same platform with the king of Israel?

It has been said that Cromwell was influenced by the evangelic spirit of his times: much more so, perhaps, than has hitherto been supposed. Previous to his introduction to public life, he lived many years in private, apparently absorbed in devotion, to the neglect, it is said, of his private affairs. In his letters, his spirit seems to be glowing for the progress of what he regarded as the pure faith. If his own accounts are true, of which we have no reason to entertain any doubt, he offered up numerous and fervent prayers for the prosperity of the Protestant faith, and the downfall of antichrist. Even amid the din of the camp, he could wield theological arguments against the Scotch clergy, represented by Carlyle as the severest reprimand they have ever received. But these concessions will only serve to divest him of the character of arch-hypocrite, under which he has been made so frequently to appear. Further than this, they can be of no force, except to place him among a class of individuals who have too much Christianity to be classed entirely with the world, and too much of the world to be placed on the side of Christianity. Such a rank is not an arbitrary one. It is the same which many of a congenial spirit with him, often regarded as champions of Christianity, are beginning to occupy. It is more and more felt that Christianity recognizes no heroes, except such as a Paul, a Luther, a Martyn, who forsaking all they have, and renouncing all confidence in the flesh, seek to regenerate the world by the Ever-lasting Word; that a Constantine, a Gustavus Adolphus, a Henry IV., have no claims to a Christian character, based merely upon their Christian policy or their Christian warfare, and if they are to be canonized at all, their merits must be founded upon different considerations entirely. Geologists inform us that the skeletons of huge, misshapen monsters have been dug from the earth, so unlike the present races of animals, that it is difficult to decide, whether they belong to the present, or are the remnants of a former world. We suppose that the position of Cromwell and others like him, with reference to Christianity, is somewhat similar to that of these animal giants in reference to the present order of things. Whether they belong to the Christian world, or are entirely exterior to it, at all events they occupy the dark and isolated position of the mammoth, the megalosaurus, and the iguanadon in the natural world, which fortunately for us have become extinct.

The character which we have been discussing is very important, owing to its bearings upon modern times. Our most enlightened political institutions took their rise in the seventeenth century, and hence for ages to come, the Cromwellian period will engage the study of the scholar and the Christian. How important then that the literature of that time should be pure and according to truth! If Cromwell is to be regarded in the light of a pure and elevated Christian, his example will be, and it ought to be imitated. But how direful the consequences, if this opinion be founded on error! It was Achilles, the hero of Homer's song, who formed the charac-ter of Alexander, whilst the hero of Macedon became the exemplar of Charles XII., king of Sweden, and justly styled the madman. But would we desire another Cromwell? Then let us cultivate a pure literature of Cromwell, and our circumstances most likely will never become so straitened, as to render his presence in our midst necessary or desirable.

But Cromwellian Christianity has its imitations, affinities in our days already, as it has had in all ages of the Church. There is a species of Christianity now abroad in our land, that has all the zeal of a Cromwell himself, but does not seem to possess any clearer consciousness of the divine power of Christianity than its prototype. We notice a manifest impatience among many with the regular developments of Providence in bringing about its ends, and an appa-rent forgetfulness that the gospel works as leaven, in the improvement and refinement of the human race. Owing to the fearfully intense activities now at work, the improvement of society is no longer permitted to be carried on as a regular growth, but must necessarily be hastened by a kind of high-steam pressure. Human appliances, often carried to violence, are employed without regard to the hidden principles of life, that are enfolding themselves in society, and bidding fair to yield an abundant crop. The sword has not as yet been unsheathed, and standing armies have not as yet been summoned as a backing to argument and reason, but how often has it been attempted to coerce public opinion, and employ it as a rod! How much of the thinking of our days is performed by voluntary associations! The most marked form, perhaps, which Cromwellianism has assumed in our days is represented to us in *modern abolitionism*, that is, the abolitionism of the extreme *left side*. Here we meet with Cromwellian zeal and impatience in abundance, and at the same time a practical denial of a vital Christianity. Our precious institutions, the freest and the best which the world has witnessed, are too corrupt to embody their ideals of perfection. Changes in the constitution, the dissolution of the Union, or if it must be, steel itself, alone can realize their views of the kingdom of God. According to these chivalrous reformers, we may wait till the day of doom for a better era, if we must rely upon the mere preaching of the fundamentals of Christianity. If Cromwell were permitted to revisit our earth, and to settle in America, it is not unlikely that he would know where to find sympathy, and how to turn our distractions to account. Happy is it for America that her military characters, know how to enjoy their honors, and to cultivate the arts of peace.

SMITHSBURG. MD.   T. A.

ART. XXIII.—THE CLASSIS OF MERCERSBURG.

THIS body held its annual meeting lately in Greencastle. In

ecclesiastical occasions in the history of the church to which it belongs. The meeting was full. The best spirit prevailed among its members. Less time than usual was lost on the dull formalities of mere outward business, and more room in consequence allowed for strictly church transactions. Questions of deep theological interest were brought forward for discussion, not in any cold abstract view, but under the pressure of the most direct and urgent practical want. These discussions were conducted with unusual earnestness and animation, and no small amount of spiritual ability; while, at the same time, the zeal to which they gave rise, was happily tempered and governed by the true spirit of Christian charity and peace. We know not that we ever attended an ecclesiastical meeting, in which what seems to us to be the proper idea of such an occasion, might be said to have been, on the whole, better sustained. Among other good things, the Classis resolved, with the help of God, to carry up its sub-scription towards the endowment of the Theological Seminary, to the mark of at least *Ten Thousand Dollars.* More than half of this sum had been secured within its bounds previously; under the reasonable expectation that the other parts of the church would have been stimulated by such noble example to come up also, with a moiety at least of the same liberality, to the completion of the work; in which case the endowment would have been long since out of the way, and the Seminary placed on a sure and firm foundation. By some strange fatality, however, the example seems rather to have worked just the other way; some of the Classes even, of which we might have hoped better things, making use of it, apparently, as a reason for sitting still and doing almost nothing. All this formed no inconsiderable temptation to anger as well as discouragement. Happily, however, this temptation was surmounted, and sorrow became tributary, by the grace of God, to the sacred interest of piety and love. The Classis fell back on the vast solemnity of the cause at stake; counted the cost as in the presence of God; and calmly concluded to shoulder again its own full proportion, and more, of all that still remained to be done, as though it had done nothing before, trusting in God, by such "coals of fire," to move finally the tardy energies of the church at large, to some corresponding zeal. Indeed the feeling seemed to be, in the end, that if it were found *necessary*, the Classis would even dare, in God's name, to shoulder, single-handed and alone, the entire work, so far as it remains still incomplete. No such necessity, however, is likely to exist. The action which has since taken place on the part of the other Classes, may be taken as a full guaranty that the endowment will now be consummated by the church as a body. Never before has there appeared so much union of mind, and determination of will, and consciousness of strength, in the body at large. All this, as carrying direct respect to the institutions at Mercersburg, is highly encouraging and full of significance. It shows that they are *not* at war with the true genius and spirit of the German Church; that they have not led the way within it to discord and disunion; that in proportion precisely as their real character is understood, they find a responsive chord of sympathy and love and truth through the whole length and breadth of its communion. Such a testimony, coming in such form, is well entitled to consideration, and ought not to pass without grateful notice.

Our object, however, in referring to the Classis of Mercersburg, is not merely nor mainly to bring into view the interesting fact now mentioned. The whole action of the Classis, at its last meeting, deserves to be commemorated, as forming a significant advance in the direction of a sound and healthy church consciousness, in this particular section of our Reformed Zion. As illustrative of this general fact, we note particularly two very important results, which were reached with great unanimity after the most full and earnest discussion; namely, the rejection of the Albright ordination as invalid, and the full affirmation of the old catechetical system, as the true and only legitimate order of the church, in opposition to the theory and fashion of religion, by which in modern times it has been so generally brought into disuse, or turned into an idle form.

The first question came up, in connection with an application from a most worthy and pious minister of the Albright connection, to be taken under the care of the Classis as a candidate for ordination in the German Reformed Church. The request in such form could not, of course, relieve the Classis itself from the

responsibility of deciding either for or against the validity of his
ordination as it stood before, and so indirectly, for or against the
right of that body to be recognized as a part of the true Christian Church.   This was felt very properly to be a most momentous and solemn issue ; and much was urged, with great plausi-
bility and force, in favor of a comprehension of this sect in the
general Protestant Church, and against any action in this case
which must imply the contrary.   The Albright body, it was said,
must be allowed to include in it some true piety ; Christ, we may
trust, will own many who belong to it for his own dear people;
the doctrines of grace are acknowledged in it, the authority of
the Bible, justification by faith, the influences of the Spirit, &c.;
and how should we then, without a breach of charity, delibe-
rately proceed to unchurch them as a sect in the presence of the
whole world ?   Must we not, to be consistent, unchurch also other
sects ?   And how in the end could we assert the validity of any
Protestant ordination at all, over against the exclusive claims of
the Church of Rome ? Must we not maintain the universal priesthood of Christians, as the only ground on which to justify the
Reformation ; and why should not this universal priesthood be
of as much avail to legitimate the ministry of Jacob Albright
and his successors, as it is acknowledged to be in favor of Luther
and Zuingli and Melancthon and Calvin ? All this was earnestly
and powerfully pleaded, on the floor of Classis.   On the other
side, however, it was urged, that if the Church be a divine fact,
schism must be also a most real and sore evil, which we are bound
to make account of just as much as we make account of heresy;
that in such case, we have nothing to do with charity or courtesy,
but are called in the fear of God to bear manful testimony to the
truth ; that if it be a solemn thing to unchurch a body of professing Christians, it is a thing no less solemn, to fling the doors
of the Church wide open, and thus virtually turn it into nothing
but a word and a name ; that in the providence of God, the Classis was here called to face a question, on whose decision the most
vast consequences might be found to hang in time to come ; that
the Albright body never had any call to become a church ; that
its ministry started from nothing, and was of no force ; that it
was a solemn duty to bear this testimony to the Albright Breth-

rerſ themselves, and that to refuse to do so must involve great unfaithfulness to the world generally, encouraging people to make no account of the danger of falling into schism in any way, but rather to take it for granted that all religious connections are alike good and alike safe. Pains were taken, besides, to show that the case of the Reformation was in no proper sense parallel with the rise of this upstart sect; that the universal priesthood of Christians involves not at all the power of starting a new church in every corner and on any occasion; and that Protestantism must be considered a failure outright, if it carry no force in its constitution sufficient to distinguish it here from the universal prostration of all bounds and metes on the side towards the open world.

In the end, an almost unanimous vote was given, with unusual heartfelt solemnity, in favor of the petition for new ordination, and so, as before said, against the validity of the Albright ministry—virtually declaring that body to be no part of the proper Church of Christ. No question was raised in regard to the baptism of the applicant. This had taken place, not among the Albrights, but at an earlier date in the Roman Catholic Church, whose ordinances, notwithstanding the great corruption of that communion, have been regarded as valid by the Protestant Church generally, from the beginning. The vote now mentioned, was taken with only four *non liquets,* and not a single negative. The lay delegates, to a man, and apparently without the least hesitation, gave their voice firmly and fully in its favor.

As to the correctness of the decision, there ought not, we think, to be the least doubt. There might be cases presented, where it would be exceedingly difficult to bring the question of church character to any such practical resolution; but no such difficulty can be allowed to hold in the case here brought into view; unless, indeed, we choose to give up all faith in the divine constitution of the Church, under any view, which would be virtually to dismiss the whole question from the start, as one of no meaning or worth. If the Church be of any force at all outwardly, as an object of faith and trust, and if schism in the old ecclesiastical sense, is to be regarded as still possible, in any shape, it must be plain that such self-constituted upstart bodies as the Albright Brethren, the followers of John Winebrenner, &c., have no right

or title whatever to be recognized as any part of the heavenly
corporation.   According to its own account of itself, (Rupp's
Hist. of Rel. Denom. 2nd edition p. 274ff.) the Sect of the Albrights, (Albrechts-leute,) took its rise about the year 1800, not
quite fifty years ago, " in one of the middle free States of America."   One Jacob Albrecht, an illiterate man, of obscure origin
and connections, became awakened to a sense of his sinful state,
and " after a long and very severe struggle, received at last, by
faith in the Son of God, the remission of his sins and the spirit
of adoption."   Gradually he gained notoriety as an exhorter,
made disciples, and finally " after a very severe conflict respecting
his call to the ministry, commenced travelling as a preacher; in
which vocation we are told, God richly blessed his labors, by giving him many souls for his hire.   " Having now continually a
feeling and tender regard for the Germans of this country, as
among them true Christianity was at that time at a very low ebb,
and almost extirpated, he united himself in the year 1800, with
a number of persons, who by his preaching had been awakened
and converted to God, into a Christian society.   This is the
origin of the Evangelical Association.   In the year 1803, this
society resolved upon introducing and instituting among and for
themselves, an ecclesiastical regulation.   Jacob Albright was
therefore elected as the presiding elder among them, and duly
confirmed by the other preachers, and by their laying on of hands
ordained, so as to authorize him to perform all transactions that
are necessary for a Christian society, and becoming to an evangelical preacher.   They unanimously chose the sacred Scriptures
for their guide, &c."   How is it possible to recognize such a body,
self-originated within the last half century in a corner of Pennsylvania, as part and parcel of the Holy Catholic Church, the
mystical one and universal Communion of the Creed, which
started in Christ eighteen centuries ago, and against which, we
are told, that the gates of hell can never prevail!   If Jacob Albright had a right to originate a new church in this way, every
pious Tom, Dick and Harry in the land, has a right to do the
same thing, and to make himself also, in like style, the fountain
and source of a new ministry—provided, only, he can find a few
simple disciples to submit themselves to his ghostly authority, and

lay their hands upon him afterwards in confirmation of his commission. Thus in the end, each Christian family might set up for the dignity of a separate Christian denomination, and have its own ministry and sacraments in its own way. It is worse than idle, in any such view, to pretend any faith in the Church at all, as a divine historical institution. We believe in the universal priesthood of Christians, as we believe also in their universal kinghood; but for this very reason, we have no faith in the idea of a particularistic atomistic exercise of any such high function in either case. The priestly power starts in Christ, and from him passes over to his body the Church, to be exercised from its life as a whole, through organs created for this purpose, and not to be snatched away by profane hands for the use of any and every sect, which may take it into its head to set up a separate priesthood and kinghood in its own name. Is it asked then, how we are to justify the Reformation, and vindicate the validity of our Protestant ministry? The answer is short. Not by any outward succession in the case of the ministry, nakedly and separately considered; but certainly not by any theory either, which overthrows the necessity of a true historical succession in the life of the Church, and makes it competent for any body of Christians, under any circumstances, to start an entirely new church. It is the life of the Church as such, the life of the Church as an organic historical whole, which alone can fully legitimate and clothe with power the needful organs of this life, and their necessary functions. If then we must admit some disturbance in the ordinary law of ministerial succession at the Reformation, it does not follow at once that the succession itself for this reason fell to the ground; the true succession lay in the life of the Church as a whole; and if it can be shown that *this* gave birth to the Reformation, it must be allowed to have been sufficient at the same time to make good, in the way of inward reproductive force, any *unavoidable* defect that was found to attend, in this revolution, the outward genealogy of the Protestant ministry. After all, it is the Church, the presence of Christ's life in his Body, which supports the true line of the ministry, and not the line of the ministry that upholds mechanically the being and authority of the Church. On this broad principle, we justify the Reformation; It was the product of the old Catholic Church itself; the central consciousness of the Christian world had been struggling towards it for centuries before; it was, in the end, the organic outburst plainly of the life of Christianity, as an objective historical whole, which simply laid hold of the Reformers, and brought itself to pass by them as its organs, without any calculation of their own. In no other view can it be successfully defended; and on this principle, accordingly, we find no difficulty in distinguishing between it and all minor religious revolutions and secessions, that seek to shelter and excuse themselves under its august shadow. Let them show a like necessity for their appearance, in the organic life of the Church as a whole. What a parody on every such imagination, is presented to us in the free and independent rise of the *Evangelische Gemeinschaft*, the self-unchurching brotherhood of Jacob Albright! Was it the power of Christianity, in its universal organic life, that gave birth to *this* mushroom? That would be indeed the mountain laboring to produce a mouse. Did the enigma of centuries and ages, which had lain like a heavy burden on the heart of the Church before, come to its magnificent solution finally in this small spiritual phenomenon, the mission of such a man, the creation of such a sect! There is absurdity in the very thought. The thing rose in a corner; it had no historical necessity; it came no one can tell whence, and so it is fast going also, no one can tell whither. There is no room for any rational comparison here with the Reformation; and so not the least reason for fearing that the honor of this great interest may be brought into jeopardy, by allowing the full truth to be both spoken and acted in so plain a case. Luther was the organ of the Church; Jacob Albright was the subject of mere private fancy and caprice. No deep, general force, the accumulated world-sense of ages, came to its uncontrollable and necessary outbreak in his person. He had no call to form a religious denomination. His sect is no birth of the Church, but a schismatic denial of its objective historical authority from beginning to end.

In these circumstances, the Classis had no right to shrink from the solemn decision it has been called to make; as it should have no wish either, now that it is made, to conceal or disguise its true purport and sense. The action took place, without haste or passion, under the most calm conviction of duty, and in full view of the critical responsibilities involved in it on all sides. In no other way, could true Christian fidelity have been shown towards the Albright Brethren themselves. We owe it to the souls of those who are led away by this delusion, to warn them plainly of their danger. The Church is bound moreover by duty to her own children, not to keep silence in regard to so great an interest. If she have no faith in herself, no power to condemn and abhor schism in any quarter, how can we expect those who are growing up in her bosom, to place any true value on their birthright, or to make any account of her authority? We are sorrowfully and solemnly persuaded, that the unfaithfulness of the Church just here, forms one of the greatest evils under which the Christian world is made to suffer at the present time. A sound church faith, on the part of the Church herself, by which she may be enabled firmly to assert her own *divine* prerogative over against all merely human associations or sects, is necessary to authenticate fully her commission itself, and forms at the same time, an indispensable element in the power of the Christian salvation, which is administered by her hands.

No less important, as regards right church feeling, was the general ground taken by the Classis on the subject of what is called the *system of the catechism*, as it stood in the original practice of the Church. It is generally known, that this had been widely supplanted a few years since, by another system altogether, which for the sake of a name, may be denominated the *method of the anxious bench;* under the influence of which, even the excellent institution of *confirmation* itself, was in danger of losing altogether its meaning and credit. Happily, this tendency has received a check, and it is now common, on all sides, to honor the Catechism again, and observe at least the form of Confirmation. It would be a great mistake, however, to suppose all done here which the case requires, by a mere outward transition from the use of the anxious bench to the use of the catechism. All turns at last on distinguishing properly between the inward life and genius of the two systems, which these shibboleths are employed thus outwardly to define. It is quite possible to put away the

bench, and bring in the catechism, and still remain bound altogether to the theory of religion, of which the first only, and not
the second, is the natural sign and type. The great thing needed,
is some true insight into the difference that exists between the
two schemes of religion which underlie the different tendencies
in question, and an inward return thus, with love and faith, to
the "old paths" from which the practice of the Church has so
widely swerved. Much was gained in this way, at the last meeting of the Mercersburg Classis, by means of resolutions and discussions brought to bear from various sides on this point. It was
encouraging here also, to find, that on a fair understanding of the
questions at issue, the judgment of the body, and especially the
instinctive sound feeling of the elders *always*, went fully in favor
of the old church spirit, and in opposition to the foreign way of
thinking, which has been seeking to drive it from its place. It
was felt that to shake off the power of that foreign system effectually, something more is necessary than to change a few outward
forms, and a few watchword phrases for the lips. The result of
all, we trust, has been a general clearer apprehension than before,
of the true design and significance of the old Reformed practice;
its dependence on the idea of the Church, as a divine organization; its relation to the conception of sacramental grace; a more
solemn sense of the real membership of baptized children in
Christ's kingdom; and of the duty and privilege of treating and
training them accordingly; a much larger faith in the high import of educational religion, the use of the catechism, as a direct
preparation for the second sacrament, and the true solemnity of
Confirmation as the necessary and proper completion of the holy
sacrament of baptism. All this implies, of course, a great deal
more than a polite toleration simply of the church system, in the
way of appendage only to its unchurchly opposite. That may
be taken as the hardest fate of all for this system, when men who
have no power to understand it at all, but are completely satura-
ted with the other scheme, pretend, notwithstanding, to tack it
externally to their own favorite theory, in the way of compliment
merely and condescension. How far this wrong has been carried
in our own church, and more still a great deal in the Lutheran,
need not here be said.   N.

ART. XXIV.—THE "BEAUTIFUL RIVER."

BY ROB'T P. NEVIN.

I.

There breathes the force of untold eloquence,
 O RIVER, in that wondrous voice thou hast!
No sound doth leap to seize the pausing sense,
 Or hold, aroused, the slumbering echoes fast
 That haunt the cover of thy chambers vast;
And yet thy silence with o'erwhelming power
 Doth speak the mysteries of dark centuries past,
By old bequeathment made thy proper dower,
When KINGS controlled, and native PRINCES strode thy shore

II.

Oh! that, high inspiration won, 'twere mine
 To interpret the wild meaning thou dost bear,
And give it utterance with a voice like thine!
 Vain wish! The mountain rill that stirs the air
 With vaunting song, doth more of import share
Than man may fathom; yet its clamorous boast,
 Which solitude e'en owns and answers there,
Abroad upon thy mightier bosom tost,
Without an image left is in oblivion lost.

III.

Strong River! thou of all that God has made
 To crown the grandeur of this scene, alone
Maintain'st thy primal glory undecayed!
 Lake—moor—hill—forest—mountain reared of stone—
 Where are the strength and grace they claimed their own?
Eternal seeming once, thy transience bred
 A theme of scorn to feed their mockery's tone;
But now the appointments of their pride are fled,
And time and thou in changeless destiny are wed.

IV.

Thus to forecast the unseen end of Fate,
   Would Prescience, erringly yet aiming, strive!
Thus pampered Power, vain in its high estate,
   And fixed establishment, assume to live
   Unchanged through change; as though the shocks that rive
The world besides, were impotent to rend
   Its flattered rule—thence-sprung derivative!—
Or Revolution, sinew-stripped, could lend
No arm to wield defeat, or shape an altered end!

V.

The old world had its dynasties: they were;—
   Reared monuments to fasten firm their fame;—
Erected temples, that each distant heir
   Thenceforth might prize the grandeur of their name?
   They were, but only were.   New eras came,
New thrones, new empires; and the old
   Lost e'en the memory of their former claim,
Or held it in enigmas darkly told,
A mystery to wonder at, but not unfold.

VI.

And here upon thy shores were kingdoms sprung!
   Through spanning cycles of unreckoned date,
Though seeming slenderly their tenure hung,
   They reached, o'erliving in bold estimate
   The length of lordlier realm, or nobler state.
Coeval with the rise of thine, arose,
   Oh, Tiber Queen!—a star, its more than mate—
The LENNAPE's!*—high towering when the close
Befell, that thence decreed thee Memory's and thy foes'.

---

* The Ienni Lennape, as their name purports, claim to be the "original
men" of the continent. Their territory at the time of the discovery of the
New World, lay between the Hudson and Susquehanna rivers, on either
shore of the Delaware. They afterwards migrated to the Ohio Valley.

VII.

Like thee they had their mighty—known apart:
   Men famed around the "fires" and in the field,
The proved in speech, the tried in arm and heart,
   Whose worth, with honor's zeal, love's faith, to shield,
   Down through tradition's channel ran revealed.
And favored bards their victories too have sung,
   In anthems through the columned forests pealed,—
Alas! whose temples, arch by arch o'erflung,
May ring response no more, like as of old they rung!

VIII.

The grand-sire with the youth, at even-tide,
   Intent to shape aright his pliant prime
For manhood meet, hath ta'en him at his side,
   And from examples of the ancient time,
   Portrayed the picture of a life sublime:
Hath decked his scalp-tuft with an eagle's plume,
   Plucked from his own brow, marked with the groove and time,
The seal of valor stamped in age's room,—
And left its story and its lesson with the 'loom.

IX.

Dark maids by moonlight in the shadowy wold,
   The fervor of a suitor's lips have felt
In tones heroic, nor in dalliance, told.
   His fairest plea the trophies in his belt:
   His valued boast the stroke his fathers dealt.
In tale historic with ancestral pride,
   Rehearsed how oft a vanquished foe had knelt;
What arm compelled—whose fate the Braves that died,—
Made these his cause—and so the warrior wooed his bride.

X.

Such the devoir of Gratitude to Worth,
   And what superior tribute, held or spent,

Could crave ambition from the wealth of earth?—
   The quarry's prize by Genius shaped, and lent
   To fill a niche, or rear a monument?—
The lettered page—the pictured woof of art?
   Cold mockeries, whose fashioned grace is meant
To serve the framer's, not the subject's part;
When Taste may sate its longing—never move the Heart.

XI.

In their rude sepulchres the dead are roomed!
   The tiller's share hath torn the generous sod
Sheltering their sleep; and o'er their bones inhumed.
   Unweeting and unheeding feet have trod:—
   Profaned and trampled they, whose name have awed
A peopled continent! What then?—Their dust
   Was dust—the rest beyond is known to God.
Living their race lived they, in sainted trust,
And passing passed—even as others have, and must'

XII.

And who, when all he loved, or wished to love
   Of kind and country, friends and home, are gone.
His hearth-stone cold—mute woodland, glen and grove,
   Where childhood's laughter with its leaping tone
   Had burst, and manhood's eloquence had flown .
Oh, who would longer live, nor choose to fade.
   A nameless thing, unpillared and unknown.
Than dwell, beyond his race's durance stayed,
A foeman's boast—a vanquisher's exultance made

XIII.

Roll on. O River! in thy power and pride'
   Thy voice hath spoken. and its solemn peal
Hath reached my soul.   Here. bending o'er thy tide,
   Devout Emotion, worshipping. would kneel,
   And from the fervor thou hast given to well,

Pour out its offering—this bosom here
   Yield all of life's vain longing it may feel,
Planning alone the purer end to bear—
Like thine, heaven's smile to win—its blessed brightness wear.
   PITTSBURGH, May, 1849.

ART. XXV.—THE SAINTED DEAD.

HEAVEN; or An Earnest and Scriptural Inquiry into the abode of the Sainted Dead. By the *Rev. H. Harbaugh*. Philadelphia: William S. Young. 1849. pp. 245. 12mo.

A very popularly written volume on a popular and interesting theme; which needs only to be known generally, we think, to find many readers, and which, when it is seriously read, can hardly fail to leave behind it a salutary religious impression. "For several years," the author tells us, "my mind has been specially directed towards the heavenly world. In gathering information on this interesting subject, I was surprised to find that so littttle had been written directly on it. I have also found, since my own mind has been employed on this subject, that there are many to whom it has been a subject of like interest, and who eagerly read what professes to throw light upon it. I have therefore ventured to offer this volume as a contribution to this department of pious inquiry, hoping that the reading of it may be as much blest to the hearts of those who read it, as I feel the writing of it to have been to me. Any book that will serve, in any degree, to draw the realities of the eternal world, especially of heaven, nearer to us, is not written and read in vain." The work, of course, is more practical than philosophical, designed to serve the purposes of believing piety rather than to minister food for curious speculation. At the same time, the writer shows himself to be possessed of a good deal more learning and philosophy too, than we meet with in many who put forward much larger pretensions in this form. Mr. Harbaugh is constitutionally a thinker, and not a mere dull retailer of other men's thoughts. The habits of the preacher and the pastor, both vocations in which he is known to excel, are not allowed with him to mar the sympathies and affinities of the scholar ; and the present production, in this view, is certainly very creditable to his literary character and powers. and carries in it also good augury for the time to come. The author has a certain advantage for the *popular* discussion of the subject he has here taken in hand, in his temperament and age. The first includes a broad dash of mysticism ; to the second he is indebted for an exuberance of imagination, which riper age will be apt considerably to tame ; both qualifications well suited to help the mind forward, in such an excursion as is here made, over the confines of time and sense, into the world of unseen mystery that lies beyond. There is nothing dark, however, nor particularly transcendental, in the style of the work. Its poetry is not prose run mad, or mounted on stilts into the region of clouds, but clear sensible thought and speech, which as a general thing all sorts of readers may readily enough comprehend. Mr. Harbaugh uses a pen, which is at once both fluent and correct.

Is Heaven a *Place? Where* is it located ? Do the saints pass into it *immediately* at their death ? In what *correspondence* is it to be regarded as standing with earth ?—These are the great cardinal questions, on which is made to hinge both the contents and plan of the book. In order to assert and make clear what is held to be the truth, in each case, as taught in the Bible, an examination is taken of the different theories and opinions that come into conflict with what is thus approved, for the purpose of setting them aside. This opens a broad free field for discussion, with full opportunity for bringing into view a good deal of curious and interesting matter, which is well adapted to illustrate the difficult bearings and connections of the general subject.

We have been requested by the amiable and excellent author

himself, to exercise our critical censorship on his work without
mercy; under the supposition, as it would seem, that the view
especially which it takes of the state of the dead, between death
and the resurrection, might not be found to suit our catholic theology; with which, at the same time, the reigning tone of the
work may be said fully to accord, especially in the importance it
attaches to the christological fact as the central ground of all true
religion.   On close inspection, however, we find no such room
for disagreement here, as we were at first led to expect and fear.
We should be very sorry certainly, to stickle for the notion of
an intermediate *place*, the conception of a definite fixed locality
in the centre of the earth or elsewhere for the outward comprehension of the departed dead; and still more so, to contend for
any such conception, as excluding the idea of paradise on the
one hand, and of hell on the other, in the case of the righteous
and the wicked.   The old Jewish representation of Sheol and
Hades, must be regarded of course as an outward picture or symbol of the truth in this case, and not as its very form.   It is only
with the inward and necessary substance of what it expresses as
presented to us in the Bible, that the christian faith is properly
concerned.   This is the fact of an intermediate *state*; the question of *place* is one of comparative insignificance, in regard to
which it is perhaps not possible to come to any satisfactory conclusion; the question of *state*, it seems to us, we have no right
to be in doubt about, or to decide except in one way.   The Scriptures teach a middle state, from beginning to end.   It is explicitly affirmed in the Creed.   It has ever been held, as a necessary
part of the Christian faith, by the Church Catholic.   It enters
essentially into the whole scheme of Christianity, and cannot be
torn from it without marring and spoiling its structure throughout.
Christianity knows nothing of an abstract redemption for the soul
separately considered, and makes no account of the so called
immortality of the soul apart from the body.   Its salvation is for
the *man*, whose nature stands in the union of both.   It requires
the resurrection accordingly to consummate its own process;
this reaches forward from the start to such full triumph over death,
and can never be counted complete till it comes to that issue.
The period then between death and the resurrection falls within

the process of redemption, (Rom. viii. 23; I. Cor. xi. 23, 51–56; I. Thess. iv. 14,) and not beyond it. It is not in the way of mere pageantry and show, that Christ is to bring the dead saints out of their graves at his second coming; that will be the natural and necessary end of the *life*, which is lodged in them now as the members of his mystical body. To conceive of the Christian redemption as something *done* at death, and all beyond as outward accident and circumstance only belonging to the heavenly state, is necessarily to wrong the whole gospel. It turns our salvation into an abstraction and strips it of its true concrete glory as revealed to us in the Creed. The intermediate state is not the heavenly state, in the full and proper sense, but belongs rather, we must say, to the economy of our present life, the world of mortality *through* which "the saints on earth and all the dead," as one blood ransomed communion, are steadily passing to that higher form of existence, "the glorious liberty of the children of God," as it is to be reached by all together finally through the portals of the resurrection.

But are not the spirits of the saints with Christ, after they leave the body? We reply, they are; and in this respect, the New Testament view of the disembodied state, in the case of the righteous, goes far beyond the idea of Sheol, as it prevails throughout the Old Testament. We may, if we choose, denominate their felicity the happiness of the heavenly world itself, and in such view speak of them as having passed into glory and as now dwelling in paradise. In all this, however, we are bound to make a broad distinction still between their condition and that of the saints after the resurrection. Heaven can not be the same thing, for souls out of the body, and souls carried through this relatively naked stage to the full redemption and liberty that lie beyond. It is the resurrection which winds up the drama of salvation, and opens the way for "the new heavens and the new earth wherein dwelleth righteousness." The intermediate state, even if it be supposed to hold within the same local bounds, can have no common measure with the resurrection state. The two states must form of necessity, two separate and distinct worlds. Sameness of place, in such a case, is of no account.

All this now may be said to be virtually admitted in Mr. Har-

baugh's book itself; although he takes a great deal of pains appa-
ently, to set aside the doctrine of the middle state entirely. It
is however, a question of place with him in the end altogether,
and not properly a question of state. His object is to make out
that the souls of believers do at their death pass into glory; which
involves to his mind, an entrance locally into a certain fixed
region called heaven, the same that is to be occupied by saints
after the resurrection. But in all this, he simply locates the theatre of the intermediate state in heaven, instead of giving it a
locality in the under world, or some where else. The state itself
he is still forced to acknowledge and allow. His disembodied
spirits exist in heaven on very different terms, from those which
hold in the case of the full and proper heavenly life, as it is to
be reached after the resurrection. They have no clear sense or
apprehension of the realities around them; no full self-consciousness, answerable to their local condition; it is a potential rather
than an actual occupancy they have of heaven after all, like that
of the present world by the infant still unborn. It is a state
"analogous to, but, of course, higher than a state of ordinary
sleep, with active dreaming." Nay, farther it is allowed to be,
under this form, an inward preparation, "celestial pupilage," for
the resurrection life, carrying out and completing the preparation
previously begun in the body. "While the saint is in this world,
in the body, he becomes conversant with material things, and
habituated to them; now, in the other world, in a disembodied
state, previous to the resurrection, he will become conversant
with and habituated to purely spiritual existence, so that after
the resurrection, when soul and body are again united, he will
be able to hold converse and communion with either material or
immaterial existences at pleasure." But what less, we ask, is all
this, than the very idea of the middle state itself, which the author
seeks to exclude? Locate it where we please, in hades or in
heaven, the fact remains at last substantially the same. The
state between death and the resurrection, as it differs widely from
our present life, differs widely also from the life that is to follow.
It is not heaven itself, in the full sense, as it is to be revealed
hereafter; but an undeveloped, relatively embryonic condition,
rather, according to this book, in which souls are matured by ·

inward exercise for that higher order of glory. We find no occasion then, to defend the reality of the intermediate state, against
Mr. Harbaugh; for he himself allows it, in language which all
must confess to be sufficiently strong.

We think, however, that he obscures the true force and value
of the doctrine, by insisting too far on the local identity of the
two states which he owns to be so materially different in their
interior constitution. Heaven of course involves the conception
of *place ;* but we have no right to think of it as holding only
under such local relations and limitations, in this form, as are
found to characterize our present mortal life. The idea of place
may admit far other modes of relation to it, than any of which
it is possible for us now to form a conception. Place itself becomes
what it is, by the way in which it is occupied and apprehended;
a new sense imparted to us, (like sight for instance to the consciousness of a world born blind,) might of itself be sufficient
to change our existence, immeasurably more than a translation
without it to the most remote part of the universe. So it is
quite easy to conceive of the whole theatre and form of our existence undergoing a revolution, first at death and then again at the
resurrection, without any vast migration in space after our present fashion of thinking, which nevertheless may involve in each
case such a universe of change as no image of any such mere
outward migration can even adequately represent. The idea of
state here is of incomparably more account, than the notion of
place ; for the simple reason that this last must necessarily be
conditioned, in its whole real determination, by the powers and
capabilities which are comprehended in the first. The Scriptures certainly open to our contemplation thus three states, in the
case of man, which are very differently related to our world,
while yet they all belong to the same grand process of space and
time for which the world serves as a theatre. The idea of this
process requires the full triumph of humanity, according to the
proper sense of Gen. i, 26; Ps. viii, 5–8, and Heb. ii, 5–10, over
all the limitations with which it is called to struggle in the world
as it now stands. This end is reached by redemption. Hence
a *mortal state,* doomed to sink under the law of sin and death ;
an *intermediate state,* in which the reign of death continues,

but all is ripening at the same time for the outburst of a higher
life; and finally a *resurrection state*, in which this mortal shall
put on immortality, and man stand forth as the perfect and last
sense of this earth, organically conducted to its own glorious consummation by Him who made it in the beginning for such use.
What more the idea of Heaven as introduced by this last state
may include, into what new relations and correspondences it may
bring its happy inmates with other spheres and climes of God's
universe, either immediately or at some subsequent epoch, we
know not; the Scriptures shed no clear light on what lies beyond.
But so much at all events the idea includes, as related to what
lies on this side; Heaven is the true end and issue of the problem
which God is conducting to a solution in the world as it now
stands, and the very form in which at last the stream of its history is destined to roll the full volume of its sense into the ocean
of light, and holiness and love, which it is formed to seek from
the beginning.

The doctrine of the intermediate state of course then is no
point of curious speculation merely, but a most deeply practical
interest for Christian faith.   In proportion as it falls out of view,
the historical *realness* of the new creation in Christ Jesus is made
to suffer in the mind of the Church.   A living christology, a
quickened sense of the mystery of the Church, must ever require
it as a necessary part of its consciousness and hope.   It is only
an *abstract* Christianity which finds it easy to part with it altogether, or that turns it into a nullity, by erasing all real distinction between the state before the resurrection and the state after
it.   Such abstraction, however, strips in this way the doctrine
of the resurrection itself of its significance, and so far saps the
very foundations of the Christian faith.

But the subject is too broad for us, to pretend to take it up
here at all in its details.   We may find occasion possibly to
return to it, as a direct and separate theme, some time hereafter.

Some have an invincible propensity to confound the idea of
a middle state with the idea of a probation after death, purgatory,
&c.   But the two conceptions are by no means the same.   The
first is taught in the Creed, and we are bound to believe it.   The
question, whether *any* of the human race will have a probation

extended to them after death, is one which our Church allows us not to meddle with in any positive way. Mr. Harbaugh, if we take his meaning right, consigns the untold millions of the heathen world to hopeless perdition. This, however, is going too far; we have no right to affirm absolutely, one way or the other. Infants, dying such, Mr. Harbaugh of course considers saved, without any such probation as implies the possibility of their being lost. Still he would admit, no doubt, that this salvation must include an evolution of reason and will in a human way; the knowledge of Christ in some way preached or made known; and a free closure, as the old divines say, with the terms of life presented in his person; otherwise all would become magic.

On the subject of the Church, as we have before said, as well as in its whole christological theory, the little volume before us is far enough removed from the abstract spiritualism, which has become so common in our modern divinity. One great object of the writer seems to be indeed, to expel such spirituality of the mere intellect from our minds, and to make us feel that the mystery of the new life, as it is unfolded to us in Christ, is no less real, and concrete and near to the world as it now stands, than are the palpable existences that surrounded us in the sphere of sense.　　　　　　　　　　　　　　　　　　　　　N.

ART. XXVI.—MORELL'S PHILOSOPHY OF RELIGION.

THE PHILOSOPHY OF RELIGION. By *J. D. Morell, A. M.*, Author of the *History of Modern Philosophy*, etc. New York: D. Appleton & Co. Philadelphia: Geo. S. Appleton. 12mo. pp. 359.

THE author of this work has come recently into favorable notice by his History of Philosophy; which is, undoubtedly, the most successful attempt that has yet been made, to exhibit in English form an intelligible outline of the marches and countermarches, achievements and exploits, of modern mind, in the regions of pure thought. The difficulty with these historical sketches among us generally is, that they are wholly outward and mechanical in their character; the product of a purely empirical reflection, which has never come to understand what speculation means, much less to have any inward sympathy with its processes and wants; and which affects, accordingly to take the size and measure and contents of a system of philosophy, much as some shrewd Yankee understanding, made up of lines and figures, would go about the business of constructing a table of statistics. No wonder that the whole subject should be turned more or less, in this way, into solemn caricature and nonsense; especially, if the case require a transfer of thoughts out of one language over into another, the profound ideas of Kant, for instance, or Schleiermacher, or Hegel, from German over into commensurate and fairly intelligible English. Such translation is, under any circumstances, a most difficult and delicate task; but in the province now before us, the difficulty approaches the character of desperate impossibility. At all events, no power can overcome it, even in part, that does not involve an actual entrance into the world of thought which is to be described, and a living reconstruction of its forms and relations in the life of the reporter. Only as the thoughts are thus truly mastered and made his own, and are brought in this way to force out for themselves a proper utterance and representation in the language he speaks, can it ever be possible for him to mediate at all between them and the thinking of other minds. Such qualification for writing a history of philosophy, Morell must be allowed to possess in a rare degree. He has himself a deeply philosophical mind; feels the necessity and dignity of speculation; owns within himself the authority of a divine call to think. His philosophy has taught him to look with reverence to the thinking of others; he has read and studied much, with living insight into systems and books; he has become widely catholic thus and free, without losing at the same time his own separate independence. No one can charge him with a disposition to undervalue or wrong the claims of English philosophy; he is far enough removed from all blind veneration for what is foreign, whether French or German, as such; while, however, the claims

of such foreign thought, are recognized in full as they ought to
be, and made to receive their just tribute of respect.   The writer
shows himself well at home in the deepest and most abstruse
processes of German speculation, and exercises certainly a fine
tact and skill in bringing them to proper statement in his own
language.

In the work before us, he may be said to break ground in a
field, which for this country, as well as England, is still in a great
measure new and strange.   To many, indeed, the whole subject
may seem to be one which we have no right to touch.   They
can admit a philosophy of sleep, a philosophy of storms, nay,
even a philosophy of hats and shoes, but they will hear of no
philosophy of religion.   The worst of it is, however, in all this
case, that a very stubborn theory of religion is found to underlie
notwithstanding, the whole judgment which it represents; only
this is not the fruit of any true reflection or inquiry, but the product altogether of blind accident and tradition.   Those who think
least about the nature of religion, are apt to be most *notional* in
their way of apprehending it, and most stiff at the same time, in
contending for their own poor scheme of notions as identical with
the very truth of the Bible itself.   It is just the tyranny of such
miserable *unphilosophy*, affecting on all sides to be the deepest
and last sense of divine things, which makes it in the highest
degree desirable and necessary to introduce into the sphere of
Christianity the emancipating power of a philosophy of religion
in its true sense.   The general object then of this work of Morell, is one which we highly approve.   The inquiries here brought
into view, as lying at the threshold of all sound theology and
opening the way to a properly free and manly christian life, are at
this time, especially, most worthy of general serious attention.   It
is high time, that we should aim at something deeper in regard
to them, than the oracular off-hand divinity of our common religious newspapers.   It is high time, that the tyranny of men who
will neither think themselves, nor allow others to think, should
be resisted, and, if possible, brought to an end.   *Protestantism*
is a holy thing against all such dead traditional authority, whether
in the Church of Rome or on the outside of it; an authority,
which takes God's truth into its own keeping as an outward ab-

straction and deposit, and so turns the whole into a treadmill of
notions, in whose rotatory track the universal world must be forced
to move, if possible, to the end of the ages.

We do not mean, of course, to make ourselves responsible
here, in any way, for Morell's system of thoughts as a whole.
There are positions in his book, which we are by no means prepared to endorse and accept as our own.   Altogether it makes too
small account of Christian doctrine, and is not sufficiently *realis-
tic* and concrete in its view of the Church.   But the value of
such a work does not turn exactly on the full orthodoxy of its
contents, or on their full agreement rather with any current creed
by which they may happen to be tried.   There are writers, whose
very errors are much more wholesome than the bed-ridden truths
presented to us by others; as having their seat and fountain in
the region of earnest living thought; as serving to unsettle the
dull habit of mere presumption and tradition; and as ministering
too, not only outward occasion, but powerful inward stimulus
and help also, to the difficult business of thought in our own
minds.   It is in view, particularly, of this sort of value belonging to it, the power it carries with it, independently of its own
conclusions right or wrong, to rouse and stimulate inquiry in
others, that we consider this volume of Morell deserving of recom-
mendation.   We would be glad to know that the work is widely
read and studied.   Fortunately, it is of a character which is likely
to confine its influence very much to those who have some power
to think for themselves, and are able thus to "prove all things"
for the purpose of "holding fast that which is good."   For a
large class even of our theological public, it can have very little
sense or significance one way or another; the field it traverses is
for them, in a great measure, away over the sea, and far out of
sight; they only wonder that any should trouble their heads with
questions and perplexities, which they find it so easy themselves
entirely to overlook or forget.   For such, however, as are capable of understanding it, and on this account likely to read it, the
book will be found both opportune and profitable.

. The following few passages may be taken as specimen extracts,
suited to show something of the author's style and spirit, and well
worthy besides of being looked at, and borne in mind, simply for
their own aphoristic interest:

"That Germany has given rise to much that is opposed to real Christianity,, and subversive of all genuine faith in God, is, unhappily true: but it has not been at all more fruitful in schemes of Infidelity than our own country: nor has it encouraged by any means so largely as we have the grovelling spirit of a utilitarian and materialistic philosophy. The only difference is, thatf whilst *our* unbelievers have nurtured the spirit of Infidelity in a low, vulgar, and unimposing form, *theirs* have stormed the fortresses of the faith with an array of learning, and a mental intensity, to which we can make but small pretension. But it should not be forgotten, that, where learning can be a bane, there it can also be an antidote; and such assuredly it has been in Germany. They who are unacquainted with the literature, the criticism, and the Christian philosophy of that country, can easily afford to despise it; but I can soberly, say, that amongst all those who have taken the pains to read, mark, learn, and inwardly digest the best productions of the German mind, I never knew *one* (and I have known many) who did not esteem the privilege of doing so amongst the greatest he had ever enjoyed. It is common to speak particularly of the *mysticism* of the German theologians. Such an opinion, I am bold to say, is, in the great majority of instances, only accounted for on the principle, that every thing appears mystical to us before we comprehend it. But if there are any number of theologians in the world who have less than ordinary title to the charge of mysticism, that number is to be found amongst the German writers; for they, of all others, have been the most fruitful in historical research, in keen-sighted criticism, and in the development of the fixed laws of our spiritual nature."—*p.* 14, 15.

—

"Sure I am, that if the germs of religious Rationalism exist any where in our country,—if there are principles possessed by any party which involve in them all that the most uncompromising Rationalist could demand, those germs and those principles are to be found amongst the strenuous assertors of the doctrine of private judgment *in its intellectual acceptation*, although that doctrine may be coupled *at present* with the most perfect orthodoxy of theological opinion. It is not my intention to offer here the evidence of what I now affirm; it will be found, I trust, sufficiently expounded in various portions of the work itself, and particularly in the chapter upon *Certitude* in the domain of religious truth. I merely design by these few remarks to repel, in the outset, the charge of Rationalism, and to whisper into the ears of those most likely. perhaps, to prefer it, the admonition, to be quite sure of the soundness of *their own* principles, and to it that they do not themselves secretly foster in their own bosom the viper. which they imagine to be inserting its poison only into the heart of others."—*p.* 18.

—

"Putting together, therefore, the generic character of our intuitions on the one side, and the rise of more subtle philosophical methods on the other, we see that there are sources of progressive development in both the elements out of which theology is constructed. The only idea we would impress upon the mind of every reader is, that *development* does not imply any organic *change* in the real and essential elements of Christian truth. Different as the seed in its first germination may be in all appearance from the perfect plant, yet the latter is simply the unfolding of what that seed at first implicitly contained. And so is it with the development of Christian theology in the world. In whatever degree the Christian life has been really awakened, there must have been some real perception of Divine truth; and to whatever extent logical appliances may be used, yet they cannot *alter*, but only *mould* the material which is there given. The increase of spiritual discernment, and the more subtle analysis of philosophical methods, do but tend to bring the truth into a fuller realization and a more scientific form. Under these influences it must march onward in its course until it ushers in the glorious period of the purified Church, and the promised rest of a regenerated world."—*p.* 201, 202.

—

"The exposition we have given of the nature and elements of Christian theology, offers a complete solution of the phenomena which have so often appeared in the history of Christianity, when the moral consciousness of an age gets beyond its recognized theology, so that the one can no longer satisfy the requirements of the other. The theology of an age naturally embodies itself in books, catechisms,, or Church symbols, where of course it remains stereotyped and fixed; in the meantime, however, the living consciousness of the Church ever unfolds as age after age rolls on, and adds new experiences of the scope and the power of Christian truth. The inevitable result of this is, that those who take their stand *pertinaciously* upon the formal theology of any given period, remain stationary, as it were, in the religious consciousness of this period, while that of the age itself goes so far beyond them, that their theology is no longer an adequate exponent of the religious life of the times, and can no longer satisfy its just demands. Since the time of the Reformation, the religious consciousness of Europe, unfolding the principles then started, has been advancing more and more towards the religious conception of Christianity; and in consequence of this we find the dogmatic theology of the earlier portions of this era unable to satisfy the moral and spiritual requirements of the present age. The effect of this is seen in the struggle which is manifestly taking place between those professed theologians who insist upon abiding strictly by the ideas, and even the phraseology of the past, and between the minds which represent the advancing spirit of the age, unchecked as they too often are by a due reverence for antiquity. Party struggles like these have unhappily the tendency to drive both sides for a time into the extreme position of antagonism, so that the one falls back entirely upon ancient authority, while the other thoughtlessly sets it at defiance. The only consolation we have is, that truth always pursues its course midway between such extremes."—*p.* 223, 224.

" Whatever of life there is now in the religion of our country, we hold to be owing to causes quite distinct from the enforcement of a complete formal theology in the Confessions of our Churches. In the Church of England, true piety has developed itself far more through her prayers and such-like appeals to the deeper religious intuitions of the people, than through the enforcement either of the Catechism or the Articles. The Nonconformist Churches, it is well known, owe their vitality to the development of a purely sponta- neous and experimental piety coincident with the rise and the spread of Methodism; and lastly, Scotland, which, under the rigid incul- cation of a formal Calvinistic theology on the part of the Church, had sunk into that dreary state of religious lethargy, from which various circumstances have now conspired *partially* to arouse it,— Scotland, I say, with its mechanical formalism and its vast under- currents of infidelity, will soon have to choose between the alterna- tive of opposing a free and expansive theology to the pressing wants of the age, or relapsing deeper than ever into the moral death of a dialectical dogmatism, and all the dread results it ever brings in its train."—*p.* 249, 250.

———

" We find, therefore, as a matter of logical necessity, that the theory of religious certitude which throws the whole decision upon the interpretation of the letter of Scripture, insensibly merges into the very foundation-principle of Rationalism; for in one case, as in the other, the individual reason is the final appeal. And this result, be it observed, perfectly coincides with the facts of history; for nearly all the Rationalism of modern times has based itself upon biblical interpretation, and appeals even to the Scriptures themselves as a verification of its conclusions. 'Is, then, the Bible so indefi- nite,' it might be said, 'that we cannot arrive at any *certitude* as to what it really contains? Surely it is all very simple, and he who runs may read.' But, alas! so says the very next theorist we meet with; and so says a third; and so they say each and all. The term simplicity, as applied to truth, is very indefinite and very deceptive. Every man's system imbibed in infancy and moulded to all his hab- its of thought, seems *to him* the plenitude of simplicity; it is only when we have broken the spell of such habits and associations, that we begin to see what an abyss there is in ideas which we looked upon as the most elementary truths; only then that we begin to find out, that some human *system* has really moulded the Bible to our under- standings, far more than the Bible has ever served as data for us to construct our system. As a moral agency, indeed, nothing can be more definite, nothing more simple than the Bible; and nothing will lead the sincere student by a shorter course to a satisfactory result; but viewed as a basis of *scientific* truth, the case is very far otherwise. Little do they consider who proclaim so loudly the doctrine of private judgment or private interpretation *as an intellectual principle*, what lies concealed in it *now*, and what may come forth from it hereafter.   Once give the individual principle full play, and whatever be the result of a man's speculations on the Bible, you have not a word wherewith to resist him.   *His* individual judgment is theoretically as good as your own, and if he be a keener logician than yourself, a thousand to one but he will beat you utterly out of the field, and set up his logical Rationalism completely over the head of your logical orthodoxy.

The conclusion, therefore, to which we come is this, that the letter of the Bible cannot be the basis of religious certitude ; and that even if we did arrive at certitude through its mere verbal *interpretation*, the actual test would still be the *reason* of the interpreter."— *p*. 286, 287.

"The age in which we now live, an age universally fruitful in independent thinking, is fast driving the question of reason and authority as held by the Protestant world to a point.   Multitudes fully conscious of the logical untenableness of their ordinary profession, have been impelled to one or the other extreme.   Some, following out the principle of individualism, have seen it land them in the lowest abyss of Rationalism ; while others, naturally shrinking from such a result, have thrown themselves into the arms of absolute authority.   On this spectacle the Christian world is now gazing, and many is the throbbing heart which is asking, at the hands of the Protestant Church, in which its faith has been nurtured, an intelligible solution of this al'-important question."—*p*. 319.

N.

ART. XXVII.—Tyler's Tacitus.

The Histories of Caius Cornelius Tacitus, with notes, for colleges, by W. S. Tyler, Professor of Languages in Amherst College. New York: D. Appleton & Co. Philadelphia : Geo. S. Appleton. 1849.

Prof. Tyler happily avoids the two extremes to which annotators upon the Classics are exposed, a prolixity on one side that rides its author to death, and a brevity on the other that leaves every real difficulty unexplained, and expounds only what is already clear. His elucidations, for a writer so concise as Tacitus, are not too copious, neither are they too sparse. An introductory essay he gives us, in the first place, abridged from the Prolegomena of L. Döderlein to his edition, on the characteristic style of Tacitus, which very much conduces to the proper understanding of his author throughout. In his own notes, he is always more suggestive than diffuse. While he neglects not the dry solutions of all grammatical difficulties, he endeavors, at the same time, by all proper information and alluring arts, to carry the reader into a lively sympathy with the author and his times. Especially is this his object in his Preliminary Remarks. In drawing a comparison, however, at the close of these, between the two great Latin historians, while he justly prefers the style of Livy, but gives, for graphic delineation of character, the palm to Tacitus, we wonder that he goes no further. We are somewhat surprised that he sets not forth the superior accuracy, diligence of research, and freedom, in a great measure, from national prejudice, exhibited in the works of Tacitus, contrasted with the great deficiency in these essential requisites of a faithful historian, which we are made to feel in the many discrepancies and Roman partialities that come before us in the writings of the earlier author.

From the greater number of editions of the Germania and Agricola of Tacitus, published of late in the United States, we would infer that these books are more read in our colleges than the. Histories. Of these too, Prof. Tyler, some years ago, has given us, perhaps, the best edition. It is certainly very pleasing to be made acquainted with some of the peculiar traits of our respectable savage ancestors, of whom we have no reason to be ashamed, and to observe also the gentle satire of Tacitus in quietly contrasting the rude but healthful morals of the German and Britons, with the refined vices of his own countrymen; but, after all, it is in his Histories that the excellence of this author shines forth preëminent. It is in describing the turbulent commotions of his own times, when the mighty empire was already being tossed by those conflicting elements, which, in after times, resulted in its dissolution, himself the while no unconcerned spectator, that the strength of his tragic genius is best displayed. As no good American edition of the Histories, so far as we are aware, has before been published, those generally in use being very inapposite and deficient in their annotations, the present volume of Prof. Tyler, we think, supplies a desideratum. We trust it may lead to the more general and thorough study of this superior work of the old Latin historian.

W. M. N.

THE

MERCERSBURG REVIEW.

SEPTEMBER, 1849.

NO. V.

ART. XXVIII.—Restitution of All Things.

By these words is indicated a period and a condition, which occupies a prominent place in Revelation, and which always has been, and should ever be, dear to the hearts and hopes of Christians of this period. "God hath spoken" oracularly, "by the mouth of all his holy prophets, which have been since the world began." Were there no other reason to urge us to an investigation of this future state of "all things," the fact that it forms the great burden of prophecy in all ages, would of itself, be sufficient. Whatever God hath spoken, deserves to be studied with diligence and prayer. But, especially, we should study profoundly and prayerfully what "he hath spoken," in so many different ways, and by so many different instruments, "by the mouth of *all* his holy prophets," men of the most exalted piety and profoundest wisdom—men admitted to the secrets of God, and his commissioned organs of communication to his creatures, in every age, "since the world began," till these extraordinary channels of revelation were closed. Surely a theme which occupies so large a portion of Revelation, should also legitimately occupy a large place in the thoughts and anticipations of God's people.   There is a glorious vision, similar in its general outlines, which seemed always to be before the eyes of ancient seers, when by Divine illumination they passed from the sphere of the present and visible, into the region of the invisible and the spiritual.   Individual peculiarities arising from idiosyncrasies of mind, or different points of vision, may be detected in all the prophets, but no one familiar with the glorious scenery of the world of prophecy, can fail to observe that one and the same great panorama was before them. *Invisibilia neque mutant, nec decipiunt:* Eternal realities do not vary with fleeting centuries.   Things seen and temporal only, are subject to change.

Surely, also, what God hath thus spoken, " at sundry times and in divers manners," it is his will that we should understand, as well as study, at least, so far as correct apprehensions are connected with full development of Christian character and the more perfect performance of duty.   God " hath made known to us the mystery of his will, according to the good pleasure he hath purposed in himself," not to gratify our fancies or stimulate our curiosity merely, but that thereby " the man of God may be perfect, thoroughly furnished unto every good work," yea, brought to the " measure of the stature of the fullness of Christ."

With these convictions, let us explore, under the guidance of the spirit of Revelation, " *the times of the restitution of all things.*"

" Restitution," in the original, is an exceedingly expressive word, its full meaning being, the restoration to its original state, of any thing which has been marred, thrown down or perverted. This application of the word to " all things," conveys by evident implication, a terrible truth, which ought to be distinctly kept in view in all our investigations, viz : that there has been an universal marring, degradation and perversion. Without this assumption, Revelation is is an enigma, and restoration has no meaning. " All things," as God made them, were " very good ;" not only good in themselves, but in their mutual relations and connexions. Nature, as we usually denominate the external circumstances of man, sea, earth and sky, harmonized with man, and man with nature.   Like different, but accordant parts, of some glorious choral symphony, the work of a master mind, man and nature together, constituted the actualization of one great idea of the infinite mind. But "sin entered the world, and death by sin, and so death passed on all men, because all have sinned," and derangement, degradation and disorder in "all things," for sin always and everywhere produces confusion, disorder and wretchedness. Man still remains, and so does nature, but the original glory and, especially, the original harmony·is gone—the beautiful ideal exists no longer. This fact of derangement and perversion, is not only testified explicitly in God's word, and made the basis of the whole scheme of restitution, but it is attested also by history and observation, ocular demonstration and awful experience, in every age. All the powers of man's nature have been implicated in the disorder introduced by sin. It has touched and tainted his understanding, his conscience, his affections, and his active energies: he feels its perverting influence in his religious instincts, his capacities for science and art, society and government. From the deteriorating influence of sin on the intellectual faculties of man, we find error in a thousand forms and in every age, and in reference to every subject. Everlasting truth is objectively and immutably the same, but the rays of truth, as they come from "the Father of lights, with whom is no variableness or shadow of turning," fall on mental optics, humid with prejudice, distorted by interest, or blinded by passion, and instead of "truth in the inward parts," the beautiful and blessed correlative of the objective reality, there is error in Protean forms and almost numberless varieties. From the perversion of man's religious instincts, we find a prolific growth in every period of Idolatry, Superstition, and Persecution. The pages of human history, devoted to the vagaries of the human conscience, the wild, fantastic freaks of conscientous wickedness, are among the saddest demonstrations of the perverting influence of sin on the nature of man. Science also, in its investigations and applications, owing to the influence of sin, has seldom or never been ancillary to piety as it was designed to be, in the original structure of "all things." In the world of science, He "for whom, and by whom, and to whom, are all things," is not "all in all," and consequently the key-note that would keep everything harmonious, is wanting. "The princes of this world," in prosecuting their researches, have often perverted genius, the most glorious gift of God to self-deification. They have wandered amidst the immense and magnificent building, till they have forgotten the Builder. "Star-eyed science" has gone to the verge of creation to bring back "tidings of despair." The various departments of art—poetry, painting, sculpture, architecture—constitute a glorious theatre for man's noblest powers, in the exercise of which he is permitted most to resemble the Creator. In all these, however, we perceive the perturbing and perverting influence of sin, the awful source of all confusion. In artistic efforts, the governing idea, which would give symmetry and perfection, to a greater or less extent, has been lost. God has been dethroned; the infinitely little, instead of the infinitely great, has been made central. The master spirit of evil, envious of all that would glorify God and elevate man, has too often guided the pen, the pencil and the chisel. In the same way, man's power of organization, as manifested in civil, social and ecclesiastical structures in every age, give sad evidence of the same fact. Government, in every age, even the best forms of it, is but an illustration and acknowledgement of imperfection and disorder. It can modify mischief, restrain rampant passion, reconcile, to some extent, conflicting interests, and *play off* one set of passions against another. It displays great ingenuity in arresting and keeping in check the destructive tendencies and elements of human nature. But, after all, it is not, it never has been, and if left in man's hands alone, it seems never likely to be "very good," as God originally made "all things" and doubtless purposed them to be in their actual working. Society, in the same way, viewed as the result of man's powers of construction, has in every age, and in none more than our own, given evidence of wrong and disorder. It favors the few and degrades the many; arrays different elements of the social fabric in fierce hostility, or concealed, but not less fearful jealousy against each other. The social machinery, however perfect in theory, works badly in fact, and though the best powers of man have been expended in mending and remodeling, it still seems radically defective, manifesting friction in almost every part. At this advanced period in the experiment of reconciling the antagonisms of society, except where the persuasive power of Christianity has rectified its evils, notwithstanding all the theories invented and labor expended, society still very much resembles Bunyan's Slough of Despond. Civilization, without the influence of Christianity, brings so many new diseases, vices and luxuries, as almost to counterbalance its advantages. And then what jarring and collision does the history of the race exhibit in the attempt to adjust the relative jurisdiction of the church and state—to settle the proper centre of unity, to ascertain and carry out practically God's *beneplacitum*, in regard to the controlling power, the righteous earthly vicegerency of the only acknowledged sovereign.

" All things," the human understanding, the human conscience, human passions, science, art, society, government, have manifested the marring, perverting, degrading influence of the apostacy, and therefore need restitution—putting back to their original position. And not only so, but " the whole creation also," is implicated mysteriously in man's sin and participates in the disorders it has introduced, and as really needs restitution. However philosophy or theology may attempt to explain the fact, or atheism and irreligion ridicule the assertion, it is true that " the whole creation groaneth and travaileth in pain together," in full sympathy with fallen man, " even until now." It has " been subjected to vanity," brought into a state altogether abnormal, does not accomplish its original design, " not willingly" or by any fault of its own, " but by reason of him that subjected the same," either Satan by his successful wiles, or man by his sin. Man, who was designed to be, in the original idea and ultimate purpose of the great designer, the lord and glory and crown of the creation, disordered and degraded it with himself when he fell. A touch of God's punitive finger turned the earth from its Paradisaical to its present state, and the restitution of all things cannot be complete till the creation itself is " delivered" by the same power " from the bondage of corruption," and made participant " in the glorious liberty of the sons of God."

Now, granting what is thus implied in the meaning of the word, that " all things" have been marred and perverted, and need restitution, and that God's ultimate purpose embraces " the

restitution of all things," it is pertinent and exceedingly interesting to inquire, to what condition will "all things" be restored?
The most natural and easy reply, unless there is something contradictory or impossible in the idea, would be, "all things" will
be brought back to their original state, with only such abatements
and exceptions as grow necessarily out of the long continued
previous existence of perversion and degradation. "All things"
are to be set right, and made to subserve the end originally designed in their creation and long continuance. The original
harmony is to be reproduced; the beauty which evoked the song
of the sons of God, and the shout of the morning stars, is to be
made visible; after the terrible episode of perversion, stretching
from Paradise to the times of restitution, there is to be an actualization of the original idea of the infinite mind, obvious to
principalities and powers in heavenly places, and to the everlasting confusion of the gloomy author of this long protracted period
of mystery and darkness. The strict meaning of the phrase
itself, selected by infinite wisdom, would guide us to this conclusion. "The times of the restitution of all things," indicates a
period, in the general, when the disorder, degradation and perversion occasioned by sin, in all the various particulars specified,
in man and nature and their mutual relations, will be rectified,
and the original wisdom of the infinite Creator will be vindicated,
and the archetypal idea of his mind, blurred and clouded by
the adversary, will shine forth to the joy of the higher order of
intelligences.

To recur for a moment to the specifications already given, in
"the times of the restitution of all things," Error, in all its Protean shapes, the result of the perversions of the human understanding, will be replaced by "truth in the inward parts." The
human mind will be in beautiful correlation to objective truth,
"like the cope of heaven imaged in a dew-drop." Superstition,
Idolatry, and the spirit of Persecution, whose vast structures have
been linked with governments and guarded by power apparently
invincible, arising from the perversions of man's conscience and
religious instincts, shall pass away. Science, in all its departments and applications, shall be sanctified by the uses which it
is made to subserve. Art, redeemed from its prostitutions, and

no longer under the guidance of the genius of evil, or viewed with jealousy by the children of light, as necessarily Satanic and essentially selfish, will be consecrated to its true and glorious purpose—the honor of God and the perfect development of man. The secret of social evils will be discovered and removed, and the ideal beauty of society which exists in heaven, where the will of God is done perfectly and universally, will be seen even on earth. Government, in church and state, and in their mutual relations, will be conformed to the everlasting principles of God's word, and accomplish God's original intention, his own glory, and man's true happiness. Man's physical structure will undergo great changes, adapting him to this new state of things "The days of God's people, shall be like the days of a tree." "His elect shall long enjoy the work of their hands." "A child shall die an hundred years old," and so short a period of earthly existence, shall be a curse compared with the usual longevity enjoyed.

It will be a period, moreover, marked by most striking changes in individual human character, and in all human institutions and practices. The "lion," in human form and power over others, "shall be turned into the lamb." "The tiger" in ferocity, "shall eat straw like an ox." Men as poisonous and pestiferous in their social and moral influence as "the asp," and bewitching to evil as "the basilisk," shall become innoxious even to the simple and credulous. "The child shall play," fearlessly and harmlessly, with "the hole of the asp," "and put his hand," without peril of pollution, "on the cocatrice' den." Without designing to deny that great literal changes may not occur in verification of these predictions, surely they are designed also to adumbrate intellectual and moral changes in human beings. Men whose fury broke through all restraints of law, and despised all penal sanctions, shall then become so docile "that a little child shall lead them."

Then also, either by the progressive perfection of science and art in their bearings on the appliances of human comfort, or by man's increased control over the elements that surround him and occasion his inconveniences, or, possibly, by some direct interposition of Heaven, like that which made earth prolific of briers and thorns after the apostacy, "the creature itself shall be delivered from the bondage of corruption," and made accordant with

that " manifestation of the sons of God," towards which its " earnest expectation" in every antecedent age has been directed.

It is a period, more particularly, when " God manifest in the
flesh," our Lord Jesus Christ, by whom and for whom "all
things" were created and are sustained, who built them originally
as a theatre for his glory, and who purposes not to be defeated
by the perversions introduced and perpetuated by the great adversary, when perfect humanity, allied to Divinity, the perfection
of Beauty, shall have the right place in human affairs, personal
scientific, artistic, social and civil, as well as directly religious.
The only right position for such a Person is, " all in all."   " He
shall reign from sea to sea, and from the river to the ends of the
earth."   " His law shall go forth from Zion and judge," adjust
all international differences, " among the nations of the earth."
" Nations shall learn and practice war no more," when "the Lord
is Lawgiver, Judge and King."   " Every knee shall bow and
every tongue confess that He is Lord to the glory of God the
Father;" all men, of all nations, shall " do all things, whether
they eat or drink, and whatsoever they do," in his name ; all that
man is, all that man possesses, and all that he can become, under
these propitious influences, intellectually, socially and morally,
will be gladly devoted to the praise of Him who allied himself
to our humanity to purchase the privilege in that nature of being
" Head over all things."   " Things in heaven and things in
earth" shall be gathered together in one, in blessed harmony under
this head.   The elder born of creation, shall gladly come into
that subordination to humanity, against which " the arch-angel
ruined," originally rebelled.   The religious differences of earth,
shall all be reconciled in a glorious unity, of which the ancient
reconciliation of Jew and Gentile, was but a type, and the Mediator
have a dominion in the universe, of which the supremacy of the
first Adam in this little earth, was a symbol.   Then will be seen
the consummation of the original compact, in view of which, he
said: " Lo, I come to do thy will, oh God !" and the realization
of that unutterable " joy that was set before him," as the ultimate result of his incarnation, and agency, and victory.   " All
things shall be put under him," " whether they be things in heaven, or things on earth, or things under the earth."   Not only

shall all the wheels of nature move at his bidding and result in his glory, and the armies of angels be " ministers to do his pleasure," but also the complicated machinery of the social and civil structures of the earth, the results of human science, the glories of human art, the treasures of human genius, the powers and passions of the human soul, fearful and wonderful, and even yet but partially developed, redeemed from their perversions and degradation, shall be inscribed with " Holiness to the Lord." The present position of the Lord Jesus Christ, is expectant and interimistic. Between the purchase and the actual possession of the kingdoms of the world, he is waiting at the right hand of the majesty of God, till the earth is made his footstool and all things are put in subjection under him. " Sit thou on my right hand," says the Everlasting, " till I make thy foes thy footstool." " Whom the heavens must receive till the times of restitution of all things." "Then cometh the end."

A careful collation of the Old Testament with the New, brings us to the conclusion, that " the times of the restitution of all things," synchronizes in point of time, and is tantamount in meaning to " the dispensation of the fullness of times," or completion of the purposed cycles of our world, and also, with "the new heavens and earth wherein dwelleth righteousness," described by Peter, and " the New Jerusalem coming down from God out of heaven," and constituting " the tabernacle of God with men," portrayed in the Apocalypse. If this be allowed, then it is plain that this period of universal rectification will have this earth of ours for its theatre—the very place which has witnessed the long protracted history of perversions, occasioned by the entrance of sin and the wiles of the adversary—the field of his conflict will be the seat of his dominion, the earth which once drank his blood as a sufferer, shall witness his triumphs as a conqueror. When the objects of the interimistic period are accomplished, then, on this theatre, a footstool made ready by antecedent operations, the original purpose of God in Christ, will take effect, and all things be restored.

Intimately connected with this, another fact ought to be mentioned, which is distinctly intimated in Scripture, i. e., that the latter stages of this preparatory period, of putting " all things"

under their legitimate Head, will be characterized by scenes of
convulsion and confusion, hitherto unparalleled.   The old order
of things, so long continued, and entrenched with so many prejudices, watched with Satanic vigilance, and guided by Satanic
power, will "pass away," we are led to apprehend, " with a great
noise."   The true practical relations and applications of Christianity, contemplated in the original plan of God, to individual
man, to science, art, society and government, the full enthrone-
ment of Christ, as "all in all," the universal supremacy of the
Law of God will not come to pass and be established, without
revolutions more marked and marvellous than any that have yet
occurred.   "There will be wonders in heaven above, and signs
in the earth beneath, blood and fire and vapor of smoke, the sun
shall be turned into darkness, and the moon into blood, before
that great and notable day of the Lord come.".   When "the
great voice comes from the temple of heaven, from the throne,
saying, It is done ; there are contemporaneously voices, and thun-
ders and lightnings, and a great earthquake, such as was not since
men were upon the earth, so mighty an earthquake and so great."
"When we see these things beginning to come to pass," instead
of doubting the coming of the times of restitution, we are commanded to "lift up our heads for our redemption," the consummation of all God's plans "draweth nigh."   When the "heavens and the earth are passing away," and "the elements melt-
ing with fervent heat," then we are specially encouraged to look
for the inauguration of "new heavens and a new earth, in which
dwelleth righteousness."

For aught we know to the contrary, and very probably, indeed,
from the obvious tenor of some portions of prophecy, there may
be also, towards the catastrophe, more direct interposition of visible, almighty agency, to "cut short the work in righteousness,"
and greatly "hasten the coming of the day of the Lord."   Beyond even all the extraordinary appliances of modern invention,
by which thought travels invisibly, with electric rapidity, and
time and distance are almost annihilated, which are doubtless to
have their highest significancy and true purpose from these connexions, God himself may set his hand to the work and apply a
momentum to the machinery, beyond our present powers of com-

putation, and thus roll round with a rapidity beyond our usual calculations, " the times of the restitution of all things."

However this may be, and " the time of the end" alone can fully decide, " it shall be done"—" the dispensation of the fullness of times," will come, " The mystery of God will be finished," and over the finale, " as the Lord liveth" and is faithful, " the sons of God shall shout for joy," as certainly as they "sang together" at the birth of creation, and at the incarnation of creation's King. What " God hath spoken by the mouth of all his holy prophets since the world began," long looked for and prayed for, the vision of ancient seers, the theme of many a song, the hope of the noble and good, in every age, the solution of earth's enigma, the vindication of the great Author and Governor, will then be a blessed reality, and in the glories of the evening time, the long and lovely Light of the close, " the former troubles will be forgotten." " Behold, I create new heavens and a new earth, saith the Lord, and the former shall not be remembered or come into mind."

The subject we have thus imperfectly presented, is, by no means, to be regarded as a mere speculation—a beautiful theory, having no connection with Christian character and present duty. On the contrary, it has immense moral significancy and practical influence, or we could not feel justified in dwelling upon it. Every Christian, and especially, every Christian minister, should as clearly as possible apprehend, from the materials given in the Scriptures and by the use of his best powers of mind, the certainty and nature of this period, " spoken by the mouth of all God's holy prophets which have been since the world began." If God has made " known to us the mystery of his will," in regard to the final scenes of the great Drama, surely correct and enlarged views must exert a blessed influence on our character and conduct. They would serve to calm our needless perturbations. They would elevate our often ignoble and unworthy aims. They would introduce us into the atmosphere where men of God, in ancient times, lived and moved and had their being, and by which their high and exalted characters were formed.

According to the views we entertain of the nature of this period, and the instrumentalities by which it is to be accomplished, will be the measure of our personal interest, also, in the improvement and perfection of systems of philosophy, in the researches of science, the applications of art in its varied departments, and the reformatory plans, bearing on the social and civil polity of our race. If the plan of God, in the ultimate triumphs of Christianity on the earth, embraces the sanctification and consecration of all these, and is designed to show that the past history of the earth has been a perversion of good, and not an evolution of essential evil in these things, how can human intellect be better employed than in tracing the true bearings of science, art, society and government, on the ultimate consummation? If science is necessarily atheistic; if poetry has no possible influence in developing piety; if art is essentially Satanic and its glories can never be inwrought into the service of God; if the æsthetic and the divine in man, are invincibly contradictory; then, what a dark enigma is past history, how perplexing is the present, and how gloomy in prospect is the future? From different views of this subject and the duties it imposes, equally good men, to all appearance, and of harmonious sentiments in the vital doctrines of religion, come to diverse conclusions, in regard to their obligations to labor for the scientific elevation, artistic excellence, æsthetic improvement, social amelioration, and temporal well-being of their fellow creatures. Without speaking positively on this point, we may say, that it is of great moment that our views of this subject should be correct and scriptural, not resulting from prejudice, or a tame submission to authority, or a lazy acquiescence in commonly received opinions, but a full and prayerful personal investigation. It is not consistent with Christian courtesy or conscience, indeed, that those who have given this subject no study at all, should dogmatically pronounce sentence of condemnation on those who have given it their best efforts of mind and affections of heart, however different be their conclusions.

The desideratum of our times, is a setting forth of the true practical applications of Christianity, as they are to be actualized in the times of restitution of all things, in the points we have specified. And if professing Christians and, especially, ministers, would retain their hold on the world and bring them under the power of the gospel, they must develope, in their lives, a practical exemplification of Christianity in its present palpable influence, in bestowing mental elevation, social equality, and universal happiness on our race! In the united church of the future, doubtless, there will be embraced whatever elements of excellence now belong to any of the separate divisions. "The middle wall of partition" and prejudice, must be taken down. The Protestant must allow that the Catholic system is not Satanic in origin, and injurious only in operation. The Catholic must come to admit, that the Reformation was not of the devil, and has secured a blessed advancement in the truth. The Puritan must allow sincerity to the churchman, and acceptance of his service by God, even though he employs art in its highest efforts to assist him in his devotions. And the churchman must accord to the Puritan the praise and veneration due to his rugged virtue and loyal love of truth. By some means, to us now unknown, all diversities will be reconciled in one blessed brotherhood, in the times of restitution.

We deem it of equal importance, that Christians should cherish "the full assurance of faith," in regard to this period, as well as "the full assurance of understanding." After we have satisfied our minds from diligent and prayerful perusal of God's word, as to what God hath promised "by the mouth of all his holy prophets," then we should have our hearts established in the persuasion, that "whatsoever he hath promised, he is able also to perform." In reference to all that is embraced in the long series of predictions, the burden of so great a part of the book of God, and, especially, all the specifications we have shown to enter into the purpose of God, even such as are most staggering to sense and mere carnal reason, we should ask ourselves: "Is anything too hard for God?" "Because it is marvellous in the eyes of the remnant of this people, should it therefore be marvellous in mine eyes, saith the Lord of Lords?" If the everlasting Author of "all things," had a definite "intent" in creating them "by Jesus Christ, according to his eternal purpose," and he has made known to us in general outline, at least, what that intent and purpose is, should we not believe that he "will work all things," even to the glorious consummation, "according to the counsel of his will," however to us his movements may be mysteriously slow? Against all appearances to the contrary, and notwithstanding all the plausible reasonings of the adversaries of truth, the Christian is privileged, "in hope, to believe against hope," as the father of the faithful did, that "the times of the restitution of all things," which God hath purposed, will surely come to pass at the period before appointed. If faith wavers at this point, it would be far more consistent to give up the whole testimony of Scripture. Why believe in the present waiting position of the Lord Jesus Christ, at the right hand of God, and yet refuse or fear to believe that result, in expectancy of which he is seated there, according to the oath and covenant of the Eternal Father? The same document, stamped throughout with the same attestation of divinity, affirms both the one and the other. Infidelity, which rejects the whole testimony of Revelation concerning Jesus Christ, and which affirms that there is no living Lord Jesus at the right hand of the majesty on high, and that there never will be any other consummation of earth's cycles, than that which the living forces of nature and man's agency can accomplish, is more consistent than the partial faith, that believes the first and yet staggers at the last. This crowning consummation is indispensable to make the whole testimony complete, and to take away the otherwise inexplicable mystery which hangs over God's purposes and proceedings towards our race. Such faith as this, not only greatly honors God, who has made this revelation and is pledged to verify it in his future providence, and glorify himself thereby, but it is eminently adapted to develope our own characters and qualify us for our duties. Christian faith, when fully matured, and when it becomes the habit and all-encircling atmosphere of the soul, rather rejoices to exercise itself simply on Divine testimony, away from outward auxiliaries, as one has beautifully remarked, in illustrating a kindred subject, even as the ivy, accustomed to lean for support on some exterior and more substantial object, when it finds none such, or outtops them in its growth, towers in its trust, straight towards heaven. Such faith, in reference to this part of Divine testimony, without aid from sense or surrounding scenes, will most speedily perfect the sanctification and most thoroughly subserve the usefulness of the soul in which it dwells.

Once more: every Christian should endeavor, earnestly and practically, to carry out the convictions of his mind and persuasions of his heart, in reference to this period, by corresponding efforts. He is privileged, not only to "look for," but also, to "hasten the coming of the day of God." Whatever special and miraculous agencies God may have reserved to himself, towards the winding up of the great scheme, beyond all question, he has chosen instrumentalities which are to be employed by his children at present. The present and constant duty and privilege of every child of Light is, to the whole extent of his ability and influence, and by his whole expenditure of effort and means, in the use of whatever talents have been committed io his stewardship, to strive to rectify the evils, perversions and pollutions, occasioned by sin, and which manifest the still unbroken supremacy of the God of this world. Every Christian is bound to do all he can, in his sphere, to have all things restored, just as if on his exertions alone, the ultimatum was dependent. He must, as far as lieth in him, enlighten human ignorance, correct human error, strive to eradicate bigotry, superstition and persecution from the earth; he must do his part to have science sanctified to God's service, art made subservient to religion, society cured of its evils, and government in church and state and in their mutual interactions, brought into accordancy with God's will and the eternal principles developed in his word.

Believing that the ideal traced in God's word, as the counterpart of the original purpose and archetypal idea, existing eternally in the Divine mind, is ultimately and certainly to be actualized, and actualized on the earth; and that "for this intent he created all things by Jesus Christ," and has heretofore continued them in being, every one who has been brought into "the fellowship of this mystery," should make it his great business and ambition in life, to actualize and exemplify this restitution, first of all, in his own character, and then, as far as his influence goes, in all the departments and relations of human life, in all lands, throughout the world. In his own personal character, in his family, in the sphere of his influence, the village, city, country or continent he can mould, the age he can elevate or refine, he should be striving perpetually and by every energy of his soul, to bring all to approximate as nearly as possible to "the times of restitution." Whether he has devoted himself to science, or is enamoured of art; called to study the social system, linked with the civil institutions of the land or age, or directly devoted to the service of God and truth in the work of the ministry; every one has a work to do, in co-operation with the great God and glorious Mediator, in which he may be animated by the loftiest motives, blessed with the purest happiness, and assured of the most complete success: he may be a worker-together with God, in bringing to pass "the times of the restitution of all things, which he has spoken by the mouth of all his holy prophets which have been since the world began."

PITTSBURGH, Pa.   D. H. R.

ART. XXIX.—REVERENCE IN WORSHIP.

REVERENCE rests on two feelings as its ground-work—love and fear; and is the result of a well-balanced and living union of these two feelings. Love, to exalt in the mind the object of worship, and to draw sweetly towards it. Fear, to hold the spirit at a respectful distance in courteous obeisance. These two feelings are essential to reverence. Love without fear becomes disrespectfully familiar; fear without love becomes cold, formal and slavish. Love and fear united and blended in just proportion, suspend the worshipping spirit at a proper distance from the object of worship, in affectionate and yet respectful adoration. In this way the spirit is bound to the object of worship by a cord of love, and yet made to stand at bay by that feeling which esteems the object of worship superior to itself, without which no worship is possible. To use a figure derived from a well-known law in nature, Love is a centripetal and Fear a centrifugal force, which unite in holding the spirit in its true orbit, and cause it to move in silent and majestic harmony around God, its centre. The same idea is also beautifully exhibited in the position of prayer customary among the ancients, in their approach to God. The worshipper stood, with his hands stretched out towards heaven, as if for help, but at the same time, with the palms away from himself, as though he would ward off the help for which he was imploring. What a significant attitude!

That love and fear, in their Scripture sense, have such a connection, and are capable of such an union as has now been predicated of them, is evident, from the fact that they are used as convertible terms. To fear God, is to love him; and to love him, is to fear him. Love, in Scripture, is always understood to include a filial fear; and fear, if approved, always includes a filial love.

As reverence requires two feelings in us, so it also requires that we should contemplate God as the object of worship, under two general aspects—his Majesty and Goodness. We must be sensible of his majesty, in order that we may exalt him in our minds; we must at the same time, be sensible of his goodness, lest we be driven back from him in despair. An apprehension of his majesty alone, creates *awe ;* an apprehension of his goodness alone, creates *presumption.* While we recognize him on the one hand, as sitting on the circle of the heavens, holding the universe in balance, we must recognize him, at the same time, moving among the lilies of the field, to clothe them in colors of beauty, among the birds of the air, giving them food, and in the habitations of men, giving them their daily bread. In short, Sinai and the Cross, the Judge and the Father, must both be before us, in order to educe feelings of true reverence.

The wicked cannot, hence, be truly reverent. The feeling of filial love love being wanting, then fear is transformed into a slavish awe. They can only think of God as a judge, standing over against them with stern majesty. Hence, how often do we hear Him called, in the language of carnal wisdom,* Jove, Great

---

* The names applied to God, at the commencement or close of our National and State Messages, are very significant when carefully observed in connection with the sources whence they emanate.

First Cause, Sovereign Ruler, and many more such names are constantly applied to him. It is only from the lips of true faith that, first, "GOD THE FATHER," and then "ALMIGHTY, MAKER OF HEAVEN AND EARTH," flows naturally and sweetly. The wicked, however polite and refined, fear God, under whatever form his existence is conceived of by them; under the influence of this fear, they are either driven away from God, or induced to withstand him in secret and presumptuous opposition; but never, until fear and love are wedded in gracious union, is reverence possible.

Without reverence, all worship must be radically defective. This must be evident from what has now been said; but will appear still more clearly when we carefully consider how, and how many, other frames of heart are connected with it or dependent upon it.

Without reverence, God cannot be steadily kept before the mind as an object supremely worthy of worship. As a feeling of reverence subsides, so fast does God sink into such an one as the professed worshipper himself. Then, of course, what the idea of worship involves—namely, that the object of worship should be exalted in the mind—is entirely wanting. When the Psalmist would incite us to worship, he first introduces God to us in his high and holy majesty:—"The Lord reigneth; let the people tremble: he sitteth between the cherubims; let the earth be moved. The Lord is great in Zion; and he is high above all people." After this representation of the object of worship, he exhorts: "Exalt the Lord our God, and worship at his footstool;" giving at the same time, a reason, to incite our love: "for he is holy." The reader's observations will have been abundantly sufficient to confirm the fact, that low ideas of God are always connected with a worship correspondingly low, presumptuous, and irreverent.

This is not all. Where reverence is wanting, there is not only on the one hand, a low conception of God as the object of worship, but necessarily, also, too high an idea of himself in the mind of the worshipper. These two go together; as God sinks, man rises. Only high thoughts of God, will give us low and humble thoughts of ourselves. When Job heard of God by the hearing of the ear, he was not properly humbled, and kept uttering things too wonderful for him, and things which he understood not; but when he saw him in his majesty, he abhorred himself and repented in dust and ashes. It is, then, that which exalts God, that also, humbles man. Here we may see also, how reverence, as related to humility, becomes the basis of many Christian graces. Meekness, submission, penitence, a tender sense of guilt and unworthiness, and that entire spirit of self-renunciation which prepares us to make a full offering of ourselves to Christ, and fully to receive him; all these cannot exist without it. Reverence cannot be wanting in our minds without its place being filled with pride, presumption, and a heaven-daring spirit of self-sufficiency and independence—a spirit which feels

"————At home
Where angels bashful look!"

God has laid the law, upon which reverence for himself is claimed, at the foundation of all laws. "I am the Lord thy God, which have brought thee out of the land of Egypt, out of the house of bondage. Thou shalt have no other Gods before me." Here he, first of all, claims for himself absolute respect. This claim is grounded upon two reasons. First, because he is the Lord their God, and second, because he had done them good, bringing them out of the house of bondage. The first inspires fear, as a Sovereign, the second love, as a God of goodness. These two feelings, as we have seen, are the elements of reverence.

While in the first table of the law he lays in his claim to reverence, in the second he makes provision for its cultivation. The same feelings, love and fear, are involved in the relation of parents and children, as exhibited in the first commandment of the second table. "Honor thy father and thy mother." This honor requires the same two elements, love and fear. To honor presupposes superiority in the person to be honored, this at once exalts him in the mind and inspires fear; it also implies a discovery of excellence and goodness, which inspires love. Thus, then, the command to honor our parents, demands of us to fear and love them, which two feelings constitute reverence. It would not have been sufficient, if we had been commanded, merely, to love our parents, for this does not necessarily involve superiority in them; neither would it have been sufficient, had we been commanded to fear them, for this would have made them tyrants and us slaves. The command as it is, destroys the one-sidedness of each, by uniting them in one feeling, which includes both.

Thus by making the relation between us and our parents similar to that between us and God, the feelings of the child are, from infancy, set in that direction which leads to true reverence towards God. The training of the child in the duties which its relations to the parent in the family require, is, at the same time, a training which will induce it constantly to rise, in the same way, and for the same reasons, into true reverence towards its Parent in heaven. "We have had fathers of our flesh which corrected us, and we gave them reverence: shall we not much rather be in subjection unto the Father of spirits and live?" We find also by observation that reverence towards God and towards our parents generally go together. The child that has reverence towards its parents from proper motives, will, if its parents are pious, naturally pass those feelings on and up through the parent to the parent's God. On the other hand, where a child, proudly and presumptuously, breaks loose from its relations to earthly parents, it is also, in the same spirit, breaking loose from God, and a downward way to profligacy, shame and abandonment, is before it. Many parents, who, by improper training of their children, or by being themselves unworthy of receiving the reverence of their children, have made this experiment to a full and bitter satisfaction. While others, who have sought to deserve the reverence of their children, and been diligent in training them to it, have had verified in their blessed experience the promise that the same God which is our God, is also, surely the God of our children, if we keep his covenant, and remember his commandments to do them.

To what has now been said of the nature and cause of reverence in worship, must also be added an important *condition* upon which its eduction and growth depends. It is this:—The supernatural and mysterious, as they necessarily enter into the constitution of the objective in worship, must be sensibly apprehended and felt by the worshipper. It is only when the worshipping spirit enters the awful twilight, which lies along the verge of the unseen, which is but the shadow of eternal realities cast over into time, that it feels itself under the influence of a spirit of reverential worship. A faith without mystery, is not only impossible in the nature of things, but where such a faith is fancied to exist, all reverence is excluded. In so far, then, as the transactions of worship are believed and felt to lie with one side in the mysterious unseen and unknown, and as forming thus the media in which contact and union between God and man is accomplished, so far will reverence enter as an element in worship. When God came down to communicate with Moses on Sinai, he ordered that bounds should be set about the mountain, beyond which the people should not pass upon awful peril; so there is, in all our communications with God in worship, an *awful border*, on the one side of which, God displays his majesty and mercy, and on the other side, we, as worshippers, make our humble and reverent approach. There we lift up holy hands in prayer for grace, and when blest, retire with humble gratitude and thanksgiving. Even the smiles that play upon our Father's countenance, when we look up bending at his footstool, are but as the rainbow in an impenetrable cloud, having as a back-ground the mysteries of Deity. "He holdeth back the face of his throne, and spreadeth his cloud upon it."

Deep reverence is an element which solemnly underlies and pervades the ancient Jewish worship. This, as soon as mentioned, is felt to be true by any one familiar with the Old Testament. A feeling, which amounts almost to awe, steals over the mind of the reader as he peruses the history of their wonderful worship. When we stand and gaze upon the smoking altars of the patriarchs, in the deep and quiet valley, or on the lonely mountain-top, we feel at once its solemn sublimity. When we enter the tabernacle in the wilderness, we feel our spirits deeply subdued by a sense of Jehovah's awful nearness. When we enter the magnificent temple at Jerusalem, where all their solemnities centre, and cast our eyes towards the holiest place, the admonition rushes in upon the spirit through all the senses: "Draw not nigh hither: put off thy shoes from off thy feet; for the place whereon thou standest is holy ground!" Every thing with which the devout Jew was conversant in worship, lay with one side in the awful darkness of mystery, while the other was only illuminated with the soft and holy light of consecration. The very ground upon which he walked, and which he tilled for his daily bread, was holy—the soil of the promise. The wells, springs and streams were sacred, reflecting still to him who gazed into them, the faces of generations dead! The valleys were sacred in their minds, for over them, ages ago, had floated the incense-breathing cloud of patriarchal sacrifice. Sacred were the mountains, Moriah, Horeb, Carmel, Lebanon, and many others, often in the days of their fathers, wreathed and crowned with the smoke of burnt-offering. Sacred were many places which marked the footsteps of Jehovah's presence in former years, and perpetuated some signal favor received by the fathers at His hands. Sacred were the Levites, a holy tribe, standing always between God and the people, and moving, during the hours of public worship, in reverential and mysterious solemnity, around the smoking altar. Sacred was their sanctuary, and most sacred the Holiest place and the high-priest, who alone dare lift the veil and pass behind it where the Shekinah of God's presence dwelt. What feelings must all this have inspired! Who could stand in the outer court, in the solemn twilight, and witness devoutly the evening or morning sacrifice, without being filled with the deepest reverence; especially, if he remembered the facts on record, that when at times, there was wicked irreverence and presumption on the part of priests or people, God burst forth upon them in some terrible judgment, as in the case of Korah's rebellion, (Num. xvi.,) and the presumption of Nadab and Abihu, the sons of Aaron. (Lev. x.)

This feeling, as it reigned in the minds of Jewish worshippers, is strongly and beautifully expressed in many passages. " Serve the Lord with fear, and rejoice with trembling." " The Lord is in his holy temple: let all the earth keep silence before him."

In the New Testament, the scenery of divine revelations, though not so awfully clouded with " blackness, and darkness, and tempest," still confronts the spirit of the worshipper with earnest, mysterious, and unearthly solemnity. Though the stern and frowning imagery which robed Jehovah's brow on the Mount, when the hosts of Israel trembled around its base, and even

Moses exceedingly feared and quaked, is illuminated with more gracious smiles in the face of the Anointed, yet he is still a consuming fire, and we are are commanded " to serve God acceptably, with reverence and godly fear." Being made " priests unto God," in the privileges of the New Testament, we are thus transferred from the outer court of the sanctuary into the " holy place," where priests serve, and have, therefore, only one veil between us and the "Holy of Holies," into which our High-priest has entered, we ought only so much the more to take the shoes from our feet, and feel as in the soul-subduing shadow of the divine presence.

In the New Testament, equally as in the Old, we feel ourselves in the mysterious *border-land,* where the natural and supernatural meet and exchange their sympathies. In the Saviour's person, the Shekinah is embosomed; not, however, entirely veiled, but blazing forth at times through the veil of his servant-form, making devils and men tremble, while they stand aghast, exclaiming: " This is the Son of God!" When he stands near the grave of Lazarus whom he loved, weeping tears of sympathy with Mary and Martha, he is a sight to draw the heart in love towards him; when a little after, he exclaims, "Lazarus, come forth!" and the dead obeys his voice, there is a majesty which inspires fear. Both these manifestations together, make him an object of reverence. This is only one among many instances, where these two aspects of his character are exhibited in connection. Along his path of wonders and of mercy, spirits good and bad, half-visible, bend in on all sides, and break full in upon our sight when called or commanded. The dead lift up their heads out of their realms of silence, when some divine power proceeding from him is felt with prophetic wakings in their drowsy dominions. Fig trees wither when he frowns; palm trees cast their branches under his feet when he triumphs; the waves of Galilee crouch, like young lions, at his feet, when he spreads his hands over them; and when he dies, the heavens and the earth put mourning on. All this, and much more, shows that the New Testament is not destitute of those elements which are the constituents of true and deep reverence.

There is, moreover, no reason why there should not *now* still the same reverence pervade our spirits in worship. Though the visible displays of God's nearness are not before us in the same form, yet they are no less real.   It is certainly not the character-istic of the dispensation of the spirit in the Church, which is " rather glorious," that it sunders God and his worshippers farther apart!   Rather ought we not to feel that these more coarse and sensible media have disappeared between God and us, for the very purpose of bringing us more really, more awfully, and if children more sweetly near him?   Proper reflection on this fact alone ought to generate reverence even more than visible displays of his majesty and nearness.   Our transactions with God, in the acts of worship, though the fact is not so tangible to the senses, involve the very same things now as they did in any previous age and under any dispensation.   The promise of the Saviour: Lo! I am with you, assures those who believe of his continued nearness. The declaration of Christ to Nathaniel: Hereafter ye shall see heaven open and the angels of God ascending and descending upon the Son of man, indicated what the Church might expect in its future history, and what its relation to the unseen world should be.   Christ, in his presence on earth, is the antitypal Ja-cob, to whom the above passage evidently alludes, lying at the foot of the mystic ladder which connects heaven and earth in divine and angelic communication.   The Church is the Bethel where, though the drowsy soul feels it not, the child of faith exclaims: How dreadful is this place! this is none other but the house of God, and this is the gate of Heaven!   The Church is thus still felt to be the awful habitation of God on earth.   " The Lord is in his holy temple."   The solemn sacraments and ordi-nances which transpire before our eyes in the sanctuary, are still, as of old, God's transactions with men.   Those who have faith to feel them real, still see in them the face of the Lord as it shines upon them out of Zion, the perfection of beauty, exclaiming rev-erently: " O come, let us worship and bow down: let us kneel before the Lord, our maker."   Even sinners in the sanctuary feel an awful shadow, which wakes their fears, settles down upon their spirits, forcing them to utter in their hearts: " O God! thou art terrible out of thy holy places!

While we are thus confronted, under the new dispensation,

with such solemn and mysterious realities on the objective side
of worship, to command our reverence, there are considerations
no less solemn, tending to the same end, in the internal or subjective relation of the worshipper to God.   Our relation to the
third Person in the adorable Trinity, under the dispensation of
the Church, is such as to bring our spirits most wonderfully into
the sphere of the divine presence, the proper consideration of
which should, at once and forever, exclude every light and frivolous feeling and overwhelm us with reverence.   " What! know
ye not that your body is the temple of the Holy Ghost which is
in you ?   If any man defile the temple of God, him shall God
destroy : for the temple of God is holy, which temple ye are !"

Reverence towards God in worship, can only be given through
the media of his manifestations and communications.   These
media are in the sanctuary and connected with it.   Through
them, and by means of them, God is worshipped ; these, then,
are to be reverently approached by those who approach God in
worship through them.   Thus reverence to God in worship, involves farther, reverence for sacred places, sacred persons, sacred
seasons, and sacred things.   When we say of any thing that it
is sacred or holy, we do not mean, of course, that there is any
change wrought upon its substance or essence, but we do mean
that *its relation to God and man is changed.*   Not to recognize
this new relation in which it is caused to stand, but to treat it as
" common," is a desecration which incurs God's most jealous dis-
pleasure.   So, for instance, to eat the consecrated bread and to
drink the consecrated cup, though the essence of neither is changed, without " discerning the Lord's body," is to eat and drink
condemnation.   " What God hath cleansed, that call not thou
common."   That is sacred and holy which has been taken out
of the sphere of nature in which it originally stood, and has had
a place assigned it in the sphere of grace, and is thus henceforth
constituted a medium of communication with God.   In this sense
God has constituted sacred places, persons, seasons, and things ;
and as such, the worshipper who would be reverent will recognize them.

" Reverence my sanctuary : I am the Lord !"   The Scriptures
teach God's omnipresence ; but they teach just as clearly his *spe-*

cial presence. His omnipresence is alike to all men and things; his special presence is his gracious and merciful relation to man through Christ, the Spirit and the Church. The very idea of religion, involves a manifestation of God's presence different from his omnipresence. The very wants of a fallen world, when it deeply feels its estrangement from God, heave up to heaven like a world-sigh from the bosom of humanity: "Oh! that thou wouldest rend the heavens, that thou wouldest come down!" God did come down.

The places where God specially manifested himself to man, were in all ages constituted sacred, and men afterwards stood on that place meditative and mute, or passed it with a slow and reverent tread. Jacob designated the place of his vision with a stone set up as a pillar, upon which he poured the oil of consecration; and it was ever afterwards Bethel—the house of God—the gate of heaven. The place where the tabernacle rested, was always a holy place, and was approached as such by all who worshipped there. The land, the hill, the city, where the temple stood, was holy; and the Psalmist never kindles into higher inspiration than when he describes its superiority over all other spots in the earth. "His foundation is in the holy mountains. The Lord loveth the gates of Zion more than all the dwellings of Jacob. Glorious things are spoken of thee, O city of God." The temple's holy inclosures were guarded by the most solemn prohibitions. (Ecc. v. 1, 2.) Here the contrite worshipper, like the publican, stood "afar off," and cast his penitent but hopeful eyes first towards the veil of the holiest place, and then heavenward, and smote in anguish upon his burdened breast, exclaiming: "Lord be merciful to me, a sinner!" To this place the hearts of pious Jews were bound in undying remembrance and affection. By the rivers of Babylon, they would see their right hand paralized and their tongue stiff and still, rather than cease to remember Zion.

Is none of this sacredness now still to attach to the sanctuary? Why then did the Saviour, the author of the new Dispensation, drive the money-changers and men of merchandize from the temple with such holy indignation? Why did the Apostle reprove so sharply the irreverence of those at Corinth, who despised the

church of God, mixing things sacred and profane, and command
that all things should be done decently and in order, as he had
also ordained in all the churches; and why did he write so carefully to Timothy, that he might know how to behave himself in
the house of God? No, the cultivation of this feeling in the Jewish mind, was intended, like their whole *cultus*, as a preparation
for their admittance into a dispensation more spiritual, where the
same reverence would be required, only with more of love and
less of awe.   The consecration of a house of worship, then, is not
an empty ceremony, but a solemn invitation to God to make it
his peculiar dwelling place, and, at the same time, a transfer of
it from the sphere of nature into the sphere of grace.   It has its
precedent in the consecration of the Temple of Solomon, is ancient in the history of the church, and is involved in the very
idea of a sacred place.   A house of worship may just as easily
be conceived of as existing without being built, as to be a sacred
place without consecration : it *is* consecrated, if not formally, yet
by the very use to which it is, or ought to be exclusively devoted.
It is impossible, if we have any sense of religion, to divest ourselves fully of the feeling that eternal realities are nearer us in
the sanctuary than in all the earth beside.   What the worshipper
feels there, is not the effect merely of "the dim religious light,"
but a certain mysterious sense of divine presence which prevails
high over all his arguments and his philosophy.   It is nowhere
seen that piety becomes lovely and humble in proportion as this
feeling is banished from the mind.

It is easy to argue that the New Dispensation is spiritual, that
God is everywhere present, that neither in Samaria's mountains
nor at Jerusalem, is the place where men ought to worship, that
the temple of God is each pious heart, and the only acceptable
service an inward worship of spirit and truth, that the kingdom
of God is not a kingdom that cometh by observation, that it is
not in outward form but in inward power; this, and much more,
sounds well, and is, also, in its proper sense, true.   Let it, however, be well remembered, that the same arguments will destroy
everything outward and objective in worship; yea, the sacraments
themselves, must yield before this force of spirit against forms,
and we land at last in Quakerism, or in some other form of mystic

spiritualism which the history of the church has so often weighed in the balances and found wanting.

I cannot refrain from introducing here a passage from a very popular and useful book by a living author, showing how the temple was reverenced among the Jews. Who will find fault with their strictness;—who will not rather admire it, and wish that its like might be found among worshippers now?

" No person was allowed to enter the ground of the temple with a staff in his hand, or with scrip on, or with money in his purse, as if he were coming to a place of worldly business; neither might he go in with dust on his feet, but must wash or wipe them beforehand; nor might he spit upon the sacred pavement anywhere; nor might he pass *across* it, when going to some other place, because it happened to be the nearest way; all which things would have been disrespectful. Nor was any light or careless behaviour, such as laughing, scoffing, or idle talking, allowed to be indulged, as being unseemly and irreverent, in such a place; but those who came to worship were required to go to the proper place, with leisure and sober step, and there to stand during the service, each with his feet close together, his face turned towards the sanctuary, his eyes bended downward to the ground, and his hands laid one over the other upon his breast, having no liberty, in any case, to sit down, or lean, or throw his body into any careless posture whatever. What a pity it is that such a regard to reverence, in outward carriage, is found in so small a measure in most Christian churches! How little sense, alas, do the great multitude of those that visit the sanctuary now, seem to have of God's presence, even in his own house, as they come, with light and careless movement, into its solemn courts, and as they attend with all manner of outward indifference upon its sacred services, bearing on all their looks the image of a worldly spirit, and in their whole deportment, showing more regard to themselves than to their Maker! Especially, what a spectacle of irreverence is often displayed in the time of prayer: what roving of the eye, indicative of roving thought within; what show of listless languor and weariness, that denotes a mind empty of all interest in the business of the place; what unseemliness of posture and manner, such as *sitting* without necessity, *leaning* this way and that

way, *lolling* in every self-indulgent attitude, *changing* positions
with continual impatience, etc.; all evincing the little impression
that is felt of the high solemnity and importance of the duty,
and the little apprehension that is entertained of the presence
and the majesty, and the infinite glory of the Being that is worshipped, before whom the seraphim are represented as standing,
with their faces and their feet covered, as they cry, in continual
adoration, HOLY, HOLY, HOLY, IS THE LORD OF HOSTS!"[*]

Reverence in worship involves also reverence for sacred persons. God's manifestations *to* man, have always been, more or
less, *through* man. All God's general revelations are at last
summed up and made special, through man as an intelligent
medium—creation's High-priest—and his revelations to *all* men
are always first revelations to *some* men. If this were the proper
place, it would be easy to show how wise, philosophical, and
benevolent this arrangement is, and how necessarily grounded
in the nature of the relation of our race to God. At present,
however, it is sufficient to refer to the fact that this is the plan
which God has always pursued in his dealings with our race; he
calls out of the mass of men those whom he intends to constitute
the representatives of his will to men, and to be the intelligent
media between man and God.

As among the Jews, so still, there are the Levites, who stand
between the altar and the worshippers. The office of the ministry, is a MINISTRY, not only in name, but in fact. The minister is the mouth of God to man, and the mouth of man to God.
The office which he holds is the investment of ministerial grace
and authority. He does not act from men, nor by men, but by
Jesus Christ, for men. No one can take this office to himself.
The people cannot invest him with the power of a minister who
is to serve them in this office. The gift must be received, as Timothy received it, by the laying on of hands, from those who had it
before. When he stands, properly commissioned, in his place,
the minister can say: I was not called to this place by the vote
of members, but by the ordination of ministers; my office came
to me, not through the members, but through the body; I come

* Nevin's Biblical Antiquities. Vol. 2, p. 158-9.

from God to man. "Paul, an apostle, (not of men, neither by men, but by Jesus Christ, and God the Father, who raised him from the dead)." Those who have the office in this way, may well, with Paul, magnify it. They are to be honored, and even doubly honored, if they exercise authority in the church well, and are to be esteemed very highly for their work's sake. They are God's representatives. By them he makes covenants with the people; by them he blesses and curses, binds and looses, pardons and retains sins. (Matth. xvi. 19, and xviii. 18.) In their hands are the keys of the kingdom. At their lips men are to receive the law, and from their hands the sacraments. Their responsibilities are heavy, their accountabilities awful, and their duties arduous! God, however, is their protector, as they are his ambassadors. Their persons are precious before his eyes. "Touch not mine anointed, and do my prophets no harm!" While the herald of Jesus stands up before the face of a gainsaying world, and lifts up his hand over the people, whether to reprove or bless, the hand of Jesus hangs over his head a banner upon which is written the fearful declaration :—"He that despiseth you, despiseth me : and he that despiseth me, despiseth him that sent me!" Let all men read and heed, at their peril.

The minister, as a sacred person, therefore, comes before the people with awful claims upon their reverence and respect. His holy prerogatives may not be invaded with capricious and bold presumption, neither may his claims be independently set aside. Even the youth of Timothy must not be despised by them over whom the Holy Ghost has made him overseer. God's high-priest must not be reviled, even by Paul, though he may be thought a white-walled hypocrite. Those in Moses' seat are to be recognized in their offices, though they say and do not. There ought to be plain evidence that God has disowned a minister, and that he is really a wolf that did not come in at the door, before we exclaim : "God shall smite thee!"

If this be the character of the ministerial office, these the relation they who hold it sustain to God, and this their solemn mission to men, it will readily appear that no reverence to God can exist without including due, though, of course, subordinate, reverence to his anointed ministry. Is this reverence shown him?

alas! By many, who would not be willing to be called infidels, he is treated, to say what is mildest, as a necessary evil in the community. By others he is treated, either with rude coldness and neglect, or with rude familiarity, which is no better. There is even a certain class of professors of religion, who immodestly and irreverently thrust themselves, if not into his place, at least, out of their place. Then, there is that every-day-still treatment, which manifests itself in so many small details, exceeding the bounds of propriety so little, yet so plainly, that it is not easy to assign to them on paper a local habitation and a name, but which nevertheless serve to show the general spirit which characterizes the age in which we live. Even children seem often to take a delight in showing how far they are above the superstition of thinking one man better than another in a free country! To do this, they will either swear in his presence, or address him with boyish familiarity. This irreverence, on the part of children, towards God's ministers, is, perhaps, the best index to the general spirit which reigns in this respect. The manner in which they are accustomed to hear ministers spoken of, and, perhaps, even the example of parents, must be regarded as a cause of its existence in their minds. Need it be said that the prevalence of this spirit is like blight to all true piety? The space which intervenes between disrespect to ministers and disrespect to God, is not broad, and is most naturally and easily crossed.

Reverence for sacred seasons, has also been mentioned as being necessarily included in true reverence towards God in worship. It has already been affirmed that, in the very nature of things *special and gracious* manifestations from God to man, necessarily involve God's special presence in some *place*. It must also be seen, from what has just been said of sacred persons, that God's special and gracious dealings with the whole race of men, necessarily involves special dealings with *some* particular ones of the race: and hence they are sacred persons. So also, God's special and gracious dealings with man, must necessarily involve the idea of special *times*. If God ever, as he does, condescend to descend from *general* to *special* dealings with us, he must do it at some *time*: hence we have sacred *seasons*.

Besides the want in our nature which seems to call for them, they are made to hold a sacred place in our minds and hearts, by their actual existence, by the command of God, through all ages. Sabbaths and holy-days are co-ordinate with all our ideas of religion. That there is a necessity in our nature, not only fallen but unfallen, for a Sabbath, is evident from the fact that it was instituted in Paradise, when man was still in his holy nature; even God himself rested on the seventh day. The Saviour also tells us, that "the Sabbath was made for man, and not man for the Sabbath." There was a need of it in man's physical, mental, and moral nature, and to meet this want the Sabbath was made. Time, that heaves under the burden of its mission, like the ocean, must, like it also, have its ebbs. Time, like space, must have its creations, marking, at intervals, its secret and sublime flow to relieve the monotony: hence the Sabbath.

Religion, too, needs a Sabbath. As it needs special places in which to present its claims, so it needs also, special times, when it can interrupt the world's onward flow, and challenge its attention to its interests. Without a *Lord's day*, the church would beg in vain for the time she needs to instruct the world, and to praise her God. On that time, too, he is especially near to his worshippers. The very quietude of the Sabbath, is as the still small voice of his presence. We ask then, reverence for this day. God demands it, and he demands it in very intimate connection with reverence in his temple worship. "Ye shall keep my Sabbaths, and reverence my sanctuary: I am the Lord." He demands it in his law given on Sinai, which shows it to be immutable as the declaration: "I am the Lord thy God!" Many of the judgments which he sent upon the Jews, were for profaning or neglecting his Sabbaths. It could easily be shown also, that the prosperity of religion and a proper reverence for the Sabbath, have always been companions; and that the same spirit which respected not its sacredness, dared also, at the same time, invade the sanctuary, and lay its uncircumcised hands upon all the holy mysteries of religion.

It would lead us too far, to enter into a formal discussion of the claims which the sacred festivals of the church have upon our reverence. The Old Testament had its Sabbaths beside *the* Sabbath. It would be well for those who are in the habit of set-

ting aside the claims of the Church Festivals *ad captandum* to
ask once, seriously, whether those of the Old might not have
been a shadow of some things to come, the substance of which
is to be found in the New Dispensation—whether the New Testament does not, instead of abolishing by demolishing, only elevate into a higher and freer form, the institutions of the Old—or
is there, indeed, a shadow without a substance? If this were
found to be true, we should then have found a rational reason,
why these festivals exist, and have existed, in the church; for it
is not every one that can believe that they sprang, Minerva-like,
into the church, from the head of some bold corrupter, "while
men slept!" Then, also, we might find a proper home for that
feeling which seems to be inherent in man, or at least shows itself
spontaneously in connection with religious want, which now seeks
to relieve itself in religious anniversaries, quarterly and protracted
meetings. If religion must have something of the kind, why
not accept of it as it is presented to us, in its germs at least, from
apostolic times, in the sacred festivals, mournful and joyous, of
the ecclesiastical year? The Athenians worship an "unknown
God," but when Paul declares one that is known to them, they
hesitate; so here, Christians reverence "special seasons," but
when the church presents such seasons to them, as the legitimate
nurslings of her own bosom, they hesitate, and even ungratefully
reject them as phantasma moving hastily away in the twilight of
superstition.

True reverence towards God in worship, requires also reverence
for sacred *things*. Sacred things, the church has, as means of
grace. The word of God, as uttered in the church, ought not,
when confirmed by the Bible and the symbols, to pass just as
one man's opinion, but as God's will, purely presented under the
direction of him who said to his ministers: "Lo! I am with you
always, even to the end of the world." Yet how is often the
word of God listened to! One sleeps. Another lounges. A third
divides his attention between the sermon and any thing else that
may claim it. A fourth gets up and makes for the door, not
only in the midst of a sermon, but in the midst of a sentence!
One, more polite, sits and mentally calls to the tribunal of his
judgment and taste, the language, gestures, tone and general

appearance of the minister.   Another, listening for a while attentively, with his eyes intently fixed on the pulpit, is subtilly diverted by an idea, towards the ends of the earth ; he roves and specu-
lates amid profit and loss, while his previous intent attitude is still
preserved, and he sits staring vacantly at the minister.   In short,
who could mention all the improprieties, more rude or more polite,
which are manifest in most of our congregations, showing plainly
that the spirit of reverential worship is not there.

Prayer and singing, especially, in the great congregation, is
wickedly daring without reverence.   The attitude of the body,
as well as the frame of the spirit, ought to be such as becomes
those who are coming professedly near to God.   Not only does
the idea of praise and prayer require us to recognize God as very
near us, but we profess also to believe that our prayers and praises
are the product of the Holy Ghost in us!   As prayer in the congregation should be as the voice of one man, so ought their outward position to present a devout uniformity.   But what do we
see ?   Sitting, standing, reclining, reposing, shifting, gaping, gazing, talking, smiling—and what remains else of this public insult
to the God of heaven, in whose presence angels show the deepest reverence!   Similar improprieties might be mentioned as
being commonly exhibited in singing.   The feeling that these
exercises are solemn transactions with God, seems but little
manifest.

As an especial mystery underlies the sacraments, they claim,
and ought to inspire special reverence.   Holy Baptism is only
exceeded in mysterious solemnity by the holy Supper.   The
communion of Christ's body, and the communion of his blood,
in the coldest sense in which these words can be understood, still
places their significancy beyond the reach of reason, into the
sphere of faith and mystery.   How awfully, upon the ear of
the communicant approaching the altar, fall these words : "Whosoever shall eat this bread, and drink this cup of the Lord, unworthily, shall be guilty of the body and blood of the Lord!"
Well is the solemn admonition, and the reason on which it rests,
immediately added: "Let a man examine himself, and so let
him eat of that bread, and drink of that cup.   For he that eateth and drinketh unworthily, eateth and drinketh damnation to

himself, not discerning the Lord's body." If the high-priest trembled when he entered the Holy of Holies, ought not the Christian worshipper approach with the deepest reverence the sacramental altar.

Then too, as minister, to stand between the altar and the worshipper to administer his holy supper! Who is sufficient for these things? The minister, who feels his position, must have more boldness than becomes one in such a place, who can perform this service without those humble tremblings which would make even a cherub look lovelier if engaged in such transactions! It is only the assurance, that the symbols before us are at once the medium and pledge of life, pardon, peace and reconciliation, that invites and encourages our approach. If it were not for this, we would rather, like the publican, stand afar off and smite our breasts in penitent anguish; but when this fact is apprehended by faith, how sweetly does it still the painful tremblings of our awe-struck spirits and calm them in the meltings of love. Here, in the holy supper, justice and mercy meet and embrace each other, mingling themselves in one peaceful stream of life and love, while the worshipper feels the alternatings of penitent fear and pardoning love, filling his soul with reverence and humble worship.

This would now be the place to draw a full-length portrait of the spirit of irreverence, and to designate it in its details, as it reigns in the church in this age and country. This, again, might naturally lead us to an attempt to find out its cause; and then reflections might be made as to the nature and necessity of a cure. This, however, must, for want of time and room, be deferred, if not entirely, to some future time.

H. H.

ART. XXX.—UNIVERSAL HISTORY.—INTRODUCTION.[*]

§. 1.   *Conception of Universal History.*

IN its most comprehensive signification Universal History is simply a biography of humanity.   This general definition will be modified and restricted by the peculiar method the historian may adopt in his representation of the subject.

Treated chronologically, it is the perspicuous narration of the most remarkable events connected wi h the rise and progress of the human race, arranged in the order of time in which they happened.

Treated pragmatically, it is not only an exhibition of the various fortunes which have befallen the human family from creation to the present time, but also of the springs and consequences of all great historical movements, as they have been produced by the harmonious interworkings of Providence and that law of nature, which by divine appointment presides over the growth of society and never contradicts, or thwarts the intentions, of Deity.

Surveyed from a more elevated scientific point of view, it is the representation of the progressive advancement of human life towards the realization of its original destiny, so far as it has been brought into actual being, in the course of the world s history.   In accordance with the teachings of Holy writ, the true dignity of man consists in his bearing and preserving, in undiminished splendor, the image of God in which he was created.   By virtue of his original structure which demands a living communion with Deity, he never could have accomplished the end of his existence had he not been elevated into fellowship with the divine nature, in the Word made flesh.   It is the duty of the historian to delineate the progressive restoration in man of God's image effaced by sin, and to point out the relation which the different periods of history, both before and after the incarnation, sustain to this great mystery.

§. 2.   *Limitation of this Conception.*

As in the sphere of nature the innumerable forms of its endlessly

---

[*] From an unpublished Manual of Universal History, by Rev. W. J. Mann, of Philadelphia, from which other extracts also may appear in the pages of this Review.   Translated from the German by J. S. E.

diversified life do not receive from the natural philosopher an equal share of attention, so in the department of history, it is not necessary for the historian to enter into a minute detail of every unimportant occurrence, or to describe the actions of every particular man. It is a law of universal force in the operations of nature that, whilst no isolated form of existence among its manifold productions, ever embodies the complete life of the species to which it belongs, some of them, on account of their general character, approximate more nearly than others to a full representation of any given species. The idea of a regular and uninterrupted growth of society, demands the application of the same law to the history of persons and of families, of races and of states. By attentively observing the movements of this principle, as it operates through human agencies, the historan may obtain an infallible guide in his investigations which will enable him to form an accurate judgment concerning the historical importance of any particular age, or nation, and to assign to every period its proper position.

§. 3.   *The Relation of Universal history to Special history.*

Universal history has for its object a faithful delineation of the rise and progress of human life under all its forms, political and mental, moral and spiritual. In distinction from this, Special history selects a particular period, and gives an extended and minute detail of its relation to a preceeding era, and its peculiar adaptation for the promotion of the interests of society generally. Monography constitutes a third department of history. It sometimes happens, that history assumes an aristocratic character, and reveals its power through the agency of single individuals, or of a body of men, or of a particular state. A description of history under this form, falls within the sphere of Monography.

§. 4.   *A more precise Definition of the Object of Universal history.*

Humanity then, in the various manifestations of its inward strength as expressed in its thoughts, in its mental and physical activity, in its actions and its sufferings, constitutes the subject of Universal history.   The motto of the historian is: *nihil humani a me alienum puto.*   Whilst that only which has actually happened, falls within the province of history, we must not reject as valueless myths, which, however deceptive they may be in themselves, are the media through which the spirit of an age reveals its intellectual and religious chara-ter. It is only by forming a clear and correct estimate of the Past, in its various relations, that we can be properly qualified to judge the historical position the Present occupies. Whatever served to unfold the character of a particular age, or nation; whatever imparted to the course of events a distinctive direction and evolved out of these events, as their necessary result, a particular form of life; is peculiarly valuable to the student of history.   This rule requires the historian to devote special attention to the different stages of civilization, to the characteristic features of entire nations, particularly their form of government, their art, their religion, their science, and the character of their most prominent leaders, and to omit extraneous or accidental circumstances which exerted no influence, neither retarding nor advancing the interests of society.

§. 5.   *Preparatory and Auxiliary Studies.*

These include particularly the ancient languages, together with every science in any way connected with the events of the Past: such as astrology, hermeneutics, ancient geography, &c.   As the conception of Universal history can be grasped only by those persons who occupy such an elevated intellectual position as enables them to comprehend the significance of the Past, we must not expect to find historians among those nations which constituted no essential factors of history, and took no part in the progress of the human race towards its ultimate design.

§. 6.   *Of the Sources of Universal history.*

Of the greatest importance are ancient written documents, comprising not only histories composed at an early period, but also written accounts of events, occasional historical remarks, acts, and ordinances, inscriptions, coins, &c., together with the artistic productions of ancient times, and, in general, all the remains, which serve to unfold the character of the human family at any particular period.   As oral sources, we may mention popular traditions which, though not to be regarded as the offspring of capricious imaginations, must nevertheless be investigated with the most searching criticism, and used with great caution.

§. 7. *Selection and Arrangement of the Materials of Universal history.*

The chronological method of arranging the materials of history according to years and centuries, in order to obtain a comprehensive view of all the most important events, which are going on at the same time, in different parts of the world, partakes of too external and mechanical a character to merit adoption. It dismembers the various parts of one and the same historical problem, and breaks up abruptly the organic connection of events which do not terminate with a particular century, but extend their influence into the succeeding one. Divested of that shallow conception, which perceives in history nothing but a fortuitous concurrence of events, or an accidental linking of a certain number of actions by the arbitrariness of fate or the caprice of chance, the historian must recognize the active interposition of an overruling Providence which conducts the history of the world, in accordance with a predetermined plan, from one degree of perfection to another. History does not move on in its course blindly and lawlessly, but is governed at every period of its progress, by a fixed law emanating from the mind of Jehovah himself. Thus considered, it is the progressive revelation of a divine thought in the constitution of the world, revealing its presence in different modes, as the circumstances of an age and the necessities of men may require. With these manifestations of a divine plan, as they appear in the successive phases of history, the historian must be acquainted; and as he delineates the gradual growth of society, he must select those particular times for epochs, when human life sprung the bands of its former existence and entered upon a new and more perfect probation, when important events finished their course and fulfilled their meaning, when fresh spiritual energies, operating upon human nature, turned the current of history into a different channel. As one nation in the vigorous exercise of its spiritual and physical capacities, may advance with more celerity in the solution of its vocation and attain to a high state of civilization, before another may have been brought to perceive its mission, it is evident that the historian cannot break the thread of his narrative, and dam the everwidening stream of history by confining it within the narrow bounds of centuries, until those nations, which occupy the rear rank, shall have advanced to a level with their neighbors, who may have surpassed them by several centuries, perhaps, in the cultivation of their natural resources. In order to comprehend the full significance of such advanced stages of civilization, especially, in their relation to the interests of the entire human family, and the difference between them and inferior forms of culture, we will assign to these latter a secondary place, and invest the former with the primary importance they severally deserve. For the peculiar position of any nation in the great chain of nations, depends neither upon its age, nor the duration of its existence, nor upon the extent of its population, nor the quantity of its actions, but upon their quality, as they embody, and introduce into real life elements, which will contribute to the advancement of history.

In strict accordance with these principles, we will direct our attention, in the first place, to the Oriental world—the cradle of humanity and the theatre of the tender buddings of its childhood. Generally speaking, the Orient was characterized by the decided predominance of the sensual over the spiritual element. His original righteousuess dissolved by the fall, man became oppressed by a heavy night of the profoundest darkness which the feeble lights of Eastern genius never could dissipate. Even those nations, whose importance justly claim the attention of the historian, were enslaved in the most miserable bondage. Their political systems suffused with the same slavish spirit, depressed most effectually the first risings of personal liberty, and degraded the primitive dignity of man, while carnal, materialistic pursuits dwarfed his moral strength. Even the most magnificent and intellectual labors of particular individuals in the sphere of art, of religion, and of science, could not transcend the bounds of sense, nor elevate the age to a loftier position.

The Grecian and Roman systems of culture, by recognizing the claims of personal liberty and impelling it into vigorous activity, awakened 'in the minds of men the slumbering consciousness of their primeval glory. In opposition to the prevalent conceptions of the world, by which it was regarded as standing in no connection whatever with the purposes of Providence, they inculcated the idea that the universe was governed by moral laws, conspiring together for the attainment of moral ends; lifted, in this way, our common nature above the contracted bounds of Eastern civilization, and carried it forward to a nobler position. Private judgment once released from the crushing weight of tyranny, displayed its activity in the generation of the idea of free citizenship and in the formation of confederated free states. These refusing to yield allegiance to the dictates of a single arbitrary will, framed political and religious organizations that secured the rights of the individual, and consolidated them into a compact unity, subject to some general authority.   In the exercise of personal freedom, the Grecians matured the richest fruits in the sphere of. arts and sciences.   An intense struggle to unfold the idea of the beautiful, to express thought in such a way that its form and contents would perfectly harmonize, to mirror forth through a statue with complete transparency, the inmost beatings of a thought so that its outward form would be alive with the idea itself, characterized the production of the Grecian mind.   In no other country was the purely *classic* form of art cultivated to such an extent, and crowned with such complete success. The religion of the Greek was marked by the same general character. He never came to the mournful consciousness of the terrible moral disharmony of his nature; in the contemplation of the beautiful artistic productions of his classic imagination, he saw in them reflections of his own supposed internal harmony, and, in this way, divested sin of its native ugliness.   Even after the dissolution of its political independence, Greece, by means of its refinement and polished literature, wielded an immense influence on the character and destiny of the human family, and served, in several respects, to prepare the way for the introduction of Christianity.

As the culture of the Grecians exhibited its beauty particularly in the sphere of feeling, of imagination, and of reason, so the Romans, with their eyes directed to the other side of our constitution, endeavored to master the problem of life by cultivating the powers of the finite Understanding and the energies of the determined Will. Hence the precise accuracy they manifested in the regulation of the various relations of civil life, and their political sagacity in securing the subordination of every individual enterprise to the promotion of the grand design of their state organization.   The invincible power thus acquired, enabled them to humble the pride of surrounding nations and to remove obstructions that might have retarded the introduction of Christianity, which was destined to re-organize the social fabric and teach the true principles of government.

Judaism, as a religion of revelation, enters into more intimate communion with Christianity, than the theological systems of Greece and Rome, which were the product of the natural understanding, unassisted by any special supernatural light.   Under the influence of the Jewish dispensation, man was brought to stand in the immediate presence of his Maker, and confronted with the terrors of his

justice. In the struggle to meet the demands of the law by cultivating holiness of heart, and to rescue himself from the thraldom of
sin by the sacrifice of appointed victims, he attained to a complete
knowledge of his character as a sinner, and of his moral inability
to deliver himself from the curse of the law. His endeavors to obtain a state of inward freedom, in the form of moral perfection, were
rendered abortive by the diseased condition of his spiritual nature;
his soul, overflowing with earnest desires for the revelation of the
Messiah, trusted in the promises of Jehovah as the sole ground of
salvation.

Judaism, as the religion of repentance, having for its object the
awakening of a knowledge of sin and a consequent necessity for
deliverance from its power by the operation of the law and the successive revelations of prophecy, must be regarded as a divinely instituted economy, designed to prepare the way directly for the manifestation of Christianity. The classical world, on the other hand,
as we behold it struggling with the great problem of life, and endeavoring, in the exercise of simply natural powers, to redeem suffering
humanity from the misery that afflicted it, and then expelling its
last expiring energies in a piercing cry for redemption, must be
considered a negative preparation for the same end.

As an entirely new spiritual principle, totally distinct from every
moral agency previously at work, Christianity now enters the very
heart of the world's history; proclaiming itself "joyful news" to all
nations, having for its object the rescue of man from the curse of
selfishness and the degrading tyranny of unbridled passion. His
spiritual freedom once secured, external liberty would follow as its
natural and necessary result. Christianity, however, does not bear
this regenerating character in the form simply of an outward divine
revelation, but in virtue of a new and heavenly *life* which it infuses
into the heart of man. Thus considered, it is not only a revelation
of the divine essence, but, at the same time, also, the complete and
richest manifestation of human nature. Christ, who is the centre
of this revelation, may, with great propriety and truth, be called the
Mediator between heaven and earth, because, in his own person,
he reconciled divinity with humanity. His incarnation introduced
a divine life into the process of the world's history, communicated
to it an entirely different direction from what it had previously, and
caused the nature of man to revolve around a heavenly centre. The
absolute triumph of the spirit over the flesh, or the redemption of

the world, was not simply announced by Him in the form of an abstract doctrine, but was actually accomplished, once for all, in His own person. He "is the key that unlocks the sense of the world's history." To become available for the purposes it was designed, the fullness of this salvation thus revealed, must be naturalized and incorporated in the life of humanity as an essential element of its character. Indeed, it may be affirmed without any hesitation, that since the time of Christ, every important historical event which contributed to form the character of society, bears a decided religious tendency, and that the entire process of the world's history present a successive series of struggles on the part of human life, to appropriate to its own use the blessings of this redemption. As all the nations of antiquity had performed their respective missions and expended their strength without having effected any positive salvation ; as a new historical epoch demands fresh energies, vigorous enough to fulfill its design ; Providence, after the dissolution of the old framework of society, brings upon the stage of action the Germanic nations, in, and through whom, particularly, Christianity exhibited its transforming and educational efficacy. Those nations, which obstinately refused to admit the light of revelation, and to recruit their exhausted strength by an admixture of Germanic elements, rapidly degenerated into Mohammedanism—a species of Paganism modified and refined, to some extent, by Christian and Jewish ideas. From the contest with this turbulent and devastating power, which concentrated for a final struggle the remaining energies of Heathenism, and strove to maintain its ascendency by worshipping the sensual and extinguishing the moral, the Germanic nations came forth conquerors with invigorated strength. In the Occident, Christianity displayed its regenerating power in subjecting the Northern barbarians to a process of education and, in the course of time, engaging their talents in the service of the Church, and elevating them to the rank of world monarchs.

This historical advance beyond the condition of ancient society, before terminating its activity, progresses through two epochs, which, though perfectly distinct from every previous period, coincide in this, that all the truly significant events which go to make up their distinctive character, can be referred to a Christian view of the world as their source. In the first, Christianity appears as a monarchical power, embodied in the will of the Church, considered as the representative of the divine will itself, that commands and compels the individual

to yield implicit obedience to her dictates. Such ecclesiastical supremacy, though liable to grievous abuse, rests, nevertheless, upon
the important thought, that the Church, so far as she is the depository of a divine revelation, carries in her constitution the power of
truth and the force of authority. This truth, however, conceived of
during the Middle Ages, under a predominantly outward form, led
men to undervalue the internal spiritual nature of Christianity, enforced the legalism of the Old Testament dispensation, and opened
the door for the entrance of Jewish and Heathen practises. In accordance with the law of divine Providence, and the necessities of
our human nature, which call forth into operation the purposes of
Heaven, a powerful reaction ensued, diametrically opposed to the
tyranny of ecclesiastical authority, .On this account it is, that the
period beginning with the Reformation and extending to the present time, has been characterized by such a large amount of individual activity in the sphere of religion. Christianity is no longer
regarded as an outward compulsory power, demanding a blind and
slavish obedience, but as a matter of personal experience, which
overcomes the individual by the force of conviction, converts the
law into a principle of free personal activity, in his own consciousness, and makes him a willing subject of the Church. The recognition of the right of private judgment, as the only means to bring
Christianity into contact with single persons, and to prepare the
world for a thorough reformation, gradually undermined the tyrannical government exercised by the Church over the State. As only
those Germanic nations, which were least adulterated by impure
foreign elements, were qualified to comprehend this profound conception of religion, they constitute, accordingly, during the progress
of this period, the chief factors of the historical process.

§. 8. *Utility of Universal history.*

Though it does not comport with the dignity of science to measure its worth by the extent of its utility, because it posesses, in itself considered, independent of its practical application, merit
enough to claim the attention of the highest intellect, still, the
historian need not fear any disparagement of his subject by instituting an investigation into its practical value.

As Universal history embraces within its compass the results of
human thought in every department of human knowledge, and con-
tes the proper basis for the formation of a high state of culture,

it posesses, in the first place, a universal value. Its study enables
an individual to recognize himself as an essential link in the great
chain of the human race, and to perceive in particular phenomena,
manifestations of the general life of humanity. In a certain sense,
history may be regarded as the judge of the world. For if it have
not yet passed sentence upon its actions, it constitutes, in all its
parts, a preparation for the final judgment; pointing with overpow-
ering efficacy to Him, who sits enthroned in the heavens far above
"the rage of the heathen, and the vain imagining of the people,"
clothed with majesty and holiness and, in the exercise of a Father's
love, endeavoring to rescue man from his deep degradation. History
is the mirror, in which the workings of individual life become visible.
Its special utility, therefore, consists in its furnishing us with sound
and wholesome counsel based upon the experience of past ages, in
the solution of the particular vocation Providence may have assigned
us. Even the relations of practical life in their final tendencies,
cannot be clearly discerned, without a comprehensive knowledge
of history. As it proves the Present to be the necessary and legitimate offspring of the Past, and discloses the internal connection
that subsists between different epochs of history, he, who aspires to
the command of a beneficial influence on his age and on posterity,
whether in the sphere of the State, or of the Church, or of art, or of
science, must cultivate an intimate acquaintance with the life of the
Past; otherwise his activity, regulated by a partial and defective view
of life, will terminate its results with his own existence: struggling
in vain against the progressive march of history, he will sink into
oblivion, his life having been wasted in disturbing and retarding the
true interests of humanity.

ART. XXXI.—Biographical Notices of Dr. Nisbet.

It is not too much to say, that the pulpit may be regarded as
at once a faithful exponent of the character of an age, and as

tributary, in a great degree, to its formation. If we could know in any given case, precisely what sort of religious ministrations prevail in any country, or at any period, we should have the best imaginable clue to the general habits of thought and feeling and action for which that country or period is distinguished. And, on the other hand, if the general character and condition of a community were to be made known to us, we should be able to find in it many significant indexes to the prevailing tone of public religious instruction. Nor is this a difficult matter to be accounted for. The pulpit, in its legitimate range of influence, includes the interests of the life that now is, as well as that which is to come. If it is designed to speak to man chiefly concerning his immortal destiny, it still acts by innumerable indirect and nameless influences, in moulding the opinions and habits of men on other subjects, and in modifying and carrying up the structure of human society.

If the influence of the pulpit is so great, its history, or the history of those by whom its character, at different periods has been determined, cannot reasonably be regarded with indifference. It is due, as well to general intelligence, to history, even to philosophy, that the greater lights of the pulpit should be kept shining through some faithful and enduring record, after they have passed under the great extinguisher—death, as it is to their own memories and to the gratitude of those who survive them. It is not only a grateful, but a profitable office, to call up these illustrious dead men from their graves, to put ourselves into communion with them in respect to the past, and thus to render their wisdom and experience availing to the intellectual and spiritual growth of ourselves and the men of our generation, and of posterity.

We trust, therefore, it will not be thought an unprofitable use of our pages, if we occasionally devote a share of them to the commemmoration of some of the departed worthies of our American pulpit. Notwithstanding the ministry in this country has, in some respects, greatly improved with advancing years, it is, by no means, certain, that in *every* respect the change has been for the better; and, unless we greatly mistake, there are some honored names in the past, from which any period might gather additional illumination. The individual whose name we have placed at the head of this article, certainly belongs to the number who deserve to be gratefully commemorated. We do not say, that he was, in all the qualities essential to the highest ministerial usefulness, the best model; but we do say, that considering his whole character and his whole history, few ministers in this country have a better claim to be remembered than he; and, we may add, considering that his entire field of labor on this side the water, was in Pennsylvania, there is, perhaps, no work on which it more fittingly devolves, than ours, to pay a brief tribute to his memory.

Charles Nisbet, was the third son of William and Alison Nisbet, and was born at Haddington, in Scotland, January 21, 1736. His elder brother, Andrew, was a minister of the established church, and was settled in the parish of Garvald, in the Presbytery of Haddington. Of the occupation and circumstances of his father, little more is known than that they were not such as to enable him to defray the expenses of his son's education, beyond a bare preparation for the university. But, notwithstanding the son was thus early cast upon his own resources, so intense was his thirst for knowledge, that he was enabled to accomplish his favorite object with comparatively little difficulty. He entered the University of Edinburgh, in 1752, and, at the same time, made an engagement as a private tutor, by means of which, he was enabled to meet the expenses of his whole college course. He is supposed to have graduated in the year 1754, in the eighteenth year of his age.

From the University, he passed immediately to the Divinity Hall, in Edinburgh, where he continued a diligent and successful student six years; during which time he supported himself chiefly by his contributions to one of the popular periodicals of the day. There still remain among his private papers, some records of his religious exercises at that time, which show that if he was enthusiastically devoted to theology, as a science, he was, nevertheless, an earnest and devout christian. He was licensed to preach the gospel by the Presbytery of Edinburgh, on the 24th of September, 1760.

His first engagement as a stated preacher, was with the church in the Gorbals of Glasgow. The congregation stipulated, in addition to the salary promised in their call, to furnish him with a house; but as he had no family to occupy a house, they failed to fulfil this part of their engagement. After having remained with them about two years, he received a call from the church of Montrose, which he thought proper to accept. On taking leave of his congregation, he, with his wonted aptness, preached to them from Acts, xxviii. 30: "And Paul dwelt two whole years in his own hired house, and received all that came in unto him."

The church of Montrose, was a large and intelligent one, and the right of patronage of the parish was vested in King George III. Mr. Nisbet was ordained on the 17th of May, 1764, by the Presbytery of Brechin, within the bounds of which he had his pastoral charge. Notwithstanding he was settled as co-pastor with the Rev. John Cooper, yet the advanced age and consequent infirmities of his colleague, devolved upon *him* nearly the whole amount of pastoral duty. He addressed himself to his work, however, with great energy and success, and quickly won, not only the respect, but the admiration of his extensive and influential charge.

About two years after his settlement in Montrose, he was married to Miss Anne Tweedie, a daughter of Thomas Tweedie, Esq., of Quarter, about thirty miles south of Edinburgh. An attachment had existed between them for twelve years; but their marriage had been postponed from prudential considerations. Another distinguished personage was married at Montrose, about the same time; and as they were both in private, friends of the celebrated Dr. Beattie, Professor at Aberdeen, he composed on the occasion, a beautiful poem, which he styled *Epithalamium Montrosianum.*

Not long after, Mr. Nisbet's settlement at Montrose, Dr. Witherspoon, then pastor of the church at Paisley, was chosen to succeed Dr. Finley, as President of Princeton College. His first impression was that he could not accept, and his first answer was in the negative. But Mr. Nisbet, though at that time only thirty-one years of age, was the person whom Dr. Witherspoon recommended as more suitable to fill that important station, than any other within his knowledge. The Dr., however, on more mature reflection, concluded to accept the place; and though his answer in the negative had already been communicated to the trustees of the college, yet, on receiving an intimation of a change in his views, they immediately renewed the appointment, and he forthwith signified his acceptance of it. Witherspoon had had something to do in conducting Nisbet's early studies, and they always remained firm friends, until death separated them.

It is well known that, at the time when Mr. Nisbet entered the ministry, the Church of Scotland was divided into two parties—the *orthodox* and the *moderate*—a division which, in a modified sense, at least, continues to this day. Mr. Nisbet was uniformly and decisively associated with the orthodox party; and though that party was then considerably in the minority, yet, in several instances, with the vigorous coöperation of Dr. Witherspoon, he made himself deeply felt in the General Assembly, and even succeeded in carrying certain measures which were regarded as adverse to the interests of the opposite party. One or two of his speeches in the Assembly have been preserved, which may be considered as models of eloquence in an ecclesiastical deliberative assembly; unless, perhaps, some might think them more highly spiced with wit than consists with the decorum due to such an occasion.

In the year 1771, Mr. Nisbet wrote a review of Wesley's system of doctrine, which was, at that time, attracting considerable attention from the theologians of Scotland. The article, which however, was not published till several years afterwards, discovers a remarkably comprehensive and discriminating mind, though it deals with both the system and its author with no inconsiderable severity. Had the article been written at a later period, it has been thought by a competent judge who knew Dr. Nisbet well, that it would have borne a somewhat different character.

Mr. Nisbet, in common with many other distinguished men of his country, justified the claims of the American Colonies which brought on the war of the Revolution. And in the progress of the struggle, he hesitated not boldly to proclaim his views both in public and private; and sometimes with such scathing irony that the partizans of government, while they could hardly repress a smile, were yet burning with indignation. He showed himself, also, the earnest friend of reform in the established church. The Patronage Act, especially, he opposed with great zeal, and in 1782, he drew up a series of resolutions, which were adopted at a large meeting in Montrose, designed to procure the repeal of that act and restore to the church the right to choose their own ministers. But, notwithstanding he was so often found, in reference to matters of church and of state, and of both united, on the unpopular side, his varied talents and acquirements, in connection with his acknowledged sterling integrity and worth, secured to him a very general and substantial popularity.

In 1783, the degree of Doctor of Divinity was conferred upon him by the trustees of Princeton College;—an honor, which it is said, would probably have been conferred by the same institution at an earlier period, but for the temporary interruption of friendly intercourse between this country and Great Britain, occasioned by the war of the Revolution.

In 1783, a new college was founded at Carlisle, Pennsylvania, called Dickinson College, in honor of the celebrated statesman, John Dickinson, who, at least, nominally, took the lead in its establishment. In April, 1784, Dr. Nisbet was chosen President of this institution; and his acceptance of the office was urged by Mr. Dickinson, Dr. Rush, and others, with great importunity. He was quite aware that the enterprise must involve serious difficulties, though there were some of which he was not, and could not be aware, till he should learn them by experience. After having had the invitation sometime before him, and looked at it in various and somewhat conflicting lights, he at length, in opposition to the judgment of many of his best friends, signified his acceptance of it, and shortly after set about preparing for his voyage to America.

He sailed from Greenock, with his family, on the 23d of April, 1785, and landed at Philadelphia on the 9th of June following. He brought with him his wife, two sons, and two daughters, having buried four children previous to his leaving Scotland. Having remained a few weeks in the family of Dr. Rush, of Philadelphia, and in the meantime, made a short visit to his old friend Dr. Witherspoon, at Princeton, he set out for Carlisle, and reached it amidst the usual patriotic demonstrations of the Fourth of July.

He was received by the assembled multitude with the most marked testimonies of respect; and on the next day was formally inducted to his new office. His inaugural discourse,—the only discourse he ever allowed to be printed—was designed to illustrate the importance of the union between learning and piety. It was considered as well worthy of its accomplished author.

Scarcely had Dr. Nisbet entered on the duties of his office, before he and several of his family were attacked with a violent fever, from which their recovery was very difficult and gradual. The Doctor himself suffered more severely than any of the rest; and after a confinement of several months, during which he was utterly inadequate to any mental or bodily labor, he had so far yielded to discouragement as to resolve on returning to his native country. Accordingly, on the 1st of October, succeeding his arrival, he tendered to the Board of Trustees of the college, the resignation of his office; which, however deeply regretted by them, they, on the whole, felt constrained to accept. As the season was unfavorable to a voyage across the ocean, he determined to postpone his return until spring; in the meantime he had so far regained his health and spirits, that he consented to be re-appointed to his office, and accordingly, on the 10th of May, 1786, he was unanimously elected a second time President of the college Though it was some time before his health was fully restored, yet it was never afterwards seriously interrupted, till the approach of the malady that many years afterwards closed his life.

As soon as his health would warrant his return to vigorous labor, he not only resumed his official duties, but pursued them to an extent which would have seemed an overmatch for any constitution. He immediately commenced the preparation and delivering of four different courses of lectures:—one on Logic, another on the Philosophy of the Mind, a third on Moral Philosophy, and a fourth on Belles Lettres, including interesting views of the principal Latin and Greek Classics. Each of these lectures was written, so far as it was written at all, on the evening immediately preceding the delivery; but his mind was such a store-house of well-digested and admirably arranged material pertaining to every subject, that a few hints only, committed to paper, were all the preparation that he needed for a meeting with his class.

In addition to the amount of labor already referred to, he yielded to a request of several of the graduates of the college, who had in view the Christian ministry, to give them a course of lectures on Systematic Theology. He was accustomed to deliver one of these lectures every day in the week, except Saturday and Sunday, while the college was in session; and the whole course consisted of four hundred and eighteen lectures, and extended through a period of somewhat more than two years. They were all written out and read with great deliberation, so that each student might take them down from the lips of the lecturer. He did not claim for them the merit of entire originality, but frankly told his students that he availed himself freely of the writings of the most approved theological authors. After this course was completed, he delivered another, consisting of twenty-two lectures, on the pastoral office; and these also, were taken down by the students in the same manner as before.

Besides his onerous labors in connection with the college, he regularly preached in the Presbyterian church in Carlisle, alternately with the Rev. Dr. Davidson, who was at that time its pastor. His services here, as well as in the college, were very generally and highly appreciated.

At the first commencement in the college, which occurred on the 26th of September, 1787, there were nine young men admitted to the degree of Bachelor of Arts; and the institution, in its constantly increasing popularity, showed the influence of its distinguished Head. It must be admitted, however, that Dr. Nisbet's expectations in coming to this country, were by no means, fully answered. Notwithstanding the great object of the Revolution had been gained in our national independence, yet the intellectual, moral and, in some respects, the civil interests of our country had suffered greatly in the struggle; and he found such a state of things here as it was hardly possible for him to anticipate. He came when the elements were in a chaotic state, and were susceptible of the influence of any vigorous and plastic hand. His letters to his friends in Scotland, breathe a feeling of disappointment; but he was not unwilling to submit to some inconvenience and self-denial for the sake of doing something to mould the character of an infant nation.

In the spring of 1792, Dr. Nisbet paid a visit to Gov. Dickinson, in honor of whom the college was named, and who then resided at Wilmington, Delaware.   The Governor, who felt himself in some degree responsible for unredeemed pledges made to Dr. Nisbet previous to his leaving Scotland, received him with every mark of hospitality and respectful attention ; and the visit seems to have been mutually and highly gratifying.   On the first evening after the Dr.'s arrival, the conversation turned on the probable effect of an earnest prosecution of the study of the physical sciences on the religious character; and such was the impression made on the mind of the Governor by the remarks of his distinguished guest, that at the close of the conversation, he said to him :—" Doctor, what you have said would form an invaluable octavo volume ;—I would give a large sum to have it in that form."   The Governor urged him to pay him an annual visit; and Dr. Nisbet shortly after his return home, received notice that Mr. Dickinson had deposited five hundred dollars in one of the banks of Philadelphia, subject to his order, to meet the expense of the visits which he had solicited.   The President was not slow to avail himself of this proffered generosity, and, accordingly, for several years afterwards, paid an annual and most welcome visit to his illustrious friend.   His journeys were always made on horseback.

In the year 1793, Dr. Nisbet was subjected to some peculiar trials, in consequence of what was called the " Whiskey Rebellion "—a rebellion in Pennsylvania, occasioned by the tax laid by the Government of the United States on ardent spirits.   Feeling that it was one of those occasion on which the pulpit had a just right to be heard, Dr. Nisbet, while the tumultuous scene was in progress, preached a sermon that was designed to discountenance the rebellious procedure, and that contained some sarcastic allusions that gave great offence to the insurgent party.   A few days after, when a company of the rebels came into Carlisle from the adjacent country, to erect a Whiskey or Liberty Pole, serious apprehensions were entertained, that Dr. Nisbet's house would be assailed by the mob; and several respectable individuals offered to remain in it for the purpose of aiding in its defence, if there should be occasion; but the Doctor declined their offer, on the ground that their presence might serve to invite an attack.　The result, however, justified the apprehension of his danger; for the mob were actually on their way to accomplish a work of destruction upon his dwelling, when they were met by some one who informed them that the President's younger daughter was seriously ill, and were persuaded in consequence of this information, to forego their contemplated outrage.

Early in January, 1804, Dr. Nisbet took a severe cold, which grew into a fever and inflamation of the lungs, and finally terminated his life.　He died on the 18th of the month, after an illness of less than three weeks.　During the greater part of the time, his bodily sufferings were intense, but his patience and fortitude were most exemplary.　Even after he lost the power of conversing with those around him, his mind was evidently absorbed in communion with his God.　He died with "Holy, Holy, Holy!" upon his lips, having, within three days, completed the sixty-eighth year of his age.　His funeral was attended by a large concourse, who evinced the most affectionate respect for his memory, and an appropriate sermon, delivered on the occasion by the Rev. Dr. Davidson.

Dr. Nisbet left a widow, who survived him more than three years, and died in the hope of a better life, May 12th, 1807.　He left four children.　The eldest son, Thomas, who had been graduated at the University of Edinburgh, died shortly after his father.　His second son, Alexander, after graduating in Dickinson College, studied law, and settled in Baltimore, where for many years, he has held the office of Judge of the city court.　The eldest daughter, Mary, was married in 1790, to William Turnbull, Esq., a native of Scotland, but at that time, a resident of Pittsburgh, and survived her father about twenty years.　The youngest daughter, Alison, who was married to Dr. Samuel M'Coskry, an eminent physician of Carlisle, in 1795, was left a widow in 1818, and is still (1849) living.　Her only surviving son is the Rt. Rev. Samuel M'Coskry, Bishop of the Protestant Episcopal Church in the Diocese of Michigan.

Dr. Nisbet's valuable library, consisting of many of the rarest works, fell into the hands of his two grandsons, Bishop M'Coskry and Henry C. Turnbull, Esq., who, with highly commendable liberality, presented it to the Theological Seminary at Princeton.

Dr. Nisbet, while in Scotland, was in intimate relations with many distinguished individuals in that country, and he maintained a constant correspondence with several of them after he came to America. Among his most devoted friends, were the Countess of Leven, a lady distinguished for her intelligence and piety; the Earl of Buchan, well known in this country as Washington's correspondent; and the Rev. Dr. John Erskine, of Edinburgh, for a long time a leader of the orthodox part of the established church. The latter left as a legacy to Dr. Nisbet, a considerable part of his library; but before the fact was known in this country, the venerable legatee had departed.

We shall not attempt anything like a minute or philosophical analysis of Dr. Nisbet's character, while we are well aware that it might very properly form the subject of an elaborate and highly instructive essay. He possessed one of those singularly constituted and yet highly gifted minds, which are found only here and there in the history of an age, and which form an appropriate study for those who would contemplate human nature in its diversified ramifications. He is one of the men who serve to relieve the otherwise monotonous character of human society, one whom even an ordinary curiosity might have craved to see, and of whom it is no wonder that the few surviving ones who knew him, love so well to speak. We regret that we can say nothing concerning him, but what others have said before; and yet we have no doubt of the correctness of our impression concerning his character, as we have received them from several of his most intimate friends. And his character was so transparent as well as so unique, that, so far as we know, there was never among those who had an opportunity of judging, much difference of opinion in respect to it. The most full, and we doubt not, the most faithful, account of Dr. Nisbet, that has yet appeared, is from the pen of the venerable Dr. Miller, whose intimate personal acquaintance with this remarkable man, as well as his accurate and acknowledged impartiality, pointed him out as the most suitable person to embody his recollections of him in a permanent record.

In his person, Dr. Nisbet was a little below the middle stature, and in early life was rather slender, but before he arrived at middle age, became somewhat corpulent, and continued so as long as he lived. The change is said to have come over him suddenly, as if under the influence of disease; and yet his health never really suffered in consequence of it. He always possessed great bodily agility, and in early life performed feats in this way that would seem almost incredible. With the exception of occasional attacks, of what would now probably be called *dyspepsia*, his health was for the most part uninterrupted.

In the intellectual world, he might almost be said to be a prodigy. The two characteristics by which he was most distinguished were memory and wit, while in some others he was highly reputable—even eminent. It were scarcely too much to say of him, that he never forgot anything which he had read or heard. He would master even a difficult work with most surprising rapidity; and when it was once in his mind, instead of making a mere temporary lodgment there, it became a perfect fixture—apparently as permanent as the mind itself. The consequence of this remarkable power of memory, in connection with a thirst for knowledge which amounted to a perfect passion, was, that it was difficult to start a subject with which he was not familiar, difficult to name an author which he had not perfectly at his command. It is said of him, that on one occasion he was dining with a party of friends, and one of them, being somewhat ambitious of displaying his classical knowledge, quoted as an illustration of something that came up, several lines of the Iliad in the original Greek. When he had finished his quotation, said the Dr., "well mon, go on; what you have left is just as good as what you have taken;" but the *scholar* was obliged to own that he had gone as far as his knowledge would carry him. The Doctor then took up the passage where his friend had left it, and went on at very considerable length, with the most perfect ease and freedom.

His wonderful wit constituted him at once a terror and an attraction; for while every body loved to listen to it, there were few who did not dread coming under its lash. In general, it took the form of playful good humor, but if occasion required, it could become the channel of terrific and scathing rebukes. One or two of his speeches delivered before the General Assembly of the Church of Scotland, which are still preserved, show that sport with him sometimes became no sport; and that he knew how to make a joke the vehicle of a thunder-bolt. If all his witticisms that tradition has brought down to us were gathered into a volume, it is not easy to say what length they would run; and we are free to acknowledge, that they do not constitute the class of his sayings that we think most worthy to be perpetuated. We will, however, mention a few of the many anecdotes that survive concerning him, which may serve to illustrate this trait of his character.

Dr. Nisbet was once asked, how he could define modern philosophy. His reply was, "It consists in believing everything but the truth, and exactly in proportion to the want of evidence; or, to use the words of a poet, in making windows that shut out the light and passages that lead to nothing." The following colloquy is said to have passed between him and Dr. Mason of New York, in reference to his very infrequent attendance on the meetings of the General Assembly at Philadelphia. It occurred at Philadelphia while the assembly was in session:—"Well Doctor," said Dr. Mason, I find you sometimes come to Philadelphia during the sessions of the General Assembly." "Yes," said he, "I am not a member, but I like to meet my friends, and see a little of what is going on." *Mason.*—"Do you not sometimes go into the assembly, and listen to its proceedings?" *Nisbet.*—Yes, I sometimes go in for the *benefit of hearing*, and then I come out for the *benefit of not hearing.*" *Mason.*—"Well, Doctor, which is the greater benefit?" *Nisbet.*—"Indeed, mon, its hard to strike the balance." Dr. Green, of Philadelphia, on a certain occasion, had had a very fine horse stolen from a pasture in the neighborhood of the city: Dr. Nisbet happening to be with him a day or two after, adverted to the circumstance of his loss. "So," said he, "I understand you have lost your horse." "Yes, Doctor," said Dr. G., "the night before last, a thief fancied him, and I fear I shall never see him again." "No doubt," said Dr. N., "it was done by one of the sovereign people; he was taken without your leave by a pure act of sovereignty. But, sir, it was only a forced loan; it was an act of practical liberty and equality; the rascal thought that you had been riding long enough, and that by all the laws of equality, it was his turn to ride now; and so he made use of his liberty to appropriate to himself a part of your property without your consent." At a certain time when he was a member of the General Assembly, the weather being very warm, and the sunny days of temperance not having yet come, a pitcher of beer was brought in and placed near the moderator's chair. The moderator being very thirsty, began to drink, and kept on drinking, till Dr. Nisbet, who was in a similar predicament, began to think that the cup was in danger of being exhausted; whereupon he jumped up, and in the best possible humor cried out,—" I hope the mo*th*erator does not mean to drink all the *bare*, because he's the *mooth* of the body!"

As a preacher, Dr. Nisbet was confessedly eminent, though it is much to be regretted that he has left so little from which we can form an estimate of his power in the pulpit. His sermons are said to have been full of weighty, well-digested and well-arranged thought, and to have been delivered in a simple and effective manner, but without any of the graces of oratory. In early life he was accustomed to write a considerable portion of what he delivered, but as he advanced in his course, he wrote nothing beyond the merest skeleton, and more frequently did not write even that. It is said that his own family did not know when he made his preparation for the pulpit, or even that he made it at all, except as his sermons evidently showed the most mature thought. On one occasion, he was found in the congregation of a brother clergyman, who had preached during the Sabbath morning on a particular subject, and promised to resume it in the afternoon. He asked Dr. Nisbet to take his place in the second service; and he complied with the request to the letter; for, not only did he preach, but took up the subject which his brother had discussed in the morning at the very point where he left it, and carried it through in the most felicitous manner, and without the semblance of embarrassment.

In his theological opinions, Dr. Nisbet was a strict conformist to the confession of faith in the Presbyterian church and the Assembly's catechism. He was, however, not only tolerant, but liberal towards Christians of other communions, and cordially extended the hand of Christian fellowship to all whom he considered as holding the grand peculiarities of Christianity.

As a theological teacher, he was regarded as among the most accomplished and most successful of the day.   Several of the greater lights of our American pulpit, some of whom still shine, while most of them have sunk in death, were trained for the ministry under his instruction and superintendence.   Dr. Miller, who enjoyed the benefit of his lectures and of a most unreserved intercourse with him for a considerable time, even now in his old age, easily kindles into a glow of affectionate and grateful feeling, whenever his venerated teacher and friend happens to be the subject of conversation.

As the President of the College, Dr. Nisbet had to contend with many difficulties, some of which grew out of the fact that the institution was then just struggling into life, and others, perhaps, from his having been trained under the influence of foreign institutions.   His fidelity in the discharge of duty, his devotion, to the interests of literature and religion, in connection with the institution-over which he was called to preside, it is believed that no one ever questioned ; and if his career in this department of labor were less brilliant than his fame as a scholar and a divine might have led us to expect, it was doubtless to be referred chiefly to causes that were beyond his control.   We now and then meet with some veteran who graduated with him, and if allusion is made to the fact, it is pretty sure to bring over his countenance a smile of exultation.

Dr. Nisbet, with his unrivalled powers of wit and sarcasm, had a warm, benevolent, generous heart.   He was quick to listen to the tale of sorrow, and always on the alert to perform offices of kindness and goodwill.   He could not brook the spirit of meanness or cunning ; frank and generous himself, he looked with profound disapprobation on the least departure from stern integrity.   To his friends he was always more than welcome ; to his family he was everything.   Nature and grace was each a liberal contributor both to his greatness and goodness.   He was a great light in the firmament of exalted minds : but it was his love of truth and love of Christ that threw over his character its most hallowed and sublime attraction.

ART. XXXII.—The Lutheran Confession.

The Evangelical Review. Edited by *William Reynolds*, Professor in Pennsylvania College. With the assistance of Dr. *J. G. Morris*, Prof. *H. T. Schmidt*, Rev. *C. W. Schaeffer*, and Rev. *E. Greenwalt.* Vol. I. No. 1. July, 1849. Gettysburg. Neinstedt.

With many others, we welcome the appearance of the new Quarterly here announced It is in all respects worthy of the very respectable auspices under which it is ushered into the world. Its outward appearance must command general admiration and respect; while the solid and substantial character of its contents, is such as to deserve and justify fully the care thus taken for their genteel representation.   Without the show of any effort or undue pretension, the present number of the publication serves well to reveal a portion of the strength it has to rely upon for its support in time to come, and carries in it a fair guaranty that its work will be prosecuted with vigor and effect.   The plan of the Review is liberal and judicious; its spirit is that of earnest faith, apparently, seeking to speak the truth in love; while the qualifications of its worthy and excellent editor, in particular, make it certain that it will be conducted wisely, to the credit of the Lutheran Church, and to the benefit, also, we trust, of the Church at large. We are glad to learn that it meets wide patronage and favor, and wish for it a still more extended prosperity in this way hereafter.

We welcome this Review, because its banner is unfurled in favor of true *Lutheranism*, in the bosom of the American German Church.   It proposes, indeed, to make itself open and free ground, to a certain extent, for the exhibition and discussion of all the conflicting tendencies which enter at this time into what is sometimes denominated American Lutheranism as a whole; tendencies far enough aside, in some cases, as we all know, from the only true life of the Church as embodied in the Augsburg Confession.   This, in the circumstances, may be all right and good.   Still, it is not meant, of course, that the Review itself is to be indifferent to all these tendencies alike, or, what would be the same thing, alike favorable to them all, in its reigning char-

acter and tone.   It is understood to go decidedly for the standards, and the true historical life, of the Lutheran Church.   This
does not imply, indeed, that it is to make common cause with
the stiff exclusive pedantry of the *Altlutheraner*, technically so
styled; who come before us in the German Church, as a fair
parallel to the similar petrifaction which is presented to our view
in the pedantry of the Scotch Seceders.   What lives must move.
The Review proposes no substitution of dead men's bones for
what was once their living spirit.   But this spirit itself it will
seek to understand and honor, with due regard to the wants of
the Church as it now stands.   It will not be ashamed of the
Augsburg Confession.   It will speak reverently, at least, even
of the Form of Concord, as well as of the great and good men
to whom it owes its origin.   It will not dream of sundering the
stream of Lutheranism from its human historical fountain in the
sixteenth century, by the miserable fiction of an American Lutheranism in no living and inward connection with the Lutheranism of Europe; the *name* thus made to be everything, and
the substance nothing.   It will not stultify Luther himself, by
professing to accept his creed and magnify his name, while the
very core of all, his sacramental faith, without which his creed
had for himself no meaning or force, is cast aside as a silly impertinence, deserving only of pity or contempt.   The Review
proposes to stand forth, in one word, as the representative of true
bona fide Lutheranism, in the old sense, as it was held, for instance, by Melancthon, in the age of the Reformation, and as it
is held now by many of the best and most learned men in Germany.   This it proposes to do here on American ground, in full
face of the unsacramental thinking with which it is surrounded
on all sides, and in full view of the scorn, open or quiet, that is
to be expected at its hands.   In all this, as already said, we unfeignedly rejoice.   We are glad that Lutheranism has found an
organ, after so long a time, to plead its own cause before the
American Church; and we are glad it has found an organ which
promises to plead this cause so ably and well.

   Are *we* then Lutheran? Just as little as we have become Roman.   As we stand in the bosom, externally, of the *Reformed*
Church, we find in it, also, the only satisfactory resting place at

present, for our faith. With vast allowance, inwardly, in favor of others, conscientiously embosomed in a different confession, we feel that the Reformed principle, particularly as it comes to what seems to us to be its truest and best expression in the Heidelberg Catechism, is the only one in which we can fairly and fully acquiesce. We believe, indeed, that Lutheranism and Reform, the two great phases of the Protestant faith, may be so brought together with mutual inward modification, that neither shall necessarily exclude the other, that each rather shall serve to make the other more perfect and complete; and we earnestly long for this union; but so long as the antithesis, which, in itself, thus far, has been real and not imaginary only, is not advanced to this inward solution and reconciliation, we are in principle Reformed, and not Lutheran. In particular, we are not able at all to accept Luther's idea of Christ's presence in the eucharist. With Calvin, and the Heidelberg Catechism, we hold the mystery itself, and abhor the rationalistic frivolity by which it is now so commonly denied; but the *mode* of it we take to be such as fairly transcends all local images and signs. It is accomplished in the sphere of Christ's Spirit only, mirifically for faith.

Why, then, it may be asked, should we find such satisfaction in an enterprise, which has for its object expressly the vindication of Lutheranism, and that is likely to be so powerfully felt in its favor? The question is fair, and deserves a fair answer.

We look upon Lutheranism, in the present stadium of Christianity, as a necessary part of the constitution of Protestantism. Our idea of Protestantism is, that the two great confessions into which it was sundered from the start, the Lutheran and the Reformed, grew with inward necessity, out of the movement itself, carrying in themselves thus a relative reason and right, of the same general nature with what must be allowed in favor of the Reformation itself. In this respect, that first grand rent is, by no means, parallel with the sectarian divisions of the present time; for they are palpably, to a great extent, the product of mere self-will, without any truly objective necessity, and as such, in the highest degree irrational. Protestantism includes in itself, two tendencies, both of which enter legitimately into its life; while each, at the same time, seems to involve at last the destruction of the other. This only shows, however, that the truth of it must hold at last, in some way, in such a union of these forces as shall make them to be one. The two original confessions come not thus by accident, but by the logical law, we may say, of the vast fact of Protestantism itself; with a necessity, however, which is not absolute, but only relative, and so interimistic, and which is destined, accordingly, in due time, to pass away in their inward amalgamation; a result which will involve, also, no doubt, a full conciliation of the Protestant principle, as a whole, not with Romanism as it now stands, but still with the deep truth of Catholicism, from which, by abuse, the Roman error springs. All which may our Blessed Lord hasten, in his own time and way. The case being thus, it is plain that Lutheranism can never give the full sense of the Protestant Church, by carrying out simply its own life in a separate and one-sided way; but it is just as plain, also, of course, that this is quite as little to be expected from the Reformed confession, under a like exclusive view. This seems to us to be well nigh a self-proving axiom, for such as have any true faith in the Reformation as God's work, and any true insight into the constitutional reason of the two confessions as its immediate and necessary product. We can have no patience with any man's pretended faith in this great movement, who can allow himself to think of either side of it, the Lutheran or the Reformed, as meaningless and false; and who can imagine thus, that the completion of Protestantism is to consist in the complete stultification of either interest, to make room for the wholesale glorification of the other, as naked and sole mistress of all truth in the case from the beginning. The Reformed Church can never fulfil its mission, either in theology or practical piety, without the Lutheran. Its perfection must stand in the end, not, of course, in passing over to the original Lutheran stand-point, nor yet in keeping up a perpetual war with it as Rome with Carthage; but still, just as little either in forgetting its existence, and pushing out pedantically the Reformed principle its own way, in full ignorance, or in full contempt, of the counterpoise it is bound to acknowledge on the opposite side. The only sufficient and rational adjustment of the antithesis which holds between the two confessions, is such as shall do justice to the full weight of the antithe-

sis itself, by bringing its two sides into such harmony, that each
shall be the complement of the other.   The problem in the case
is not to denounce and damn, nor yet to ignore and forget, but
in love to reconcile, and so surmount the opposition that is found
to be really and truly in the way.

   With any such view as this, it is not possible, of course, to be
satisfied with the reigning habit of our American Protestantism,
as it now stands.   The old confessional antithesis, which was
felt to be so deep and vital in the age of the Reformation, has,
with us, apparently, gone almost entirely into oblivion.   Few
understand it, and few, consequently, take any interest in it whatever.   It is regarded widely as an obsolete folly.   The age is
supposed to have got beyond it, and to stand on higher ground.
Now this would be very well, if our supposed advantage in such
form were the result of a true inward mastery of the old theological question itself, or system of questions rather, which gave so
much trouble to our ecclesiastical ancestors.   But this is not the
case.   The old controversy has been silenced simply, not settled,
in favor of one side, without any regard to the rights of the other;
and the consequence is, accordingly, a one-sided declination, also,
of the interest thus favored, away off from its own true and proper orbit.   We have among us confessional divisions still; but
they are not founded at all in the original Protestant separation.
That is, for the most part, no longer thought of at all, or thought
of only as one particular rent, (now out of date,) among a score
of other rents, more nearly affecting the consciousness of the present time.   To a large part of our theology, the term *Reformed,*
as it enters into the original history of Protestantism, is no longer
intelligible.   How many ministers even, with regular education,
take it for the designation simply of some fragmentary interest of
the German Church, as we find it sometimes applied, for instance,
to particular secessions, such as the Reformed Methodists, Reformed Presbyterians, &c., with no sense whatever, as it might
seem, of its true generic signification, as applied in the beginning
to the whole confession, which in Switzerland, France, Holland,
England, Scotland and Germany, was thus distinguished from
the other great confession bearing the name of Luther.   Such
want of familiarity with the old sense of the title, is itself a proof,

however, that the sense of the fundamental distinction or issue in Protestantism, to which it refers, has also passed away. Not only the name, but the idea, also, of the *Reformed* confession, as related to the Lutheran, has grown strange to the main part of our religious thinking. We have, ordinarily, a much more active sense for the subordinate issues, exhibited in Methodism, for instance, or Secederism, or Newschool Presbyterianism, &c., in their relations to other sects. The primary confessional interest of Protestantism is gone, by the virtual failure among us of one whole side of the antithesis on which it once turned. Lutheranism has been in this country a perfectly foregone cause. Our Protestantism has planted itself wholly on the Reformed side of the old confessional line; in such a way, however, as to make no account of any such line; with the assumption, rather, that the ground thus taken covers the whole sense of Protestantism, and that it offers no other field properly for theological distinctions. So, of course, with our sect spirit universally. Our evangelical christianity, in general, however, shows in this respect the same character. The true Lutheran element has no place in it whatever. Luther would not feel himself at all at home in our churches. Take Puritan New England, which in some sense rules our religious life. Luther is glorified by it, of course, on all sides; but how few there understand him, or have any real sympathy with his soul. The Protestantism of New England, is the extreme left, we may say, of the Reformed wing of this faith, to which the very existence of Lutheranism has come to be a mere word. The predominant feeling with it has been, that the history of theology in this country, since the days of Jonathan Edwards, downwards, may be taken as the comprehension, in substance, of all that is important in its history since the Reformation, or before it; that all other theology, at least, must be measured and tried by this; and that no school or tendency is worth minding much, that comes not near to it in some way, in its formulas and tones. Even the old *Reformed* theology, of foreign lands, has found but small respect or study at the hands of this self-sufficient and self-satisfied spirit. But how much less the old Lutheran theology? And yet, what is Protestant theology, as a science, if no account be made in it of the vast achievements of the Lutheran Church? We have had experience in this case, as well as room for observation; and we know that a good theological education is not supposed generally to need any reference whatever to this old Lutheran divinity, except in the way of outward polemic notice, here and there, as in the case of other false systems. Our reigning theology feels itself to be absolutely complete in the Reformed shape only, and goes, for the most part, on the broad assumption that all else is now, and ever has been, sheer unbiblical fancy, which, if a minister have some knowledge of, in antiquarian style, it is well, but which, at the same time, he may be ignorant of just *as* well, for all solid purposes in his profession.

In these circumstances, unfortunately, the Lutheran Church itself in this country, heretofore, has had almost no power to make its voice heard, in favor of the interest it was called historically to represent. The entire German Church, both Reformed and Lutheran, has been long prevented by outward circumstances, from entering into the full possession and free use of its proper native resources, so as to do itself justice in the midst of the simply English tendencies with which it has been surrounded. In this way, to American Christianity in general, Lutheranism as here existing, has seemed a perfectly insignificant element in our religious history. And then, to make the matter worse, our Lutheranism itself, and it must be acknowledged too, the very best part of it, religiously considered, dissevered, in a great measure, from its own history, fell in largely with this way of thinking, learned to undervalue itself, and sought in the same measure to win favor and respect by ceasing to be Lutheranism altogether, except in outward form and name. We have had thus the strange spectacle of the Lutheran confession throwing itself clear over the line by which it was originally distinguished from the Reformed, and not only making common cause with this in its general principle, but actually taking the lead, oftentimes, in the work of pushing out this principle to its worst extreme consequences on the opposite side. No wonder that the whole interest should be so widely treated, in this state of things, as a theological nullity. One whole side of Protestant theology has been thus, here in America, as good as extinct; and it has been taken for granted, in every direction, that it was absolutely full and complete, in the form simply of the other side.   Our theological questions, it is well known, turn almost exclusively on this assumption; being started and reasoned upon for the most part from Reformed premises *only*, as if no body could dream now of including anything beyond these in the conception of Protestantism.   On such a question, for instance, as that of sacramental grace, the mystical force of the holy sacraments, one which was felt to lie at the ground of christianity itself in the sixteenth century, it is common now to make no account whatever of the Lutheran faith, (as little as of the Roman Catholic,) but just to go forward gravely as though it had never existed, or never had entered confessionally into the life of the Reformation at all!   The necessity of coming to any right understanding with it on so vital an interest, is not felt at all nor acknowledged; but on the contrary, it is taken to be a test and mark of truth, rather, to get as far off from it as possible, and to show the utmost possible independence of its authority, as something wholly foolish and false.

Now this involves, of course, a gross insult upon the American Lutheran Church itself, which is only made worse by the kind courtesies that may seem to go along with it, at least, in part.   It is as though New England should say: "Good Lutheran friends, we hold your old confessional stand-point, so far as we have thought it worth while to look at it, (a needless trouble, however, for our own faith, *we* go by the Bible,) to be no better than arrant nonsense, and Luther himself, (glorious man,) a poor dolt, for making so much noise and fuss about it as he did.   But we do' not burden *you*, of course, with any such obsolete folly. *American* Lutheranism, like all else American in this wonderful nineteenth century, is quite too clever for that.   We smile upon you as evangelical in our own sense, and shall be pleased to have you smile upon us as your very good friends, in return."   But this is not all, nor the worst, in this case.   Such vast wrong done to one whole side of Protestantism, whose rights are just as legitimate and clear, historically, as those of the other, must of necessity infer vast wrong to this also, as having no power to remain true to itself in any such isolated and abstract view.   We hold it for a fixed maxim, that the genuine Reformed tendency can

continue to be genuine, only in connection with the Lutheran
tendency, with which it divided in the beginning the universal
force of the Protestant movement.   It can never complete itself
by falling away from this entirely, losing all sense of its presence,
treating it as an impertinent and senseless nothing; this must
amount at last to a falling away from Protestantism itself.   It
can become complete, (as Lutheranism, also,) only by recognizing the weight that actually belongs to its twin-born counterpoise,
and so leaning toward it as to come with it finally into the power
of a single life, that shall be neither one nor the other, separately
taken, but both at once thus raised to their highest sense.   A
Christianity, then, that ignores and rejects in full the Lutheran
element, can never be sound and whole.   The Reformed habit
of thought wins no favor in our eyes, from being *so* Reformed
as to have lost all sympathy with the old Lutheran theology, all
power possibly of understanding at all what this means.   On the
contrary, all such abstraction fills us with misgiving and distrust.
We have no faith in a religion, that takes half the Reformation
for the whole.   We have no disposition to sit at the feet of a theology, that yawns over the vast confessional interest of the sixteenth century, as a stale and tedious thing; that takes no pleasure, of course, in the true central church questions of our own
time, all revolving as they do, more or less, round the same deep
problem, and struggling towards its solution; but gives us instead,
the formulas and shibboleths only, of some single denomination,
a mere fragment of the Reformed section of Protestantism at best,
as the quintessence and *ne plus ultra* of all divinity.   No such
theology can be safe.   It tends, with inward necessity, towards
rationalism, or the region of thin void space.   It must, in due
time, cease to be Reformed, as well as Lutheran, passing clear
over the true Protestant horizon altogether, with imminent hazard
of losing finally even its form of sound words, as far as this may
go, in a system that resolves all mystery into sheer abstraction,
and owns the supernatural only as an object of thought.

What we have now said, may suffice to explain, how it is that
we are led to hail, with unaffected hearty satisfaction, the appearance of the Gettysburg Evangelical Review, set as it is, and we
trust also powerfully and efficiently set, for the defence of what

is comprehended for our common Protestantism in the great and mighty confessional interest of Lutheranism. We consider it important in this view by itself; but we consider it important still more, as a sign and evidence, one large sign among many others as yet less notable, that the American Lutheran Church, not dead heretofore but sleeping, is about now to shake off its theological slumbers, and address itself as a strong man to the work of its own true and proper mission, in the general problem of American Christianity. It were a burning shame, in such a country as ours, that the Church of Luther, as such, should *not* be heard and felt in the ultimate constitution of the national faith. It were, besides, however, a deep and irreparable loss to this faith itself, not to be completed in this way. All who take an intelligent interest in American Christianity, must deprecate the idea of its being permanently divorced, as it has been, for instance, thus far in New England, from the deep rich wealth of the old Lutheran creed. Our Reformed theology needs above all things, just now, for its proper support and vigorous development, the *felt* presence of the great Lutheran antithesis, as it stood in the beginning. It can never prosper, in any manly style, without this condition. What can a purely Methodist, or Baptist, or Puritan theology ever be worth, when weighed in the balances of true science, under any such pedantically abstract character? The very conception of such merely sectarian divinity, as something thus scientifically complete within itself, is preposterous. Let Lutheranism, then, by all means, flourish, for the sake of that which is not Lutheran. We bid the Evangelical Review God speed.   J. W. N.

ART. XXXIII.—The Triumph of Love.

A HYMN—FROM SCHILLER.

[The following is a literal translation of one of Schiller's most beautiful lyric poems. An attempt has been made to preserve, as far as possible, the spirit and flow of the original. This has been done by employing accent alone, without regard to rhyme, or the number of feet. That the English language will admit of such a measure, is clearly shown by the successful efforts of Southey, Shelley and Coleridge. To translations of lyric poetry (in which great freedom is ever allowed), whether from the Greek, or from the German, it seems peculiarly adapted. In such cases, rhyme is a clog too heavy even for the strength of genius, and plain prose too tame. Something between the two, therefore, is easier for the translator, and more likely to give those, for whom translations are intended, a better idea of the original.]

HAPPY through Love
The Gods—through Love
  Men are like Gods.
Love makes Heaven
More heavenly—the Earth
  Like unto Heaven.

Once behind Pyrrha's back,
  Poets agree,
Out of rock-pieces sprang the World,
  Men out of stone.

Of rock and stone their hearts,
  Their souls of night,
From heaven's flame-tapers in-
  To glow ne'er fanned.

Not yet with softest chains of roses
Bound their souls young Amorets;
Not yet with songs the tender Muses heaved
Their bosoms, nor with harmony of strings.

Ah! yet around themselves
Wound they no loving garlands!
Drearily fled the Springs
  Toward Elysium.

Ungreeted climbed Aurora
  Out of the Ocean's lap;
Ungreeted sank the Sun
  Into the Ocean's lap.

Wildly wandered they through groves,
'Neath the misty moonbeams' light:
   They dragged an iron yoke.
Gazing upon the gallery of stars,
   As yet the secret tear
    Sought for no god.

*   *   *   *

Lo! from the blue flood rises
Heaven's daughter soft and mild,
   Drawn by the Naiads
   To intoxicated shores.

A youthful May-impulse
Glides through, as morning twilight,
   At the almighty *Be*,
   Air, Heaven, Sea and Earth.

The eye of the sweet day laughs
In the midnight of gloomy woods:
   Odorous Narcissi
   Bloom under her feet.

Already sang the nightingale
   The first song of Love;
Already murmured fountain-falls
   In tender bosoms, Love.

Thrice-fortunate Pygmalion,
Already melts thy marble, glows!
   God Amor, Conqueror!
   Embrace thy children!

*   *   *   *

Happy through Love
The Gods—through Love
   Men are like Gods.
Love makes Heaven
More heavenly—the Earth
Like unto Heaven.

*   *   *   *

'Mid the golden nectar-foam,
Like a pleasant morning dream,
An everlasting pleasure-band
Fly the days of the Gods.

Throned on a lofty seat
Jove brandishes his bolt;
Olympus shrinks afraid
At the angry shaking of his locks—

To the Gods leaves he his throne;
Lowers himself to a son of Earth;
Sighs an Arcadian through the grove;
The tame thunder at his feet;
Sleeps, rocked on Leda's pillow;
The Titanqueller sleeps.

The majestic steeds of the Sun
Through the wide realm of Light
The golden rein of Phœbus guides;
On nations falls his rattling arrow.
   His white sun-steeds,
   His rattling arrows,
'Mid Love and Harmony,
Ha! how willingly forgot he!

   Before the wife of Jupiter
     Bow the Uranides;
   Proud before her chariot-throne
     Bridle up the peacock-pair;
   With the imperial golden crown
     Decks she her ambrosial hair.

   Beautiful Princess! Ah Love
   Dreads to near thy Majesty
     With the sweet impulse!
   From her proud heights.
     The Queen of the Gods
   Must beg the charmèd girdle
     From the Fetteress of Hearts.

     *   *   *   *

     Happy through Love
     The Gods—through Love
       Men are like Gods.
     Love makes Heaven
     More heavenly—the Earth
       Like unto Heaven.

     *   *   *   *

Love lightens the Realm of Night.
To Amor's sweet sorcery
     Orcus submits.

Friendly looks the black King,
When Ceres' daughter smiles on him.
Love lightens the Realm of Night.

Heavenly in Hell resound,
And constrain the wild Guard
   Thy songs, O Thracian!
Minos, in his visage tears,
The torment-sentence mitigates.

Fondly round Megæra's cheeks
The wild snakes kissed themselves;
No longer lashed the scourge;
Hunted up by Orpheus' lyre,
The vulture fled from Tityus;
Softer here upon the shore
Rushed Lethe and Cocytus.
They listened to thy lays, O Thracian!
Love thou sangest, Thracian.

    *   *   *   *

    Happy through Love
    The Gods—through Love
      Men are like Gods.
    Love makes Heaven
    More heavenly—the Earth
    Like unto Heaven.

    *   *   *   *

Through eternal Nature
Scents her flower-trace,
Waves her golden wing.
Beamed on me from the moonlight not
The eye of Aphrodite?
Not from the sunny hill?
Smiled not from the sea of stars
The Goddess on me here?
Star, and sun, and moonlight
Moved not my soul.
Love, Love only smiles
Out of the eye of Nature,
As out of a mirror.

Love murmurs the silver brook;
Love teaches it a softer flow.
Soul breathes she in the woe
Of plaining nightingales—
   Love, Love only lisps out
    The lute of Nature.

Wisdom with the sun glance,
Great Goddess, treads back,
    Gives way to Love.
Never to Conqueror, or Prince
Bendedst thou the knee, a slave!
    Bend it now to Love.

Who up the steep star-path
Before thee went heroically
      To the seats of Godhead?
Who rent the Holy Place,
Shewed thee Elysium
Through the chinks of the grave?
Called *she* not us hither
That we might be *immortal?*
Seek even the Spirits
A master without her?
    Love, Love only leads
    To the Father of Nature,
    Love only to the Spirits.

        Happy through Love
        The Gods—through Love
          Men are like Gods.
        Love makes Heaven
        More heavenly—the Earth
          Like unto Heaven.

                                    T. C. P.

ART. XXXIV.—THE SECT SYSTEM.

*History of all the Religious Denominations in the United
    States: containing authentic accounts of the rise, progress,
    faith and practice, localities and statistics, of the different
    persuasions: written expressly for the work, by fifty-three emi-
    nent authors belonging to the respective denominations. Sec-
    ond Improved and Portrait Edition.* Harrisburg, Pa: Pub-
    lished by John Winebrenner, V. D. M. 1848. 8vo. pp. 598.

THE idea of this work is ingenious. Our ordinary Histories of Religions, it is well known, besides being in general seriously defective in other respects, have never been able to satisfy completely the different sects of which they give an account. However impartial the compiler may have supposed himself to be, he had his own standpoint, as the Germans say, which affected more or less all his observations, his own theological spectacles that gave both shape and color somewhat to every object which came within the range of his vision. How could a rigid Calvinist do justice to a body of Arminians, or be content to sit for his own picture under the hands of a limner belonging to any such blear-eyed tribe? How could an Episcopalian be expected to speak of Presbyterianism with becoming reverence and respect; or how could a Presbyterian be trusted to set forth, without distorting prejudice or passion, the claims and doings of Episcopacy? Even Buck's Theological Dictionary, with all its popularity, was found to be greatly defective in this view; while the rapid march of sectarianism, besides, especially on this side of the Atlantic, called loudly for additions and improvements, which it became always more difficult and delicate to make with due satisfaction to the parties concerned. In these circumstances, it occurred to our worthy and respected friend, *I. D. Rupp*, Esq., of Lancaster, Penna., to project and publish an entirely new work in this line, in which every denomination, instead of taking its picture from abroad, should be permitted to paint itself according to its own pleasure and liking; the whole to be constructed, as the almanac-makers say, for the horizon of the United States, as distinguished from that of all the world besides. "A work thus prepared," it was supposed, "must be entirely free from the faults of misrepresentation, so generally brought against books of this character." The thought was certainly felicitous, so far as that particular desideratum went; it met approbation and favor on all sides; the requisite number of pens, each pledged to do honor to its own sect, were soon set in motion; and in the course of two years, April, 1844, the *He Pasa Ecclesia*, as it was called, or Church Universal, made its appearance, with all befitting order and solemnity, in the literary world. Its success was such as to do full credit to the originality and ingenuity of its plan. Each sect was content to let all others glorify themselves, while it was allowed the privilege of glorifying itself before the public in the same way.   None found occasion to quarrel with a mirror, which so faithfully gave them back their own image according to their own mind.   The book became thus the joint product and property of the sects represented in it, and gained, at the same time, a clear passport to circulate among them indiscriminately as it best could.   This circulation proved to be both large and profitable, which is a great object, we all know, in every enterprise of this sort. A very considerable part of the first heavy edition, as we are informed, made its way to England.   As a business interest, at all events, the importance of the work is fully established.   We have it, accordingly, stereotyped now, and done up in holiday style, as a second improved edition, under the auspices of Mr. Winebrenner, V. D. M., (by interpretation, *Minister of the Word of God*); who himself figures conspicuously in the book, both as the founder and historiographer of one of its sects, (one among the "fifty-three eminent authors" mentioned on its title-page,) with the honor of a portrait to signalize such double distinction. How the work got into his hands, and out of the hands of its original projector and proprietor, we are unable to say.   We know only that Mr. Rupp has felt himself in some way wronged in the case, and that he proposed, not long since, to re-occupy the field with another publication, on the same general plan, but of more complete and thorough execution.   The list of sects, which stood as before given, between forty and fifty, was to be considerably enlarged; to do full justice to the fruitful history of our country, the new work was to contain "authentic accounts of upwards of *seventy* religious denominations," that have belonged to it thus far.   This design, we presume, has fallen to the ground; the other enterprise being too fully master of the field, to allow under any similar form, a safe and successful competition.   So this "History of Denominations," as it now stands, with Mr. Rupp's name extinguished and Mr. Winebrenner's made to flourish in its stead, would seem to be fairly seated upon the saddle as a sort of popular text book and standard for reference, in the department it pretends to fill.   It is in the way of being most extensively disseminated.   Agents are called for in every part of

the United States, to promote its sale. Printed on good paper,
"embellished with 24 splendid portraits," handsomely bound
"with gilt backs and embossed sides," it is retailed at the rate of
$2 50 per copy, allowing, no doubt, a fair profit all round to those
who take the trouble of placing it thus widely in the hands of
the public.

We are willing to acknowledge, that we made very small account of this book when it first came in our way. It was not to
be imagined, of course, that a work got up in such *omnibus* style
could be trusted at all, as a faithful and competent survey of the
general field it proposed to represent. However unsatisfactory a
history of sects might be, from the standpoint of any one of them
affecting to be the centre, the case was not likely to be materially
improved by allowing every sect to play in turn the same central
part in its own favor. Such a course might, indeed, promote
the popularity of the work, by enabling it to tickle the vanity of
all parties; but it could not insure at all its truthfulness as to any
part, nor its scientific worth as a whole. The idea of a history
requires it to be as much as possible objective, and independent
of all personal references and interests; whereas, in this case, full
rein was given to the principle of subjectivity, to shape and fashion everything, at each turn of the kaleidoscope, according to its
own accidental pleasure. The original editor, accordingly, seems
not to have expected a true and complete history of sects in this
way, but only a more successful *approximation* to something of
the sort than had been reached on the old plan. It is admitted
that each writer "may have been influenced by a bias, natural
to many, to present the *beauties of his own faith* in glowing
colors;" but for all this due allowance must be made by the intelligent; and out of the data, here outwardly brought together,
the unprejudiced reader, it is hoped, may have it in his power to
draw his own conclusions, as to the whole, in some safe and sufficient way. This has some force. It goes, however, to confirm
what we have just said of the worthlessness of any such literary
salmagundi, viewed as a veritable History of religious Denominations; and it was in this view that we were disposed to look
upon it in the beginning, as now said, with rather more contempt
than heartfelt respect. We had no ambition to have it in our

library; and, to speak the plain truth, when called upon by a strenuous agent, not long since, who insisted on making us buy a copy of this second improved edition, with pictures, gilt backs and embossed sides, we took it finally, more to get rid of the application, (the book is reasonably cheap,) than for the sake of any comfort or satisfaction we expected to find in its ownership.

But we were wrong. That first judgment was quite too hasty and sweeping; and we have been brought to entertain since, a much more favorable feeling towards the work thus forced into our hands. Allowing it to be as valueless as now represented, for the purposes of a scientific text-book, or dictionary, of the widely extended sphere it proposes to fill, are there not other sides and aspects under which it may still deserve to challenge our careful regard; and this too, in the most close connection, indirectly, at least, with the highest interests of religion and science? We had no right to take it for a veritable and proper History of Sects, in the true sense of any such title; and then to hold it responsible for flaws and defects, offences and shortcomings, that might be found to attach to it under this high view. In the nature of the case, it could be no such history. How could the "fifty three *eminent* authors belonging to the respective denominations," described in it, (Mr. Winebrenner himself, Shem Zook, Joe Smith, and others,) be expected all to conspire in any such idea and scheme, as would be necessary to impart to it the philosophical unity, rotundity and wholeness, which a complete work of this sort must be felt to require? But aside from any such high character as this, there are other very important uses plainly enough to be derived from a work so constructed, which should be taken, in truth, as its proper end and meaning, and on the ground of which it has a full right to circulate at large in the republic of letters. These uses have come to seem so considerable in our eyes, the claims of the book to our respect, on this ground, have so diverted our attention from the wrong relations in which we were disposed to look at in the beginning, that we may be in danger now, possibly, of being carried too far, by natural reaction, in our estimate of its merits. Our prejudice is fairly converted into a sort of fond partiality. We positively like the book, and would not consent to part with it easily. Though no

History of Religious Denominations, exactly, in the sense of an Ullmann or a Neander, it is, in its own way, a most interesting and valuable Commentary on the Sect System, which both Ullmann and Neander would read, no doubt, with no small amount of instruction and profit. In this view, the conception of the work is such as to do credit to the mind from which it sprang. It was well, aside from all bibliopolistical ends, to give this moral Babel an opportunity of speaking for itself; and now that it has thus spoken, it is well to lend an ear to the cataract of discordant sounds that is poured forth from its tongue. There is much to be learned from it for a seriously thoughtful mind; something directly; and a good deal more in the way of suggestion and silent circuitous meditation. What a world of pensive reflection is furnished by Catlin's Indian museum? This exhibition of American sects is not quite as complete; but as each tribe paints *itself*, the whole gallery of portraits wins, in the same general view, a monumental interest which it could not well have in any other way, and is likely to be gazed upon with curious admiration hereafter, when the sects themselves, in most cases, (it is to be trusted,) shall have passed away, with the Pottawottamies, into mere memory and song.

It was a happy thought, to add in this second edition the twenty four lithographed pictures of "distinguished men in the different denominations." This is a decided improvement, worth itself almost the price of the book; for the pictures are good in their kind, and may be taken we believe, as very fair and truthful images of the men they represent. They have in this way a double value; they make the book *pictorial*, which is a great point nowadays in the art of popular literature; and, they serve to shed, at the same time, a true *historical* light on its contents, which is not the case with the "splendid illustrations" that enter commonly into the texture of these pictorial publications. We have no taste, we confess, for such fancy prigments, redolent of trade far more than of divine art; however well suited they may be to capture the eye of children, young or old. The "Pictorial Bible" especially we hold in absolute dislike as something worse than a money-making humbug, and would not be willing to make use of it even if it were given to us in the way of a free

present. But the case is very different, where pictures exhibit
to us the actual forms of history itself, and bring us thus into
contact with its true original spirit and life. In the case before
us particularly, a good likeness may be of itself a window to let
in light on a whole world of facts, which finds its significance
mainly in the man whose personality is thus presented to our
view. The face of a sect hero, in some instances, may be of
itself a key, to unlock the interior sense of the sect. At all events,
after reading the account of a new religious movement in this
form, we like to have it in our power to turn to the picture of its
leading representative, whether living or dead; we seem to catch,
by means of it, a more vivid impression of the history; the face
of the man becomes a type, to explain and illustrate the genius
of the denomination. Altogether then we are pleased with these
portraits. They have already fixed themselves in our mind,
and we frequently revert to them, in the view now mentioned,
as subjects for profitable contemplation. With some of them,
we were familiar before; but the greater part of them have been
introduced to us, for the first time, by this book. Here is the
smooth quiet face of Pope Pius IX., well worthy of being considered in connection with the outward troubles of his pontificate.
Here are the well known images of Luther and Zuingli, and
Calvin, all strikingly significant of the high and solemn mission
they came to fulfil, in the work of the Reformation. Here are
Menno Simon, and Emanuel Swedenborg, and Count Zinzen-
dorf, and George Fox, (a rich face to study,) and the Rev. John
Wesley. Then we have a number of more modern heads; of
American growth; some of which happily " remain unto this
present," though others are fallen asleep. Interesting among
these are the portraits of the Rev. Richard Allen, " Bishop of the
First African M. E. Church of the U. S.," (Bethelites,) and the
Rev. Christopher Rush, who represents another African M. E.
Church of like independent organization. Elias Hicks again is
a face to study — a psychological gem, worthy to stand close by
the side of the original founder of Quakerism. You seem to
read there the very sense of his system, the inward light run out
into the most outward rationalism, the flesh ironically parading
its own powers and pretensions as the highest law of the spirit.

We love also to gaze upon the features of Jacob Albright. The
man's face is a voucher in full for the simple honesty of his character. It is serious, humble, and wholly without guile. We
doubt not his well-meaning zeal. But, alas, what a countenance
for a Moses of God's Israel, as compared with the face of Luther!
David Marks, the Free Will Baptist, and William Miller, of *Mil-
lerite* fame, are also worth inspection. Last, though of course
not least, deserves to be mentioned the full bust, and particularly
speaking face of John Winebrenner, V. D. M., the present
publisher of this book himself; to whom we are indebted for the
idea of these " splendid portraits of distinguished men," and who
has the honor besides, as we here learn, of being the originator
of a sect styling itself the " Church of God," (about the year
1825,) one of the heroes thus of his own book; to say nothing
of the distinction which belongs to him as the historiographer
of his sect, one of the " fifty-three eminent authors," as before
noticed, to whose united paternity the book before us refers itself
on the title page. Mr. Winebrenner's portrait may be said to
go beyond all the rest, in a certain self-consciousness of its own
historical significance and interest. It has an attitude, studied for
dramatic effect; an air of independence; an open Bible in the
hands; in token, we presume, that Winebrennerism makes more
of this blessed volume than any other sect, and that it was never
much understood till Mr. Winebrenner was raised up at Harrisburg, in these last days, to set all right, and give the " Church of
God" a fresh start, by means of it, out of his own mind.

This professed regard for the Bible, however, is by no means
peculiar to Mr. Winebrenner. It distinguishes the sects in general; and just here is one important lesson offered for contemplation, by the pages of this work. The Adventists or Millerites
(p. 41,) own " no other creed or form of discipline than the written word of God, which they believe is a sufficient rule both of
faith and duty." The Baptists, (p. 49,) " adhere rigidly to the
New Testament as the sole standard of Christianity," and take
the Holy Scripture for " the only sufficient, certain and infallible
rule of saving knowledge, faith and obedience, the supreme
judge by which all controversies of religion are to be determined,
&c." So the Freewill Baptists, p. 78; the Free Communion

Baptists, p. 85; the Old School Baptists, (p. 87,) who oppose "modern missionism and its kindred institutions" as unscriptural; the Six Principle Baptists, p. 90; the German Baptists, p. 92; the Seventh Day Baptists, "who have no authentic records by which they can ascertain their origin other than the New Testament," p. 95, and who tell us that the church can never contend successfully "with catholicism, even in our own country," till the lesson is fairly learned, that the "Bible *alone* is the religion of Protestants," p. 103; the German Seventh Day Baptists, who (p. 110,) "do not admit the least license with the letter and spirit of the Scriptures, and especially of the New Testament—do not allow one jot or tittle to be added or rejected in the administration of the ordinances, but practice them precisely as they are instituted and made an example by Jesus Christ in his word." The Sect of the Bible Christians, as their name imports, "believe it to be the duty of every one, in matters of faith, (p. 124,) to turn from the erring notions, and raise traditions that are to be found in most of the denominations of professing Christians, and to draw their principles directly from the bible" The "Christians," constituted about the beginning of this century by the confluence of three different streams of independency, reject all party names to follow Christ, take the Bible for their guide, (p. 166,) and carry the principle of shaping their faith by it so far, that a doctrine which cannot be expressed in the language of inspiration they do not hold themselves obligated to believe;" and a strange *system*, it must be allowed, they make of it in their way. The "Church of God," as called into being by Mr. Winebrenner, (p. 176,) "has no authoritative constitution, ritual creed, catechism, book of discipline or church standard, but the Bible"—with a short manifesto or declaration simply, showing what the Bible, according to Mr. Winebrenner's mind, must be taken clearly to mean. The Congregationalists, of course, appeal to the Scriptures (p. 281,) "as their only guide in all matters both of faith and polity;" though they do but speak in the name of all the sects, when they say, somewhat curiously in such company, speaking of creeds and confessions: "By the Bible they are to be measured, and no doctrine which cannot be found in it is to be received, however endeared to us by its asso-

ciations, or venerable by its antiquity. This strict adherence to
the Scriptures, as the only rule of faith and practice, must necessarily prevent many of those erroneous opinions, and that credulous reliance upon tradition, which are too apt to characterize
those who follow the Bible only at second hand." In the enterprise of Alexander Campbell to reconstruct the church, a. 1810,
which has given rise to the Disciples of Christ, (or Campbellite
Baptists,) it was laid down as a fundamental maxim, (p. 224,)
" that the revelations of God should be made to displace from their
position all human creeds, confessions of faith, and formalities of
doctrine and church government, as being not only unnecessary,
but really a means of perpetuating division." The Albright
Sect, a. 1803, "unanimously chose the sacred Scriptures for their
guide in faith and action, (p. 275,) and formed their church discipline accordingly, as any one may see who will take the pains
to investigate and examine the same." So in other cases. However they may differ among themselves in regard to what it teaches,
sects all agree in proclaiming the Bible the only guide of their
faith ; and the more sectarian they are, as a general thing, the
more loud and strong do they show themselves in reiterating this
profession.

All this is instructive. It sounds well, to lay so much stress
on the authority of the Bible, as the only text-book and guide
of Christianity. But what are we to think of it, when we find
such a motley mass of protesting systems, all laying claim so vig-
orously here to one and the same watchword? If the Bible be
at once so clear and full as a formulary of Christian doctrine and
practice, how does it come to pass that where men are left most
free to use it in this way, and have the greatest mind to do so,
according to their own profession, they are flung asunder so perpetually in their religious faith, instead of being brought together,
by its influence apparently, and, at all events, certainly in its
name? It will not do to reply, in the case, that the differences
which divide the parties are small, while the things in which they
agree are great, and such as to show a general unity after all in
the main substance of the Christian life. Differences that lead
to the breaking of church communion, and that bind men's consciences to go into sects, can never be small for the actual life of

Christianity, however insignificant they may be in their own nature. Will it be pretended, that the Bible is friendly to sects; that it is designed and adapted to bring them to pass; that they constitute, in short, the normal and healthy condition of Christ's Church? It is especially worthy of notice, that one great object proposed by all sects, in betaking themselves, as they say, to the exclusive authority of the Scriptures, is to get clear of human dogmas and opinions, and so come the more certainly to one faith and one baptism. They acknowledge the obligation of such unity, and just for this reason call upon the Christian world to come with them to the pure fountain of God's word, as having, no doubt, that it is to be secured in this way. Winebrennerism, Campbellism, Christianism. &c., are all based, (we doubt not, honestly,) on a design to "restore the original unity of the Church;" and for the accomplishment of this object, they hold it, most of all, necessary, "that the Bible alone should be taken as the authorized bond of union and the infallible rule of faith and practice," to the full exclusion of every creed or formulary besides. This however, as we have seen, is just what all our sects are eternally admitting and proclaiming as their own principle. There is not one of them, that is not disposed to take the lead, according to its own fancy, in such wholesome submission to the Holy Scriptures; and the great quarrel of each with all the rest is just this, that they are not willing like itself, to sacrifice to this rule all rules and tradition besides. How does it happen then that the sect distraction has not been prevented or healed by this method, but is found to extend itself perpetually in proportion to its free and untrammelled use? When Congregationalism tells us, (p. 201,) that its principle of strict adhesion to the Bible, in the sense now noticed, serves to shut out divisions, it tells us what is palpably contradicted by the whole history of the sect system from beginning to end. However plausible it may be in theory, to magnify in such style the unbound use solely of the Bible for the adjustment of Christian faith and practice, the simple truth is, that the operation of it in fact is, not to unite the church into one, but to divide it always more and more into sects. The thing is too plain to admit any sort of dispute. The work before us is a commentary in proof of it throughout. Clearly, then, the prin-

ciple in question requires some qualification.   No one can intelligently study this book of sects, without finding occasion in it to distrust the soundness in full of a maxim, which all sects proclaim,
with equal apparent sincerity, as lying at the foundation of their
theology, and which is so plainly at the same time the main prop
and pillar of their conflicting systems.   We must either admit
a limitation in some form to the principle, *No creed but the Bible*, or else make up our minds at once to the hard requirement
of accepting this array of sects as the true and legitimate form of
the Christian life, equally entitled to respect and confidence in all
its parts.

The full misery of the case becomes more evident, when we
connect with it the idea of *private judgment*, in the full sense, as
the necessary accompaniment and complement of the exclusive
authority thus attributed to the Scriptures.   This, we may say,
is always involved in the maxim, under its usual sectarian form ;
since the admission of any controlling influence whatever from
beyond the individual mind, must serve of itself materially to
qualify the maxim, changing it indeed into quite a new sense.   It
is easy enough to see, accordingly, throughout this book, that the
supreme authority of the Bible, as it is made to underlie professedly the religion of all sects, is tacitly, if not openly, conditioned
always by the assumption that every man is authorized and bound
to get at this authority in a direct way for himself, through the
medium simply of his own single mind.   We have a somewhat
rampant enunciation of the whole maxim, on page 512, in behalf of the Cumberland Presbyterians, in which, no doubt, however, the sects generally would without any hesitation concur.
" The supremacy of the Holy Scriptures," it is there said, " and
the right of private judgment, have long been the great governing
principle of all evangelical Christians.   These abandoned, and
there is no excess, extravagance, or superstition, too monstrous
for adoption.   The Bible must be the supreme rule of faith and
practice, or else it will be converted into fables and genealogies,
unless we grant to the many the privilege of thinking for themselves, we must grant to the few, or one, the power of infallibility."   An open Bible and private judgment, the only help
against excess, extravagance and superstition, in the name of re-

ligion! So say the Cumberland Presbyterians. So say the Baptists, through all the tribes of all their variegated Israel, from Maine to California. So the followers of Winebrenner, the Albright Brethren, and, in one word, every wild sect in the land. And why then are they not joined together as one? Why is Winebrenner's "Church of God" a different communion from Campbell's "Disciples of Christ;" and why are not both merged in the broad fellowship of the "Christians," as the proper ocean or universe of one and the same Bible faith? Theory and fact here, do not move, by any means, in the same line. The theory, however, still requires, in these circumstances, that the fact, such as it is, should be acknowledged to be right and good. Private judgment in religion is a sacred thing, which we are not at liberty to limit or restrain in any direction, but are bound to honor as the great palladium of piety, in every shape it may happen to assume. The Congregationalist, then, has no right to quarrel with the results to which it conducts the honest Baptist; and the honest Baptist again has just as little right to find fault with the use made of it, by the Albright Brethren, or the African sect of the Bethelites. This principle of private judgment, the hobby of all sects, places all plainly on the same level, and unless men choose to play fast and loose with their own word, opens the door indefinitely for the lawful introduction of as many more, as religious ingenuity or stupidity may have power to invent.

The principle, in truth, is absurd and impracticable, and such as always necessarily overthrows itself. We find, accordingly, that the glorification of it in the sect world, is very soon resolved into mere smoke. Just here we encounter first, on a broad scale, the spirit of hypocrisy and sham, which enters so extensively into the whole constitution of sectarian christianity. Every sect is ready to magnify the freedom of the individual judgment and the right of all men to read and interpret the Bible for themselves; and yet there is not one among them, that allows in reality anything of the sort. It is amusing to glance through the pages of this auto-biography of Religious Denominations, and notice the easy simplicity with which so many of them lay down the broad maxim of liberty and toleration to start with, and then at once go on to limit and circumscribe it by the rule of their own narrow horizon ; proving themselves generally, to be at once unfree and illiberal, in proportion precisely to the noise they make about their freedom.   The " Church of God," according to her V. D. M., at Harrisburg, has no constitution, ritual creed, catechism, book of discipline, or church standard, but the Bible.   This she believes to be the only creed or text book, which God ever intended her to have.   " *Nevertheless*, it may not be inexpedient," we are told (p. 176,) " *pro bono publico*, to exhibit a short manifesto, or declaration, showing her views, as to what may be called leading matters of faith, experience and practice ;" and so we have a regular confession of 27 articles, (p. 176–181,) all ostensibly supported by proof from the Bible as understood by Mr. Winebrenner, fencing in thus her " scriptural and apostolical" communion, and of course fencing out all who, in the exercise of their private judgment, may be so unfortunate as not to see things in precisely the same way.   This is only a specimen of the inconsistency and contradiction which characterize sects in general. Their common watchword is : The Bible and Private Judgment ! But in no case do they show themselves true to its demands. It is always, on their lips, an outrageous lie, of which all good men should feel themselves ashamed.   What sect in reality, allows the Bible and Private Judgment to rule its faith ?   Is it not notorious that every one of them has a scheme of notions already at hand, a certain system of opinion and practice, which is made to underlie all this boasted freedom in the use of the Bible, leading private judgment along by the nose, and forcing the divine text always to speak in its own way ?   It is of no account, as to the point here in hand, that sects agree to tolerate one another politically ; the want of religious toleration is enough of itself to falsify their pretended maxim of following simply the Bible and private judgment.   It shows plainly that this maxim is *not*, at least, the measure of their religious life, but that some other rule is required to keep it to its particular form and shape.

But there is a vast chasm also, in the political or outward toleration itself, as it may be called, to which the sect system affects in general to be so favorable.   It is full of zeal, apparently for human freedom in every shape, the rights of man, liberty of conscience, and the privilege of every man to worship God in his own way.   The Independents claim the merit of opening, in regard to all these great interests, a new era in the history of the human race; but they had no toleration originally, for the Quakers and Baptists; and both these bodies, accordingly, carry away the palm from them on this ground, as having by their patient testimony done far more signal service to the cause of religious freedom. Roger Williams is taken by his sect to be the father emphatically of our American Independence (p. 57,); and it is of the first Baptists in particular, we are told, that these words of Hume in favor of the Puritans stand good: "By these alone the precious spark of liberty was kindled, and to these America owes the whole freedom of her constitution." But, alas, the regular Baptists, themselves have been found continually prone to assert, in one shape or another, the old tyranny over conscience; on which account it has been necessary for one new sect after the other to take a fresh start in the race of independence, so that one is left quite at a loss in the end to know, to which of all the number, the modern world should consider itself most deeply indebted for its full democratic emancipation in the affairs of religion. In Rhode Island itself, under the free charter of Roger Williams, the Seventh Day Baptists, (p. 97,) had to endure much for the right of differing from their more othodox neighbors; " a hostile spirit was soon raised against the little band and laws were enacted severe and criminal in their nature ; John Rogers, a member of the church, was sentenced to sit a certain time upon a gallows with a rope about his neck, to which he submitted." So the German Seventh Day sect in Pennsylvania, protests loudly against all legislation, that would force it in any way to keep a different sabbath than its own, and claims the honor of standing with this question, in the very Thermopylæ of American freedom. "The great principle, we are told, (p. 122,) for which the Seventh Day People are contending—*unfettered religious liberty*—is alike dear to all the churches of the land; it belongs equally to all denominations, however large or however small." The "Christians" sprang from the same idea of independence. One portion of them styled themselves at first characteristically "Republican Methodists," p. 165 ; another grew out of " a peculiar travel of mind in relation to sectarian names and human creeds," on the part of one Dr. Abner Jones, a Baptist of Vermont; a third broke away from the Presbyterian Synod of Kentucky, at the time of the great revival, to escape "the scourge of a human creed." As a general thing, sects are loud for liberty, in the more outward sense, and seem to be raised up in their own imagination for the express purpose of asserting in some new way what they call liberty of conscience. But all history shows that they are bold for this liberty only in their own favor, and not at all in favor of others. It is not enough in their case that they acquiesce in the independence of other sects as already established; their maxim of private judgment, if they were honest, should lead them to throw no obstruction whatever in the way of new sects, starting out of their own bosom. Even if they might not feel bound to retain such divergent tendencies in their communion, they ought, at least, to recognize the perfect right they have to make their appearance, as legitimately flowing from the proper life of Christianity, and instead of laying a straw in their way, should assist them rather to develope their force, and stand out as new phases of religion in the general sect system to which they belong. Nothing short of this deserves to be considered true toleration, on the ground professedly occupied by private judgment sects. Where, however, do we meet with any such sect, whose practice is governed by any such rule?

The truth is, as any one may see who has any familiarity at all with the character and history of sects, that no more unpropitious atmosphere for liberty and independence can well be conceived, than that which they everywhere tend to create. Those precisely which make the greatest boast of their liberty, are as a general thing, the least prepared either to exercise it themselves or to allow its exercise in others. The sect habit, as such, is constitutionally unfree. All true emancipation in religion begins only where the power of this habit has begun to be broken, and the sense of a true catholic Christianity is brought to reign in its place. Each sect has its tradition; in most cases, a very poor and narrow tradition; the fruit of accident or caprice in the history of its founder, conditioned more or less by the outward relations in which he was called to his apostolic mission; a certain scheme of notions and words, passing over always more and more to the character of dead mechanical gibberish and cant; to whose authority all are required to swear, within its communion, and whose little circle or ring none may transgress without losing cast. Take, for instance, the small community of the Albright Brethren. Is it not just as much bound in this respect, full as servile and full as intolerant, to say the least, as the Church of Rome? Is it not, in its way and measure, a papacy, a would-be ecclesiastical domination, which seeks as far as possible to nullify and kill all independent thought and all free life? It is full indeed of professed zeal for Protestant liberty, free inquiry, an open Bible, universal toleration, the right of all men to think for themselves, and all such high-sounding phrases; but we must be simple enough, if we can be led for a moment to take such professions for anything *more* than so much sound. The liberty of the sect consists at last, in thinking its particular notions, shouting its shibboleths and passwords, dancing its religious hornpipes, and reading the Bible only through its theological goggles. These restrictions, at the same time, are so many wires, that lead back at last into the hands of a few leading spirits, enabling them to wield a true hierarchical despotism over all who are thus brought within their power. All tends to crush thought, and turn the solemn business of religion into a sham. True spiritual independence must ever be an object of jealousy in such a communion, as much so fully as in any popish convent. Let a generous minded man begin really to think for himself, by rising above the life of the mere sect, and it matters not how much he may have of the Spirit of Christ, or how truly he may reverence God's word, he will fall into suspicion and condemnation; and if true to himself, must find it necessary in the end to quit the association altogether, the victim of reproach and persecution, for those very rights of conscience, whose special guardianship the little brotherhood has been affecting to take almost exclusively into its own hands. This is only an instance, to exemplify a general fact. All sects, in proportion as they deserve the name, are narrow, bigoted and intolerant. They know not what liberty means. They put out men's eyes, gag their mouths, and manacle their hands and feet. They are intrinsically, constitutionally, incurably popish, enslaved by tradition and prone to persecution. The worst of all schools for the formation of a true manly character, is the communion of such a sect. The influence of sects is always illiberal; and it should be counted in this view a great moral calamity, in the case of all young persons, especially, to be thrown upon it, in any way, for educational training.

The book before us illustrates instructively the *unhistorical* character of the sect system. The independence which it affects, in pretending to reduce all Christianity to private judgment and the Bible, involves, of necessity, a protest against the authority of all previous history, except so far as it may seem to agree with what is thus found to be true; in which case, of course, the only real measure of truth is taken to be, not this authority of history at all, but the mind, simply, of the particular sect itself. The idea of anything like a divine substance in the life of Christianity, through past ages, which may be expected of right to pass forward into the constitution of Christianity as it now stands, is one that finds no room whatever in this system. A genuine sect will not suffer itself to be embarrassed for a moment, either at its start or afterwards, by the consideration that it has no proper root in past history. Its ambition is rather to appear in this respect *autochthonic*, aboriginal, self-sprung from the Bible, or through the Bible from the skies. "A Six Principle Baptist," we are told, p. 88, "who understands the true principles of his profession, does not esteem it necessary to have his tenets through the several ages of the church. He is fully persuaded, however early or generally other opinions may have prevailed, that those principles which distinguish him from other professions of Christianity, are clearly taught and enjoined by the great head of the Church, in the grand commission to his apostles." This language suits all sects. If the past be with them, here and there, it is all very well; but if not, it can only be, of course, because they are right, and the universal past wrong; for they follow (multifariously) the Bible, which is the only infallible rule of faith and practice. The Baptists glory in having no succession before the Reformation, except by occasional gleams and flashes athwart the darkness of the middle ages, here and there, in out-of-the-way crevices and corners, produced by sects and fragments of sects, of whom almost nothing is known, and concerning whom,

accordingly, all things may be the more easily *guessed*. But
what of that? Every congregation has power to originate a new
christianity for its own use, and so may well afford to let that of
all other ages pass for a grand apostacy, if need be, to keep itself
in countenance. In the same spirit, one Baptist sect is continually rising after another, and setting in motion a new church,
without the least regard to the " want of fellowship" proclaimed
against it by the body it leaves behind. " It makes no difference
to me who disowns me," cries Mr. Randall, in the face of such
an exclusion, p. 75, " so long as I know that the Lord owns me;
and now let that God be God who answers by fire, and that people be God's people, whom he owneth and blesseth." This, in
his own words, " is the beginning of the now large and extensive
connection called *Freewill Baptists.*" Hear another tribe:
" Every denomination (p. 95,) is proud of tracing its origin back
to its founder. But not so with the Seventh Day Baptists.
They have no authentic records by which they can ascertain
their origin, other than the New Testament." Hear again the
" Christians," self-started in Kentucky, A. D. 1803. " As they
had taken the Scriptures for their guide, pedobaptism was renounced, and believers baptism by immersion substituted in its
room. On a certain occasion, one minister baptized another minister, and then he who had been baptized, immersed the others."
So Roger Williams himself, (p. 57,) the father of American Ana-
baptism, " in March, 1639, was baptized by one of his brethren
and then he baptized about ten more." Jacob Albright, of course,
had quite as much right to originate a new ministry, (p. 275,) in
the same way; which, however, is very much like a man pretending to lift himself up from the ground by his own breeches
or boot-straps. So throughout. The idea of a historical continuity in the life of the Church, carries with it no weight whatever
for the sect consciousness. It is felt to be as easy to start a new
Church, as it is to get up a new moral or political association
under any other name.

This turns, of course, at bottom, on a want of all true and steady
faith in the Church itself as such. The Church is declared in
the Creed to be an object of faith, a necessary part of Christianity. As such it is a divine supernatural fact, a concrete reality,

an actual objective power in the world, which men have no ability whatever to make or unmake at their own pleasure. In this form it defines itself to be one, holy, catholic and apostolical. To be apprehended at all as it is, it must be apprehended under these attributes, as the inseparable adjuncts of the fact which faith is here brought to embrace. To conceive of the Church as an institution *not* holy, not formed for holiness and not requiring it, would be at once to give up its existence altogether as affirmed in the Creed. And just so it must lose its true power for faith, if it be conceived of as *not* one and universal and historical, not formed for all this, and not demanding it throughout as an indispensable part of its idea. Only where such a sense of the Church prevails, can the danger and guilt of schism be felt at all, or any hindrance be raised at all to the easy multiplication of sects. In its very constitution, accordingly, the sect spirit is an unchurchly spirit. It turns the Church into a phantom; values it at best only as an abstraction; transforms the whole high and awful mystery into the creature of its own brain. The book before us is full of evidence and illustration, in regard to this point. Sect Christianity is not the Christianity of the Creed, or at best it is this Christianity under a most mutilated form. Of this proof enough is found in the fact that wherever the sect spirit prevails the Creed falls into disuse. It may be still spoken of respectfully perhaps when spoken of at all; but what sect repeats it, or recognises in it the mirror of its own consciousness? The Creed has become almost universally a dead letter, in the religion of sects. There are, no doubt, thousands of so called evangelical ministers in our country at this time, to say nothing of their congregations, who could not even repeat it correctly, were they called on suddenly to do so, as a test of their Christian knowledge.

As thus unchurchly, the sect system tends to destroy all faith in the holy sacraments. No one can well fail to be struck with this, in studying its own account of itself in this History of Religious Denominations. Our view of the sacraments is always conditioned by our sense of the mystery comprehended in the idea of the Church, and forms thus, of course, at the same time, a simple, but sure, touchstone of our faith in the Church itself. The idea of divine sacraments, mystically exhibiting the supernatural realities they represent as things actually at hand, and the idea of a divine Church as proclaimed in the Creed, go hand in hand together.   The sect mind, therefore, in proportion as it has come to be unchurchly and simply private and individual, is always necessarily to the same extent unsacramental.   The forms of the sacraments may be retained, but the true inward meaning of them is more or less lost.   One broad and most instructive evidence of this, is found in the fact that the sect spirit left to itself, invariably runs towards the baptistic theory; which proceeds throughout on the assumption, that the sacraments carry in their constitution no objective mystical force whatever.   It is not by accident, merely, that almost every new sect that rises, is led, sooner or later, to reject infant baptism; the sect principle flows legitimately to this result, and it can never, indeed, stop short of it without inconsistency and contradiction.   The Baptists take Christian baptism to be a sign only (p. 46) of Christian profession, which has no significance except as it is preceded by the grace it represents, as something previously at hand in the person who receives it; in which view, naturally enough, they contend that it can never be applied, with propriety, to unconscious infants. The Lord's supper, of course, (p. 52,) is only another sign of the same sort.   This is plausible; falls in with common sense; and we are not surprised to hear, accordingly, that where mixed communion prevails in some parts of England, (p. 67,) " the sentiments and practice of the Baptists are so far introduced among the members of pædobaptist churches, that comparatively few of their pastors can say very much against the Baptists."   The thing doth eat like a cancer; sending its roots oftentimes far in advance of its open presence, where the true substance of sacramental faith is gone and only the form of it left in its room.   Mr. Winebrenner makes the " Church of God" believe in " three positive ordinances of perpetual standing"—sacraments have a wonderful tendency to rationalize themselves into mere *ordinances* in the sect vocabulary—" viz : *Baptism, Feet washing,* and the *Lord's supper*" (p. 178).   All for believers only, and not for children. We find a much better triplicity of Protestant sacraments, if we *must* have three, in the creed of the African Methodists, (p. 403,) where they are made to be, " the Lord's supper, Baptism, and

Holy Matrimony"—the last left without any farther definition. Campbellism started in pædobaptist connections, on the broad basis of the Bible and justification solely by Christ's merits, not meaning to add a new sect to those already existing, (p. 225,) but hoping rather to put an end to sects. In due time, however, the baptistic question came in its way. Thomas Campbell, father of Alexander, undertook to preach it right, according to his old Scotch Seceder faith; but the Bible and private judgment proved too strong, to be ruled down in such style. His discussion "convinced a number of his hearers, (p. 226,) that the practice of infant baptism could not be sustained by adequate scripture evidence;" and worst of all "his son and coadjutor, Alexander, especially," was after a full examination of the subject, led to the conclusion, not only that the baptism of infants was without Scriptural authority, but that immersion in water, upon a true profession of faith in Christ, alone constituted Christian baptism." On conferring with his oldest sister, she was found to be already on the same ground; and by the time a Baptist minister was at hand to immerse them, strange to say, the old gentleman himself, and a considerable part of his congregation, had become so " forcibly impressed with the same convictions," that they were all prepared to go together into the water. This is curious and instructive. With the premises of Campbellism, which are the premises of all unhistorical, unchurchly Christianity, it could not honestly come to any other conclusion. The wonder is not, that such Christianity should run so often into this baptistical rationalism, the next thing to the Quaker spiritualization of the sacraments into sheer nothing; but rather, that it should be able in any case, to stop short of it as the natural end of its thinking. Look, for instance, at the pains taken, p. 488, 48 in the name of the New School Presbyterian Church, to set aside the whole idea of anything like a true supernatural force mystically lodged in the Church itself; ordination only the " recognition of one whom God has *already* by his providence and grace put into the ministry;" no intrinsic force in *any* rite; no grace in union with the outward symbols of either sacrament, (all in plump opposition to the Westminster standards); no other influence from them, other than " that which results from a wise adaptation for enforcing truth, by striking symbols, and creating hallowed associations!" Surely it needs no very great depth of thought to see, that all such constitutionally unsacramental religion can owe it only to the most dead outward tradition, if it is kept in any case from passing over in due form to the Baptist ranks. Its pædobaptism is little better than a solemn sham.

Another striking feature of sect Christianity, which finds ample illustration in Mr. Rupp's book, is the tendency it has to drive all religion into a system of outward notions and abstractions. It is apt indeed, as we all know, to lay great stress on its practical and spiritual character. But its spirituality and practicality lack the force, that belongs properly to a truly divine life. They hold not so much in the actual apprehension of divine realities by faith, as in the mere notion of them by the imagination. They come not so much to an inward living union with the very life of the soul, as they are accepted by it rather in an external, mechanical way, as something different altogether from itself and out of itself. Religious truth so apprehended is always abstract, and not concrete. Sect Christianity, which makes so much of the individual mind and so little of all that is objective, can never avoid these abstractions. The individual mind, in its view, must take truth out of the Bible; there it is offered in an outward way, for this purpose; we have only to satisfy ourselves first, rationally, that the Bible is inspired; all turns afterwards on extracting from it our faith and practice. The idea of a living revelation in the Bible, which must authenticate it and unfold its true sense, is but dimly, if at all, perceived. The Bible is turned thus into an outward Jewish rule, and religion is made to have its merit mainly in the acknowledgment of its authority under such view. The text, and nothing but the text, becomes its motto and hobby, which it is ready to harp upon continually in praise of its own dutiful obedience. It needs no great sagacity to see, from the Bible itself, that this is *not* the way in which it proposes itself as our rule of faith and practice. It is not made like a catechism; it is no formal directory of things to be done and things to be left undone. It goes on the assumption throughout that Christianity is a living fact, a divine reality, which must be expected to act out its own significance in a free way, and through the medium

of whose self-interpreting life only the Bible can come to its true
application and force.   But all this the spirit now before us most
obstinately ignores.   It affects to go by line and plummet; and
all sorts of exegetical violence and trickery are resorted to, for
the purpose of saving to appearance, in its own favor, the credit
of its own false and servile maxim.   The result is pitiful dishonesty, and endless crimination and altercation, on all sides.   The
most heartless and hollow of all theological controversies, are those
which turn on this unhistorical and outwardly mechanical use
of the Scriptures.   Congregationalism affects in this way to be
the *very* truth of the New Testament, as it lies open to plain
common sense.   The Baptists, however, charge it with being
false to its own principle, in allowing infant baptism, for which
there is no rule or precedent, but at most a presumption only, in
the sacred rule book; and beyond all controversy the Baptists
here are right.   If Christianity be such an abstract letter, " the
law of baptism" must be taken as a positive institution whose
whole worth lies in our obediential respect to the authority pre-
scribing it, and which we have no right, therefore, to stretch a
particle beyond what is expressed in the precept.   But we have
other Baptists again, who charge the regular Baptists with being
themselves unfaithful to the Protestant rule; and who find it
necessary, accordingly, to become more Bible stiff still.   The
Seventh Day Baptists, for instance, can find no express authority
in the New Testament for the change of the Sabbath to the first
day of the week; which indeed can be found there by nobody
else, as little as any such authority for the baptism of infants.
It is all in order, therefore, when we hear them say in true Baptist and Jewish style: " This Sabbath he has imposed upon us
by a power which belongs to himself alone; and it is perpetually
obligatory on us to sanctify *that day*, until He himself abrogates
us from the service" (p. 121,).   Full as conclusive, certainly, as
the everlasting changes rung on the same string, in opposition to
the comprehension of infants, in Christ's covenant.   With equal
consistency, these Bible Christians " celebrate the Lords's supper
at night, in imitation of our Saviour; washing at the same time
each other's feet, agreeably to his command and example."
Among other Bible proofs for the perpetuity of the original Sab-

bath, they refer us to the texts: " The Sabbath was made for man," and " The Son of Man is Lord even of the Sabbath day," (p. 104, 107,) ; precious exemplifications of the abstract method now under consideration ; though, in truth, not a whit worse than a great many stereotyped tricks of the same sort in use with more respectable denominations, by which an incidental expression, oftentimes of the most ambiguous interpretation, is gravely made a peg on which to hang the whole weight of a doctrine or institution, which it is counted downright heresy to dispute.

Altogether, sect christianity has a wonderful propensity to substitute the abstract and mechanical for the living and concrete, on all sides ; as might be extensively illustrated from the book before us, if the limits of our present article allowed. It must ever be so, where the sense of the historical, objective, sacramental and churchly, in the fact of Christianity, is wanting, and the ultimate measure of it sought in the exercises of the single mind separately considered. " Christianity," says Campbellism, p. 231, " is a system of religion and morality instituted by Jesus Christ, principally taught by his Apostles, and recorded in the New Testament. It has for its immediate object the amelioration of the character and condition of man, morally and religiously considered. It consists in the knowledge, belief and obedience, of the testimony and law of Jesus Christ, as taught by his apostles and recorded in the New Testament—Are not law and obedience, testimony and faith, relative terms, so that neither of the latter can exist without the former? . . . Is not testimony necessarily confined to facts, and law to authority?   . Wherefore, in every case, faith must necessarily consist in belief of facts ; and obedience in a practical compliance with the expressed will or dictates of authority. By facts, is here meant, some things said or done. *Conclusion* : Upon the whole, these things being so, it necessarily follows, that Christianity, being a divine institution, there can be nothing human in it ; consequently, it has nothing to do with the doctrines and commandments of men ; but simply and solely with the belief and obedience of the *expressly recorded* testimony and will of God, contained in the holy Scriptures, and enjoined by the authority of the Saviour and his holy prophets upon the Christian community." This must be allowed to express well, what may be styled the reigning theory of Christianity among our modern sects. But now, with all due respect to Mr. Campbell, (who has this honorable apology, indeed, in our mind, that he has made more conscience of following out his principle to its proper consequences, than many others, who denounce his consequences,while they make common cause with him in his principle); with all due respect, we say, to President Campbell, this is not Christianity, but in its best view Judaism; and when made to stand for the conception of Christianity, it always involves, though it may be under the guise of an abstract supernaturalism, the very power of Rationalism itself; which only needs suitable scientific sea-room, to run out finally into all the results of its past significant and truly instructive history in Germany. Of this we have not a shadow of doubt. Christianity is no such outward statute-book of things to be believed and things to be done. It is " the law of life in Christ Jesus." It is a new constitution of grace and truth starting in Christ's *person*, and perpetuating itself in this form, as a most real historical fact, by the Church. The difference between this conception and the other, (Moses and Christ, John i. 17, John the Baptist and Christ, Matth. iii. 11, ix. 11,) is very great; and we only wish that Mr. Campbell, and many others, could be led to revolve it solemnly and earnestly in their minds. What if it might be found to be the true Ariadne thread in the end, that should conduct them forth from the horrible sect labyrinth into the clear sunlight of catholicity, which they have been so unsuccessfully struggling to reach in a different way.

There is much besides to be learned from this History of Denominations, for the right understanding and appreciation of the sect spirit. We are admonished, however, by the length of our article, to dwell no farther at present on details. What we have to say farther, will be presented hereafter in the form of certain general reflections, which come over us painfully from the contemplation of the subject as a whole.

J. W. N.

ART. XXXV.—HORÆ GERMANICÆ, *or Hymns from the German, in the metres of the originals.*

No. 1. A version of "*Lobe den Herren, den mächtigen König der Ehren.*"

[This well known hymn was composed by Joachim Neander, born in Bremen, anno 1610, where he also died as pastor, in 1680. He was an intimate friend of Spener. He composed quite a number of hymns, some of which he himself set to music.]

PSALM CIII., 1–5.

Praise thou the Lord, the omnipotent monarch of glory;
Join in, my soul, with the heavenly choir in their story!
　　　　Come and partake;
　　　Psaltery and Harp also wake,
　　　Sing the Creator's great glory!

Praise thou the Lord, who e'er ruleth and guideth all surely;
Over life's pathway, so fearful, he leads thee securely;
　　　　Ever he sends
　　　Mercies and blessings and friends;
　　　Then from thy heart thank him truly.

Praise thou the Lord, who hath fearfully, wonderf'lly made thee;
Health hath vouchsafed, and when heedlessly falling hath stayed thee;
　　　　Fainting and weak,
　　　When not a word thou couldst speak,
　　　Wings of his mercy did shade thee.

Praise thou the Lord, who thy life hath so visibly guided,
Streams of free grace, in his Son for thy sin hath provided;
　　　　Plain to thy view,
　　　God, the Almighty and True,
　　　Ne'er from his child is divided.

Praise thou the Lord, and forget all his benefits never;
Swell the loud chorus, ye chosen, till broad as a river,
　　　　Upward it stream;
　　　Soul, O forget not this theme,
　　　Praise him, O praise him for ever.

No. 2. A version of "*Ach sey mit deiner Gnade.*"

[Composed by Carl Bernhard Garve, a clergyman of the Moravian Church, born near Hanover, anno 1765, and died at Herrnhut, 1841.]

2. Cor. xiii. 13.

THY grace be ever with us,
   O Jesus, Blessed Lord!
'Gainst Satan's wiles defend us,
   And help divine afford.

Thy love be round about us,
   O Father, Gracious God!
Without its cheering presence,
   This World's a dreary road.

With thy communion bless us,
   O Spirit, Heavenly Dove!
While pilgrims here we wander,
   And in the realms above.

No. 3. A version of "*Der du noch in der letzten Nacht.*"

[Composed by Count Zingendorf, the founder of the Moravian Church, born anno 1700, and died 1760.]

JOHN xiii., 34, 35.

O thou, who on that mournful eve,
   When death was near at hand,
Didst speak once more of Christian *love*
   Unto thy chosen band:

Remind thy Church, which else, alas!
   Dissensions might ensnare,
The union of thy children was,
   Thy last command and prayer.

No. 4. A version of "*Ich sag es jedem, dasz er lebt.*"

[Composed by Frederick Von Hardenberg, better known as Novalis, born 1772, died 1801.]

2. Cor. v. 17.

I say to each that Jesus lives;
    He to his Father rose,
And sent his quickning Spirit dawn
    To give us true repose.

I say to each, let each the joy
    To other friends afford,
That soon in every land will down
    The Kingdom of the Lord.

Now to our souls this vain world seems
    Like as a Father-Land;
But the new Life will snatch us hence,
    Enraptured, from its hand.

No. 5. A version of "*Hallelujah! Schöner Morgen.*"

[Composed by Benjamine Schmolk, born in 1671. In his old age, like Milton, he became blind. He died in 1737.]

Deut. v. 12.

Hallelujah! Lovely Morning,
    Lovelier far than words can say!
Here I feel no care nor sorrow,
    Yes, this is a heavenly day.
Rich abundance here of joys,
All my inmost soul employs.

Sabbath, full of light and beauty,
    Day of sweetest rest to me!
In these dark and barren journeys,
    With thy calm serenity,
Thou dost drive away distress,
O thou day of blessedness.

How I feel my Father's blessings,
    On me fall as morning dew!
While his heavenly, verdant pastures,
    Burning with desire, I view.
O this sacred morning hour,
Hath a rich refreshing power.

Rest, then, all my world employments ;
  To another work I haste,
For I need my freest powers,
  In the highest God to rest.
Nought beseems this holy day,
Save to bless my God and pray.

In the silence of devotion,
  Will I keep my heart awake ;
Of the highest, truest treasures,
  In their fullness I'll partake ;
For my Jesus, to my heart,
Will the word of life impart.

Lord, encourage my endeavors,
  And do thou prepare my taste ;
Truth and comfort thence obtaining,
  Let me to my manna haste :
Thus within my ready mind,
Shall thy word its echo find.

Bless the teachings of thy servants ;
  All their fear of man displace ,
And with those who to thee listen,
  Make thy covenant of grace.:
Thus accepted at thy throne,
Deign their prayers and praise to own.

Grant that I this day may finish,
  As it is this morn begun.
Bless and animate and cherish,
  Thou, who art thy people's sun,
Till perfected, I and they
Hail th' eternal SABBATH-DAY.

J. H. G.

ART. XXXVI.—Historical Development.

" We fear that this phrase " historical" is connected in their minds
with the doctrine of development, of which also they speak a good
deal, and which we consider the thing in the world most irrecon-
cilable to the true idea of an historical Church. We ourselves do
not see how development is to work without the aid of an infallible
earthly head of the Church. We think it has worked very badly
with the aid of such an head ; but that was because the head was
not really infallible. It seems to us that continued progress requires
a continual standard to which to appeal. If we have an infallible
living teacher upon earth, to whom we can go, and upon whose decisions we can rely, the doctrine of development may be safe ; but
it will be useless. But a development, independent of such a teacher, must be continually in danger of going wrong, as we find that
most actual developments of Church doctrine have. Now, if we
have not an infallible living authority to protect us; we must substitute for it some fixed standard, by which the development is to be
tried. But progress is of the essence of development, and it must
get beyond any fixed standard. They will come to differ. Which
are we to follow ? If the fixed standard, why not adopt it at once,
and say nothing of development ? If development, how are we to
know that we are right ? What is theology but a science, like the
human sciences ? What has become of Revelation ? We have no
difficulty in answering these questions for ourselves. We adhere to
the fixed standard, the Scriptures as interpreted by the consent of
the whole Church, Catholic as well in time as in space. But this
fixed standard is utterly incompatible with development. All sects,
in the true sense of the word, have developed away from this standard. All " sectarianism," in the true sense of the word, is nothing but a development, which has introduced a new doctrine not
conformed to this standard."—*True Catholic.*

The passage here quoted, forms the conclusion of an article
on " Sectarianism," in the April number of the True Catholic,
(a most respectable Episcopal Magazine published in Baltimore,)
which winds up with a short friendly notice of " what has been
called the Mercersburg School." We use it as a convenient occasion, for fixing attention on the true force of the question to which
it refers.

What is *historical* development? Not fact added to fact, or
thought to thought, in an outward way. Still less movement
from one position to another wholly new and different. But
growth, evolution from within, organic expansion. All *life* im-

plies such movement. History has no other sense. It is the
revelation of an idea, or spiritual fact, in *time ;* the very form,
in which the orignal *wholeness* of such a fact is brought to pass,
the only form in which it *can* come to pass. So in the case of
the single man. So in the case of every nation. And shall we
then hold the Church, the inmost sense of man's life, to be a
dead outward *traditum ?* God forbid. It is historical ; not because it is the same thing forever, like a mountain or a sea ; that
would be the very opposite of history ; but because it is the power of a divine fact, which is forever growing itself more and more
into the consciousness, the interior life of the world, (a process that
implies new forms and stages of its apprehension continually,)
and which can never be complete till the whole thinking and
working of humanity shall appear transfused with its glorious
reconstructive power ; something, God knows, to which even
the Church itself, in its best and palmiest state, has never yet
been able to attain.

What do the friends of Christianity mean, when they deny
development. Can they deny *change ?* Not surely without the
derision of all history itself. The Church of the fourth century
is *not* one in form with that of the first ; the Church of the sixteenth century again is different from both. Rome pretends the
contrary, in her own favor. But the pretense is monstrous. What
Protestant denomination, however, can carry through any similar
plea ? Is modern Presbyterianism identical with past Christianity, in all ages before the Reformation or in *any ?* is modern
Methodism ? is modern Episcopacy ? All intelligent and candid men know the contrary, and are coming to confess it more
and more. And what are we to say then of such change ? Must
it all be set down as apostacy and corruption ? Let those shoulder this dread alternative who see proper to do so. We gladly
embrace, for our part, (as the only escape from it,) the idea of
organic development, by which, through all changes, we are allowed to believe the Church, *one*, holy, catholic and apostolical,
from the beginning onward to the last day.

Such development requires no " infallible earthly head," for
its direction and conduct ; just as little as a living oak needs to
be built up by line and compass. An outward authority of this

sort, supposed to supersede the free working of the intelligence and will of the Church itself, would be the source of petrifaction and stagnation only, not of development. This implies freedom, ethical activity, life poised upon itself as a principle and centre. It is just the stability system, which in every shape turns into mechanism and leads to popery.

Christianity, it is true, has its "fixed standard" in the Bible. But the standard is not itself Christianity, the thing it is to try and measure. *That* is a divine fact, from Christ onward, out of the Bible and beyond it. The Bible is its norm. But what then? Must it be stationary, to be normal? All life has its fixed norm, which, however, embraces it not as something fixed and at rest, but as a fact in motion, the succession of different states, and stages in time. Does the developement of a plant, carry it "beyond its fixed standard"? The Bible is the fixed standard of Christianity, not as the whole depth and compass of its sense may be supposed to have been at hand in the consciousness of the Church from the beginning; for this has not been the case, and is very far from being the case even now; but as furnishing the divine mirror by which this sense is to be tried and recognized us true, through all stages of its growth into the actual life of humanity by the Church. The piety of a child is very different from that of a full grown man; and yet the Bible is the *fixed* standard of the entire *movement*, by which the first gradually ripens into the second.

"What has become of Revelation?" *Can* a revelation, we ask in return, be really in the world as a *mere* outward authority, be it living pope or dead book of whatever name; but to be so in any real sense *must* it not, along with the letter, enter into the actual consciousness of the world also, the very process of its inward being, as "spirit and life"? And how is this to be effected save in a *human* way, or through a mighty process of history, by which ages shall be required to evolve into full apprehension and power, the vast interior fulness of the Christian principle, the "great and wide sea" of truth that lies before us in the Bible? Surely to be *historical* at all, Christianity must be in the world under the form of history, which itself implies organic life and growth, and not with the form simply of Pompey's Pillar or the Pyramids. **N.**

ART. XXXVII.—Address to the Suffolk North Association of Congregational Ministers, *with Sermons on
the Rule of Faith, the Inspiration of the Scriptures, and the
Church*, by *J. P. Lesley*, Minister of the First Evangelical
Church, Milton, Mass. 1849. Crosby & Nichols, 111, Washington st., Boston.

This Address is valuable as an indication of the true spirit of
the reigning Puritan orthodoxy. The Author has been hardly
dealt with. He is an injured man. His rights as an individual
and a Christian, have been trampled under foot. And in this regard, his energetic protest has significance and weight, both against
the Presbytery of Philadelphia, that withdrew his license, and
the Suffolk North Association of Congregational Ministers, that
refused to grant him even an examination *de novo*. The whole
proceeding was an act of tyranny.

Although we are not willing to endorse all Mr. Lesley's opinions, and are widely separated from him in our views of the
church and church power, yet, as receiving great wrong, we sympathize with him, and are free to confess that we admire his sincerity and manly independence.

The ostensible reasons for the course pursued by these ecclesiastical bodies were not based on immorality, or unfitness, or
contumacy, but on doctrinal differences concerning the theory of
Inspiration and the relation of Science to Revelation. But the real
" head and front of his offending" lay, no doubt, in his enlarged
and liberal spirit, and his resolution not to be bound by dead tradition.

To preserve due harmony between Freedom and Authority
is an exceedingly difficult problem in every sphere. But it seems
to be more so in the Church than in the Family, or in the State.
That She, holy and catholic, is possessed of divine authority,
which cannot be resisted without sin, admits of no question : that
this authority may be grossly abused to the destruction of individual liberty is also clear. That the Individual has rights to be
sacredly respected, and may exercise his private judgment in stout
resistance of the abuse of power, we are not dispose to deny :
but, on the other hand, the lawless setting up of particular pri-

vate judgment in defiance of the Universal Church is manifestly schismatical, sectarian, and as much to be hated as prelatical despotism itself. And this is the character of the so highly belauded Private Judgment, which, according to the Puritan Recorder, makes it right for any "Tom, Dick, or Harry" to manufacture a religion of his own fresh from the Bible, just as though the naked letter of the Bible, and not the Person of our Lord and Saviour, Jesus Christ, were the principle of Christianity, just as though all past history were a lie, and the Church hitherto a complete failure.

And here, as everywhere, extremes meet. True Freedom holds only in the element of Authority. The extreme of the one runs over into the extreme of the other; the wrong use of Private Judgment into the wrong use of Power. In short, Private Judgment, in the common sense, is at bottom tyrannical. As directed against churchly ideas, it is loud and vehement enough, in behalf of the Individual; grants him the broadest license; asserts the perfect right of the most obscure and ignorant Thomas, Richard, or Henry to erect his standard boldly in the face of the whole Christian world; boasts continually of the sufficiency of the pure Bible, untrammelled by tradition; and makes common cause with every infidel Ronge, and every renegade monk, who, from the vilest motives, may heap up slanders against his Spiritual Mother. But, like that Charity, which, while it sheds tears over the real, or imaginary woes of some antipodal heathen tribe, lets Want stand vainly pleading at its own door, this Private Judgment is bounded by lines of longitude and latitude. It is private only as opposed to something without; for let a truly independent thinker make his appearance in its midst, one, who puts in practice fearlessly this acknowledged right of judging for himself by the Scriptures, and behold the result—martyrdom, to all intents and purposes! The case of Mr. Lesley affords a very striking illustration. A young man of unblemished moral character, pious, sincere, earnest, gifted with eminent talents, a ripe scholar, trained in the Theological School of Princeton, well versed in Natural science, his manners polished, and his views enlarged by extensive travel and intercourse with men, because he dares to differ in some few points, and these non-essential, from the received, stereotyped tradition, has his good name blasted by vague, intangible whispers in secret, and in public by the mysterious insinuations of the religious newspapers, which, with their accustomed magnanimity, refuse to publish any explanations or defence. O Shame, where is thy blush? O Private Judgment, where thy boasted tolerance? where thy contempt of tradition? Strange, that men, who advocate private judgment so strenuously in theory, should deny it thus in practice! Strange, that men, who disclaim all tradition should be thus slavishly bound by it! Strange, that men, who express an utter abhorrence of the tyrannical use of power should yet prove tyrants themselves. But then, it is so natural for us to see the mote in our brother's eye, whilst we forget the beam in our own.

The greatest insult that can possibly be offered to the reigning orthodoxy is to maintain that there can be anything *new* in Theology. And here was Mr. Lesley's error. It starts back horror-struck from the idea of progress. All the metes and boundaries of Belief are mapped out and settled forever. Doctrine has received its last finishing touch. Not an iota can be added; not an iota taken away. Our tradition is *the* tradition. All forms of thinking must come rigidly up to our measure, must lie down on our Procrustean bed. All churches, Episcopal, Reformed, Lutheran, Roman Catholic, Greek, and Nestorian, must eventually be swallowed up in ours, which, being normal and pure, shall continue fixedly the same on to the Millennium, and still further. This is the prevailing consciousness, and wo to that man, who ventures to confront it! He is regarded with distrust from Maine to Louisiana. The stigma of heresy is fastened on him immediately. It is breathed about quietly from mouth to mouth, and slaughters his reputation like an invisible sword. Private Judgment condemns him, and the aggregate Private Judgment of all Puritanism, in this direction, is a Tyrant more awful than the Holy Father himself in the days of his proudest glory. That "fatal imposture and force of names falsely applied," by which evil is called good, and good evil, is brought to bear against him with tremendous effect. Germanism and Popery, that "word of fear," that bugbear, so like the ghost, or monster, seen by the timid cowboy in the dusky wood! are the favorite terms. In them is included all imaginable wickedness. Far better were it for a theological candidate to be guilty of open crime, than to be so unfortunate as to see the least good in either. And whoever venerates the Church as the Body of Christ, and upholds the idea of progress in Christian life and doctrine, must expect to be considered as incurably tainted, and receive one or the other of these dreaded names. And then, not Piety can shield him, nor Innocence save him. He is subjected with prompt severity to the ecclesiastical rack, and must succumb, or be excommunicated. Noble young men, not a few, have suffered from the workings of this Inquisitorial Engine.

The real cause of this crying evil seems to be in a departure from the ancient faith of Christendom. Doctrine, in a certain fixed traditional form, is foisted in as the principle of Christianity, in the room and stead of the Person of our adorable Saviour. His living presence in his Body the Church is not recognized. Hence tradition is dead and mechanical. Hence spring all the disorders, which vex and divide the Christian world. For, if our faith were strong in the living power of Christ within, in his promises to be with us *alway* to the end of world, in the energy of the Holy Spirit, there would be no cowardly shrinking as though every change brought destruction along with it. The power of the Christian life, both in the individual and in the body, would be rested on as fully capable of resisting damnable heresy, just as the life of the tiny polyp, in tropic seas, is capable of resisting and even gathering nourishment from waves that batter down the hardest rocks. Popery would then be honestly encountered and answered, not anathematized. Germanism would be studied and understood, not met with blind, wholesale condemnation. All departments of Art and Science, and Common Life would be subjected to, and filled with Christianity, and not stand widely asunder from it as they now do. In one word, Authority and Freedom would be both universal.

But as long as the faith of the ancient Church, as embodied in the Creed, and devoutly acknowledged by the Reformers, and incorporated in their symbolical books, is suffered like some Phidian sculpture, to lie buried in the dust of ages and forgotten, we need not hope for any cure. The law of dissolution must do its work. The organism that ceases to grow must cease to live. Nature is inexorable. Though it harden to stone, yet like an

Alpine glacier, it will be compelled to slide slowly down over the edge of the precipice. And the reigning orthodoxy has unconsciously thus slidden, by the weight of its icebound tradition, from the ground of its own symbols, and must slide much further, unless God in his mercy prevent.

We are sorry that Mr. Lesley, in the defence of his lawful rights, has been driven into absolute independency. The blame lies not on him, but on those who did the unchristian act. Yet such isolation cannot be pleasant. In the heart of every believer there exists a strong yearning for communion with the Universal Church—that Church, which has lived in history from the beginning. Separation from her is painful. It carries with it a sense of contradiction. If She is now, She has ever been, since the Incarnation of her Lord. And if the power of her life be worth anything, it ought to be strong enough to bind men together with closer ties than those found either in the Family, or in the State. In Christ Jesus, all are *one*, not merely by virtue of an invisible unity, for the spirit of unity ever by its own law seeks to make itself actual, and, rather than continue as an abstract notion, will overlook much that is imperfect. Our Blessed Lord obeyed Scribes and Pharisees, because they sat in Moses' seat. If we are willing to be as tolerant as He, there is no necessity for complete isolation. **T. C. P**

ART. XXXVIII.—MANUAL OF ANCIENT GEOGRAPHY AND HISTORY, by *Wilhelm Pütz*, principal tutor at the Gymnasium of Düren. Translated from the German. Edited by the Rev. *Thomas Kerchever Arnold*, M. A., Rector of Lyndon, and late Fellow of Trin. Col. Cam. Revised and corrected from the London edition. New York: D. Appleton & Co. Philadelphia: G. S. Appleton. 1849.

IT is difficult for an author to render a manual of universal history at the same time concise and attractive. The ground to be gone over is so extensive and his time so limited, that he cannot describe it in all its parts. He must deal in generalities. He cannot enter into details. Writers of this class, too, it must be said, have generally not had a proper apprehension of the nature of history, and on that account, their books are dryer than they should be. A nation, they are aware, may have its growth and decline, but of an onward improving march in the universal life of mankind, they have no idea. Between successive dynasties and ages, with them, the only connecting chain is chronology. As a manual of ancient history, this work is in advance of any thing that has preceded it. It does not, to be sure, enter ostensively into the philosophy of history, but from its judicious and systematic arrangement, it has a strong bearing that way. It suggests, at any rate, and leaves room for the teacher to philosophize. 'Of every country, in the first place, it gives the prominent geographical features, briefly, but graphically delineated, and then are recorded its historical transactions. If no other benefit were derived in this way, than the transporting in imagination of the student, back amid the transactions to be described, by making him familiar, in the first place, with the countries, this method would be preferred; but it is also the most natural and synthetical. From the situation and natural advantages of a country, the pursuits of its people receive always, more or less, their peculiar bent; and by the character of its scenery, whether sombre or cheerful, whether plain or romantic, whether abounding in deserts, interspersed with lakes, or set off with mountains, their own characters and dispositions, especially in early times, are very much modified and influenced.

Another peculiar trait of this volume is, the introduction, at the close of the historical account of each country, of a paragraph descriptive of its Literature and Fine Arts. As these are always intimately connected with the religion of a nation, and are, in fact, its highest efflorescence, they are the best criteria of its civilization and advancement. They tell us much of its deepest thoughts, its sublimest imaginings. Not only from the literature and music of a people, can we judge of their peculiar tastes and dispositions. From their sculpture, painting, and architecture, moreover, those mute sources of history, is spoken to us a language deep and even more graphically descriptive of their characters than that of words.

This manual, we believe, is well adapted to supply a pressing want in our schools and colleges. Though necessarily concise, it is still sufficiently attractive and interesting. It contains much in little space judiciously arranged, and, without doubt, is the best elementary hand-book of ancient history that has yet been published.

W. M. N.

THE

MERCERSBURG REVIEW.

NOVEMBER, 1849.

NO. VI.

ART. XXXIX.—THE SECT SYSTEM.

HISTORY OF ALL THE RELIGIOUS DENOMINATIONS, &c., *Second improved and portrait edition of Rupp's work, published by John Winebrenner, V. D. M.* Harrisburg, Pa.

Second Article.

1. Our sect system is exceedingly *irrational*. We can conceive of divisions in the church that might be in a certain sense rational and necessary, and so capable of some scientific representation. The original distinction of Protestantism from Catholicism, and the resolution of the first again into the two great confessions Lutheran and Reformed, have this character. They have their ground in the idea of Christianity itself; they form necessary *momenta*, or moving forces, in the process by which this idea is carried forward to its final completion; they can be studied accordingly, and understood, in the way, for instance, of comparative symbolism. But nothing of this sort can be affirmed of our reigning modern sects. No idea underlies them, by which they can be said to have a right to exist. Their appearance is in defiance and scorn of all such objective reason. It is their boast, to be sprung for the most part of mere private judgment and private

will. They start generally, by their own confession, in the
most outward and accidental occasions. A Jacob Albright is
awakened, and finding no congenial religious connections immediately at hand, makes his subjectivity the basis of a new sect,
which in due time swells into an evangelical church. A John
Winebrenner takes it into his head, that every body is wrong but
himself, and being put out of the old church, complacently offers
himself to the world as the nucleus of a new one, that may be
expected to work better. Elder Randall is pushed aside by the Regular Baptists, and forthwith originates the Freewill Baptists. Mr.
Cowherd (p. 124,) is led to inculcate the doctrine of abstinence
from the flesh of animals, as well as total abstinence from all in-
toxicating liquors, " on the testimony of the Bible," and has many
other private fancies besides on the same testimony ; and so we get
the *Bible Christian Church ;* still happily in the wilderness and
out of sight. Dr. Abner Jones, of Vermont, has " a peculiar travel of mind in relation to sectarian names and human creeds,"
and to rectify the evil sets in motion a sect of his own, which
falls in afterwards with two other equally providential accidents,
and helps in this way to form the body calling themselves " Christians." And so it goes, to the end of the chapter. Can anything
well be more accidental and capricious, than the rise of sects in
this way ? Who does not see, that we might as reasonably have
five hundred in such form, as fifty or sixty ? Have there not
been hundreds of men, who had just as much vocation in their
circumstances as Albright or Winebrenner, to found new churches,
that might have had just as much character and meaning too, as
theirs, or possibly a good deal more ? It is the easiest thing in
the world to moot new questions in religion, scores of them, that
might just as fully justify division as half of those that have
already led to it, provided only the proper zeal were got up in
some quarter to push them out to such extreme, " for conscience'
sake," and to put honor on the Bible.   Will any pretend to reduce
such a system to any sort of intelligible method or scheme ? It
has none. . It is supremely irrational, so far as all inward reason
goes, by its very constitution. We might as well pretend to sys-
tematize and genealogize the clouds, driven hither and thither by
all conflicting winds. It is a chaos, that excludes all science.

Who will dream here of a Sect Symbolism, generically unfolding the inward sense of each upstart body, as related to all the
rest and to the whole system, its historical necessity, its comple-
mental contribution to the full idea of Protestantism? Who
will find it needful for the right understanding of theology, to
pursue the history of its doctrines through the mazes of our present
sectarianism, as held, for instance by the United Brethren, the
Cumberland Presbyterians, and all manner of Baptists; in the
same way that all true theology does require undoubtedly such
a prosecution of doctrines, through the life of the ancient Greek
Church, the life of the Roman Church, and that of the original Protestant Church under both its grand confessional distinctions. Take one wing only of the system, the Scotch Secession,
which has been accustomed from the first to make the greatest account of its own *theological* significance, in this way; and
what after all, we ask soberly, is the value of all its witnessings
put together, in this country, for the cause of universal Christianity, whether in theory or practice? Is there any inward reason
in its divisions and subdivisions, its abortive unions and consequent new sections, till the whole has become a tangled web in the
end which it is a perfect weariness of the flesh to pretend to unra-
vel? Altogether we have some ten or twelve bodies in this country,
(possibly more,) conscience split for the glory of God, who stand
unitedly, while severally excluding one another, not only on the
Bible, the sure foundation of all sects, but on the Presbyterian
sense of the Bible also as embodied in the Westminster Confession. *Can* there be any meaning or reason in such a phenomenon? Has historical theology any real interest whatever in the
questions that lie between Old Covenanters, New Covenanters,
Associate Seceders, Associate Reformed Seceders, and Reformed
Associate Reformed Seceders, clear out to the tip end of orthodoxy
in the last *wee* Associate Presbytery of Pennsylvania? To ask
the question, is to provoke a smile. Who understands this field
of church history? Who cares to thrust himself into its briery
waste? Do these sects understand themselves? Is there, in truth,
anything in them *to be* understood; or that is likely to weigh a
feather hereafter, under any separate view, in the mind of God's
Universal Church? Alas, for the *unreason* of our reigning sect
system!

2. The evil just noticed is greatly aggravated by the considederation, that very few sects remain *constant* at all to their own origin, or make it their business to understand and maintain them. If this change were the result of a true inward process, serving to develope the sense of some mission they had at first, it might be all very well; but every body may easily enough see, that this is not the case. The movement is altogether negative and outward, and amounts to nothing. Once formed, the body floats hither and thither according to circumstances, till finally its original moorings are lost sight of almost entirely; only it still carries its old name and has gradually accumulated a certain historical substance of its own, a body of recollections and traditions, shibboleths and hobbies, prejudices and pedantries; whereby all manner of selfish interests and ends are enlisted for its support, and room made for a few men in the saddle, by humoring its fancies, to rule and guide it almost at their pleasure. Thus the original irrationality of sects is made for the most part more irrational still, looses any little grain of reason it may have had at first, by the meaningless fluctuations of their subsequent history. The starters of a sect, fifty years afterwards, in many cases, would hardly recognize their own progeny. Happy is the sect, that is able to define at all its own distinctive position, or that can give any show of reason whatever for its existence, under such form as it actually carries. In the great majority of cases, this cannot be done even by the ministers themselves. And then as to the people, poor sheep in the hands of their leaders and pastors, what can *they* be expected to know of their own denominational " whereabouts," or of its rational necessity, in the general pellmell of conflicting " persuasions" with which they are surrounded? As a general thing they know nothing about it.

3. The system is constitutionally *tyrannical.* Every sect pretends indeed to make men free. But only consider what sects are; self constituted ecclesiastical organizations, called forth ordinarily by private judgment and caprice, and devoted to some onesided christian interest, under perhaps the most superficial and narrow view; educated polemically to a certain fanatical zeal for their own separatistic honor and credit; and bent on impressing their own " image and superscription," on all that fall be-

neath their ghostly power. Are these the circumstances that favor liberality and independence? The man who puts his conscience in the keeping of a sect, is no longer free. It might as well be in the keeping of a Roman priest. In many cases indeed this were far better. Have the Baptists no traditions? Is there no slavery of intellect and heart among the United Brethren? Pshaw! The very last place in which to look for true spiritual emancipation, the freedom of a divinely, self-poised catholic mind, is the communion of sects.

4. The narrowness and tyranny of the sect spirit, unfriendly to all generous christian life, is of fatal force in particular against the cultivation of *theology*, without which in the end it is not possible for the church to have any true prosperity. Theology can be no science, except as it has to do with the whole of Christianity, and is thus at once both churchly and historical in the full sense of these terms. The sect life, by its very conception, kills it, by turning it into a petrifaction or causing it to evaporate in the way of thin abstraction. Facts here are very plain. Sects, as they actually exist, have no theology, save as now mentioned; the miserable residuum only, so far as it may have any value at all, of the church life they had to start upon in the beginning, carried along with them as a mere outward tradition. Sects have no pleasure in theology, as a science. It has nothing to expect from this quarter. It is no libel on our American sects in particular, to say that they have not thus far contributed anything at all to the advance of this most noble and excellent of all sciences; and it needs no prophet's gift to say, that they never will do so in time to come. If any service has been rendered to it in any quarter, it has been by such as have been able to surmount the system in some measure, forcing their way upwards into a more catholic region. No sectarian theology can ever be of any permanent value.

5. The sect plague has no tendency to work out its own *cure ;* unless it be in the way of a deadly malady, that ends itself by ending the life on which it has come to fasten. It is vain to look for a reduction of the number of sects, by their voluntary amalgamation. No two have yet been able to make themselves one. The difficulty is not in their theological differences. These

are for the most part of very little practical force; with the great mass of the people, we may say, indeed, of absolutely no force at all. In nine cases out of ten it is a matter of sheer accident, that this man is an Albright and his neighbor a Cumberland Presbyterian, that one phase of the Baptist faith prevails here and another phase of it ten miles off. All this, however makes no matter; and it would make very little matter, if it were brought to be never so clear that the causes of separation in any case had completely fallen away. There would still be no union. It is the curse of the system, that it can never of itself break the chains it has thus forged for its own slaves. On the contrary, it tends perpetually from bad to to worse. It is easier by far to divide one sect into two, than it is to splice two sects into one. There is not the least reason to expect accordingly, that the system will ever reform itself into any better shape. Is is plain moreover that it has no necessary end; on the contrary, its capabilities and possibilities are indefinitely boundless. No multiplication of sects can exhaust the principle from which they spring.

6. It is well to note how generally the sect system adheres to the article of *justification by faith*, and how prone it is to run this side of Christianity out to a false extreme, either in the way of dead antinomianism or wild fanatacism. With many persons, at this time, the test of all soundness in religion is made to stand in the idea of salvation by grace as opposed to works, Christ's righteousness set over to our account in an outward way, and a corresponding experience more or less magical in the case of those who receive it, which goes under the name of evangelical conversion. But now it falls in precisely with the abstract mechanism of the sect mind, to throw itself mainly on this view of religion, to the exclusion or at least vast undervaluation of all that is comprised in the mystery of christianity as the power of a new creation historically at hand in the church. It is common for sects, accordingly, to make a parade of their zeal, in such style, for the doctrines of grace and the interests of vital godliness; and this is often taken at once for a sufficient passport in their favor, as though any body of religionists professing faith in free justification and violent conversion, must needs be part and parcel of Christ's Church, however unchurchly in all other

respects. But surely for a sober mind, it should be enough to expose the fallacy of such thinking, to look over the array of sects which is here presented to our view, and see how easy it is for almost the whole of them, if need be, to legitimate their pretensions in this way. All fragments of the Scotch Secession of course are one here. however divided in their "testimonies" at other points. They make election the principle of christianity, turn justification by faith into a complete abstraction, and so nullify the law in one form, only to come too generally under the yoke of it again in another. The Baptists, through all their divisions, meet here also as on common ground ; with antinomian tendency in one direction ; with a tendency to fanatacism in another direction ; but with common intolerance, all round, to every view of religion that is not found to harmonize with their own abstract scheme. The Winebrennerians hold justification by faith without works, (p. 177,) and are great in their way for revivals and wholesale conversions. So of course the Albright Brethren (p. 277.) So the United Brethren in Christ (p.564.) These and other sects indeed ambitiously strive to outdo one another, in the business of saving souls in the most approved style, "getting them through" as it is called, according to the abstract scheme now noticed. The one grand requisite for fellowship in the Campbellite communion is, (p. 225,) "an entire reliance upon the merits of Christ alone for justification ;" it is founded we are told, (p. 223,) "upon the two great distinguishing principles of the Lutheran Reformation, *viz:* the Bible alone as the rule of faith, to the entire exclusion of tradition, and the relying only upon that justification that is obtained through faith in Jesus Christ." Even the "Chrstians," with no faith in Christ's divinity, and the Universalists too, when it suits, can go in for some sort of abstract magical justification, and on the strength of it bring into play the common revival machinery with quite good success. All this surely deserves to be well laid to heart. There are, it is but too plain, "depths of Satan" here, as well as in other quarters, against which we need to stand solemnly on our guard. Let no one feel that it is safe to go with a sect, simply because it may seem to be *evangelical*, (O most abused word,) in this quacksalvery style. What can it be worth, if it be dissociated wholly from the old church consciousness embodied in the creed ?

7. For one who has come at all to understand the constitution of this abstract supernaturalism, it can produce no surprise to find the sect system marked universally by a *rationalistic* tendency. A Rationalism that denies the supernatural altogether, and a Supernaturalism that will not allow it to enter into any concrete union with the natural, are at bottom much of the same nature; and the last needs only the force of true consecutive thinking always, to pass over peacefully into the arms of the first. Sects start usually in abstract supernaturalism, with an affectation of hyper-spiritual perfection. But the rationalistic element comes at once into view, both in their thinking and practice. This is clearly exemplified in the Baptistic scheme, as already noticed; a divine statute book, outwardly certified to be from heaven; christian *laws* drawn forth from it in a like outward way; the mechanism of salvation brought nigh to men all outwardly again, in the form of thought or credited report; its application magically affected by an outward impulsion from God's Spirit, carrying the soul through a certain process of states and feelings. No sacramental grace. No true union with the life of Christ. So with sects generally. Their idea of private judgment; their notion of religious freedom; their low opinion of the sacraments; their indifference to all earnest theology; their propensity to drive religion by might and by power, rather than by the still small voice of God's Spirit; all betray a rationalistic habit of mind, and lean inwardly to still more decidedly rationalistic consequences and results. When Mr. Campbell makes Christianity to be " simply and solely," (p. 233,) the belief of certain testimony, and obedience to certain laws, outwardly offered to men in the Bible, what less is it, we ask, than the very genius of Rationalism itself; although most of the other sects probably would accept the same definition, as altogether satisfactory and sufficient. The sect life tends to destroy faith, as it is notoriously unfriendly also to every thing like reverence. It is not strange at all to see it running out into " Christianism ;" or to hear, in certain quarters, of converts being taken into the church, (so called,) without baptism ! There is too much reason to fear, that the virus of a low vulgar insensibility to the divine fact of Christianity has come to pervade the popular mind, in some sections of our country,

under the forms and shams of this unchurchly religionism far beyond what most persons have ever been led to imagine or suspect.

8. It is encouraging however, as well as curious, to see how the sect system is made to lend *testimony* throughout, against itself, to the idea of the Holy Catholic Church; not unlike the devils in the New Testament, who were forced to acknowledge Christ, while fighting against him or fleeing from his presence. Every sect, in spite of itself, is forced to acknowledge, at least indirectly, the necessary attributes of the Church, as one, holy, catholic, and apostolical. It cannot be a *mere* particular corporation, society or persuasion, however much in some views it may seem disposed to be nothing more. To stand at all, it must put on the character of a church, and then carry out as it best can what this character is felt by a sort of inward necessity, to imply and require. Some sects openly claim the prerogatives and powers of the Universal Church, as belonging to themselves alone, in such a way as to exclude all that is not of their own communion ; and this certainly is the most consistent course. Generally however no such claim is made ; but the sect professes to look upon itself only as a tribe of the true Israel, a section or wing in the sacramental host of God's elect. And yet it goes on, in these circumstances, to arrogate to itself within its own bounds full church powers ; such powers as have no meaning, except as conditioned by the idea of a catholic or whole church ; powers which cannot be fairly asserted, without virtual limitation upon the equal independence of sister sects. The inward ecclesiastical economy of every sect, as to its ordinations, admission of members, church censure, supervision of both faith and practice, &c., is so ordered as to involve throughout the assumption of an absolute and final and exclusive supremacy in matters of religion. The idea of the Church, however dimly and obscurely present, will not allow it to be otherwise. It *must* be one and universal, the *whole*, that of necessity excludes all beyond its own sphere. In this way every sect, so far as it can be called a church at all, becomes necessarily a caricature of the catholicity with which it pretends to make war, and so, like every other caricature, bears witness to the truth, which is thus distorted by it and brought into con-

tempt. In some cases, we have surprising confessions in favor of the true idea of the Church, where they might seem to be wholly out of place. Mr. Winebrenner (p. 175,) insists on visibility, unity, sanctity, universality and perpetuity, as the necessary attributes of the church "An invisible church that some divines speak of,' he tells us, "is altogether an anomaly in christian theology" So again: "The union of sects, into one general evangelical alliance, or into one human organization diverse in character, faith and practice, from the one true church of God, as characterized in the Bible, we have no belief in nor sympathy for." So we meet in Mr. Alexander Campbell many traces of a sound and right feeling here, which we may well regret to find overwhelmed again, and made of no effect, by the power of the unhistorical sect mind which is allowed after all to prevail in his system.

9. The posture of sects, being such as now described, involves them unavoidably in endless *inconsistency* and *contradiction.* There is a lie always at the bottom of it, from which it can never fully make its escape. It is the part pretending to be the whole, while it proclaims itself still to be nothing more than a part. The sect acknowledges the christian consciousness to be something deeper, more comprehensive, more absolutely necessary and real, than its own modification of it as a sect; and yet, this modification, the relative and partial sect consciousness, is in fact exalted above the other and clothed with powers which appertain of right only to the idea of christianity in full. The sect wills itself above the church, calls itself modestly *a* church, as one of many; but then goes on, almost in the same breath, to play itself off as *the* church, virtually sinking all other catholicity into a fiction as opposed to such high usurpation. Here is a tremendous contradiction, which runs through the entire system. The very features it is most ready to quarrel with in Romanism, it thrusts upon us again in new shape as its own. It hates church tradition; will hear of no binding force in church history; but straightway manufactures a log chain of authority in the very same form, out of the little yesterday of its own life, which it binds mercilessly on the neck of all its subjects. It will have no saints nor fathers; but forthwith offers us instead its own foun-

ders and leaders, and makes it well nigh blasphemy to speak a
word in their dispraise. It is great for private judgment; which it
takes mighty good care however to regulate, by bit and bridle, to
one single track, and that generally of the most narrow sort. It is
loud for the Bible, an open Bible, the Bible *alone ;* but only as
read through the medium of its own theological habit, and wo to
the wight who may presume to read it in any other way. So
throughout. The very things it protests and fights against in the
church of Rome, it is ready the next moment to assert in its own
favor, under some altered form ; only with this difference that
the old *catholic* truth which in every case underlies the Roman
abuse, is with sects generally treated as part of that abuse itself,
so that the new exercise of power brings no such sacred sanction
along with it for the pious heart. It is counted dreadful that the
church should be placed under the *human* headship of the pope,
or of a pope and council ; but has not every sect its human
headship—whether one man, five men or twenty is of no account
—whose supremacy is complete in all its religious affairs, only
by its own confession *without* right divine ? This headship,
moreover, with all its pretended humility, is in no case slow to
assume the exercise of divine powers. Popery, we are told with
horror, presumes to fix doctrines, make laws, use keys &c., all in
virtue of its own right and power, instead of simply following
the letter of the Bible. And what sect, we ask, is not continually doing the same thing, in substantially the same way ? Has
not each sect its system of doctrines, or at least of notions, derived through its own prophetical headship, its particular founder
and standing leaders, from the divine record, and legislated into
authority by its own circle of reading and teaching, as absolutely
as any faith that prevails in Rome ? Has it not besides its *index
expurgatorius* too, in fact if not in form, its particular world of
religious thought hedged in carefully by its approved books and
tracts, or possibly by a powerful " book establishment" even, that
contrives to monopolize in great measure the business of thinking for the body at large ? Rome, it is said, dares to create ecclesiastical rules, ceremonies, rites, &c. And what sect is it, that has
not done the same thing ? The Holy Church Catholic, by its
very idea, includes in itself the whole power of the Saviour's

Mediatorial life, under its three functions, prophetical, priestly and kingly. To say that these functions are exercised by Christ only under an outward and separate form, and that the Church, his mystical Body, does not also include them in her constitution as " the fullness of him that filleth all in all," is a profound absurdity; an absurdity so profound indeed, that no religious body can assert it, and still claim to be a church, without at once falling into the most gross practical contradiction; that, namely, of repudiating the true powers of christianity in the only view in which they *are* true, and then trying to force them into its service again under another form that involves of necessity what is wrong and false. In claiming church rights and church powers accordingly, and in pretending to exercise church functions and satisfy church wants, every sect does in truth lay claim to a true prophetical, true priestly, and true kingly character, at the same time; as without all this, the other pretension is reduced to empty smoke. That is, every sect puts itself forward as an infallibly safe expositor of the true sense of Christianity and the Bible, a perfectly trustworthy and sufficient depository of God's grace and the sure medium of reconciliation with him for sinners, the legatee in full of the commission of the keys as originally given to Peter and his fellow apostles. And yet on the other hand, no such divine powers are acknowledged, as necessary at all to constitute the Church; and other sects are allowed to have just as much right to play prophet, priest and king, in the same ecclesiastical style, as the body in question; which at once turns all such exercise of church functions into a merely human assumption, resting on no general necessary ground whatever, that is, into the very essence of popery itself. In such perpetual self-contradiction is the sect system doomed everywhere to move, by trying to uphold the conception of the Church, while it shows itself at war with all the attributes that enter into its constitution.

Every sect, in claiming to be a church, claims rights and powers which it has no ability whatever, to make good, and invites a faith and trust for which it can offer no sort of commensurate ground in its actual constitution. Take, for exemplification, the large and respectable body of the Narraganset Brethren. Of its origin, tenets and ways, the case does not require that we should speak. Enough that it rose in the way of protest against errors and defects which were supposed to prevail in the rest of the Christian world, threw itself on the sole guidance of the Bible, and has all along shown itself very zealous for evangelical religion and its own revivals. It allows now that there are other churches besides itself in the world; that the sects generally, are such churches; and is ready indeed, on fit occasion, to make a great parade of liberality and toleration, in the way of shaking hands with other denominations, to express what it conceives to be the "communion of saints." Still it puts itself forward, for all who can be induced to listen to its claims, as the comprehension in full of what the idea of the Church requires; that is, it arrogates to itself prerogatives and resources, which are absolutely universal in their nature, and as such exclusive of every like claim in any other quarter. The sect calls on all men, as they value their salvation, to take refuge in her communion. She does not simply offer them the Bible, but along with it her own tradition also, her sacraments, her ministrations of grace. She is not content to make them christians, but seeks to make them also Narragansets. Her mission is to spread and build up Narragansetism. This for her is identical with absolute and complete Christianity; she expects the whole world to become Narragansets, if not before, at least in the blessed millenium. This same feeling she tries to infuse into every soul, that falls within the range of her ecclesiastical domain; and she exacts from them accordingly, at the same time, full faith in her separate sufficiency for all church purposes and ends. She assumes in regard to them the full stewardship of Christ's house. She makes herself responsible for their souls, engaging if they do but trust her guidance and care to see them safe into heaven. She carries the keys of the kingdom of heaven, to bind and to loose, to open and shut, at her own pleasure. All this implies *universal* validity in her acts, validity for all men and not simply for some men; and in no other view can it ever be the object of Christian faith and trust. But see now the contradiction of the whole case. Narragansetism does not pretend to assert these universal powers in a truly universal way, but only within a given circle, the compass namely of her own membership. It is the church, with all its divine resources, for one man who has got into its communion, but not at all for another, his neighbor, who belongs to another communion. It is charged with the salvation of one it may be in a family, where all the rest are cared for in a wholly different way. It exacts a faith and obedience of one, which it never thinks of requiring in the case of another. It calls for sacrifices and services in the first case, all for the glory of God in the promotion of Narraganseism, which it never dreams of demanding or exacting in the second. Its privileges and opportunities are for Narragansets only, not for Christians generally, save as they are willing to put on the Narraganset livery, and so make this to be identical with the profession of Christ. The censures of the sect too are taken by herself to be of universal force for those on whom they fall ; although acknowledged to be of no force whatever, should it be pretended to hurl them over the sect fence, into any part of the Christian world that lies beyond. Thus one man is excommunicated, put out of the whole church, by a power which would be only laughed at if it undertook to disturb in the least the ecclesiastical relations of another, close beside him, only within another communion, involved in precisely the same offence. Nay, the man who is thus amenable to Narraganset jurisdiction to day, may to-morrow clear himself of it completely by taking letters of dismission from his sect, with all its universal powers, and passing over to the jurisdiction of some other evangelical body, which exercises the same universal powers, with equal independence, in like circumscribed and particularistic style.

How *can* church powers carry with them any truly necessary and universal force, such as all church faith is felt to demand, exercised in this arbitrary and conventional way? Plainly, in this whole order of things, the church has no necessary existence whatever, but is the creature and product simply of the men who belong to it, with such powers as they may be pleased to lodge in it for present use. There is a sore contradiction here in our whole sect system, the thorn of which those only can fail to feel sharply, who have never yet been brought earnestly to reflect on the true nature of the Church itself. No wonder that sects find it hard often to distinguish themselves from mere voluntary societies, in the service of morality and religion. No wonder, that their sacraments sink so readily into rationalistic signs, and that the assertion of supernatural objective powers, as something immanent in the constitution of the Church itself, is apt to fill them with offence. It is hard indeed to conceive of all this in the communion of a sect, which I am at full liberty to forsake to morrow, if I so please, for the communion of another. How can I yield to such a body ever, as such, the faith and homage that are due to the Church as a divine reality, and which crave the presence of this Church in full as a necessary object, to make room for their exercise? If I may thus leave one sect, why not twenty; and if twenty, why not all? On what principle of common sense am I bound to confine my ecclesiastical vagrancy to the range of actually existing sects, (accidents as they are too generally at best,) instead of bidding adieu at once to the whole of them, and originating a new communion, more to my taste, in the bosom say of my own house? To all such questions the sect system can make no satisfactory reply. It tends, with inward necessity from the beginning, to subvert completely the whole idea of the Church.

10. It is owing in part at least, no doubt, to the vast inward lie which the sect system thus carries in its very constitution, that its influence is found to be so *unfavorable actually to honesty and godly sincerity*, in the case of those who surrender themselves to its power. This is a wide subject, which we will not pretend here to take up in its details. All experience however shows, that the sect mind, as such, has a strange tendency to run into low cunning, disingenuous trickery and jesuitic policy. Religion degenerates with it into a trade, in which men come to terms with God on the subject of their own salvation, and lay away their spiritual acquisitions as a sort of outward property for convenient use. The object is required to bend and bow to the subject; becomes a thing indeed for private appropriation, and under such partial apprehension is made to stand falsely for what is the whole. Sect piety is constitutionally unequal, inconsistent, fantastic and pedantic. It never has been, and never can be, sound, calm, full, catholic and free. By the very falsehood of substituting the sect for the Church, it is involved necessarily in hypocrisy, which reaches always with fearful power at last into its entire life. It has a tendency universally to run into sham.

It abounds notoriously in cant. It is full of hollow pretensions, phrases and forms that have parted with all life. It delights in all sorts of quackery. Nor is this dishonesty confined to the sphere of religion; it is very apt to infect the whole life. Hypocrisy towards God begets naturally unfaithfulness towards men. It is not meant of course to charge all sectarian christianity with the moral defect now noticed. We speak only of the *tendency* it has this way. Good men, in the bosom of a sect, may rise superior to the danger; but in doing so, they lay aside to the same extent the sect consciousness itself, and are brought into conflict thus with its ordinary pretensions and claims. On all sides, however, we have examples enough of the bad power, which belongs to the system in the general view here presented. This book of sects sheds no small amount of illustration on their habit of carnal policy and jesuitic calculation. Still wider evidence of it is to be found every day, in our common sectarian religious press. What sectarian paper is trusted beyond the limits of its own denomination, on any question involving sectarian interests and relations? It seems almost the necessary character of every such publication, to be disingenuous and unfair; without thought, it may be, or premeditation; which itself, however, serves only the more fully to show how completely natural such want of catholic integrity is, for the whole system out of which it so easily and readily springs.

11. It is truly amazing, that any person should pretend to justify the sect system, as either agreeable to the true idea of Christianity or conducive to its interests. Some, however, still do so openly; while a much larger number would seem to acquiesce in the thought, indirectly, at least, and by implication. Every such imagination, however, is itself, but a sign and proof of the evil nature of the system, for which it thus seeks to raise an apology; for it carries in itself, we may say, the principle of annihilation in the end, for all that is comprehended in the faith of the holy catholic church. Not only is our sect system in flat contradiction to the letter of the New Testament; it is at war besides with the divine constitution of Christianity itself. It wrongs the idea of the Church, withdraws it as an object of faith from the Christian world, and in this way mars and spoils the symmetry, and full-

ness, and force, of the Christian life throughout. The bad fruits of the system, in this view, stare us in the face from all sides. Our theology is sickly, lame and lean. Our piety is angular and hard, running much into narrow technicalities and traditionary forms. Every denomination has its own small world of theory and experience, which it affects to regard as universal Christianity, without the least account of the other little worlds of like sort, with which it is surrounded. It is gross falsehood, to say that the influence of sects on one another is wholesome, and favorable to the general cause of Christianity. Their emulation is not holy; and any gain that may seem to come of it, is no better than "the hire of a whore or the price of a dog" brought into the house of the Lord, which he has declared to be an abomination in his sight (Deut. xxiii. 18). It is not by any such rivalry and strife, that the glorious gospel may be expected to prevail in the world. All zeal for religion is rotten, and will be found at last to stink, that springs not from a true interest in religion for its own sake. Our sects do not love each other. Their relation to each other, at best, is one of indifference. To a fearful extent, it is one of quiet malignity and hatred. What sect takes any active interest in the welfare of another, rejoices in its prosperity, sympathizes with its griefs and trials, makes common cause with it in its enterprises and works? Every body knows, rather, that the charity of sects stops short for the most part with the lines of circumvallation that surround for each one its own camp, and that it is cold as winter towards all that lies beyond. The jealousies and collisions of sects, not loud, mainly, but in the form rather, of quiet still fanaticism, are the source of endless religious mischief throughout the land. Altogether the system is a plague that calls for mourning and lamentation in every direction.

12. For one who has come to make earnest with the church question, and who has courage to face things as they are in the way of steady firm thought, the whole present state of sect christianity is full of *difficulty* and *discouragement*. In the first place, it is not possible for him to identify any one sect with the idea of the whole Church. Whether he be a Methodist, or a Presbyterian, or a Lutheran, or of any other denomination, he sees clearly that it is a desperate business to think of making out a full agree-

ment with primitive christianity in favor of his own body. He owns too, at any rate that other bodies are included in the Church, as it now stands. Of course, his own is but a part of the Church, not numerically only, but also constitutionally. Hence it must be regarded, when taken by itself, as a one-sided and defective manifestation of the Christian life; and so the consciousness, or state of mind, which it serves to produce, and in which distinctively it stands, can never be rested in as evangelically complete. It is not possible thus for a true church consciousness, and the particular sect consciousness, Presbyterianism, Lutheranism, or any other, to fall together as commensurate spheres of life; the first is something far more wide and deep than the second, and cannot be asked to yield to this as ultimate in any way, without the sense of incongruity and contradiction. Then again, it becomes impossible, of course, to acquiesce in the denominational position as final and conclusive. No position can be so regarded, that is not felt to be identical with the absolute idea of Christianity, the true sense of it as a whole. What earnest minded man now seriously expects that his particular denomination, Methodist, Presbyterian, or any other, is destined to swallow up at last all other types of Christianity, and so rule the universal world? Nor is the case relieved at all, by imagining the different sects, as they now stand, to continue collectively in permanent force. It is not possible at all for a truly thoughtful spirit, to settle itself in this as the legitimate and normal state of the Church. The very sense of sect, as related to the sense of the Church, requires that the first should pass away. The whole sect system then is interimistic, and can be rightly endured only as it is regarded in this light. And yet the system itself is opposed to every such thought. It cannot will its own destruction. Every sect demands of its members a faith and trust, as we have already seen, which imply that it is to be taken as absolute and perpetual. It plays, in its place, the part of Christ's one universal Church. Here, then, is a difficulty. To cleave to the sect as an ultimate interest, in the way it requires, is to be divorced in spirit necessarily, to the same extent, from the true idea of Christ's kingdom, whose perfect coming cannot possibly be in such form. To become catholic, on the other hand, is necessarily to rise above the standpoint of the mere sect, and to lose the power thus of that devotion to its interests, separately considered, which it can never fail to exact notwithstanding, as the test and measure, in such relation, even, of universal Christianity itself. How much of embarrassment and confusion is involved in all this, the more especially as the sect system has no tendency whatever to surmount its own contradiction, but carries in itself the principle only of endless disintegration, many are made to feel at this time beyond what they are well able to express.

J. W. N.

ART. XI.—Universal History.—Antehistoric Period—The Chinese.

[In the last number of the Review was published the introduction to a Manual of Universal History, originally prepared for the use of Marshall College, by the Rev. Mr. Mann, of Philadelphia, and designed to be used as a text-book in that Institution. It contains a general outline of the principles which are illustrated in detail in the succeeding parts of the work. The introduction itself cannot be fully understood unless studied in connection with the historical facts narrated in the history of the different nations treated of. No final sentence, either of praise or dispraise, can be justly passed upon its merits, before an opportunity may be afforded for the perusal of the entire Manual.

The history itself is divided into three grand divisions: 1. The Antehistoric period; 2. The most important nations before the birth of Christ; 3. The most important nations after the birth of Christ. Under these leading divisions are arranged, in systematic order, the several nations, ancient and modern, which have in any way contributed to the progress of society towards its final end. As Christ himself is regarded as the centre of the world, ancient history must be considered as a preparation, in all its parts, for the great mystery of the Incarnation; and modern, as an expansion of it. In the department of Ancient History, great pains are taken to show how the political, social, artistic, and scientific activity of the human family, in its final tendencies, strove to effect a lasting union between God and man, but without success. Still, as struggles after emancipation from the thraldom of sin and the attainment of spiritual freedom, they must not be regarded as void of meaning. They demonstrate, beyond the possibility of contradiction, that our common human nature, in consequence of its original constitution, hungers and thirsts after a living union and communion with the fountain of Light and Life, with the Great God himself. Such a union, however, could not have been accomplished in a sudden, abrupt way. In accordance with the law of our life, which is a law of progressive growth, history moves forward through a period of 4000 years before the Incarnation—that greatest of all facts—took place. When now men had been prepared for his reception by a systematic course of education, conducted by Providence, in conjunction with human agencies, the Word became Flesh. The new life thus introduced into the very heart of the world, constitutes the governing principle of Modern History; and it is the business of the historian to point out the influence which it exerted on society at large.

That the readers of the Review may be enabled to obtain a clearer conception of the character of this Manual, it has been thought proper to continue the publication of extracts from it.]

PART 1. *The Ante-historic Period.*

§ 1. A cloud of impenetrable darkness overshadows the primitive state of man. Neither Sacred nor Profane History furnishes us sufficient and authentic materials for the formation of clear and definite opinions concerning the condition and character of the earliest society. This uncertainty arises not only from the absence of proper data and the meagreness of the chronicles we may possess, but springs immediately out of the idea of history itself. In nature the ripest bloom of vegetation and the richest fullness of the most beautiful forms of its existence, are preceded by a state of chaotic confusion, when the elemental powers are struggling in the birththroes of creation. In the idea of life is implied a progressive advance from lower to higher stages of perfection. Its beginnings, involved in a process of formation, escape the ken of the acutest observer, and successfully defy detection. In the department of nature, order succeeds to disorder, light to darkness, beauty to deformity.

Nor does this law of life terminate its activity within the narrow bounds of nature; it displays its presence in a higher form, in the province of human existence. But history is the summary of the various manifestations of mind, as they have been successively revealed at different periods, in the onward march of time. As, therefore, the beginning of our common human life lies hid from common observation, and becomes visible only after it has attained to a certain point in its growth, so in history, its earliest appearances are not characterized by any distinctive features. It is only after man has advanced to a certain position in the scale of civilization, that the certainty of history increases and its materials become authentic.

§ 2. According to the Scripture account, He who in the beginning created the heavens and the earth, made man in his own image, surrounded him with Paradasaic happiness, and invested him with sovereign authority over the inferior orders of creation. It is impossible to determine with precise accuracy the locality of the beautiful garden of Eden—the blooming cradle of our first parents, and the gloomy sepulchre of their pristine innocence. Nor can any adequate solution be given to the question which on the very vestibule of history enforces its claims upon our attention, how the human race which, according to the Biblical narrative, sprung from the same stock, could have branched out into so many distinct families, differing from each other in color, in physical organization, and in mental and spiritual endowments.

In opposition to the Pantheistic cosmological speculations of heathen antiquity, which either ascribed to matter an eternal co-existence with God himself, or regarded it as a voluntary emanation of his being, the Bible teaches that the world sprang into existence out of nothing, at the command of Jehovah, whose good pleasure it was, in this way, to reveal his Omnipotence, his Wisdom, and his Love.

Various theories have been advanced respecting the abode of our first parents. The simple fact that Mesopotamia was rendered fruitful by artificial irrigation, overthrows the hypothesis which assigns it to that country. Others bestow this honor upon Canaan, because it abounds the whole year round in palatable fruits. Numerous arguments tend to prove, that the elevated but warm and lovely Cashmere, enjoyed the privilege of nourishing our progenitors. Vide 1 M. ii., 8, 10–14.

All profound philosophers, who have made man the subject of their special study, acknowledge with one accord that the differences of color and of mind which characterize the several races, spring not so much from the influence of climate and the gradual deterioration effected by unnatural intermarriages, and other causes, as from the operation of immoral principles introduced into our nature by the Fall. This diversity consists not only in the variety of color and of size, in the formation of the skull and in the physical appearance generally, but principally and mainly, in the relative

strength of the mental capacities and in the intensity of self consciousness. Still, with this difference in full view, it would be both
unphilosophical and unscriptural to uphold the theory of a *specific*
distinction in the various branches of the human family, and to deny
the biblical account of the unity of its origin. Most recent physio-
logical and philological investigations prove, beyond the possibility
of doubt, that, whilst the races differ from each other in certain
leading characteristics, they coincide so far as to justify us in referring them all to a common origin. They may be most conveniently
divided into three distinct stems: the Ethiopian or Negro, which,
considering its general character, may be compared to the darkness
of night, the Mongol, to the faint light of dawn, and the Caucasian,
to the full blaze of day. The Malays, Hottentots, Indians, &c.,
whose influence upon the progress of society has been very trifling,
are to be regarded rather as degenerate branches of races than independent races themselves.

§ 3. From the Bible and numerous traditionary legends of various nations geographically separated, this much may be gathered
with absolute certainty: our first parents lived in a state of happy
innocency, which was destroyed by sin; in consequence of this
defection, they were driven out of the garden of Eden, and compelled to eat their bread in the sweat of their brow; with their multiplication and distribution over the earth, arose the distinction of
races and tribes; the character of their descendants was gradually
improved by the art of working in metals, by the practise of agriculture, by a gradual acquaintance with the powers of nature, and
by the purifying influence of their religion, which was divinely
appointed to teach them their dependance upon Him whose law
they had violated.

To give a minute description of the peculiar privileges our first
parents enjoyed in Paradise, does not fall within the province of
Universal History. Still, it may not be improper to mention, that
the biblical account concerning the character of Adam, cannot be
referred to any intellectual superiority, but to the purity of his
heart and the possession of inward peace with his Maker.

As regards the creation of woman, it is worthy of remark, that
whilst the Bible recognized a decided difference between the sexes
in physical organization, in mental and moral capacities, it also
teaches that this diversity is a necessary condition for their proper
union. Among the nations which flourished before the time of

Christ, females were not honored with the respect they justly deserve, but lived either in a state of absolute slavery, or shared the affections of their husbands with jealous rivals. But the rights and dignity of woman were clothed with imperishable glory by the great fact of the incarnation, and enforced upon the attention of men by the doctrines inculcated by the son of David.

According to 1 M ii. 15, the happiness of our first parents did not consist in inglorious ease, or sluggish torpidity. Within the inclosure of their celestial home, in meek submission to the will of God, they performed their appointed work without experiencing the sharp pangs of sorrow; in strains of heavenly eloquence they pronounced His high praises, uninterrupted by the wild jargon of discord. But their glory was withered by the poisonous blast of sin; the harmony of their souls was disordered, and death introduced into every department of the universe.

As man put forth his activities in a period when it was impossible to collect historical material and transmit it in writing to posterity, the numerous attempts to trace with distinct accuracy the progress of our race from its original condition, from the state of the hunter, of the fisherman, of the shepherd, to the formation of the first kingdoms, have never been crowned with complete success. In the Bible we have some satisfactory hints recorded. vide 1 M. 4. God did not permit man to run on in a course of sin without throwing in his path some obstructions; in the exercise of the most watchful solicitude, He endeavored to awaken him to a knowledge of his misery and to an intense longing after the promised Messiah, 1 M. iii. 15.

§ 4. As the deluge swept into oblivion the productions of human industry during this obscure period, it is neither necessary nor important to asscertain the precise extent of its duration. After the flood, we find the survivors of the race at Mt. Ararat, on the high table land between the Black and Caspian seas.

That this awful catastrophe which caused the destruction of nearly the whole human family really occurred, has been abundantly proved, apart from the veracity of the Bible, by the traditionary records of ancient nations. Humboldt discovered clear intimations concerning some vast flood of waters that overwhelmed the earth in ruin, in the legends of Central America.

Whatever conjectures we may entertain concerning the physical appearance of the antediluvian world—and beyond mere conjecture

we cannot go, because the flood extinguished all the manners customs, arts, sciences of this early period—we are compelled to admit
without any clear historical evidence, as a necessary result of the
laws of nature, that the surface of the earth was materially changed
by the desolation occasioned by the deluge.

§ 5. The sacred writings attribute the repopulation of the world
to the activity of Noah's three sons. From Mt. Ararat, as a starting
point, they spread in different directions; the descendants of Shem
settled in the southern and eastern part of Asia; of Ham, in the
south-western, and in the neighborhood of the Nile; of Japhet, in
the north-western part of Asia, and in Europe.

In a branch of Shem's family, was preserved the knowledge of
the true God. In 1 M. ix. 27, is recorded a prophecy of the future
historical importance of Japhet's descendants, who in the course of
time became the monarchs of the world, and were first made acquainted with the economy of the Gospel.

With the dispersion of nations, whilst they were engaged in building the tower of Babel, language, which had hitherto preserved its
unity, fell into a state of interminable confusion. A multitude of
tongues, distinguished from each other by essential differences, but
proving their common origin by many points of similarity, spread
over the earth. In the Indo-Germanic family formed by the sons
of Japhet, are included the Indian, the Greek, the Latin, the German, the Sclavonic, together with their cognate languages. This
family occupies an extensive tract of country; it reaches from the
extreme south of India to Iceland, in the north-western part of Europe, and bids fair to take full possession of America. The Shemites gave birth to the Chaldaic, the Syriac, the Hebrew, the Arabic,
together with their kindred tongues; the Hamites, to the Caanantic,
the Mongolian, the Ethiopian, and all the languages of Africa.

§ 6. Historical and geographical facts furnish convincing proof,
that the physical, intellectual and moral culture of any race depends,
more or less, upon the outward configuration of the country in which
it has settled. In the formation of human character, two influences
are continually operative. Man as spirit, stands in the closest connection with the invisible world, and is exposed to its hallowed influences; as body, he is bound to the earth and subject to changes
effected by temperature of climate, diversity of surface, beauty of
scenery. But as body and soul are only different phases of one life,
and reciprocally influence each other, it is clear that the internal

structure of man may be modified by the outward forces of nature.

Thus it is that in fruitful plains and well watered valleys, where agriculture reaches its perfection, a tranquil and peacable life prevails; in deserts and steppes, which induce a roaming habit, a pastoral life; in mountainous districts, which compel its inhabitants to obtain subsistence by hunting, a warlike and predatory disposition is engendered. The inhabitants of commodious seacoasts, who may be called the mediators between distant countries, imbibe a strong attachment to commerce and navigation; whilst the immigrant cast upon barren and inhospitable shores, who consumes his energies in endeavoring to secure a scanty livelihood by fishing, forms a hardy and robust character in continual conflict with the tumultuous elements of nature.

§ 7. The apostacy of man from God, was an apostacy from his own original dignity. Having lost the knowledge of his previous superiority over all the works of nature, and laboring with systematic zeal to efface the remembrance of his obligations to his Maker, he gave to the finite creature the worship due alone to the infinite Creator, attributed to natural powers sanctifying influences, and effectually precluded, in this way, the possibility of redemption from the curse of sin.

The three original races, however, were not involved to the same extent in the moral obliquity which characterized the heathen world generally. The descendants of Japhet, terrified by the magnficent appearances of nature, sought their protection by invoking their assistance. Captivated by the surpassing beauty of the human form and the vigor of the human intellect, they divested their gods of supernatural attributes and degraded them to the level of mere human beings. The sons of Ham whose understanding had been darkened by the worship of animals, degenerated into a miserable Feticism and clothed the idea of a supreme power with a gloomy, diabolical character. The Shemites alone, one branch of which race retained a faint remembrance of the true God, recognized in the majestic course of the planets and their brilliancy, proofs of Divine power and wisdom.

§ 8. As we are not able to determine precisely the duration of the ante-historic period, we cannot point out the particular time when it terminated. If we date the creation of the world in round numbers from 4000 A. C., the deluge happened, according to Scripture chronology, 2350 A. C.

We cannot regard as authentic sources of information, the chronological tables and genealogies in the possession of some oriental nations which have elaborated a claim to the remotest antiquity by the successive accumulation of thousands upon thousands of years. Such an incongruous and unwarrantable connection of immense periods of time, always betrays a shallow conception of history, and arises not infrequently from a very inaccurate knowledge of the significance of historical events, and a vain desire on the part of a nation to increase its claims to respect by putting on the venerable garb of old age.

§ 9. The proper sphere of history, as distinguished from the unsatisfactory accounts of the ante-historic period, begins with the time when single kingdoms assume a fixed, definite form, when the sources of information commend themselves to our notice by the certainty of their character, and are no longer accompanied with a host of fables and marvellous stories.

The primitive form of human society is the Patriarchal, in which the members of a family are subordinated to the control of the father, who presides over its interests by a kind of natural right. But this simple form of life could not always maintain its authority. In the course of time, it was succeeded by the formation of tribes or clans. These contractions, alliances for the purpose of resisting the encroachments of ambitious patriarchs, gradully enlarged the limits of government and prepared the way for the rise of independent kingdoms. With the patriarchal, or nomadic state, however, the proper sphere of history, strictly speaking, does not commence. The permanent settlement of an agricultural people in a country according with their mode of life, necessarily and imperceptibly occasioned the enactment of laws, of ordinances, and of treaties. As man advanced in the scale of civilization, new relations sprang into being which required either an improvement of previously existing laws, or the introduction of new ones. Thus, in the course of time, and in entire accordance with the natural growth of society, there arose the different occupations of life, as agriculture, hunting, &c., together with the various classes of men as hunters, shepherds, farmers, tradesmen, warriors, priests, &c., who filled these several stations. At the head of these different orders stood a particular cast, which exercised a kind of sovereign power.

•   •   •   •   •   •   •

Part II.—A.— *The Chinese.*
§ 11. *Geographical Outline.*

From the eastern and southern terminations of the high table-land which covers Central Asia, the empire of China, containing, according to the most recent computation, a population of two hundred millions of souls, stretches its immense surface southward to India, and to the Pacific ocean on the east. China proper, which here claims our attention particularly, is separated from the other countries of Asia by vast chains of mountains and uncultivated steppes, and from the rest of the world by tempestuous seas. Down from its principal western mountains, stream two mighty rivers, the Hoang Ho and the Tang tse Kiang. The country which these waters traverse, presents a soil of unparalleled fertility. The mountains of China abound in metals; it is richly provided with every species of animals and plants.

§ 12. *Influence of these Geographical Relations.*

This planet which is so admirably adapted for the residence of intelligent creatures, is the divinely appointed hall in which an intellectual and moral race are to receive their education.

In the formation of individual and national character, and in the progress of civilization, two elements perfectly distinct, but in their action reciprocal, are continually at work. As above remarked, the peculiar configuration of continents and the geographical position of particular countries, with their mountains and valleys, their lakes and rivers, exert a controlling influence on the people who inhabit them. Mere outward circumstances, however, would be insufficient to give a distinctive direction to the activities of any nation, if there were at hand no peculiar mental and spiritual constitution upon which they could operate. In passing judgment upon the character of any people, the historian must not only recognize the influence which geographical circumstances exert, but must also describe the peculiar spiritual constitution with which Providence has endowed them.

As respects China, the impress of its peculiar situation is clearly discernible. Its geographically isolated position, and the rich fertility of its soil, excite in the Chinese a feeling of self dependance and a spirit of national vanity, which causes them to treat all foreigners as barbarians. But man is formed for society; his nature can never be fully unfolded except as he cultivates domestic and international relations.   On this account it is that the Chinese, who began and carried forward, to some extent, the work of civilization, never succeeded either in unfolding their natural resources, or in advancing the general interests of society.

§ 13. *History of China.*

Next to the Hebrews, the Chinese, a branch of the Mongol race, lay claim to a prodigious antiquity.   Without pretending to discuss the justice or injustice of their claims, which have been ably defended by some historians, and as ably assailed by others, we will date the commencement of the Chinese empire, 3082 B. C.; though we are not prepared to furnish satisfactory reasons for selecting this particular time.   On account of the monotonous uniformity which characterizes its history and its complete isolation from the rest of the world, and in order to preclude the necessity of returning to its consideration, we will delineate its history from the earliest times to the present day.

The ancestors of the Chinese, like those of all other Asiatic nations, are supposed to have descended from the neighboring mountains of central Asia.   In their governmental relations, they allow themselves to be called by no national name, but sometimes assume the names of their emperors.   So extravagant is their vanity, that they imagine their country occupies the centre of the globe, and proudly dignify themselves with appellations such as "the Celestial Empire, the Middle Kingdom," &c.

Their oldest rulers discharged the functions both of teachers and lawgivers.   Of these Fu Hi and Chai Mung, who are supposed to have instructed the earliest inhabitants in agriculture, in the manufacture of silk, in writing and other useful arts, were honored with peculiar respect.   Soon after their death, the method of computing time by divisions of sixty years' duration, was introduced.

Tú, the Great, (2297 B. C.,) before whose accession to the throne an elective form of government was practised, divided the kingdom into nine provinces, and ordered charts of them to be engraved on iron plates.   His immediate successors, who were neither possessed of his political abilities, nor favored by the good fortune which generally attended his plans, exposed the empire to foreign invasions by their impolitic measures, and brought destruction upon his dynasty by their weakness, 1766 B. C.   From this period down to the present time, the government of China was successively conducted by twenty-one dynasties.

From the earliest times onward through the entire period of its existence, three influences, in their operation exceedingly injurious, retarded the prosperity of China and checked its growth. The gross licentiousness and oppressive cruelty of some of its rulers, destroyed the moral sense of the people by encouraging the indulgence of unbridled passion; the feudal system which had been framed and put into operation by the energetic Mu Mang, broke the unity of the empire by increasing beyond lawful bounds the rights and privi‐ leges of individual kings: to complete the disorder, the fierce Tar‐ tars rushed from their original abodes, and devastated the country they had unlawfully invaded.

During the third dynasty, (1122–249 B. C.,) flourished the two most profound philosophers of China, La Riam and Confucius. But their scientific investigations had no power to relieve their country from the heavy load of misery which now afflicted it. Even Con‐ fucius, though worthy of our admiration as a teacher of morals and a preserver of peace in a kingdom distracted by internal dissensions, could not move the immobility of the Chinese by the vigor of his thoughts, nor purge the immorality of their conduct by the pure precepts of his ethical system, nor rectify the disorders of their gov‐ ernment by his representation of filial piety as the root of all virtue, and the sure guaranty of good citizenship. During the fourth dy‐ nasty, (246–210,) which witnessed the erection of the Great Wall as a defence against the destructive invasions of the northern Tar‐ tars, the empire rose to a height of prosperity and glory hitherto unattained. This period of political renown was followed in the fifth dynasty, by an extensive and successful cultivation of the sci‐ ences. The historian Scema dispelled the ignorance of the age by his learned researches; the old canonical books known by the name of Ring, were collected and formed into a system; the art of print‐ ing, not with moveable types, but from blocks of wood, with charac‐ ters carved in the manner of sculpture, was invented.

The progress of Chinese civilization thus auspiciously commenced, was interrupted by the rise of civil dissensions, which again desola‐ ted the country with fearful ruin, and gave occasion for the inroads of the Topa Tartars, who conquered the greatest portion of China. In the southern provinces, which happily escaped the grasp of these invaders, the eighth dynasty was founded by Song, 420 A. D.

These civil feuds continued during the century immediately following. An account of them would be neither interesting nor profitable. A more terrible storm which had been gathering its strength many years before its appearance, poured its wrath upon the unfortunate Chinese. In the first part of the thirteenth century, the Mongols, under the celebrated Yinges Khan, invaded the empire, subverted the government, and compelled them to submit to the yoke of a foreign dynasty. But the destruction of their political independance did not in the least change their peculiar national character. With an obstinate stubborness which the severest penalties could not abate, they clung to the customs of their fathers and even induced their conquerors to adopt their laws and institutions. Pekin became the capital of the empire, and the erection of the Great Imperial canal commenced 1280 A. D.

The rule of the Mongols was of short duration. They were compelled to evacuate the country in the year 1368, by the outbreak of a revolution occasioned by a priest, who formed the resolution to deliver his countrymen from the oppression of their invaders. Soon after, 1616, the Mantchew Tartars advanced to the frontiers of China, and declared that they had been summoned by a Divine call to subjugate the country. After a series of fiercely contested battles, they succeeded in establishing their own government, and founded the twenty-second, or Tai Tsin dynasty, which still has undisputed possession of the throne. Various attempts have been made, particularly by Jesuit missionaries of the Roman Catholic Church, to bring the Chinese under the influence of the Gospel, but their obstinate adherence to old customs, and hatred to all innovations, have rendered all such laudable efforts unsuccessful. Very recently, however, the gates of the celestial empire, for so long a time closed against the inhabitants of the western world, have been unbarred; the thunder of the English cannon before the walls of Canton, may prove to have been the precursor of the final triumph of Christianity over a godless heathenism.

The name of the present emperor is Tao Kwang. He commenced his reign 1821.

The most extensive work on Chinese history, is the *Historie générale de la Chine*, par Mailla. He continues the history to the year 1736, A. D.

§ 14.   *The Character of the Chinese in general.*

Though inferior to the Mongolian and Tartar nations in courage and bodily strength, the Chinese, who are members of the same race, possess good natural endowments. The ingenuity and inventive character of their mind preserves them from falling into a state of stupid indifference; their love of order in the various relations of life, tends to the cultivation of taste; their industry promotes at least the physical welfare of the country, while the cool, calculating judgment which directs their conduct, restrains them from the commission of impolitic actions. Their complete isolation from the civilizing influences of the world at large, and the proud consciousness of being dependant alone upon their own resources for the necessaries of life, have not only inspired them with a fixed aversion to the introduction of every foreign element, and incapacitated them for examining impartially the productions of other nations and acknowledging their decided superiority, but have also effectually retarded their own progress in civilization. Their history, in this respect, furnishes clear proof that no nation, how brilliant soever its natural capacities may be, can make continuous advances in the proper cultivation of its own resources, except as it enters into living communion with surrounding nations. Providence in his wisdom has so arranged the various departments of society, that its perfection depends upon the extent of their mutual influence.

The constitutional defect in Chinese character, is an overbearing vanity which looks down upon the world with supreme contempt, and regards its inhabitants as uncultivated barbarians. Believing that no advance can be made beyond the science and art of their ancestors, the Chinese are disposed to consider the mental productions of other nations as unwarrantable innovations, which only deserve the ridicule of all great and good men No one dare presume to be wiser than their fathers were. But this sweeping judgment, if reversed, will accord better with the facts of history and approach nearer to the truth. Their childish predilection for everything which bears the impress of antiquity, may call forth a smile for their folly and provoke our wrath at the obstinacy with which they endeavor to check the onward march of history. Their sensibility is rather blunt; their imaginative powers very weak; all is the product of cold reason. They are influenced neither by the stirrings of a laudable enthusiasm, nor by a spirit of active enterprize; in the regular discharge of the ordinary duties of life, they are content to live without ever attempting to ameliorate their condition: like little children, they find most delight in games and plays, in gewgaws and gilded puppets.

From the earliest period on record, such has been the character of the Chinese; nor have they ever succeeded in advancing from this contracted state to a higher and more ennobling condition. Their violation of the wholesome laws which govern the progress of civilization, entailed upon them and their descendants the bitterest miseries. As they refused to enter into active intercourse with other nations for the purposes of self-culture, and stoutly resisted the introduction of foreign elements, in direct opposition to the designs of Providence, they degenerated into a stiff uniformity in every department of life, for lack of fresh educational elements to stir them up to renewed activity in the performance of their mission. All is at a stand-still. Even their language, which forms the basis of all true intellectual culture, because it is the organ for the expression of thought, possesses neither beauty nor flexibility, but is characterized by tedious monotony and a construction so arbitrary, as to render an acquaintance with it almost impossible. It is a law of universal application, clearly established by the facts of history, that those nations which do not strive to unfold their physical and mental resources by oft repeated efforts, and recruit their energies whenever exhausted by an appropriation of fresh material from abroad, lose all vigor, and, in the end, become what may be called historical petrifaction. Thus with the huge empire of China. It may be compared to an unwieldy machine of gigantic proportions, put in motion, not by any self-moving force, but by outward mechanical appliances, which continually produces the same effect and wastes its strength by the labor of its action. It has not only lost the results of the civilization its inhabitants obtained in those ages when they were characterized by some activity, but it has atcually been undergoing a retrograde movement. The influence which it exerts at the present day upon the progress of society, is comparatively insignificant and trifling.

§ 15. *The Private Life of the Chinese.*

Among the Chinese, males and females dress in nearly the same apparel. The Tartar emperors, who never succeeded in destroying their peculiar customs, compelled them, nevertheless, to adopt the

practice of tonsuring. The age of twenty they regard as the transition from youth to manhood. Gentlemen of education, like the
ladies of our own country, are in the habit of carrying an ornamen-
tal fan.

Females are educated in the family circle and kept in a state of
strict seclusion. At the age of ten, boys are sent to school, where
they learn to read and write. After having received instruction in
the principles of a few useful works, they begin the study of the Sacred Books which form the basis of the entire political and social
organization of China. Under the superintendence of the public
authorities, whose business it is to inquire into the progress of the
pupils, two annual examinations are instituted.

The Chinese wife lives in a state of complete retirement. Marriage contracts are formed by the parents, with the aid of some
female friend, independantly of the wishes of the parties concerned.
Various causes have tended to divest the females of China of their
natural dignity. In the eastern provinces, particularly, where the
overcrowded population induces mothers to strangle their babes at
birth, they are treated with great disrespect.

In social intercourse, the Chinese are characterized by affected
politeness and an unnatural stiffness of manners. The rules of eti-
quette, which they are bound to practice, are enforced by legal
enactments as laid down in one of their old lawbooks. Their fastidious urbanity, especially towards public officers, and pedantic
refinement, engender a cringing, slavish disposition, which destroys
proper self-respect and prepares them to become the submissive tools
of their superiors. Though extremely fond of feasts and lively
sports, their domestic life presents a predominantly serious aspect.

In obedience to the laws of their religion, which have been invariably observed from time immemorial, they pay great respect to
the dead.

§ 16. *Their Public Life—The State.*

Chinese society is composed of two leading classes, the common
people and the mandarins. The monks or priests constitute a sort
of middle class. Agriculture is the principal employment; rice the
chief product. Manufactures and trade receive a considerable share
of attention, but are generally confined to the limits of the empire.

The Kuanfu, or as the Portuguese call them, the Mandarins, em-

bracing the superior officers, the literati, and the warriors, which
are again subdivided into several distinct divisions, from the higher
class.

The form of government is an unlimited monarchy, or a pure
despotism. Divine honors are paid to the emperor, who is styled
the Son of Heaven. A chief board of officers residing at Pekin,
assisted by subordinate boards in the different provinces, conduct
the machinery of government. With each board is connected a
censor, whose business it is secretly to observe the actions of the
people and to report to the emperor all movements which may
threaten the ruin of the empire. The statute-book consists of two
hundred and fifty volumes; the army of one million of men who
possess neither strength nor courage; the navy is quite insignificant.

§ 17.   *Chinese Art.*

In the department of Art considered as the expression of the
beautiful in nature and spirit, in distinction from the useful arts
which minister rather to the wants than to the pleasures of mankind, the Chinese occupy a very low rank. Their artists, as they
never conceived a sublime idea, find most delight in the expression
of distortion and deformity. Their productions consist of grotesque,
disproportioned monsters, bearing the impress of childish folly and
disgusting beyond measure.

According to the most authentic records, the Chinese received
the first impulse to the study of art from India, 1 A. D., when they
came in contact with the religious system of Fo (Buddha). But, as
observed above, a marked feature in their character is the absence of
imagination, and an absolute inability to comprehend the real significance of an idea in its pure essence. That poetical enthusiasm
which lifts the soul above the confines of sense from things visible
into the region of things invisible, is repressed and completely destroyed by the dry, prosaic tendency of the Chinese intellect.
They are constitutionally disqualified either for the conception or
appreciation of a work of true art. They were neither captivated
with the glowing fancy of the Indian, nor stimulated to mental
activity by the profundity of his speculations. When Indian art
was transplanted to the soil of China, its glory and beauty departed.

The Indian Dagob, in the form of a water-bubble to represent the
brevity and vanity of life, furnished the model for the most impor-
ant architectural productions of China. Its proportions, however,

were considerably modified. The symbolical cupola was changed into a lofty steeple, rising up in nine successive stories, with small sloping roofs, narrowing as they approached the top; the tiles were painted with a brilliant yellow and the sides variegated with polished porcelain. The Chinese temples, which do not differ materially from the elegant mansions of private citizens, are of small dimensions. They are surrounded by rows of pillars. The roof is decorated by undulating lines, by carvings of fabled heroes and hideous figures. It is very evident from the historical remains of their artistic productions, which generally wear a repulsive, prosaic appearance, having neither grace nor justness of proportion, that the Chinese never came to an understanding of the real nature of the Fine Arts. But in the department of practical architecture, the great wall which extends along the northern frontier fifteen hundred miles in length, proves that they possessed superior skill in mechanical construction. It is said by those who have made the necessary calculations, that the materials of which it is composed would be sufficient to construct a wall of ordinary height and thickness around the whole earth. Mere accuracy of execution, however, does not by any means exhaust the conception of art. Therein precisely consists their defect, that they failed to discover the difference between useful and liberal arts, and converted the latter into mere mechanical drudgery. The artist, possessed of keen perception, whose taste has been trained to a just appreciation of the beautiful, may observe in the Chinese, as they gaze upon their works, the thought struggling up into existence, that the idea of art requires vastly more than a servile imitation of nature; but the embodiment of this thought in an outward form they never could accomplish. In the representation of domestic objects they evince an accuracy of observation worthy of praise. They paint insects, birds, fruits, and flowers, very beautifully, and render them quite attractive by the variety of their coloring. Their paintings, in many respects, resemble those of the Indians, but have not the same poetic beauty. In drawing, they are awkward and clumsey. Of perspective they have not the smallest notion. The fact that distant objects appear smaller than those immediately present, they attribute to a defect in the eyes. Of music the Chinese have ever been immoderately fond, but have neither skill in its execution nor a perception of proper harmony. Their gamut consisting of five tones, is very imperfect, the keys being inconsistent. They have no knowledge of semitones, or of counterpoint. The performance of their dra-

mas which, for the most part, are devoid of deep thought, and occupied with the representation of love scenes and harlequin tricks,
is accompanied with music and song. Their best poetical productions, consisting partly of lyric, partly of didactic compositions, are
contained in their canonical books. With novels and romances
they are abundantly supplied. It is not necessary to enter into a
minute description of their poetry. It is not characterized by any
striking beauties; its chief defect is, a barrennes of lofty ideas. The
Chinese who live in the cold region of the finite Understanding,
and never entered the territory of pure thought, cannot be expected
to excel in this department of art.

§ 18. *Chinese Science.*

Several causes have contributed to retard the progress of the
Chinese in science. Apart from the influence of their natural disposition, which has no tendency at all towards the mystic and invisible, but is best satisfied with such ideas as require no labored
thoughts, and commend themselves to an indolent mind by clear
shallowness, their language—the best exponent of a nation's mind
—on account of its poverty, its artificial arrangement and its stubborn
inflexibility, opposes a barrier almost insurmountable. It is composed
of only two hundred and seventy-two primitive roots. A variety of sig-
nifications in no wise connected by inward similarity, but denoted by
the modulation of the voice, by different methods of accentuation and
by a host of written characters, is frequently attached to the same
word. Our knowledge of Chinese science is still very limited, notwithstanding the recent learned researches of European antiquarians.
China has never been the theatre of great philosophical developments. Its learned men seldom allow their minds to be disturbed
by profound meditation on the essence of Deity, and the relation
which he sustains to the world. Their labor is expended on the
different branches of natural philosophy, on geography, on medicine,
and in the formation of scientific encyclopedias.

On the subject of Chinese literature, the Spanish Dominican
Pater Taso, who, in 1703, composed the first Chinese grammar,
deserves particular praise. In the beginning of the last century, a
lexicon was issued by the Minoret Basilius a Flemona, containing
definitions of ten thousand written characters. During the present
century Antonio Martucci, of Siena, and Julius Klaproth, of Berlin,
have thrown much light upon the antiquities of China. Of most

value, however, is the work of Abel Reumsat on the Chinese language, published at Paris, 1822.

§ 19. *Chinese Religion.*

The old religious system of the Chinese was of a simple and patriarchal character. Here, as well as in their civilization, generally, they never advanced beyond the first stage of culture. They adored one supreme, all-powerful Being; believed in the existence of Genii and protecting spirits, who were subject to His control, and placed a high value on the efficacy of prayer and sacrifices. When Confucius appeared, the ancient religion had lost its power. Gross immorality abounded. The entire nation was involved in religious and political disorders. He endeavored to correct the vices which had crept into the state by representing the prince as the father of his people, and to suppress the prevailing licentiousness by insisting on the cultivation of those practical virtues which had in former days crowned China with prosperity. His ethical system was gladly welcomed by those who mourned over the degradation of their country. After his death, his disciples, who were enthusiastically attached to his person, zealously propagated his doctrines. Contemporary with Confucius flourished another religious system of an Epicurean character. It discarded the doctrine of immortality, and sought to break the power of death by medical prescriptions. About the time of Christ, the Fo religion was transplanted to China from India. At the present day, it numbers about one million of priests, who impose upon the people the grossest superstitions.

But all the religious systems of China, that of Confucius not excepted, whose ethical precepts were certainly well adapted to promote the temporal interests of his countrymen, could not restore man to a proper moral position. We seek in vain for a recognition of the true nature of sin, which had disturbed the harmony of his soul. That, which forms the grand characteristic of all true religion —the idea of an atonement for sin, as the only means of deliverance from its power—is left out of sight altogether. There are some historians, who go so far as to consider the Fo system a perfected form of Atheism.

The question, which has of late elicited considerable discussion, whether the religion of Fo can be regarded as being identical with the Buddhism of India, admits of no satisfactory solution, on account of the defectiveness of our historical information.

§ 20. *Concluding Remarks.*

The gigantic empire of China presents the astonishing spectacle of an entire nation remaining stationary for thousands and thousands of years. Here the most modern is at the same time the most antient. Its civilization is, as it were, stereotyped. Its present condition is marked by the same features it possessed centuries ago; no improvement, no advance of society is discernable. Why this? Providence, surely, never intended that any nation should be compelled to check its growth at any particular period of its history, and become stagnant. Progression is the divinely appointed law of the Universe. But this progress depends upon certain fixed principles, and one of them is, that a nation must not surround itself with the net of selfishness, and obstinately refuse intercourse with its neighbors, but open its ports for the reception of those commodities its own territory does not supply, and enrich its own poverty by the appropriation of the rich treasures of foreign nations. The geographical isolation of China has left its seal invincibly stamped upon the social, political, intellectual and moral character of its inhabitants. On this account it is, that Chinese civilization presents a dwarfish, stunted appearance. Again, a solid and progressive civilization depends upon the healthy growth of society generally, and the gradual improvement of its individual members. These two factors must never contradict each other; the amelioration of the social system must go hand in hand with the expansion of the faculties of individuals. The predominance of any one of them tends invariably to stop the advancement of civilization. In China, the interests of the one are secured at the expense of the other. An empty tyrannical formalism rules with imperious sway, subordinating to itself every individual movement and crushing the risings of personal freedom. That spiritual instinct, the birthright of every nation, which stirs up to activity the native energies of a people, is completely destroyed. Society becomes still more unsettled, if this outward despotism stands above the common interests of the people, refuses to sympathize with their necessities and alleviate their miseries. Such is the actual condition of China. Its government is conducted by a few aristocratic families, who own no affinity with their subjects, but keep them in check with the rod of tyranny. Educated under the influence of such defective views of life, the spirit of the nation has quietly sunk into the miserable slavery of traditional laws, and fallen under the control of cruel tyrants.

ART. XLI.—A PLEA FOR OUR OLFACTORIES.

I AM not inclined to fall in with the great German critics, when they assert in their books that with the inferior senses poetry has nothing to do; that with the two superior, the visual and the auditory, it holds all its sweet converse. As regards the rest of the Fine Arts this may be true enough. Music, I admit, thrills at once the auditory nerve, and painting, sculpture and architecture throw at once their beautiful images on the *camera obscura* of the eye. The impressions created within, are fac-similes of the outward objects. . Their pleasures, therefore, may be said properly, to belong to the eye or ear. They have little to do with the other senses. But is this the case with poetry? When read aloud to us, does it impart to the tympanum of the ear its fac-similes? In the mere sound of its words does its rapture wholly consist? I am disposed to think not. Little else than the part of a telegraphic wire does the auditory nerve, in this case, perform, conveying unweetingly its despatches to the sensorium behind. Again, when silently we peruse a poem, does it impress on the retina of the eye its images, or pictures? Certainly not. Impressed there are only letters. Still further back, on the sensorium, are brought out its daguerreotypings, by the imagination. This faculty, however, has the power of setting forth, not only visions, but also fragrances. In descriptive poetry, it can make us catch the very odors of the scene portrayed. Our olfactories are wrought upon often as powerfully as our organs of sight. Our noses, to be sure, have no Fine Art of their own, addressing them immediately from without, but do they not, in poetic pleasures, participate with our eyes and ears? Do not their fancies often form the sweetest parts of a described landscape?

Of the nose, what low ideas are too generally entertained by the romantic, unreflecting portion of mankind—*ignobile vulgus!* As a mere sentinel set over the mouth, with which alone it sympathizes, they consider it! All its annoyances and abuses they remember; all its sensitive delights they forget! As a standing butt, they look upon it, if in any-wise peculiar in its shape, at which any one may be hurling his rude jests. Though in outward show, the most imposing, commanding organ, they consider it in real importance the very least; and were its virtue for them destroyed, which, in truth, I would not care if it was, considering how little they can appre-

ciate its advantages, nothing thereat they declare they would be
grieved, but rather somewhat delighted, as in that case they would
be freed from its intolerable stenches. A becoming ornament to
the countenance they admit, for they cannot deny it, that it is; but
from its position, they exclaim, how wonderfully exposed to being
tweaked! How wonderfully well adapted too, they should have
observed, for penetrating into the corols of blossoms, or for extending
its orifices over fruits or mouths of bottles, and extracting thence
their odors! Have not the eyes and ears their annoyances and
antipathies too, their ugly sights and discordant sounds? If those
addressed to the nose be more offensive, is not this indicative of its
having finer feelings? Must not its joys be, in proportion, more
lively and exhilarating? Even its professed advocates, those who
have spoken and written in its behalf, have not always seized on its
strongest points. Why does Slawkenbergius dwell so much on its
physical proportions and make so little account of its sensitive
shrewdness, as he is represented by Sterne? In that adjudged case
too, of Cowper, though, to be sure, the spectacles in fine are award-
ed to the nose, yet, why is it shown off, while wearing them thus
confirmed, the eyes shut the while, in such an asinine, ridiculous
position? In truth, that whole case is fabulous; well suited, no
doubt, to convey an instructive moral, but certainly not in character. To be putting in claims for spectacles, or any other chattel,
belonging to the eyes, is not after the modest fashion of the nose.
The grievances have always been from the other side. The Peter
robbed has generally been this organ, and the Pauls paid thereby
eyes. For inestimable favors conferred upon us by our olfactories,
we are too prone to award the whole credit to our visual organs.

Of poetry addressed to the nose, the finest specimens are not to
be met with in the ancient classics. The Greeks and Romans
indulged in many "odoraments to smell to," it is true. In liquid
odors for their heads they delighted, and their festival chaplets were
often redolent; of which things their lyric bards make honorable
mention, for which we thank them. Indeed, in their love of per-
fumes they far surpassed the moderns; but, after all, they cannot
be said, in their day, to have come to the ascertainment of the full
poetic faculty of the nose. That harmonizing of the senses, that
rendering, in descriptions, the perceptions of one more vivid by
using metaphorically for it the appropriate language of another, the
old Greek authors were not wholly ignorant of, I admit. With

them, however, the transitions were generally ascending.   To render more graphic their descriptions of speech, or music, they often
borrowed language appropriate to the eye; but they never reversed
the order.   To aid descriptions of the eye's perceptions, they never
condescended to employ the language of the ear, and certainly not
that of the lower senses.   Thus Sophocles in his Oedipus Tyrannus:

Ἔλαμψε γὰρ τοῦ νιφόεντος ἀρτίως φανεῖσα
Φάμα παρνασσοῦ————————

Shone forth just now hath the *splendent* voice
From snow-clad Parnassus————————

Indeed, their transitions were confined almost wholly to the upper
two senses, the visual and the auditory.   Into the most worshipful
society of these, they seldom suffered to pass the perceptions of
the nose.   They looked upon it as a plebeian.   It had little to do
with the ideal world.   Its tendencies were downward.   With the
satirical upturning of this organ the Romans were especially struck.
Naso suspendere adunco, was with them a favorite figure.   Nicety
of judgment too, they typified by it.   Him of shrewd intellect
they described as being *emunctæ naris.*   The internal, invisible
traits of the mind, they thus showed forth figuratively by means of
the external visible features of the senses.   As an aid to hearing,
however, already furnished with its own beautiful, external volutes,
to call into requisition the perceptions of the nose, never entered
into their fancies.   To them this would have seemed like painting
the lily, or throwing a perfume on the violet.

   It was reserved for modern bards to arrive at the full truth in this
matter.   They found out, or rather felt intuitively, that music is
only vibrations; that it does not blend with the surrounding atmosphere; that of aromatics, on the other hand, the effluvia are
mingled with the breeze; that they become of their conveying fluid
an intermixed portion, and thus are brought into actual contact
with our olfactory nerves.   Possessing, therefore, of music the
etherial sublimity, they have besides of taste the pungent reality,
without any of its grossness.   No wonder then that, from comparison with odors, music suffers not; that, in fact, its descriptions
in this way, are rendered more graphic; at any rate under the
ennobling hand of Shakespeare:

> If music be the food of love, play on;
> Give me excess of it; that surfeiting,
> The appetite may sicken, and so die.——
> That strain again;——it had a dying fall:
> O, it came o'er my ear *like the sweet south,*
> *That breathes upon a bank of violets,*
> *Stealing and giving odor.*"
>
> *Twelfth Night. Act. I. Scene I.*

Milton, too, is pleased with such comparisons. Being deprived of sight, we might at first imagine that his other senses, from being called into more frequent use, on account of his loss, had thus become more sensitive and refined; wherefore he was led often to draw from their perceptions his similes. Not in his Paradise Lost, however, nor in his Paradise Regained, do we meet with the most striking examples of these, but in his minor poems, which were written in his youth, when his fancy was in its full bloom and his organs were all complete. Not, therefore, to his being confined to fewer senses, can we attribute his tact in this way, but to his full poetic temperament. Thus, for instance, in the Masque of Comus, he says:

> "At last, a soft and solemn-breathing sound
> Rose, *like a stream of rich distilled perfumes,*
> *And stole upon the air*, that even Silence
> Was took ere she was ware, and wish'd she might
> Deny her nature, and be never more
> Still, to be so displaced."

Indeed, not to odors alone, but sometimes even to the dull sensations of touch, he dares compare music, and that too, certainly, with the finest effect; as again in the same Masque:

> "Can any mortal mixture of earth's mould,
> Breathe such divine, enchanting ravishment?
> Sure something holy lodges in that breast,
> And with these raptures moves the vocal air
> To testify his hidden residence:
> How sweetly did they float upon the wings
> Of silence, through the empty vaulted night,
> At every fall *smoothing* the raven down
> Of darkness till it smiled!"

Descriptive poetry resembles landscape painting in a measure, it is true; but instead of its addresses being confined to the eye, as is too generally supposed to be the case, of its choice passages, some of the sweetest are spoken to the ear, and the most affecting,

or certainly the raciest, to the the the nose. Indeed, of this last organ
to the pleasures, as being the most exhilarating, the true poet rises
up mostly, as it were, by a sort of climax or gradation in description. In setting forth his landscape, in the first place, he directs
our fancy to its visual objects, then he lets us hear, if he can, the
chirpings of its feathered quiristers; but last of all, to complete the
picture and lap us in Elysium, he makes us breathe besides its
fragrance. The nearest thing to eating a landscape, which, of
course, we cannot do, is, in my opinion, the inhaling of its spicy
breath. No matter, on the other hand, how charming to the eye
may be the scenery described, or melodious to the ear the chanting
of its birds, if, in the slightest degree, its air be offensive to the nose,
it can never please. Thus Chaucer, in The Floure and the Leafe,
makes his gentlewoman describe, in the first place, the surrounding
oaks and the secreted arbor set "with sicamour and eglatere" in
which she was standing; then of the song from a goldfinch on a
medlar-tree, answered by that of a nightingale, whose position was
yet unseen, she discourseth; but last of all, in the following strain
of the combined fragrance of the laurer tree and eglentere, (now
called the bay-tree and sweet-brier,) she stirreth up the sweet remembrance :

> "Wherefore I waited about busily
> On every side if I her (the nightingale) might see,
> And at the last I gan full well aspie
> Where she sat in a fresh grene laurer tree,
> On the further side even right by me,
> That gave so passing a delicious smell,
> According to the eglentere full well.
>
> Wherof I had so inly great pleasure,
> That as me thought I surely ravished was
> Into Paradice, where my desire
> Was for to be, and no ferther passe
> As for that day, and on the sote grasse
> I sat me downe, for as for mine entent,
> The birds song was more conuenient,
>
> And more pleasaunt to me by manifold,
> Than meat or drinke, or any other thing,
> Thereto the herber (arbor) was so fresh and cold,
> The wholesome sauours eke so comforting,
> That as I demed, sith the beginning
> Of the world was neuer seene or than
> So pleasaunt a ground of none earthly man."

In the same way Milton represents the arch fiend, when approaching the borders of Eden, as being struck, in the first place, with the tempting beauty of the fruits and blossoms on the branches overreaching the high verdurous wall. Then, being still too distant, no doubt, to hear its music, he is inspired next, as set forth in the following lines, by the odors wafted in its breezes:

> ————"so lovely seemed
> That landscape; and of pure now purer air
> Meets his approach, and to the heart inspires
> Vernal delight and joy, able to drive
> All sadness but despair: now gentle gales
> Fanning their odoriferous wings, dispense
> Native perfumes, and whisper whence they stole
> Those balmy spoils. As when to them who sail
> Beyond the Cape of Hope, and now are past
> Mozambique, off at sea north-east winds blow.
> Sabéan odors from the spicy shore
> Of Araby the bless'd; with such delay
> Well pleased they slack their course, and many a league
> Cheered with the grateful smell old Ocean smiles.
> So entertained these odorous sweets the fiend,
> Who came their bane."
>
> *Paradise Lost. Book IV.*

Somewhat after the same manner, but with a bolder leap, Shakespeare, in setting forth the old romantic castle of Macbeth, springs at once, not *in medias* but *in ultimas res.* Without mentioning its impressions on the eye or ear, he calls up to the imagination its whole charming appearance by touching at once on the freshness of its surrounding atmosphere. Thus discourse king Duncan and Banquo while, after having dismounted, they are walking up leisurely towards its timehallowed front, regarding, with expanded nostrils, its imposing aspect:

> "DUNCAN:—This castle has a pleasant seat: *the air*
> *Nimbly and sweetly recommends itself*
> *Unto our gentle senses.*
> "BANQUO:— This guest of summer,
> The temple-haunting martlet, does approve,
> By his loved mansionry, *that the heaven's breath*
> *Smells wooingly here.* No jutty, frieze,
> Buttress, nor coigne of vantage, but this bird
> Hath made his pendent bed, and procreant cradle:
> Where they most breed and haunt, I have observed,
> *The air is delicate.*"
>
> *Macbeth. Act I. Scene VI.*

Reader, hast thou ever feasted thine olfactories on the blossoms of that shrub which, on account of their surpassing fragrance, is known commonly by the name of the sweet-scented (*calycanthus floridus*)?   Certainly thou hast, for it is now everywhere cultivated by the tasteful in their redolent gardens.   I rejoice exceedingly that it is no exotic; that it is not confined even to the Southern States as falsely laid down by botanists in their books, but that it is the production also of mine own native county.   From my window now, far down the valley, I can catch a faint glimpse of that transcendent knob, at whose base it once bloomed abundantly.   *Troja fuit!*   Its humble growth, not continuous, but in sparse clusters or single twigs, was confined to a small tract of ground, in some places rocky, carpeted with moss or mouldering leaves, overshadowed with oaks and other trees, embracing perhaps ten acres.   It was its only region.   In all my rambles north of Mason's and Dixon's line, I never fell in with another *placer*.   Its blooming season was in May or June.   And think you, it was left unobserved "to waste its sweetness on the desert air?"   I tell you nay.   Though in its scent was its whole attractive force—a dark, brown flower, without any outward show—yet, it acted as a powerful magnet, drawing, in its season, towards its hallowed precincts, many a cavalcade of youthful votaries often from twenty miles around.   With these, once or twice, in my juvenility, I was drawn along, nothing loth.   They partook, in some degree, of the pleasantry and good fellowship of that company, described by Chaucer, which wended on pilgrimage to Canterbury.   Their riders were not grouped, however, so diversely nor promiscuously, but strung out more at length into pairs of opposite sexes.   What were prospects or Mayings or berry-gatherings in comparison?   We were going on the sublimer embassage of the nose.   Like those pilgrims of Chaucer, we too dismounted, on our way, after having come over a disclosing hill, at our "gentil hostelrie," in the mountain-shadowed village of Strasburg, that was highte the Rising Sun; where we tarried and refreshed ourselves, an hour or two, ere we diverged from the main road westward into a narrower, shadier way, conducting us toward the enchanted region.

> "Gret chere made oure hoste us everich on,
> And to the souper sette he us anon:
> And served us with vitaille of the beste."

Mine host of the Rising Sun, now enjoying thy placid retirement and green old age in that ancient neighborhood, still dost thou sympathize with me, at least in part, on these savory reminiscences. In one thing, however, thou didst come short. Though a seemly man thou "wast with alle, for to han ben a marshal in an halle," yet thou wast not perfect in all thy parts. Except as tractors to others thou caredst nothing for the shrubs. To thee, as thou toldst me *sub rosa*, they smelt like chintzes. O, most unaccountable monomania of the nose! By thine idiosyncrasy from what a paradise wast thou excluded! Into what a Pandemonium was thou thrust! To us, and to every one in his sane nasal sense, they smelt like taste of strawberry or pine-apple only transcendently more exhilarating and delicious. Tales like those told on the way to Canterbury, or, indeed, of any sort, we had none. If told at all, it was only on the charmed ground to lady's ear. I regret excceedingly, as my country's loss, that, of late years, that spot has been desecrated, cropt off and rooted up by wandering herds and flocks. How conducive were its walks to courtship and romance! How awakening to love and poetry!

I am not ashamed to own that I sometimes give myself up entirely to the soft imaginings of my nose; that, stretched beneath some umbrageous beech-tree, I permit myself to be carried away by the inspirations of that organ, swept over, like an Æolean lyre, by the passing breezes. *Amabilis insania.*

> "Audire et videor pios
> Errare per lucos amoenæ
> Quos et aquæ subeunt et auræ."

In this way, instead of being degraded, I feel myself exalted. What utilitarian careth for odors as such? *Cui bono?* he crieth aloud. We confess, they cannot be turned into any practical utility; that no man becometh fatter or richer from having feasted on them his olfactories. They improve not his health nor his outward estate. No purely practical man, therefore, we are willing to admit, nor, in fact, any inferior animal, followeth after fragrances as a good in themselves. Their uses are higher. They strengthen our imaginations and superior faculties. They convey us at once into the aesthetic regions. How absurd then in any critic to exclude their organs from the province of the Fine Arts! It was a curious fact that, on arriving at that odorating spot of the shrubs above described, the votaries generally felt disposed to lisp in numbers. A few became for the time actually improvisators; others quoted old scraps of verse, while hardly one refrained from addressing, at any rate his partner, in strains of soft but highly impassioned eloquence. The most inveterate case that came under the divine afflatus of these blossoms, was that of H. G. He was a bachelor and affluent dry-goods-merchant in the somewhat distant village of S. From his boyhood he had been brought up to worship only Mammon. With him money was the *summum bonum;* and from all fragrances he turned away his scornful nose, as being unsatisfying and designed to mislead him from the tangible.

Like Chaucer's merchant,

> "His resons spake he ful solempnely
> Souning alway the encrese of his winning."

Having set forth from S——, one pleasant May-morning, on a collecting trip to the village of Strasburg, he was overtaken on the way by a select party of his acquaintance on their annual pilgrimage to the knob. For his own benefit they impressed him into their company. Observing in him, however, symptoms of uneasiness, a disposition at one time to gallop a-head, and, at another, to lag behind, they placed him under the safe-keeping of a sprightly young widow hight Mrs. Maria T. who held him in tow. When arrived at Strasburg, he would certainly have made his escape and gone about his collecting business, but he was restrained by a prudent gentleman of the party, who took him aside and reminded how extremely improper and impolitic in him it would be to desert the widow, who, without him, would be a supernumerary. She was one of his best customers, wearing actually at the time a riding habit the materials of which had been purchased at his own store. That he might not offend her, therefore, he was induced to go along; but when arrived at the spot, he showed no out-bursts of inspiration. He gathered no shrubs; but in fact scandalized the whole party by remarking that he would just as soon collect as many hops; and indeed rather, as such blossoms were wholesome and could be turned to some profitable account. Thereupon they gave him up as a hopeless case, a man whose imagination was utterly siccated, and they took no further pains to retain him in their company; so that on returning they lost sight of him, lagging behind, before they reached Strasburg; but what was their astonishment, on the following week, to observe in the S——— Gazette, his advertisement of new goods, extending down nearly half a column, composed the whole way in most capital verse!

As "the lover, the lunatic, and the poet, are of imagination all compact," no wonder that the spot was conducive also to courtship and matrimony. For every enamored swain, in that section of country, when he wished after a winter's hard siege, to bring at length his courtship to a happy consummation, it was a prevailing usage to invite his fair one to accompany him with others on a pilgrimage to the shrubs. Should she consent to be his partner on that occasion, he was a made-up man. He had no further difficulty in the case; as proposals among the shrubs were never scorned. They were always followed by espousals. Had the ancient Greeks and Romans been acquainted with the name and virtues of this aromatic they would certainly have crowned their god of marriage, Hymenæus with it instead of the fragrant *amaracus*. That unprecedented emigration latterly of forlorn bachelors from that neighborhood, drawn away, no doubt, by the unsatisfied yearnings of their noses, to remote southern and western climes, and the increased number, consequent thereupon, of deserted spinsters now to be met with throughout that whole section of country, I feel fully persuaded, is to be attributed, perhaps entirely, as a primitive cause, to the correspondingly increased numbers of ruthless swine and horned cattle which, of late years, have been permitted to roam at large through the once blissful but now desecrated vicinity of that stupendous knob.

W. M. N.

ART. XLII.—THE RELATION OF CHURCH AND STATE.

"WHAT constitutes reality?" This is the great and fundamental question which has divided the literary world, like the physical, into two great hemispheres. According to the one mode of thought, that only is *real* and *true*, the origin, the nature, the use and end of which can be determined by the calculating understanding, and stated in just so many words. Science is nothing more than the enumeration of phenomena and facts, and their classification as may be agreed upon by the learned. "Life itself is a mere harmony, an effect." Society is merely an aggregation of individuals united from choice. Government is a full grown "*Minerva*" sprung from the head of human wisdom. The State is a social compact entered into for the mutual defence of life property and rights. The Church is but the collective body of believers, who take the Bible as the ground of their faith and rule of their life:—the Bible, however, as interpreted by each one for himself, without being in the least dependent upon tradition, or the united wisdom of the church of by-gone ages. All relations are external, more or less, mechanical and arbitrary.

Natural phenomena stand related merely through the medium of contiguity, or mental association. The different members of the state are held together by the bond of interest, and motives of expediency. The bond of union between church members, is like that between the different parts of a mechanism, held together by the force of external power; or, to say the most, it. is merely of a moral character, as, for instance, the bond of friendship. The Church and State stand related as two voluntary associations; as, for instance, the societies of Free Masons and Odd Fellows, holding each other at respectful distance, from motives of mutual jealousy, and sometimes uniting the hands of friendship from motives of policy.

We do not maintain that this utilitarian, common sense practical philosophy is utterly void of truth, but that it is greatly at fault: it is one-sided, incomplete, outward, mechanical.

According to the other mode of thought, there is a world of truth, and ideas beyond the present world—"ideas," as observed by a learned author of our day, "that are fixed and eternal, more stable than the earth, more permanent than the heavens"—ideas that were never born and can never die, and from which alone individual things derive reality, and by partaking of which they become objects of science."

The general goes before the particular; the whole before its parts. Science is the objective truth in a subjective form. Physical and metaphysical phenomena are the diagrams of the invisible and eternal. Life is an identifying principle, ever unfolding itself according to the law of its own being. Society is a concrete generality. Civil law is not the will of man expressed with reference to his temporal well-being, but the very plastic power by which the character of man is forming for a higher state of being.

The State is a divine institution, a power ordained of God, perfect in its ideal, though sadly imperfect in its real existence. Above the State is the Church, the "Body of Christ," the fullness of him that filleth all in all," "the Bride of the Everlasting Bridegroom." The subject of the present article has not come up to our view exactly as Ezekial's vision of a wheel within a wheel, neither one of which touched the other; but rather as two great organisms, each of which is the development of a life peculiar to itself, whilst the integral parts of the one are also the integral parts or members of the other. The relation of the Church and State, therefore, must be internal and necessary, hidden and mysterious, as well as external in its character. To this we can find nothing analogous in nature.

Some have supposed that the analogue is to be found in the human constitution, that the soul and body of man have each an identifying principle of their own, and that these two principles in their development interpenetrate each other so as to constitute one life. No such duality, however, exists in fact, the human body without the soul has no life, it is a mere corpse, and the soul without the body resolves itself into pure spirit, and is incomplete. The *union* of the two is essential to the idea of humanity: body and soul condition each other as form and contents. There is in all life an immanent necessity and tendency to externalize itself, to become real for something else, i. e., it develops itself in the form of body. The soul and body of man are but the internal and external sides of *one* and the *same* life.

This may serve to illustrate either the idea of the State or the Church, separately considered; but not the mysterious relation of the one to the other, not, at least, without considerable modi-

fication. Were we to adopt the utilitarian philosophy, which is
but a modification of the theory of *fluxions* entertained by the
ancient Ionian school, that views *every thing* as in a state of constant fluctuation and change—nothing for a single moment maintaining a fixed identity—no internal law or power to bind and
control the ever floating atoms of the material and moral worlds,
we must, of course, come to the conclusion that the State is a
mere structure, as Cæsar would call it, built upon the waters; a
mere police system to maintain order among the inhabitants of
the earth; a mere human regulation to secure the temporal welfare of our race. But then, according to this view, as one generation of men after another passes away, the State itself must
necessarily die, on an average, at the expiration of every thirty
years, and can only be revived again by a kind of political gal-
vanism. This view, though shallow and infidel, has found many
advocates in modern times. Civil law being nothing more than
the will of man, has no divine authority and power. In the
form of government called the Monarchy, it is but the will of
the monarch with reference to his subjects; in the Aristocratic
form of government, it is but the will of the few in reference
to the many; and in the Republican form of government it is
the will of the majority of the people expressed with reference
to the minority or the whole.

According to this view, the State has no reality: her life has
become extinct, and government has become absolute. There
may be an absolute democracy as well as an absolute monarchy.
The popular will may tyrannize, as well as the individual; and
then to speak of the relation of Church and State becomes impossible: our subject, in this case, resolves itself into the relation
of the human will to the divine, as the latter is revealed through
the medium of the Gospel.

This view is destined to give way, however, to that more elevated system of philosophy, which teaches that the state is an
institution of divine origin, that it is the natural, the necessary
and specific form under which human life, in its manifold departments, is developed and actualized.

According to Hegel, " the state is the actualness of the moral
idea;" " the divine will present in the actual form and organiza-

tion of a world unfolding spirit:" "die reiche Gliederung des Sittlichen in sich."* It is the entire human family organized, animated and bound together by a common, internal, necessary and specific law, giving form and character to all individual human life. It is, of course, obvious that the State has an outward form; it is closely allied to nature and the world of sense; it has its temporal and worldly interests to subserve. But this its external side is not to be placed in opposition to its internal life or spirit; they are the necessary complements of each other, as soul and body. The State then being the necessary form of all human life, it is impossible for man to exist or live excepting in this relation. As well might we expect the branch separated from the vine to yield its annual fruits, or the feathered songsters of the air to warble their notes of praise in the briny deep, or the finny tribes to play upon the desert sand, as for man to live separated from the general life of his race. The State therefore must be as ancient as the human family; and the history of the world is the development of State life, which increases and grows with the increase and growth of our race. The last recorded fact of the world's history will be the *consummation* of this mysterious growth.

But the internal IDEA of the State is not to be confounded with the origin of its external form. It is true, symptoms of organic life are never witnessed excepting in union with its conditions; these, however, do not contain any life giving principle: for this we must always look to a higher source. "The idea," in the language of the author already quoted, "is and ever must be *one*; but the external origin may be as various as the ever varying circumstances of mankind." The external origin may be the amplification of the family, as most of the earlier States were; it may be the social compact, of which so much is written and said; it may be the result of a long series of causes, bringing men together within geographical limits: or, as in our own country, it may be the result of revolution.

* In borrowing these convenient forms of expression from Hegel, we do not wish to be understood as having any sympathy whatever with the pantheistic tendency of his system, nor with the peculiar view of his, according to which the State is made to swallow up the Church.

It is only, however, when the mass of dry bones, thus providentially thrown together, "are clothed with sinews, muscles and flesh, and have breathed into them the breath of life, that the nation, according to the etymology of the term, can be said to have been born." Hence the multitude of the States. So also we may account for the variety of form in state government; but all these being pervaded, and animated by the general law of political life are gathered up as parts of the world embracing state organism.

According to this view, the State is constitutionally a divine power, having all the functions and characteristics of a religious institution. These functions may be denominated: the *Regal*, the *Educational*, and the *Devotional*; the first having reference more particularly to the will, the second to the intellect, and the third to the affections. In the exercise of her regal power, the State exerts a sovereign sway over the lower portions of creation. Man, viewed as an individual, is justly styled the lord of creation; yet his regal character can only hold fully in the conscious union of his race; hence the State makes all the lower kingdoms of the world tributary to herself: by her power the earth is subdued: the beasts of the forest are made to fear and tremble, and the very elements are controlled. She also sways the sceptre of dominion over her own subjects; she governs, defends and protects them: she executes upon offenders the penalty of the law, and reprieves whom she will. Whether, now, the reigning sovereignty of the State be vested in the monarch, the aristocracy, or in those set apart as rulers by the popular will, the ultimate sovereignty is vested in fundamental law as such, which exists in the world as the true representative of the Majesty in the heavens, governing alike the governor and the governed. The reigning sovereignty can only derive its authority and power from the ultimate. Here is the true ground of obedience to the "powers that be"; and only he is the free man whose will harmonizes with the divine will as thus revealed.

The Regal power of the State is inseparably connected with the Educational. Indeed, law and authority are always educational in their nature and tendency. By this we do not mean that the State merely encourages education among the masses

of the people by establishing schools, colleges, and other semi-
naries of learning, and by exercising a superintendence over
them; but that the very hidden meaning of her constitution,
the very substance of the idea, as well as the truth of nature
generally, are expressed through the medium of conscious intelligence. Man is so constituted as to take up the objective truth
in whatever form it may be revealed, to embody it in his very
constitution, and to become its living interpreter; and whilst this
in the case of the single individual, as in the instance adduced,
it is *preëminently* true of man in his conscious union with the
race. As the state organism, therefore, embodies in it the elements of understanding and reason, of conscious intelligence, it
is the living exponent of the truth: and hence no one is disposed to gainsay when a point is once settled by the united testimony of the whole world, or when it is once confirmed by the
ever living voice of the State. But there is in the subjective
truth a necessity and tendency again to become objective: i. e.,
having been reproduced in the way of reflection and thought, it
is collected in the form of literature, and becomes objective to
the present and succeeding generations. The world's literature,
therefore, may be viewed as the product of state life under this
particular form. That is, the State is constitutionally educational
in her character. Being associated with the moral universe of
God, her design and tendency is to educate man for a higher
state of society. All her outward ends, such as the preservation
of life, property, and rights, are but secondary in this.

But the moral and intellectual nature of man cannot be separated from the religious. Morality without religion has no soul:
if conformity to the law do not spring from a living principle, it
is merely outward—it is worthless. Religion, however, is devotional: therefore the state life also unfolds itself in the form of
devotion. There has ever been in the world a feeling of dependence upon the Supreme Being; and even when the knowledge
of the true God was lost, this feeling was still manifested in the
worship of the Deity as he was supposed to be enshrined in the
objects of nature and the works of art.

The devotional feeling also manifests itself in that essential
form of state religion, which still exists in Christian countries,

viz: the civil oath. The subjective truth being constantly in danger of perversion by depraved man, seeks protection in the objective and eternal. The State conscious of her dependences upon the supernatural and supreme, reverently appeals to High Heaven in this form for safety and protection. It is only possible, however, for the State to attain a full consciousness of her dependence through that medium in which God has given the fullest revelation of himself to the world, i. e., the Church. As the Church borrows her social character from the State in the form of marriage, so the State is indebted for the true idea of the oath to the Church. This is the two-fold bond of their internal union. If we may conceive of these two divine institutions under the figure of two ships upon the ocean, sailing side by side, we would say that the oath and marriage are the strong grapnels, by which they are indissolubly bound together.

Our view of the ideal State, therefore, can only hold in its union with the Church, which, we trust, will become still more apparent as we proceed.

From all that has now been said, it will follow that all the office-bearers of the State are vested with a sacred character. The civil ruler does not merely bear the the sword of utilitarian, but of vindictive justice. Lawyers, whose office it is to unfold the hidden mysteries of law and truth, are oracles of God. Magistrates, who administer the oath in civil courts, minister at the altar of the Most High.

The real State, as it is presented to our view in history, and the ideal are not isolated and separate things: they stand related as the real and ideal humanity: as the latter is actualized in the former, so the real is ever struggling onward and upward towards its final consummation in the ideal.

The world is under the dominion of sin and evil, and until this dominion be broken, it is not possible for the real state to reach her ideal. We may suppose that, by moral, intellectual, and religious culture, literature, morality, and state religion may reach an elevation hitherto unknown; but as long as the stream of life, unfolding itself in the specific form now described, is tainted with sin, the State *cannot* become complete: much less can humanity be brought into that close and intimate union with the divine nature for which it was designed in the original creation. Hence the necessity of the new creation, a still higher plastic power, viz: the HOLY CATHOLIC CHURCH. Of all powers this is the greatest and most imposing: of all bodies this divine human organism is the most perfect and complete: of all realities this is the greatest and most sublime.

In contemplating the Christian church, we must not view it as an *ideal*, supended midway between heaven and earth, for man to gaze upon and admire: neither as a separate planet spoken into being by the divine word, and inhabited by a separate order of intelligences: nor as a world suspended within reaching distance from our earth, to which her inhabitants may pass at pleasure, so as to lose their citizenship here: neither should we view it as a purely spiritual influence, which has gone out upon the great ocean of human mind to calm the turbulent waters of life: nor yet as a religious institution planted at the *side* of the State, so that we can say, the one is here and the other there: but as a higher order of divine life *in this world*, which, in its development, takes to itself a body from the elements of humanity.

The *principle* of this new life is the *Lord Jesus Christ*, the incarnate *Saviour*, who is very God and very man in one person, and in whom dwells all the fullness of the God-head bodily. In him the divine and human natures are united as they never were before. The union is *deep, mysterious* and *vital*. The growth of the Church is the development of Christ's life in the world. To attempt a separation of the Church from the person of Christ, is to attempt a separation between the soul and body: it is to destroy the very life of the Lamb's Bride. "No Christ, no Church; and no Church, no Christ." The Church is the body of Christ, and Christ is the life of the Church: they are INSEPARABLE. And as the Church life, in its development, as well as that of the State, take up *all* the elements of our nature; as the life of Christ animates the whole man, soul and body, it follows that the state life and church life flow into and interpenetrate each other: not that they are so mixed as to become something different from both: nor that the one looses its identity in the other: but the State life is purified and invigorated by that of the Church, so that it is possible by the former to reach its ideal perfection. They are one, but yet distinct. This is mysterious; but must be believed nevertheless: for to disbelieve is to deny all faith in both Church and State as present realities. Humanity may be viewed as a mysterious tree, whose roots strike deep into the ground of nature, whose wide spreading branches overshadow the whole earth, and whose top is destined to reach the highest heavens. Its growth, however, is found to be feeble and sickly: the branches spread; but they tend towards the earth. But now there is a new principle of life introduced, which, in its development, throws off and overcomes every thing that would retard its growth, and the tree of humanity, thus invigorated, rapidly tends towards its culminating point of ideal perfection. Shall we then conclude that the Church is merely a remedial agent; that her design is merely to restore to man what he lost in consequence of sin; and that the kingdom of God is to be established in the world, according to Professor Rothe, in the form of the State? The Church being constitutionally holy and catholic, we reply, is such a remedial agent: she dries up the fountains of sin and misery: she heals the diseases of our fallen nature, purifies the stream of human life: and all social relations, as well as the arts, sciences and literature generally, are sanctified by her hallowed influence: her life penetrates every form of human existence and elevates it above the sphere of sin and the flesh. It is in the Church, and in the Church alone, that the State can reach her ideal perfection. Christianity being the highest form of humanity, we may safely say, that the Church is the perfection of the State. But whilst it is possible for the State to reach her ideal in the Church, it is not possible for the Church to reach her ideal in the State. The higher may elevate the lower; but the lower cannot elevate the higher. The river may empty itself into the sea; but the ocean cannot empty itself into the river. In the relation which we designate the State, man is under the influence of a divine plastic power, which tends to a high and holy end; but in the relation which we designate the Church, man is brought into the "holiest of holies": he is brought into the *real* and *vital* union with God in the person of his only begotten Son. Whilst, therefore, the church life, and state life tend towards the same end, viz: the perfection of humanity in union with the Deity, it is possible only for the former to reach this end, or to carry man forward to the point of his final destination.   Thus the Church life, though it transfuse and purify that of the State, nevertheless maintains its distinctive character; whilst, at the same time, the State life being thus transfused and purified does not lose its identity.

They are distinct in mysterious unity.

The distinctive character of the Church will also appear, when we take into view the manner in which her life is carried forward in the world, or the manner in which it forms for itself a body. The State, as we have seen, lives and grows in the way of natural generation : every one who is born into the world is born into the State, and becomes an integral part of its complex unity. The Church lives and grows in the way of *supernatural* generation. As Christ became incarnate through the supernatural and miraculous agency of the Spirit (for he was conceived by the Holy Ghost), so his divine life is carried forward in the world, or made over to us, by the same supernatural power. "For by one Spirit are we all baptized into one body, whether we be Jews or Gentiles, whether we be bond or free, and have been made to drink into one spirit" 1 Cor. vii. 13. By the spirit accompanying the means of grace appointed in the Church, as for instance, the preached word and sacraments, the life of Christ is nourished in his mystical body. Organic Christianity, therefore, does not exclude the office work of the third person in the adorable Trinity. By the Spirit, the temple of God, which has Christ for its foundation, its life and chief corner-stone, is reared. As the elements of humanity are thus taken up and become the integral parts of this supernatural organism, it follows that the principle of sin and evil is excluded. The Church is a holy temple : holy in her origin, in her constitution, and her design. But the same may also be predicated of the ideal State, as a power ordained of God. Between the ideal Church, therefore, and the ideal State, there can be no contradiction nor conflict. They are in full and perfect harmony, the one in the other.

Of this internal union of Church and State, the history of their external relations presents but a distorted view; and it is only when the ideal relation shall have been fully actualized in the real, that the external relation can be viewed as the proper expression of the internal. Sin is the cause of all contradiction and conflict. It is this that brings man into conflict with himself; it is this that brings him into contradiction with his Maker. This is the cause of all distortion and deformity; this creates the opposition between Church and State. History presents to our view a four-fold form of relations between them. During the ages of primitive Christianity, the State actually assumed the *hostile* position towards the Church. The world, brought under the dominion of idolatry, could not tolerate the pure and holy principles of Christianity. The civil powers were arrayed against the infant Church. Persecution raged in all the terrors of fire and sword. But the superior power of the Church clothed in the armour of God, not in carnal weapons, soon appeared in signal triumph over the power of darkness; the fires of persecution were quenched in the blood of martyrs; the hostile sword stained with the blood of the saints falls powerless from the hands of the cruel oppressors. The regal authority and power of the Church come to be more extensively felt and acknowledged. Under the reign of Constantine already, Christianity became the prevailing state religion. Though the Church and State constituted, as before, two organic wholes, they sustain to each other in a more eminent degree the relations of mutual action and reaction. During the former period the church life, in the exercise of its peculiar power to overcome opposition, and to assimilate to itself everything congenial with its own nature, took to itself a peculiar form and shape; for it is the peculiar characteristic of Christianity, that it can live and grow under the most adverse circumstances and oppressive relations. It is to be expected, therefore, that, by the charge of external relation from the hostile to the friendly, which was effected by the transition of the Emperors from Paganism to Christianity, the church organization would be greatly modified. As might be expected, the supreme magistrates, who are now members of the Church and participate in her affairs, would be naturally inclined to transfer the relation they had stood in to the Pagan state religion, over to their relation to the Christian Church. "They are here met, however," as observed by Dr. Neander, "by that independent spirit of the Church, which, in the course of three centuries, had been developing itself, and acquiring a determinate shape; which would make them see that Christianity could not, like Paganism, be subordinated to the political interest." "There had in fact arisen in the Church," according to the same distinguished historian, "in the previous period, a false theocratical theory, originating, not in the essence of the Gospel, but in the confusion of the religious constitutions of the Old and New Testament, which grounding itself on the idea of a visible priesthood, belonging to the essence of the Church and governing the Church, brought along with it an uncristian opposition of the spiritual to the secular power, and which might easily result in the formation of a sacerdotal state, subordinating the secular to itself in a false and outward way." Excepting Valentinian II, the emperors entertained precisely that view of the Church, which was presented to them by tradition; having no judgment of their own, they were born along by the dominant spirit."

This theocratical theory was the prevailing one in the time of Constantine. Viewing the Church as a divine institution built on Christ and the Apostles, in which nothing could be altered by the arbitrary will of man, he regarded the voice of the Church as the voice of God. "Thus, when in the year 314, an appeal was made from the Episcopal tribunal to the Imperial decision, he declared: "The sentence of the bishops must be regarded as the sentence of Christ himself."

It was, however, when the Patriarchal reign of the Church, which is now introduced, passed over into the Papal, that it becomes a settled principle that the Church is to govern the State. In the time of Gregory VII., the subordination of the State to the Church was so deeply and extensively felt that the kings were obliged to acknowledge that they derived their authority to reign from the Pope. This is illustrated by the results of the memorable contest that arose between Henry IV. and Pope Gregory VII. Hence the numerous instances of kings and princes acknowledging their inferiority to the Chief Pontiff by holding his stirrup until he would mount his horse. This theocratical view, according to which the Church is to govern

the world, it must be owned, is not very far from the scriptural
idea.   The distortion, however, consists in this, that the life of
the Church not being fully developed in her own constitution,
and the civil and social relations of human life not being sanctified
by the spirit of Christianity, the State not being taken up into
the living *organism* of the Church, the ecclesiastical dominion of
the latter over the former is nothing more than a "*Jewish* yoke;"
it is more or less oppressive and unhallowed in its character.
Hence there must necessarily be a reaction : and accordingly,
after the Reformation of the sixteenth century, we find the
Church under the dominion of the State.

   In some countries, indeed, she is viewed as nothing more than
a police system to keep the masses of the people under proper
restraint as a kind of an instrumentality that may be most successfully employed to secure the obedience of subjects to civil
law and authority.   Let us turn to England for illustration.   According to the statute book of this country, " The king, his heirs,
&c., shall be taken, accepted, and reputed the only supreme
head of the Church of England, ... and shall order, and
correct, restrain, and amend all such errors, heresies, abuses, offences, contempts, and enormities, which by any manner of spiritual authority or jurisdiction may be restrained."   Arch-
bishops, bishops, archdeacons, and other ecclesiastical persons,
have no manner of ecclesiastical jurisdiction, but by and from
the Royal Crown.*

   The idea that the ministers of the Christian church should
receive their appointments from a worldly Prince, or that the
Church should, in any sense, be in slavish subjection to the
State, is most painful to the christian consciousness.   The fourth
and last form of relationship that comes to our view in history,
between the Church and the State, is the independent, or, for
instance, in our own country, where government offers the Church
protection, and accedes to her the right to govern herself according to the laws of her own constitution.   As Americans, it is
natural for us to suppose that this form is far superior to any of

---

* Not having access to the original, we have been obliged to take this
quotation second-handed from the book of Baptist W. Noel, on the Union
of Church and State.

those previously specified; and this too, is in perfect accordance
with our ideas of historical development and progress. To place
the Church in subordination to the State, as in England, though
our political structure rest upon far more liberal and christian
principles, or, to place the State under the dominion of the
Church, in the sense of the middle period, must certainly be
regarded as a retrograde movement. At the present stage of the
world's history, therefore, we should most heartily acquiesce in
the existing relation of Church and State in our country. It
must be evident at a single glance that, as the Church and State
are not *internally united,* as their ideal relation has not been
fully realized in an outward form, the Church is as little prepared to take the reins of State government, as the State is to
undertake the management of ecclesiastical affairs. Let us suppose that, in her present divided state, the right were acceded to
the Church to govern the world, what a painful scene of discord
and conflict must we not witness? When the Roman Catholic
Church, the most ancient of all, the only true church of God in
the world, would naturally claim the presidential chair: Then
the Episcopal Church, which is more ancient still, having only
evaded the errors and abuses of the Papacy, and which is also
the only true Church, would, of course, be entitled to the
chief magistracy. The Episcopalian form of government, however, is most warmly disputed by the Presbyterians, whose form
of government claims to be the most Scriptural, the most ancient
and withal the most republican. The Lutheran Church, too,
as the oldest daughter of the Reformation, would naturally step
forward and press the claim of priority. And all the Methodists
in the land, raising the shout:—"The reformation of Wesley
far more glorious than even that of Luther?" would appear in
formidable array. The Seceder, the Baptist, the Winebrenne-
rian, and many other sects, having inscribed upon their banners,
"The only true Church of God," would be seen going up to
Washington city, each claiming possession of the White House.
The German Reformed Church, always too modest and slow to
claim and take care of her own, we do not suppose would be
found in the number.

But when, in the glorious future, the divisions of Zion shall
all be healed, when all believers shall be baptized by their only

proper name—" Christian"; when they shall all be one, as Christ and the Father are one; when the Church shall be *one* in reality as she is *one* in idea; and when she shall have gathered up into her own constitution, animated and sanctified by her own hallowed life and spirit, all the forms and relations of human life, it becomes an interesting question: "Where then will be the State?" and "What the form of her existence?" According to our theory, she *cannot* have become extinct; but she will be found in the free and holy service of the Church. The form of her outward existence, we, of course, cannot foretell. Could we determine the form of the future Church, we might venture a conjecture; but even this is concealed from our view. But if our view be correct, that the ideal State and the ideal Church are *one*, it must follow that in the end they will be one in an outward form. The State fellowship, or communion, will be elevated into the higher form of the Church communion. The Regal power of the State will be one with that of the Church, when " Christ shall reign king of nations as he now reigns king of saints:" the civil powers, which were ordained of God, shall be gathered back into the hands of his only begotten Son, and shall be exercised in harmonious union with his glorious reign, whether personal or spiritual, in the Church. The educational function of the State will also be elevated and become one with that of the Church, which is now the only infallible interpreter of the truth, whether revealed in a natural or in a supernatural way. And every form of State religion will then be one with the pure and holy worship, whose incense shall ever come up acceptably before the throne of the great Eternal.

Christ is now (in the full meaning of the expression) "all and in all " The little stone, which was cut out without hands, having smitten the images of iron, of clay and brass, has now become a great mountain, and fills the whole earth. The small grain of mustard seed has now become a great tree, whose wide spreading branches overshadow the entire globe, and all people, of every kindred, tongue and climate, take shelter under it. We end in the " new heavens, and the new earth, wherein dwelleth righteousness."

HAGERSTOWN, Md.   M. K.

AR'T. XLIII.—WISDOM'S VOICE.

MAN *should be wise.* All nature has a tongue
To teach him knowledge, were his soul but strung
    To catch the lesson poured upon his ear.
O'er the broad world the rays of truth are flung,
To show him things in their own proper light,
    Were but the spirit eye unscaled and clear,
To read their silent meaning as it might.

All breathes with language eloquent and pure;
Tells him of change; warns him how little sure
    The light foundations of his worldly state;
And bids him seek a footing more secure,
Ere yet the slippery confidence may slide,
    And the lost spirit, roused, alas, too late,
Sink in its strength, and perish in its pride.

The solid earth he treads upon, that seems
Immoveable; its forests, plains and streams;
    Its seas, and everlasting hills sublime;
All have a voice to chide his empty dreams.
They tell of generations swept away;
    Themselves coeval with the birth of time
Yet rushing always towards the same decay.

The sun speaks to him from his awful height,
And the soft moon throned on the realm of night.
    The stars look down upon him too, as though
They sought to woo him, with their gentle light,
Upward to God. The heavens, as they shine,
    Make earth seem empty, narrow, dark and low
And point the spirit to her home divine.

The winds, the clouds, the ever-varying sky;
Hours, days, nights, months and seasons, as they fly,
    In quick succession, through their circling range;
The summer leaves that fade, and flowers that die;
The growth of ages, crumbling in decay;
    All warn us loudly of our coming change
And urge our feet to take the heavenly way.

The mighty wreck that still is going on
O'er time's broad sea; whole generations gone;
    Cities of men, and empires, buried deep
In its dark wave; the desolation done
In one brief age; the pride of nations fled;
    The mighty hurried to their last great sleep;
States rent; thrones fallen; living millions dead;

Life's rolling, heaving, ever changing ground;
The havoc years are making all around;
  The altered show that meets the sight each day;
  The places vacant where our friends were found;
Familiar forms fast sinking from our eyes;
  The graves so thickly strown upon our way;—
Sure in a world like this, man *should* be wise.

                                    N.

ART. XLIV.—Puritanism and the Creed.

THE *Puritan Recorder*, one of the most respectable and widely influential religious papers in New England, has lately uttered itself on this subject, in a succession of short articles, (called forth as it would seem, in opposition to our late view of the Creed,) which we have no right entirely to overlook. We trust at the same time, that our object in noticing them, will be rightly appreciated. We should be sorry to give way to mere polemical zeal, in such a case, for its own sake. We have no quarrel specially with the Recorder; and it is not in our mind at all, to challenge it to any sort of public argument or debate. That would require a common audience; which it is vain for us, of course, at this time, to ask or expect. Before the amphitheatre of the Recorder's public, we can be heard, for the most part, only in such form as the paper itself may see fit to allow; and we have had experience enough to know, that even where our denominational religious papers are least disposed to be consciously unfair, no sort of justice is to be hoped for, ordinarily, in this way. Our interest is in the subject, under its general aspect, and as related to theology in its broad view. We make use of the Recorder as an *occasion*, simply, for bringing home to the consideration of our readers a vastly significant interest, in a connection of actual life, near at hand, such as is suited to fix upon it their earnest attention.   There is no good reason, at all events, why a Review like ours should limit its critical interest to what is published in the form of pamphlets and books.   A large part of our literature, at present, appears in the form of newspapers. The weekly religious press, especially, has come to be of far more account for our theology, so far as we can be said to have any that is living and not dead, than all the books now produced in its service.   These are in general so mechanical, that they carry in them very little power either for bad or good.   To understand the actual religious life of the country, theoretic as well as practical, we must commune with the religious newspapers of the different sects.   They, indeed, generally disclaim scientific theology; aiming simply, as they say, to be practical; but in their own way they show themselves ready enough, notwithstanding, to settle all theological questions in the most summary off-hand style; and with the advantage of their position, the authority thus assumed is allowed very generally to prevail.   We are bound, accordingly, to have regard to them, if we would deal with the theological life of the country in a living way.   A newspaper paragraph may be of more account at times, as a text for religious discussion, than a whole sermon, or a large lettered duodecimo of three hundred and fifty pages, manufactured to order according to previous fashion and rule.

In writing upon the Creed, we ventured to say, not without hesitation in our own mind, that Puritanism is constitutionally at variance with this ancient rule, and if left to itself would fall on a very different formula to represent its faith.   The hesitation we felt in saying this, arose not from any doubt of its being the truth, but from the apprehension of its seeming to be a hard saying to others, who might not see the truth of it at once, and so be led to think our judgment unkind and harsh; just as some have considered it harsh, that we should affirm a similar falling away from the faith of the sixteenth century in the case of the holy sacraments; as though the question were one of courtesy only, and had nothing to do at all with stern historical reality. We were afraid that many might consider it a slander to charge Puritanism with being in conflict with the Creed, when it is still willing to accept the form of it at times, as orthodox and good;

the circumstance being overlooked, that in every such case the Creed is quietly filled with a new sense materially different from that which belonged to it in the beginning.* We are now, how. ever, happily discharged of all this concern. The Puritan Re- corder, in the name of Puritanism, and with intelligent insight, as it would seem, into the true nature of the question at issue, openly and boldly accepts our representation as fully correct. The Creed, in its genuine and original sense, is no true type, we are told, of the present *orthodoxy* of New England. Whatever traditional respect may have been allowed to it in the beginning, it has fallen on all sides into disuse, and is notoriously out of date. All this too is proclaimed an improvement in our general Chris- tianity; for the Creed turns out, on close examination, to be at war with the Bible, and the use of it is perilous to the interests of evangelical religion. The Puritan Recorder, in this case, is no mean witness. We are bound to respect its testimony; we do respect it in fact; and we wish it to be listened to seriously and solemnly, throughout the length and breadth of the Ameri- can Church.

"The experience of two centuries has shown," says the Recor- der, "that the Creed and Puritanism have not a kindred spirit. The first Puritans did not discard what is called the Apostles' Creed, but expressly allowed its use, and by a sort of courtesy, gave it a place beside their formularies and catechisms. It even had a place in the New England Primer. But its life and spirit never entered into the life of the Puritan churches. And, consequently, it now exists among us as some fossil relic of by-gone ages. And we look with a sort of pity upon those who are laboring to infuse life

---

* "Dr. N., who appears to be chief cyclops, and forger of thunder-bolts for what is called the Mercersburg Theology, has turned his one eye, with vulcanian glare, towards us; and launched his lightnings at our heads, for a supposed want of respect for that venerable symbol, the so-called Apos- tles' Creed. In rebuking the flippancy of a sciolist, [Dr. Bushnell,] who had spoken as if it were an undoubted fact, that this ancient form was drawn up by the Apostles, we had said that it 'was no more an apostolical inven- tion, than was Christmas pie.' In the sense in which we used the words, Dr. N., like any man of ordinary learning, fully accords with us. And we hold, as firmly as he does, that the Creed is truly apostolical in regard to the 'divine substance of its contents,' and 'as representing from the beginning the one unvarying faith of the universal Christian world.' There are other creeds, which, in the same sense, are no less apostolical."—*Boston Christian Observatory, for Sept.,* 1849: This is well, as far as it goes; but it tallies badly with the Puritan Recorder.

into it, and to set it up as a living ruler in the Church. We are free to confess, that this Creed has forsaken the Puritans, and gone over to become the idol and strength of all branches of anti-puritanism.

"And there are good reasons; for Puritanism builds on the Scriptures, and this Creed teaches, in several respects, anti-scriptural doctrines. It is true, that most of it is capable of a sense which harmonizes with the Scriptures, and so the Puritans received it, in a sense consonant with their theology—either leaving out, or putting a strained sense upon the passage which asserts that Christ descended into hell. But it is neither safe nor expedient to receive such a document, in such a perverted sense. For the document once being admitted, and its authority being made to bind the conscience, then the way is open for those who hold the errors held by its authors, to plead that we are bound to receive it in the sense which its authors gave to it, and this makes it an instrument of corrupting the faith of the gospel.

"But what are the heretical points of this Creed? We shall have space in this article for only one, and that is the doctrine of purgatory, as taught in the assertion that Christ descended into hell."— *Pur. Rec.*, *Aug.* 23, 1849.

This particular charge of teaching the doctrine of Purgatory, the article then goes on to substantiate and settle in its own brief way, without the least regard to true history, by a few hop-step-and-jump combinations, within the bounds of a paragraph measuring about one-fourth part of a single column of the paper in which it appears. Two other errors, one latent in the clause "Catholic Church," the other peeping forth from the "Communion of Saints," are laid over for subsequent dissection.

In the Recorder of the following week, Aug. 30, we have another article, nearly a column long, disposing of the second of these last mentioned errors in equally sweeping and summary style. Modern evangelical Christians, we are told, have no occasion for the clause "Communion of Saints," in their forms of belief. "The meaning which they would fit to it, is not one sufficiently prominent to have a place in so brief a confession of faith. And it is very clear that the unknown authors of the Apostles' Creed had a meaning for it, and a use for it, which we have not." And then we have historical hypothesis again substituted for historical fact, to show that the true sense of it is to be found in the superstitions of the Roman Church. "If we suppose that the Romish doctrine of the intercession of departed saints for men upon earth, and of the efficacy of prayers addressed by us to the saints in heaven, and of the efficacy of prayers offered for the dead, had obtained at the time when this phrase was added to the Creed, then we see an adequate reason for its addition." This IF, made good by the violent assumption, that the article was no part of the primitive faith of the Church, but a device added to it somewhere along in the fourth century, (a fact demanded, and so made sure, by the necessities of the hypothesis itself,) proves strong enough to hurry us, by a few strokes of the pen, into the convenient conclusion, that it was brought in purely and solely for the purpose of covering this general Roman fancy. "And *if so*, the use of the Creed by us is a snare, since, though we may find a different and true sense, which will fit the words, the historic sense has superior claims, which will not fail to be felt by many minds, that attach an authority, not to say sacredness, to the venerated document."

The first article in the Recorder of the next week, Sept. 6, calls our attention again to the "heretical points of the Creed," under the somewhat startling caption: THE HOLY CATHOLIC CHURCH A FIGMENT. In repeating the clause, *I believe in the holy catholic Church*, the early Puritan, we are told, wist not what he said. They suit not the faith of a Puritan. "Let him attach his own sense to the words, and he can utter them. But then the utterance comes from him with a sort of foreign accent and unnatural constraint. If the term 'catholic church' embrace all the elect or true believers, in all places and all times, the living and the dead, and those not yet born—that is, the spiritual or invisible church, the mystical body of Christ—very well. But if it mean that the visible church is a 'holy catholic church'—an organic body, embracing all professing Christians as one whole, in one organic brotherhood—it has no warrant in Scripture. In the light of the New Testament, the idea of a *catholic visible church* is intrinsically impossible and absurd." Christ himself, we are gravely informed, "organized no church," but committed the "organizing of *churches*" to the apostles. This they did after the day of Pentecost. The churches thus organized, however, were all equally original, independent, and complete in and by themselves. "They were not splinters nor fractions of

churches, but whole *churches.*"   In the Recorder for Sept. 13,
the subject is resumed, under the caption: "The False Theory
of the Visible Church a Hindrance to Christian Union."   Here
the Creed is charged with teaching "the phantom of an organic
catholicity of the visible Church"; on which account, says the
Recorder, as such a church "exists not in fact, nor in the theory
of the New Testament, it is not for us to recite such a creed."   It
kills "the principle of the essential independency of the churches,"
and makes sectarianism and schism to be a sin.   Only let the
public mind be well charged with this principle of atomistic
christianity, and the misery of our sect system is at once in a
great measure brought to an end.   It is the notion of catholicity,
as we have it in the Creed, that leads men to declaim against
what they call the "sect spirit."   "Let that phantom go to the
winds," and we shall see that individuals may form a new church
at any time to suit themselves, without prejudice to Christ's house.
"Let the principle of independency expand to its just proportions
in the public mind, and the right of Christians thus to organize
will be generally conceded."   Then, too, the evils of sectarian
division will in a large measure cease; "the mutual irritation
and odium of the sects comes of this false assumption," that the
Church should be outwardly one.   The same false theory it is,
which originates the reproach brought against the Church by
the surrounding world, on account of its sectarianism.   "Just
remove the phantom which dwells in the imagination as some
sacred thing, and no violence will be supposed to have been done
to a sacred thing, when, like Abram and Lot, Christians separate
for the avoidance of strife.   Take away the idol, and no sacrilege will be committed in mutilating it, and no weak consciences
will be defiled in eating what is offered in sacrifice to it."   This
may be taken, certainly, as a short and easy cure for all sorts of
schism; though one can hardly fail to see in it a certain sort of analogy with the style, in which our Socialists and Radical Reformers generally affect to rid themselves of such ethical and religious
obstructions as happen to come in *their* way.   Remove, for instance, the phantom of holy matrimony, which now dwells in
the imagination of men as some sacred thing, and no violence
will be supposed to have been done to what is sacred, when, like

Abraham and David, Christians multiply wives or concubines to suit themselves. Take away the idol, and no sacrilege will hold against it in the form either of adultery or fornication. But what if the "idol," holy matrimony in this last case, and the holy catholic church in the other, should prove to be, in the end, no phantom at all, but the very shrine of divinity itself, set up among men to be the object of their perpetual faith and veneration? The *argumentum ab utili* is then at an end. . Marriage may not be set aside, to accommodate a community of libertines; the Church may not be shorn of its original inborn attributes, to suit the humor of sects.

The Puritan Recorder, of course, assumes throughout, that the Church is no divine institution, in the form asserted by the Creed. But this at last remains simply an *assumption*. It is not proved. The writer has a certain preconception of the nature of the Church, which he finds to be contradicted by the theory of the Creed; whereupon he expects us at once to accept *his* preconception, on the authority of his own word, as the true sense of the New Testament, and so to jump with him to the conclusion, that the theory of the Creed is unscriptural, fantastic and false. We are not prepared to bow to such logic as this. The whole assumption here taken against the Creed, is gratuitous and untrue. The *idea* of the Church presented in the Creed, falls back historically to the very cradle of the Christian faith; full as much so as the idea of the incarnation itself. The one mystery in truth grows forth from the other; the idea of the Church has its necessary root in the idea of Christ. And this entire faith, of course, then, meets us in the New Testament. The conception of the Church, as a new universal or catholic creation, starting in Christ, and destined to take up the world finally into its sphere, underlies the Christian revelation from beginning to end. This conception involves, too, throughout, all the attributes which are ascribed to the Church in the Creed; unity, sanctity, catholicity; for these come not from abroad, but have their necessity in the nature of the conception itself. The Church is by its constitution one and not many; and however it may fail to actualize its own interior sense in this form, in any given stage of its history, it can never renounce this sense as

something false, but must still labor towards its full actualization as the only end in which it can be regarded as complete.
So as regards holiness; and so also as regards catholicity. The
Church can never, without infidelity, renounce her vocation
and right to be the absolute mistress at last of all spheres of our
human existence, however far short she may fall at present of
the power that is needed to make good such universal pretension.
This, of course, implies *visibility* ; however the Church may be
hindered for ages in her effort to come to a complete externalization of her divine life, as the true last sense of the world, yet
to this it must assuredly come in the end, if she be indeed this
last true sense; and the whole process of this effort itself, moreover, must include throughout the character of visibility as far
as it goes.   All this, we say, lies in the New Testament, as well
as in the faith of the primitive christian world, expressed in the
Apostles' Creed; and it is a mere play of fancy, accordingly,
when the Puritan Recorder imagines the contrary, and so requires
us to give up the article of the Creed as a pious figment.

   This, however, by the way. It is not our business here, to
interpret the New Testament, or vindicate the Creed.   We wish
simply, to fix attention on the general fact now in hand, the discrepancy which is acknowledged to hold between the true sense
of this ancient symbol and Puritanism.   It will be seen at once,
that the difference, as presented by the Recorder, is very material.
Three points are particularly singled out, in proof and illustration
of its force, namely, the descent to hades, the communion of
saints, and the idea of the holy catholic church; but the difference itself is plainly of a general character, and must be regarded
as extending to the entire Creed; for this is not made up of dis-
connected fragmentary parcels, but forms a single whole in harmony with itself throughout.   The Recorder indeed denies this,
and declares itself out of patience with us, (July 26,) for assuming, without proof, that "the Creed is the product of the first
ages of Christianity," and that it is to be considered at all "rotund and full" in its constitution; quoting Sir Peter King, to
show that it *was* a fragmentary production, after the third century.   But there is no good reason here, we think, for getting
out of patience on *that* side, however it may be on ours.   We

have never pretended that the Creed came round and full, as it now stands, from the age of the Apostles, or that it was not made to undergo some variations and additions, in the progress of its early history. We have taken pains to say just the contrary; for the purpose of planting its authority on better ground, in the conception of its organic derivation from a central principle, in the faith of the universal early Church. We have said that it *grew* forth from the primary christian consciousness, the sense of Christ as the ground and fountain of the new creation; in which view, it might be of more or less volume, and admit many varieties of expression, without any change in its essential substance; just as the ten commandments gather themselves up at last into love to God and love to man. The Creed represents truly the faith of the universal Church in the first centuries; nobody pretends that the different forms of it before the Council of Nice, involved any material divergencies of belief; and the whole stands before us in the end as an inwardly symmetrical and complete system, shooting forth from a common root, and revealing in all its parts the power of a common life. This inward, constitutional unity of the Creed, which is something very different from the unity of a catechism or a watch, we have endeavored to establish by an actual analysis of its form and plan; and we have not met with any attempt yet to show our analysis wrong. The Creed here speaks for itself. We need no outward testimony to prove its unity. All the case requires is, that we should rightly study the structure in its own forms and proportions. In this view, its roundness and wholeness are such as to make themselves felt by all serious persons. The Recorder itself, evidently feels this constitutional unity of the Creed, even while trying to make it out a bundle of fragments; and it is on this ground, accordingly, we have the candid and free admission, that the symbol, as a whole, falls not in with the proper life of Puritanism. This is undoubtedly correct. The variation may be more directly apprehensible at some points than it is at others; but it runs through the entire scope and structure of the Creed. I s genius is not that of Puritanism. The two " have not a kindred spirit." Their standpoint is different. The descent to hades, the communion of saints, the holy catholic church, we are told, belong not to the Puritan circle of thought, and must have a new sense forced upon them to sit even in a stiff way on Puritan lips. But they belong plainly enough to the circle of thought embodied in the Creed, and fall in naturally and easily with all its other articles. All these, then, must have a sense in the Creed, which is not fully owned in the same form by Puritanism. The christological confession holds under a different view. The forgiveness of sins, and the resurrection of the body, are thought of in different relations. The whole inward habit of the ancient faith, is not such as to fit at all the habit of the modern faith. Puritanism is not at home in the Creed: feels awkward in the use of it; prefers quietly to drop the use of it altogether. That is not the mould in which its faith has been cast. Its orthodoxy puts things together in another way.

But surely now the open acknowledgment of such a fact as this deserves attention. For only see how much it involves. The Creed expresses the faith, the primary religious mind or consciousness of the universal ancient Church. In this form, Christianity took its historical rise, in the living heart of the Christian world. The sense of the mystery ran into this fundamental shape from the beginning, and was made to underlie thus the whole subsequent life of the Church. All later symbols were held to be of force, only as they rested on the first. The old catholic christianity throughout had its basis in the consciousness expressed by the Creed. Its fathers, martyrs, confessors and saints, would all have shrunk with dismay from the thought of holding it in any other form. The Reformation again planted itself professedly on the same ground, the faith of the New Testament, as set forth fundamentally in the Apostles' Creed. Both the Protestant confessions, in the beginning, the Reformed as well as the Lutheran, stood here upon common ground. Protestantism was held to be, not a new faith extracted from the Bible, but the old Christian faith itself, purged from Roman corruptions; and the ancient symbols were taken, accordingly, as its necessary ground and rule, from which it was counted unlawful and unsafe to depart. The confessions and catechisms of the sixteenth century, all do homage to the Apostles' Creed, as the primary text and outline of evangelical christianity. What would

Luther have said to the suggestion, that the Creed and Protestantism had not a kindred spirit? How would such an assertion have fallen on the mind of Melancthon or Calvin? Beyond all controversy, Protestantism in its original form, supposed itself to be of one mind with the Creed, and would have shuddered at the thought of treating it simply as "the fossil relic of by-gone ages." Our modern *Puritanism*, then, by its own confession in the case before us, is something materially different from all previous Christianity, both Catholic and Protestant. The Creed does not suit it, and cannot be used by it without unnatural constraint. This, indeed, was not at once clear to the genius of Puritanism itself. It started with the idea that it still loved the Creed, and could frame its mouth easily enough to recite it on fit occasion; "by a sort of courtesy, gave it a place beside its formularies and catechisms;" allowed it even to figure, for a time, in the New England Primer. But the water and the oil refused at last to mix. The Creed lost its voice, and wasted gradually into a shadow. "Its life and spirit never entered into the life of the Puritan churches;" and now the secret is fairly out. "We are free to confess," says the respectable editor of the Recorder, "that this Creed has forsaken the Puritans, and gone over to become the idol and strength of all branches of anti-puritanism."

It is plain, then, that Puritanism, in this view, is at war at once with the Fathers and with the Reformers, with early christianity and with the christianity of the sixteenth century. However it may agree with them in many points of doctrine, abstractly stated, its apprehension of christianity as a whole, the organism of its faith, the standpoint of its religious contemplation, and so, of course, the relations and bearings under which it sees all particular truths, come before us with a quite different character. Puritanism is not original Protestantism. It is an advance on this; a real breaking away from its first life; Protestantism, we may say, self-stimulated into a sort of "second growth." The simple fact that it allows no room whatever for the *Lutheran* principle, which in the beginning divided the interest of Protestantism with the Reformed, is of itself enough to prove this for any reflecting mind. It is proved here, also, however, by its want of affinity and sympathy with the Creed. Puritanism is ready to acknowledge that the spirit of the Creed, which is the spirit of all earlier Christianity, is against it and not to its taste. It glories in setting history here at full defiance. It is *independent* in all respects, and able to stand without help on its own bottom.

We are reminded, however, that Puritanism in all this exercise of independence, is still the dutiful disciple of the Bible. What is history against the word of God; what is the voice of the Creed, in comparison with the oracles of inspiration? Why make account of Fathers and Reformers, in the presence of the Scriptures? "Puritanism," says the Recorder, "builds on the Scriptures, and this Creed teaches, in several respects, anti-scriptural doctrines." *We* are charged with denying that the Bible is a complete rule of faith, because we insist on the authority of the Creed; nay, the "main characteristic" of our theology, its "parent feature," is made to be an idolatrous devotion to this symbol, as a sort of rival to the written word. There would be full as much reason, by the way, to resolve our system into an idolatry to the idea of sacramental grace. We are quoted as saying: "The Bible is not the *principle* of Christianity, nor yet the rock on which the Church was built;" but what we say immediately after, is not allowed to follow: "The one principle of Christianity, the true and proper fountain of its being, is the person of Christ; not any written account or notion of his person, but the actual living revelation of it, as a fact, in the history of the world." This position, of course, is not to be contradicted. Still we have the same changes rung perpetually on the old string. "Puritanism draws its life directly from the Bible and the Holy Ghost," aside from all creeds or traditions. "No stopping place here between Puritan liberty and Romish inquisition; that is, between liberty to think, and the suppression of thought by force." All this, we are told, is fully and forever settled in New England. "So deeply has the conviction that the Bible is the only rule of faith, seated itself in the Puritan mind; so clearly have the reason and force of this principle been revealed to the descendants of the Pilgrims; and so fully are we all possessed of the right of private judgment in religion; that we should seem to be laboring the proof of self-evident truths, if we were to go into argument here" (*Pur. Rec. Aug. 2*).

It is a blessed thing, certainly, and at times, too, saves much trouble, for "every man to be fully persuaded in his own mind." The case, however, is one that allows liberty and inquiry; and we do not ourselves find it by any means so clear, as these whole-sale positions imply. We beg leave, respectfully, to reiterate our word: The Bible is not the principle of Christianity, nor its foundation; this is a fact, out of the New Testament, before it and beyond it, which has its *principium* in the living person of Christ; and which, in this form, must rule the interpretation of the Bible for every true believer, and not be itself ruled, through the Bible, simply by his own mind. Will this be denied even in New England? We trust not. And yet, in the face of it, what becomes of all this talk about private judgment and the Bible, as the *sole* factors of the christian faith? Christianity itself, as something far more than any private judgment, must assist me to the true sense of the Scriptures, or I shall study them to little purpose. The only question, then, is, where this help is to be found. Puritanism refers us for it at once to the Holy Ghost. Very good; we too say, only those who are taught by the Spirit can understand the things of the Spirit. But the question returns: Where and how are we placed in communica-tion thus with the Holy Ghost? Puritanism, in the case before us, assumes that the mysterry takes place in a purely private way, each christian being enlightened by abrupt illapses for himself alone. This, however, we can by no means allow. It is against nature, against revelation, and against all sound philosophy. The agency of the Spirit on men, is conditioned universally by their living relations in the world, reaches them through the medium of their social and historical life, makes itself actual in and by the spiritual organism in which they are comprehended and car-ried. The child is illuminated as a child, and not as a full grown man; the Hottentot as an unlettered savage, and not as a gradu-ate of Oxford or Cambridge. To read the Bible to purpose, then, requires still more than the momentary presence of the Holy Ghost. There must be previous education, a development of thought, an inward moral habit, in one word, a positive spi-ritual substance, to some extent, already at hand, as the fruit of history and growth, *through* which only the voice of the Spirit

can ever be heard. Will any sane mind dispute this? We think
hardly. The question, then, is not, whether the Bible shall be
our sole rule of faith, but with what inward posture and habit
we are to come to the study of the Bible for this purpose; for it
is grossly absurd to suppose, that we can ever come to it without
some such posture and habit. Puritanism has its spiritual habit,
its tradition, its theological medium, its *a priori* governing religious consciousness, in this way, just as fully as any other section
of the christian world. The point here, accordingly, is in truth,
not the Creed against the Bible; this last we all allow to be supreme; but the Creed against the inward habit and tradition of
Puritanism, which, to our view, is something quite different. It
is all idle, in such case, to raise the cry: The Bible, the Bible,
the Bible of the Lord, are WE. That is the very point which is
to be settled. Other ages have had the Bible too, to study and
follow; and it is not at once clear, why the use of it by modern
New England is to be taken as infallibly right, and all other use
of it, differing from this, as infallibly wrong. Every such assumption is suited rather to remind us of Paul's keen challenge
to the Church at Corinth: "What! came the word of God out
from you? Or came it unto you only?" Christianity is older
than Puritanism; and we see no good reason, in this case, why
the elder should serve the younger, or the past become nothing
to make all of the present. We see no good reason, in other
words, for divesting ourselves of the general consciousness of the
ancient Church, as expressed in the Apostles' Creed, and putting
on in place of it the consciousness or creed of modern New England, as the only sure medium of access to the true sense of the
Bible. We go for private judgment too, and Protestant independence; but for this very reason we wish to secure the conditions that are most favorable to their rational exercise; and it
seems to us, in this view, we confess, vastly more safe to be in
union here with the general mind of the ancient Church, than
to be in conflict with it through the authority of any other system.
Why may not private judgment stand in the bosom of the old
faith, as fully as on the outside of it? Why should our homage
to the Bible be less free and independent in the communion of
the Creed, than when we substitute for this the theological habit

of Puritanism? It comes to nothing, that Puritanism pleads in its favor the authority of the Bible, and charges the Creed with heresy. That is only its own word. Whole ages of Christianiy, thousands and tens of thousauds of God's saints, the noble army of martyrs, fathers and reformers, have thought differeutly, with one voice proclaiming the Creed as the true and proper sense of the Scriptures, the glorious ground type of the Christian faith. A mind in no sympathy with the Creed, will, of course, not find it in the Bible; just as the Unitarian fails to find there the mystery of the Trinity, and so appeals to it as *his* witness against all other orthodox authorities. But let such sympathy prevail, and at once the whole case is changed; the supposed heiesies of the venerable symbol brighten into glorious truths; and the Bible is found, with easy interpretation, to speak the same sense from every page. When the Puritan Recorder claims the witness of the Bible against the Creed, it simply asks us to accept beforehand its own scheme of religion, through the medium of which the Bible is made to speak what it pretends. We, for our part, protest that we find in it no such meaning whatever. On all the points urged by the Recorder, the Creed is in full harmony with the Bible.

It would be strange indeed, if the sense of Christianity in the age when the New Testament was formed, were a less sure medium for its interpretation, than a later habit of thought altogether different. The presumption here, is at once powerfully against Puritanism. The true standpoint for understanding the Bible, is that of the Creed; and any view that may be taken of it from any different position is of small force, as weighed against the light in which it is seen and read from this position. "To the law and to the testimony," by all means; but then to save the force of this appeal, we insist on coming to the rule in a right way. Let us have the Bible in the element of its own life. And where else can we rationally pretend to find this, if it be not allowed to start, at least, in the Apostles' Creed?

Whether any protest may be made against the declaration of the Puritan Recorder, on the part of the general Puritan interest itself, remains to be seen. We would fain trust, that there are many in New England as well as out of it, owning the power of this system, on whose feelings still the declaration must fall harshly, and who will be disposed to demur to its authority. It is of itself, however, something very significant, that so far as we have heard no such protest has been uttered as yet from any quarter. Is silence here to be construed into consent? Or does it imply, at least, indifference and apathy towards the whole subject, as one of comparatively small account in any view? Such a declaration, made from any respectable source in the name of Protestantism, during the sixteenth century, would have called out, most certainly, from all sides, a loud indignant rebuke. Now it is met, at best, with passive unconcern. Congregational New England has no voice to vindicate the authority of the Creed. Presbyterianism too is silent. Were the honor of its Shorter Catechism invaded in the same way, there would be no lack of remonstrance and complaint. And yet the Creed is the *primary* Protestant symbol, of more sacredness and force, assuredly, than any catechism.[*] From other non-episcopal bodies, of course, (if we may except the Reformed Dutch,) not even the most gentle protest was to be expected. It needs no proof that our sects generally, are without zeal for the Creed. Its historical, catholic, sacramental, mystical character, suits not their mind. There can be no veneration for the Creed, where there is no veneration for the Church.

It seems to us, however, that this is a case which is entitled to general serious consideration. We have no right to overlook it, or to pass it by as of only insignificant account. The question, whether the Apostles' Creed is of force for evangelical Protestant-

---

[*] We have heard of one Presbyterian paper, in which the Recorder's vilification of the Creed was republished, without a word of exception or censure. We meet the same portentous phenomenon in the *Lutheran Observer*, Sept. 21. It is still for this model of Lutheran orthodoxy, it seems, an open question, whether the *symbolum apostolicum* teaches false doctrine or not. While some assign it a place beyond its merits, "others as learned and pious as they," charge it with heresy, "when explained agreeably to its original design and import." On this issue, "*we* are anxious that our readers should be made acquainted with both sides of the question, and therefore lay before them the following article on the subject, taken from the Puritan Recorder." The Observer itself thus is *non liquet*.

ism, however it be answered, is a very great question, which ought not to go without a clear and full response, that may be heard and laid to heart on all sides. The Creed is a theological unit. It cannot be taken to pieces, without destruction. From its own standpoint and posture, all its articles flow with easy necessity as the proclamation of a single fact. In this form it is the primitive type of Christianity, the mould in which the faith of the gospel first took living shape in the Church. It was so acknowledged at the Reformation, as well as in all ages before. Now, we are told, it has become a fossil relic, with the spirit of which Puritanism owns no inward affinity or fellowship. Is this confession to be accepted as truth? If not, the occasion certainly requires that it should be met with some open contradiction. Puritanism should let the world know, that the Creed has *not* forsaken it, and is *not* still to be counted a dead letter only in its old confessional Primer. If, on the other hand, the confession be accepted as true, the occasion requires that a fact so strange and startling should be openly explained and made to appear right. Silence here is wholly out of place. A great theological interest is at stake. Here are two *minds*, two theological habits, the old catholic consciousness and the modern Puritan consciousness, "having no kindred spirit," each of which claims to be, not at once the Bible, (neither the Creed nor the New England Primer is *that*,) but still the only true and safe preparation for coming to the sense of the Bible, the necessary "ποῦ στῶ" for the right understanding of its divine contents. Which are we to follow? Puritanism acknowledges its own novelty, and yet requires us to quit the Creed, and cast ourselves upon its independent separate guidance instead, as the infallible rule and measure of Christianity. *I* build upon the Scriptures, it exclaims; the Creed is a human production, and teaches false doctrine; follow *me*. Truly, a very great and solemn demand! Let it be heard with all becoming seriousness and respect. Still, we tremble at the thought of such a deep rupture with the old Christian consciousness, and venture to ask: By what authority doest *thou* this thing, and who gave thee *such* authority? And this question, we say, demands a calm and clear answer; a scientific answer; an answer that may satisfy at once the yearnings of pious feeling, and the necessities of earnest theological thought.

Again we say, in conclusion, we are anxious that the *animus* of this article should not be misunderstood. Our aim is not war, but God's free truth in the spirit of love and peace. We need no angry voice, to remind us of the vast achievements and high merits of Puritanism. All that is fully and constantly before our mind. We need no outward advocate, to urge the force of its peculiar claims. We know what they are, by inborn constitutional sense. The hardest Puritan we have to do with always, is the one we carry, by birth and education, in our own bosom. But the misery of it is, for our quiet, that the Catholic is there too, and will not be at rest. In other words, we are forced to do homage to *both* tendencies, and have no power, like many, to resign ourselves wholly to the separate beck of one. According to the Boston Recorder, "there is no stopping place between Puritan liberty and Romish inquisition, between liberty to think and the suppression of thought by force." But just this we are by no means prepared to believe.* On the contrary, we are deeply persuaded that the sense of authority and the exercise of free thought go hand in hand together, and cannot be disjoined in the moral world without deep prejudice to truth. We are deeply persuaded too, in the case before us, that Catholicism and Puritanism both enter of right into the constitution of Christianity, and that neither can legitimately exclude the other. The problem of their true and proper union, is indeed one of no common difficulty; the great problem, as it would seem, for the new era of Christianity, which is now so generally supposed to be at hand. The inmost wants of the time, however, cry aloud for its solution. Blind outward authority, and mere private

---

* Romanism, in its genuine shape, takes the same ground; only planting itself on the contrary pole of the antithesis, and requiring us to accept our faith in an *ab extra* way from the hands of the Pope. Both poles, thus disjoined, come to very much the same falsehood in the end. This we hope to show more fully in our promised review of Brownson's Quarterly; and as many seem to be a little impatient with the delay of this article, we here take occasion to say, that it will appear, God willing, in our next number. Good reasons have stood in the way of its appearing sooner.

judgment, are alike insufficient as a key to the Bible. What we desire is, that this should be acknowledged, and a true conciliation at least aimed at between the great tendencies, which are here placed in opposition and conflict. It is not by the simple assertion of its own life, but in *so* asserting this life as to leave no room for the other side of religion, that Puritanism seems to us to be too often in fault. When it claims to be at once the sum and substance and end of all Christianity, the absolute sense of the Bible, and requires that all other systems, the old Catholic, the primitive Protestant, the thinking of all other times and of all other lands, shall be tested and tried by itself, or by the Bible to its particular mind, (which is just the same thing,) we cannot but feel that the claim is at war with all reason and right. Such exclusiveness involves vast wrong to the cause itself, in whose favor it is thus urged. Puritanism is bound to acknowledge the rights of other tendencies, the Catholic, the Lutheran, the original Reformed, for instance, if it would have its own acknowledged, and so coöperate efficiently in the great task of bringing Christianity to its last universal form. Let it do this, and we are ready always to sit respectfully at its feet, and drink in wisdom from its lips. We reserve to ourselves, of course, in this posture, the right of free contradiction, where it may seem to be needed; and we shall not insult it, by supposing its granite nature so soft that any such freedom can ever require an apology.

J. W. N.

POSTSCRIPT.

Though in no very immediate relation to the subject of the foregoing article, we may as well notice here as anywhere else, if we are to notice at all, the sharp dissatisfaction expressed by the Puritan Recorder, and in another quarter also, with the article in our last number, referring to the case of Mr. Lesley. It has been held up to reproach, as a direct vindication of this gentleman's opinions and course; and the attempt is made, on this

ground, to insinuate against all connected, whether nearly or re-
motely, with the Mercersburg Review, a general sympathy with
error and a wish to set aside church authority and the binding
force of creeds!

· We are sorry, that any occasion should have been furnished
by this article, however innocently, for those who seek occasion,
thus to pervert and misrepresent our true position, for the purpose
of keeping out of sight the questions of deep practical concern,
that are really at issue between us and themselves. Our interest
in these, on the score simply of their general theological significance, is so sincerely honest and earnest, that we are always made
to feel sick at heart, when we find any merely personal or party
reference thrust forward into their place, and some accidental
purely subordinate question allowed to run away thus with the
attention that should be confined to the main interest in debate.
We have no concern for the cause of Mr. Lesley whatever, and
no wish, certainly, to endorse or vindicate his views in any
way; we are very certain too, that nothing of this sort can be
legitimately saddled on the particular article to which this notice refers; still we regret, for the reason just stated, that more
care was not taken to anticipate and shut out more effectually the
possibility of its being abused into any such wrong and injurious
sense. We hope to profit by the lesson, and shall try to bear in
mind that we need the wisdom of the serpent, no less than the
simplicity of the dove, to keep at bay the *odium theologicum*,
with which unfortunately we are called too often to deal as the
substitute of zeal for the truth.

It is not true that the article in question "enters with all zeal
into the case of Mr. Lesley and his come-outer church," and
makes common cause with the man and his measures. It explicitly says the contrary, and condemns the separatistic position he
has allowed himself to take. The design of the article, as any
candid mind may easily see, was not at all to support Mr. Lesley
in his theological or ecclesiastical position; he is only an accident
in the case; the true thing proposed, was to exemplify the inconsistency and contradiction of those, who cry up *private judgment*
as a last authority in religion, and yet in this and similar cases,
are not willing to let their principle prevail beyond certain metes

and bounds of their own imposition. The very caption of the article is " Private Judgment," and its whole aim and scope is, not to magnify this, certainly, but to bring it into discredit.   How should it be imagined, then, to go in favor of such individualism, under its most rampant form? It is throughout, an *argumentum ad hominem.* It takes Puritanism, or Independency, on its own premises, and charges it in the case of Mr. Lesley, (any similar case would have answered for illustration just as well,) with palpable and gross self-contradiction.   In this view the argument is of full force.   If the Church of the Creed be a phantom, and Christianity the sense simply of the Bible, as every " Tom, Dick and Harry" in the land, *(pax verbo,)* may choose to take it, we see not, certainly, on what ground any church censure can legitimately hold against the exercise of such independency in any form.

Such we take to be the drift and purpose of this offending article.   If, however, it might be supposed by any to carry covertly a different sense, nothing could be more unfair, surely, than to lay the burden of such different sense on the general character of the Review; contradicted, as any child might see it to be, by the whole spirit and bearing of the Review itself, from the beginning.   It has been asked, whether the Church in which *we* stand would not also exclude a man for grave confessional errors.   We reply, it would do so certainly.   The uniform doctrine, moreover, of this Review has been, that the right as well as the duty to preserve the faith once delivered to the saints, resides by divine appointment in the Church.   Private judgment and independency, in the ultra Puritan sense, we do not allow, but consider rather to be in bad opposition to Christ and Christianity.   The sect spirit thus we hold to be emphatically *Antichrist.*   It is all in order, therefore, for *us* to insist on church authority and the evil of schism.   But it is not in order for those to do so, who profess to give full scope to the sect maxim: " No creed but the Bible and private judgment."   When *they*, notwithstanding, in virtue of their associated judgment, pretend to lay bit and bridle on the principle of independency where it varies from themselves, and charge it with " come-outerism," as the word goes, for being independent in such separate style, they give the lie to their own principle, and may well be called upon to explain and justify the contradiction involved in their conduct.

The "Presbyterian," we understand, finds it a bad sign against us, that we are against creeds; on the familiar adage, that men do not oppose creeds commonly till creeds come to be in opposition first to themselves. The "Puritan," on the other hand, finds it a bad sign that we make too much of creeds. "Those," we are told, "who give to the creed and tradition an authority superior to that of the Scriptures, can hardly be inconsistent in endorsing for one who denies the plenary inspiration of the Bible." These two insinuations, of course, do not cohere very well together. For any fair reader of our Review, both must be taken as simple balderdash.

We are not opposed to creeds. No one can go against creeds, who goes for the Church as an article of faith. The difficulty with us here is, not in the too little of our faith, for the taste of the dissatisfied, but in its *too much*. To oppose sects, is not to oppose creeds; but just the reverse. What is needed above all things to upset their tyrannical arbitrariness, is the sense of a true catholic tradition springing from the life of the Church, in a real way, as it has stood from the beginning. This starts beyond all controversy in the Apostles' Creed; while on this foundation it makes room for much more, in the way of historical orthodox faith, comprehended with more or less success in later symbols, Catholic and Protestant, which the Church is bound to acknowledge and respect to the end of the world. For creeds, (so called,) that affect to set aside the foundation creed of Christianity, substituting for it some original scheme of their own, we do entertain, it is true, but small admiration or regard. But such upstart faith is itself at war with the true idea of a creed. It makes no account of history, but just fancies its own system from the skies. The sect spirit is universally unhistorical, and so, to the same extent, *creedless*. Those who oppose creeds, on the other hand, (independents, radicals, come-outers,) are always unhistorical. *We* go with all our might for the idea of the Church, for the Apostles' Creed, for catholic tradition, for historical Christianity; as the only refuge and help from the horrid evils, that seem to yawn upon us continually from the abyss of the unchurchly system.

Is this to wrong the Bible? So thinks the "Puritan"; but so think not we. We have full faith in its inspiration, and own its authority to be supreme in all questions of religion. But you "give to the Creed and tradition an authority superior to that of the Scriptures?" Not at all. We give to them only an authority superior, at worst, to that of the Puritan scheme of thought, the New England tradition, so far forth as this same may be found seeking to thrust the old faith out of the way. Forced to an election between two conflicting traditions, one resting in the Apostles' Creed, and the other charging it with *heresy*, we choose the first, as on the whole more rational and safe than the second. This is the only true issue in the case. To make the Puritan tradition *per se* the same thing with the Bible, is but an impudent begging of the whole question in debate. We do not believe that Puritanism, as distinguished from the old catholic sense of the Creed, expresses at all the true sense of the Bible; and we have yet to learn by what right we are to be shut up to its authority here, that is a whit better, to say the least, than that claimed to the same purport by the Church of Rome. Why should the fathers of New England be counted more infallible, as interpreters of the Bible, than the fathers of the ancient Church in Africa or Asia Minor? Did these last love the Bible less? Had Augustine less regard for its authority than Edwards? *Why*, to show my obedience to the Bible, must I give up the Creed, and immerse my mind in the element of Puritanism only in its stead? To say: "Come to the Bible, without *any* medium," is pitiful nonsense. No man *can* come to it in that way: and the least really free in their approach to it ordinarily, are just those who are most forward to dream and talk of their freedom in any such fantastical style.

THE late meeting of the German Reformed Synod at Norris-town, is allowed, on all hands, to have been one which it was a privilege to attend. It was characterized throughout by a good spirit. Among its proceedings, the action taken on the subject of a new liturgy, is entitled to special interest. This was based on an able report, presented by the Rev. Mr. Bomberger, chair-man of a committee to which the general question had been referred a year before by the Synod at Hagerstown. The report consisted of a proper historical introduction or preamble, setting forth the general posture of the early Church, and of the Church at the Reformation. in regard to worship, and of a series of reso-lutions, issuing in favor of an immediate movement, at this time, for the formation of a liturgy suitable to the wants of the body rep-resented by the Synod. The whole led to an animated discus-sion of nearly two days, which served, far beyond all that was expected in the beginning, to bring out the result of a general substantial agreement and harmony of views. With very slight modification, the entire report was adopted. The resolutions affirm : 1. That the use of liturgical forms falls in clearly with the practice and genius of the original Protestant Church ; 2. That no reason exists in the state of the present American Ger-man Church, to justify a departure from this ancient usage ; 3. That the Liturgy now authorized is inadequate to the wants of the Church, as apart from other defects it makes no provision for *ordinary* occasions of public worship ; 4. That while the older Reformed Liturgies are in general worthy of adoption, there is still need of various modifications to adapt them fully to our cir-cumstances and wants ; 5. That the present time is as favorable for new action in the case, as any that can be anticipated here-after ; 6. That it is expedient, accordingly, to proceed forthwith in the business of providing a new Liturgy. In conformity with the conclusion thus reached, a large committee was appointed to report, at the next meeting of the Synod, a scheme or plan of such a Liturgy as the interests of the Church may be supposed to require, with certain parts made more or less complete, in the

way of specimen and rule, that may be expected to govern subsequently the construction of the whole.   It is a matter for con-
gratulation, certainly, that so auspicious a commencement is at
length made in this high and solemn work.   For two years past,
the subject has been, in a certain sense, before the mind of the
Church; in such a way, however, unfortunately, that it has not
been able to come to any fair and open discussion.   No one could
show any good reason, why the liturgical question should *not* be
treated, in the German Church, with the most unreserved freedom; and yet there has been evidently a feeling of embarrassment in venturing to approach it, and a disposition to hold it at
arm's length, which has stood thus far much in the way of a just
consideration of its rights and claims.   In the mean time, as it
now appears, the want that needs to be supplied in this direction,
has been steadily making itself to be more and more felt, on all
sides; until at length it is found, as it were, forcing its own way
to the clear utterance, from which it had been so long previously
withheld and restrained.   The preparation for a new Liturgy
has been altogether more general and deep, it would seem, than
most had before imagined.   The Synod, at the start, was by no
means clear in regard to its own mind.   Discussion, once fairly
set free, caused a whole world of fog to pass away; and the body
was taken with a sort of surprise, in the end, at the unanimity of
its views and feelings, where it had been so needlessly haunted
with the spectre of controversy and discord.   The discussion had
in all respects a happy effect.   The interest taken in it, too, by
the community, bore testimony to its importance.   Such a question, involving what pertains to the interior life of the Church,
always commands attention and respect, when treated by an ecclesiastical body in an earnest and manly way.   The more, too,
any such body can be led to exercise its interest, in this way, on
questions that enter into the real life of the Church, to the exclusion of what would suit just as well for a Temperance Society or
any other like voluntary and merely human association, the more
may it be expected to rise always in the actual dignity of its own
character, as well as in the solemnity of all its proceedings.

As the case now stands, the door is thrown open, of course,
for the most free discussion of the whole liturgical question

Not only is such discussion allowed, but it is loudly demanded and required. It is not enough here to act; we need intelligent action. It is not enough to follow a mere blind sense of want, or to obey a tendency however good; we need clear insight into our want, and rational mastery over our own movement. This cannot be without much thought, much consultation and debate. It is not enough, of course, that the ministers, and some of the elders, be satisfied; the case requires that the people, the churches generally, should have their attention turned seriously to the subject, their views enlightened, their hearts disposed and prepared for what may be done. This is indeed just one of the last cases in which any end is to be carried by management or trick. No one need fear discussion. The Church can never be hurried into a Liturgy, without her own consent; her own full, free and hearty consent; and if discussion and inquiry may serve to carry her where she would not be prepared to go otherwise, who can have a right to say that such movement is irrational or wrong. If we are to have a Liturgy at all, it is of the utmost consequence that we should have a good one; and this requires, in the first place, a true and just idea of what a Liturgy means, and in the second place, some general inward preparation for the use of one in its proper form. We have no right then, and nobody surely should have any wish to prevent the most full and free study of the subject in all its length and breadth, in order that if possible these necessary conditions of success, in so vast and solemn an enterprise, may be duly secured. We have no right to lay down limits and bounds, within which only the Church is to be considered free to exercise her liberty in this form. The entire question is open. Let the subject be examined without prejudice, or deference to surrounding prejudice, or shy jealousy of any particular *tendency*; as though a "tendency" might hoodwink a whole Church out of its sober rationality, and *we* would forestall all that, and take care of its proper liberty, by laying a bridle on its neck beforehand, to keep it from going too far! The danger here, is not in free inquiry, but in the want of it. What is most of all to be deprecated, is the formation of an unripe Liturgy; one that may fall behind the true inward demands of the interest itself, and that may fail, accordingly, to satisfy in the end the very want from which it springs. No Liturgy can go far beyond the reigning idea of worship, which it is brought in to assist and serve; and if this be still incomplete, or a confused tendency only, perhaps, which has not yet got to its own proper end, the result is likely to be a sort of buckram invention, which will sit stiffly on the Church for the time, and prove at last a mere form too irksome for its better life to endure.

Everything here depends on starting right. Our Liturgy will take its character and complexion finally, from the conception we have of the end it is designed to serve. If it is taken to be a mere outward help and convenience for the purposes of public worship, a sort of crutch to assist the decent conduct of our sanctuary devotions, it is not to be expected that we shall be able to bring it to anything better than such poor mechanical character. Better no Liturgy at all, we say from the bottom of our heart, than one produced from such a spirit and constructed on such a plan. In such case, indeed, its services must deserve to be called *forms* in the bad sense, such as can serve only to generate bondage and not freedom. A Liturgy so adopted, is like the notion of civil government, as taken by a certain school to be a prudential compact, in which men part with some of their rights to be more sure of the rest. Government, in any right view, is the form in which the very idea of our human life becomes real and complete. So we say, the very idea of worship itself demands a liturgy; this is the very form, in which it requires to hold, in order that it may come to its own most true and perfect sense. If there be no need for a liturgy in the idea of Christian worship, in itself considered; if it is to be taken at best, but as an accommodation to the necessities of the ignorant and weak, like the exercises of an infant school designed for infants only; we are ready to say, the sooner the subject is dismissed from our thoughts the better. If we are to have a Liturgy that is worth anything, we must seek it and accept it under a widely different view. We must see, that it involves no bondage, but freedom. We must embrace it, not as a burden but as a relief, not as a yoke but as a crown, not as a minimum of evil simply, but as a maximum of privilege and good. The bondage lies, of a truth, wholly on the other side. The conception of a liturgy in the true sense, as compared with our reigning unliturgical and *free* worship, is the conception of a real emancipation into the liberty of the children of God. Argument and debate here, that are not led by the idea of worship itself, but turn on other considerations altogether, whether they go for or against a liturgy, are of very small account; of just as little worth, in truth, as a controversy about art, by those who have never yet felt what art means, and for whom all artistic creations are alike destitute of inward law and soul. Worship, like art, has a life and nature of its own. It involves, in its very constitution, certain principles, elements, and rules, which must be understood and turned to right account, to make it complete. To deny this, or to have no sense of it, is to stand convicted at once of entire incompetency to say one word rationally on the subject here in consideration. Any true analysis of the nature of worship, any proper resolution of it into its necessary constituents and conditions, we have no doubt at all, must bring us to see and feel that it requires a liturgy, and that a vast loss is suffered where it is violently forced to move under any less perfect and free form. All unliturgical worship, is to the same extent, rude, cumbersome and incomplete. Nature is a divine liturgy throughout. The life of heaven, still more, is a liturgy, "like the sound of many waters," of the most magnificent and sublime order. What we need, in our present movement, is the full sense of what worship means in this view; sympathy with the music of the spheres, and with the song of the angels; the same mind that led the early Church into the universal use of liturgies, without opposition or contradiction, so far as history shows, from any quarter.   N.

END OF VOLUME I.

Lightning Source UK Ltd.
Milton Keynes UK
UKHW02n1313130218
317658UK00005B/400/P